BRYN THOMAS was born in Zimbabwe ~~~~~~ grew up on a farm. Since graduating ~~~ University with a degree in anth~~~ els have included a Saha~~~ built himself, a solo 2~~~ Andes, more th~~~ 50,000km o~~~ book, s~~~ Guide E~~~ on the Tr~~~ e old British Lib~~~ ~uent publications have ~~~~~~ *the Annapurna Region*, also from Trailblazer, and guides to ~~~~~ n for Lonely Planet.

In 1991 he set up Trailblazer, to produce ~~~~~ of route guides for adventurous travellers that has now grown to over 40 ~~~~~.

ANNA COHEN KAMINSKI (below, in Mongolia with Roger) updated the 9th edition of this book. She was born in Moscow and experienced a Communist childhood before her family moved to the West. Though she has travelled on five continents since earning her Bachelor's degree in Comparative American Studies at the University of Warwick, this is only the second time she has properly explored the country of her birth from end to end. Anna also writes for Lonely Planet and Rough Guides, covering destinations as diverse as Chile, Peru, Colombia, Jamaica and Sweden. In between travels she calls Cambridge, England, home.

Trans-Siberian Handbook

First edition 1988; **this ninth edition June 2014**

Publisher Trailblazer Publications 🖥 www.trailblazer-guides.com
The Old Manse, Tower Rd, Hindhead, Surrey, GU26 6SU, UK

British Library Cataloguing in Publication Data
A catalogue record for this book is available from the British Library

ISBN 978-1-905864-56-0

© Bryn Thomas 2014 Text and maps

The right of Bryn Thomas to be identified as the author of this work has been
asserted by him in accordance with the Copyright, Designs and Patents Act 1988

Editor: Anna Jacomb-Hood
Cartography: Nick Hill
Layout: Anna Jacomb-Hood
Chinese text: Qing Sun & Daniel McCrohan
Proofreading: Nicky Slade
Cover design: Richard Mayneord
Index: Jane Thomas & Anna Jacomb-Hood
Photographs © Anna Cohen Kaminski (unless otherwise credited)
Illustrations © Nick Hill

Quotations used in Part 5 are from the *Guide to the Great Siberian Railway 1900*.
Background information for Vladimir, Suzdal & Nizhny Novgorod was written by Athol
Yates and updated from material originally published in his *Russia by Rail* (Bradt Guides).

Important note

Every effort has been made by the author and publisher to ensure that the information
contained herein is as accurate and up to date as possible. However, they are unable to
accept responsibility for any inconvenience, loss or injury sustained by anyone
as a result of the advice and information given in this guide.

Updated information will be available on:
🖥 **www.trailblazer-guides.com**

Photos – Front cover and this page: A rare picture, taken in the early 1970s,
of the Trans-Siberian being hauled by a steam engine (© Ron Ziel)
Overleaf: Looking across Lake Baikal

Printed on chlorine-free paper by D'Print (☎ +65-6581 3832), Singapore

Trans-Siberian
HANDBOOK

BRYN THOMAS

AND

ANNA COHEN KAMINSKI

TRAILBLAZER PUBLICATIONS

INTRODUCTION

PART 1: PLANNING YOUR TRIP

PART 2: RUSSIA

PART 3: SIBERIA AND THE RAILWAY

PART 4: CITY GUIDES AND PLANS

PART 5: ROUTE GUIDE AND MAPS

APPENDICES

Dedication

In loving memory of Patricia Major, who helped found Trailblazer and was Series Editor for 19 years

From Anna: I dedicate my research to my parents, Ellen and David, without whom none of this would have been possible, and for whose loving support I am forever grateful.

Acknowledgements

From Bryn: I am greatly indebted to the numerous people who have helped me with this project since the publication in 1988 of what became, in its second edition, the book that started Trailblazer. I'm grateful to Patricia Major, for her unwavering support right from the beginning and for setting the high editorial standards. Thanks also to Jane Thomas for her extensive work in compiling the original strip maps and town plans. Nick Hill has built on her foundations with consummate skill; I'm grateful to him for the digitised maps, his excellent line drawings and also for all his research work on earlier editions. Thanks to Anna Jacomb-Hood for her continuing work on the book, this time in her eagle-eyed editing of the text as well as for typesetting and layout, and to Nicky Slade for thorough proofreading.

I'm very grateful to Anna Cohen Kaminski for further improving the book by comprehensively researching and writing the last two editions. Thanks to Qing Sun & Daniel McCrohan for the Chinese translations; James Pitkin for the seventh edition of the book; Nick Hill, John King and Neil McGowan for updating the sixth edition, Nick Hill for the fifth edition; Athol Yates for original text on Vladimir, Suzdal and Nizhny Novgorod, the accompanying railway text, the carriage plan and all his and Tatyana Pozar-Burgar's work on the fourth edition of the book; Athol Yates and Nicholas Zvegintzov for the railway dictionary, Dominic Streatfeild-James who updated the third edition (and whose wry comments survive); Doug Streatfeild-James for the Chinese words and phrases section; Neil Taylor; and Ron Ziel for the cover photograph. Thanks to Richard Mayneord for the cover design and photos.

Thanks also to the many readers who wrote in; see p528 for their names.

From Anna: I'd like to thank Bryn for giving me this incredible opportunity (for the second time!) and for his help and guidance throughout, Nick and Anna for all their hard work on the book, and Daniel for the Chinese translations.

Thank you to everyone who assisted me at home and on the road: Trevor and Marc for your jolly company in Irkutsk and Olkhon Island; Mike, the team at Khongor and Boojum for your help in Ulaanbaatar and beyond; Subo (and Chris) for keeping me company during research in Beijing and Daniel for all his help and insider tips; Neil for his insider knowledge of Moscow, Olya Keppen for opening her Moscow home to me and Masha for the memorable dinner; Anatoliy and Alexander in Krasnoyarsk for the great hospitality and a cracking tour of the dam; the best hostels and their hosts – Larisa in Ulan-Ude, 'Jack' Sheremetov at Baikaler in Irkutsk, Anya at Baikal Trail Hostel in Severobaikalsk; Tatiana at Omnomnom Hostel in Yekaterinburg; and the staff at Godzilla's in Suzdal and Soul Kitchen Junior in St Petersburg.

A request

The author and publisher have tried to ensure that this guide is as accurate and up to date as possible. However, things change quickly in this part of the world. If you notice any changes or omissions please contact Bryn Thomas (bryn.thomas@trailblazer-guides.com, or via the address on p2). A free copy of the next edition will be sent to persons making a significant contribution.

INTRODUCTION

Why take the train?

*'Best of all, he would tell me of the great train that ran across half the world
... He held me enthralled then, and today, a life-time later, the spell still holds.
He told me the train's history, its beginnings ... how a Tzar had said, 'Let the
Railway be built!' And it was ... For me, nothing was ever the same again. I
had fallen in love with the Traveller's travels. Gradually, I became possessed
by love of a horizon and a train which would take me there ...'*
Lesley Blanch *Journey into the Mind's Eye*

The spell that Lesley Blanch's 'Traveller' cast captured me, too, as it
has countless others. And after the classic film of Boris Pasternak's
love story, *Dr Zhivago*, there can be few people unaware of the
magic and romance of
crossing Russia and the **Almost 6000 miles, a seven-day**
wild forests and steppes of **journey, between Moscow and**
Siberia on the longest rail- **Vladivostok; just under**
way journey in the world – **5000 miles, five days, between**
the Trans-Siberian. The dis- **Moscow and Beijing**
tances spanned are immense: almost 6000 miles, a seven-day journey, between Moscow and the Pacific port of Vladivostok (for boat
connections to Japan); just under 5000 miles, five days, between
Moscow and Beijing.

(Above): All trains make a stop in Novosibirsk, Siberia's largest city (see p274).

INTRODUCTION

From the dazzling onion domes of Russian cathedrals (such as the 15th century **Assumption Cathedral** in Moscow, **above**) ...

Since the rail service linking Europe with the Far East was established at the turn of the 19th century, foreign travellers and adventurers have been drawn to it. Most of the early travellers crossed Siberia in the comfort of the carriages of the Belgian Wagon Lits company, as luxurious as those of the Venice-Simplon Orient Express of today. Things changed somewhat after the Russian Revolution in 1917 as it became increasingly difficult for foreigners to obtain permits for Siberia.

It was not until the 1960s that the situation improved and Westerners began to use the railway again for getting to Japan, taking the boat from Nakhodka (it now leaves from Vladivostok) for the last part of the journey. In the early 1980s travel restrictions for foreigners visiting China were relaxed and now many people have found the Trans-Siberian a fascinating and relatively cheap way to get to or from both China and Mongolia.

While the ending of the Cold War removed some of the mystique of travelling in the former USSR, Russia's increasing accessibility means that there are new travel opportunities right across the country. With foreigners no longer obliged to stay in overpriced state-run hotels, visiting the country is more

affordable than ever before.

Rail passengers inevitably absorb something of the ethos of the country through which they travel: on this train you are guaranteed to meet local people, for this is no 'tourist special' but a working service; you may find yourself draining a bottle of vodka with a Russian soldier, discussing politics with a Chinese academic, or drinking Russian champagne with a Mongolian trader.

In this jet age most of us have lost touch with the travel experience that is slow enough to give us a real concept of the geographical distance we've travelled. Quite apart from being environmentally unfriendly, to the 21st

... to former palaces (Beijing's **Forbidden City**, **above**) and temples in China and Mongolia, a journey along the Trans-Siberian gives you countless fascinating opportunities for stopping off along the way. If you make only one stopover on the journey it should certainly be **Lake Baikal (below)**, although both the Trans-Siberian and BAM lines run close to the lake in places.

century traveller air travel has become mind-numbingly routine and unexciting. To embark on a long-distance rail journey, spending days on a train and traversing thousands of miles over the planet's surface, is just as thrilling now as it was a century ago. As Eric Newby wrote in *The Big Red Train Ride*, 'The Trans-Siberian is the big train ride. All the rest are peanuts'. Nothing can change that.

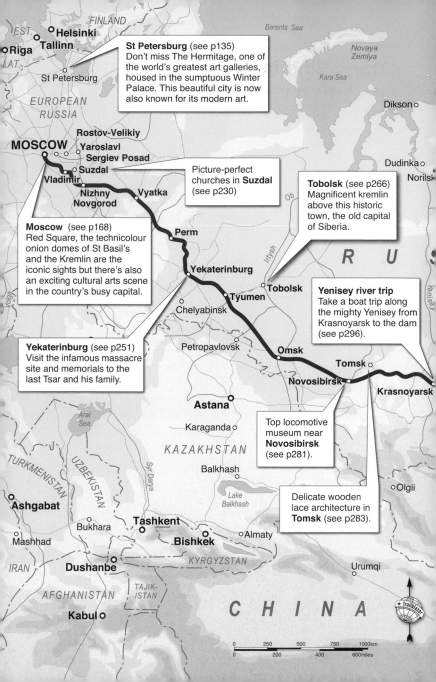

St Petersburg (see p135)
Don't miss The Hermitage, one of the world's greatest art galleries, housed in the sumptuous Winter Palace. This beautiful city is now also known for its modern art.

Picture-perfect churches in Suzdal (see p230)

Tobolsk (see p266)
Magnificent kremlin above this historic town, the old capital of Siberia.

Moscow (see p168)
Red Square, the technicolour onion domes of St Basil's and the Kremlin are the iconic sights but there's also an exciting cultural arts scene in the country's busy capital.

Yenisey river trip
Take a boat trip along the mighty Yenisey from Krasnoyarsk to the dam (see p296).

Yekaterinburg (see p251)
Visit the infamous massacre site and memorials to the last Tsar and his family.

Top locomotive museum near Novosibirsk (see p281).

Delicate wooden lace architecture in Tomsk (see p283).

Trans-Siberian Highlights
and best stop-offs along the routes

Trans-Siberian
Trans-Manchurian
Trans-Mongolian
Baikal-Amur Mainline
AYaM

Khatanga

Tiksi

FAR EAST

Magadan

Lena

 whnaya Tunguska

Yakutsk
Nizhny Bestyakh

Okhotsk

Sea of Okhotsk

S I A

SIBERIA

Bond with Russian miners travelling the **BAM railway** (see p498).

Okha

Tommot
Aldan

Neryungri

Hot springs and hiking near **Severobaikalsk** (see p411)

Komsomolsk-na-Amure

Vanino

Bratsk

Tynda

Bamovskaya

Severobaikalsk

Sovetskaya Gavan

Tayshet

Angara

Lake Baikal

Olkhon Island (see p317)

Amur

Birobidzhan

Khabarovsk

Blagoveshchensk

Fuyuan

Irkutsk

Ulan-Ude

Chita

Manzhouli

Harbin (see p376) Ice Lantern Festival (Jan-Feb).

Ussuri

Sea of Japan

Irkutsk (see p297) Southern gateway to **Lake Baikal**

Buryat culture in **Ulan-Ude** (see p319)

Harbin

Suifenhe
Zarubino

Vladivostok
Nak-hodka

ULAANBAATAR (Ulan Bator)

Naadam Festival in **Ulaanbaatar** (see p358)

Changchun

Vladivostok (see p342) Vibrant culture and the new bridge

MONGOLIA

Shenyang

Erlian

N KOREA

Nomadic stays in **Mongolia** (see p373).

BEIJING

Pyongyang

Seoul

Datong

Beijing's Forbidden City (see p386) & excursions to the **Great Wall** (see p407).

S KOREA

CHINA

Routes and costs

ROUTE OPTIONS   [see previous page for map]

Travellers crossing Siberia have a choice of three main routes: the Trans-Siberian, Trans-Manchurian and Trans-Mongolian.

The **Trans-Siberian** crosses the entire length of Siberia to the Pacific terminus at Vladivostok. The **Trans-Manchurian** travels through most of Siberia before turning south through Manchuria and ending in Beijing. The **Trans-Mongolian** also terminates in Beijing but travels via Mongolia which gives you

The Trans-Mongolian, Moscow-Beijing route via Mongolia, is the most popular

the chance to stop off in Ulaanbaatar. Out of the three, the Moscow–Beijing route is the most popular, but all three have a lot to recommend them.

Another alternative to the Trans-Siberian is the road less travelled – the **Baikal Amur Mainline (BAM)**. It runs parallel to the former but 600km to the north, between Tayshet to the west of Lake Baikal and the eastern coast of Russia.

If you want to travel on to Japan after your trip you have several options. From Vladivostok there are both ferries (mid May to December) and flights.

There are also cheaper ferry services from various Chinese ports including Shanghai, Tianjin and Qingdao, all of them within easy reach of Beijing.

Trans-Manchurian and Trans-Mongolian travellers can continue from Beijing by train round China, which has an extensive rail system as well as direct rail links into Vietnam. You can even travel back to Europe along the Silk Road on the Turkestan–Siberia (Turksib) railway.

COSTS

Overall costs

How much you pay for a trip on the world's longest railway line depends on the level of comfort you demand, the number of stops you wish to make along the way

(**Above**): Russians are generally very sociable and when you travel on trains, particularly if you're in a *platzkart* carriage, it's common to share your food with people you meet. These four travellers, three miners and a local girl visiting her relatives, plied this author with tea and caviar.

(**Below**): The train makes numerous stops along the way, giving you the opportunity to buy food on the platform from local people.

SV (1st class) compartment on an older train, containing just two berths. On newer trains each SV compartment has its own bathroom, some even with a shower.

and the time of year you travel. At times Russian Railways offer seriously discounted tickets for those prepared to ride in the less-popular top berths. If these are on offer when you want to go, and you don't mind being in a top berth, consider it a bonus; see p14 for sample fares on the main routes.

Among other big costs to factor in are transport to your departure point, transport back at the end of your journey, accommodation in Moscow, Beijing and any stopover towns, food and spending money.

The independent package deals offered by many travel agents can be better value than they might appear. Packages on the Trans-Siberian between Moscow and Beijing, including transfers and one night's accommodation in Moscow, start at about £800/US$1200, though if you travel *platzkart* (3rd class in an open-plan dorm carriage), you can get by on around £55/$80 per day travelling independently. If a super-luxurious two-week guided rail tour from Moscow to Vladivostok with en suite accommodation in private saloon cars pulled by a restored steam locomotive is more your idea of travelling, be prepared to part with around £8000/US$12,000 (see p30).

One-way flights from London to Moscow have become considerably cheaper with the introduction of easyJet flights, and can be as little at £50; one-way/return flights to Beijing cost around £390/510. The cheapest fully-inclusive Trans-Siberian holidays cost from around £1800 including flights to and from London.

Open plan *platzkart* carriage, with 54 bunks arranged in groups of six.

From New York, one-way flights cost around US$750 to Moscow and about the same to Beijing, depending on the season. The cheapest fully inclusive Trans-Siberian holidays cost from around US$4000 per person in high season, including flights.

From Australia, single flights cost as little as A$428 to Beijing or A$1350 to Moscow, depending on the season. The cheapest fully inclusive Trans-Manchurian trip costs around A$5200 per person including two nights in Moscow. A 10-day Vladivostok to Moscow budget package costs about the same with flights.

Hotel costs

The price and value of accommodation in Russia varies wildly. **Hostels** in major cities charge about US$20-35/£15-23/€17-28 per dorm bed or US$75-105/£50-70/€60-80 for a private room. **Homestays** are an option in most larger Trans-Siberian towns, at about US$45-60/£30-40/€34-47 per person per night including some or all meals. If travelling independently, you can cut costs by **CouchSurfing** (see p61). **Mid-range hotels** cost around US$90-150/£60-100/€70-110 for a single or US$110-220/£66-132/€80-160 for a double with attached bathroom. Independent travellers who search out basic rooms with shared bathrooms in cheaper hotels can expect to pay US$40-60/£30-40/€35-45 for a single or US$45-65/£32-42/€35-48 for a double. Breakfast is sometimes included in the price.

A young *provodnitsa* (carriage attendant); many are students doing summer work.

Moscow, St Petersburg, Vladivostok and Beijing are the only places with genuinely **five-star hotels** (US$645/£430/€518 or more per night) although a number of Trans-Siberian cities, including Khabarovsk and Irkutsk, have good four-star places. Hotel prices in Moscow and St Petersburg are higher than anywhere else in the country.

For more information on accommodation see pp60-62.

Train classes

Trans-Siberian train carriages are classed as either *platzkart* (3rd class), an open-plan dorm on rails, *kupé* (coupé; also called 2nd, hard or tourist class), with four-berth closed compartments; or *spalny vagon* (SV, also called 1st or soft class), with comfortable two-berth compartments, sometimes with washbasins.

Typical *kupé* compartment on a Russian train.

INTRODUCTION

❏ Train fares

Approximate sample fares (excluding any booking fees) are shown below for a non-stop, single (one-way) journey on each of the main routes across Siberia. They are what you would pay for a ticket, were you to buy it over the counter in Moscow or Beijing; those offered by some Western travel agents may cost substantially more. Prices are also subject to increase, particularly in times of high demand. At the time of writing you could get significant discounts on upper berths in platzkart and kupé, as they are less popular than bottom ones. On the non-stop trains between Moscow and Beijing you don't have the option of travelling platzkart; it's either kupé or SV. Within Russia, most trains give you all three price options.

The fares below are sample prices for the most popular trains:

● **Trans-Siberian route** (Moscow–Vladivostok with Rossiya 002)
platzkart (3rd) R10,642 = US$321/£195/€235
kupé (2nd) R16,124 = US$486/£295/€356
SV (1st) R29,928 = US$903/£548/€661

● **Trans-Manchurian route** (Moscow–Beijing with Vostok 020)
platzkart (3rd) not available on non-stop trains
kupé (2nd) US$851/£544/€656
SV (1st) US$1205/£770/€929

● **Trans-Mongolian route** (Moscow–Beijing with Pekin 004)
platzkart (3rd) not available on non-stop trains
kupé (2nd) US$732/£468/€564
SV (1st) US$1146/£732/€882

On Trans-Mongolian train Nos 003/004, however, SV compartments are four-berth and identical in layout to all other services' kupé compartments except a bit wider, so they are poor value. But these trains also have an additional '*de luxe 1st*' class: carpeted two-berth compartments with armchairs and attached bathrooms (currently still the only ones with showers on train Nos 003/004).

Few compartments are single sex. Foreigners may find themselves sharing with other foreigners if they've booked through an agency that deals mainly with non-Russians. For further details on train classes see p114.

BREAKING YOUR JOURNEY   [see map between pp9-10]

All major cities on the Trans-Siberian can be visited. If you're booking through an agency, plan carefully: once you have started on your trip, it's too late to change your itinerary. But if you travel independently you can just buy tickets as you go along, and stop off whenever and wherever you like.

> If you're booking through an agency, plan carefully: once you have started on your trip, it's too late to change your itinerary

If your trip starts in **Moscow** (see p168) you'll need several days to see the iconic sights of Russia's illustrious capital: the Kremlin, Red Square and numerous world-class museums and galleries, and sample its cosmopolitan dining scene and vibrant nightlife. A side-trip to **St Petersburg** (p136) is highly worthwhile for its splendid waterways, palaces and priceless art, or else you can choose to begin your journey there. At the other end, **Beijing** (p384) beckons with its neon, mind-bogglingly vast Tiananmen Square and the Forbidden City, proximity to the Great Wall of China and any Chinese cuisine you can think of.

In between there are the 'Golden Ring' cities of **Vladimir** (p224), one of Russia's oldest, and **Nizhny Novgorod** (p237) with an impressive Kremlin of its own, and historically rich and yet very modern **Yekaterinburg** (p251), infamous as the massacre site of the Romanov family. **Novosibirsk** (p274) is the vast capital of Western Siberia with an impressive Lenin statue and a superb locomotive museum, **Tomsk** (p282) is an interesting university town specialising in wooden 'lace' architecture and **Krasnoyarsk** (p288), situated on the slow-moving Yenisei, is the gateway to outdoor adventures in Stolby Nature Reserve. **Irkutsk** (p297), capital of Eastern Siberia, is the gateway to **Lake Baikal** (p308), the world's deepest freshwater lake and one of the great natural wonders of the world; a stay beside the lake is not to be missed. The Buryat town of **Ulan-Ude** (p319) is near Russia's largest and most colourful Buddhist monastery, and cosmopolitan **Khabarovsk** (p334) has a particularly pleasant promenade along the Amur river, as well as a cluster of good museums. **Vladivostok** (p342), the bustling home port of Russia's Pacific Fleet, is the eastern railway terminus, with a new bridge to rival San Francisco's, steep streets, spectacular views of the Golden Horn Bay and a great dining scene.

Those headed to or from Beijing may wish to stop in **Ulaanbaatar** (p353), the somewhat chaotic capital of Mongolia, and use it as a springboard for visiting the Gobi Desert, staying in gers with nomads and taking part in adventures on horseback and camelback.

When to go

The mode of life which the long dark nights of winter induce, the contrivances of man in his struggle with the climate, the dormant aspect of nature with its thick coverage of dazzling snow and its ice-bound lakes now bearing horses and the heaviest burdens where ships floated and waves rolled, perhaps only a fortnight ago: – all these scenes and peculiar phases of life render a journey to Russia very interesting in winter.
Murray's *Handbook for Travellers in Russia, Poland and Finland* **(1865)**

For many people 'Siberia' evokes a picture of snowy scenes from the film *Dr Zhivago*, and if they are not to be disappointed, winter is probably the best time to go. It is, after all, the most Russian of seasons, a time of fur coats, sleighrides and chilled vodka. In sub-

Lake Baikal in winter. When the ice forms it gets thick enough to drive across.

zero temperatures, with the bare birch and fir trees encased in ice, Siberia looks as one imagines it ought to – a barren, desolate wasteland (the train, however, is well heated). Furthermore, during the snowy months you can take part in husky sledding, snow mobile rides, ice biking and expeditions with reindeer if you choose to stop by Lake Baikal.

Russian cities, too, look best and feel most 'Russian' under a layer of snow. St Petersburg with its brightly painted Classical architecture is far more attractive in the winter months when the weather is crisp and skies clear. But if you want to spend time in any Siberian city you'll find it more enjoyable to go in late spring, summer or autumn, when outdoor conditions are more visitor friendly.

In Siberia the heaviest snowfalls and coldest temperatures – as low as minus 40°C (minus 40°F) in Krasnoyarsk and some other towns the train passes through – occur in December and January. From late January to early April the weather is generally cold and clear. Spring comes late. In July and August it is warm enough for an invigorating dip in Lake Baikal. The birch and aspen provide a beautiful autumnal display in September and October.

In Moscow the average temperature is 23°C (73.4°F) in summer and minus 9°C (+16°F) during the winter; there are occasional heavy summer showers.

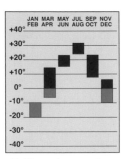

Moscow – temperature (average max/min °C)

Tourist season

The tourist season runs from May through September, peaking from mid-July to early September. In the low season (October to April) some accommodation may be closed, but you'll also find it much easier to get a booking for the train at short notice at this time and there are certain tours that are only available during the colder months (ie trekking with reindeer near Severobaikalsk, see p412). During the summer it can be difficult to get a place on the popular non-stop Moscow–Beijing route without planning several weeks ahead.

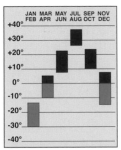

Beijing – temperature (average max/min °C)

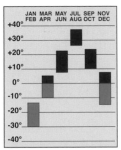

Irkutsk – temperature (average max/min °C)

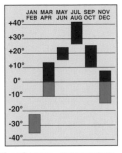

Ulaanbaatar – temperature (average max/min °C)

Best churches and cathedrals
● **St Basil's Cathedral (above,** see p172), **Moscow,** with its instantly recognisable multi-coloured domes
● **Church of the Resurrection Built on Spilt Blood, St Petersburg** (p140) – where Tsar Alexander II was assassinated in 1881
● **Church of the Intercession on the Nerl** (p230) – a beautiful, historically significant church near **Vladimir**
● **Chapel of the Revered Martyr Grand Princess Yelizaveta Fyodorovna, Yekaterinburg** (p254) – appealing little wooden memorial next to the garish church dedicated to the Romanovs

Best short hikes and treks
- **Stolby National Park** (see p295) – forested trails among incredible rock formations in the hills of Krasnoyarsk
- **Lake Baikal** (p308) – Great Baikal Trail and Frolikha Adventure Coastline Trail – trek the network of trails in the forested wilderness around Lake Baikal
- **Olkon Island** (p317) – (**opposite**)

- **Great Wall of China** – (**above**, p408) tackle the crumbling battlements at Simatai, Jingshanling and Mutianyu
- **Mongolia** – Hike to Turtle Rock in Gorkhi-Terelj National Park (p373) or ascend Bogd Khan Uul (p374) near Ulaanbaatar
- Take the hillside path (p411) overlooking Lake Baikal in Severobaikalsk (**opposite, bottom right**)

Lake Baikal

● One of the most sacred sites for the Buryat people is Shaman Rock (**right**) on Olkhon Island (see p317).

● (**Above**): *Obo* ('sacred place'), near Shaman Rock. Lengths of cloth are attached as offerings and can be any colour other than black, the colour of death.

● (**Below, left**) Hikers on a ridge at the northern end of Olkhon Island.

● (**Below, right**): Viewpoint in Severobaikalsk.

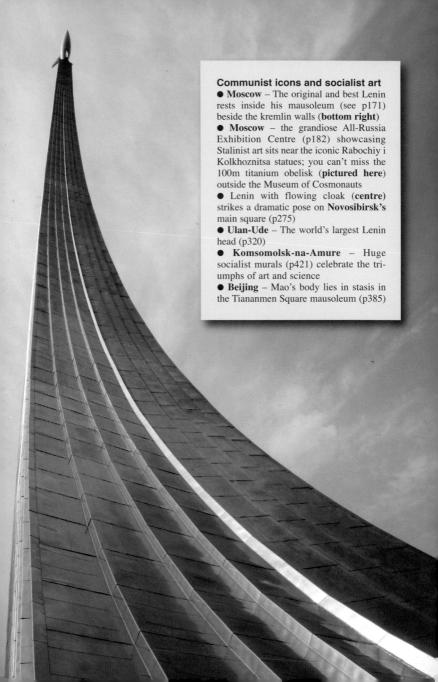

Communist icons and socialist art
● **Moscow** – The original and best Lenin rests inside his mausoleum (see p171) beside the kremlin walls (**bottom right**)
● **Moscow** – the grandiose All-Russia Exhibition Centre (p182) showcasing Stalinist art sits near the iconic Rabochiy i Kolkhoznitsa statues; you can't miss the 100m titanium obelisk (**pictured here**) outside the Museum of Cosmonauts
● Lenin with flowing cloak (**centre**) strikes a dramatic pose on **Novosibirsk's** main square (p275)
● **Ulan-Ude** – The world's largest Lenin head (p320)
● **Komsomolsk-na-Amure** – Huge socialist murals (p421) celebrate the triumphs of art and science
● **Beijing** – Mao's body lies in stasis in the Tiananmen Square mausoleum (p385)

Best modern art

● **(Above) Moscow graffiti** (see p180) giant murals courtesy of local and international street artists

● **Moscow's Gorky Park** (p177) – Garage, making artistic waves in the park

● **St Petersburg** – Erarta (see p147): bastion of contemporary art and interactive installations

● **Perm** – the best of contemporary art in the city is at PERMM (p245)

Greatest man-made achievements
- **(Above):** The immense **Golden Horn Bridge** (see p342) – Vladivostok's answer to the Golden Gate Bridge
- **Great Wall of China** (p407) – it didn't stop the invaders but still looks mightily impressive
- **Bratsk Dam** (p409) – the train lines run along the top of this immense dam
- **Yenisey Hydroelectric Dam** (p296) near Divnogorsk – the constructions along the top surely served as inspiration for AT-AT walkers in Star Wars

(**Above**): American built Ea3246, plinthed at Tynda station. (**Below**): Wooden lace window frame, Tomsk. There are still some traditional ornately-decorated wooden buildings in many Siberian towns.

Locomotives & great train rides
● The **Circumbaikal Railway** (see p311) between Port Baikal and Slyudyanka
● Tunnels, cliffs and rivers on the **approach to Beijing** (p490) along the Trans-Mongolian railway
● Taiga, snow-tipped mountains and mighty rivers along the **Severobaikalsk-Tynda** stretch (pp499-501) of the BAM
● **Seyatel Museum** (p281) – an impressive collection of locomotives 25km from Novosibirsk and **Novosibirsk's History Museum of the West Siberian Railway** (p276) with its models of Russian steam engines through the ages

Gulags and WWII
● **Perm-36** (p250) – the worst of Siberia's notorious forced labour camps
● **Germ Warfare Base; 731 Division, Harbin** (p379) – where the Japanese 'experimented' with prisoners of war
● **Museum of the Leningrad Blockade** (p145), St Petersburg – the harrowing story of a starving city

Greatest kremlins

● **Tobolsk (left)**, with its golden domes and splendid cathedrals (see p266)
● **Nizhny Novgorod** (p238) – walk its fortified walls and check out the exhibitions inside its towers
● **Rostov** (p211) – the most intimate Kremlin, where you can sleep in the former servants' quarters
● **Suzdal (below)** – 11th century kremlin (p231) surrounded by an earthen rampart

Best food and drink experiences

● Feast on every type of Chinese cuisine imaginable – from Imperial cuisine and Peking duck to Szechuan, Cantonese and Yunnan in Beijing (p401)
● Try smoked omul **(left)**, a fish endemic to Lake Baikal
● Explore the cosmopolitan dining scenes of Moscow, St Petersburg and Vladivostok
● Share the *buuz* (steamed dumplings), homemade bread, clotted cream and milky tea while staying with Mongolia's nomads

(**Left**): Omul for sale on a station platform
(**Far left**): Suzdal's famous honey mead

Best shopping

● Purchase traditional bows and arrows, felt boots, leatherwear and more at **Ulaanbaatar's State Department Store**, **Narantuul market** and **Mary & Martha Mongolia** (p371)
● Shop for tea and t-shirts near **Beijing's Drum and Bell Towers** or head for **Panjiayan Market** for antiques, Cultural Revolution relics and semi-precious stones
● Find local woodcarvings and Siberia's endemic charoite stone at **Listvyanka's lakeside market** (p312)
● Buy haute couture at **Moscow's GUM**

Top temples and monasteries
- **Ivolginsky Datsan** (**above**) – Russia's largest Buddhist temple complex (see p326)
- **Gandan Monastery** (p356) – Ulaanbaatar's most impressive Buddhist monastery
- **Lama Temple** (p388) – clouds of incense and dragon-decorated roofs in Beijing
- **Ganina Yama** (p261) – a wooded spot 16km from Yekaterinburg where the murdered Romanovs are worshipped as saints

Best palaces
- St Petersburg's **Yusupov Palace** (p143), where conspirators tried to murder Rasputin
- Beijing's **Summer Palace** (p390) – the luxurious lakeside retreat of the emperors
- **Tsarskoye Selo** (p149) – the sumptuous retreat of the tsars at Pushkin
- **Forbidden City** (p386) – the palaces of Chinese emperors don't come any grander than this (**below**)

Exotic cultures and festivals

● **(Above)** In Mongolia join a trip from **Ulaanbaatar** and spend time with the Tsaatan reindeer herders (see p373); in Russia trek with the Evenki into the mountains near **Severobaikalsk** (p412)

● In July, attend **Naadam Festival (below)** – Mongolia's archery, horse racing and wrestling extravaganza (p358)

● Join the chilly celebrations around the spectacular otherworldly ice sculptures at **Harbin's Ice Lantern Festival** (p379)

PLANNING YOUR TRIP

Bookings and visas

INDIVIDUAL ITINERARIES OR ORGANISED TOURS?

Note that regulations governing the issuing of Russian visas are particularly susceptible to change. Check the latest situation with your embassy or through the organisations listed on pp28-37.

Fully independent travel

Travelling independently is not difficult and is the best way to gain an insight into the 'real' Russia. Getting a tourist or business visa allows you to wander around freely and as of 2013 it has become even easier to purchase Russian intercity and even international rail tickets yourself, online.

For a tourist visa, together with your visa application you must present confirmation of (mostly fictitious) hotel bookings, furnished by a registered Russian tourist organisation. Various agencies and hotels can do this for you (see pp23-4). Some will furnish documentation of accommodation for the duration of your visa, in exchange for your booking only your first night's stay with them. Once you have your visa and are registered with the organisation that's sponsoring you, or one of their affiliates, you are free to travel wherever you want, irrespective of what the documentation says.

Although few Russians outside the large cities speak English, this shouldn't put you off. Many Russians are friendly and generous, and learning a bit of basic Russian before you go will help communication.

Semi-independent travel

This is a popular way for foreigners to travel on the Trans-Siberian. A specialist agency makes all accommodation and train bookings (with or without stops along the way), providing you in the process with the documentation needed for obtaining a Russian tourist visa. You choose departure dates and the number and length of stops, in effect designing your own trip. Once in Russia you're usually on your own, although some agencies offer guides to meet you at the station and help you organise your time in stopover cities. You'll often get good-quality accommodation in Moscow as part of the deal. Numerous travel agents can make these arrangements (see pp28-37), or you can deal directly with locally based Trans-Siberian specialists such as Monkey Business in Beijing (see p36) and Hong Kong (see p37).

Group tours

Some visitors (predominantly retirees) come to Russia in organised groups. Going with a tour group certainly takes much of the hassle out of the experience, but it also means there isn't much room for doing your own thing and, unless you go on an expensive tailor-made tour, you can be stuck with travellers you may not get on with. Most tours are accompanied by an English-speaking guide from the moment you set foot in the country until the moment you leave. See pp28-37 for information on tour companies.

ROUTE PLANNING

Main services

The table opposite is a summary of some major Siberian train services. For timetables and other details see pp507-12, but note that timetables are subject to change. There may be occasional one-hour variations on account of differences between countries in implementing Daylight Saving Time.

❏ **What if I don't want to do it all by train?**

Of course you needn't sit in a train for a week to see Siberia or Mongolia. It's quite feasible to fly to or from an intermediate point and travel only part of the way by train. Major airports along the Trans-Siberian which have nonstop air connections with Moscow, Beijing or other international hubs include the following (the prices quoted are for one-way flights):

● **Yekaterinburg** (Moscow daily, from US$120; Frankfurt 3/week, Prague and Cologne weekly)

● **Novosibirsk** (Moscow daily, from US$150; Frankfurt and Hanover almost daily in summer, from US$360; Beijing 3/week, from US$430; Seoul weekly, from US$420)

● **Irkutsk** (Moscow daily, from US$300; Tokyo weekly, from US$700; Tianjin, Shenyang and Dalian weekly, from US$550)

● **Vladivostok** (Moscow daily, from US$150; Harbin weekly, from US$320; Seoul 4/week, from US$550; Osaka weekly, from US$650; Tokyo 2/week, from US$540; and Hanoi weekly, from US$580)

● **Ulaanbaatar** (Moscow 4/week, from US$650; Beijing 1-2/day, from US$240; Tokyo weekly, from US$820; Seoul 10/week, from US$490).

Outbound air tickets are generally easy to buy a few days ahead (but see the note below about the Naadam Festival).

If you wish to break up your train journey, you can book tickets for specific route segments online at 🖳 www.rzd.ru; Trans-Siberian specialist agencies such as those listed on pp28-37 can also arrange rail tickets for specific segments, although buying these on arrival is quite feasible and gives you more flexibility to alter your plans. You needn't book more than a day ahead for short segments, but you may need more time for longer ones such as Irkutsk–Moscow. Sleeping berths may be scarce on services not originating in your proposed departure town. From October to April it's easy to book almost any train at short notice.

Possibilities include: No 005/006 Ulaanbaatar–Moscow, No 023/024 Beijing–Ulaanbaatar, No 025/026 Novosibirsk–Moscow and No 361/362 Ulaanbaatar–Irkutsk. Certain services and times get heavily booked – eg those to and from Ulaanbaatar around Mongolia's Naadam Festival in mid-July.

❏ **Not the Trans-Siberian Express!**
Travel writers often wax lyrical about the fabled 'Trans-Siberian Express' but in fact no **regular** train service of that name exists. While the British generally refer to their trains by a time (eg 'the 10:35 to Clapham'), the Russians and Chinese identify theirs by a number (eg 'Train 003' from Beijing to Moscow). As in other countries a few crack services have been singled out and given names, but 'Trans-Siberian Express' is not among them. 'Trans-Siberian', 'Trans-Mongolian' and 'Trans-Manchurian' are, however, common terms for the main **routes** across Siberia and between Moscow and Beijing.

The train which runs all the way from Moscow to Vladivostok is the 002, and going in the other direction it's the 001; both services are also called the *Rossiya*. The 020 covers the full Trans-Manchurian route from Moscow to Beijing, while in the other direction it's the 019; these are both called the *Vostok*. Trains on the Trans-Mongolian route between Moscow and Beijing, and most other long-distance services, are identified only by number.

There are now, however, some luxurious special tourist trains (see box p30).

Local times are given in the table below but note that official Russian timetables use **Moscow Time** only.

The trains that run across Siberia are working services used by local people, and they're very popular. On most routes they run to capacity, especially in summer (when additional services may be laid on). Buying tickets as you go along isn't too difficult, as some Russians usually leave it to the last minute, but booking in advance means getting the berth you want. Barring travelling in peak season, if you book a day before you want to travel, you'll probably get what you want on the shorter sections, but you'll need to book further in advance if you want a ticket for the whole route or for a longer section such as Irkutsk–Moscow.

Train	Leaves	on	at	Arrives	on	at
001 *Rossiya*	Vladivostok	Odd days	04:25	Moscow	Day 7	05:52
002 *Rossiya*	Moscow	Even days	13.50	Vladivostok	Day 7	13:10
033 (Mongolia)	Beijing	Wed	08:05	Moscow	Mon	13:58
043 (Mongolia)	Moscow	Tue	21:35	Beijing	Mon	14:04
005	Ulaanbaatar	Tue Fri	14:25	Moscow	Tue Sat	13:58**
006	Moscow	Wed Thur	21:35	Ulaanbaatar	Mon Tue	06:40**
019 *Vostok* (Manchuria)	Beijing	Sat	23:00	Moscow	Fri	17:58***
020 *Vostok* (Manchuria)	Moscow	Sat	23:45	Beijing	Sat	05:46***
023 Beijing		Tue	08:05	Ulaanbaatar	Wed	13:20
024 Ulaanbaatar		Fri	07:15	Beijing	Fri	14:04

** **005**: *January to March & November to December once every two weeks, weekly from June to mid October and not running at all April & May;*
006 *as above but weekly June to September.*
*** *not running at all January to May.*

❏ NATIONAL HOLIDAYS AND FESTIVALS

When planning your trip it is worth taking into account national holidays and major festivals as these often have an effect on the ability to get train tickets and also to book accommodation.

RUSSIA
National holidays If a national holiday falls on Thursday, Friday and Saturday may also be holidays. If a holiday falls on Saturday or Sunday, Monday will be a holiday.

- 1 January: **New Year's Day**
- 7 January: **Russian Orthodox Christmas Day** – midnight church services everywhere.
- 23 February: **Defenders of the Motherland Day**
- 8 March: **International Women's Day**
- Late April/early May: **Paskha (Russian Orthodox Easter)** – midnight church services on the Easter Sunday in Russia, followed by eating of *paskhlny keks* (Easter cake) and exchanging of painted Easter eggs.
- 1 May: **Day of Spring and Labour** (formerly May Day or International Working People's Solidarity Day). The following work day is also a holiday.
- 9 May: **Victory Day**, military parades are held in Russia's big cities to commemorate the end of WWII (known in Russia as the 1941-45 Great Patriotic War).
- 12 June: **Russia Day**, commemorating the 1990 declaration of Russian sovereignty
- 7 November: **National Reconciliation Day** (formerly the Anniversary of the Great October Revolution) – military parades taking place on Moscow's Red Square and in other big cities.
- 12 December: **Constitution Day**
- 31 December: **New Year's Eve**, celebrated with raucous parties everywhere.

Many businesses tend to be closed the few days after New Year and many Russians have taken to celebrating Christmas on December 25 as well.

Festival and events Below are the best of the festivals that you might come across during your travels:
- Late February/early March: *Maslenitsa* **(Pancake Week)** – in Russia, the end of winter celebrated with folk shows and lots of pancake-eating before Lent.
- June: **White Nights** – parties, theatre and concert performances when the sun does not fully set on St Petersburg.
- June: **Maitreya Buddha Festival** – held at the Ivolginsky Datsan near Ulan-Ude.
- June: **Surkharban (Buryatiya Folk Festival)** – horse-riding and wrestling at the hippodrome in Ulan-Ude.
- Late December/January: **Russian Winter Festival** – troika rides and folk performances in Moscow and Irkutsk.

CHINA
National holidays It is not a good idea to travel on or around the following: 1 May, the week-long holiday following National Day or over the Chinese New Year as many places tend to close, demand outstrips supply with regard to train tickets and prices shoot up dramatically.

- 1 January: **New Year's Day**
- January/February: **Chinese New Year** – the biggest holiday of the year, with feasts and traffic chaos as people make their way home. It is on 19 February 2015, 8 February 2016, 28 January 2017 and 16 February 2018.

China – National holidays *(continued)*
● 8 March: **International Women's Day**
● 1 May: **International Labour Day**
● 4 May: **Youth Day**
● 1 June: **International Children's Day**
● 1 July: **Birthday of the Chinese Communist Party**
● 1 August: **Anniversary of the founding of the People's Liberation Army**
● 1 October: **National Day**

Festival and events Below are the best of the festivals that you might come across during your travels:
● 5 January-15 February: **Harbin Ice & Snow Festival** – a month of other-worldly ice sculptures and competitions in Harbin, China.
● March or April: The **birthday of Guanyin**, the Chinese Buddhist Goddess of Mercy – a good time to visit Buddhist temples. The birthday falls on the 19th day of the second moon.
● mid-May: **Great Wall Marathon** – book your spot in advance if you want to run one of the world's toughest marathons that involves scaling steep sections of the Great wall of China (💻 www.great-wall-marathon.com).
● June: **Dragon Boat Festival** – racing of colourful boats along China's larger rivers – a festival dating back at least 2500 years.

MONGOLIA
National holidays Constitution Day, International Women's Day and Mongolian Republic Day are generally normal working days. Book travel and accommodation well in advance if travelling during the Naadam Festival, as both get booked.
● 1 January: **Shin Jil (New Year's Day)**
● 13 January: **Constitution Day**, commemorating the adoption of the constitution on 13 January 1992
● January/February: **Tsagaan Sar (Lunar New Year)**; Mongolian New Year, celebrated during a three-day holiday
● 8 March: **International Women's Day**
● 1 June: **Mother and Children's Day**
● 11-13 July: A three-day public holiday during **Naadam Festival**, see below
● 26 November: **Mongolian Republic Day**
● 31 December: **New Year's Eve**, celebrated with raucous parties everywhere.

Festival and events Below are the best of the festivals that you might come across during your travels:
● Mid-March: **Camel Polo Winter Festival** – involves camels and polo in Ulaanbaatar.
● June: **Roaring Hooves Festival** – an international music festival (💻 www.roaringhooves.com) held in the Gobi Desert, Ulaanbaatar and elsewhere in Mongolia.
● 11-13 July: **Naadam** – Mongolia's biggest festival (see box pp358-9) involving horse races, archery and wrestling.
● August: **Mongolia Bike Challenge** – mountain-biking rally (💻 www.mongoliabikechallenge.com) that covers 1500km of some of Mongolia's best scenery.
● September: **Gobi Marathon** – a tough 42km marathon in the Gobi Desert (💻 www.gobimarathon.org).

PLANNING YOUR TRIP

❑ **The longest journey**
If it's a long-distance rail-travel record you're after, begin your journey in Vila Real
de Santo António in southern Portugal, cross Europe to Moscow, take the Trans-
Mongolian route from there to Beijing and continue to Ho Chi Minh City (Saigon) in
Vietnam – a journey of 17,852km (11,155 miles).

For an even longer journey you'll have to wait until the proposed 103km tunnel
under the Bering Strait goes ahead. If it really does you'll be able to travel all the way
from London to Mexico City via Moscow, Irkutsk, Magadan, Fairbanks and
Vancouver – approximately 25,500km (16,000 miles).

Moscow to Vladivostok

There are many trains on the line between Moscow and Vladivostok, but the
001/002 *Rossiya* train is the top choice for speed and service, though it's also
noticeably more expensive than slower trains. There are other very good trains
which cover shorter segments; these increase your options if you are making
stopovers along the way.

There are ferries from Vladivostok to Japan and Korea in the summer
months (see box p352).

Moscow to Beijing: Trans-Manchurian or Trans-Mongolian?

You have two route choices between Moscow and Beijing: the Trans-
Mongolian route via Ulaanbaatar in Mongolia, and the Trans-Manchurian route
via Harbin in China. There are advantages and disadvantages with each.

The Trans-Manchurian train is the 019/020 *Vostok*, while the Trans-
Mongolian Moscow–Beijing service is the 003/004 (sometimes shown as 0033/
0043), although there are additional, shorter-distance options including the
023/024 (Beijing–Ulaanbaatar) and 361/362 (Irkutsk–Naushki–Ulaanbaatar).
Only the 003/004 offer de luxe 1st class carriages (see p114), although travellers
who opt for kupé will find these carriages identical on both routes. Unless
you're American, Israeli or Indian you need a Mongolian transit visa on this
route, even if you do not stop along the way. The Trans-Mongolian journey
takes about 12 hours less than the Trans-Manchurian.

Despite long-standing Trans-Siberian lore, there's no difference between
the restaurant cars on the two routes as these are supplied by the country
through which you're travelling. Both trains have weekly departures in each
direction. Summer is the most difficult time to book a place on long-distance
trains on either route, so make arrangements several months in advance.

Stopping off in Mongolia If you're taking the Trans-Mongolian route,
breaking your journey in Ulaanbaatar is highly recommended, particularly for
stays with nomad families outside Ulaanbaatar, trips into the Gobi and visits to
Khuvsgul Nuur, Lake Baikal's smaller cousin in northern Mongolia.
Ulaanbaatar is the headquarters of numerous tour agencies who can arrange all
trips and relevant permits.

Side trips

There are numerous possibilities for side trips by rail, including on the **Siberian BAM Railway** (from Tayshet, Khabarovsk or Skovorodino) and the **Turksib Railway** (from Novosibirsk), with links via the Turksib to the **Kazakhstan–China Railway**. See pp109-11 for more on all these lines. From **Blagoveshchensk** (see p473), on a spur off the Moscow–Vladivostok line at Belogorsk, you can cross the Amur River by boat to Heihe in China. With onward connections via Harbin, this little-known alternative to the Trans-Manchurian line is actually the cheapest land route from Moscow to Beijing at present.

A branch line runs from Sibirtsevo, near Vladivostok, via Ussuriysk to Pyongyang in **North Korea**, although at the moment these services are not for tourists. For visitors, the only way to enter North Korea by rail is via Beijing. From Beijing it's also easy to continue by rail into **Vietnam**; it's a three-night journey.

VISAS

Visas are required of most foreigners visiting Russia, Mongolia and China. Getting a Russian visa is reasonably straightforward, but the process is still con-voluted. It's straightforward to get either a Chinese visa or Mongolian visa. Visa regulations do change, so check with relevant embassies.

Russian visas must be obtained in one's country of residence. Chinese visas are also easiest to obtain in your home country rather than a third-party coun-try; applying elsewhere requires exceptional amounts of paperwork and can be very time-consuming. Mongolian visas may be obtained easily in most coun-tries, but you may require an invitation if you apply outside your country of res-idence. None of the visas can be acquired at land borders and visas for all three countries are valid for entry within three months of issue, so you have to time your applications to coincide with your proposed trip.

Visa agencies

The following can assist you with applying for visas for all three countries: **Visa HQ** 🖳 www.visahq.co.uk; **Monkey Business** see p36; **Express to Russia** 🖳 www.expresstorussia.com; **Visa Link** 🖳 visalink.com.au; **IVDS** 🖳 www.vi sum-dienst.de; **Action Visas** 🖳 www.action-visas.com.

❑ **Health insurance requirements**
Citizens of countries signatory to the Schengen Convention (Austria, Belgium, Denmark, Finland, France, Germany, Greece, Iceland, Italy, Luxembourg, Netherlands, Norway, Portugal, Spain and Sweden) and from Israel, Estonia and Switzerland who apply for a Russian visa are officially required to produce proof of medical insurance valid in Russia. This is hardly enforced. Some embassies don't ask at all, while others will accept just about any insurance document. In any case, it pays to have comprehensive health insurance when travelling across Russia.

To apply for Russian invitations in particular, contact: **Way to Russia** (⌨ waytorussia.net) or **Visa Able** (⌨ www.visaable.com).

Russian visas

A Russian visa is a one-page form stuck directly into your passport, containing your passport information, entry and exit dates, and the name and registration of the organisation that has invited you. It is best to apply at the embassy or consulate in your home country. Check their requirements online before applying, but typically, in addition to a completed visa application form (now available online at ⌨ https://visa.kdmid.ru), you need a passport valid for six months, an invitation/confirmation document, accommodation voucher(s), a passport-sized photo and the visa fee.

If you're starting your trip in Beijing, it's simplest to get your visa in your home country, though the Russian consulate in Beijing (⌨ www.russia.org .cn/eng) and the Russian Embassy in Hong Kong (⌨ www.russia.com.hk) may also issue transit, tourist and business visas since the visa application rules have recently been simplified.

The visa fee depends on where you apply, your nationality, the type and duration of the visa, and how quickly you want it. For Americans a single-entry tourist visa costs from US$130, for British nationals from £48, and for EU citizens from €35, depending on the country. Processing takes five working days, although you can get a next-day service by paying more.

● **Tourist visa** Tourist visas are non-extendable and issued for up to 30 days, with single-entry and double-entry versions. A tourist visa requires an invitation (see opposite).

If you want to stay longer than 30 days you'll need to apply for a business visa or another type of visa. If heading west when leaving Russia, bear in mind that many trains into Eastern Europe cross the border after midnight, so make sure your visa is still valid.

● **Business visa** Business visas are issued for 3, 6 or 12 months and can be single entry, double entry, or multiple entry; they are valid for up to 90 days' travel within a six-month period. You'll require an invitation from a registered Russian business or from a specialised visa agency, such as VisaHQ.

Business visas are actually easier to arrange than tourist visas because you don't need to book accommodation. They're ideal for travellers who want a longer stay in Russia and you don't have to be a business visitor to apply for a business visa, but they are slightly more expensive to obtain than a tourist visa. A 3-month single entry business visa for Americans/British/some EU citizens costs US$130/£96/€35.

● **Private visa** This visa is for foreigners who are invited by Russian friends or relatives, is valid for three months and can be single or double entry. However, it can take a long time to obtain and is a lot of work for your relatives and friends (Russian nationals only), so it's far easier to apply either for a tourist or business visa.

● **Transit visa** Transit visas are normally given only to those who are in transit through Russia; for those transiting by air, visas are issued for only 72 hours. For non-stop Trans-Siberian journeys, whether originating in Moscow, Ulaanbaatar or Beijing, you can get 10-day visas which allow you to travel on the Trans-Siberian, stay in Moscow for a few days (if coming from the east) and then leave. If starting in Moscow, you may not linger there at the beginning of your trip. You may have to show your Russian rail ticket, and sometimes your onward ticket, when applying for the visa.

Visa invitations To get a tourist visa to Russia, you must first obtain an invitation ('visa support') or equivalent document (*podtverzhdenie* подтверждение) confirming your accommodation details while in Russia, plus one or more vouchers (*order* ордер) confirming payment for this accommodation. These documents may be issued by specialised visa agencies (see p23), travel agents (see pp28-37), as well as hotels or hostels registered to do so with the Russian Ministry of the Interior. The documents must all state your passport details, itinerary and duration of stay, along with the inviting organisation's address and registration number. If you're going on a package tour, your travel agent will organise everything and you'll see very little of this paperwork.

Although an itinerary must be specified, the visa doesn't list your proposed destinations, allowing independent travellers to visit places on the spur of the moment. Most travel companies will issue an invitation/confirmation only for the days for which you have paid to stay with them, but some will confirm accommodation for the duration of your visa in exchange for your booking just your first night's stay with them, leaving you free to go where you like after that.

Most travel agencies as well as hostels and hotels in Moscow (see pp196-9) and St Petersburg (see pp160-2) also offer visa registration (see below).

Visa extensions Tourist visas may not be extended at all, whereas extending other types of visas is both time-consuming and expensive. Exceptional circumstances (ie serious illness) may be taken into consideration as a legitimate reason for overstaying by a day or two, but avoid this at all costs by arranging a visa for a longer period than you might actually need. If you don't think that 30 days will be enough for you, seriously consider applying for a 90-day business visa.

Visa registration All visitors to Russia must register their visa within seven working days of arrival. Visas must be registered at least once during your trip. Registration is done with the Upravlenie Federalnoye Migratsionnoy Sluzhby (UFMS) – though not on Wednesdays – and most hotels and many hostels offer this visa-registration service either for free or for around £10 (US$15/€11). If your accommodation does not offer visa registration, you may need to use the services of an agency or do it yourself – a difficult process – at a post office (see 🖥 www.waytorussia.net/RussianVisa/Registration.html).

Technically, you must register within seven working days in any town that you stay in – a rule that's contradictory in nature. For example, if you stay in a town for two days without registering and then move on, you're technically breaking the rules, yet the same rules allow you seven days to register, so in that respect, you haven't broken them. In practice, as long as you register on arrival in Russia and hold on to your train, bus and plane tickets to prove that you didn't stay for seven working days in any of the places along the way, you shouldn't have any trouble, even if you hadn't managed to register more than once.

Mongolian visas

Mongolian **tourist visas** are issued for up to 30 days. There are single- and double-entry versions; for UK citizens a single-entry visa costs around £40 and takes 2-5 working days (£60 if processed in a day); a double-entry visa costs

PLANNING YOUR TRIP

❏ Embassies and consulates

● **Britain** VFS Global (🖥 ru.vfsglobal.co.uk; Russia Visa Application Centre, 15-27 Gee St, London EC1V 3RD, and 16 Forth St, Edinburgh EH1 3JX) processes visa applications on behalf of the Russian Embassy (🖥 www.rusemb.org.uk). Applications are accepted online, by post, or in person; the process for the latter is fairly speedy (8.30am-3pm Mon-Fri; passport collection 5-5.30pm).

The **Chinese Visa Service Application Centre** (🖥 www.visaforchina.org; 12 Old Jewry, London, EC2R 8DU; 9am-3pm Mon-Fri; passport collection 9am-4pm) is separate from the Chinese Embassy (🖥 www.chinese-embassy.org.uk). There are Chinese consulates in Manchester (🖥 manchester.china-consulate.org) and Edinburgh (🖥 edinburgh.china-consulate.org).

The **Mongolian Embassy** (🖥 www.embassyofmongolia.co.uk) is at 7 Kensington Court, London W8 5DE (drop-off and collection 10am-noon Mon-Fri).

● **USA** The consular office of the **Russian Embassy** (🖥 www.russianembassy.org) is at 2641 Tunlaw Road, NW, Washington DC 20007 (9am-12.30pm Mon-Fri). There are also consulates in San Francisco (2790 Green Street, CA 94123), New York (9 E 91st Street, NY 10128), Seattle (600 University Street, Suite 2510, Seattle, WA 98121) and Houston (1333 West Loop South, Suite 1300, Houston, TX 77027).

The consular office of the **Chinese Embassy** (🖥 www.china-embassy.org) is at 2201 Wisconsin Ave NW, Suite 110, Washington DC 20007. There are consulates and visa offices in New York (520 12th Ave), Chicago (100 West Erie Street), Houston (3417 Montrose Boulevard), Los Angeles (3rd Floor, 500 Shatto Place) and San Francisco (Visa Office Consulate General of the PRC, 1450 Laguna Street).

The **Mongolian Embassy** (🖥 www.mongolianembassy.us) is at 2833 M Street NW, Washington DC 20007 (9am-noon Mon-Fri) and there's also a consulate in San Francisco (465 California street, Suite 200).

● **Canada** The Russian Visa Centre of the **Russian Embassy** (🖥 www.rusembassy .ca) is at Suite 505, 294 Albert Street, Ottawa, Ontario (9.30am-12.30pm). There are consulates in Montreal (🖥 www.montreal.mid.ru) and Toronto (🖥 www.toronto .mid.ru).

The Visa for China Application Centre (🖥 www.visaforchina.org) of the **Chinese Embassy** (🖥 ca.china-embassy.org) is at Suite 1501, 393 University Avenue, Toronto, Ontario; 250-999 West Broadway, Vancouver, BC; and Suite 200, 855, 8th Avenue, SW, Calgary, Alberta. All three centres are open 9am-3pm on weekdays for submission of applications and 9am-4pm for collection. The **Mongolian Embassy** (🖥 www .mongolianconsulate.org.au) is at 151 Slater St, Suite 503, Ottawa.

£55/75. Transit visas are available for stays of three days and cost from £35. Embassy officials may ask to see an onward (eg Russian or Chinese) visa.

Mongolia has **consular offices** along the route of the Trans-Siberian, in Irkutsk (p302), Ulan-Ude (pp322-3) and Beijing (p397). The application process is straightforward. You'll need to apply in person with a passport valid for at least six months, one or two photos and the visa fee.

Citizens of the USA may stay in Mongolia up to 90 days without a visa, but if they plan to stay longer than 30 days, they must register with the authorities within seven days of arrival. Israeli citizens can stay up to 30 days without a visa.

● **Australia** The **Russian consulate** (⌨ www.sydneyrussianconsulate.com) is at 7-9 Fullerton St, Woollahra, NSW 2025 (9.30am-12.30pm Mon-Thur).

There are Chinese Visa Application Centres (⌨ www.visaforchina.com.au) affiliated with the **Chinese consulates** in Sydney: Level 5, 299 Elizabeth Street; Perth: Ground Floor, 256 Adelaide Terrace; Brisbane: Part Level 4, 140 Ann Street; Melbourne: Ground Floor, 570 St Kilda Road; and Canberra: Suite 201, Level 2, Canberra House, 40 Marcus Clarke Street. All are open for submission of documents and collection Mon-Fri 9am-3pm.

The **Mongolian Embassy** (⌨ www.mongoliaconsulate.com.au) is at 23 Culgoa Circuit, O'Malley, Canberra, ACT 2606; the consulate section is open 9am-5pm.

● **New Zealand** The **Russian** consular office (⌨ www.newzealand.mid.ru) is at 57 Messines Rd, Karori, Wellington; the consular section is open Mon-Fri 9.30am-1pm. The Visa Office of the **Chinese consulate** (⌨ www.chinaconsulate.org.nz) is at 630 Great South Rd, Greenlane, Auckland. Document submission is Mon-Fri 9am-noon; collection is 2-4pm.

Mongolia's Honorary Consulate (⌨ www.mongolianconsulate-nz.com) is at 86 Kings Crescent, Lower Hutt 5010, Wellington; the consulate section is open Mon-Wed 10am-3pm by prearranged appointment.

● **South Africa** The consular office of the **Russian Embassy** (⌨ russianembassy.org.za) is at 316 Brook St, Menlo Park, Pretoria (Mon-Fri 8.30-11.30am). There is also a consulate in Cape Town: 8 Riebeek St.

The **Chinese Embassy** (⌨ www.chinese-embassy.org.za) is at 225 Athlone St, Arcadia, Pretoria. There are consulates in Durban: 45 Stirling Crescent, Durban North; Cape Town: 25 Rhodes Avenue, Newland; and Johannesburg: 25 Cleveland Road, Sandhurst, Sandton; these are open Mon-Fri 8.30-11.30am.

There is **no Mongolian embassy** in South Africa.

● **Japan** The consular division of the **Russian Embassy** (⌨ www.rusconsul.jp) is at 2-1-1 Azabudai, Minato-ku, Tokyo 106-0041. There are consulates in Osaka, Niigata, Hakodate and Sapporo. Since January 2013 all applications for a visa in Japan need to completed online and then the form needs to be printed out and taken to the embassy with the relevant supporting documents.

The **Chinese Embassy** (⌨ www.china-embassy.or.jp/chn) is at 3-4-33 Moto-Azabu, Minato-ku, Tokyo 106-0046. The **Mongolian Embassy** (⌨ www.mn.emb-japan.go.jp) is at 21-4 Kamiyama-cho, Shibuya-ku, Tokyo 150-0047.

It may be possible to pick up a 30-day tourist visa at Ulaanbaatar's airport or at the land border if travelling by train, but it's best to get a visa in advance.

It's possible to **extend your visa** for up to 30 extra days in Ulaanbaatar. If you intend to stay in Mongolia for more than 30 days, regardless of whether you need a visa or not, you must **register** within seven days of arrival (see pp364-5).

Chinese visas

Most foreigners require a visa to visit China (with the exception of Hong Kong). **Tourist visas** are generally given for up to 30 days, although if you apply for a shorter period you may only be granted a visa for the period you request. At the time of writing, total costs (including visa fee) for a single-/double-entry visa are £66/81 for UK citizens and US$208/208 for US citizens.

One-month **extensions** are easy to arrange in most cities within China through the Foreign Office Branch of the Public Security Bureau.

The process of getting a visa is straightforward at most Chinese embassies. In addition to your passport and the application form you'll need one photo, the visa fee and the processing fee. Note: same-day or next-day turnaround is not available. The list of places you wish to visit on the application form is merely a formality; it's not checked and doesn't limit you to those places. You must apply for your visa at the consulate under whose jurisdiction your place of residence falls (with the exception of Hong Kong, where it's also possible for foreigners to get visas); fees and requirements vary from place to place.

Something to bear in mind before planning a trip is that if your profession can be interpreted as 'media' in any way, there's an additional restriction: you may only apply for a Chinese visa a month before you wish to travel, regardless whether it's for business or pleasure, whereas other tourists may apply up to three months before they wish to enter China. It's possible to collect your visa in person; having your passport and visa sent back to you by post may take up to three weeks.

Other visas

If you are starting from Beijing and planning to continue westward through Europe after you leave Moscow or St Petersburg, depending on your own nationality you may need transit visas for some countries bordering Russia, including Belarus. At the time of writing, nationals of most countries need a visa to visit or transit Belarus.

Citizens of EU countries and the US can visit Ukraine visa-free for up to 90 days.

MAKING A BOOKING IN BRITAIN

While it is relatively straightforward to organise an independent or semi-independent journey on the railway if you have the time and the inclination, a number of travellers benefit from an agency's expertise when it comes to drawing up an itinerary, arranging stopovers and accommodation along the way and providing advice and support. The following companies offer Trans-Siberian,

Trans-Mongolian and Trans-Manchurian, as well as more general Russia tour packages.

● **Go Russia** (☎ 020-3355 7717, 🖳 www.justgorussia.co.uk) offer a variety of Trans-Siberian packages as well as a large number of adventure, eco and cultural tours and language courses. They also hold monthly seminars about Russia in London.

● **Great Rail Journeys** (☎ 01904-734061, 🖳 www.greatrail.com) offer a 19-day Trans-Siberian tour including a visit to Warsaw and with travel from Moscow to Vladivostok on the Golden Eagle Trans-Siberian Express (see box p30) – in summer and in winter – and a 20-day tour on the Tsar's Gold Private Train in summer; shorter trips excluding Warsaw are also available, as are tailor-made trips.

● **IntoRussia** (formerly Intourist; ☎ 0844-875 4026, 🖳 www.into-russia.co.uk) has over 70 years' experience booking trips and can help arrange all aspects of a journey on the Trans-Siberian, Trans-Mongolian or the Trans-Manchurian as well as tailor-made and luxury journeys. They can also arrange visas and a variety of tours in Russia and China.

● **Intrepid** (freephone ☎ 0808-274 5111, 🖳 www.intrepidtravel.com) offer a 21-day Trans-Mongolian experience from Russia to China and a 16-day Trans-Siberian trip as well as many other tours in Russia, China and Mongolia.

● **On the Go Tours** (☎ 020-7371 1113, 🖳 www.onthegotours.com/Trans-Siberian-Railway) caters for all budgets, offering tours in different parts of the world, including the western section of the Trans-Siberian, themed tours of Russia and tailor-made tours.

PLANNING YOUR TRIP

❏ **Getting to Russia or China from Britain**
There are daily **flights** to Moscow with several major airlines, starting at around £129/197 one way/return. However, budget-carrier easyJet offers one-way fares to Moscow Domodedovo (see p192) from around £50.

Flying to Beijing is more expensive: at least £390 one-way, £510 return. STA Travel (🖳 www.statravel.co.uk) and Trailfinders (🖳 www.trailfinders.co.uk) are both good travel agencies when it comes to searching for the cheapest airfare. Both do discounted flights for students and people under 26. Other good websites to try are Flight Centre (🖳 www.flightcentre.co.uk), Ebookers (🖳 www.ebookers.com) and Skyscanner (🖳 www.skyscanner.net).

The Man in Seat Sixty-One (🖳 www.seat61.com – see box p43) has very useful information on the numerous **rail** options available, including taking the Eurostar from London to Brussels and then a direct two-day train via Berlin, Warsaw and Minsk, Belarus, to Moscow, though having to get a Belarus visa can significantly increase the overall cost. Alternatively, you can hop on a St Petersburg train in Warsaw and go via Vilnius (with a change of train) instead. The Deutsche Bahn Travelservice (🖳 www .bahn.co.uk) can book a one-way ticket from London to Moscow for as little as £213 (advance purchase), depending on the season and availability.

Tickets to a range of European cities can be booked through Rail Europe (🖳 uk .voyages-sncf.com/en), Eurostar (🖳 www.eurostar.com), or DB Bahn (🖳 www.bahn .co.uk).

● **Railbookers** (☎ 020-3327 0800, 🖳 www.railbookers.com) can arrange tailor-made journeys from Moscow to Beijing as the classic journey or in luxury on either the *Tsar's Gold* train or the *Golden Eagle*; see box below.

● **Real Russia** (☎ 020-7100 7370, 🖳 www.realrussia.co.uk) See p33.

● **Regent Holidays UK** (☎ 020-7666 1244, 🖳 www.regent-holidays.co.uk) specialise in individual and group train tours, including the Trans-Siberian, Trans-Mongolian and BAM railways and pricier tours on the *Tsar's Gold* train (see box below).

● **Russia Experience** (☎ 0845-521 2910, 🖳 www.trans-siberian.co.uk) offer a variety of packages for budget and mid-range travellers and can help book accommodation and train tickets.

● **Russian National Tourist Office** (London ☎ 020-7985 1234, Edinburgh ☎ 0131-550 3709, 🖳 www.visitrussia.org.uk) can help book accommodation in Russia, offers various tours of the country and provides a visa service.

● **Sundowners Overland** (☎ 020-8877 7657, 🖳 www.sundownersoverland .com) have specialised in overland journeys across Asia for 50 years and offer everything from independent/tailor-made journeys to group tours and for all budgets on either the Trans-Siberian, Trans-Mongolian or Trans-Manchurian. Under the name **Vodka Train** (🖳 www.vodkatrain.com) they also offer loosely

---

❏ **Luxury private trains**
● The **Golden Eagle Trans-Siberian Express** is Russia's version of the Orient Express. On most journeys the train is pulled by a fully restored steam (P36) loco-motive. Accommodation is provided in three classes: the Imperial Suite, which includes a private guide at stops en route, and Gold and Silver class. The carriages are air conditioned and all compartments have en suite facilities with showers as well as flat-screen TVs. The train also offers fine dining and extensive wine lists.

The Golden Eagle is operated by Golden Eagle Luxury Trains Ltd (☎ 0161-928 9410, 🖳 www.goldeneagleluxurytrains.com); a two-week escorted tour from Moscow via Ulaanbaatar to Vladivostok (or vice-versa), including several nights in luxury hotels, costs from £9695 per person if travelling as a couple or from £13,995 if travelling solo. There are regular summer departures and occasional 'Winter Wonderland' tours, plus an annual July trip to Ulaanbaatar for the Naadam festival. Tours can either be booked direct with Golden Eagle, or through a number of other agencies.

● The **Tsar's Gold** train sleeps up to 200 passengers in air-conditioned carriages with four categories of accommodation: standard (which has three levels); Nostalgic Comfort (with a shower for every two cabins); Bolshoi; and Bolshoi Platinum (facil-ities are en suite for both the Bolshoi categories). The train has four restaurant cars so it is possible for all passengers to eat at the same time and the menu comprises tradi-tional Russian and international dishes. There is no dress code. In the evening the restaurants turn into a bar and lounge. On-board lectures in a variety of languages are offered. The Tsar's Gold operates between Moscow and Erlian; between Erlian and Beijing passengers change to a chartered Chinese train which only has standard level carriages.

Both of these trains can be booked by many of the agencies listed here.

---

structured, unescorted group journeys for people aged 18-35, with young local guides at stopover towns.
● **Steppes Travel** (☎ 0845-075 6079, 🖳 www.steppestravel.co.uk) offer tailor-made individual Trans-Siberian itineraries and tours, plus options for Moscow, St Petersburg and the Russian Far East.
● **The Trans-Siberian Travel Company** (☎ 020-8816 8925, 🖳 www.thetranssiberiantravelcompany.com) can book everything from the journey on whichever route and in whichever direction you prefer as well as either the *Tsar's Gold* and/or *Golden Eagle* luxury trains (see box opposite); in addition they offer a variety of tours in Russia, China and Mongolia.

Budget travellers booking from Britain should note that they can also arrange Trans-Siberian rail tickets through specialist agencies in China (see pp36-7) and Russia (see pp32-3).

MAKING A BOOKING IN CONTINENTAL EUROPE
From France
● **Espace Transsiberien** (☎ 09 70 46 18 03, 🖳 www.espace-transsiberien.com/fr) offer a range of Trans-Siberian tours.
● **Les Connaisseurs du Voyage** (☎ 01 53 95 27 00, 🖳 www.connaisseursvoyage.fr) specialise in tours of the world, including Trans-Siberian and Trans-Mongolian trips.

From Germany
● **Die Bahn** (🖳 www.reiseauskunft.bahn.de) With Deutsche Bahn's switched-on, multilingual travel service, you can make Trans-Siberian rail bookings and train bookings from Germany to Moscow online or by phone.
● **Gleisnost** (🖳 www.gleisnost.de) offers train journeys along the Trans-Siberian and Trans-Mongolian railways, and can organise ferry connections from Vladivostok to Korea and Japan.
● **Lernidee-Erlebnisreisen** (☎ 30-786 000 33, 🖳 www.lernidee.de) Journeys on trains and rivers. Siberian itineraries range from a 2nd-class ticket on the Moscow–Beijing train to stopovers in Mongolia (three nights including full board, with English-speaking guide).
● **Pulexpress** (☎ 30-887 1470, 🖳 www.pulexpress.de) Book Russian rail tickets and have them delivered with this official agent of Russian Railways.

From the Netherlands
● **Rusreis.nl** (🖳 www.rusreis.nl) Recommended by a reader as excellent value and helpful with their itinerary via Kazan.
● **Tozai Travel** (🖳 www.tozai.nl) Itineraries for individual travellers, including five different Netherlands to Beijing routes via Moscow.
● **Trans-Sputnik Nederland** (🖳 www.trans-sputnik.nl) Specialist in Trans-Siberian, Trans-Mongolian and Trans-Manchurian train tickets.
● **VNC Asia Travel** (🖳 www.vnc.nl) Group tours from Moscow to Beijing, with stopovers in Irkutsk and Mongolia, trips that take in the Naadam festival and journeys on the *Tsar's Gold* train (see box opposite).

❑ **Getting to Russia or China from continental Europe by air**

Numerous major and budget airlines from mainland Europe fly to Moscow and Beijing. Standard one-way/return fares from major cities tend to be around €90/135 to Moscow and €430/600 to Beijing.

In **France**, good budget flight websites to try are Last Minute (💻 www.last minute.fr) and Nouvelles Frontières (💻 www.nouvelles-frontieres.fr). From **Germany**, good travel agencies include STA Travel (💻 www.statravel.de), Just Travel (💻 www.justtravel.de) and Travel Overland (💻 www.traveloverland.de).

To get to Moscow or Beijing from **the Netherlands**, try NNVS Reisen (💻 www .nbbs.nl) or Cheap Tickets (💻 www.cheaptickets.nl) – both in Dutch. In **Spain**, Barcelo Viajes (💻 www.barceloviajes.com) is a good starting point, while in **Italy**, CTS Viaggi (💻 www.cts.it – in Italian) does discount air fares for students.

From Continental Europe to Moscow by train

Deutsche Bahn (DB Bahn; German Rail) has some of the best (and oldest) rail connections with Russia. There is a daily (June-Aug; Tue/Fri/Sun the rest of the year) train **from Berlin** (departure from Lichtenberg Station) to Moscow at 9.03pm, taking 25 hours. This is the *Moskva Express* and sleeping cars are attached for the St Petersburg route. Book your ticket via DB Bahn (💻 www.bahn.de). Since late 2011 the *Trans-European Express*, run by Russian Railways, has linked **Paris** with Moscow once again (3-6/week, around 60hrs).

From Minsk, Belarus, there are numerous daily trains to Moscow (11 hours, 20/day) and St Petersburg (15hrs, 3/day): however, you'll need a Belorussian visa.

Trains **from Warsaw** to Moscow (18-21hrs, 2/day) and Warsaw to St Petersburg (29hrs, daily) also go through Belarus, so you'll need a transit visa.

From Estonia there are trains to Moscow (15hrs, daily) and St Petersburg (6 hours, daily), as well as 6-7 express buses between Tallinn and St Petersburg. **From Helsinki, Finland,** there are trains to St Petersburg (3½-6½hrs, 3/day), including the high-speed *Allegro*, as well as a daily service to Moscow (13½hrs).

There are daily overnight trains **from Riga, Latvia**, to Moscow (16 hours) and St Petersburg (13hrs), as well as a couple of buses daily to both cities with Ecolines (💻 www.ecolines.net). **From Lithuania's Vilnius**, there are trains to Moscow (15hrs, 3/day) and to St Petersburg (15½hrs, 2/day). The Moscow-bound trains go via Minsk, Belarus, requiring you to have a Belorussian transit visa.

From Ukraine, there are frequent services to Moscow from all major cities, including: Kyiv (9½hrs, 18/day), Lviv (23hrs, daily), Odessa (23hrs via Kyiv, daily), Kharkiv (13hrs, 12/day) and Sevastopol (25hrs, daily). There are also daily trains to St Petersburg from Lviv (31hrs via Vilnius) and Kyiv (24hrs).

There are also regular services to Moscow and St Petersburg from **Amsterdam**, **Budapest**, **Prague** and **Vienna**.

From Russia

Almost all the hostels and hotels have travel desks and provide visa support and travel services. You could also try:

● **IntoRussia, formerly Intourist** (💻 www.intourist.com) can provide visa support, book train tickets, accommodation and tours. Branches in Moscow are at: Noviy Arbat 2, Moscow 119019 (☎ 495 783 1814) and at Sokolnitseskaya 4A, Moscow 107113 (☎ 495 926-43-87).

● **Real Russia** (☎ 499 653 8574, 🖳 www.realrussia.co.uk) Visas, accommodation, transfers, tours, excursions and more. Also East West Link (☎ 495 374 6562) for train tickets and visas.

If you are booking your tickets yourself in Russia or China you may find the sample booking forms on p128 (Russia) and pp132-3 (China) useful.

From Scandinavia

● **Eco Tour Production** (☎ 498 487 105, 🖳 www.nomadicjourneys.com) is a Swedish partner with Ulaanbaatar-based Nomadic Journeys (see p372); Eco Tour can also help with train journeys starting from Ulaanbaatar.

● **Intourist Norway** (🖳 www.intourist.no) can arrange tickets for all Russia routes (in either direction) as well as visas and accommodation.

MAKING A BOOKING IN NORTH AMERICA

From the USA

● The **China National Tourist Office** (🖳 www.cnto.org) has branches in New York and Los Angeles.

● **Go to Russia Travel** (☎ 1-888-263-0023, 🖳 www.gotorussia.net) This specialist company – with offices in Atlanta and San Francisco – offers both individual travel assistance (including flights and visa support) and package tours.

● **Mir Corporation** (☎ 1-800-424-7289, 🖳 www.mircorp.com) offer a range of individual and small-group escorted tours on the Trans-Siberian, with homestay or hotel accommodation; they also offer the *Golden Eagle Trans-Siberian Express* and the *Tsar's Gold* (see box p30).

● You can get information from the **Russian National Tourist Office** (🖳 www .russia-travel.com) as well as visas and plan your trip.

● **Sokol Tours** (☎ 1-724-935 5373, 🖳 www.sokoltours.com) can arrange visas, train tickets and book accommodation; they also operate several tours in Russia.

● The **Society of International Railway Travelers** (🖳 www.irtsociety.com) is a membership organisation which organises de luxe train trips all over the world, including Trans-Siberian journeys with the *Golden Eagle* (see box p30).

PLANNING YOUR TRIP

❏ **Getting to Russia or China from North America**

● **From the USA** Numerous airlines fly from the US to Russia. From New York, return flights to Moscow cost around US$920 in high season. Korean Air has flights from several west-coast cities, including Los Angeles, via Seoul to Vladivostok for around US$2400 return, but it is often cheaper to fly from LA via Moscow. One-way flights to Beijing start at about US$750 from New York or US$1300 from Los Angeles.

A major budget airfare specialist is STA Travel (🖳 www.statravel.com), with offices all over the country.

● **From Canada** From Vancouver, Toronto and Montreal, fares to Moscow and Beijing tend to be somewhat pricier than from major US cities. You're looking at paying around C$1300 for a return flight to Moscow from Montreal or C$1630 from Vancouver, and around C$1300 from Vancouver to Beijing.

A reputable travel agency specialising in discounted student fares is Travel CUTS/Voyages Campus (🖳 www.travelcuts.com).

● **Travel all Russia** (☎ 1-800-884-1721, 🖳 www.travelallrussia.com) can arrange visas and book train tickets; they also offer group tours on the classic routes as well as all the luxury private trains (see box p30).

From Canada
● **Adventure Center** (☎ 1-800-228-8747, 🖳 www.adventurecenter.com) Worldwide journeys, including a range of individual and group Trans-Siberian and Trans-Mongolian adventure tours.
● **China National Tourist Office** (🖳 www.tourismchina.org) has a branch in Toronto.

MAKING A BOOKING IN AUSTRALASIA

From Australia
● **Beyond Travel** (☎ 02-9080 0400, 🖳 www.beyondtravel.com.au) can arrange Trans-Siberian travel packages starting in Moscow, St Petersburg, Vladivostok or Beijing, including stopovers, transfers, accommodation, sightseeing, flights and visa support.
● **Intrepid Travel** (🖳 www.intrepidtravel.com) offer small group adventures for all budgets, including 21-day Moscow to Beijing via Ulaanbaatar tours.
● **Russian Travel Centre** (☎ 02-9262 1144, 🖳 www.eetbtravel.com) can arrange Trans-Mongolian and Trans-Manchurian trips, with options for home-stay accommodation.
● **Sundowners Overland/Vodka Train** (☎ 1300 559 860, 🖳 www.sundowners overland.com) specialise in overland journeys across Asia (see pp30-1).
● **Travel Directors** (☎ 1300-856 661, 🖳 www.traveldirectors.com.au) Recommended Trans-Siberian specialist agency offering high-quality, upmarket tour packages, along with basic visa support.
● **Travman Tours** (☎ 1800-338 007, 🖳 www.travman.com.au) is Australia's CITS representative; can arrange westwards rail tickets from China and various China tours.

From New Zealand
● **Adventure World** (☎ 0800-238-368, 🖳 www.adventureworld.co.nz) New Zealand's biggest adventure-travel wholesaler offers individual and group Trans-Siberian, Trans-Mongolian and Trans-Manchurian journeys.

❑ **Getting to Russia or China from Australasia**
● **From Australia** From Sydney you can get to Moscow via Beijing with Air China for around A$1600 return. To Beijing, flights are around A$1400 return, though you can get cheaper bargains from Melbourne and the Gold Coast via budget carrier Air Asia – as little as A$428 one way – with the additional advantage of not being penalised for a one-way flight. The best agencies for cheap air fares are STA Travel (🖳 www.statravel.com.au) and Flight Centre (🖳 www.flightcentre.com.au).
● **From New Zealand** you'll find similarly priced fares to Russia and China. STA Travel (🖳 www.statravel.co.nz) and Flight Centre (🖳 www.flightcentre.co.nz) offer some of the best deals on air fares.

❑ **Getting to Russia or China from Japan and South Korea**
● **From Japan** There are frequent **flights** from Tokyo to Moscow; expect to pay
around ¥60,000/100,000 one-way/return. There are several weekly flights from
Tokyo and Osaka (Kansai) to Beijing for around ¥25,000/58,000 one way/return.
There are also flights from Tokyo to Vladivostok and Khabarovsk (from around
¥34,000/65,000 one-way/return).

Reputable travel agents include STA Travel (🖳 www.statravel.co.jp) and Across
No 1/HIS Travel (🖳 www.no1-travel.com).

In addition to flights you have several options for travel **by ferry** from Japan.
You may sail to the Russian port of Vladivostok (see box, p352), or to Chinese ports
within easy reach of Beijing: Shanghai or Tianjin.

The Chinese-run **Japan-China International Ferry Co** runs weekly ferries to
Shanghai, with departures from Osaka or Kobe on alternate weeks on Tuesdays,
arriving in Shanghai on Thursdays. One-way fares range from ¥20,000–50,000 for a
berth in a shared Japanese-style room, with 10% discounts for students and a 40%
discount on return trips. The journey takes approximately 48 hours. With the advent
of the high speed Beijing–Shanghai railway, journeys between the two cities take as
little as 9 hours. **China Express Line** sails weekly between Kobe and the Chinese
port of Tanggu, near Tianjin, a 48-hour trip, departing on Fridays and arriving on
Sundays (48hrs). One-way fares start at ¥20,000, with a 10% discount for students.
From Tianjin it's a 30-minute train journey by high speed 'Hexie' train to Beijing.

See 🖳 www.seejapan.co.uk for more details. **Tickets** for most services can also
be bought from branch offices of JTB (Japan Travel Bureau) and KNT (Kinki Nippon
Tourist).
● **South Korea** There are frequent **flights** from Seoul to Moscow (from around
666,000/977,000 won one-way/return), as well as Siberian cities such as Khabarovsk
and Vladivostok (from around 340,000/508,000 won one-way/return).

● **Innovative Travel** (☎ (03-3653 910, 🖳 www.eetbtravel.com) is associated
with Russian Travel Centre (see opposite).
● **Sundowners Overland/Vodka Train** (☎ 0800-770156, 🖳 www.sundow
nersoverland.com) specialise in overland journeys across Asia (see pp30-1).

MAKING A BOOKING IN SOUTH AFRICA

● **STA Travel** (🖳 www.statravel.co.za) in South Africa has branches in
Johannesburg, Pretoria, Bloemfontein, Durban and Cape Town, and can assist
with booking Trans-Siberian tickets.

MAKING A BOOKING IN JAPAN

● **Euras Tours Inc** (☎ 03-5562 3382, 🖳 www.euras.co.jp) is a friendly, effi-
cient agency handling bookings for rail journeys to Europe with a choice of itin-
eraries combining flights, ferries and trains, directly into Russia or via China.
They have offices in Tokyo and Osaka.
● **M. O. Tourist Co Ltd** (🖳 www.mo-tourist.co.jp) Ferry and plane tickets to
Russia as well as tours.

MAKING A BOOKING IN CHINA

From Beijing

In the summer trains fill up quickly, so if you plan to spend some time travelling around China, make Beijing your first stop and get your onward travel nailed down. Once you've made your train reservations (see pp130-4) and paid your deposit, do the rounds of the embassies and collect your visas. You'll need RMB (yuan) as well as crisp US dollar cash, and a stock of passport photos.

Alternatively you may be able to reserve a place on the train while you're in Shanghai (ask at the travel bureau in Peace Hotel). Shanghai has a Russian consulate but no Mongolian consulate.

● **Monkey Business** (☎ +86 10-6591 6519, 🖳 www.monkeyshrine.com) Chief 'Monkey' is André and he and his team have put thousands of budget travellers on trains across Siberia. They'll organise everything (including visa support) and also sell some individual packages from Beijing to Moscow and a wide range of stopover options (eg Mongolia, Irkutsk, Lake Baikal and Yekaterinburg). They can even book a journey from Moscow to Beijing. See also p398.

❏ **Getting to Russia or China from South-East & Central Asia**
● **From South-East Asia** There are numerous **flights** from Singapore to Beijing; STA Travel (🖳 www.statravel.com.sg) is a good starting point when looking for discounted fares. In Bangkok, budget travellers can try STA Travel (🖳 www.statravel .co.th) or head for Khao San Rd, lined with competitive travel agencies. There are direct flights from Bangkok to Moscow, Novosibirsk and other major Russian cities with Aeroflot and S7, as well as seasonal charter flights to Vladivostok, Khabarovsk and other Siberian cities. From Vietnam, there are weekly flights between Hanoi and Vladivostok as well as flights to Beijing.

There are direct **trains** from Hanoi to Beijing, taking around two days. While it's not possible to get to China by rail from Thailand, you can take a bus from Bangkok to Ho Chi Minh City via Cambodia, and from Nong Khai in the north of Thailand to Hanoi via Laos, and continue by rail from there.
● **From Central Asia** From Ulaanbaatar, there are frequent **flights** to Moscow and Beijing with MIAT and Air China, respectively. There are numerous flights to Moscow from the capitals of various Central Asian republics, such as Almaty in Kazakhstan, Tashkent in Uzbekistan, Dushanbe in Tajikistan and Bishkek in Kyrgyzstan.

Moscow and Novosibirsk are both served by **trains** from Almaty, Kazakhstan; Bishkek, Kyrgyzstan; Tashkent, Uzbekistan and Dushanbe, Tajikistan. From Moscow, there are also train services to the currently troubled Caucasus area.
● **Getting to Russia from China by air** There are many direct flights from Beijing to Moscow, as well as Irkutsk, Khabarovsk, Vladivostok and Novosibirsk. There are also several weekly flights from Shanghai and Hong Kong to Moscow, and from Harbin to Khabarovsk and Vladivostok. Russian airlines flying to/from China include Aeroflot, Transaero and S7. The Hong Kong to Beijing route is served by Air China and China Southern Airlines.

● **CITS Beijing** (☎ +86 10-6522 2991, 🖥 www.cits.net) CITS is China's official tourist agency and buying rail tickets from them is the cheapest and quickest way besides purchasing them yourself at the railway station. Staff tend to be fluent in English and helpful. See also p399.

Online booking is also possible. Reliable Chinese companies dealing exclusively with train ticket bookings are 🖥 www.chinatraintickets.net, 🖥 www.china-train-ticket.com or 🖥 www.travelchinaguide.com. While you end up paying a small mark-up fee, the tickets are conveniently delivered to your hotel or place of lodging.

Embassies in Beijing You really should get your Russian visa before arriving in China though it may also be possible to arrange visas in Beijing.

For the Trans-Mongolian route, most nationalities need a Mongolian visa as well as a Chinese one; exceptions include Americans and Israelis. However, try to get your visas before arriving in China to avoid the language-barrier/paperwork complications. If you're continuing through Europe after Moscow you may also need a transit visa for Belarus or Ukraine (see p28).

For information on embassies in Beijing see p397.

From Hong Kong
Hong Kong can be a good place to arrange a ticket or stopover package on the Trans-Siberian. Most visitors do not require a visa to enter Hong Kong and it's possible to organise your visa to mainland China here.

Agencies here offer a range of services and booking with them from abroad is usually no problem. Several travel agencies in the Nathan Rd area can arrange tickets with a few weeks' notice. Some will sell you a voucher to exchange in Beijing for a reserved ticket. Others sell you an open ticket with a reservation voucher, leaving you to get the ticket endorsed by CITS in Beijing; don't accept an open ticket without a reservation voucher. But to visit any Russian cities apart from Moscow you'll need a tourist visa and therefore visa support.

● **Monkey Business** (🖥 www.monkeyshrine.com – see opposite) is very experienced in Trans-Siberian travel and offers a full range of services and goes under the name Moonsky Star Ltd. If you want to make advance plans, get in touch with their Beijing office (see p398).

What to take

The best advice today is to travel as light as possible as pretty much anything you're forgotten can be purchased in the larger cities.

CLOTHES

For summer in Moscow and Siberia pack thin clothes, a sweater and a raincoat. In most hotels you will be able to get laundry done, often returned the same day.

Take shirts and tops of a quick-drying cotton/polyester mixture if you are going to wash them yourself.

Winter in Russia and northern China is extremely cold, although trains and most buildings are kept well-heated: inside the train you can be warm enough in a thin shirt as you watch Arctic scenes pass by your window. When you're outside, however, a thick winter overcoat is an absolute necessity, as well as gloves and a warm hat. It's easy to buy good-quality overcoats/jackets in Beijing. If you're travelling in winter and plan to stop off in Siberian cities along the way, consider taking thermal underwear and ridge-soled boots. At other times of the year your shoes should be strong, light and comfortable; most travellers take sturdy trainers. On the train, though, Russians wear flip flops or slippers.

LUGGAGE

If you're going on one of the more expensive tours which include baggage handling, take a suitcase. Those on individual itineraries have the choice of a rucksack (comfortable to carry for long distances), a zip-up holdall with a shoulder strap or a frameless backpack. It's also useful to take along a small daypack for your camera, books etc. Since bedding on the train and in hotels is supplied you don't need to take a sleeping-bag, although some travellers prefer to carry their own sleeping-bag liner. Never travel with an ounce more than you absolutely need. Few people will have luggage weighing 35kg but be aware that is the limit in compartments and if travelling from Beijing this rule is likely to be applied.

GENERAL ITEMS

Useful items

A **moneybelt** is the best way to safeguard your documents and cash. Wear it underneath your clothing and don't take it off on the train, as compartments are very occasionally broken into. A good pair of **sunglasses** is necessary in summer as well as in winter, when the sun on the snow is particularly bright. A **Sigg flask** or thermos which can take boiling water is very useful, as is a **mug** (insulated is best), **fork/spoon/knife set** and a **universal adaptor**.

The following items are also useful: adhesive tape, ball-point pens, business cards, camera and adequate capacity memory cards for a digital camera, torch (flashlight), umbrella, games (cards, chess – the Russians are very keen chess players – Scrabble etc), toilet paper, calculator (for exchange rates), notebook or diary, penknife with corkscrew and can-opener (although there's a bottle opener fixed underneath the table in each compartment on the train), photocopies of passport, visa, air tickets, etc (keep them in two separate places), spare passport photographs for visas, sewing-kit, string (to use as a washing-line), tissues (including the wet variety), universal bath plug (Russian basins usually don't have a plug), washing powder (liquid travel soap is good) and multi-purpose travel body wash that doubles as shampoo. A compass is useful when looking at maps and out of the window of the train. Earplugs can be a bonus both on the train and in noisy Chinese hotels. Don't forget to take a good book (see pp41-3).

If you are going to Beijing consider taking a face mask – the kind cyclists in big cities wear – to protect you from the worst of the smog.

It's also a very good idea to bring things to show people: **photos** of your family and friends, your home or somewhere interesting you have been. Looking at photographs, especially of people, is a great way to break the ice when you don't speak much of the local language.

Gifts

The Russians are great present givers (see box p76) so if you are invited as a guest to a local home take a box of chocolates, a bottle of wine or, better, bring things that are harder for Russians to get, such as souvenirs of your country. Foreign coins and badges are also good, as Russia is full of collectors.

Provisions

Travellers expecting lavish meals in dining cars are doomed to bitter disappointment; though the menus in Russian restaurant cars are sometimes long, often they'll only have a few items on the list. However, there's no need to panic and bring a rucksack filled with food as it is much easier nowadays to get provisions in Western-style supermarkets in the big cities and also at the stations you stop at (see pp122-3). A recent development also is the arrival of food-peddling ladies who walk up and down the carriages, selling savoury cakes, crisps, chocolate, instant noodles, soft drinks and beer, so you won't go hungry. However, if there is anything you feel you can't live without – particular brands of things such as Marmite or Vegemite – and it is easy to carry do bring it.

Medical supplies

You may consider bringing aspirin or paracetamol; sunscreen lotion; DEET-infused insect repellent and a compact mosquito net (vital if you're travelling in summer); antiseptic cream and some plasters/Band Aids; a medical kit containing sterile syringes and swabs for emergency medical treatment. Note that some Western brands of tampons and condoms are not always easily available in Russia or China, so bring your own if you favour a particular kind. Bring an extra pair of glasses or contact lenses if you wear them. You may want to take along something for an upset stomach but use it only in an emergency, as changes in diet often cause slight diarrhoea which stops of its own accord. For vaccination requirements, see pp44-5.

The above items can be purchased in pharmacies all over Russia, as well as in Ulaanbaatar and Beijing, but if you're after specific brands, your best bet it to bring them from home.

Mobile phones, laptops and other digital media

Pretty much every traveller and local brings a **mobile phone** on the train, and these can be charged using outlets in the carriages; platzkart carriages tend to have one socket at either end that supports 220v; there are also a couple placed at berth 7 and 27. If you have an unlocked tri-band or quad-band phone and you are spending some time in Russia, it pays to pick up a SIM card from a Russian mobile company (see p67-8).

PLANNING YOUR TRIP

The number of travellers using **laptops, iPods, MP3 players, iPads, smartphones, Kindles and tablets** in Russian trains is increasing, even in *platzkart*, so if you bring one along, unless you're travelling in a particularly remote area (ie the BAM) you won't be terribly conspicuous.

Photographic equipment

Digital cameras are the norm in Russia, major Chinese cities and Ulaanbaatar. Batteries can be charged on board from outlets in the carriages, but bring extra batteries as these outlets are few and far between. Every city along the route has digital print shops and in most internet cafés the staff will burn your photos onto a CD for you if you bring a USB cable. Many travellers on long journeys carry portable hard drives for storing photos.

If you shoot with film, bring more than you think you'll need. Don't forget to bring some faster film for shots from the train (400 ASA). It's wise to carry all your film in a lead-lined pouch (available from camera shops) if you are going to let them go through X-ray machines at airports.

See p75 for notes about taking photographs in Russia and p121 for information about taking photos from the train.

MONEY

(See also pp65-6) With certain exceptions, you will have to pay for everything in **local currency** (roubles in Russia, RMB/yuan in China, tugrik in Mongolia). Russian hotels have to accept roubles, even though some set their rates in dollars or euros.

There are abundant, well-signposted, 24-hour international **ATMs** in all major cities along the Trans-Siberian, and in Beijing. Most accept Visa, MasterCard and other major cards and offer cash withdrawals from your own account in local currency. In Russia, the one bank that seems to accept most cards is TransCreditBank; you'll find its ATMs at all major railway stations.

Cards are accepted by many hotels and a growing number of guesthouses, restaurants and shops. But there are many times when **cash** is essential, for example when you can't pay by card eg for visa fees at many embassies and in Mongolian restaurant cars on the Trans-Siberian. So, it's essential to have a stash of cash; by far the most useful currencies in Russia, Mongolia and China are US dollars and euros, though pounds sterling are also widely accepted. See p65 for details of towns and cities in Russia where other currencies are commonly accepted. Carry only a small amount in your pocket and the rest safely under your clothing in a moneybelt. Keep a second stash somewhere else for emergencies.

Travellers' cheques are quickly becoming obsolete and carrying them is, in general, more hassle than it's worth, but if you do they are accepted in the following order: American Express, Thomas Cook and Visa; forget taking other brands. Instead, it's worth getting a **cashcard** with a company such as Eurochange (🖳 www.eurochange.co.uk), as you can use it as a regular bank card to withdraw money and you can store up to five different currencies on it.

BACKGROUND READING

A number of excellent books have been written about the Trans-Siberian railway. Several are unfortunately out of print, though they're often available through inter-library loan or second-hand on ▣ www.amazon.com. The following are well worth reading before you go:

● *Journey Into the Mind's Eye: Fragments of an Autobiography*, by Lesley Blanch (1988), is a fascinating book: a witty, semi-autobiographical story of the author's romantic obsession with Russia and the Trans-Siberian Railway.

● *To the Edge of the World: The Story of the Trans-Siberian Railway* by Christian Wolmar (Atlantic Books, 2013) is a modern history of the railway entertainly told by an expert rail historian who regularly appears on TV and on the radio in the UK. Highly recommended.

● *To the Great Ocean* by Harmon Tupper (1965, out of print) was the first detailed history of the building of the railway. It's a fascinating, well-written read – if you can find a copy.

● *The Trans-Siberian Railway: A Traveller's Anthology*, edited by Deborah Manley, is well worth taking on the trip for a greater insight into the railway and the journey, through the eyes of travellers from Annette Meakin to Bob Geldof. If you can't find it in a bookshop it's available from ▣ www.trailblazer-guides.com.

● *Guide to the Great Siberian Railway 1900*, by AI Dmitriev-Mamanov (David and Charles 1971, out of print but facsimile reprint available since 2009), a reprint of the guide originally published by the Tsar's government to publicise their new railway. Highly detailed but interesting to look at.

● *Peking to Paris: A Journey across two Continents*, by Luigi Barzini (1973, new edition 1986), tells the story of the Peking to Paris Rally in 1907. The author accompanied the Italian Prince Borghese and his chauffeur in the winning car, a 40hp Itala. Their route took them across Mongolia and Siberia and for some of the journey they actually drove along the railway tracks.

● *The Big Red Train Ride*, by Eric Newby, is a perceptive and entertaining account of the journey he made in the Soviet era, written in Newby's characteristically humorous style.

● *Through Siberia by Accident*, by Dervla Murphy, is a warm and witty account of this very readable adventurer's travels in Siberia and the BAM region in 2003-4.

● *In Siberia*, by Colin Thubron, is the best modern book for background on Siberia and certainly one you should either read before you go or take with you on the trip. Thubron's excellent earlier travelogue, *Among the Russians*, was written after his travels in Soviet times.

● *Asia Overland: Tales of Travel on the Trans-Siberian and Silk Road* by Bijan Omrani (Odyssey, 2010) has an interesting section on the Trans-Siberian.

● Paddy Linehan's *Trans-Siberia* (2001) is an easily readable account of a trip; the contemporary flavour shines out a-plenty and you quickly warm to the author's unpretentious style.

PLANNING YOUR TRIP

● *The Princess of Siberia* (1984) is Christine Sutherland's very readable biography of Princess Maria Volkonskaya, who followed her husband Sergei Volkonsky to Siberia after he'd been exiled for his part in the Decembrists' Uprising. Her house in Irkutsk is now a museum (see p300).

● *As Far As My Feet Will Carry Me* (1955, reprinted 2003) is the true story of the escape of German prisoner of war, Clemens Forell, from the Siberian Gulag where he was serving a 25-year hard-labour sentence. It's a gripping adventure tale.

● *Into The Whirlwind* is Eugenia Ginzburg's powerful account of how in 1937 she was arrested and falsely charged as a Trotskyite revolutionary as part of Stalin's purges, and sentenced to exile in Siberia. The sequel, *Within the Whirlwind*, is no less moving; it describes the 18 years she spent in a Gulag, her fate shared by hundreds of thousands of Russians. Essential reading.

● *Stalin's Nose: Travels Around the Bloc*, by Rory Maclean (1992) Maclean explores the former Eastern Bloc in a battered Trabant with his elderly aunt Zita and a pig named Winston. He recounts the histories of some of his more notorious relatives, providing in the process a surreal, darkly humorous commentary on communism and its demise.

● *Lenin's Tomb*, by David Remnick (1993), is an eyewitness account of the heady Gorbachev era by this articulate former *Washington Post* correspondent.

● *Between the Hammer and the Sickle: Across Russia by Cycle*, by Simon Vickers (1994), is a highly entertaining account of an epic bicycle journey from St Petersburg to Vladivostok in 1990. Out of print.

● *East of the Sun: The Conquest and Settlement of Siberia* by Benson Bobrick (1993, reprinted 1997) A readable narrative of Russia's conquest of Siberia, a saga which in colour and drama rivals the taming of the American West.

● *Around The Sacred Sea: Mongolia and Lake Baikal on Horseback* by Bartle Bull (1999) In 1993 Bull and two photographers rode north from Mongolia into Siberia and around Lake Baikal, partly a Boys-Own adventure and partly to report on the growing environmental threat to the lake after the collapse of the USSR. The result is an engaging true-life adventure story.

● *The Conquest of a Continent: Siberia and the Russians*, by American historian W Bruce Lincoln (1993), captures the ambition and cruelty of Cossacks, fur trappers and military adventurers in the region.

● *A People's Tragedy: The Russian Revolution 1891-1924*, by British historian Orlando Figes (1997), is a scholarly work of social and political history that brings this turning point in Russia's history to life. Winner of the 1997 NCR Book Award.

● *A History of Twentieth-Century Russia* by Robert W Service (1997) The eminent British scholar of Russian history looks back at the entire Soviet experiment, from the rise of communism to the collapse of the USSR.

● *Holy Russia*, by Fitzroy Maclean (1979, out of print), is probably the most articulate and readable of many summaries of European Russian history and includes several topical walking tours.

● *Brezhnev's Folly: The Building of BAM and Late Soviet Socialism* by Christopher J Ward (2009) is a very readable analysis of the BAM project.

The above books are the impressions of foreign scholars and visitors; for a Russian perspective on the Russian mind and soul, try some of the following:

● Dostoyevsky's thought-provoking, atmospheric *Crime and Punishment* (set in the Haymarket in St Petersburg).

● Tolstoy's *War and Peace*.

● Mikhail Bulgakov's surreal masterpiece, *The Master and Margarita*.

● *Dr Zhivago* by Boris Pasternak (whose grave you can visit in Moscow).

● *Memories from the House of the Dead*, a semi-autobiographical account of Dostoyevsky's life as a convict in Omsk.

● *A Day in the Life of Ivan Denisovitch* by Alexander Solzhenitsyn, detailing 24 hours in the life of a Siberian convict.

● *The Gulag Archipelago* by Alexander Solzhenitsyn.

❏ Internet resources

Many travel agents have their own websites, some with useful links; see pp28-37.

● **RZD** – 🖥 pass.rzd.ru Website in English and Russian about Russian railways. Search for timetables, routes, and book tickets.

● **The Man in Seat Sixty-One** – 🖥 www.seat61.com For information on rail travel anywhere in the world this is the best site there is. Helpful for planning rail trips to and from Russia. Includes a comprehensive section on the Trans-Siberian with lots of useful links.

● **Way to Russia** – 🖥 www.waytorussia.net A good commercial site about travelling in Russia. The information is comprehensive and reasonably up to date. See also p24.

● **Railway Ring** – 🖥 parovoz.com A venerable site for Russian rail fanatics, with an English version and exhaustive links to other sites on railways in Russia, the Baltic States and elsewhere in the CIS.

● **Library of Congress Russian Info** – 🖥 lcweb2.loc.gov/frd/cs/rutoc.html In-depth Russian history, culture, religion, politics etc: the online version of a book published by the LOC under its Country Studies/Area Handbook Program (1996).

● **Russian Museums directory** – 🖥 www.russianmuseums.info A useful site listing all the museums in Russia with a town-by-town search facility and weblinks to a number of the museums listed.

● **Russia Today** – 🖥 www.einnews.com/russia An excellent round-up of Russian news and analysis, though you have to be a subscriber.

● **Dazhdbog's Grandchildren** – 🖥 www.ibiblio.org/sergei Russian folklore, traditions, culture, myths; many useful links too.

● **Buryatia government page** – 🖥 egov-buryatia.ru Buryatia government page covering Buryatia's history, culture and more.

● **The Red Book** – 🖥 www.eki.ee/books/redbook/foreword.shtml Scholarly, sobering research (1991) on the ethnic minority communities of the ex-USSR, with lots about 'endangered' Siberian native peoples.

● **Trans-Siberian Web Encyclopedia** – 🖥 www.transsib.ru/Eng Lots of Trans-Sib memorabilia, pictures of stations and trains. However, it hasn't been updated much since 2005.

● **Russian Cuisine** – 🖥 www.ruscuisine.com Russian recipes and more.

For information on locomotives, *Soviet Locomotive Types: The Union Legacy* by AJ Heywood and IDC Button is very thorough. It's out of print, but can be obtained second-hand via Amazon.

Other guidebooks
Other rail guides to Russia include *Siberian BAM Guide: Rail, Rivers and Road* by Athol Yates (also from Trailblazer but stocks are low).

Health precautions and inoculations

No vaccinations are listed as official requirements for Western tourists visiting Russia, China or Mongolia. A number, however, are listed as 'advisable'.

Vaccination services and travel advice is available throughout the UK through **MASTA clinics** (🖳 www.masta-travel-health.com) and **Nomad Travel Clinics** in London, Manchester, Bristol, Cardiff and Bath (🖳 www.nomadtravel.co.uk). Your GP may be able to give you some of the recommended inoculations, but you'll have to make an appointment with either of the above for the less-common ones.

In the USA the **Center for Disease Control and Prevention** (🖳 www.cdc.gov) is the best place to contact for worldwide health information.

RECOMMENDED INOCULATIONS

● **Tetanus** A booster is advisable if you haven't had one in the last 10 years: if you then cut yourself badly in Russia you won't need another.

● **Diphtheria** Ensure that you were given the initial vaccine as a child and a booster within the last 10 years. The World Health Organisation recommends a combined diphtheria-tetanus toxoid (DTT) booster.

❏ **Health and travel insurance**
Wherever you're travelling you should have comprehensive health insurance; most travel agents or tour operators can provide this but it is worth checking different providers to get the best level of cover for the cost. Some nationalities need **health insurance** before they can get a Russian visa (see box p23).

The UK has reciprocal **health-care agreements** with some countries, including Russia, but not China or Mongolia. Treatment in state hospitals in Russia is free on production of your passport (prescribed medicines need to be paid for); but given the state of most Russian hospitals you're advised to arrange proper health insurance and go to a private clinic if you get ill. EU and EEA citizens will get free or reduced cost treatment (for anything that becomes necessary during a trip) in the Czech Republic, Estonia, Finland, Germany, Hungary, Latvia, Lithuania, and Poland on production of an EHIC. However, visitors are always advised to have comprehensive travel/health insurance as well.

● **Hepatitis A** Those travelling on tight budgets and eating in cheaper restaurants run a risk of catching infectious hepatitis, a disease of the liver that drains you of energy and can last 3-8 weeks. It's spread by infected water or food, or by utensils handled by infected persons. Gamma globulin antibody injections give immediate but short-term protection (2-6 months). A vaccine (trade names Havrix or Avaxim) lasts for twice that time (and up to 10 years if a booster is given within 6-12 months).

● **Tick-borne encephalitis** A viral infection of the central nervous system that is incurable. Those venturing into forests in Siberia and even Western Russia are strongly advised to get a vaccination against tick-borne encephalitis, as the number of cases has increased over the last few years and infected ticks have spread west over a wider area.

● **Japanese B Encephalitis** It's well worth getting this vaccination if you're looking to spend a month or longer in Siberia and the Russian Far East as Japanese B Encephalitis cannot be treated and a high percentage of cases result in brain damage or death.

● **Malaria** If you plan to visit rural areas of south-western China you may be at risk of malaria, a dangerous disease which is on the increase in parts of Asia. You may need **anti-malarial tablets** starting before you go and continuing for weeks after you leave the malarial zone; check the type you need with your travel clinic.

● **Rabies** Consider a pre-exposure **rabies** vaccination course, particularly if you're going to be dealing with animals, cycling, caving or hiking in remote areas. Also bear in mind that in parts of Russia, Mongolia and China there can be vicious stray dogs. The injection course involves three vaccinations over 21 days minimum, so give yourself plenty of time. Even after vaccination, if you've been scratched or bitten you'll still require two booster injections ASAP; the initial vaccination course simply buys you more time.

● **Other** Ensure you've had recent **typhoid**, **polio** and **tuberculosis** boosters. If you're planning to go off the beaten track it's advisable to have a vaccination against **meningococcal meningitis**. If you're arriving from Africa or South America you may be required to show a **yellow fever** vaccination certificate.

MEDICAL SERVICES

Those travelling with tour groups will be with guides who can contact doctors to sort out medical problems. Serious problems can be expensive, but you'll get the best treatment possible from doctors used to dealing with foreigners. If you're travelling independently and require medical assistance, contact one of the hospitals recommended in this book.

Large hotels in China usually have a doctor in residence. In Beijing, Shanghai and Guangzhou (Canton) there are special hospitals for foreigners. Take supplies of any prescription medicine you may need. Medical facilities in Mongolia are quite limited and some medications are unavailable, so it may be better to travel to Beijing if you require serious medical treatment.

2 RUSSIA

Facts about the country

GEOGRAPHICAL BACKGROUND

The Russian Federation includes over 75% of the former USSR, but even without the other old Soviet republics it remains the largest country in the world, incorporating 17.175 million sq km (over 6.5 million square miles) and stretching from well into the Arctic Circle right down to the northern Caucasus in the south, and from the Black Sea in the west to the Bering Strait in the east, only a few kilometres from Alaska.

Russia is twice as big as the USA; the UK could fit into this vast country some 69 times.

Climate

Much of the country is situated in far northern latitudes; Moscow is on the same latitude as Edinburgh, St Petersburg almost as far north as Anchorage, Alaska. Winters are bitter: the coldest inhabited place on earth, with temperatures as low as -68°C (-90°F), is Oymyakon, in Yakutia in north-eastern Siberia.

Geography is as much to blame as latitude. Most of Russia is an open plain, stretching across Siberia to the Arctic; while there is high ground in the south, there are no northern mountains to block the cold Arctic air which blows across this plain. To the west are the Urals, the low range which divides Europe and Asia. The Himalaya and Pamir ranges beyond the southern borders stop warm tropical air from reaching the Siberian and Russian plains. Thus isolated, the plains warm rapidly in summer and become very cold in winter. Olekminsk, also in Yakutia, holds the record for the widest temperature range in the world, from -60°C (-87°F) to a breathtaking summer high of 45°C (113°F). Along the route of the Trans-Siberian, however, summers are rather milder.

Transport and communications

Railways remain the principal means of transport for both passengers and goods, and there are some 87,500km of track in Russia. The heaviest rail traffic in the world is on certain stretches of the Trans-Siberian, with trains passing every few minutes. The **road network** is comparatively well-developed and ever-growing; more and more people own cars, particularly in the larger cities.

Russia's **rivers** have historically been of vital importance as a communication network. Some of these rivers are huge and even navigable by ocean-going ships for considerable distances. But ice precludes year-round navigation so **air travel** has gradually taken over.

Landscape zones: flora and fauna

The main landscape zones of interest to the rail traveller are as follows:

● **European Russia** Flora and fauna west of the Urals are similar to those elsewhere in northern Europe. Trees include oak, elm, hazel, ash, apple, aspen, spruce, lime and maple.

● **Northern Siberia and the Arctic** The *tundra* zone (short grass, mosses and lichens) covers the treeless area in the far north. The soil is poor and much of it permanently frozen. In fact *permafrost* affects over 40% of Russia and extends down into southern Siberia, where it causes building problems for architects and engineers. Wildlife in this desolate northern zone includes reindeer, arctic fox, wolf, lemming and vole. The birdlife is richer, with ptarmigan, snow-bunting, Iceland falcon and snowy owl as well as many kinds of migratory water and marsh fowl.

● **The Siberian plain** Much of this area is covered in *taiga*, a Russian word meaning thick forest. To the north the trees are stunted and windblown; in the south they form dark impenetrable forests. More than 30% of all the world's trees grow in this zone. These include larch, pine and silver fir, intermingled with birch, aspen and maple. Willow and poplar line rivers and streams. Much of the taiga forest along the route of the Trans-Siberian has been cleared and replaced with fields of wheat or sunflowers. Parts of this region are affected by permafrost, so that in places rails and roads sink, and houses, trees and telegraph poles often keel over drunkenly. The fauna here includes species once common in Europe: bear, badger, wolverine, polecat, ermine, sable, squirrel, weasel, otter, wolf, fox, lynx, beaver, several types of rodent, musk deer, roebuck, reindeer and elk.

● **Eastern Siberia and Trans-Baikal** Much of the flora and fauna of this region is unique including, in Lake Baikal, such rarities as the fresh-water seal. Amongst the ubiquitous larch and pine there grows a type of birch with dark bark, *Betula daurica*. Towards the south and into China and Mongolia, the forests give way to open grassy areas known as *steppes*. The black earth (*chernozem*) of the northern steppes is quite fertile and some areas are under cultivation.

● **The Far Eastern territories: the Amur region** Along the Amur River the flora and fauna are similar to those of northern China and it is here that the rare Amur tiger (see box p479) is found. European flora, including trees such as cork, walnut and acacia, make a reappearance in the Far East.

A BRIEF HISTORY OF RUSSIA

The first Russians

Artefacts uncovered in Siberia suggest that human history in Russia may stretch back much further than previously believed: 500,000 or more years.

In the 13th millennium BC there were Stone Age nomads living beside Lake Baikal. By the 2nd millennium BC when fairly advanced civilisations had emerged here, European Russia was inhabited by Ural-Altaic and Indo-European peoples. In the 6th century BC the Scythians (whose magnificent gold-work may be seen in the Hermitage, see pp138-9) settled in southern Russia near the Black Sea.

Through the early centuries of the 1st millennium AD trade routes developed between Scandinavia, Russia and Byzantium, following the Dnieper River. Trading centres (including Novgorod, Kiev, Smolensk and Chernigov) grew up along the route and by the 6th century AD were populated by Slavic tribes known as *Rus* (hence 'Russian').

The year 830 saw the first of the Varangian (Viking) invasions and in 862 Novgorod fell to the Varangian chief Rurik, Russia's first sovereign. Oleg of Novgorod, Rurik's successor, founded Kievan Rus, the first united Slavic state, in 882.

Vladimir and Christian Russia

The great Prince Vladimir (978-1015) ruled Russia from Kiev and was responsible for the conversion of the country to Christianity. Until then Slavs worshipped a range of pagan gods and it is said that in his search for a state religion Vladimir invited bids from Islam, Judaism and Christianity. Islam wasn't compatible with the Slavs' love of alcohol and Judaism didn't make for a unified nation. Vladimir chose Christianity, had himself baptised at Constantinople in 988AD, and ordered the mass conversion of the Russian people, with whole towns being baptised simultaneously.

The 11th century was marked by continual feuding between his heirs. It was at this time that the northern principalities of Vladimir and Suzdal were founded.

The Mongol invasion and the rise of Muscovy

In the 1230s the Golden Horde brought a sudden halt to economic progress in Russia, burning towns and putting the local population to the sword; the first Russian town to fall was Ryazan in 1237. By 1244 Kiev was under their control and the Russians establishing a new political centre at Muscovy (Moscow), further north. Moscow was picked as a site almost by accident; rulers of Moscow had very few male heirs so the principality did not need to be split among heirs, as was the case with other places.

All Russian principalities were obliged to pay tribute to the Mongol khans but Muscovy was the first to challenge their authority, 130 years after the invasion. The revolt was crushed, but by the end of the 1400s Moscow, under Ivan III, gained control of the other Russian principalities and shook off the Mongol yoke.

Ivan the Terrible (1530-84)

When Ivan the Terrible came to the throne he became Tsar of All the Russians and by his successful military campaigns extended the borders of the young country. The first ruler to declare himself Tsar of All the Russians was his grandfather, Ivan III; by marrying the niece of the last Byzantine Emperor he got the right to call himself Caesar (Tsar) and Moscow – the Third Rome. Since then Russian rulers have borne the title 'Tsar'.

Ivan the Terrible was as wild and bloodthirsty as his name suggests: in a fit of anger in 1582 he struck his favourite son with a metal staff, fatally injuring him (a scene conjured up by Ilya Repin in one of his greatest paintings). Ivan was succeeded by his mentally retarded son Fyodor, but real power rested with the regent, Boris Godunov. Godunov himself later became Tsar, ruling from 1598 to 1605.

The early 17th century was marked by dynastic feuding which ended with the election of Michael Romanov (1613-45), first of a line that was to rule until the Revolution in 1917.

Peter the Great and the Westernisation of Russia

Peter I (1672-1725) well deserves his sobriquet, 'the Great', for it was his policy of Westernisation that helped Russia emerge from centuries of isolation and backwardness into the 18th century. He founded St Petersburg in 1703 as a 'window open on the West' and made it his capital in 1712. During his reign there were wars with Sweden and Turkey. Territorial gains included the Baltic provinces and the southern and western shores of the Caspian Sea, Russia was proclaimed an empire and recognised as a world power.

Catherine the Great and the empire's expansion

Catherine the Great led a coup against her own husband, thus becoming the supreme ruler of Russia, and conducted extensive campaigns of a more romantic nature with a series of favourites in her elegant capital. Peter's extravagant

---

❏ An English Tsarina for Ivan Vasilyevich?

In Elizabethan times there were diplomatic and trading links between England and Muscovy whose emissaries and merchants came to London 'dripping pearls and vermin' while Englishmen went to Moscow. Indeed the Tsar had occasion to complain of the behaviour of some of them thereby eliciting a tactful letter from the Queen.

Elizabeth's diplomatic skills brought about a peace between Ivan Vasilyevich and John, King of Sweden, and the former was so grateful to her that 'imagining she might stand his friend in a matter more interesting to his personal happiness, he made humble suit to her majesty to send him a wife out of England'. The Queen chose Anne, sister of the Earl of Huntingdon and of royal Plantagenet blood, but the lady was not willing to risk 'the barbarous laws of Muscovy which allowed the sovereign to put away his czarina as soon as he was tired of her and wanted something new in the conjugal department. The czar was dissatisfied and did not long survive his disappointment', dying in 1584. He is better known to history as Ivan the Terrible and his reputation may well have affected the Queen's thinking when she sorely tried Tsar Boris Godunov's patience with her diplomatic procrastination over his attempts to get an English bride for one of his sons.

(Sources: *The Letters of Queen Elizabeth*, ed. Harrison; *Lives of the Queens of England*, Agnes Strickland; *History of England from the Accession of James II*, Lord Macaulay; Camden's Annals). **Patricia Major**

RUSSIA

building programme in St Petersburg continued under Catherine II (1762-96). During her reign, Russia extended her territory to the west, gaining parts of Poland, and proving victorious against the Crimean khanate, thus extending her boundaries to the Black Sea. Successful in the Russo-Turkish Wars against the Ottoman Empire, by the early 19th century, Russia also made significant land gains in Transcaucasia.

Alexander I and the Napoleonic Wars

In 19th-century Russia the political pendulum swung back and forth between conservatism and enlightenment. The mad Tsar Paul I came to the throne in 1796, only to be murdered five years later. He was succeeded by his son Alexander I (1801-25) who was said to have had a hand in the sudden demise of his father. Alexander abolished the secret police and lifted the laws of censorship. Given the growing unrest among the peasants, some historians believe that he would have freed the serfs had the aristocracy not objected so strongly to the idea, though the majority disagree. In 1812 Napoleon invaded Russia and Moscow was burnt to the ground by its inhabitants before he was pushed back over the border.

Nicholas I, Alexander II, and Alexander III

Nicholas I's reign began with the first Russian Revolution, the Decembrists' uprising (see p89), and ended, after he had reversed most of Alexander's more enlightened policies, with the Crimean War against the English and French in 1853-6. Nicholas was succeeded by Alexander II (1855-81) who was known as the Tsar Liberator, for it was he who finally freed the serfs. His reward was his assassination by a student in St Petersburg in 1881. He was succeeded by the repressive Alexander III, who feared assassination, given his father's fate, and during whose reign work began on the Trans-Siberian Railway.

Nicholas II: last of the Tsars

The dice were heavily loaded against the unfortunate Nicholas. He inherited a vast empire and a restless population that was beginning to discover its own power. In 1905 his army and navy suffered a humiliating defeat at the hands of the Japanese. Just when his country needed him most, as strikes and riots swept through the cities in the first few years of the 20th century, Nicholas's attention was drawn into his own family crisis. It was discovered that Alexis, heir to the throne, was haemophiliac. The Siberian monk, Rasputin, ingratiated his way into the court circle through his ability to exert a calming influence on the Tsarevich. His influence over other members of the royal family, including the Tsar, was said to be vast.

October 1917: the Russian Revolution

After the revolution in 1905, Nicholas agreed to allow the formation of a national parliament (Duma), though its elected members had no real power. Reforms came too slowly for the people and morale fell further when, during WWI, Russia suffered heavy losses.

By February 1917 the Tsar had lost control and was forced to abdicate in favour of a provisional government led by Alexander Kerensky. But the Revolution that abruptly changed the course of Russian history took place in

October of that year, when the reins of government were seized by Lenin and his Communist Party. The Tsar and his family were taken to Yekaterinburg in the Urals, where they were murdered (see pp252-3). Civil war raged across the country, with the White pro-monarchist movement fighting against the new regime's Red Army, and it was not until 1920 that the Bolsheviks brought the lands of Russia under their control, forming the Union of Soviet Socialist Republics (USSR). Lenin created the Cheka (secret police) – a terrifying state organ that mercilessly cracked down onto any opposition, putting 'Iron Feliks' Dzerzhinsky in charge of it. The Cheka was the predecessor of the dreaded KGB and the current FSB.

The Stalin era and World War II

After Lenin's death in 1924, Joseph Stalin deftly outmanoeuvered more likely successors, such as Leon Trotsky, to become the Soviet Union's undisputed leader until his death in 1953, systematically destroying any opposition along the way. During the Great Terror in the 1930s, a climate of fear and distrust prevailed, with neighbours, family members and friends denouncing each other for crimes real or imaginary. Millions were sentenced to hard labour in the Gulags, which provided much of the workforce for ambitious building projects. Political repression came to a head in the Great Purge of 1937-38, in which thousands of 'enemies of the people' were exiled or executed, including many prominent military leaders accused of plotting against Stalin. The combination of rapid social and economic changes, as well as collectivisation – major restructuring of the agricultural system whereby productive peasants were stripped of land, which was then combined to make vast collective farms – led to the famine of 1932-33. The USSR was transformed from a backward agricultural country into an industrial world power at massive cost to its own people.

In 1939, the Molotov-Ribbentrop Non-aggression Pact was signed with Nazi Germany, the two powers dividing Poland and the Baltic States between them. When Hitler broke the non-aggression treaty and invaded Soviet territory, the USSR rallied in spite of enormous losses and played a vital part in the defeat of the Nazis during WWII, extending its influence to the East European countries that took on Communist governments after the war.

Khrushchev, Brezhnev, Andropov and Chernenko

After Stalin died in 1953 Nikita Khrushchev became Party Secretary and attempted to ease the strict regulations which governed Soviet society, dismantling Stalin's cult of personality. Between 1957 and 1961, the USSR became the leader in space exploration, with Yuri Gagarin becoming the first man to orbit the earth.

In 1962 Khrushchev's installation of missiles in Cuba almost led to war with the USA. He was forced to resign in 1964, blamed for the failure of the country's economy and for his clumsy foreign policy. He was replaced by Brezhnev who continued the USSR's policy of adopting friendly 'buffer' states along the Iron Curtain. He ordered the invasion of Afghanistan in 1979 'at the invitation of the leaders of the country', a quagmire that the Soviet forces became stuck in for a decade.

RUSSIA

When Leonid Brezhnev died in 1982, he was replaced by the former head of the KGB, Yuri Andropov. Andropov died in 1984 and was succeeded by the elderly Konstantin Chernenko, who managed a mere 13 months in office before becoming the chief participant in yet another state funeral.

Gorbachev and the end of the Cold War

Mikhail Gorbachev, at 54 the youngest Soviet premier since Stalin, was unanimously appointed by the Politburo in 1985 and quickly initiated a process of change known by the terms *glasnost* (openness) and *perestroika* (restructuring). He is credited in the West with bringing about the end of the Cold War (he received the Nobel Prize in 1990) and while it was widely acknowledged before he came to power that things had gone seriously wrong, he played a key role in the changes that took place in the USSR.

Gorbachev launched a series of bold reforms: Soviet troops were pulled out of Afghanistan, Eastern Europe and Mongolia, political dissidents were freed, laws on religion relaxed and press censorship lifted. These changes displeased many of the Soviet 'old guard,' and on 19 August 1991, a group of senior military and political figures staged a coup. Gorbachev was isolated at his Crimean villa and Vice-President Gennadi Yanayev took over, declaring a state of emergency. Other politicians, including the President of the Russian Republic, Boris Yeltsin, denounced the coup and rallied popular support. There were general strikes and, after a very limited skirmish in Moscow (three casualties), the coup committee was put to flight.

The collapse of the USSR

Because most levels of the Communist Party had been compromised in the failed coup attempt, it was soon seen as corrupt and ineffectual. Gorbachev resigned his position as Chairman in late August 1991 and the Party was abolished five days later.

The Party's collapse heralded the demise of the republic it had created and Gorbachev began a desperate struggle to stop this happening. His reforms, however, had already sparked nationalist uprisings in the Baltic republics, Armenia and Azerbaijan. Despite his suggestions for loose 'federations' of Russian states, by the end of 1991 the USSR had split into 15 independent republics; Gorbachev deserves full credit for letting the USSR dissolve with almost no bloodshed. Having lost almost all his support, Gorbachev resigned and was relieved by Yeltsin.

Yeltsin and the 1990s

Elected in the first direct presidential election in Russian history in June 1991, Yeltsin's years in power were nothing if not turbulent. After the collapse of the Soviet Union, almost half of Russia's population was plunged into poverty practically overnight, as their life savings became worthless. Rapid privatisation followed, with control of former state enterprises going to private individuals with insider connections in the government. A massive brain drain, with many thousands of professionals emigrating, and a capital drain, with wealthy Russians investing abroad, led to an economic crisis, which in turn led to the collapse of the social services. On 22 September 1993 Yeltsin suddenly dissolved parliament and declared presidential rule, which led to a standoff between Yeltsin and the Congress, culminating in the siege of the White House, its electricity lines cut and the building stormed by troops faithful to Yeltsin, resulting in the death of 171 people.

Besides political unrest, the 1990s saw the rise of criminal gangs and violent crime, not to mention the ongoing guerrilla war between Chechen rebel groups and the Russian military since Chechnya declared independence in the early 1990s.

Putin's Russia

His government plagued by accusations of corruption (Yeltsin's daughter became part of the presidential team) and he himself plagued by ill-health (or alcoholism), on New Year's Eve in 1999, to everyone's surprise, Yeltsin resigned and handed presidential power to his prime minister of four months, Vladimir Putin, practically an unknown, his name put forward by mathematician-turned-billionaire-businessman Boris Berezovsky who fancied himself a kingmaker (and who committed suicide in the UK in 2013, having fled into exile after falling out with Putin). Three months later Putin won the presidential election with just 52.5% of the vote, pledging to clean up Russia and transform it into a 'rich, strong and civilised country'. He was partially true to his word, the economy growing due to high oil prices, and the overhaul of the tax system making it simpler to operate and harder to avoid, though Putin's past career as a KGB spy has clearly left him with authoritarian tendencies, and he has shown himself to be no friend of free speech, with independent newspapers hounded and their reporters killed – most famously, Anna Politkovskaya who was shot in broad daylight in 2006 on Putin's birthday, something viewed by many to be too much of a coincidence. To date, there are only a couple of independent publications left in the Russian Federation that don't toe the party line. Most worryingly, the Duma approved a law giving the president the right to declare a state of emergency and close down political parties whenever he sees fit to do so.

Continuing violence in Chechnya spilled beyond its borders, with a series of deadly apartment-block bombings in Moscow and other Russian cities blamed on Chechen terrorists (though evidence has come to light that leads some to believe that the bombings were carried out by the FSB and blamed on the Chechens to unite a frightened population behind the new president), and by early 2000 much of Grozny, the Chechen capital, had been razed to the ground by Russian troops. Armed conflicts in the Northern Caucasus were brought to international attention particularly during the October 2002 Moscow theatre siege and during the Beslan school shootings in 2004, both incidents resulting in hundreds of deaths which could have been avoided. These and the September 11 attacks in the USA gave free rein to Putin's hard-line approach in Chechnya, with no solution in sight.

Under Putin, Russia began flexing its muscles, earning international condemnation. The arrest of oil tycoon Mikhail Khodorkovsky at gunpoint on a Siberian airport runway in October 2003, later sentenced to nine years in prison for tax evasion (with the sentence extended until 2014), led to more criticism in the West, as it was an open secret that Putin had made a deal with the oligarchs: they could operate in peace as long as they didn't interfere in politics and Khodorkovsky was known to harbour political ambitions. In November 2006, former FSB (federal security service) agent turned whistle-blower, Alexander Litvinenko, died an excruciating death from polonium radiation poisoning in a London hospital. Overwhelming evidence suggests that it had been a KGB hit job; the Kremlin refused to extradite the suspected murderer, thus souring Russian-British relations.

On 1 January 2006, the very day Russia took over chairmanship of the G8 group of industrialised nations, Russia cut its gas exports to Ukraine after that country failed to reach an agreement with Gazprom over a proposed rate hike. The cut-off negatively affected gas flow in Eastern and Western European countries as well, and tarnished Russia's image as a reliable energy and trade partner.

A law passed in January 2006 made it more difficult for foreign non-governmental organisations to operate in the country. The Kremlin has said it suspects some NGOs may harbour spies. And in December 2006, bowing to pressure from the Russian government, Shell Oil offered to hand over its controlling interest in the US$20 billion Sakhalin-2 energy project to state-owned Gazprom. This was widely viewed in the West as a strong-armed tactic reminiscent of Russia's days as a state-controlled economy.

The Medvedev interlude

As the constitution prevented Putin from running for a third consecutive presidential term, Dmitrii Medvedev was elected President of Russia on 2 March 2008. Medvedev nominated Putin as Prime Minister, but there was no question either abroad or in Russia as to who actually held the power. Furthermore, one of Medvedev's acts as President was to amend the constitution, changing all future presidential terms from four years to six years.

In Putin-like displays of firmness, Medvedev made the controversial decision to attack Georgia following unrest in the Caucasus that resulted in a Georgian offensive against Southern Ossetia, a Russian territory. Georgia claimed to have been provoked by Russian military exercises along the border and after the signing of the peace agreement, it turned out that Russia had appropriated some of Georgia's territories.

In September 2010, Medvedev sensationally sacked Yuri Luzhkov, the mayor of Moscow for 18 years, citing 'loss of confidence', after bitter feuds erupted between the Kremlin and Luzhkov's Moscow city government. Corruption was cited as another reason for ending Luzhkov's undisputed reign of the capital, during which his wife, the third richest woman on the planet, is said to have amassed almost $3 billion, though it is widely believed that it was because Luzhkov overstepped the mark and treated the President with contempt.

Unrest continues to plague the Caucasus border areas, with small-scale terrorist acts occurring quite frequently; the damning December 2010 Wikileaks report accused Russia of being a 'kleptocracy' where organised crime acts under the protection of the government, bribing is rampant, the judicial system and the police are in cahoots with the mafia and the rule of law is applied very selectively indeed.

Putin, back again

In 2013, a teary-eyed Putin was once again elected President when Medvedev chose not to run for a second term, which surprised no one. However, before he was inaugurated, tens of thousands of Russians took to the streets to protest what they deem to be unfair elections and the lack of choice they got. The way the political system works now, it is practically impossible for anyone who might challenge the status quo to even be in the running, as there are now convoluted rules and regulations in place that are almost impossible to follow. The rules have been amended so much over the past decade that the president is the only one to be directly elected by the people; most other public roles are appointed by the ruling party. The constitution is altered at will to suit the powers that be, the most recent example being the decision to take away the Prosecutor-General's power to appoint regional prosecutors and give them to the president instead. So now the president will decide who shall and shall not be prosecuted; so much for an impartial judicial system.

Russians are quite pessimistic about the state of the country, many complaining about the lack of jobs for newly qualified professionals, which still results in a brain drain, the endemic corruption that permeates every level of government, and lack of investment in the country by Russia's wealthiest citizens who prefer to invest abroad.

In spite of security fears and a few teething troubles (new hotels not completed in time for the Games, a glitch affecting one of the Olympic rings during the opening ceremony), the Winter Olympic Games in Sochi in February 2014 went relatively smoothly and by the end the host country topped the medal table.

In February 2014, Ukraine's president, Viktor Yanukovich, was ousted after months of protest. Subsequently, Putin declared that the new Ukrainian government was 'illegal' and that therefore he was no longer obliged to honour the 1994 treaty that bound Russia to respect Ukraine's borders. Furthermore, he stated that Russia was obliged to defend Russian citizens resident in Ukraine against aggression from 'fascists and anti-Semites'. In the turmoil that followed, Crimea was annexed by Russia after a hastily-held referendum and, as we go to press, key government buildings in eastern Ukraine have been taken over by armed pro-Russia forces.

ECONOMY

Russia has vast natural resources and in this sense has the potential to be an extremely rich country. It has the world's largest reserves of natural gas as well as deposits of oil, coal, iron ore, manganese, asbestos, lead, gold, silver and copper that will continue to be extracted long after most other countries have exhausted their supplies. Russia's forested regions cover an area almost four times the size of the Amazon basin. Yet owing to gross economic mismanagement under communism and continuing corruption since the privatisation of state industries, the country has experienced severe financial hardship, particu-

RUSSIA

larly in the 1990s, and had been a recipient of Western aid. However, the high oil and natural gas prices over the past few years have given a much-needed boost to the economy, even if there's a wide gap between the country's wealthiest citizens and the rest of the population.

THE RUSSIANS

Russia is the ninth most populous nation in the world with an estimated 143.5 million people. The country's population was in decline for 15 years for a number of reasons – drug use, alcoholism, sexually transmitted diseases and deteriorating medical care among suggested causes, but also due to people's life choices: women choosing a career over having a family. Slow population growth has been taking place since 2009, though average life expectancy is 72 years for Russian women and just 59 years for men. To counter the downward trend in birth, the Russian government has recently started offering financial incentives again for families with more than two children, echoing the 'hero mother' of the Soviet era.

A high proportion of Russia's people (81%) are ethnic Russians. The rest belong to nearly 100 ethnic minorities, the most numerous being Tatars (3.9%), Ukrainians (1.4%), Bakshir (1.1%) and Chechens (1%). In the former USSR it was never wise to refer to people as 'Russian' because of the many other republics they might have come from; there's still a world of difference between 'Russky' (a person of Slavic descent who is also a Russian citizen) and a 'Rossiyanin' (a citizen of Russia who may belong to a number of different ethnicities. Racial intolerance, sadly, is a fact of Russian life, particularly in large cities with visible ethnic minorities.

Russia is divided into *oblasts* (the basic administrative unit), *krays* (smaller territories) and *autonomous republics* (special territories containing ethnic minority groups such as the Buryats in Siberia). Siberia is part of the Russian Federation and exists only as a geographical, not a political, unit, though occasionally there are talks of Siberia breaking away and becoming autonomous – usually spurred on by the fact that Siberia produces most of Russia's mineral wealth, yet the revenue seems to flow out of Siberia to the capital.

GOVERNMENT

Russia moved briskly down the political path from autocracy to 'socialist state', with a period of a few months in 1917 when it was a republic. From November 1917 until August 1991 Russia was in the hands of the Communist Party, and until September 1993 it was run by the Congress of People's Deputies. This 1068-seat forum was elected from throughout the USSR. At its head sat the Supreme Soviet, the legislative body, elected from Congress. Since only Party members could stand for election in Congress, only Party members could ever run the country.

The approval of a new Russian Constitution in December 1993 means that the country is now governed by a European-style two-tier parliament – the Duma – very similar to that of France. The head of state is the Russian president, currently Vladimir Putin. Again.

Despite the theory, Russia is far from democratic. The power of the country is vested in a few hundred chief executives of huge corporations who picked up enormous wealth through the corrupt privatisation of state enterprises. These so-called 'oligarchs' now monopolise the media, gas and oil, military production and banking sectors, in effect controlling the entire Russian state. With these monopolistic and in many cases criminal power merchants securely lodged in the Kremlin, true democracy is a long way off. Under Putin's autocratic control the situation has not changed; in fact, presidential control has tightened over the judiciary system and the free press.

EDUCATION AND SOCIAL WELFARE

Education and health care are provided free for the entire population but standards are much higher for those who opt for private healthcare. **School** is compulsory between the ages of seven and seventeen, with the result that Russia has a literacy rate of 98%. Although funding for research is currently at an all-time low, until a few years ago the country ploughed some 5% of national income directly into scientific research in its 900 universities and institutes. Russia's present inability to maintain its scientists has led to a severe brain drain; certain states in the Middle East are very keen for Russian scientists to help them with their nuclear programmes.

The national **health-care** programme is likewise suffering through a lack of funds. Russia has produced some of the world's leading surgeons, yet recent outbreaks of diseases extinct in the developed world have demonstrated that health services here were never comprehensive. The most publicised epidemic in the last few years has been diphtheria, with the death of hundreds of Russians who should have been inoculated at birth. While the wealthy have access to state-of-the-art medical equipment and very high health-care standards in private hospitals, the state hospitals tend to be grim, understaffed places, where nursing staff must be bribed to do their jobs properly.

Recent government programmes aim to stabilise living standards, gradually reduce poverty and mass unemployment, and create conditions for real growth in income, but the majority of the population is not optimistic about their chances of success.

RELIGION

Russia was a pagan nation until 988 when Tsar Vladimir ordered a mass conversion to Christianity. The state religion adopted was that of the Greek **Orthodox Eastern Church (Russian Orthodox)** rather than Roman Catholicism. After the Revolution religion was suppressed until the late 1930s when Stalin, recognising the importance of the Church's patriotism in time of war, restored Orthodoxy to respectability. This policy was reversed after the war and many of the country's churches, synagogues and mosques were closed down. Labour camps were filled with religious dissidents, particularly under Khrushchev, though some old people, who no longer had anything to lose, continued to display icons in their homes without facing much persecution.

Gorbachev's attitude towards religion was more relaxed and the 1990 Freedom of Conscience law took religion off the blacklist. In 1991 Yeltsin even legalised Christmas: Russian Christmas Day, celebrated on 7 January, is now an official public holiday again. Numerous churches have been restored to cater for the country's estimated 50 million Orthodox believers. In 1997 the Cathedral of Christ the Saviour, demolished by Stalin to make way for a public swimming-pool, was rebuilt in Moscow (see p179). The new cathedral was the setting for a magnificent service on 20 August 2000 in which Tsar Nicholas II and his family, the more famous victims of communism and the Revolution, were made saints in an elaborate canonisation ceremony.

As well as Russian Orthodox Christians there are also about 1.4 million **Roman Catholics**. The number of **Christian sects** is also growing. Sects as diverse as the so-called '**Old Believers**' (who split from the Orthodox church in the 17th century), Scientology and Jehovah's Witnesses are looking for converts here. This has worried some Russians and on 14 June 1993 the Supreme Soviet passed an amendment to the Freedom of Conscience law banning foreign organisations from recruiting by 'independent' religious activities without permission.

Although the number of **Muslims** has fallen with the independence of the Central Asian Republics, there are still about 11 million in Russia, who now face the discrimination traditionally set aside for Jews. The Russian government has become very keen on the 'war on terror' and voiceless migrant workers, most of whom come from the impoverished Central Asian republics, are subject to horrific treatment by the police and ultra-nationalist gangs.

Russian Jews, historically subject to the most cruel discrimination, have been less trusting of the greater religious freedoms. Their position has been made even more uncomfortable by the recent growth of Russian neo-Nazi groups and by the canonisation of the last tsar, a confirmed anti-Semite. In 1990 more than 200,000 Jews moved to Israel, pouring in at a rate of up to 3000 per day. By 1998 over half a million had left, though there are still large Jewish communities in Moscow and St Petersburg.

In Buryatia, the centre of **Russian Buddhism**, many monasteries have reopened. Since all are a long way off the tourist track, they have not been kept in good repair as museums, unlike churches in European Russia.

Religious freedoms have also brought a growth in **animism** and **Shamanism**, particularly in Siberia.

Practical information for the visitor

ESSENTIAL DOCUMENTS

(Also see Part 1: Planning Your Trip) One 19th-century English traveller who left his passport and tickets behind in London still managed to travel across Siberia carrying no other document than a pass to the Reading Room at the British Library. These days, you couldn't get away with that.

The essential documents are your passport, a Russian visa and, if appropriate, a visa for the countries you'll be entering after Russia. If you are travelling with an organisation which has issued you with vouchers to exchange for accommodation or train tickets, don't forget these. **Always carry a photocopy of your passport when you are in Russia**: if the police stop you and you don't have it on you, you'll be fined, and you may not wish to trust them with the actual document. As backup, you may wish to scan your passport page and visa and email the scans to yourself.

It's also worth bringing photocopies of your Russian visa. Note that, in theory, **all visas must be registered within seven business days of your arrival in each Russian city** (see pp25-6).

ARRIVING IN RUSSIA

Customs allowances: entering or leaving the country

You should not have any problem bringing into Russia any items for personal use or consumption, including modest amounts of spirits or wine. You need a special permit to export 'cultural treasures', a term used to include almost anything that looks old or valuable. Paintings, gold and silver items made before 1968, military medals and coins may attract the attention of customs officials and may be confiscated or charged at 100% or more duty if you do not have a permit from the Ministry of Culture.

Customs declaration forms

At the Russian border you will be given a Customs Declaration Form (*tamozhennaya deklaratsiya*, таможенная декларация) on which you have to declare all the money and luggage you are carrying. These days it's largely a formality and it's unlikely that the border guards will check a foreigner's luggage.

China no longer requires visitors to fill in a separate customs form and neither does Mongolia.

Border-crossing procedures

Border-crossing procedures on the train may take anywhere from three to seven hours. The first step is for immigration and customs officers of the country you are leaving to check passports and visas and collect customs forms. At the Mongolian and Chinese borders, they may disappear with your passport for half an hour or so, before coming back and dishing them out. The compartments are then searched by border guards, though the searches usually consist just of a quick glance inside the luggage compartments. On the other side of the border the entire procedure is repeated.

As rails in Russia and Mongolia are of a wider gauge than those in China and most of Europe, bogies have to be changed at the borders. The carriages are lifted individually and the bogies rolled out and replaced. Passengers are sometimes allowed off the train during this time, in which case you can wait at the border station. If you do get off, carriage attendants won't normally let you get back on before the official boarding time, which is when the train returns to the station to pick up the passengers. Don't leave valuables behind.

During the entire border-crossing procedure the train's lavatories remain locked. This is not purely for security reasons since changing the bogies requires workers to operate beneath the train.

WHERE TO STAY

There's now a wide range of places to stay in Russia: everything from youth hostels and B&Bs to luxurious boutique hotels and international hotel chains.

Types of accommodation

Hostels More and more cities in Russia – including St Petersburg, Moscow, Vladimir, Suzdal, Nizhny Novgorod, Yekaterinburg, Tyumen, Novosibirsk, Tomsk, Krasnoyarsk, Irkutsk, Ulan-Ude, Khabarovsk and Vladivostok – have opened up bona-fide hostels, making budget travel that much easier. Most hostels come with oodles of useful information on the city, free wi-fi and internet use, and (occasionally) free breakfast. Many offer a range of services – from booking your onward travel to arranging city tours and staff tend to be bilingual, since backpacking and staying in hostels is a Western phenomenon that's only just catching on with budget Russian travellers.

Dormitory beds cost about US$20-35/£15-23/€17-28, while doubles may cost US$75-105/£50-70/€60-80. A number of places in St Petersburg and Moscow belong to Hostelling International (HI; 🖳 www.russia-hostelling.ru), so it could be worthwhile investing in an HI card for the discount. Information on hostels can also be obtained from Hostels.com (🖳 www.hostels.com) or the similar Hostelworld.com (🖳 www.hostelworld.com).

Bear in mind that many hostels consists of apartments inside multi-storey apartment buildings and that there's rarely a sign outside, making them tricky to find. Make sure you write down the exact address, door code (if given) and phone number of the hostel just in case you get lost.

Homestays These can be organised in most cities along the Trans-Siberian for US$45-60/£30-40/€34-47 per person per night including some or all meals, with additional charges for any tours, ticketing, transport or other services. You are matched to your host according to the language you speak.

A reliable agency is Host Families Association (HOFA; 🖳 www.hofa.ru); the association is based in St Petersburg.

Budget hotels These places are usually clean and basic, with a café or basic restaurant but no other conveniences. Rooms are simple with a TV and fridge and either an attached or shared bathroom. The best rooms are referred to as *lux* ('luxury'); unlike the mid-range hotels, here it just might mean that the room is more spacious; it won't necessarily have better facilities.

Most places now provide toilet paper, soap and a clean towel the size of a handkerchief. Bathrooms are usually clean but will still have Soviet plumbing. Sink and bath plugs are rare, so it's wise to carry your own universal plug. During the summer, many budget hotels may be without hot water for up to four weeks (more in some Siberian cities), as hot water is centrally supplied and pipes must be cleaned annually. The staff rarely speak English, but are either helpful towards foreigners or freaked out by them.

Basic hotel rooms cost US$40-60/£30-40/€35-45 for a single or US$45-65/£32-42/€35-48 for a double.

Resting rooms Most railway stations offer resting rooms (*komnaty otdykha* комнаты отдыха) where you can stay overnight or even just for a few hours; they tend to charge for 3, 6, 12 or 24 hours, or sometimes by the hour. Some require you to have an onward train ticket. These rooms are basic – expect nothing but a bed and a power socket – but clean and comfortable, some with TVs, and fall into the category of single, twin, four-bed room or six-bed room, usually with shared bathrooms. Some resting rooms charge extra for use of hot shower. Solo travellers staying in anything other than a single will find themselves sharing with strangers of the same gender. The lux rooms tend to have en suite bathrooms, TV and fridge. For 12 hours, lux rooms generally cost US$50/£35/€40, while beds in a shared room generally cost US$20/£15/€18.

CouchSurfing & Airbnb The brainchild of an American student, **CouchSurfing** (⌨ www.couchsurfing.org), the free global hospitality/cultural-exchange scheme that's particularly popular with travellers in their late teens, 20s and 30s has really taken off in Russia, and in all large cities you will find numerous English-speaking hosts happy to put you up or at least meet up and hang out with you. Staying with a knowledgeable local can really transform your experience and give you valuable insight into today's Russia. You have to be a member of ⌨ www.couchsurfing.org, and it's a good idea for you to rack up several positive ratings by hosting travellers yourself before you ask to surf someone's couch. Pick your host carefully, choosing someone with multiple positive ratings and making sure you know exactly what kind of accommodation's on offer and don't forget to be an ideal guest. The only downside to Couchsurfing is that your hosts will not be able to register your visa for you, meaning that you'll have to find a travel company that does, though this is easily arranged in larger cities.

In Russia's larger cities, particularly in Moscow and St Petersburg, many people offer private rooms and even apartments under the **Airbnb** (⌨ www .airbnb.co.uk/s/Russia) scheme but that you might have to stay outside the city centre to get a bargain.

Mid-range hotels These are mostly solid Soviet-era hotels, which have been renovated to offer features such as wi-fi and cable TV, Rooms are divided into standard single/double, 'improved' single/double, *polu-lux* (junior suite) and *lux* (suite) categories. Anything other than a standard room will be larger and more comfortable. In some hotels there may be a *dezhurnaya* (floor attendant) – a Soviet-era throwback – often an elderly female busybody, who seems to spend most of her time drinking tea in a little den and keeping an eagle eye on all that happens on her floor.

Over the last few years, a good range of brand-new business hotels has sprung up, with modern bathrooms and good, functional rooms with all the mod-cons, and often English-speaking staff. The same is true of some new mini-hotels and mid-range boutique hotels that you'll find in larger cities; these are well-run, Western-style establishments with efficient service. The staff can usually help you make travel arrangements.

In Moscow and St Petersburg standard hotel rooms cost US$120-360/£80-240/€95-270 and in other cities US$90-150/£60-100/€70-110 for a single or US$110-220/£66-132/€80-160 for a double with attached bathroom.

Top hotels Many are owned by large Western chains such as Marriott and Radisson, though Moscow and St Petersburg in particular boast some luxurious hotels inside historical buildings restored to a very high standard.

The rooms come with all mod-cons and luxurious touches, such as Jacuzzis in bathrooms. Facilities may include restaurants, travel agencies, money exchange, gym, spa, sauna and swimming pool. The staff tend to be multi-lingual. Luxury chains aside, in Moscow and St Petersburg you'll also find concept boutique hotels. Truly luxurious hotels are found in Moscow, St Petersburg and some of the other larger cities and prices are what you would expect in the West – around US$645/£430/€518 per night. In the country, a town's only 'luxurious' option may be a renovated Soviet monstrosity.

LOCAL TRANSPORT

If you're booking an independent trip through an agency, you may be encouraged to purchase 'transfers' so that you will be met at the airport or station on arrival and taken to your hotel. Prices tend to be high, but transfers are more reliable than comparably priced taxis. If travelling on a budget, local public transport is more than adequate.

For information about booking tickets for rail travel in Russia see pp124-9, for Mongolia see p130, and for China pp130-4.

Metro, buses, trolleybuses and trams
The **metro** is a cheap and efficient way to get around, with trains every few minutes. In Moscow it's worth using the metro just to see the grand older stations, which have ornate ceilings, gilded statues, Communist mosaics and enormous chandeliers.

Russian metro stations are deeper underground than their Western counterparts in order to double as bomb shelters, so their escalators are long and swift. The one at St Petersburg's Ploshchad Lenina station rises 59m (194ft). At street level, metro stations are indicated by a large blue or red 'M'. Lines are named after their terminal stations, as on the Paris metro. Where two or more lines intersect, the transfer station may have more than one name, one for each line. As trains move off from the station, the next station is announced. The counter above the end of each tunnel indicates how long it's been since the last train left. Besides Moscow and St Petersburg, you'll find a metro system in Novosibirsk, Yekaterinburg, Nizhny Novgorod and Kazan. See p520 for useful station signs.

Every major city has a comprehensive and inexpensive **bus** service (fixed-fare and often very crowded) and usually also **trolley-buses** and **trams**. Most

❑ **The most useful travel app**
Google Maps: eat your heart out! Russia's 2Gis (🖥 www.2gis.ru) is a travel app like no other: it allows you to upload interactive maps of many major cities (including most along the Trans-Sib), zoom in on every building, every street, and click on any public transport stop to find out exactly which buses/trams depart from there and at what time, as well as select specific public transport routes to see exactly where they go. If you want to see if there are hotels/restaurants/pharmacies/hairdressers near your exact location, you can do that too. It is also updated monthly. The only catch is that it's all in Russian, but if you have a smartphone, you can still make use of it.

buses/trolleybuses/trams have conductors who go around collecting fares and dishing out tickets. In Moscow, you may use multi-ride tickets on all forms of public transport; you have to press the ticket to the scanning device.

Taxis
In Russia, official taxis are safer than unofficial ones. You'll recognise the former by the green 'for hire' light. Although they have meters, not all use them. Agree on a price before you even get in since once the driver realises you're a foreigner, he'll bump it up accordingly. Ask a local beforehand what the taxi trip should cost and don't be afraid to haggle. Most Russians book taxis over the phone; just pop into any large hotel and ask them for help in ordering a taxi. Unofficial taxis are pretty much any car willing to give you a lift. If you don't like the look of the driver, don't get in.

In Ulaanbaatar, flag down any driver and settle on a price. In both Mongolia and Russia it's a good idea not to put your luggage in the boot as the driver may hold it for ransom and demand more money.

In China, few taxi drivers speak English, so have your destination written down in Chinese characters. Taxis are metered; you'll find the rate per kilometre on a sticker on the rear side window. With motorcycle, motor tricycle and pedal tricycle taxis, you have to agree on the price beforehand.

Hitchhiking
Hitchhiking (*avtostop*) is widely practised in Russia, particularly amongst young people. Drivers will readily give you a lift; if you stand in the street with your arm outstretched someone will pull over and ask where you want to go. However, if you try to hitch a ride in a city, they'll expect payment (even though it is illegal), which essentially makes them a cheaper version of the official taxis. Outside the cities, you can easily catch a lift along motorways, at truck stops and next to traffic police stations or anywhere where drivers have to slow down. Have some gifts at the ready and be prepared to be sociable.

The usual precautions apply: women shouldn't hitchhike alone and if you don't like the look of the driver or the car has more than one occupant, don't get in. Don't put your luggage in the boot (trunk) or your driver could simply pull away when you get out to retrieve it.

RUSSIA

Hitching in Mongolia is common, particularly in the countryside, but you're expected to pay the driver, so there's little difference between hitching a ride and waiting for infrequent public transport.

Domestic flights

Domestic flights are a quick and efficient (if somewhat expensive) way of covering long distances if you don't wish to ride the Trans-Sib all the way, and there are frequent flights between Moscow and all major Russian cities, though Russian airports tend to be inefficient and chaotic. Safety standards among smaller, older Russian airlines are reasonable, though it's better to use one of the larger carriers such as Aeroflot (🖥 www.aeroflot.com), S7 (🖥 www.s7 .com) or Transaero (🖥 www.transaero.com). You can book tickets online with most Russian airlines.

In Mongolia, there are flights from Ulaanbaatar to destinations around the country with Aeromongolia (🖥 www.aeromongolia.mn), EzNis (🖥 www.eznis airways.com) and MIAT (🖥 www.miat.com).

China is covered by numerous airlines, such as Air China (🖥 www.airchi na.com.en), China Eastern Airlines (🖥 www.ceair.com) and China Southern Airlines (🖥 www.csair.com). You can check timetables on websites such as 🖥 www.ctrip.com.

Boat

Most of the cities you will visit are built on rivers and short trips on the water are usually possible. In St Petersburg the most interesting way to reach Peterhof is by hydrofoil. Cruise boats from Moscow and St Petersburg stop at various Golden Ring cities along the way. From Irkutsk you can get to Lake Baikal by boat up the Angara River and also to various destinations on the lake's shore, though schedules are not terribly reliable.

There are also some long-distance options: for example, trips up the Yenisey from Krasnoyarsk to Dudinka, or between Omsk and Tobolsk along the Ob and Irtysh rivers, from Khabarovsk to Komsomolsk-na-Amure along the Amur and from Yakutsk along the Lena.

ELECTRICITY

In Russian cities electricity is 220V, 50 cycle AC and the same is true in China and Mongolia. Sockets require a continental-type plug or adaptor; in Russia and Mongolia they are designed to accommodate the two European-style round prongs, whereas in China, plugs come in four designs: two round prongs, as in Europe, two flat prongs, as in the USA, three-pronged round pins as in Hong Kong and three-pronged angled pins as in Australia. It's best to bring a universal adaptor.

Most train carriages have two sockets (one opposite the provodnitsa's cubbyhole and one at the other end, by the toilets) that can be used to charge mobile phones and such; form an orderly queue.

TIME

Russia spans nine time zones and on the train you will be adjusting your watch by an hour almost every day. Russian railways run entirely on Moscow Time, listing the departure and arrival times on timetables accordingly. All station clocks show Moscow Time, so it can be disconcerting to cross the border from China at breakfast-time, only to be informed by station clocks that it's just 2am.

Moscow Time (MT) is four hours ahead of GMT/UTC. This used to be its summer time but thanks to Medvedev **Russia** is now permanently on this time (though this may yet change). Following the railway timetable system, throughout the route guide times are shown in relation to Moscow Time; those for the main cities are: Novosibirsk (MT+3), Irkutsk (MT+5), Khabarovsk (MT+7) and Vladivostok (MT+7). For times relative to GMT/UTC, add four hours to MT. Local time in Novosibirsk (MT+3), for example, is GMT/UTC + 7. In the city guides section of this book, local times are used.

Most of **Mongolia** and all of **China** are both GMT/UTC + 8 and since neither observes summer time the time stays the same throughout the year.

MONEY

(See also p40). The basic unit of Russian currency is the rouble (рубль), which is divided into 100 kopecks (копейки). There are 10 and 50-kopeck and 1, 2, 5 and 10-rouble coins; banknotes come in denominations of 10 (which are being phased out, see box p290), 50, 100, 500, 1000 and 5000 roubles.

The rouble is the only legal currency in Russia. Upmarket hotels and restaurants may quote prices in US$ or euros but will expect payment in roubles. Some Russians still change their roubles to euros or dollars for security, although as the rouble has been fairly stable over the last few years, they are gaining confidence in their own currency.

You may have difficulty getting change from large denomination notes in pretty much anything that is not a large supermarket. Hoard your coins and small-denomination rouble notes for use on public transport, museums and luggage storage facilities. (There is no need to hoard small denomination notes in either Mongolia or China.)

For details about money, exchange rates and the currency in **Mongolia** see p66 and p364 and for **China** see p66 and p398.

What to bring

Euros and US dollars are the easiest currencies to exchange throughout Russia. Pounds sterling and a few other non-EU currencies can be changed in Moscow, St Petersburg, and some other major cities; Swedish kronor are widely accepted in St Petersburg, while Japanese yen and Chinese RMB/yuan are easily exchanged in Khabarovsk and Vladivostok.

Foreign banknotes must be as new, crisp and clean as possible, because older ones, especially if they're torn, soiled or have writing or ink stamps on them, are likely to be rejected.

In Mongolia, all major currencies are readily exchanged for tugriks at currency exchanges; the same is true in China.

Exchanging currency

You can easily find currency exchange services along main streets (visible by their fluorescent exchange rates posted outside) and also inside hotels and banks in major cities, though hotels tend to offer worse rates than either currency exchange services or banks. Avoid the currency exchange by the baggage reclaim section at Moscow's Domodedovo Airport like the proverbial plague.

Exchange facilities are plentiful in Ulaanbaatar and in Beijing.

❏ Rouble exchange rates

To get the latest rates of exchange see 🖳 www.xe.com/ucc.

	Rouble
Aus$1	R33.11
Can$1	R32.41
China Y10	R57.18
Euro€1	R49.41
Japan ¥100	R34.94
Mong T100	R2.02
NZ$1	R30.62
Sing$1	R28.41
S Africa R10	R33.64
UK£1	R60.04
US$1	R35.74

Credit/debit cards and ATMs

Credit cards – especially Visa and MasterCard, less readily American Express and Diners Club – are now accepted in many of Russia's upmarket shops, hotels and restaurants. In most cities, including those along the Trans-Siberian, it's easy to find an ATM (банкомат) where a range of debit cards can be used for rouble cash advances. You may find, however, that some Russian banks do not accept cards from some foreign banks, regardless of whether they sport the relevant symbols or not, so keep a supply of cash on you for emergencies. TransCreditBank (Транскредитбанк) ATMs are found at all major railway stations and tend to accept all foreign Visa and MasterCards.

In **Mongolia**, credit cards are accepted by top end hotels and travel agencies, but there's usually a 3% surcharge. Cash advances are free with Visa, but MasterCard can incur charges of up to 4%. In **China**, you can use credit cards and debit cards to withdraw money and to pay at top hotels, but foreign cards are used less frequently to pay for purchases.

Tipping

In **Russian restaurants**, the tip is generally up to the customer's discretion. In more upmarket restaurants in large cities, it's typical to tip up to 10% for good service. **Guides** should receive a tip of around 10% of their daily rate.

In **China**, tipping is not done at all, unless you're tipping a porter in a high-class hotel. In **Mongolia**, tipping is not essential but appreciated; rounding up the bill is fine.

POST AND TELECOMMUNICATIONS

Internet and wi-fi

With the proliferation of free wi-fi in cafés, restaurants, bars, hotels and hostels across Russia and in Ulaanbaatar and Beijing, and increased use of smartphones, tablets, iPads and notebooks, internet cafés are fewer in number, though some can still be found in major Russian cities, Ulaanbaatar and Beijing. For those with their own laptops, pre-paid 3G and 4G modems can be purchased from most mobile phone stores in Russia.

In Russia, internet access tends to be cheapest at post offices. In China, be prepared to produce ID when using an internet café and even to have your photo taken. Social media that's common in the West (Facebook, Twitter) is forbidden in China though can still be accessed via proxy servers. In Mongolia, internet cafés are plentiful in Ulaanbaatar but outside the cities, getting online is practically impossible.

Post
Airmail to and from the UK takes about a week, and two weeks to the USA. Outgoing mail is generally reliable, whilst incoming mail is less so. To send a parcel from Russia you must have it wrapped and sealed with a wax stamp at the post office. Post offices are typically open 8am-8pm, and the larger cities have 24-hour post offices.

On international mail from Russia addresses may be written in English and in standard Western format but it is helpful to write the country name in Cyrillic: UK: Великобритания; USA: США; Canada: Канада; Germany: Германия; Australia: Австралия; New Zealand: Новая Зеландия.

For mail to Russia and domestic mail the address should be in Russian and follow this format: Six-digit postal code; Name of city or town; Street name, with house number set off by a comma; Name of addressee; followed below by the return address.

If you wish to send something urgent or valuable out of Russia, Mongolia or China, use one of the courier companies such as DHL (💻 www.dhl.com) and FedEx (💻 www.fedex.com) that have branches in the capitals and large cities.

Mail **from China** takes around a week to reach international destinations, and it's possible to send letters from many hotels. Post offices tend to be open 9am-5pm daily. **Mongolian post** is reliable but can be slow, and letters and postcards must be sent from the post office.

Telephone
The country code for Russia is 7. To make an international call dial 8, then wait for a second tone and dial 10 followed by the country code and number. To make a long-distance call, dial 8, followed by the area/city code and number. If calling abroad from a mobile phone, dial + followed by the country code and phone number. Note that city codes and phone numbers in Russia often change.

The main mobile phone companies in Russia are MTS (💻 www.mts.ru), Beeline (💻 www.beeline.ru), Megafon (💻 www.megafon.ru) and Skylink (💻 skylink.ru). SIM cards cost as little as R300 and you can top up your credit

RUSSIA

| **Emergency numbers** | Fire ☎ 01 | Police ☎ 02 | Ambulance ☎ 03 |

either by buying top-up cards from kiosks or by walking into any mobile phone store and using a self-service top-up machine: pick your network, type in your number, choose the amount of credit you'd like to add, insert the cash and receive confirmation of the top-up via text.

There is good mobile phone reception all along the Trans-Sib and increasingly so in rural areas. Roaming costs can be quite expensive, but all networks offer a tariff that allows you to pay the same across all of Russia's regions.

To call from street telephones (*taksofon*) that are fast becoming obsolete you need a prepaid telephone card (*kartochka dlya taksofona*); these are available from kiosks and metro station ticket windows. Different types of taksofon take different brands of card. You can use street phones to make local, domestic and international calls, but it can be cheaper to get phonecards in a variety of units, available in shops and kiosks, that can be used from landlines or call centres to call abroad. At a call centre (междугородный телефон) you leave a deposit with the cashier who will assign you a booth from which you make your call. Pay the balance after the call.

More and more travellers carry smartphones and other wi-fi enabled devices that allow them to make use of the proliferation of wi-fi hotspots to make free calls abroad via Skype.

FOOD AND DRINK

There's more to Russian cuisine than borsch and chicken Kiev, which you'll discover as soon as you spend time off the train. Yes, Russian food tends to be solid and hearty, but it's moved far, far beyond the stereotypes of the Soviet era and its influences span the entire former Soviet Union – from the Baltic States via the Caucasus and Central Asia to the Far East, with Georgian (see box p71), Armenian and Tatar cuisines adding spice to an otherwise rather bland palate. Today, Russians look even further afield; in large cities you'll find Indian, Thai, Chinese and Japanese restaurants cheek by jowl with Russian ones, and the menu of your typical Russian restaurant these days tends to include the Holy Trinity of shashlyk, pasta and sushi.

As for Russian food itself, you're bound to encounter all manner of vegetables and grains, grown in the rich dark soil of this vast land, converted into tasty soups, salads and breads; all manner of fish from Russia's many lakes, rivers and seas, seafood from the Pacific and Northern Oceans, and every kind of meat you'd expect (and some you wouldn't: wild game, for example).

Breakfast

When Russians eat at home, the first meal of the day may include fruit juice, cheese, eggs, *khleb* (bread), *varenye* (jam), *kefir* (sour yoghurt drink), *tvorog* (cottage cheese) or different types of *kasha* (porridge) – from oatmeal or buckwheat to millet or rice. The aforementioned tvorog is particularly delicious when fried up as *syrniki* (cottage cheese fritters), served with *smetana* (sour cream), honey or jam.

Zakuski and salads

Russian hors d'oeuvres (*zakuski*) – typically something to eat as an accompaniment to vodka or beer – consist of some or all of the following: cold cuts of meat, sliced salami, *bliny/blini* (small/thin pancakes), sausages, salmon, pickled herring, paté and caviar. Salads range from simple cucumber and tomato and the classic *selyodka pod shuboi* ('herring in a fur coat' – salted herring under layers of beetroot, pickles, egg and mayonnaise) to vegetable salad with beef tongue or chicken livers, mushroom salad, smoked salmon salad, Greek salad and Caesar salad.

Soups

Soups can make a meal in themselves, accompanied by a stack of brown bread. Best known is the originally Ukrainian but now firmly associated with Russia *borsch* (beetroot soup) which often includes other vegetables (potatoes, cabbage and onion), chopped ham and a swirl of *smetana* (sour cream); the veggie version is *postny borsch*; otherwise it's typically made with beef stock. *Solyanka* is a delicious, hearty soup with smoked meats, pickles, olives, lemon and honey, with just the right mix of salty, sweet and sour. *Shchi* (cabbage soup) is the traditional soup of the proletariat and was a favourite of Nicholas II, who is said to have enjoyed only plain peasant cooking, to the great disappointment of his French chef. *Okroshka* is a chilled soup of meat, vegetables and *kvas* (a

❏ You don't eat meat?!

Vegetarian cooking isn't widely practised in much of Russia and with the exception of big cities like Moscow and St Petersburg, where you can find vegetarian restaurants, and a few Hare Krishna-style Asian restaurants throughout the country, there aren't many venues dedicated to vegetarians. Nevertheless, vegetarians can manage in Russian restaurants if they choose carefully, but they shouldn't rely on the waiter's imagination or assistance! In this book we've noted restaurants offering a number of vegetarian options with a [V].

Amongst **appetisers**, *shchi* (cabbage soup) is often meatless; Georgian sulguni cheese is very similar to Greek halloumi and is usually served grilled; carrot, tomato and cucumber salads are also available.

Main courses are harder; one option is to order a double portion of a starter found on almost every Russian menu: *Julienne*, also known as *griby v smetane* – wild mushrooms baked in cream sauce. Omelettes are another option, if a horribly predictable one. Perversely, you can often do better in cheap cafés than in fine restaurants because meatless food is regarded as rather down-market. Items to look for in cafés are *piroshki* (dough-pastries with fillings like onion, cabbage or carrot), *vatrushki* (cream-cheese pastries) and *vareniki* (dumplings filled with potato, mushroom, cabbage, cottage cheese or sour cherry). You can almost always find *blini* or *oladyi* (different kinds of Russian pancakes) served with either sour cream or jam.

In **Georgian restaurants** *lobio* (spicy bean stew) is a vegetarian mainstay, and a few Georgian places also serve *achma* (a kind of cream-sauce lasagne), as well as *khachapuri* (cheese-filled bread). Finally, Russians love of **Italian food** means that Italian restaurants are to be found in every city, with reliable pasta backup options as a result.   **Neil McGowan**

❑ **Black gold – Russia's caviar**
The roe of the sturgeon is becoming more expensive as the fish itself becomes rarer. Four species are acknowledged to produce the best caviar: beluga, sterlet, osyotr and sevruga, all of them from the Caspian and Black Seas. To produce caviar's characteristic flavour (preferably not too 'fishy') a complicated process is involved. The female sturgeon is stunned with a mallet, her belly slit open and the roe sacs removed. The eggs are washed and strained into batches of uniform size. The master-taster then samples the roe and decides how much salt to add for preservation.

Processed caviar varies in colour (black, red or golden) and also in the size of the roe. Red caviar comes from salmon and is far cheaper than the rarer black kind. Caviar is either eaten with brown bread or served with sour cream on *blinis*.

A recent report from the World Wide Fund for Nature (WWF) warns that the sturgeon is on the brink of extinction because of aggressive fishing by Russia. The report says that up to 90% of caviar is now obtained illegally, so if you do wish to take some 'black gold' home with you (tourists are permitted 250g of caviar per person), make sure you purchase sealed jars, only from shops and not from peddlers, and only if they are sealed with a CITES (Convention on International Trade in Endangered Species) label, which is an international trade-control measure designed to curtail sturgeon poaching.

beer-like brew made from fermented bread). *Rassolnik* is a soup of pickled vegetables and *ukha* is a hearty soup that contains fish and potatoes.

Fish and seafood
Fish common in Russia include *selyodka* (herring), *pahltoos* (halibut), *syomga* (salmon) and *osetrina* (sturgeon), but you may come across numerous other varieties, including *shchuka* (pike), *karp* (carp) and any number of river fish, often encountered in smoked and dried form at train stops and city markets. One to look out for as potential Trans-Sib provisions are tins of smoked *shproty* (sprats), a smaller cousin of the sardine. Fresh fish are steamed, fried, baked, boiled and come with a variety of sauces. Around Lake Baikal you can try *omul*, the famous Lake Baikal fish, which has a delicate flavour; smoked *omul* is also very good. Seafood such as *grebeshki* (scallops), *krevetki* (prawns), *kal'mar* (squid) and *oostritsy* (oysters) grace the menus of many restaurants. In the Far East, you can try *krahb* – the giant crab from the frigid waters of Kamchatka.

Meat
Popular Russian mains include *kotleta po kievsky* (chicken Kiev), *beef Stroganoff* (named after the wealthy merchant family – Stroganov – who financed the first Siberian explorations in the 1580s), *zharkoye* (meat and vegetable hot pot served in a clay pot), and the ubiquitous *shashlyk* – spiced skewers of grilled pork, veal, lamb, beef, chicken or chitterlings.

From Siberia come *pelmeni*, small dumplings typically filled with meat (but sometimes also mushrooms, fish or even seafood), served in a broth, boiled and topped with soured cream or fried. Other regional specialities you're likely to encounter include *plov* (rice with mutton and spices) and *lagman* (spicy meat and noodle soup) from Central Asia, *vareniki* (large Ukrainian dumplings filled either with meat, potatoes, mushrooms, cottage cheese or sour cherries), *salo* (pig's fat preserved with salt and spices) – another Ukrainian favourite, and *buuzy*, *pozy* or *manty* – large, steamed meat dumplings favoured by Buryat and Uzbek people.

Decent steakhouses have popped up in all major cities, but you're not likely to find steak tartare on their menus.

In supermarkets you will find a wide range of *sosiski* (frankfurter-like sausages) and *sardelki* (fat sausages), as well as excellent *kolbasa* (salami) and other smoked-meat products.

Something for the sweet tooth

On many menus you'll encounter ice cream (*morozhenoye*) and fruit compote (tinned fruit floating in a large dish of syrup). Other options may include delicious *blinis* with sour cream and jam; sweet varieties of *vareniki* (see above)

❏ **The Caucasian invasion**

Out of all the culinary delights contributed to the Russian table by the former Soviet republics, pride of place goes to **Georgian dishes**. Their rich, distinctive flavours are largely due to the use of the *khmeli-suneli* spice mixture and liberal use of ground walnuts and walnut oil. Grilled meats feature prominently, flavoured with fresh herbs, such as coriander, parsley and dill and often sprinkled with pomegranate seeds. Georgian cooking also makes excellent use of offal; some of the more adventurous dishes involve simmered calves' or sheep's brains with tomato and herbs.

There is a wealth of aubergine and other vegetable dishes for vegetarians, as well as the ubiquitous *khachapuri* (circular bread topped with melted sulguni cheese). A number of meat dishes are traditionally cooked and served in a *ketsi* (кеци, a shallow clay dish). Typical dishes you may come across include:

● *basturma* – marinated, grilled beef or lamb
● *buglama* – baked lamb with vegetables
● *chakhokhbili* – spicy chicken stew
● *chikhirtma* – sour chicken soup
● *churchkhella* – an elongated, lumpy-looking, chewy sweet that consists of walnuts or hazelnuts on a string, encased in dried grape juice.
● *dolma* – stuffed grape leaves
● *kharcho* – traditional beef soup with rice and walnuts
● *khinkali* – large steamed, meat-filled dumplings
● *kuchmachi* – hearts, livers and kidneys, cooked up with herbs in a ketsi
● *lavash* – Georgian flatbread
● *pakhlava* – Georgian take on baklava, the sticky flaky pastry with honey
● *pkhali* – savoury vegetable paste, made with spinach, beets, cabbage and more
● *satsivi* – cold chicken dish with walnut sauce
● *shilaplavi* – like pilau rice with lamb, only wetter
● *tsiplyonok tabaka* – chicken fried with garlic and spices

And what is Georgian food without **Georgian wine**? Particularly well-known for its reds, Georgia's repertoire includes Saperavi, Khvanchkara, Akhasheni, Mukuzani, while standout whites to look out for are Ereti, Tsinandali, Alaverdi and Alazanskaya Dolina.

tend to be eaten as a main course rather than dessert. Fresh fruit is readily available from street vendors. The menus of most restaurants now also include cheesecake, tiramisu, pannacotta and other Eurocentric favourites. In bakeries, you'll find *pirozhniye* (cakes with lurid icing and cream); Russian-made chocolate and *pechenye* (biscuits) are sold everywhere.

Bread
Russian bread, the cornerstone of Russian cuisine, served with every meal, is wholesome and delicious. Over 100 different types are baked in Moscow alone, ranging from white to rye to black sourdough similar to German pumpernickel, not to mention sweet croissant-type creations and poppy-seed rolls. If you're packing for the train, note that brown bread stays fresh much longer than white bread, which goes stale after a day or two.

Drinks
Non-alcoholic Most popular is **tea**, traditionally served black with a spoonful of jam or sugar. Milk is not always available so you may want to take along some powdered creamer. Russians have been brewing **coffee** since Peter the Great introduced it in the 17th century, but the only coffee you'll find on the train is the cheap instant stuff. Café chains such as Traveler's Coffee serve an excellent range of global coffees and loose-leaf teas – all at European prices or higher. *Kefir* (sour yogurt drink) is readily available at most canteen-style eating options.

Bottled **mineral water** is available everywhere, often carbonated, with the more expensive brands such as Narzan and Borzhomi tasting rather strongly of all those natural minerals that supposedly have medicinal properties.

There are several varieties of sugary bottled **fruit juice** (*sok*), with Coca Cola and other **soft drinks** found everywhere, as well as home-grown varieties such as Takhun. Freshly squeezed juices have made their way onto menus under the English word 'fresh'; just pronounce it with a Russian accent! A summer/autumn favourite is *mors*, a particularly pleasant drink made from cranberries or seahawthorn berries.

You should also try *kvas* (a semi-fermented mixture of stale brown bread, yeast, malt sugar and water that tastes like a cross between Coke and Guinness). A popular summer cooler sold on the streets, its alcohol content is so low as to be unnoticeable.

❏ **Drinking water**
Although tap water is safe to drink in most Russian cities (apart from St Petersburg, see box p163), delicate Western stomachs may still react to it, so it's wise to stick to bottled mineral water or boiled water to be on the safe side. In Irkutsk and Listvyanka you can safely drink the tap water, which comes directly from Lake Baikal.

On the train, boiled water is always available from samovars in each carriage.

In Mongolia and China, drink only boiled or bottled water; thermos flasks of boiled water are routinely provided on trains and in hotels.

❏ **Vodka and how to drink it**
Be warned that the standard vodka measure in Russia is *sto gram* (100g), compared to 25g in the UK. Vodka is traditionally served ice cold and drained in one go from a shot glass. Men are expected to down in one, but a woman is usually excused. It can be easy enough to drink but it will quickly catch up with you. If you find yourself being invited to join group festivities by some Russians, you may be asked to give a toast and you should take this seriously – a short speech about your subject is enough.

A shot of vodka tends to be followed immediately by *zakuski* (see p69): a popular Russian saying is that 'only drunkards drink without food'. If someone flicks their throat with their forefinger, it usually means 'How about a drink?'. It can be difficult to refuse and Russians can be very insistent, so you can try only drinking a little. If, however, you don't wish to drink at all, and people are being pushy, a drastic tactic guaranteed to get you left alone (and turn you into a social pariah) is to claim that you're an alcoholic (*Ya alkagolik/ya alkagolichka* (m/f).

Alcohol

In a land synonymous with vodka, there's a considerable amount of **beer** drinking going on and beer actually outsells the 'firewater'. Russian beer is cheap and readily available and the most popular brands, such as Baltika, comes in huge 2-litre bottles; there's a growing number of microbreweries across the country and international beers are also available.

Vodka (see box above) is distilled from wheat, rye or potatoes, largely according to the 40% alcohol-to-water ratio patented in 1894 by Dmitry Mendeleyev (the inventor of the periodic table) and is normally drunk straight. If you tire of the original product, there's a range of flavoured vodkas to sample, including *limonnaya* (lemon), *vishnyovaya* (cherry), *pertsovka* (pepper) and *klyukovka* (cranberry). One reader (Warren) wrote to advise making your own flavoured vodka: 'Mix vodka, local strawberries, carbonated water and sugar and you have yourself a cocktail we called the 'Siberian Sling'!

Do not be tempted to drink **samogon** – homemade firewater that takes the place of vodka for the destitute, alcoholic contingent; it can be made of poisonous substances, such as cleaning fluid.

Russian **wine** (check out 🖥 www.russiawines.com) comes in *sladkoye* (sweet) and *polusladkoye* (semi-sweet) dessert-wine varieties, rather sweet for the Western palate, as well as *sukhoye* (dry) and *polusukhoye* (semi-dry) reds; dry whites are thin on the ground. **Russian shampanskoye (champagne)** is a sparkling white that doesn't taste like actual champagne and tends to be very cheap. Far superior to Russian wines are the Georgian ones (see box p71), which are well worth seeking out.

Russians also have a love of **konyak** – brandy, the best of which is produced in the Caucasus and with Armenian konyak considered the finest.

WHERE TO EAT AND DRINK

With the exception of provincial backwaters, Russian cities offer a large range of quality restaurants, fast-food joints, cafés and self-service cafeteria-type

---

❏ **Buying your own food**

A Russian **supermarket** (супермаркет) has everything you would expect a super-market to have, though outside the big cities the choice may be more limited. Prices, particularly in big cities, are on a par with Western ones.

A *produktovy magazin* (продуктовый магазин) is a **grocery store** that sells a limited range of fresh vegetables, fruit, bread, meat, eggs and manufactured products. Because the products are kept behind a counter, you don't get much chance to inspect the merchandise; if you don't speak Russian, all you can do is point at what you want.

A **market** (*rynok* рынок) can be anything from clusters of old people selling gar-den produce at metro exits to a large covered market with dozens of stalls offering a plethora of fruit, vegetables, dairy products, home-made honey and meat.

---

eateries – most with prices to match the West. **Tips** (see p66) of 10% are not expected everywhere, but they are certainly appreciated.

Restaurants tend to be open daily from around 11.30am or noon until 10.30 or 11.30pm. In some upmarket restaurants you may find **cover charges** of up to 10% added to your bill.

Cafés open earlier – at around 8am – and stay open until 9pm or so. The cheapest places to eat are **self-service cafés** (*stolovaya*), serving salads, meaty mains, soups and tea; a meal will set you back about US$6. In most cities there are also Western **fast-food chains** such as McDonald's, Pizza Hut and KFC, plus Russian derivatives such as Russkoye Bistro and Teremok (serving blini with a multitude of fillings). Cafés, particularly the likes of the Traveler's Coffee chain, serve a good variety of world teas, coffees, cakes and light meals – salads, sandwiches, pasta.

Restaurant service and deciphering menus

In restaurants, **service** varies wildly: in more cosmopolitan cities, serving staff have caught on to the idea of Western hospitality and waiters tend to be polite, cheerful and helpful. Out in the boondocks you do occasionally get surly throw-backs to the Soviet era who look you up and down as you enter, decide that you're not worth their time and go back to looking at their mobile phone, and eventually deign to serve you.

Many restaurants in large cities are used to foreigners and most **menus** will come with an English translation or at least with pictures to point at. In self-service cafés you just take what you want or point at what you want. If you get invited to eat out with a group of Russians, expect a protracted, jolly, alcohol-fuelled evening.

TOILETS

You may have heard frightening tales of public toilets in Russia, Mongolia and China. Some of them are very true. In Russia, Ж (*zhensky*) stands for 'women's' and M (*muzhskoi*) stands for 'men's'. Even in the larger cities, it pays to have some toilet roll on you; some public toilets will give you a miserly portion of low-grade loo roll in exchange for the entrance fee, but others may not.

Many public toilets in Russia and China have old-style squatter loos, with the exception of toilets in nice shopping centres, good hotels and fast-food places, which have Western-style toilets. Note that the plumbing in most Russian cities cannot cope with toilet paper, which you must deposit into the malodorous basket next to the toilet instead. If staying with nomads in rural Mongolia, you will become intimately acquainted with very basic latrine pits, where there is no toilet paper, no sink and often no door. Outdoor privies are also common in rural parts of Russia and China, including Olkhon Island on Lake Baikal.

MAGAZINES AND NEWSPAPERS

Two free, visitor-friendly, English-language newspapers worth looking out for in their respective cities are the daily *Moscow Times* and the twice-weekly *St Petersburg Times*. They're easy to find in hotels, hostels, cafés and supermarkets frequented by foreigners; for English-language publications in China see p397 and in Mongolia see pp363-4. Western news magazines such as *Time* and *Newsweek* are sold at hotels used to receiving mostly international guests.

PHOTOGRAPHY

Particularly in Russia, but in all three countries **it's not a good idea to photograph** official-looking buildings, military/security infrastructure; on occasion you may even be prevented from taking pictures of railway stations by security personnel. Taking pictures from the train used to be forbidden but now it's OK, although it would be wise not to get trigger-happy at aerodromes, military installations or other politically sensitive areas.

Remember that in Russia, as in most other countries, **it's considered rude to take pictures of strangers**, their children or possessions without asking permission. Often people are happy to have their picture taken but you must always ask. This is particularly the case during political demonstrations or rallies. A useful phrase is 'Mozhno vas snyat?' (Можно вас снять?) meaning simply, 'Can I take a photo of you?' If you do take photos of a person always offer to send them copies and, if they accept, make sure you follow through with your promise; ask them to write down their address for you. Photography – particularly flash photography – is banned in many **museums**. In Russia and China, taking photos inside **churches and temples** is discourteous and therefore normally discouraged; taking a photo of someone in front of an icon is considered disrespectful. In Mongolia, museums ask for extortionate photography fees and photography inside monastery buildings is forbidden.

If travelling in winter always carry your camera inside your pocket or elsewhere near your body, as batteries get sluggish in the intense cold.

R U S S I A

❑ **Abbreviations**
★ = Author's favourite; **sgl** = single; **dbl** = double; **twn** = twin; **trpl** = triple; **lux** = luxury room; **apt** = apartment; **pp** = per person; **[V]** = vegetarian;
Street names: Russia see box p80; Mongolia see box p366; China see box p397.

CRIME AND ANNOYANCES

Russia is generally as safe (or as dangerous) a place to travel as New York or London; the vast majority of **crime** in big cities tends to be pickpocketing, particularly on public transport and in other crowded places. Tourists are rarely singled out for muggings, though incidents have occurred in small towns as well as big cities across the country. Most of the victims have been men walking alone at night. When you go out at night, go in a group and if you are on your own, consider taking a taxi, even if the distance is short, especially if you would have to walk through a poorly lit area.

❏ RUSSIAN CUSTOMS, ETIQUETTE AND SUPERSTITIONS

Customs and etiquette

● Wine, cake, chocolate or flowers are traditional gifts if you're invited to dinner in someone's home. A small gift for any children is also appropriate. If you bring flowers be sure the number of flowers is uneven: even numbers are for funerals.

● Shaking hands or kissing across the threshold of a doorstep is considered to bring bad luck.

● Take off your gloves when shaking hands.

● Be prepared to remove your shoes upon entering a home. You will be given a pair of slippers (*tapki*) to help keep the apartment clean.

● Smoking is common and accepted in Russia.

● Be prepared to accept all alcohol and food offered when visiting friends; this can be quite a lot. Refusing a drink or a toast is a serious breach of etiquette. An open bottle must be finished.

● Be prepared to give toasts at dinners, etc. Be careful, the vodka can catch up with you.

● Dress up for the theatre. Check in your coat and any large bags at the garderobe.

● Russian men still expect women to act in a traditional manner. It's bad form for a woman to be assertive in public, to carry heavy bags if you're walking with a man, to open doors, uncork bottles or pay your own way in social situations.

● In a Russian Orthodox church women should cover their heads with a scarf or hat and wear a skirt. Men should remove their hats.

Superstitions

Russians remain remarkably superstitious; many of the following were once also common elsewhere in Europe:

● Never light a cigarette from a candle. It will bring you bad luck.

● Do not whistle indoors or you will whistle away your money.

● Never pour wine back-handed, it means you will also pour away your money.

● A black cat crossing your path is bad luck.

● A woman who finds herself sitting at the corner of a table will be single for the next seven years.

● If you spill salt at the table you will be plagued by bad luck unless you immediately throw three pinches over your left shoulder.

● If someone offers you good wishes, or if you are discussing your good fortune, you must spit three times over your left shoulder and touch (knock on) wood to keep your good fortune.

Be sensible about your safety. Keep a low profile and don't advertise loudly that you're a foreigner, especially in clubs or bars. Don't dress ostentatiously or wear expensive jewellery. Most hotel rooms are secure, though petty pilfering may occur in the cheaper places and hostels, so put any valuables in a safe if there is one. A moneybelt for your passport, credit cards, travellers' cheques and foreign currency is essential. Also see the box on p120.

Racism is a problem in Russia, particularly in the bigger cities, so if you're non-white in appearance, you should show particular vigilance when walking around at night, as right-wing skinhead gangs have been known to pick fights with anyone who doesn't look Russian. Racial violence does occur with alarming frequency, particularly against the darker-skinned illegal immigrants from the Central Asian republics; perpetrators are never punished by police, the police often being the guilty party themselves. Anti-Semitism, sanctioned by the Soviet state, is still very much present, with anti-Semitic and plain ol' racist statements made even by well-educated Russians, and with ultra-nationalist right-wing factions frequently trying to stir up the population by playing on their fears of Russia being overrun with foreigners.

Make sure you have your passport (or a photocopy of it), visa and other relevant documents on you, because the police may treat you with suspicion and look for an excuse to fine you.

City traffic can be downright dangerous, particularly in Ulaanbaatar and big Russian cities, with some drivers ignoring traffic lights and pedestrian crossings, so watch out.

One of the biggest **annoyances** is that, in all three countries people are not very good at **queuing**. This means that standing politely to one side won't get you very far; if boarding public transport in cities you should be prepared to elbow your way into the throng. **Spitting** on the street is something you'll find prevalent in China, and to a lesser degree in Russia and Mongolia. It's anything but discreet, so don't be surprised to see even pretty girls in designer gear loudly clear their throats and gob like a football player. You may also see people in China and Mongolia press down on one nostril in order to blow the contents of the other onto the pavement.

Mosquitoes abound in the summer in all three countries, so pack your DEET-infused insect repellent and a compact mosquito net, as they can be a health threat as well as an annoyance in certain parts.

ENTERTAINMENT

Nightlife and cultural life in Moscow and St Petersburg is as varied as in large Western cities, as is the case in Beijing. These cities have lots of nightclubs and bars, but it really helps to have local friends to show you the best places. In smaller towns your major options are the hotel bars and clubs, which often stay open late. Most provincial cities also have a modern 'megaclub' which combines a disco, bowling alley, bar and restaurant; these places are very popular with locals and pick up late in the evening.

RUSSIA

❑ Event tickets
Tickets for most events can be purchased from 🖥 www.eventful.com or from relevant venue websites.

Traditional cultural activities such as opera, theatre, ballet or the circus are easy to attend, particularly in Moscow and St Petersburg. Performances usually start early: between 6pm and 7pm.

Ballet
Many of the world's greatest dancers have been from Russia's Bolshoi and Kirov companies. Some defected to the West including the Kirov's Rudolf Nureyev, Russia's most famous ballet star, who liked to say he was 'shaken out' of his mother's womb on the Trans-Siberian as it rattled towards Lake Baikal.

If you're a ballet aficionado, don't miss the chance of a night at the magnificent Bolshoi Theatre; the season runs from September to May, but even in summer there are performances by smaller companies.

Opera and theatre
In the past, opera was encouraged more than theatre as it was seen as politically neutral. Glasnost, however, encouraged playwrights to dramatise Russian life as it is, rather than as the government wanted people to see it. This has led to a number of successful theatre groups opening in Moscow and St Petersburg. It's easy enough to attend opera performances in Moscow and St Petersburg, but for theatre, the vast majority of performances – from Shakespeare's plays to experimental, contemporary works – tend to be in Russian only. If you're travelling with children, there are also several puppet theatres which are highly recommended.

Cinema
In the 1980s the Soviet film industry benefited from the greater freedoms that came with glasnost. In early 1987 one of the most successful and controversial films was *Is It Easy To Be Young?*, which was deeply critical of the Soviet war in Afghanistan. In the 1990s the pessimism of the people towards life is reflected in films made in the country.

Little Vera (1990) is the story of a provincial girl who sinks into small-time prostitution and finally drowns herself (Gorbachev walked out of it saying he disapproved of the sex scenes). In *Executioner* (1991) a female journalist takes on the mafia in St Petersburg and loses.

The 1994 film *Burnt by the Sun*, by director Nikita Mikhalkov, set in the mid 1930s just before Stalin's Great Purge, won the grand prize at the Cannes Film Festival as well as the Academy Award for best foreign-language film.

The 1997 film *Brother*, featuring a sparse crime tale reminiscent of French new wave, signalled a new era in Russian movie-making. Also notable is 2002's dreamlike *Russian Ark* by director Alexander Sokurov. Consisting of a single

90-minute camera shot moving through St Petersburg's Winter Palace, it was the world's second-ever unedited feature film.

In 2004, *Nochnoi Dozor* ('Night Watch'), part one of a fantasy horror film trilogy, directed by Timur Bekmambetov, was an international hit. Shot in Karelia, the 2006 film *Ostrov* ('The Island'), directed by Pavel Lungin, scripts the life of a fictional 20th-century sailor-turned-monk and focuses on Orthodox spirituality, while Valery Todorovsky's 2008 release, *Stilyagi* ('Hipsters'), is a musical that explores the lives of Soviet youth obsessed with fashion in the 1950s. Alexei Popogrebski's thriller *Kak Ya Provyol Etim Letom* ('How I Ended This Summer'), set at a polar station on a remote island in the Arctic Ocean, won the Golden Bear award at the 2010 Berlin Film Festival.

In 2012, Alexander Mindadze's *Innocent Saturday*, about the Chernobyl disaster, received the Grand Prix at the Brussels International Film Festival, while Fyodor Bondarchuk's *Stalingrad*, about the eponymous WWII battle, in 2013 became Russia's first big-budget IMAX and 3D film.

Nowadays Western films are everywhere, particularly Hollywood blockbusters. With the exception of several arts cinemas in Moscow and St Petersburg, foreign films are dubbed into Russian.

Rock concerts and sports matches

Moscow in particular hosts many big international artists and bands – either in stadiums or venues such as the Kremlin State Palace. Sports-wise, football is hugely popular, as is ice hockey in winter. Football fans may wish to catch FC Spartak or FC Dynamo at a home game at the Luzhniki Stadium and Arena Khinki, respectively.

SHOPPING

Moscow and St Petersburg boast some of the country's grandest and most luxurious department stores and designer shops; if you have the money, you can buy anything from haute couture and Russian music CDs to military memorabilia and regional handicrafts. Note that brand-name clothing is likely to be more expensive than in Europe and the States, but it's worth seeking out items by local designers such as Kira Plastinina, Anybody's Blonde, Bessarion, Homo Consommatus and Ludmilla Radchenko.

❑ **Opening hours**
Large **department stores** are open from 9am to 8pm Monday to Saturday. **Smaller shops** have a wide range of times, opening anywhere between 8am and 11am, closing between 8pm and 11pm.

All **museum/gallery** opening times mentioned refer to the peak season June-August; outside peak season, opening times are reduced. Throughout the year museums/galleries stop selling entrance tickets an hour before closing time.

Standard opening hours for **restaurants** are 11.30am/noon to 11.30pm/midnight; **cafés** generally open earlier and close earlier.

RUSSIA

What to buy
Handicrafts and kitsch souvenirs These include attractively decorated black lacquer *palekh* boxes (icon-painters started making them when religious art lost popularity after the Revolution); finift (see box p213) jewellery from Rostov; enamelled bowls and ornaments; embroidered blouses and tablecloths from the different regions; large black printed scarves; guitars and *balalaikas*; lace tablecloths and handkerchiefs; jewellery and gemstones from Siberia and the Urals – particularly items made of charoite (a purple stone endemic only to Siberia; see p276), malachite and jasper, and painted wooden ornaments including the ubiquitous *matryoshka* dolls which fit one inside the other. Modern variations on the matrioshka include leaders of the former USSR, The Beatles, Putin and even Barack Obama. You can also find the ubiquitous McLenin's T-shirts and other pseudo-Communist clothing.

Military memorabilia and paintings It's difficult to find genuine Communist memorabilia these days, but there's still plenty of military memorabilia on sale: anything from hats and hip flasks to diving suits and medals. Check what you're buying carefully as it might not be genuine. This is equally true with the old banknotes you can buy.

If you buy antiques or valuable paintings, you need to have a permit from the Ministry of Culture in order to export it from the country – easily organised by reputable shops.

CDs Russian music runs the gamut from pop to doom metal. Bands that have been around for decades but still pack the music venues include Mashina Vremeni (Time Machine), Gosti iz Budushchevo (Guests from the Future) and Mumiy Troll. A popular young female vocalist is Alsu, while popular male vocalists include Philip Kirkorov, Nikolai Baskov and one-time Eurovision winner Dima Bilan. Alla Pugacheva is an older female singer with a loyal following, particularly among women over 50. Newer acts include reggae artists 5nizza, dance-club stars Dr Bronx and Natali, rockers Graydanskaya Oborona, pop artist Lyapis Trubetskoi, rapper Basta and punkers Krasnaya Plesen. Top Russian DJs include Nina Kraviz, Hard Rock Sofa, Feel and Alexander Popov.

❏ **STREET NAMES GLOSSARY**

Russian	Cyrillic	Abbreviation	English equivalent
bulvar	бульвар	бул (bul)	boulevard
gostinny dvor	гостинный двор		shopping arcade
most	мост		bridge
naberezhnaya	набережная	наб (nab)	embankment
ploshchad	площадь	пл (pl)	square
prospekt	проспект	пр (pr)	avenue
pereulok	переулок	пер (per)	lane/side street
shosse	шоссе		highway
ulitsa	улица	ул (ul)	street

SIBERIA AND THE RAILWAY

Historical outline

EARLY HISTORY

Prehistory: the first Siberians

Discoveries at **Dering Yuryakh**, by the Lena River 100km south of Yakutsk, have indicated that man has lived in Siberia for far longer than had previously been thought. Archaeologist Yuri Mochanov, who led excavations there in the 1980s and 1990s, believes that the thousands of stone tools he found embedded in geological stratum dating back over two million years suggests human habitation stretching back this far, which would place the site on a par with Professor Leakey's discoveries in East Africa. It's a highly controversial theory as it would mean that initial human evolution also occurred outside Africa. Western archaeologists who have studied the material believe, however, that it cannot be more than 500,000 years old; that would still give the Siberians an impressively long history.

There is evidence of rather more recent human life in the Lake Baikal area. In the 13th millennium BC, **Stone Age nomads** roamed round the shores of the lake, hunting mammoths and carving their tusks into the tubby fertility goddesses that can be seen in the museums of Irkutsk today. Several sites dating back to this early period have been excavated in the Baikal area; the railway passes near one at the village of Malta (see p456), 85km west of Irkutsk.

There is far more archaeological evidence from the **Neolithic Age** (12th to 5th millennia BC) and it shows that nomadic tribes had reached the Arctic Circle, with some even moving into North America via the Bering Strait (then a land bridge) and Alaska. These northern nomads trained dogs to pull their sledges, but remained technologically in the Stone Age until Russian colonists arrived in the mid-17th century.

In the south, several **Bronze Age cultures** emerged around the central parts of the Yenisey River. Afanassevskaya, south of Krasnoyarsk, has given its name to the culture of a people who lived in this area in the 2nd millennium BC and decorated their pottery with a characteristic herringbone pattern.

The first evidence of permanent buildings has been found near Achinsk, where the Andronovo people built huge log cabins in the

1st millennium BC. Excavations of sites of the Karassuk culture, also dated to the 1st millennium BC, have yielded Chinese artefacts, indicating trade between these two peoples.

Early civilisations

The **Iron Age sites** show evidence of more complex and organised societies. The clear air of the Altai Mountains has preserved the contents of numerous graves of the 2nd century BC Tagar culture. Their leaders were embalmed and buried like Egyptian pharaohs with all that they might need in the afterlife. In their burial mounds archaeologists have found perfectly preserved woollen blankets, decorated leather saddles and the complete skeletons of horses, probably buried alive when their masters died.

In the 3rd century BC **the Huns** moved into the region south of Lake Baikal where their descendants, the Buryats, now live. The Huns' westward progress continued for five centuries until the infamous Attila, 'The Scourge of God', having pillaged his way across Europe, reached Paris where he was defeated in 452 AD.

The ancestors of the Kyrgyz people were **the Tashtyks** of Western Siberia, who built large houses of clay (one found near Abakan even has an under-floor central heating system), moulded the features of their dead in clay death masks and decorated their bodies with elaborate tattoos. The tiny Central Asian republic of Kyrgyzstan, south of Kazakhstan, is all that remains of a once-mighty empire that stretched from Samarkand to Manchuria in the 12th century.

In the following century **the Kyrgyz** were defeated by the rapidly advancing Mongols. **Chinggis Khan's Mongol empire** grew to become history's largest land empire, including the Tartars of South Russia and the peoples of North Asia, Mongolia and China.

The first Russian expeditions to Siberia

In medieval times Siberia was known to Russians only as a distant land of valuable fur-bearing animals. Occasional expeditions from Novgorod in the 15th century became more frequent in the 16th century, after South Russia was released from the Mongol grip by **Tsar Ivan the Terrible**. Ivan's seizure of Kazan and Astrakhan opened the way to Siberia. Yediger, leader of a small Siberian kingdom just over the Urals, realised his vulnerability and sent Ivan a large tribute of furs, declaring himself a vassal of the Tsar.

Yediger's son Kuchum was of a more independent mind and, having murdered his father, he put an end to the annual tribute, proclaiming himself Tsar of Siberia. Ivan's armies were occupied on his western frontiers, so he allowed the powerful Stroganov family to raise a private army to annex the rebel lands. In 1574 Ivan granted the **Stroganovs** a 27-year lease on the land over the Urals as far east as the Tobol River, the centre of Kuchum's kingdom.

Yermak: the founder of Siberia

The Stroganovs' army was a wild bunch of mercenaries led by an ex-pirate named Yermak, the man now recognised as the founder of Siberia. They crossed the Urals and challenged Kuchum, gaining control of his lands after a struggle that was surprisingly long considering that Russian muskets faced only swords and arrows.

On 5 November 1581 Yermak raised the Russian flag at Isker, near modern Tobolsk, and sent the Tsar a tribute of over 2500 furs. In return Ivan pardoned him for his past crimes, sent him a fur-lined cape that had once graced the royal shoulders, and a magnificent suit of armour. Over the next few years Yermak and his men were constantly harassed by Kuchum, and on 16 August 1584 were ambushed as they slept on an island in the Irtysh. The story goes that Yermak drowned in the river, dragged under by the weight of the Tsar's armour. Yermak's name lives on as the top brand of Russian rucksack.

The quest for furs

Over the next 50 years **Cossack forces** moved rapidly across Siberia, establishing *ostrogs* (military outposts) as they went and gathering tributes of fur for the Tsar. Tyumen was founded in 1586, Tomsk in 1604, Krasnoyarsk in 1628 and Yakutsk in 1633. By 1639 the Cossacks had reached the east coast.

Like the Spanish Conquistadors in South America they dealt roughly with the native tribes they met, who were no match for their muskets and cannon. The prize they lusted after was not gold, as it was for the Spaniards in Peru and for later Russian adventurers in Siberia, but furs. In the days before fur farms, certain pelts were worth far more than they are today; from the proceeds of a season's trapping in Siberia a man could buy and stock a large farm with cattle and sheep. The chances of a Russian trapper finding his way into and out of the dark, swampy forests of the taiga were not very high, but quite a few did it.

Khabarov and the Amur

In 1650 a Russian fur merchant named Khabarov set out from Yakutsk to explore the Amur region in what is now the Far Eastern Territories, fertile and rich in fur-bearing animals. Khabarov found the local tribes extremely hostile, as the Russians' reputation for rape and pillage had spread before him. He and his men committed such atrocities that the news reached the ears of the Tsar, who ordered him back to the capital to explain himself. Bearing gifts of fur, he convinced the Tsar that he had won valuable new lands which would enrich his empire. The local tribes, however, appealed to the Manchus, their southern neighbours, who sent an army to help them fight off the Russians. The Tsar's men were gradually beaten back. Periodic fighting went on until 1689, when the Russians were forced out of Manchuria and the Amur by the Treaty of Nerchinsk.

18th-century explorers

Peter the Great became Tsar in 1696 and initiated a new era of exploration in the Far East. By the following year the explorer **Vladimir Atlasov** had claimed Kamchatka for Russia. In 1719 the first scientific expedition set out for Siberia. Peter commissioned the Danish seaman **Vitus Bering** to search for a northern sea-passage to Kamchatka and the Sea of Okhotsk (unaware that such a route had been discovered by Semyon Deshnev 80 years earlier). However, the Tsar did not live to see Bering set out in 1725.

Between 1733 and 1743 another **scientific expedition**, comprising naval officers, topographers, geodesic surveyors, naturalists and astronomers, made detailed charts of Russian lands in the Far East. **Fur traders** reached the Aleutian Islands and in 1784 the first Alaskan colony was founded on Kodiak Island by **Gregory Shelekhov** (whose grave is in the cemetery of Znamensky Convent in Irkutsk). Russian Alaska was sold to the United States in 1868 for the bargain price of two cents an acre.

THE 19TH CENTURY

There were two developments in Siberia in the 19th century which had a tremendous effect upon its history. First, the practice of sentencing criminals to a life of exile or hard labour in Siberia was increased to provide labour for the mines and to establish communities around the military outposts.

The exile system (pp86-90), which caused a great deal of human misery, greatly increased the population in this vast and empty region. Secondly, and of far greater importance, was the building of the Trans-Siberian Railway in the 1890s (see pp98-101).

Colonisation

By the end of the 18th century the population of Siberia was estimated to be about 1.5 million people, most of whom belonged to nomadic native tribes. The policy of populating the region through the **exile system** swelled the numbers of settlers, but criminals did not make the best colonists. The government therefore tried to encourage **voluntary emigration** from overcrowded European Russia. Peasant settlers could escape the bonds of serfdom by crossing the Urals, although Siberia's reputation as a place of exile was not much of an incentive to move.

As the railway penetrated Siberia, the transport of colonists was made easier. Tsar Alexander's emigration representatives were sent to many thickly populated regions in European Russia in the 1880s, offering prospective colonists **incentives** including a reduced rail fare (six roubles for the 1900km/1200-mile journey) and a free allotment of 27 acres of land. Prices in Siberia were high, and colonists could expect to get up to 100% more than in European Russia for produce grown on this land. Many peasants left Europe for Siberia after the great famine of 1890-91.

Further exploration and expansion

Throughout the 19th century scientists and explorers continued to make expeditions to Siberia. In 1829 an expedition led by the German scientist, **Baron von Humboldt**, already famous for his explorations in South America, investigated the geological structure of the Altai plateau in southern Siberia.

In 1840 the estuary of the Amur was discovered, and colonisation was encouraged after **Count Muravyev-Amursky**, Governor General of Eastern Siberia, annexed the entire Amur territory for Russia, in flagrant violation of the 1689 Russo-Chinese Treaty of Nerchinsk. But the Chinese were in no position to argue, being threatened by the French and British as well as by internal

The Siberian Boundary Post (circa 1880) In this melancholy scene, friends and relatives bid exiled prisoners farewell beside the brick pillar that marked the western border of Siberia on the Great Post Road.

troubles in Peking. By the Treaty of Peking (1860) they ceded the territory north of the Amur to Russia, and also the land east of the Ussuri, including the valuable Pacific port of Vladivostok.

THE EXILE SYSTEM

The word 'Siberia' meant only one thing in Victorian England and 19th-century Russia: an inhospitable land of exiled murderers and other evil criminals who paid for their sins by working in its infamous salt mines. While some of the first exiles sent over the Urals did indeed work in salt mines, most of them mined gold, silver or coal.

By 1900 over a million people had been exiled and made the long march to the squalid and overcrowded prisons of Siberia.

George Kennan

In 1891 a book entitled *Siberia and the Exile System*, written by George Kennan, was published in America. It exposed the truly horrific conditions under which prisoners were kept in Siberia and aroused public opinion in both America and Britain. Kennan was a journalist working for the *New York Century Magazine*. He knew Siberia well, having previously spent two years there. At that time he had been unaware of how badly convicts were treated and in a series of lectures before the American Geographical Society had defended the Tsarist government and its exile system.

When his editor commissioned him to investigate the system more thoroughly, bureaucrats in St Petersburg were happy to give him the letters of introduction which allowed him to venture into the very worst of the prisons and to meet the governors and convicts.

The government doubtless hoped that Kennan would champion their cause. Such had been the case with the Rev Dr Henry Landsell who had travelled in Siberia in 1879. In an account of his journey, *Through Siberia*, Landsell wrote that 'on the whole, if a Russian exile behaves himself decently well, he may in Siberia be more comfortable than in many, and as comfortable as in most of the prisons of the world.' After the year he spent visiting Siberian prisons, Kennan could not agree with Landsell, and revealed the inhumanity of the exile system, the convict mines and the terrible conditions in the overcrowded prisons.

The first exiles

The earliest mention of exile in Russian legal documents was in 1648. In the 17th century exile was used as a way of banishing criminals who had already been punished. In Kennan's words: 'The Russian criminal code of that age was almost incredibly cruel and barbarous. Men were impaled on sharp stakes, hanged and beheaded by the hundred for crimes that would not now be regarded as criminal in any civilised country in the world, while lesser offenders were flogged with the knut (a whip of leather and metal thongs, which could break a man's back with a single blow) and bastinado (cane), branded with hot irons, mutilated by amputation of one or more of their limbs, deprived of their tongues, and suspended in the air by hooks passed under two of their ribs until they died a lingering and miserable death.' Those who survived these ordeals were too mutilated to be of any use so they were then driven out of their villages to the lands beyond the Urals.

Exile as a punishment: the convict mines

With the discovery of valuable minerals in Siberia and in light of the shortage of labourers, the government began to use criminals to work the mines. Exile was thus developed into a form of punishment and extended to cover a range of crimes including desertion, assault with intent to kill and vagrancy (when the vagrant was of no use to the army or the community). According to Kennan, exile was also a punishment for offences that now seem nothing short of ridiculous: fortune-telling, prize-fighting, snuff-taking (the snuff-taker was not only banished to Siberia but also had the septum between his nostrils torn out) and driving with reins. Traditionally Russian drivers rode their horses or ran beside them: reins were regarded as too Western, too European.

Abolition of the death penalty

In the 18th century the demand for mine labour grew, and the list of crimes punishable by exile was extended to include drunkenness and wife-beating, the cutting down of trees by serfs, begging with a pretence to being in distress, and setting fire to property accidentally. In 1753 the death penalty was abolished (for all crimes except an attempt on the life of the Tsar) and **replaced by exile with hard labour**. No attention was given to the treatment of exiles en route, who were simply herded like animals over the Urals, many dying on the way. The system was chaotically corrupt and disorganised, with hardened murderers being set free in Siberia while people convicted of relatively insignificant offences perished down the mines.

Reorganisation in the 19th century

In the 19th century the system became more organised but no less corrupt. In 1817 a series of *étapes* (**exile stations**) was built along the way to provide overnight shelter for the marching parties. They were nothing more than crude log cabins with wooden sleeping platforms. **Forwarding prisons** were established at Tyumen and Tomsk from where prisoners were sent to their final place of exile. From Tyumen convicts travelled by barge in specially designed cages to Tomsk. From there some would be directed on to Krasnoyarsk or to Irkutsk, a 1670km (1040-mile), three-month march away. Prisoners were sent on to smaller prisons, penal colonies and mines. The most infamous mines were: on the island of Sakhalin, off the east coast, where convicts dug for coal; the gold mines of Kara; and the silver mines of Nerchinsk.

Records were started in 1823 and between this date and 1887, when Kennan consulted the books in Tomsk, 772,979 prisoners had passed through on their way to Siberia. They comprised *katorzhniki* (hard labour convicts), distinguishable by their half-shaved heads; *poselentsi* (penal colonists); *silni* (persons simply banished and allowed to return to European Russia after serving their sentence); and *dobrovolni* (women and children voluntarily accompanying their husbands or fathers). Until the 1850s convicts and penal colonists were branded on the cheek with a letter to indicate the nature of their crime. More than half of those who crossed the Urals had had no proper trial but were exiled by 'administrative process'. As Kennan states: 'Every village commune has the right to banish any of its members who, through bad conduct or general worthlessness, have proved themselves obnoxious to their fellow citizens.'

Life in the cells
The first prison Kennan was shown on his trip in 1887 was the Tyumen forwarding prison. He records the experience thus: 'As we entered the cell, the convicts, with a sudden jingling of chains, sprang to their feet, removed their caps and stood in a dense throng around the *nari* (wooden sleeping platforms) "The prison" said the warden, "is terribly overcrowded. This cell for example is only 35 feet long by 25 wide, and has air space for 35, or at most 40 men. How many men slept here last night?" he inquired, turning to the prisoners. "A hundred and sixty, your high nobility", shouted half a dozen hoarse voices ... I looked around the cell. There was practically no ventilation and the air was so poisoned and foul that I could hardly force myself to breathe it in.'

The hospital cells
None of these dreadful experiences could prepare Kennan for the hospital cells, filled with prisoners suffering from typhus, scurvy, pneumonia, smallpox, diphtheria, dysentery and syphilis. He wrote afterwards: 'Never before in my life had I seen faces so white, haggard, and ghastly as those that lay on the gray pillows in the hospital cells ... As I breathed that heavy, stifling atmosphere, poisoned with the breaths of syphilitic and fever-stricken patients, loaded and saturated with the odor of excrement, disease germs, exhalations from unclean human bodies, and foulness inconceivable, it seemed to me that over the hospital doors should be written "All hope abandon, ye who enter here".'

From the records he discovered that almost 30% of patients in the prison hospital died each year. This he compared with 3.8% for French prisons of the time, 2% for American prisons and 1.4% for English prisons.

Corruption
As well as the inhuman conditions he saw in the prisons, Kennan found that the whole exile system was riddled with corruption. Bribes were regularly accepted by warders and other officials. One provincial administrator boasted that the Governor of Tobolsk was so careless that he could get him to sign any document he was given. As a wager he wrote out The Lord's Prayer on an official form and placed it before the Governor, who duly signed it. The St Petersburg government was too far away to know what was going on in the lands beyond the Urals.

Many high-ranking officials in Siberia were so tightly bound by bureaucratic ties that change was impossible, even if they desired it. An officer in the Tomsk prison confided in Kennan: 'I would gladly resign tomorrow if I could see the (exile) system abolished. It is disastrous to Siberia, it is ruinous to the criminal, and it causes an immense amount of misery; but what can be done? If we say anything to our superiors in St Petersburg, they strike us in the face; and they strike hard – it hurts!'

Political exiles
Life for the so-called 'politicals' and 'nihilists', banished to prevent them infecting European Russians with their criticisms of the autocratic political system that was choking the country to death, was generally better than that for other prisoners. Many came from aristocratic families and, once out of prison, life for them continued in much the same way as it had west of the Urals.

The most famous political exiles were the '**Decembrists**', men who took part in an unsuccessful coup in 1825. Many were accompanied into exile by their wives. Some of the houses in which they lived are now preserved as *dom* (house) museums in Irkutsk (see p300). Kennan secretly visited many of the politicals in Siberia and was convinced that they did not deserve to be exiled. He wrote later: 'If such men are in exile in a lonely Siberian village on the frontier of Mongolia, instead of being at home in the service of the state – so much the worse for the state.'

A few politicals were sentenced to exile with the native Yakuts within the Arctic Circle. Escape was impossible and life with a Stone Age tribe must have seemed unbearable for cultured aristocrats who had until recently been part of the St Petersburg court circle.

Temporary abolition of the exile system
The exile system was abolished in 1900. But, however corrupt the system and inhuman the conditions in these early Siberian prisons, worse was to come only

Political exiles, many of whom came from aristocratic families, were free to adopt whatever lifestyle they could afford within the confines of Siberia, once they had completed their prison sentences.

30 years later. Under Stalin, **vast concentration camps** were set up, in European Russia as well as Siberia, to provide a huge slave-labour force to build roads, railways and factories in the 1930s and 1940s. Prisoners were grossly overworked and undernourished. The **mortality rate** in some of these camps is said to have been as high as 30%. Reports of the number of people sentenced to these slave labour camps range from 3 million to 20 million. Some researchers place the death toll up to the late 1950s as high as 18 million.

Early travellers

VICTORIAN ADVENTURERS

The Victorian era was the great age of the gentleman (and gentlewoman) adventurer. Many upper-class travellers spent the greater part of their lives exploring lesser-known regions of the world, writing long and often highly readable accounts of their adventures and their encounters with the 'natives'. Siberia attracted almost as many of this brave breed as did Africa and India. Once travel across the great Siberian plain by normal forms of transport of the time (carriage and sledge) had been tried, some resorted to such new-fangled inventions as the bicycle (RL Jefferson in 1896), the train (from 1900) and the car (the Italian Prince Borghese in an Itala in 1907). Some even crossed the country entirely on foot.

THE GREAT SIBERIAN POST ROAD

Before the railway was built there was but one route across the region for convicts, colonists or adventurers: a rough track known as the Great Siberian Post Road or *Trakt*. **Posting stations**, where travellers could rent horses and drivers, were set up at approximately 40km (25-mile) intervals.

Murray's 1865 *Handbook for Russia, Poland and Finland* tells travellers: 'Three kinds of conveyances are available: the *telega*, or cart without springs, which has to be changed at every station, and for which a charge of about 8d is made at every stage; the *kibitka* or cart (in winter a sledge) with a hood; and the *tarantass*, a kind of carriage on wooden springs which admits of the traveller lying down full length and which can be made very comfortable at night. The two latter vehicles have to be purchased at Perm, if the *telega*, or postal conveyance be not accepted. A *tarantass* may be bought from £12 to £15.'

❏ **Travel by tarantass**
Kate Marsden, a nurse travelling in 1894, recalled the agony of days spent in a tarantass in the following way: 'Your limbs ache, your muscles ache, your head aches, and, worst of all, your inside aches terribly. "Tarantass rheumatism" internal and external, chronic, or rather perpetual, is the complaint.'

George Kennan called the **Imperial Russian Post System** 'the most perfectly organised horse express service in the world'.

The discomforts of Siberian travel
Since a visit to Siberia could rarely be completed in a single season, most travellers had the opportunity to try the various modes of transport used in summer and winter. While most found **the sledge** more comfortable than **the tarantass**, no 19th-century travelogue would be complete without a detailed description of the tarantass. This unique vehicle had a large boat-shaped body, and travellers stored their belongings on the floor, covering them with straw and mattresses on which they lay. This may sound comfortable, but when experienced at speed over atrocious roads and for great distances, by contemporary accounts it was not. SS Hill wrote in 1854: 'The worst of the inconveniences arose from the deep ruts which were everywhere ... and from the necessity of galloping down the declivities to force the carriage upon the bridges. And often our carriage fell with such force against the bridges that it was unsafe to retain our accustomed reclining position ...'.

The driver (yamshchiki)
The driver (*yamshchik*) of the tarantass or sledge was invariably drunk, and had to be bribed with vodka to make good time between post stations. Murray's 1865 guidebook thoughtfully includes in its Useful Russian Phrases section '*Dam na vodki*' ('I will give you drink money'). **Accidents were commonplace**; RL Jefferson (on a trip without his bicycle in 1895) wrote that his yamshchik became so inebriated that he fell off the sledge and died.

The same fate befell one of Kate Marsden's sledge-drivers who had gone to sleep with the reins tied around his wrists. She wrote: 'And there was the poor fellow being tossed to and fro amongst the legs of the horses, which, now terrified, tore down the hill like mad creatures ... In a few minutes there was a fearful crash. We had come into collision with another tarantass and the six horses and the two tarantasses were mixed up in a chaotic mass'.

The horses
Sledges and tarantasses were pulled by a *troika*, a group of three horses. These were small furry specimens, 'not much larger than the average English donkey', noted RL Jefferson. They were hired between post stations and usually belonged to the yamshchik.

SS Hill was shocked at the way these animals were treated by the local people. He remarked: 'The Arab is the friend of his horse. The Russian or Siberian peasant is his severe master who exacts every grain of his strength by blows accompanied with curses ... lodges him badly or not at all, cares little how he feeds him, and never cleans him or clips a hair of his body from the hour of his birth to that of his death.' Horses were worked literally until they died. RL Jefferson recalls that two of his animals dropped dead in harness and had to be cut free.

(**Above**): Until the building of the Trans-Siberian, the Great Post Road formed the life-line for hundreds of tiny communities such as this. (**Below**): There were few bridges on the Road – crossing frozen rivers and lakes was treacherous in early winter and spring.

Dangers

Travel in Siberia was not only uncomfortable, it was also dangerous. **Wolves and bears** roamed the forests and when food was scarce would attack a horse or man (although you were safe in a tarantass). In the Amur region lived the world's largest cat, the **Amur tiger**. Just as wild as these animals, and probably more dangerous, were the *brodyagi*, **escaped convicts** in search of money and a passport to readmit them to Europe.

Dirt and disease

As well as the discomfort of the 'conveyance' and the dangers along the Trakt, travellers were warned about the dirt and disease they could encounter. RL Jefferson wrote: 'No wonder that Siberia is looked upon by the traveller with abhorrence. Apart from its inhabitants, no one can say that Siberia is not a land of beauty, plenty and promise; but it is the nature of its inhabitants which make it the terrible place it is. The independence, the filth and general want of comfort which characterise every effort of the community, serve to make a visit to any Siberian centre a thing to be remembered for many years and an experience not desirable to repeat.'

Hotel rooms were universally squalid. Kate Marsden gives the following advice to anyone entering a hotel bedroom in Siberia: 'Have your pocket handkerchief ready ... and place it close to your nostrils the moment the door is opened. The hinges creak and your first greeting is a gust of hot, foetid air.'

Insects

Especially in the summer months, travellers were plagued by **flies and mosquitoes**. Kate Marsden wrote: 'After a few days the body swells from their bites into a form that can neither be imagined nor described. They attack your eyes and your face, so that you would hardly be recognised by your dearest friend.'

At night, travellers who had stopped in the dirty hotels or posting stations were kept awake by **lice, bedbugs and a variety of other insects** with which the bedding was infested. RL Jefferson met a man who never travelled without four saucers and a can of kerosene. In the hotel room at night he would put a saucer filled with kerosene under each bed-leg, to stop the bugs reaching him in bed. However, Jefferson noted that: 'With a sagacity which one would hardly credit so small an insect, it would make a detour by getting up the wall on to the ceiling, and then, having accurately poised, drop down upon the victim – no doubt to his extreme discomfort.'

Bovril and Jaeger underwear: essential provisions

RL Jefferson (see 'Jefferson's Bicycle Jaunts', pp95-6) never travelled without a large supply of Bovril and a change of Jaeger 'cellular' underwear – 'capital stuff for lightness and durability' he wrote after one long ride on his Imperial Rover bicycle.

Kate Marsden shared his enthusiasm for Dr Jaeger's undergarments: 'without which it would have been quite impossible to go through all the changes of climate; and to remain for weeks together without changing my clothes', she wrote. On the subject of provisions for the trip, Murray's guidebook recommended taking along **basic foodstuffs**. Miss Marsden packed into her tarantass 'a few boxes of sardines, biscuits, some bread, tea and one or two other trifles which included 18kg (40lb) of plum pudding'.

❏ KATE MARSDEN VISITS SIBERIAN LEPERS

Miss Marsden was a nurse with a definite mission in Siberia. In the 1880s she learnt, through travellers' accounts, of the numerous leper colonies north of Yakutsk. There were rumours of a special herb found there which could alleviate the symptoms of the disease. After an audience with Queen Victoria, during which she was given useful letters of introduction, she travelled to Moscow. She arrived in mid-winter, wearing her thin cotton nurse's uniform and a white bonnet, which she immediately exchanged for thick Russian clothes.

Crossing Siberia

After meeting the Empress Maria, who gave her 1000 roubles for her relief fund, she started on her long sledge ride. It was not a dignified send-off – 'three muscular policemen attempted to lift me into the sledge; but their combined strength was futile under the load'. She got aboard eventually and was soon experiencing the extreme discomfort of Siberian travel. She said it made her feel more like 'a battered old log of mahogany than a gently nurtured Englishwoman'.

Distributing tea, sugar and copies of the Gospels to convicts in the marching parties she encountered along the Post Road, she reached Irkutsk in the summer. She boarded a leaky barge on the Lena River north of Lake Baikal, and drifted down to Yakutsk, sitting on the sacks of potatoes with which the boat was filled. Of this part of the journey she wrote: 'Fortunately we had only about 3,000 miles of this but 3,000 miles were enough'.

Her goal was still a 3200km (2000-mile) ride away when she reached Yakutsk. Although she had never been on a horse before, this brave woman arranged an escort of 15 men and rode with them through insect-infested swamps and across a fiery plain, below which the earth was in a constant state of combustion, until she reached the settlement of Viluisk.

The lepers of Viluisk

On her arrival the local priest informed her that 'On the whole of the earth you will not find men in so miserable a condition as the Smedni Viluisk lepers'. She found them dressed in rags, living in hovels and barely existing on a diet of rotten fish. This was in an area where, in winter, some of the lowest temperatures in the world have been recorded. Unfortunately she did not find the herb that was rumoured to exist there but left all the more convinced that finances must be raised for a hospital.

Although she managed to raise 25,000 roubles towards the enterprise, her task was not made any easier by several individuals who took exception to her breezy style of writing, accusing her of having undertaken the journey for her own fame and fortune. Some even suggested that the journey was a fiction invented so that Miss Marsden could collect charitable sums for her own use. In the end she was forced to sue one of her defamers who wrote a letter to *The Times* describing her journey as 'only a little pleasure trip'.

Nevertheless she achieved her aim: a hospital opened in Viluisk in 1897. It still stands and her name is still remembered in this remote corner of Russia.

SS HILL'S *TRAVELS IN SIBERIA*

This account of Hill's Siberian adventures was the result of a journey made in the early 1850s to Irkutsk and Yakutsk. Armed with a pistol loaded with goose-shot (the law forbade a foreigner to shoot at a Russian, even in self-defence), he travelled by tarantass and lived on *shchi* (soup) and tea most of the time. He makes some interesting observations upon the **culinary habits of the Siberians** he met along the way.

He records that on one occasion, when settling down to a bowl of shchi after a long winter's journey, 'we found the taste of our accustomed dish, how-ever, today peculiar'. He was made aware of the main ingredient of their soup later, 'by the yamshchik pointing out to us the marks of the axe upon the frozen carcass of a horse lying within a quarter of a verst of the site of our feast'. In some places even tea and shchi were unavailable and they could find only cedar nuts ('a favourite food article with the peasants of Eastern Siberia'). He ate bet-ter in Irkutsk, where, at a dinner party, he was treated to *comba* fish, 2m (6ft) in length and served whole. 'I confess I never before saw so enormous an animal served or cooked whole save once, an ox roasted at a 'mop' in Worcestershire', he wrote later. He was shocked by the behaviour of the ladies at the table, who, when bored, displayed 'a very droll habit of rolling the damp crumb of rye bread ... into pills'. He remarks with surprise that in Siberian society 'a glass of milk terminates the dinner'.

JEFFERSON'S BICYCLE JAUNTS

RL Jefferson was an enthusiastic cyclist and made several bicycle journeys to Siberia in the 1890s. A year after cycling from London to Constantinople and back, he set out again from Kennington Oval for Moscow on his Imperial Rover bicycle. Twelve hours out of Moscow, a speeding tarantass knocked him down, squashing the back wheel of his 'machine'. Repairs took a few days but he still managed to set a **cycling speed record** of just under 50 days for the 6890km (4281-mile) journey from London to Moscow and back.

His next ride was to the decaying capital of the Khanate of Khiva, now in Uzbekistan. The 9700km (6000-mile) journey took him across the Kyrgyz Steppes in south-west Siberia, along the coast of the Aral Sea and over the Karakum Desert. When the bicycle's wheels sank up to their axles in the sand, he had the Rover lashed to the back of a camel for the rest of the journey. While in Central Asia he lived on a diet of boiled mutton and *koumis* (fermented mares' milk). He travelled in a camel-hair suit (Jaeger, of course) and top boots, with a white cork helmet to complete the outfit.

Across Siberia

Jefferson made two more trips to Siberia. In *Across Siberia by Bicycle* (1896), he wrote that he left Moscow and 'sleeping the night in some woodman's hut, subsisting on occasional lumps of black bread, bitten to desperation by fearful insects, and tormented out of my life during the day by swarms of mosquitoes, I arrived in Perm jaded and disgusted'. He then cycled over the Urals and through the mud of the Great Post Road to Yekaterinburg. Here he was entertained by the Yekaterinburg Cyclists' Club whom he described as 'friends of the wheel – jolly good fellows all'.

Declaring that 'from a cyclist's point of view, Russian roads cannot be recommended', he abandoned his Rover in 1897 for the adventure described in *Roughing it in Siberia*. With three chums he travelled by sledge from Krasnoyarsk up the frozen Yenisey ('jerking about like peas in a frying pan') to the gold mines in Minusinsk district, spending several weeks prospecting in the Syansk Mountains.

Building the railway

The first railway to be built in Russia was Tsar Nicholas I's private line (opened in 1836) which ran from his summer palace at Tsarkoye Selo (Pushkin) to Pavlovsk and later to St Petersburg, a distance of 23km (14 miles). The Tsar was said to have been most impressed with this new form of transport and over the next 30 years several lines were laid in European Russia, linking the main cities and towns. Siberia, however, was too far away to deserve serious consideration since most people went there only if they were forced to as exiles. As far as the Tsar was concerned traditional methods of transport kept him supplied with all the gold and furs he needed.

PLANS FOR A TRANS-SIBERIAN RAILWAY

Horse-powered Trans-Siberian Express?

The earliest plans for a long-distance railway in Siberia came from foreigners. Most books which include a history of the Trans-Siberian give passing mention to a certain English engineer, if only because of his wildly eccentric ideas and his unfortunate name. Thus it is a **'Mr Dull'** who has gone down in history as the man who first seriously suggested the building of a line from Perm across Siberia to the Pacific, with carriages being pulled by wild horses (of which there were a great many in the region at the time). He is said to have formally proposed his plan to the Ministry of Ways of Communication who, perhaps not surprisingly, turned it down.

In fact the Englishman's name was **not Dull but Duff** and it's not only his name that has been distorted through time. His descendants (John Howell and William Lawrie) have requested that the story be set straight. **Thomas Duff** was an enterprising adventurer who went to China to seek his fortune in the 1850s. He returned to England via Siberia, spending some time in St Petersburg with wealthy aristocratic friends. Here he was introduced to the Minister of Ways of Communication and it was probably during their conversation that he remarked on the **vast numbers of wild horses** he had encountered on his journey. Could they not be put to some use? Perhaps they might be trained to pull the trains that people were saying would soon run across Siberia. It is unlikely that this remark was meant to be serious but it has gone down in history as a formal proposal for a horse-powered Trans-Siberian Express.

More serious proposals

At around this time the American Perry McDonough Collins was exploring the Amur River, having persuaded the US government to appoint him as commercial agent in the region. After an enthusiastic welcome by Count Muravyev-Amursky, Governor-General of Siberia, Collins set off to descend the Amur in a small boat. Collins envisaged a trade link between America and Siberia with vessels sailing up the Amur and Shilka Rivers to Chita, where a railway link would shuttle goods to and from Irkutsk. He sent his plans for the building and financing of such a line to the government but they were rejected. His next venture, a telegraph link between America and Russia, also failed but not before he had made himself a considerable fortune.

It took a further 20 years for the government to become interested enough in the idea of a Siberian railway to send surveyors to investigate its feasibility. Plans were considered for lines to link the great Siberian rivers, so that future travellers could cross Siberia in relative comfort by a combination of rail and ship. European lines were extended from Perm over the Urals, reaching Yekaterinburg in 1878.

Tsar Alexander III: the railway's founder

In 1881 Alexander III became Tsar and in 1886 gave the Trans-Siberian project his official sanction with the words: 'I have read many reports of the Governors-General of Siberia and must own with grief and shame that until now the government has done scarcely anything towards satisfying the needs of this rich, but neglected country! It is time, high time!'

He was thus able to add 'Most August Founder of The Great Siberian Railway' to his many other titles. He rightly saw the railway as both the **key to developing the land beyond the Urals** and also as the **means to transport his troops to the Amur region** which was being threatened by the Chinese. When the commission looking into the building of the new line declared that the country did not have the money to pay for it, the Tsar's reply was to dismiss it and form a new one.

THE DECISION TO BUILD

The new commission took note of petitions from Count Ignatyev and Baron Korf, the Governors-General of Irkutsk and the Amur territories, respectively. They had proposed rail links between Tomsk and Irkutsk, Lake Baikal and Sretensk (where passengers could board ships for the journey down the Shilka and Amur Rivers to the coast) and for the Ussuri line to Vladivostok. Baron Korf considered it imperative for the Ussuri line to be built as soon as possible if the valuable port of Vladivostok was not to be cut off by the advancing Chinese. The Tsar took note and declared: 'I hope the Ministry will practically prove the possibility of the quick and cheap construction of the line'.

Surveys were commissioned and detailed plans prepared. In 1891 it was announced that the Trans-Siberian Railway would indeed be built and work would start immediately. It was, however, to be constructed as cheaply as possible using thinner rails, shorter sleepers and timber (rather than stone) for the smaller bridges.

The route
The railway commission decided that the great project should be divided into several sections, on which work would commence simultaneously. The **West Siberian Railway** would run from Chelyabinsk (the railway over the Urals reached this town in 1892) to the Ob River where the settlement of Novo Nikolayevsk (now Novosibirsk) was being built. The **Mid-Siberian Railway** would link the Ob to Irkutsk, capital of Eastern Siberia. Passengers would cross Lake Baikal on ferries to Mysovaya, the start of the **Transbaikal Railway** to Sretensk. From there they would continue to use the Shilka and Amur River for the journey to Khabarovsk, until the **Amur Railway** could be built between these towns. The **Ussuri Railway** would link Khabarovsk with Vladivostok.

There were also plans for a shortcut from the Transbaikal area to Vladivostok, across Manchuria. This would be known as the **East Chinese Railway**.

Nicholas lays the foundation stone
After the decision to start work, the Tsar wrote the following letter to his son, the Tsarevich, who had just reached Vladivostok at the end of a tour around the world: 'Having given the order to build a continuous line of railway across Siberia, which is to unite the rich Siberian provinces with the railway system of the interior, I entrust you to declare My will, upon your entering the Russian dominions after your inspection of the foreign countries of the East. At the same time I desire you to lay the first stone at Vladivostok for the construction of the Ussuri line forming part of the Siberian Railway ...'.

On 31 May 1891 Nicholas carried out his father's wishes, filling a wheelbarrow with earth and emptying it onto what was to become part of the embankment for the Ussuri Railway. He then laid the foundation stone for the station.

RAILWAY CONSTRUCTION

Construction phase 1 (1891-1901)
● **The Ussuri, West Siberian & Mid-Siberian railways (1891-98)** Work started on the Ussuri line (Vladivostok to Khabarovsk) some time after the inauguration ceremony and proceeded slowly. In July 1892 construction of the West Siberian line (Chelyabinsk to the Ob River) was begun. In July 1893 work started on the Mid-Siberian line (Ob River to Irkutsk).

The West Siberian reached Omsk in 1894 and was completed when the rails reached the Ob in October 1895. The Ussuri Railway was completed in 1897. In the following year the final rails of the Mid-Siberian were laid, finally linking Irkutsk to Moscow and St Petersburg.

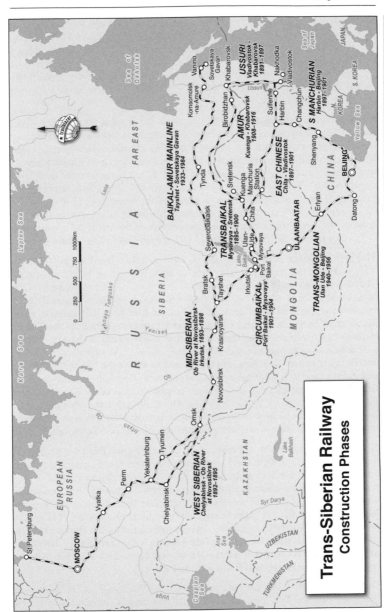

Trans-Siberian Railway
Construction Phases

● **Transbaikal Railway (1895-1900)** The rail link between the Lake Baikal port of Mysovaya and Sretensk on the Shilka River was begun in 1895. In spite of a flood which swept away part of the track in 1897, the line was completed by the beginning of 1900.

Passengers could now travel to Irkutsk by train, take the ferry across Lake Baikal and the train again from Mysovaya to Srtensk, where steamers would take them to Khabarovsk.

● **East Chinese Railway (1897-1901)** Surveys showed that the proposed Amur Railway between Sretensk and Khabarovsk would be expensive to build because of the mountainous terrain and the large supplies of explosives required to deal with the permafrost. In 1894 the Russian government granted China a generous loan to help pay off the latter's debts to Japan. In exchange a secret treaty was signed which allowed Russia to build and control a rail link between the Transbaikal region and Vladivostok, across the Chinese territory of Manchuria.

Every difficulty encountered in building railways in Siberia (severe winters, mountains, rivers, floods, disease and bandits) was a feature of the construction of the East Chinese Railway, begun in 1897 and opened to light traffic in 1901.

The labour force The greater part of the Trans-Siberian Railway was built without heavy machinery, by men with nothing more than wooden shovels. They nevertheless managed to lay up to 4km (2½ miles) of rail on a good day. Most of the labour force had to be imported as local peasants were already fully employed on the land. They came not only from European Russia but from as far away as Italy and Turkey. Chinese coolies were employed on the Ussuri Railway but overseers found them unreliable and terrified of the Amur tigers with which the area was infested.

The government soon turned to the prisons to relieve the shortage of labour, and gangs of convicts were put to work on the lines. They were paid 25 kopecks (a quarter of a rouble) a day and had their sentences reduced – eight months on the railways counted for a year in prison. The 1500 convicts employed on the Mid-Siberian worked hard but those brought in from Sakhalin Island to work on the Ussuri line ran riot and terrorised the inhabitants of Vladivostok.

Shortage of materials On many parts of the Siberian Plain engineers discovered that although there were vast forests, the trees were unsuitable for use as sleepers (ties). Timber had to be imported over great distances. Rails came from European Russia and some even from Britain. They were shipped either via the Kara Sea (a southern extension of the Arctic Ocean) and up the Yenisey River to Krasnoyarsk, or right around the continent by boat to Vladivostok (which took two months). From here, when work started on the Transbaikal line in 1895, materials were shipped up the Ussuri, Amur and Shilka Rivers to Sretensk (over 1600km/1000 miles). Horses and carts were scarce in Siberia and these, too, had to be brought in from Europe.

Difficult terrain When the railway between St Petersburg and Moscow was being planned, the Tsar took ruler and pencil and drew a straight line between the two cities, declaring that this was the route to be followed, with almost every town by-passed. For the Trans-Siberian, Alexander ordered that it be built as cheaply as possible which is why in some places the route twists and turns so that expensive tunnelling might be avoided.

There were few problems in laying foundations for the rails across the open steppeland of the Siberian Plain, but cutting through the almost impenetrable forests of the taiga proved extremely difficult. Much of this area was not only thickly forested, but swampy in summer and frozen until July. Consequently the building season lasted no more than four months in most places. Parts of the route in eastern Siberia were locked in permafrost and, even in mid-summer, had to be dynamited or warmed with fires before rails could be laid. The most difficult terrain was the short line around the southern end of Lake Baikal, the Circumbaikal Loop, which required over 200 trestles and bridges, and 33 tunnels.

Conditions For the workers who laboured in Siberia, conditions were hardly the most enjoyable. All were far from home, living in isolated log cabins that were not much cleaner or more comfortable than Tyumen's squalid prison, graphically described by George Kennan in *Siberia and the Exile System* (see p86). Winters were very long and extremely cold. The brief summer brought relief from the cold but the added discomfort of plagues of black flies and mosquitoes in the swamps of the taiga. There were numerous outbreaks of disease. Workers on the East Chinese Railway were struck by bubonic plague in 1899 and cholera in 1902. In many places the horses were wiped out by Siberian anthrax.

There were other dangers in addition to disease. In Manchuria and the Amur and Ussuri regions, the forests were filled with Amur tigers for whom the occasional railway labourer no doubt made a pleasant snack. In Manchuria construction camps were frequently raided by *hunghutzes* (bandits) who roamed the country in gangs of up to 700. As a result the Russian government was obliged to allocate considerable money and manpower to the policing of the region.

There were several setbacks that no one could have foreseen. In July 1897 severe flooding swept away or damaged over 300km (200 miles) of track near Lake Baikal on the Transbaikal line, also destroying settlements and livestock. Damage was estimated at six million roubles. In other areas landslides were caused by torrential rainfall.

Construction phase 2: Reconstruction (1898-1916)

As the first trains began to travel over the newly laid tracks, the shortsightedness of building the railway as cheaply as possible soon became clear. Many of the materials used in its construction were either substandard or unsuitable to the conditions they were expected to withstand. The rails, less than half the weight of those used in North America and fashioned of inferior quality iron, soon bent and buckled and needed replacing. The ballast under the sleepers was far thinner than that put down on the major railways of Europe. As a result the ride in the carriages was bumpy and uncomfortable and speed had to be kept down to 13mph for passenger trains, 8mph for freight. Foreign engineers proclaimed the whole system unsafe and were proved correct by the frequent derailments which took place.

In 1895 Prince Khilkov became Minister of Ways of Communication. On a tour of inspection along the West and Mid-Siberian lines he quickly realised the need for a massive rebuilding programme. Extra trains were also needed to transport the hundreds of thousands of emigrants who were now flooding over the Urals. In 1899, 100 million roubles were allocated for repairs, work which would have been unnecessary had sufficient funds been made available from the start.

● **The Circumbaikal Loop Line (1901-1904)** In 1901 work began on the 260km (160-mile) Circumbaikal Loop Line around Lake Baikal's southern shore. The initial project had been shelved in 1893, the terrain considered too difficult. Passengers used the ferry service across the lake but it was soon found that the ships couldn't cope with the increased traffic. The situation became critical at the start of the Russo-Japanese war in 1904 when troops and machinery being sent to the East by rail were delayed at the lake. Construction of the new line continued as quickly as possible and by the end of the year the final section of the Trans-Siberian was opened. Passengers were at last able to travel from Calais to Vladivostok entirely by train.

● **The Amur Railway (1907-1916)** The original plans for a railway from Sretensk to Khabarovsk along the Shilka and Amur Rivers were abandoned because the route would entail expensive engineering work. After the Russo-Japanese war in 1904-5, the government realised there was a danger of Japan taking control of Manchuria and the East Chinese Railway. As this was the only rail link to Russia's naval base at Vladivostok, it was decided that the Amur Railway must indeed be built.

Work began at Kuenga in 1908. There were the usual problems of insects, disease and permafrost but with the rest of the railway operational, it was easier to transport labour and materials to the area. When the bridge over the Amur at Khabarovsk was finished in 1916, the Trans-Siberian Railway was at last complete. Since 1891 over one billion roubles had been spent on building all the sections (including the East Chinese line).

THE FIRST RAIL TRAVELLERS

Rail service begins

As each of the sectors of the Trans-Siberian was completed, a rail service was begun. To say that there were teething troubles would be a gross understatement: there was a shortage of engines and carriages, most of the system operated without a timetable and there were frequent delays and derailments along the shoddily constructed line. Nevertheless, to attract foreign travellers, luxury trains and 'Expresses' were introduced. Those run by the government were known as Russian State Expresses while another service was operated by the Belgian Compagnie Internationale des Wagons-Lits. In 1900 the Ministry of

Ways of Communication published its English-language *Guide to The Great Siberian Railway*.

Early rail travellers

When **RL Jefferson** set out to investigate the Minusinsk gold-mining region in 1897, he was able to take the train (travelling this time without his bicycle but no doubt taking along a good supply of Bovril and Jaeger underwear) as far as Krasnoyarsk. The first Englishwoman to travel the entire length of this route was **Annette Meakin**, who in 1900 took her aged mother along for company. They travelled via Paris to see the Siberian display at the Paris Exhibition (see box below). Having crossed Siberia, they went by ship to Japan and then on to North America, crossing that continent by train, too. Having circumnavigated the globe by rail, Miss Meakin recorded her experiences in the book she called *A Ribbon of Iron*. Two years later **Michael Myres Shoemaker** took *The Great Siberian Railway from St Petersburg to Pekin* (the name of his account of the journey). He wrote enthusiastically: 'This Railway will take its place amongst the most important works of the world ... Russia is awakening at last and moving forward.'

It is interesting to compare the descriptions these travellers give of the trains they took, with the carriages displayed at the Paris Exhibition as well as with the service operated today by Russian Railways.

The carriages

In gushing prose, advertising brochures informed prospective Trans-Siberian travellers that the carriages in which they were to be conveyed would be of a standard equal to those used by European royalty. In addition to the luxurious sleeping compartments and dining cars shown at the Paris Exhibition, there would be a bathroom with marble bathtub, a gymnasium equipped with

---

❏ The Paris Exhibition

The Russian government was keen to show off to the world the country's great engineering feat and at the Paris 'Exposition Universelle' of 1900, a comprehensive Trans-Siberian exhibit was staged. Amongst photographs and maps of Siberia, with Kyrgyz, Buryat and Goldi robes and artefacts, there were several carriages to be operated by the Belgian Wagons-Lits Company on the Great Siberian Railway. They were furnished in the most sumptuous style, with just four spacious compartments in the sleeping carriages, each with a connecting lavatory. The other carriages contained a smoking-room done up in Chinese style, a library and music-room complete with piano.

In the two restaurant cars, decorated with mahogany panelling and heavy curtains, visitors to the exhibition could dine on the luxurious fare that was promised on the journey itself. To give diners the feeling of crossing Siberia, a length of canvas on which was painted a Siberian panorama of wide steppes, dense taiga and little villages of log cabins, could be seen through the windows. To complete the illusion, the painted panorama was made to move past the windows by mechanical means.

Visitors were intrigued and impressed and more than a few soon set off on the epic trip. The reality, they were to discover, was a little different from what they experienced at the exhibition.

a stationary bicycle and other exercising machines, a fire-proof safe, a hair-dressing salon and a darkroom equipped with all the chemicals a photographer would need. The carriages would be lit by electric lighting, individually heated in winter and cooled by under-floor ice-boxes in summer.

Although more than a few of those luxurious appointments, which they had seen in the carriages of the Siberian exhibit in Paris, were missing on their train, Annette Meakin and her mother found their accommodation entirely satisfactory. The ride was not so comfortable from Mysovaya on the Transbaikal Railway. Only fourth-class carriages were available, and the two ladies were forced to take their travelling rugs and picnic hamper to the luggage van, where they spent the next four days.

Travelling in 1902, Michael Myres Shoemaker was very impressed with the bathing arrangements on the train and wrote: 'I have just discovered that there is a fine bathroom in the restaurant car, large and tiled, with all sorts of sprays, plunges and douches. This bath has its separate attendant and all the bath towels you may demand.' He was less enthusiastic about his travelling companions, a French Consul and family whose fox terrier 'promptly domesticated itself in my compartment'.

The restaurant car At the Paris Exhibition visitors were led to believe that a good part of the enjoyment of travelling on the Trans-Siberian would be the cordon bleu cuisine served in the restaurant car. It was claimed that the kitchens were even equipped with water tanks filled with live fish. The waiters would be multilingual and a truly international service was promised.

Travellers found this to be something of an exaggeration. Annette Meakin reported the existence of a Bechstein piano and a library of Russian novels in the restaurant car. Shoemaker wrote: 'The restaurant car is just like all those on the trains of Europe. There is a piano, generally used to hold dirty dishes. There are three very stupid waiters who speak nothing save Russian. The food is very poor.'

Travellers were warned by guidebooks that there were occasional food shortages on the trains and were advised to take a picnic hamper. The Meakins found theirs invaluable on their four-day jaunt in the luggage van. In fact during the service's first four years there were no restaurant cars. RL Jefferson wrote that at meal-times the train would stop at a convenient station and all passengers (and the engine-driver) would get off for a meal at the station.

The church car Behind the baggage car was a peculiar carriage known as the church car. It was a Russian Orthodox church on wheels, complete with icons and candelabra inside, church bells and a cross on the roof, and a peripatetic priest who dispensed blessings along the way. This carriage was

---

'The Siberian express is a kind of "Liberty Hall", where you can shut your door and sleep all day if you prefer it, or eat and drink, smoke and play cards if you like that better. An electric bell summons a serving-man to make your bed or sweep your floor, as the case may be, while a bell on the other side summons a waiter from the buffet ... Time passes very pleasantly on such a train.' **Annette Meakin** *A Ribbon of Iron*

detached at stations and settlements where churches had not yet been built and services were conducted for railway workers and their families.

Transport of emigrants

While foreign visitors discussed whether or not their accommodation was all that the Paris Exhibition had led them to expect, emigrants travelled in the unenviable conditions described by RL Jefferson: 'The emigrants' train is simply one of the cattle trucks, each car being marked on the side "Forty men or eight horses". There are no seats or lights provided, and into each of these pens forty men, women and children have to herd over a dreary journey of fourteen or fifteen days ... They have to provide their own food but at every station a large samovar is kept boiling in order to provide them with hot water for their tea.' By the end of the century they were crossing the Urals to Siberia at the rate of about a quarter of a million peasants each year.

Stations

Little wooden station buildings mushroomed along the railway. Russian stations were traditionally given a class number from one to five. Of the stations listed in the official *Guide to the Great Siberian Railway*, none was of the first class and the majority were no more than fifth class. Beside most stations there towered a water-tank to supply the steam engines; many of these towers, their eaves decorated with ornate fretwork, can still be seen today. Most of the larger stations had their own churches and resident priests. If the train did not have a church car, stops would be made for lengthy services at these railside churches, especially on the eve of important saints' days.

> Travelling in 1901, John Foster Fraser reports, in *The Real Siberia*, that locals did good business on the platforms selling 'dumplings with hashed meat and seasoning inside ... huge loaves of new made bread, bottles of beer, pails of milk, apples, grapes, and fifty other things'.
> This is still true today.

RL Jefferson found that in the early years of the railways, the arrival and departure of every train at a Siberian station was quite an event, being 'attended with an amount of excitement that it is hard to associate with the usually stolid Russian. Particularly is this so in Eastern Russia where railways are new and interesting.' A man 'performs a terrific tintinabulation on a large suspended bell. All the conductors blow whistles.' Jefferson goes on to explain that none of the passengers was allowed out of the train until the engine driver had got down and shaken hands with the station-master and his staff.

Bridges

Although the rails were badly laid and of poor quality, the bridges that were made of stone were built to such a high standard that many are still in use today. They were largely the work of Italian masons, who laboured throughout the winter months: the bridge-building season, since no work could be done on the snow-covered line. Many labourers succumbed to hypothermia in temperatures as low as -40°C, dropping to their death on the ice below.

In winter, where bridges had not been finished when the railway lines reached them, engineers had the brilliant idea of laying rails across the ice. The sleepers were literally frozen onto the surface of the river by large amounts of water being poured over them. When RL Jefferson's train reached the track laid across the Chulim River, passengers were made to get out and walk, in case the train proved too great a weight for the ice to bear. He wrote: 'As it passed us we felt the ice quiver, and heard innumerable cracks, like the reports of pistols in the distance, but the train got across the centre safely.'

Delays

Because the original line was so badly laid, the ride in the carriages was rough and uncomfortable and speed had to be kept down. There were frequent derailments and long delays. Annette Meakin complained: 'We stopped at a great many stations; indeed on some parts of the route we seemed to get into a chronic state of stopping'. 'All day long at a dog trot,' wrote Shoemaker, 'Certainly no more than ten miles an hour.' Over some sections the train went so slowly passengers could get out and pick flowers as they walked along beside it. Still, the delays did give one time to catch up on current affairs, as Miss Meakin observes when her train was delayed for four hours ('a mere nothing in Siberia') at Tayga. She writes: 'As we sat waiting in the station the good news was brought that Mafeking had been relieved.'

Breakdowns

These were all too frequent. A wait of 24 hours for a new engine was not regarded as a long delay. Annette Meakin recorded the following incident: 'Outside Kainsk the train stopped. "The engine has smashed up," said a jolly Russian sailor in broken English. "She is sixty years old and was made in Glasgow. She is no use any more" ... The poor old engine was now towed to her last berth ... I had whipped out my "Kodak" and taken her photograph, thinking of Turner's "Fighting Temeraire".'

Cost of the journey

The *Guide to the Great Siberian Railway* informed its readers that, for the journey from London to Shanghai: 'The conveyance by the Siberian Railway will be over twice as quick and two and a half times cheaper than that now existing' (the sea passage via the Suez Canal). The cost of a first-class ticket for the 16-day journey was to be 319 roubles. From Moscow to Vladivostok the price was 114 roubles.

THE RAILWAY IN THE 20TH CENTURY

After the Revolution (1917-18)

'When the trains stop, that will be the end,' announced Lenin, and the trains, the Trans-Siberian included, continued to run throughout those troubled times.

When the new Bolshevik government pulled out of WWI in early 1918, a Czech force of 50,000 well-armed men found themselves marooned in Russia, German forces preventing them from returning to western Europe. Receiving permission to leave Russia via Vladivostok, they set off on the Trans-Siberian. Their passage was not a smooth one, for the Bolsheviks suspected that the Czechs would join the White Russian resistance while the Czechs suspected that the Bolsheviks were not going to allow them to leave. Violence erupted, several Czechs were arrested and the rest of the legion decided to shoot their way out of Russia. They took over the Trans-Siberian line from the Urals to Lake Baikal and travelled the railway in armour-plated carriages.

The Civil War in Siberia (1918-20)

At this time Siberia was divided amongst a number of forces, all fighting against the Bolsheviks but not as a combined unit. Many of the leaders were nothing more than gangsters. East Siberia and Manchuria were controlled by the evil Ataman Semenov, half-Russian, half-Buryat and supported by the Japanese. He charged around Transbaikalia murdering whole villages and, to alleviate the boredom of these mass executions, a different method of death was adopted each day. Then there was Baron General von Ungern Sternberg, a White Russian commander whose cruelty rivalled that of Semenov.

The Americans, French, English and Japanese all brought troops into Siberia to evacuate the Czech legions and to help Admiral Kolchak, the Supreme Ruler of the White Government based at Omsk. Kolchak, however, failed to win the support of the people in Siberia's towns, his troops were undisciplined and in November 1919 he lost Omsk to the Bolsheviks. He was executed in Irkutsk in early 1920 and the Allies abandoned the White Russian cause. The Japanese gave up Vladivostok in 1922, leaving all Siberia in Communist hands.

Reconstruction (1920-39)

After the Civil War the Soviet Union set about rebuilding its battered economy. High on the priority list was the repair of the Trans-Siberian line, so that raw materials like iron ore could be transported to European Russia. The First Five Year Plan (1928) set ambitious goals for the expansion of industry and agriculture. It also included new railway projects, the double-tracking of the Trans-Siberian and the building of the Turk-Sib, the line between Turkestan and Novosibirsk. Work began on two giant industrial complexes known as the Ural-Kuznetsk Combine. Iron ore from the Urals was taken by rail to the Kuznetsk Basin in Siberia, where it was exchanged for coal for Ural blast furnaces. For all these giant projects an enormous, controllable labour force was needed and this was to a large extent provided by prisoners from the corrective labour camps.

World War II (1939-45)

Siberia played an important backstage role in the 'Great Patriotic War', as Russians call WWII. Many factories were moved from European Russia to Siberia and the populations of cities such as Novosibirsk rose dramatically. The Trans-Siberian's part was a vital one and shipments of coal and food were continuously despatched over the Urals to Europe throughout the war years.

In the **21st century** work continued on the BAM (see p109) and the AYaM (see p110) and there are plans to build a line to Magadan.

STEAM LOCOMOTIVES IN SIBERIA

In 1956 the USSR stopped producing steam engines and official policy was to phase them out by 1970. As with most official plans in the country, this one overran a little and a second official end of steam was announced for 1987, when the number of locos stood at over 6000. Some of these were sold as scrap to Germany and Korea but many were stored as a 'strategic reserve' in remote sidings and used very occasionally for shunting work; there are some to be seen along the Trans-Siberian line (see the Route Guide for locations). In 2000, however, it was decided not to retain steam engines within these strategic military reserves so numbers are now falling fast. Each of the country's 32 railway administrations is allowed to keep just 10 steam engines so now there are probably no more than 320 working steam locos in the whole of Russia. In northern China there are numerous steam engines still at work.

In 1836 Russia's first locomotive, a Hackworth 2-2-2, was delivered to St Petersburg to pull the Tsar's private carriages over the 23km (14 miles) of six-foot gauge track to his palace at Tsarskoye Selo. The Russians have always been (and still are) conservative by nature when it comes to buying or building engines. Usually large numbers of a few standard locomotives have been ordered so there's not much of a range to be seen even today. They seem to be uniformly large, standing up to 5m (17ft) high, and larger than British locos, partly because the Russian gauge is almost 9cm (3½ inches) wider than that used in Britain.

They are numbered separately by classes, not in a single series and not by railway regions. If variations of the class have been built, they are given an additional letter after the main class letter. Thus, for example, the first type of 0-10-0 freight locomotive was Class E and those of this class built in Germany were Class Eg. Classes you may see in Siberia include the following (Roman alphabet class letters given in brackets; * = very rare):

● **Class O (O)** The first freight trains on the Trans-Siberian route were pulled by these long-boilered 0-8-0 locos (55 tons) which date back to 1889. The 'O' in the class name stands for *Osnovnoi Tip* meaning 'basic type'. Production ceased in 1923 but as late as 1958 there were 1500 of these locomotives still at work.

● **Class C (S)*** 2-6-2 (75 tons) A highly successful passenger engine. 'S' stands for *Sormovo*, where these locos were built from 1911. **Class Cy (Su)** ('u' for *usileny*, meaning 'strengthened') was developed from the former class and in production from 1926 to 1951.

● **Class E (Ye)** 2-10-0 1500 Ye 2-10-0s were imported from the USA in 1914.

● **Class Эу/Эм/Эр (Eu/Em/Er)*** Subclasses of the old type (E) 0-10-0, 80 tons, built in Russia from 1926 to 1952. The old type E was also produced in Germany and Sweden, as Esh and Eg subclasses.

● **Class Ea (YeA)*** 2-10-0 (90 tons) Over 2000 were built in the USA between 1944 and 1947 and shipped across the Pacific.

● **Class Л (L)** 2-10-0 (103 tons) About 4130 were built from 1945 to 1956.

● **Class П36 (P36)** 4-8-4 (133 tons) 251 were built between 1950 and 1956 – the last express passenger type built for Soviet Railways. 'Skyliner'-style, fitted with large smoke-deflectors, and painted green with a cream stripe. Preserved examples at Sharya, Tayga, Sibirtsevo, Skovorodino, Belogorsk, Mogzon and Chernyshevsk.

Classes **O, C/Cy, E (O, S/Su, Ye)** have all disappeared from the steam dumps but you will see the occasional one on a plinth.

For more information refer to the comprehensive *Soviet Locomotive Types – The Union Legacy* by AJ Heywood and IDC Button (1995, Frank Stenvalls/Luddenden Press). There's also a good deal of information about Russian trains on the internet; a good place to start is ▣ **www.transsib.ru/Eng/** – the Trans-Siberian Railway Web Encyclopedia.

OTHER RAILWAY LINES LINKED TO THE TRANS-SIBERIAN

BAM – a second Trans-Siberian
In the 1930s another Herculean undertaking was begun on the railways of Russia. The project was named the **Baikal-Amur-Mainline (BAM) БАМ** (see pp498-504): a second Trans-Siberian railway, 3140km long, running parallel but to the north of the existing line. It was to run through the rich mining districts of northern Siberia, providing an east–west communications back-up to the main line. Work began in Tayshet and the track reached Ust Kut on the Lena River before the project was officially abandoned at the end of WWI. Much of the 700km of track that had been laid was torn up to replace war-damaged lines in the west. Construction continued in secret, using slave labour until the Gulags were closed in 1954. In 1976 it was announced that work on the BAM was **recommencing**. Incentives were offered to collect the 100,000 strong work-force needed for so large a project. For eight years they laboured heroically, dynamiting their way through the permafrost which covers almost half the route, across a region where temperatures fall as low as -60°C in winter. In October 1984 it was announced that the way was open from Tayshet to Komsomolsk-na-Amure. Although track-laying had been completed, only the eastern half was operational (from Komsomolsk to Bamskaya, where traffic joined the old Trans-Siberian route).

By 1991 the whole system was still not fully operational, the main obstacle being the Severomuysk Tunnel, bypassed by an unsatisfactory detour with an impressive 1:25 gradient. It took from 1981 to 1991 to drill 13km of the 15.3km of this unfinished tunnel in the most difficult of conditions. Many were already questioning the point of a railway that was beginning to look like a white elephant. Work has more or less stopped now; the main sections of the line are complete but traffic is still infrequent. The BAM was built to compete with shipping routes for the transfer of freight but the cost has been tremendous: there has been considerable ecological damage and there is little money left for the extraction of the minerals that was the other reason for the building of the railway. It is possible to travel along the BAM route starting near the north of Lake Baikal and ending up at Khabarovsk. Rail traffic on the BAM line currently remains far below capacity, with about six trains per day plying the route. According to Russian Railways, by 2009 the BAM was carrying about 12 million passengers and 12 million tons of cargo each year, though its total capacity is around 18 million.

The BAM was saved from oblivion when Kremlin Chief of Staff, Dmitry Medvedev, discussed developing the Russian Far East in an April 2005 interview. However, he also mentioned the BAM as the sort of **wasteful project** that should be avoided. 'We do not need yet another huge construction project with an unpredictable outcome, as happened with BAM' he said. The BAM was meant to give development in Siberia a much-needed boost. But rather it has become another export route to sell Russian resources abroad. The line is now used to send crude oil from small fields near Irkutsk to China at a rate of 10,000 tons per month. Oil is loaded onto trains at Ust-Kut and sent to Komsomolsk-na-Amure and then on to the port of Vanino.

However, with the AyaM having now reached Nizhny Bestyakh as well as plans to move much of the freight traffic from the main Trans-Siberian route onto the BAM, traffic on the BAM may increase significantly in the coming years. Renovation of the Komsomolsk-na-Amure–Sovetskaya Gavan section began in 2009 to reinforce the line for the extra traffic and is due to finish in 2016.

Though plans conceived in the 1950s to build a tunnel to connect the BAM with Sakhalin Island have since been abandoned, there is now talk of building a bridge instead to connect the island to the mainland and even more ambitious talk of then connecting Sakhalin Island to the Japanese island of Hokkaido, either via a tunnel or a bridge, to allow a direct land transport link from Japan to Asia and Europe.

Through Siberia by Accident (2005) is Dervla Murphy's entertaining account of her travels in the region.

AYaM and Little BAM

The **AYaM** АЯМ (**Amuro-Yakutskaya Magistral**) is the **Amur-Yakutsk Mainline**, built to connect Tynda on the BAM with Yakutsk in the north. The project was scheduled for completion at the same time as the BAM but construction has been fraught with both engineering and financial difficulties. As of 2011, the rails had been laid as far as Nizhny Bestyakh, the town across the Lena River from Yakutsk, with passenger services due to commence by the end of 2013. Nizhny Bestyakh is due to be the starting point for the railway branch that will eventually run as far as Magadan, though that's not projected for completion for a decade or so. At the time of writing, decisions were being made regarding the prospective bridge connecting Yakutsk to Nizhny Bestyakh – whether that will be a railway bridge or a regular automobile bridge, to connect the railway to the port of Yakutsk in order to transport freight more efficiently. The building of the bridge commenced at the end of 2013.

Little BAM Малый БАМ is the 180km rail link between the Trans-Siberian at Bamovskaya and Tynda, the start of the AYaM.

Turkestan–Siberia (Turksib) railway

The Turksib links Novosibirsk on the Trans-Siberian with Almaty in Kazakhstan, a journey of 1678km. From there it's possible to continue on into

Western China. The line was constructed in the 1930s to make it easier to transport grain from Siberia and cotton from Turkestan between these two regions.

Kazakhstan–China railway

In September 1990 a rail line was opened between Urumqi in north-west China and the border with Kazakhstan, opening a new rail route between east Asia and Europe via the Central Asian Republics. China built this link to create the shortest Eurasian rail route (2000km shorter than the Trans-Siberian) between the Pacific and the Atlantic, enabling freight to be transported faster and more cheaply than by ship. This means that it's now possible to travel along the ancient Silk Route by rail, through the old Central Asian capitals of Khiva, Bukhara and Samarkand and the Chinese cities of Dunhuang, Luoyang and Xi'an.

Turkey-Kazakhstan–Iran railway

In May 1996 a 295km cross-border railway line was officially opened between Mashhad in Iran and Saraghs and Tejen in Turkmenistan. This line, it was said, was the forerunner of a network that would join land-locked Central Asia to the Persian Gulf and, via Turkey, to the Mediterranean. The potential was there for a new Silk Route between southern Europe and the Far East, cutting travel times by up to 10 days. Six years later the line had reached northwards via Turkmenabat (Turkmenistan) and Tashkent (Uzbekistan) all the way to Almaty (Kazakhstan), and southwards to Tehran (Iran). In March 2002, with great fanfare, a weekly service was inaugurated for the 3300km, 70-hour Almaty–Tehran journey. But a month later it was suspended, apparently over disagreements about right of way through Uzbekistan.

It's currently possible to take the modern, efficient Trans-Asian Express that runs weekly from Ankara to Tehran (provided you get an Iranian visa).

Sakhalin railway

The island of Sakhalin (north of Japan) is currently linked to the Russian mainland by rail ferries operating between Vanino and Kholmsk. Steam specials are occasionally run on the island's 3ft 6in-gauge rail system.

A line to Korea

In 2001 negotiations began in earnest to extend the Trans-Siberian Railway into Korea, forming an even more profitable link between Europe and Asia. In 2002 North and South Korea announced they would cooperate in rebuilding the Trans-Korean Railway, with Russia bankrolling part of the project to pay off its US$1 billion debt to South Korea. Bridging Korea's DMZ (Demilitarised Zone) was the first step in extending the Trans-Siberian to the tip of the peninsula.

North Korean Railways trains run from Moscow to Pyongyang (2/month). Also, there are two Russian carriages running to Pyongyang from Moscow (4/month); these extra carriages are attached to the 001/002 Moscow–Vladivostok *Rossiya* and run as far as Ussuriysk, near Vladivostok, where they detach and follow the branch line to Tumangan, where there's a change of train to Pyongyang. At the time of writing, these services were not approved for foreign passengers and foreigners wishing to visit North Korea have to do so via Beijing.

Riding the Trans-Siberian today

THE TRAIN

Taking a train across Russia is a thoroughly enjoyable experience. Trains tend to be comfortable, well-geared up towards long-distance journeys and very punctual, which is particularly impressive considering the distances many travel.

Engines

If you're counting on being hauled across Siberia by a puffing steam locomotive you will be sadly disappointed. Soviet Railways (SZD), now Russian Railways (RZD), began converting the system to electricity in 1927. The work was completed in 2002 and today the Trans-Siberian line is entirely electrified (25kV 50Hz ac, or in some cases 3kV dc).

Passenger engines are usually Czech Skoda ChS4T's (line voltage 25kV 50 Hz; max output 5200kW; max speed 180kph; weight 126 tonnes) or ChS2s (3kV dc; 4620kW; 160kph; 126 tonnes), or Russian-built VL10s, VL60's or VL65s. On the Moscow–St Petersburg route the latest Czech-built engines are used: the CS200 (3kV dc; 8400kW; 200kph; 157 tonnes) and the CS7 developed from it. The most common freight engines are the large VL80S and the newer VL85.

Elsewhere on the Russian system where electrification is incomplete, and for shunting duties, diesel rather than steam engines are likely to be used, typically Russian-built 2TE10L/M/V (with overhanging windscreens) or sometimes 2M62U or 3M62U twin or triple units. If you're continuing on the Trans-Mongolian or Trans-Manchurian route, it is quite likely that a steam loco will be hitched to your carriages at the China border, at least for shunting duties; see pp108-9 for identification information and class numbers.

Carriages and carriage attendants

Many **carriages** in use are of East German origin and solidly built. There are doors at both ends and the only place where passengers may smoke is in the

---

❏ **Carriage keys**
On our train (No 006) there were a large number of Mongolian traders who proved to be very entertaining. They had managed to obtain a carriage key so that they could unlock the loo door after it had been locked. They would always oblige us with a quick unlock when we asked. We did notice that this carriage key looked familiar and it may be worth advising British travellers to try taking their British Gas meter cupboard key with them since it looks as if it is identical.   **Andrew Wingham** (UK)

Note from updater: If the toilets have been locked because the train is travelling through a populated area, unlocking them there is not a good idea because they are supposed to be locked for hygiene reasons (see p118). However, the same key can be used to unlock windows on some trains, so can still be useful.

(unheated) area between the carriages, where the windows never open, letting stale smoke into the carriage whenever the door is opened. The smoking area rule is strictly enforced.

Carriages are heated in winter (to a very warm 22-26° Celsius) and air-conditioned in summer; platzkart carriages in firmenny trains have ventilation systems (you may need to ask the provodnitsa to switch it on) as well as windows that open, whereas on older trains, you have to make do with just the windows. The air-conditioning system works on the pressure difference between the inside and outside of the carriage and takes about an hour to get going, so all carriage windows must be kept shut. One's initial instinct is to throw them open, and carriage attendants wage a constant battle to keep them closed. The air-con is not always very effective.

Radio is sometimes piped into the kupé compartments from the attendant's den to act as a wake-up call if you're about to arrive at your destination.

Each carriage is staffed by two **attendants** (female *provodnitsa* or male *provodnik* in Russian, *fuwuyuen* in Chinese), whose 'den' is a shoebox-sized compartment at the end of the carriage. One works the day shift, while the other works the night shift. Their duties include collecting your tickets, letting down the steps at stations, coming round with the mop and bucket, cleaning the bathrooms, keeping the carriages heated by shovelling coal in (on some trains), selling you tea (without milk) or instant coffee, and, according to the rule book, providing you with chess and checkers to keep you entertained (good luck with getting them to do that!). The attendants also maintain the **samovar** (see box) which is opposite their compartment.

Carriage attendants are often either students, earning some cash in summer, or career carriage attendants who tend to be middle-aged, often disgruntled and with very set ideas about how their carriage is run. (Note: the former are generally much more easy-going).

The coal-fired **stove-samovar** (*batchok*) provides a continuous supply of hot water in each carriage. Savvy travellers stock up on instant pot noodles at stations.

Train types

A regular long-distance train (**skory poyezd скорый поезд**) falls into one of two categories: *firmenny* or regular passazhirskiye poyezda (passenger train). The term **firmenny (фирменный)** refers to certain train services, including all international trains and many domestic ones. They typically have names (ie the 001/002 is the *Rossiya*) and tend to be newer, arrive and depart at more convenient times, stop at fewer stations, have cleaner carriages with slightly more comfortable berths and are equipped with bio-loos rather than the old let's-dump-it-all-on-the-track loos. Other long-distance trains are simply known as **passazhirskiye poyezda пассажирские поезда**; they have similar facilities but tend to be a little slower (and therefore cheaper).

If you're travelling short distances (ie between Moscow and Rostov or between Perm or Yekaterinburg and Kungur, you may take an **elektrichka электричка**, also known as **prigorodny poyezda пригородный поезда** – a local train connecting a big city to its suburbs and nearby towns. These have seats only, and tickets tend to cost less than platzkart berth tickets for the same distance.

Timetables for **suburban trains** usually run on local time rather than Moscow Time, but double check!

Classes of service

There are four main classes on Russian long-distance trains, though on the vast majority of trains that ply the Trans-Sib, you're only likely to encounter the top three. Some firmenny trains consist entirely of SV and kupé carriages.

SV/1st class *SV* (*spalny vagon*, literally 'sleeping car'; also called *myagky* 'soft' or lux) has comfortable, two-berth compartments which sometimes have washbasins. On a few firmenny trains (some Moscow–St Petersburg services and some Moscow–Kazan trains) each SV compartment may have its own shower and toilet.

On the Trans-Mongolian trains Nos 003/004 (0033/0043), SV compartments are *four*-berth and identical to all other services' kupé compartments except they are 16cm wider, so they are conspicuously poor value. But these particular Trans-Mongolian trains also have an additional de luxe 1st class, whose two-berth, carpeted, wood-panelled compartments have wider bunks, armchair, wind-down window and attached bathroom with rudimentary hand-held shower. Otherwise you still have to share facilities at the end of the corridor, but since SV carriages on most routes are rarely sold out, it does mean a significantly shorter bathroom queue.

Some SV compartments come equipped with TV, which you can unplug and use the socket to charge up your own electronic devices. Not all long-distance trains have SV carriages. SV berths tend to be almost twice the price of kupé berths.

Kupé/2nd class *Kupeyny or kupé* (coupé; also called 2nd class) refers to carriages with nine enclosed four-berth compartments which are found on all long-distance trains. These tend to be compact, with a fold-down table, but with enough room to move around and with ample storage space for each traveller. Kupé compartments share bathrooms at the end of the carriage.

Kupé berths can be twice as pricey as platzkart berths.

Platzkart or platzkartny/3rd class *Platzkartny* or platzkart (3rd class) is the most basic of sleeping carriages, an open-plan arrangement of doorless compartments, each with four bunks in tiers of two plus another two bunks – top and bottom – along the wall of the corridor. The bottom side bunk converts

TYPICAL CARRIAGE EXTERIOR

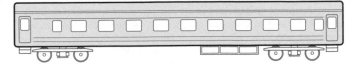

SV CARRIAGE INTERIOR

Bathroom   Attendant's compartment   Nine closed compartments with two berths each   Bathroom

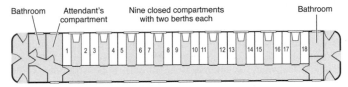

KUPE CARRIAGE INTERIOR

Bathroom   Attendant's compartment   Nine closed compartments with four berths each   Bathroom

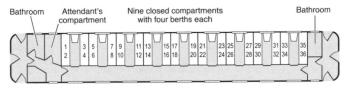

PLATSKART CARRIAGE INTERIOR

Bathroom   Attendant's compartment   Nine open compartments with six berths each   Bathroom

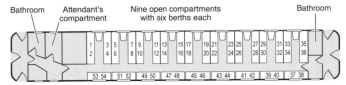

into a table and chairs. These dorm carriages sleep 54 people and, as in kupé, passengers share facilities at the end of the carriage.

The advantage of platzkart carriages, particularly in summer, is that they tend to be better-ventilated than kupé compartments as they have windows that open rather than an inadequate ventilation system, and your kupé neighbours may insist on keeping the compartment door closed at all times. Also, if you're a solo female traveller, it may well be preferable to travel in an open-plan carriage rather than share an enclosed space with three male strangers; some kupé compartments are female-only, but they may sell out.

Travelling 3rd class is a great way to interact with Russians, who tend to be sociable. However, depending on the length of the journey and the passengers in your particular carriage, on some stretches you may also contend with rowdy socialising, passengers who play tinny pop music on their mobile phones for the entertainment of all around, and small children running up and down the carriage. With all the pros and cons weighed up, we conclude that platzkart is as comfortable a way to travel as kupé on long-distance journeys, particularly if you choose your berth wisely (see box below). Platzkart berths tend to cost roughly half the price of kupé berths. Platzkart is not available on some *firmenny* trains.

Obshchiy/4th class

Obshchiy (meaning general) signifies platzkart carriages with unreserved seating only; each platzkart bottom berth seats three people.

If you're forced to travel long distance in obshchiy – not something we'd recommend, but sometimes it's the only way to get from Vladivostok to Komsomolsk-na-Amure in summer when all other options sell out – do what savvy locals do: waste no time and climb up onto one of the redundant top bunks, using it as a sleeping berth with no bedding. You'll only find obshchiy on some slower long-distance trains.

❏ The Woman in Berth 51 or Choosing Your Dream Platzkart Berth

You can't really say you've truly adjusted to life aboard a Russian long-distance train until you find yourself in your platzkart berth, with your luggage stowed and your pyjamas on, eating smoked fish and drinking tea, while the other passengers are still boarding the train. So, which berth to go for: bottom, top, side bottom, or side top?

First, the platzkartny carriage: it's basically a dormitory consisting of 54 places, and divided into lots of six, with the main entrance, the provodnitsa's 'room', a toilet and the samovar at one end (or just a samovar if it's a firmenny train), and another toilet (two toilets on a firmenny) and smoking area at the other. You have two lots of two bunks facing each other and sharing a table with another two across the aisle, stretching along the wall. Each berth comes with its own advantages and disadvantages. The end closest to the provodnitsa is the choice end of the carriage, though if you get a berth closest to the end, your sleep may be disturbed by the light that's perpetually on by the provodnitsa's cubicle. (See graphic on p115.)

● **Bottom berth** The most popular and the most likely to sell out. You will have easy access to the luggage compartment underneath the bunk, a window seat and prime access to the table. However, you may also have to socialise constantly with the person opposite and will have nowhere to escape to if your companions happen to be rowdy.

● **Top berth** Less popular. You will be unable to sit up due to the storage shelf directly above and getting up on the bunk may be difficult for the athletically challenged. It can also be a real nuisance trying to get your luggage up to the top shelf. When not sleeping, you will have to perch on the bottom bunk and may be drawn into conversations/beer drinking/caviar consumption. However, you can crawl up to the top bunk and escape unwanted companions at any time. You will have the readiest access to the window and if you're a fresh-air fiend and you get there early enough, you can open it and then pull out your top bunk so that no one will be able to close it without first dislodging you from your sleeping area. The window issue is null and void if the provodnitsa has beaten you to it and locked it.

❏ Bedding

SV, kupé and platzkart berths all come with mattresses and pillows; in platzkart, you just have to find the nearest mattress rolled up on the storage shelf or top bunk.

Bedding (two sheets, a pillowcase and a hand towel) tends to be included in the price of SV berth tickets and kupé berth tickets, particularly on *firmenny* trains. If you're buying a ticket online, tick the 'with linen' box if you want it included in the final price. Even if you don't opt for bed linen but later change your mind, you can pay the provodnitsa for a bed linen set once you board the train (the cost is the same either way: R111.50 in platzkart or R119.50 in kupé).

Luggage

Each passenger can take up to 35kg of luggage with them for free on the Trans-Siberian, though in practice, this is only enforced in Beijing as baggage is weighed before you are allowed onto the platform. On Russian trains, passengers often board with enormous suitcases and boxes.

The Trans-Siberian is a popular way for Australians and New Zealanders to return home after living in London, because baggage allowances are virtually

● **Bottom side berth** Less popular than the regular bottom but perfect for those under the height of 5ft 5 inches; any taller and your legs will stick out into the aisle. Woe betide you if you get the dreaded berth No 37 at the toilet end of the carriage, where stale cigarette smoke filters through and you're repeatedly disturbed by everyone on their way to the loo or to have a smoke. At least 80% of your fellow passengers are smokers; you do the maths.

Since the bottom side bunks stretch along the corridor and convert into two seats and a table during the day, you have no luggage storage area of your own. However, you have easy access to the luggage compartment underneath the bottom bunk near you; rush on to the train first in order to claim it. Alternatively, if you have a rucksack, you can place it on the bunk and sleep with your legs on either side, thus solving the luggage-storage problem. Bottom side berths nearest to the provodnitsa's cubicle (53 & 54) are rarely available as they are occupied by bags of bed linen.

You also have a choice window seat though this might be a problem if the top side bunk is occupied and you have to chase the other person off the chair opposite you when you wish to turn it into a bunk.

● **Top side berth** The least popular of the lot. You don't have much of a view; the luggage shelf above you is difficult to reach (and usually occupied by rolled up mattresses) and unless you're happy to spend your entire journey lying down, your only options are to perch like an unwanted guest on one of the bottom bunks or a side bottom seat. Only acceptable as an overnight option; not good for long-distance travel, particularly if the train is full.

Avoid berth No 38 at the toilet/smoking area end of the carriage like the proverbial plague.

What about **berth 51**? It happens to be this updating author's favourite: it's close to the provodnitsa's end of the carriage, to the samovar and to the exit, allowing for maximum ventilation.

unlimited. But if you're departing from Beijing you must box up any excess baggage, with a limit of one box per ticket; note that the box travels in a separate carriage. Bring only the excess to the Luggage Shipment Office (8am-noon, to the right of the main station) in Beijing at least 24 hours before departure, along with passport, ticket and customs entry declaration.

In your compartment, luggage can be stored either in the box or space under the bottom seat, in the free space beside the box, in the space above the door (kupé) or in the luggage racks above the top bunks (platzkart).

Bathing on the train

Sadly, the marble bathtub (ingeniously designed not to overflow as the train rounded a corner) and the copious hot water and towels that Michael Myres Shoemaker (see p104) enthused over in 1902 are no more.

On some Russian *firmenny* trains there are now extra carriages attached beside the restaurant car which include one compartment with a **shower cabinet** in it. Charges vary from train to train but expect to pay around R150; you need to tell the staff in advance that you wish to use it so that they can turn on the water heater. The Chinese-run Trans-Mongolian (Train Nos 003 & 004) doesn't currently include a shower cabinet although their older-style de luxe 1st class compartments have hand-held showers.

Kupé and platzkartny passengers have to make do with a wash in one of the 'bathrooms' at each end of every carriage. This is a small cubicle with a stainless steel basin and lavatory. In old-style trains, to flush the lavatory, fully depress and hold the foot pedal, and the contents fall out onto the track (hence staff having to lock toilets when the train enters a residential area; see box p112). Firmenny trains tend to have both toilets at the end of the carriage furthest away from the provodnitsa's cubicle and bio-loos. Note that unless they contain the new-style bio-loos they are often locked for up to 20 minutes before and after major station stops.

The taps on the basin are operated by pushing up the little lever located under the tap outlet. Hot water is very rarely available. There's a socket for an electric razor but you may need to ask the attendant to turn the power on. Bring

---

❏ Bathing in a Chinese spittoon

A week was a short time to go without a bath in Siberia, we were told, but this didn't make the prospect any more appealing. I read somewhere that in pre-Revolution days most Russian peasants spent the whole winter without having a bath.

Shopping for supplies on a freezing December afternoon in Beijing before we left, we resolved to find some kind of bucket or basin to facilitate washing on the train. In one shop we found weighty china buckets with bamboo handles. We settled for something smaller, an enamel spittoon (diameter 9ins/23mm) which turned out to exactly fit the basin in the train. It could be filled from the samovar in the corridor (to the astonishment of the Chinese passengers who knew the true purpose of the utensil) and it greatly simplified the process of washing, without having to queue for the shower.

a **universal plug**, or a spittoon (see box opposite), and a **sponge** or **flannel**, just in case you do decide to 'shower'.

One way of having a 'shower' in these bathrooms is to fill the basin with hot water from the samovar, and use a mug to scoop out water and pour it over yourself, or else buy a detachable travel shower head from an outdoor equipment store before setting out. Don't worry about splashing water around as there is a drain in the floor. The bathrooms are generally kept clean.

Restaurant cars

One of the myths that has sprung up amongst prospective travellers is that you get better food on the Chinese (Trans-Mongolian) train. As with most international rail travel, restaurant cars belonging to the country through which the train is travelling are attached at the border. Regardless of which train you're on, when you're passing through China you eat in a restaurant car supplied by Chinese Railways; at the border with Mongolia this is replaced by a Mongolian restaurant car; and while the train is in Russia, meals are provided by a restaurant car from Russian Railways.

Note that the Trans-Mongolian usually has no restaurant car between the Russian border and Ulaanbaatar. Regional trains such as the Irkutsk–Ulaanbaatar service may have no restaurant car at all. Bearing this in mind it is always worth taking along fruit, bread, cheese, salami; instant porridge and instant noodles are good for a hot meal, as there's always reliable boiling water in every carriage. See also box below.

● **Russian restaurant car**   Russian restaurant cars are run as private franchises, so service, food quality, prices and opening hours are highly unpredictable. Staff shop en route for whatever provisions they can find, so menus are unpredictable too.

On entering the car you may be presented with a menu, almost invariably in Russian. The menu may be extensive but only have a few items available; the only available dishes will be indicated by a pencilled-in price or added in an indecipherable scrawl. The choice may include egg or tomato salad with sour cream, *shchi* (cabbage soup with meat), *solyanka* (a thick meat soup), meatballs with either mash or macaroni, beef stroganoff, the ever-present *bifstek*, or rice and boiled chicken. Payment is in roubles only.

You can buy tea and instant coffee from the provodnitsa. Banned for several years, alcohol is now sold on trains. In fact you may find your restaurant car offering little more than crisps, instant noodles, chocolate bars and biscuits, plus

---

❏ **Wandering food sellers**
These days, you don't have to rely just on the restaurant cars and the food you've brought with you for sustenance; most trains have 'trolley ladies' wandering up and down the carriages with offerings of pizza, deep-fried meat/cabbage pie, soft drinks, crisps and beer. The food offered is generally mediocre but it is filling and costs roughly the same as food sold on the platform.

fruit juice, vodka, beer (pricier than on station platforms), or chilled Russian champagne, with no cooked food in sight. Some screen bootleg videos.

Russians think of the restaurant car as little more than a bar; since most bring their own provisions, few eat a meal in one. You may find everything overpriced at first, but service may get cheaper and friendlier the more you return. On popular tourist services the restaurant car is a good place to meet other foreigners.

❏ Safety tips

There are many stories of crime on the railways, however, a few simple precautions will substantially reduce your chances of anything untoward happening to you.

● **Lock your compartment door** from inside when you go to sleep, using both the door-handle lock and the flick-down lock; your Russian companions will do this anyway. The railways are currently installing a plastic device known as a *blokirator* to further thwart break-ins, mainly on *firmenny* trains, both kupé and SV. It immobilises the locking handle in the locked position and is allegedly so effective that even some attendants cannot outwit it from outside. 'Best piece of information I managed to get from Russians on the train was on safety in the carriage – an explanation about the secondary door lock; the main door lock can be undone with a standard triangular UK gas meter box key (worth taking with you). I was recommended to put a cork in the second door catch to stop it being opened with a knife. Therefore worth taking a cork with you' (Will Harrison-Cripps, UK). On some *firmenny* trains electronic locks have been installed that require a swipe key to get into the compartments.

● At night, **put your bags under the sleeping berth** or in the space above the door. It is not necessary to lock them, but don't leave them lying around either.

● **Padlock your luggage** if travelling solo and *platzkart*, before stepping out at one of the stops.

● **Dress down** and always carry your valuables on your person. Stash non-essentials only in shoulder bags, and just a few roubles and US dollars in your wallet. Money and documents should be in a **money belt** under your clothing; even sleep with it on.

Some tips for when you leave the train, especially in larger towns and cities:
● **Change money only at kiosks and banks**.

● Keep a **pocket torch** (flashlight) handy as many entrance halls and stairways are unlit. This is especially important in winter when it gets dark very early.

● **Never enter a taxi which is carrying anyone other than the driver** Take a good look at the driver and the car; if you're in any doubt, wave it on. Taxis ordered by telephone or through organised services at hotels are often a better bet.

● **A common scam** is for someone to drop a roll of cash and then to act as if they are searching for it. If you pick it up and return it, you may then be treated with mock suspicion and asked to show your own cash. A nimble-fingered thief can then slip notes out of your own wad of cash.

● **Street urchins** can be the most visible and aggressive thieves. If you don't ignore them they'll swarm around you like bees, begging and even grabbing your legs or arms to distract you, and before you realise it they'll have opened your bag or pulled out your wallet. Their 'controller' is often a dishevelled-looking woman with an infant in her arms. If you're approached, don't look at them but walk away quickly. If you fear you're becoming a victim, go into a shop or towards a group of Russians, who will usually send them packing.

● **Mongolian restaurant car** With luck you'll get a smart new Mongolian restaurant car. Generally the main differences from Russian restaurant cars are that here you're likely to get a menu in English, nearly everything comes with mutton, and you pay in US dollars or Mongolian tugriks though Chinese yuan may be accepted at bad exchange rates. Delicacies include mutton goulash or beefsteak with egg on top, omelette for breakfast, and tea, coffee and soft drinks. Mongolian beer is recommended.

● **Chinese restaurant car** Travellers tend to agree that Chinese restaurant cars have the best food, the widest choice and the best service. The cars are well-used, which is a good sign. You might get a breakfast of eggs, bread, jam and tea, there are usually noodles available; for lunch or supper you can typically choose from dishes such as tomato salad, cold chicken or sauté chicken with peanuts, fish, sweet and sour pork, sauté beef or aubergine with dried shrimp.

Drinks include beer, soft drinks and mineral water. Payment is in yuan (renminbi) and US$ are sometimes accepted.

Photography from the train

Taking photographs from the train is permitted. However, the problem is to find a window that isn't opaque or one that opens. They're usually locked in winter so no warmth escapes. Opening doors and hanging out will upset the carriage attendants if they catch you; if one carriage's doors are locked try the next; remember that the kitchen car's doors are always open. Probably the best place for undisturbed photography is right at the end of the train: 'No one seemed to mind if we opened the door in the very last carriage. We got some great shots of the tracks extending for miles behind the train'. (**Elizabeth Hehir**, The Netherlands).

See also p40 for help with what photographic equipment to bring and p75 for general notes about photography in Russia.

LIFE ON THE TRAIN

If travelling practically non-stop from Moscow to Vladivostok or Beijing, most people imagine they'll get bored on so long a journey, but you quickly settle into a certain rhythm of life on board the train and find plenty to occupy your time.

As well as looking at the scenery, sleeping, exploring the train from top to bottom, trying to take photos, making tea, and getting out at each stop to see what food there is on offer, you can have monosyllabic conversations with inquisitive Russians, meet other Westerners, read, play cards or chess, or visit the restaurant car. Some Russians can be very sociable with foreigners and may insist you share their food. To refuse would be rude. You should obviously offer some of your food as well, though often it will not be accepted as they will see you as their guest.

The Trans-Siberian time warp

During his trip on the Great Siberian Railway in 1902, Michael Myres Shoemaker wrote: 'There is an odd state of affairs as regards time over here. Though Irkutsk is 2,400 miles from St Petersburg, the trains all run on the time of the latter city, therefore arriving in Irkutsk at 5pm when the sun would make it 9pm. The confusion en route is amusing; one never knows when to go to bed or when to eat. Today I should make it now about 8.30 – these clocks say 10.30 and some of these people are eating their luncheon.'

You will be pleased to know that this has not changed. The entire system operates on Moscow Time (same as St Petersburg Time), and all long-distance timetables list Moscow Time. Crossing the border from China after breakfast, the first Russian station clock you see tells you that it's one o'clock in the morning! The restaurant car, however, runs on local time. Passing through as many as seven time-zones, things can get rather confusing. The answer is to ignore Moscow Time and reset your watch as you cross into new time zones (details in the Route Guide). Just add or subtract the appropriate number of hours every time you consult the timetable in the train corridor.

Stops

The timetable near the provodnitsa's cubicle shows all the stops (or all the major stops) that the train will be making, as well as the timing and length of stops. Passengers are only allowed off the train if the stops are longer than 10 minutes; do not be tempted to jump off at shorter stops as you will incur the provodnitsa's ire. If you wander off during a longer stop, make sure you're back several minutes before the train is due to leave and always have your passport on you. If a train is running late, the length of time spent at major stops will be curtailed, so check with the provodnitsa exactly how much time you have.

RAILWAY STATIONS

Food at the stations

It's wise to buy some provisions before you get on the train, especially if you're travelling a long way without a break. However, at many of the stops along the Trans-Siberian locals turn out on the station platform to sell all manner of foodstuffs: fruit, vegetables and even entire cooked meals (cabbage rolls, freshly boiled potatoes with dill, pancakes filled with cottage cheese, boiled eggs and fresh bread, smoked fish, salted cucumbers and berries).

Often, the best selection of edible goodies is found at smaller stations, whereas at main stations you can pick up instant noodles, chocolate and soft drinks but little else. Some travellers have reported upset stomachs after eating platform food so you should take care with salads, cold meats and fish and anything that looks as if it has been

❏ **Facilities at railway stations**
At all major stations, you should come across the following facilities:
● luggage storage room (see opposite) and/or luggage lockers
● toilets
● resting rooms (see p61)
● ATMs – particularly the reliable TransCreditBank (see p66)
● waiting room; larger railway stations have de luxe waiting rooms (R60/hr)
● automatic ticket vending machines; these also enable you to check timetables (see p127)
● vending machines selling food and drink

sitting around for too long. Generally, if the food is hot you should be fine; all fruit should be washed.

Kiosks sell bread, crisps, chocolate, fizzy drinks, instant noodles and beer.

Some of the best spots for food that we found during the update of this book were Ilanskaya (good variety of home-cooked food) and Tobolsk (great for smoked fish, nuts and berries). This may change, as occasionally vendors are chased off the platforms as security regulations change.

Luggage storage

All major railway stations have luggage storage facilities, be they a storage room камера хранения or luggage lockers автоматические камеры хранения.

Using one of the *avtomaticheskie kamery khranenia* (**combination-lock luggage lockers**) is quite straightforward. Put your bag in the locker, deposit the amount of money required (exact change is sometimes necessary), and firmly close the locker door. Collect the receipt with the code that you'll later need to input to open the door. Note down your locker number and don't lose the code!

Using a locker is cheaper than leaving your luggage on numbered spaces on shelves in the luggage room if you're leaving more than one piece of luggage, as you only pay for one locker; otherwise you have to pay for two luggage room spaces.

If there are no lockers, leave your luggage with the **luggage room** attendant. Produce your passport and pay a set fee according to the size of your luggage. You may have to produce your ticket if you're just come off the train or an onward ticket if you're boarding later on in the day. Your luggage will be allocated a number; don't lose the luggage tag you're given as you'll need it later to claim your luggage. If possible, carry exact change: the luggage room attendant will love you for it. The luggage rooms at major railway stations are open 24 hours. Check opening times regardless as there might be scheduled staff breaks of 30-60 minutes that coincide with your train's departure.

Each luggage room has its own rules. In some, you pay a set sum (typically around R150) for sutki сутки (24 hours). Others charge for kalendarniye sutki календарные сутки (midnight to midnight) when you are charged for an additional 24 hours from midnight onwards. Note that some work according to local time, while some might count midnight according to Moscow Time. Have fun!

Though they're largely obsolete (we only saw some in Tynda), you may also come across some **old-fashioned lockers**. To use one, buy a token from the luggage room attendant. On the inside of the locker door is a set of four dials, on which you select your own combination of three numbers and a Cyrillic character.

Before you shut the locker, write down the locker number and your chosen combination. Then insert the token, close the door and twirl the knobs on the outside. To get your bags out, set the combination on the knobs and wait two seconds until you hear the electric lock click back (some lockers require you to put in a second token before this happens).

BUYING A TRAIN TICKET

If you're looking to travel on one of the non-stop *firmenny* trains either from Moscow to Vladivostok, or Moscow to Beijing, you will need to purchase your tickets well in advance, particularly if you're travelling during peak season (see p16). If, however, you're planning to stop in various Russian cities en route, in many cases you can get away with buying a ticket a couple of days in advance, or sometimes even on the same day.

There are three main ways of purchasing a ticket direct: online; from a ticket machine at the station; or – the dreaded last resort – from a non-English speaking ticket seller at the station, for which you'll have to find the correct window and use the handy form we've prepared but for this option you can only pay in cash (roubles). The fourth, and largely unnecessary option is to purchase through a ticket agency, which results in markups of up to 30%.

Long-distance domestic and international tickets can only be purchased 45 days in advance, whether online or at a ticket office; for the latter, at the larger railway stations, look for prigorodny zal пригородный зал (suburban train hall)

❏ DECIPHERING A TRAIN TIMETABLE

All stations feature timetables, revised twice a year, with departure and arrival times for long-distance trains set to Moscow Time. For local (suburban) trains, departure and arrival is usually set to local time.

Train timetables usually provide the following information: train number and category, frequency, arrival and departure times as well as the departure and arrival cities. These timetables can seem a bit of a conundrum at first glance, so we're here to help you make sense of it.

Train number
Номер or номер поезда (nomer or nomer poyezda): slower trains tend to have higher numbers eg 01 for a fast train, 973 for a slow train.

Type of train
● Скорый (skory – fast train) Some of the skory trains tend to be 'name trains', eg the firmenny *Tomich* between Moscow and Tomsk.
● Пассажирский (passazhirsky – passenger train)
● Пригородный (prigorodny – suburban or local train)

Frequency of departure
● ежедневно (yezhednevno – daily)
● чётные (chyotniye – even days)
● нечётные (nechyotniye – odd days)
● отмен or отменён (otmen or otmenyon – cancelled)

Days of the week are indicated either by a number (ie 1 = Monday, 3 = Wednesday) or by abbreviations (Пон = Mon, Вт = Tue, Ср = Wed, Чт = Thurs, Пт = Fri, С = Sat and Вск = Sun).

Bear in mind the **time differences**: in Vladivostok, a train leaving, say at 19.30 on a Monday is, in fact, leaving at 2.30am on a Tuesday because of the +7 hours' time

❏ Fares

Long-distance train tickets are good value; prices are worked out according to distance travelled and class of ticket. Costs for a 24-hour journey are approximately:

- SV: US$260-325/£160-200/€190-235
- kupé: US$130-180/£80-110/€95-130
- platzkart: US$65-100/£40-60/€45-70
- obshchiy: US$30-50/£20-30/€25-35

At the time of writing, RZD was offering online discounts of up to 20% for certain routes on kupé and SV tickets and further discounts for top berths in kupé, as top berths are less popular than bottom berths. Tickets for firmenny trains cost about 1¼ to 1½ times the cost of a non-firmenny ticket.

or пригородные кассы (suburban train ticket windows) – either buy your ticket from the window or from an automatic ticket machine (автомат).

Buying online

The easiest way to purchase tickets is to do so online. The Russian Railways website 🖥 www.rzd.ru is now fully bilingual, accepts foreign credit and debit

difference. If a train normally leaves, say, on even days, months with an odd number of days, where two odd days follow one another, throw the timetable off, so look for the all-important **footnotes** at the bottom of the timetable that indicate that the train will only be running on even days between certain dates (eg 15/VI – /31/VIIIЧ means that it'll be running on even days between mid-June and the end of August. Sometimes the frequency is dictated by time of year, so a train running on odd days all summer may start running only on Mondays and Wednesdays in autumn (again, look for indications in the footnotes).

Arrival and departure times

Long-distance train times are shown in a 24-hour format and usually in Moscow Time (Московское время Moskovskoye vremya).

For **suburban trains**, departure and arrival is usually indicated in local time (местное время, mesnoye vremya).

- время отправления (vremya otpravleniya – departure time)
- время отправления с начального пункта (vremya otpravleniya s nachal'nova punkta – departure time from the train's starting point)
- время прибытия (vremya pribytiya – arrival time)
- время прибытия в конечный пункт (vremya pribytiya v konechny punkt – arrival time at final destination)
- время в пути (vremya v pootee – duration of the journey)

Journey distance

Some timetables show расстояние (rastoyaniye) – distance in km (kilometres) from the point of departure. If it's a train with Moscow as one of its two points of origin, distances will be calculated from Moscow. These calculations are not terribly accurate, though they occasionally correspond with the km markers you'll see en route (see pp426-7).

cards and allows you to see exactly which berths are free in the carriage of your choice. RZD also offer online discounts on certain routes if you buy a kupé or an SV ticket, and further discounts if you opt for a top bunk in kupé.

You need to **set up a user profile** in order to purchase tickets. Once a ticket is purchased you cannot change it but **you can cancel** the ticket online under 'My Orders'; the money will be refunded to the card/bank account you used to pay for it within 30 days (though normally far quicker); if you cancel you lose approximately R100-150 on each such transaction, depending on the ticket price. The only exception to online refunds is if you purchase a Sapsan ticket at a special online discount and then wish to cancel your ticket; you have to fill in specific paperwork (in Russian) requesting a refund and send it, along with the receipt for the ticket, to a specific Moscow office.

You also need to **print out your ticket** as you can't board without one. Either use your computer to print the voucher with the barcode (click on 'Ticket Form' next to the purchase in question under 'My Orders'), or make a note of the 14-digit ticket number at the top of ticket voucher. You will then need to print it using one of the automatic ticket machines found at every major station; for this you'll need to enter your passport type and number, and then either scan the barcode under the red light or enter the 14-digit ticket number.

The screen may not always be cooperative; sometimes you really have to stab at the onscreen digits with your finger to get them to register. If no machine is working, you'll have to get it printed out at one of the ticket windows; for

---

❑ **Getting to that train on time**

If you're looking to board a long-distance train, do not leave it till the last minute, as the larger Russian stations have several tracks which may involve taking an underpass or overpass. Also, trains can consist of more than 20 carriages, so you actually have to find the correct carriage indicated on your ticket (carriages tend to be in numerical order, but sometimes you might find, say, carriage No 17 next to carriage No 24). If you're at the train's station of origin, you may start boarding up to 30 minutes before departure; if you're catching a train at one of the intermediate stations and it's a short stop, it pays to be on the platform in advance.

First, find the departure board and make sure you're looking at **отправление** (**otpravleniye – departure**) rather than прибытие (arrival). Underneath, it should indicate the following:

• **No поезда (No poyezda)** – train number
• **Категория (kategoriya)** – type of train, ie скор skory (fast) or пасс passazhirsky (passenger)
• **Станция назначения (stantsiya naznacheniya)** – destination
• **Отправление (otpravleniye)** – departure time
• **Платформа (platform)** – platform number
• **Путь (put')** – side of platform; eg platform No 3 can have platform No 5 or 6 either side of it)
• **Опоздание (opozdaniye – lateness)** If a train is running late, its expected arrival time is indicated here.

that, you'll need your passport and your ticket voucher (or number). At some stations (Moscow, St Petersburg, Yekaterinburg, Kazan, Nizhny Novgorod, Novosibirsk and Vladivostok) there are dedicated exchange points for vouchers; elsewhere, you'll have to go up to a regular ticket window.

Some routes (ie Moscow to St Petersburg) accept **'paperless' tickets**; e-registration is available when you board at the initial station of the service. Just show your email confirmation and passport to the provodnitsa; there's no need to print an actual ticket.

Using an automatic ticket machine

The railway stations for all the cities mentioned in this guide are now equipped with automated ticket machines, most of which work. You can either use them to purchase tickets, print out tickets you've purchased online (see p125), or look up train timetables.

Regardless of whether you're using the machine to look up train availability or to purchase a ticket, you will first have to insert your credit or debit card and enter your PIN. Do not be alarmed; your card will not be charged unless you actually purchase a ticket.

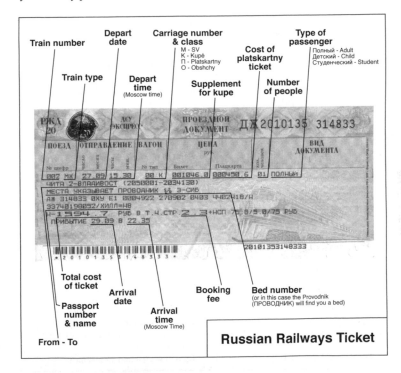

TRAIN INFORMATION AND TICKET-BUYING FORM

Please help me.

I don't speak Russian.

Please read the question I point to and
    write the answer or...

* = circle your answer.

Q = question / A = answer

MT = Moscow Time

Information

Q. When is the next train with available
    SV* kupé* platzkartny* spaces
    to ....?

A. The train No is ....
    It departs at .... : ...... (MT).

Q. Are there SV* kupé* platzkartny*
    tickets to ....
    on train No ....?

A. Yes / No

Q. When does the train depart and
    arrive?

A. It departs at .... : .... and
    arrives at .... : .... (MT).

Q. How much does a SV* kupé*
    platzkartny* ticket cost?

A. It costs .... roubles.

Q. Which ticket window should I go to?

A. Ticket window No ....

Q. What platform does train
    No .... leave from?

A. Platform No ....

Buying tickets

Q. May I buy .... SV* kupé*
    platzkartny* tickets to ....
    on train No ..... leaving on ....?
    (DD/MM/YY format, eg 31/12/15)

A. Yes, it costs .... roubles.

A. No.

Q. Why can't I buy a ticket?

A. There is no train.

A. The train is fully booked.

A. You must buy your ticket at
    window No ....

A. You can only buy a ticket .... hours
    before the train arrives.

Printing tickets

Q. Could you please print my ticket?

Thank you for your help.

Будте любезны, помогите мне.

Я не говорю по-русски.

Прочтите вопросы на которые я
    укажу, и напишите ответ, или
    * = обведите свой ответ.

Воп. = вопрос / Отв. = ответ

МВ = Московское Время

Информация

Воп. Когда следующий поезд со
    свободными местами (СВ*
    купе* плацкарт*) до ....?

Отв. Номер поезда ....
    Отправляется в .... : ....(МВ).

Воп. Есть ли свободные места
    (СВ* купе* плацкарт*) до ....
    в поезде номер ....?

Отв. Да / Нет

Воп. Когда поезд отправляется и
    прибывает?

Отв. Отправляется в .... : ....
    и прибывает в .... : .... (МВ).

Воп. Сколько стоит билет в СВ*
    купе* плацкарт*?

Отв. Билет стоит .... рублей.

Воп. К какой кассе мне подойти?

Отв. Касса номер ....

Воп. С какой платформы
    отправляется поезд номер ....?

Отв. Платформа номер ....

Покупка билетов

Воп. Можно ли купить ... (СВ* купе*
    плацкарт*) билет до ....
    на поезд номер .... который
    отправляется до ....?

Отв. Да. Билет стоит .... рублей.

Отв. Нет.

Воп. Почему я не могу купить билет?

Отв. Нет поезда.

Отв. Нет мест.

Отв. Вы должны купить билет в
    кассе номер..............

Отв. Вы можете купить билет за
    .... часов до прибытия поезда.

Распечатывание билетов

Воп. Распечатайте, пожалуйста, мой
    билет.

Большое спасибо за помощь

❏ **Ticket buying for non-Russian speakers**

If you can't speak enough Russian to buy a ticket, write what you need on a piece of paper as shown below. The clerk will usually write down a suggested train number and departure time and hand it back to you. Say *Da* (Yes) and you'll get the ticket. Check that the time the clerk writes down is Moscow Time by pointing to it and saying *Moskovskoye vremya?* For more complex enquiries use the form opposite. If there's a long queue, however, it would be better to transcribe the question you need answered from that form onto a piece of paper (see below) rather than trying to get the clerk to look through the whole page.

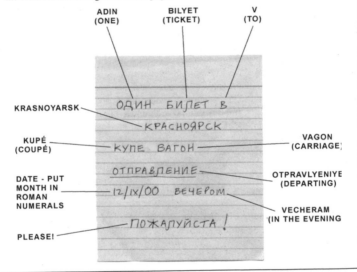

- ADIN (ONE)
- BILYET (TICKET)
- V (TO)
- KRASNOYARSK
- KUPÉ (COUPÉ)
- VAGON (CARRIAGE)
- DATE - PUT MONTH IN ROMAN NUMERALS
- OTPRAVLYENIYE (DEPARTING)
- VECHERAM (IN THE EVENING)
- PLEASE!

ОДИН БИЛЕТ В
КРАСНОЯРСК
КУПЕ ВАГОН
ОТПРАВЛЕНИЕ
12/IX/00 ВЕЧЕРОМ
ПОЖАЛУЙСТА !

Buying at a ticket window

If, by chance, you find yourself in a situation where you have to purchase a ticket from a ticket window – the least efficient choice, as queues tend to be slow – there are usually several ticket windows (*kassa* касса) to choose from, depending on your destination and possibly on whether you want a same-day or advance-purchase ticket. If the choice is not obvious, seek out the сервис центр (service centre), found at most major railway stations, where the staff often speak a little English and can book your ticket for a fee of R250 or so.

At the window you'll need to tell them your destination, train number, date of departure and compartment class: Л (L = two-berth *SV*), М (M = four-berth *SV*), К (K = *kupé*), П (P = *platzkartny*), О (O = *obshchiy*), either verbally or in writing (see above). Printed tickets (see p127) contain not only information about the train but also your name and passport number, which will be checked when you board the train. If you're buying for someone else you have to present their passport.

BUYING A TRAIN TICKET IN MONGOLIA

Mongolian trains tend to be the same in layout as Russian ones, so you can opt for a kupé or platzkartny berth. If you're buying an international ticket in Ulaanbaatar, you have to book in advance – up to 10 days before departure. See p371 on booking tickets in Ulaanbaatar.

BUYING A TRAIN TICKET IN CHINA

If you're planning on travelling by train in China and if your travels include the Beijing (via Harbin) to Chita route or any long-distance route to a popular destination it's best to reserve ahead, particularly if travelling during the Spring Festival (January/February), around May 1st, October 1st, or at the end of August when students are going back to university and all the desirable tickets – soft sleeper, hard sleeper and soft seats – sell out very quickly. Hard sleeper and soft sleeper tickets have to be bought several days in advance.

The fare is calculated according to distance, class of train, availability of air-con, class of ticket and positioning of your bunk. You can look up up-to-date train timetables (within China) at 🖥 www.chinatravelguide.com.

If you don't speak any Mandarin you can use the form on pp132-3 to help. If, however, you don't want to face the bedlam that large railway stations in China often represent, you can buy your ticket online from KCRC (🖥 www .mtr.com.hk) for trains originating in Beijing, Shanghai or Hong Kong (no markup) or alternatively book your ticket through an agency (see pp36-7) at extra cost. Payment at railway stations is in cash only, whereas agencies accept credit cards as well.

Tickets for most long-distance journeys go on sale 2-10 days in advance at railway stations and designated ticket offices, though a proportion is made available from travel agencies a day before they go on sale elsewhere. D and Z train tickets (see opposite) go on sale 10-20 days before the travel date. In big cities, such as Beijing and Shanghai, ticket windows at railway stations are open 24 hours.

If you're looking to do the Trans-Manchurian/Mongolian with Beijing as your starting point, it's actually easier to get Beijing–Moscow tickets than Moscow–Beijing, though tickets for trains passing through Ulaanbaatar and Chita still sell out quickly in summer, and it may be easier to buy tickets for trains going via Manchuria.

If you need to travel on specific dates, you have to book in advance via one of the travel agencies (see pp398-9) and have the tickets delivered to your accommodation; many hostels and hotels can help you book tickets. International tickets may be purchased up to 40 days before travel.

Classes of service

On Chinese trains, there are five classes of tickets:
● **Soft sleeper** (ruan wo 软卧) – comfortable, air-conditioned, lockable compartments with four bunks and bed linen provided; the best ones are found on recent D- and Z-class trains. This class sometimes sells out, so book early.

• **Hard sleeper** (ying wo 硬卧) – doorless compartment with 6 bunks in three tiers; bed linen provided. Half the price of soft sleeper berths. The bottom bunk tends to be more expensive. However, the middle bunk is best, as the top ones are cramped and people crowd on the bottom bunks during the day. Available on T-, K- and N-class trains. Also book early, as this is the most popular class.

• **Soft seat** (ruan zuo 软座) – Divided into first-class and second-class categories on D-, C- and G-class trains. First class consists of two seats abreast, with power sockets and TV. Second class is marginally less comfortable.

• **Hard seat** (ying zuo 硬座) – only found on T-, K- N-class and some Z-class trains. The seats are padded but carriages are often noisy, dirty and packed with people like sardines in a barrel, as most Chinese can only afford this class of travel.

• **Standing** (zhan piao 站票) – If you haven't managed to score a ticket in advance during national holidays and peak season, this may be your only option.

Hard and soft seats are fine for a short journey but hard seats in particular are not recommended for overnighters as you won't get much sleep due to the clamour, the light, the occasional smoke (though smoking is officially forbidden in carriages, it's not always strictly enforced), and the scores of souls unlucky or desperate enough to possess standing tickets, otherwise known as 'hell on rails'. If you find yourself among their number, and you're fast enough, you may manoeuvre yourself into a free luggage rack or try sleeping on top of your luggage on the floor, though you may wake up covered with a blanket of sunflower seed shells.

Fares
Sample one-way ticket prices for the Beijing to Moscow trains are roughly US$810-910 for hard sleeper, US$1100 for soft sleeper, and US$1200-1400 for de luxe soft sleeper.

Between Beijing and Harbin one-way tickets cost roughly RMB154/244/280/429 for hard seat/soft seat/hard sleeper/soft sleeper. Between Shanghai and Beijing one-way ticket prices are around RMB555/934 for hard seat/soft seat.

Which train?
Chinese trains are divided into roughly three categories:

• **Bullet trains** G High-Speed Electric Multiple Units (EMU) Train, Gaotie (高铁), the fastest train available (380km/hr) ; **C** – Intercity EMU Train, Chengji Lie Che (城际列车); and **D** – Electric Multiple Units (EMU) Train (250km/hr), Dongche (动车).

• **Express trains** Z – Direct Express Train, Zhida (直达), no stops, very fast; **T** – Express Train, Tekuai (特快), few stops and fast; and **K** – Fast Train, Kuaiche (快车), few stops and fast.

• **Slower trains** Pukuai (普快) and Puke (普客) – These have few facilities and stop at all the stations so are best avoided.

All trains, apart from international ones, depart daily.

TICKET BUYING FOR NON-CHINESE SPEAKERS

If you don't speak Mandarin, you can use the form below for train departure-related queries. However, if there's a long queue, you're better off going to the ticket office that deals with foreigners as your fellow Chinese travellers may not be terribly patient with you, or else book your (marked-up) ticket via an agency on pp36-7.

NOTE: **soft sleeper** (软卧)   **hard sleeper** (硬卧)
            soft seat (软座)   **hard seat** (硬座)

Train information and ticket-buying form

Please help me.   我需要您的帮助

I don't speak Mandarin.   我不会讲中文

Please read the question I point to   请您查看我所指向的问题，
    and write the answer or....   写下您的回答或者..........
    * = circle your choice.   圈出您的回答

Q = question 问题 / A = answer 回答

Information

Q. When is the next train   请问下一班通往 ……..........
    with available   的并且有
  soft sleeper* / hard sleeper*/   软卧* / 硬卧*/
  soft seat* / hard seat*   软座* / 硬座*
  spaces to ....?   车票出售的旅客列车什么时
                                          候发车

A. The train No is ....   车次是 …...............................
It departs at .... : ....   发车时间是 …......... : …..........

Q. Are there soft sleeper*/   请问通往 (A)…................... 的
    hard sleeper*/   (B)…......................
    soft seat* / hard seat* tickets   次旅客列车有没有
    to (A).......................   软卧* / 硬卧*/
    on train No (B)..................?   软座* / 硬座* 车票出售

(A) …………..................... is for destination (B)………. is for train number

A. Yes 有 / No 没有

Q. When does the train depart and   请问该次列车的发车时间和到
    arrive?   达时间是

A. It departs at .... : .... and 该次列车的发车时间是
    arrives at .... : ....   …… : …….
                                          到达时间是 ……… : ……......

Q. How much does one
   soft sleeper* / hard sleeper* /
   soft seat*/hard seat* cost?

请问一张
软卧* / 硬卧*/
软座* / 硬座* 的票价是

A. It costs .... yuan.

票价是 .... 元

Q. Which ticket window should
   I go to?

请问我应该在哪个售票窗
口买票

A. Ticket window No ....

售票窗口.............号

Q. What platform does train
   No .... leave from?

请问.......... 次旅客列车从哪个
站台发车

A. Platform No ....

站台............号

Buying tickets
Q. May I buy *A*........ soft sleeper*/
   hard sleeper* / soft seat* / hard seat*
   tickets to *D*......................
   on train No *C*...............
   leaving on *B* ....?

请问我可不可以买
B........................ 年
B........................ 月
B........................ 日
A .... 张
C .... 次通往
D................................. 的
软卧* / 硬卧* / 软座* /
硬座车票

(*A* is for the number of tickets wanted; *B* is for the date in the order of
YYYY/MM/DD; *C* is for the train number; *D* is for the destination)

A. Yes, it costs .... yuan
A. No.

可以，总票价是..............元
不可以

Q. Why can't I buy a ticket?

请问为什么我不能买票

A. There is no train.

没有你想搭乘的车次

A. The train is fully booked.

车票已售完

A. You must buy your ticket at
   window No ....

你需要在第............
号售票窗口买票

A. You can only buy a ticket
   .... hours before the train arrives.

你只能在列车到站前提前
.... 小时买票.

Thank you for your help.

谢谢您的帮助

Which ticket window?

At **Beijing's** main railway station and at Beijing West there used to be English-speaking ticket offices, but that's no longer the case. Sometimes one of the windows will have a 'for foreigners' sign on it, and the seller will speak some English, but otherwise either have a Chinese speaker write down for you what it is you need, or use our handy question-and-answer sheet.

If you're buying a ticket in **Shanghai**, at the main railway station there are two ticket halls – one for same-day tickets (main building) and the other for advance tickets (on the east side of the square); there should be an English-speaking ticket window in the latter. You can also buy tickets to major destinations (cash only) using the bilingual ticket machines to the east of the same-day ticket hall.

Which ticket?

At the window you'll need to tell them your destination, train number, date of departure and compartment class (see pp130-1) either verbally or in writing (see pp132-3). There are several types of long-distance tickets but the most common is a short computer-printed one. It contains information such as the train number, time of departure, carriage and seat number.

Chinese Railway Ticket

St Petersburg
Санкт Петербург

'It is in Russia – but it is not Russian!' exclaimed Tsar Nicholas I to his visitor, the Marquis de Custine. The remark speaks volumes: the city was conceived as one to rival any European city. Russia has always wanted to be seen as an equal, first by European powers, and then by world powers – a statement that is as true today as it has been for the past three centuries.

St Petersburg, more Western in appearance and with a more relaxed feel to it than the uncompromisingly Russian Moscow, is named after the patron saint of its founder, Tsar Peter I 'the Great', a man who had toured Europe, who wrote fluently in eight languages and who felt his illiterate, unwashed forebears were a shaming heritage. The city was created as a 'window to the West', a face Russia could proudly show the world, and remained the capital until the Soviet era. It can hardly be coincidence that Vladimir Putin, architect of post-Soviet Russia's rediscovered pride in its image abroad, is a St Petersburg lad.

Though not officially part of the Trans-Siberian railway, St Petersburg is nevertheless connected to it and an excellent place to either start or finish your journey, if only to experience a part of Russia that's markedly different from the rest of the country. Built on multiple waterways, with opulent palaces – former residences of nobles and former rulers – St Petersburg has a wealth of world-class museums, a lively art and music scene and nightlife to rival the capital. This city, which has played a pivotal role in Russia's history, particularly in the 20th century, which suffered unimaginably during WWII but managed to recover, epitomises for many Russians that key quality of the 'Russian character': stoicism.

'The Northern Capital'
Petersburgers persistently refer to their city as the 'Northern Capital' (or more conversationally as 'Peter', while to the older generation it remains 'Leningrad'). The criteria for its location were strategic rather than climatic. At the same latitude as the Orkney Islands or North Dakota, winter photos taken before about 10am or after 2pm will show the city in half-darkness, while summertime darkens for only a few hours of twilight – down to about 45 minutes during

June's 'White Nights' celebrations. Biting winter gales off the Gulf of Finland give way in summer to armies of hungry (but non-malarial) mosquitoes.

St Petersburg (population: 5,028,000) was Russia's first paved city. These paving-stones were a legacy of Catherine the Great; it is said that they were swept clean each day by prostitutes arrested the previous night. Their modern-day successors escape such duties, and with Soviet potholes to add topographic interest, sturdy footwear is recommended. Winter ice isn't removed but crushed, turning the city into an unofficial skating-rink from October until April. Bring ridge-soled boots.

HISTORY

Imperial glories

At the turn of the 18th century Peter the Great finally defeated Sweden in the Great Northern Wars campaign inherited from his father. Sweden's navy had once sailed unopposed down Russia's rivers and Peter, determined never to be thus humiliated again, in 1703 ordered construction of a defensive garrison, the St Peter and Paul Fortress, on the banks of the River Neva. Russia had no navy, so shipyards were needed too. Peter detested Moscow and he made the decision to simply abandon Russia's backward, shambling capital and move the title here. Swedish PoW labour and bottomless reserves of cash saw a complete new city rise in just nine years. By 1712 this was the new Russian capital, and Peter was styling himself not merely 'Tsar' but 'Imperator'.

Falconet's riverside Bronze Horseman statue, the city's virtual trademark, bears the legend *Petrus Primus – Katerina Secunda*, a Latin double-entendre which not only translates their titles but reminds us that 'Peter was first – and Catherine followed through'. The glory-days of the Russian Empire were under a woman born in Germany as Princess Sophie of Anhalt-Zerbst, now known to the world as Catherine the Great. St Petersburg flourished during her reign, benefiting from her skills at empire-building and statesmanship, and her private passions for architecture, the arts, fine conversation, the Russian language, cavalry officers and horsemanship. Once clear of the threat of Napoleonic France, Catherine's successors ruled over Europe's wealthiest empire, from a capital barely a century old. The fortunes to be made here attracted Europe's highest achievers. The city showcased the neoclassical architecture of Rossi, Rastrelli and Karl Ton. Home-grown writers such as Pushkin, Gogol, and Dostoyevsky vied with visitors like Balzac, and Anton Chekhov wrote *Uncle Vanya* and *The Seagull*. The Imperial Opera commissioned Verdi to write *Don Carlos*. Mikhail Lomonosov, the poet and scientist considered the father of modern Russian literature, was made rector of a new University, and Dmitri Mendeleev conceived his Periodic Table of Elements. Yet in most of Russia, serfs worked the land in conditions bordering on slavery to pay for all this. Change was inevitable, but was resisted until it took control of events by itself.

St Petersburg to Leningrad and back again

It was not only the working classes who envied the wealth and privilege of St Petersburg. Any Russian not of noble birth or military inclination found himself excluded from the capital – even a century before the Revolution of 1917 Gogol was satirising the capital's wealth and social iniquities in his surreal tales *The Nose* and *The Overcoat*. Most of Dostoyevsky's writing depicts St Petersburg as a force wrecking the lives of its inhabitants. In 1881 Tsar Alexander II was blown to pieces by anarchists in the very centre of the city.

A bungled attempt to quash a protest over the price of bread in January 1905 led to the 'Bloody Sunday' massacre in Palace Square. In February 1917 Tsar Nicholas II retired to private life, with effective power transferred to a provisional government. Armed attempts by aristocratic cavalry officers to return Nicholas to the throne created an atmosphere of panic and havoc. This played into the hands of Trotsky's Bolsheviks, who in October 1917 arrested the provisional government and declared Soviet Power under a leader freshly returned from exile in Switzerland, Vladimir Ilyich Ulyanov, better known under his adopted name: Lenin. Lenin returned all governmental functions to Moscow – and left them there, making the change of capital official in 1918. Between 1914 and 1924, the city was briefly known as Petrograd. The Imperial capital was left to fall into genteel decay. Gentility descended into barbarity during WWII: for 900 days the city – renamed Leningrad in 1924 after Lenin's death – was besieged and nearly a quarter of the population died of hunger, disease or bombardment. Yet the Communists, resentful of their own Imperial past, starved the city of resources after the war, preferring to develop new industrial centres in Russia's interior. Perversely, this policy – and boggy terrain unconducive to high-rise building – saved it from the excesses of Soviet planning, but left it in a state of disrepair. Little time was wasted, however, in renaming the city St Petersburg within a year of the fall of communism.

St Petersburg today

Millions of roubles were invested in the country's second wealthiest city in time for its tricentenary celebrations in 2003 and some investment has continued, thanks to the efforts of the two local lads: current president and former president, respectively: Vladimir Putin and Prime Minister Dmitrii Medvedev. Though one may argue that it was an insufficient effort given the decades of neglect, few visitors will fail to be impressed by the city's somewhat tarnished grandeur, which served as inspiration to some of Russia's leading literary figures. St Petersburg – now with a population of some five million – gives the impression of a lively, growing city, though the older buildings in the historical centre are still under threat, many already demolished to give way to new building projects.

A particularly wonderful time to be in St Petersburg is during the White Nights in the summer, when the sun sets very late and the city seems to be in a permanent state of celebration, though every season holds its own attractions.

WHAT TO SEE AND DO

★ The Hermitage Эрмитаж   [see Map 1]

The director of the Hermitage once said: 'I can't say that the Hermitage is the number one museum in the world, but it's certainly not the second.' No visit to St Petersburg should omit the Hermitage (Dvortsovaya pl 2 Дворцовая пл 2, **M**

CITY GUIDES & PLANS

Nevsky Prospekt Невский Проспект, 🖳 www.hermitagemuseum.org, 10.30am-6pm Tue-Sun, until 9pm Wed; adults/students with valid ISIC card R400/300, free admission for all visitors first Thur of month; photos/video R200), combining the city's two must-see attractions. Most famously, this is one of the world's biggest and most splendid collections of fine art. As a bonus, it is housed in the grandest rooms of the former **Winter Palace Зимний Дворец** of the Tsars, Europe's wealthiest royal family.

The collection began with 225 paintings presented to Catherine the Great by a Berlin-based Russian banker named Gotskovsky, the first of many to gain Imperial promotion by sending artworks home to Her Majesty. Catherine displayed them in her Hermitage, a purpose-built annexe of the Winter Palace added by the Italian architect Rastrelli in his 1762 remodelling of the complex.

The collection swelled with gifts from foreign rulers seeking favour or trade agreements, and officers and civil servants looking for a quick promotion. Some pieces were eventually shifted to the Russian Museum. But the greatest, and most controversial, of the Hermitage's acquisitions came after 1917 with the 'nationalisation' of the private collections of Russia's aristocracy and bourgeoisie. The massive collection now numbers more than three million catalogued works housed in five interconnected buildings. All the state rooms, private chambers and servants' quarters of the Winter Palace, plus the Old and New Hermitage buildings, cannot display more than half the items at one time. This is also a research centre, with priceless works from ancient Rome, Greece, and Egypt amongst many others, and experts on archaeology and ancient cultures in residence.

There is so much to see here that a single visit can only scratch the surface. Many visitors make several visits, following themed routes. The museum comprises the following main departments:

- **Prehistoric Art**, including the exquisite Scythian gold collection
- **Antiquity**, including Ancient Greece and Rome
- **The Treasure Gallery**, comprising the Gold and Diamond Rooms, tracing the respective jewellers' crafts from well before the birth of Christ up to the 20th century (tickets cost R300 for each room and are purchased at the same time as the main entrance ticket)
- **Western European Art**, which draws some of the biggest crowds
- **Oriental Art**, including the Middle East, China, Japan and Central Asia
- **Russian Culture**.

There are also special sections including **armaments** and **numismatics**; and, of course, the extraordinary 'collection' represented by the setting itself, including grand marble halls with gilded columns, mosaic floors and immense crystal chandeliers.

CITY GUIDES & PLANS

Most casual visitors follow a well-trodden path combining Western European Art and the most impressive of the Palace State Rooms. The goal of many is the superb French Impressionist collection, which is on the top floor on the Dvortsovaya pl (Palace Sq) side. The museum is so vast that it's easiest to navigate by looking out of the windows and using the river and Palace Square as landmarks.

You enter via the splendid **Jordan Staircase**. Of the **State Rooms**, don't miss the Malachite Hall, designed by Brullov, with its enormous vases made of the semi-precious stone, and the adjacent Small Dining Room, where the 1917 revolutionaries arrested the Provisional Government (who had made the Palace their headquarters). Perhaps most impressive are three adjacent rooms: the Royal Throne Room, the Great Banquet Hall and the Gallery of Heroes of 1812, the last decorated with over 1000 portraits of officers who served in the Napoleonic campaign. Various stories are told about the missing canvases – that their subjects died before the portraits were finished or, more credibly, that they were subsequently disgraced by their involvement in the 1825 Decembrist plot to depose Nicholas I. And if the permanent collections were enough of a draw in themselves, there are also **themed bi-monthly temporary exhibitions**, recent ones including 'Bauhaus architecture in Tel Aviv' and 'Contemporary Japanese Art'.

For **guided tours**, call ☎ 571 8446. To avoid the queues you can buy tickets online at 🖳 www.hermitageshop.org/tickets for US$17.95 (one-day ticket), valid for the Hermitage complex only, or US$25.95 (two-day ticket) also valid for temporary exhibitions at the former General Staff Building Бывшее Здание Главного Штаба and at Menshikov Palace Меншиковский Дворец, and for the period art and furniture at the Winter Palace of Peter the Great Зимний Дворец Петра Великого; also for the Porcelain Museum Музей Фарфора (otherwise entry is R100 for each one).

State Russian Museum Русский Государственый Музей   [Map 1]

Given the size of the Hermitage collection, it seems almost impossible that there could be another art museum of similar scope anywhere in the world – but there is, just halfway down Nevsky pr in the former Mikhailovsky Palace. The State Russian Museum (ul Inzhenernaya 4/2 ул Инженерная 4/2, **M** Nevsky Prospekt or Gostinny Dvor, 🖳 www.rusmuseum.ru, 10am-6pm Wed & Fri-Mon, Thur 1-9pm, entrance to Mikhailovsky Palace only adult/student R350/150; entrance to other branches adult/student R300/150, joint ticket, valid for three days for both branches, adult/student R600/300; photos R100), the country's **first public art gallery**, has four branches, the main one being the former Mikhailovsky Palace, with its maze of beautifully decorated rooms. While the Hermitage contains almost uniquely non-Russian works, the Russian Museum is home to the finest of the country's own Old Masters.

The original collection, which opened in 1895, is displayed in chronological order around the palace, while work from the turn of the 20th century is in the adjacent **Benois Wing**. You begin with icons and applied art from as early as the 12th century, including those by legendary 14th-century master Andrei

Rublyov. The heart of the collection, however, is the work of Russian painters of the 18th to mid-19th centuries, rarely exhibited abroad. Don't miss the chance to see Brullov's *The Last Days of Pompeii*, Vasnetsov's over-the-top

---

❏ A walk down Nevsky prospekt Невский проспект   [Map 1]

Nevsky prospekt (pr) has been the main shopping street and the most fashionable place to be seen in St Petersburg since the city's founding. A walk along this grand street, past palaces and churches, over canals and beside faded buildings is a walk through the history of the city itself. Nevsky pr starts near the **Admiralty Building** **Адмиралтейство** and, as you walk south-east from here, you can identify the buildings by the numbers beside the doors.

● **No 7** Gogol wrote *The Government Inspector* here in the 1830s.

● **No 9** This building was modelled on the Doges' Palace in Venice, for the Swedish banker Wawelberg.

● **No 14** A blue and white sign here, dating from the WWII Siege of Leningrad, advises pedestrians to walk on the other side of the street during shelling.

● **No 17** This impressive building, designed by Rastrelli and completed in 1754, was once the palace of the wealthy Stroganov family (see p82). Although they are more famous for the beef stew named after them, it was the Stroganovs who initiated the conquest and colonisation of Siberia by sending their private army to the Urals in the 1570s.

● **No 18** The **Literaturnoye Kafe** was Pushkin's favourite. It's worth seeing but tends to be packed with tourists. The entry fee covers high-class entertainment such as violin concerts.

● **No 20** The former **Dutch Church**, built in 1837.

● **No 24** Once the showrooms of the court jewellers Fabergé (creators of the golden Easter eggs now on display in the Kremlin).

● **No 28** The former showrooms of the Singer Sewing Machine Company with their trademark (a glass globe) still on the roof.

● On the southern side of Nevsky pr stands **Kazan Cathedral** **Казанский Собор** (Kazanskaya pl 2, **M** Nevsky Prospekt, 10am-7pm daily, services 10am & 6pm daily) designed by Voronikhin and completed in 1811. Prince Peter Kropotkin, writing in 1911, called it 'an ugly imitation on a smaller scale of St Peter's in Rome'. The large, domed cathedral is approached via a semi-circular colonnade with statues at either end. The one on the left is Mikhail Kutuzov, who prayed here before leading an army to fight Napoleon. After the 1812 victory over the French the cathedral became a monument to Russia's military glory.

In an act of supreme tastelessness the Soviets turned it into a Museum of Atheism. Part of the cathedral still houses exhibits on the history of religion, while the rest has been returned to the Orthodox Church.

KAZAN CATHEDRAL

● Looking north along Griboyedov Canal you'll see the pseudo-Old Russian style **Church of the Resurrection** **Церковь Воскресения Христова**, whose multicoloured onion domes are reminiscent of St Basil's in Moscow. It's also called the Church of the Resurrection Built on Spilt Blood as it's erected on the spot where Alexander II was assassinated in 1881.

medieval heroes, or Aivazovsky's boiling seascapes. Perhaps the finest of all are the portraits of Ilya Repin, whose monumental *The State Parliament* fills a whole room and depicts the last Tsar, Nicholas II, with his ministers.

• **No 31** This building housed the **City Duma Бывшая Городская Дума** (Municipal Council) in Tsarist times. The tower was used as a fire lookout. Opposite the Duma is Mikhailovskaya ul, running north into pl Iskusstv (Arts Square). In the former Mikhailovsky Palace on the square is the **State Russian Museum** (see p139), home to over 300,000 paintings, drawings and sculptures. **Mussorgsky Theatre Театр Мусоргского** (the former Maly Theatre, Малый Театр), where opera and ballet are performed, and the **St Petersburg State Philharmonia Филармония** are near the museum. **Grand Hotel Europe Гранд Отель Европа** (see p162) is a short distance away at Mikhailovskaya ul 32.

• **No 32** In the **Church of St Catherine Екатерининская Церковь** is the grave of Stanislaw Poniatowski, the last King of Poland and one of Catherine the Great's lovers. Local artists sell their sketches and watercolours outside.

• **Gostinny Dvor Гостиный Двор**, the city's largest department store, fills the entire block between Sadovaya ul and Dumskaya ul. This is the place to splurge on upmarket items alongside fashion-conscious New Russians. **Passazh**, across the street, was the city's first privately owned department store and has a range of goods similar to any large Western department store. There is a large supermarket (see p164) in the basement. From the street you can see a **statue of Catherine the Great**, surrounded by her lovers (or 'associates' as some guides coyly put it) in the middle of **pl Ostrovskogo**, referred to as Catherine Gardens. In the park behind this is **Pushkin Theatre** and on the western side of the square you'll find the **National Library of Russia**, filled with over 31 million books.

• **No 56 Eliseyevsky Gastronom** was a delicatessen in Tsarist times, rivalling the Food Halls at Harrods. After the Revolution it became Gastronom No 1 and the ornate showcases of its sumptuous interior were heaped with jars of boiled vegetables. It is now called Yeliseyev Emporium Coffee Shop and Western delicacies are on offer here (see Where to eat p163); it is also a wonderful example of classic St Petersburg interior design.

The building on the south side of the street beside the Fontanka 'Canal' (properly River Fontanka) is known as **Anichkov Palace Аничков Дворец**, after the nearby **Anichkov Bridge** with its famous equestrian statues.

MOSKOVSKY RAILWAY STATION

• **No 82 Art Gallery of the Masters' Guild** (Gildiya Masterov) offers a good range of contemporary art, tapestries, ceramics, batik, jewellery and glassware by well-known artists.

• It's 1km from here to pl Vosstaniya where **Moskovsky station** (see p157) is situated.

• From pl Vosstaniya it's 700m to the end of the avenue at pl Aleksandra Nevskogo where you will find **Alexander Nevsky Monastery Монастырь Александра Невского** (Map 2), with seven churches in its grounds.

CITY GUIDES & PLANS

Other branches (all on Map 1, pp150-1), which host excellent temporary exhibitions, such as contemporary photography and a recent collection of paintings by Sylvester Stallone, are found at the **Marble Palace Мраморный Дворец** (ul Milionnaya 5/1, **M** Nevsky Prospekt), the nearby **St Michael's Castle Михайловский Замок** (ul Sadovaya 2, **M** Nevsky Prospekt or Gostinny Dvor) and **Stroganov Palace Строгановский Дворец** (Nevsky pr 17, **M** Nevsky Prospekt).

St Petersburg by boat

Peter the Great imagined his city as the 'Venice of the North', and many of its finest buildings are meant to be approached by water. A boat ride (see Tours p160) along the city's canals and rivers can be an excellent way of seeing the sights, although you'll need to make sure to take an English-language tour.

Sights on most routes include **St Isaac's Cathedral** (see below); the **Church of the Resurrection** (see p140); **Mariinsky Theatre Мариинский Театр**, the blue-and-white home of top-rated opera and ballet (see p165); **Mariinsky Palace Мариинский Дворец**, built without stairs for the invalid Princess Marie, and now the City Hall; **Kazan Cathedral** (see p140); and **Yusupov Palace** (see opposite). Some trips also go out onto the Neva.

Don't miss a **night boat tour** in summer: the sight of the city's many lit-up bridges being raised (see box below) is spectacular. Locals claim that if you make a wish just as a bridge is raised, it will come true.

St Isaac's Cathedral Иссакиевский Собор [see Map 1]

St Isaac's Cathedral (Isaakievskaya pl 4 Иссакиевская пл 4, **M** Admiralteyskaya, 11am-7pm closed Wed; colonnade 11am-5pm, closed 2nd Wed of each month; 🖥 www.cathedral.ru, museum inside the cathedral R250, colonnade R150), its interior decorated with mosaics, paintings and gold trim, is one of the largest cathedrals in the world and its colossal bronze dome dominates the city skyline. Its 40-year construction, completed in 1859, was the life's work of French architect Nicholas Montferrand (whose petition to the Empress to be buried there was refused on the grounds that he was Roman Catholic). It's well worth climbing the 262 steps up the colonnade for the expansive view of the city.

Near the cathedral is **Senatskaya Square Сенатская Площадь** (formerly called Decembrists' Square Площадь Декабристов), scene of the ill-fated 'patriotic rebellion' of 14 December 1825. It's now dominated by Etienne-Maurice Falconet's **Bronze Horseman Медный Всадник**, an equestrian monument to Peter the Great erected in 1782 by order of Catherine the Great.

❏ **Bridge raising**

St Petersburg is a working port and shipping must pass. It does so at night from May to September when the waterways aren't frozen; **all** the city's bridges are raised from approximately 2am until 5am. There is no alternative way home if you are caught out; you just have to wait. There are no commuter boat services even in daylight hours and the metro shuts down at midnight.

Great Choir Synagogue Большая Хоральная Синагога
[Map 1, pp150-1]   The second largest synagogue (Lermontovsky pr 2 Лермонтовский пр 2, **M** Sadovaya, Sun-Fri 8am-8pm, service 10am Sat, 🖥 www.jewishpetersburg.ru) in Europe, its splendid Great Hall accommodating up to 1200 worshippers, remains an important focal point for the city's Jewish community. On the premises you'll also find a ***kosher restaurant*** and a shop where you can purchase unique rabbi *matryoshkas*.

Yusupov Palace Юсуповский Дворец   **[Map 1, pp150-1]**
This stately building (nab Reki Moiki 94 наб Реки Мойки 94, **M** Sadovaya/Sennaya Ploshchad, 11am-5pm daily; 🖥 www.yusupovpalace.ru, adult/student R500/380, including audioguide in English) is famous as the place where in 1916 the ersatz monk Rasputin was poisoned by his dinner host, young Viscount Felix Yusupov, stabbed and shot by Yusupov's cronies and thrown through the ice of the Moika Canal. Rasputin proved to be remarkably resilient; the cause of death was drowning, but not before he managed to claw through a substantial chunk of the ice.

  The palace is an opulent, splendidly decorated building inside, especially its private theatre. To venture into the cellar where you'll find wax figures of Rasputin and the plotters and hear the story of his murder, you either have to join a daily Russian-language tour (1.45pm daily, R380), or book a tour in English in advance (☎ 314 3239, R600).

★ Peter and Paul Fortress Петропавловская Крепость   **[Map 1]**
Begun in 1703, the city's first stone structure (**M** Gorkovskaya Горьковская; fortress open 6am-11pm in July and August, except Wed and last Tue of month; limited hours the rest of the year; museums 11am-6pm, until 5pm Tue; 🖥 www.spbmuseum.ru, entrance to fortress grounds is free; entrance to all main attractions R370) was built to keep Swedish invaders out and was subsequently used to keep prisoners in. Its impregnable **Trubetskoy Bastion Трубецкой Бастион** (10am-7pm daily, R130) served as a Tsarist political prison, with a roster of dissident inmates including Dostoyevsky and Gorky (who survived) and Lenin's elder brother Alexander (who was hanged for treason). After the revolution and up until 1924 the bastion held inmates from privileged classes.

  Time your visit to see the noon-day cannon fired from the ramparts. The highlight of the fortress is the **SS Peter and Paul Cathedral Петропавловский Собор**, built in 1712 to a height of 122.5m, where most of Russia's rulers from Peter the Great to Nicholas II (see box p144) are buried, with its splendid chandeliers and pink, green and gold frescoes. Climb the **bell tower** (6am-9pm daily, R150), for a good, if somewhat restricted panoramic view and to see the unique bell collection. During the Blockade, several courageous citizens risked their lives to climb up the bell tower spire and paint it grey.

  Also well worth visiting is the **Commandant's House Комменданский Дом** (11am-7pm, closed Wed, R130), featuring the history of the city, enhanced by some interactive displays, period costume, early cinema equipment and a most remarkable dolls' house.

CITY GUIDES & PLANS

❏ **The Romanov Reburial**

Despite considerable controversy, July 1998 saw the remains of the Romanov Royal Family transferred for reburial in SS Peter and Paul Cathedral from the abandoned mineshaft near Yekaterinburg where they had been hidden after the murder in 1918.

The list of those who had much to lose from this event was numerous. Hardline Communists feared the backlash that the story would cause. The City of Yekaterinburg fought long and hard to hold on to the relics (and the tourist trade they brought in). The City of Moscow argued they should be buried in the Kremlin with the earliest Tsars. President Boris Yeltsin felt a lump in his throat – 30 years previously the Communists had razed the holding-place in Yekaterinburg where the murders took place, and as Yekaterinburg's mayor he'd signed the orders himself. Even the Russian Orthodox Church winced: in their haste to damn the Communists for the murders, they'd rushed in in the 1920s to authenticate a set of remains in Paris (purchased for a tidy sum) which had been worshipped as holy relics for nearly 50 years, and were now shown up as fakes.

Then there were the embarrassed relatives of the late 'Anna Anderson', the woman who'd hoodwinked even close intimates of the Royal Family that she was the escaped Princess Anastasia, rightful Tsarina (her body was subsequently DNA-tested at the behest of greedy relations and shown to be Franziska Schanzkova, a Polish refugee). Last but not least, Fox Motion Pictures had just released a full-length animation, *Anastasia*, showing her not only escaping but marrying the sensitive young soldier who'd pulled her not-quite-dead body from the corpses, and finding happiness in America…

As you enter the Cathedral take a sharp right before the inner doors, to an anteroom where an official plaque declares that you are surrounded by the complete, authenticated and indubitable remains of those killed in Yekaterinburg on 16 July 1918. Even with such a definitive statement (which sidesteps a short tally of bones, and the whereabouts of the Royal valet, chambermaid and physician who also fell in the hail of bullets), this was to be a burial that refused to go easily to the grave. Opening the catacombs to inter Nicholas with his forebears, workmen found a 'last laugh' from the Communists, who had piped concrete into the foundations to prevent any further burials. Ceremonies were delayed whilst digging equipment blasted enough space for the funeral urns.

With a date set and foreign dignitaries invited (including the British Royal Family, cousins of the Romanovs), Yeltsin's Vice-President Boris Nemtsov went to the Finance Ministry with his budget for the rites, commemorative stones, VIP reception – in all, around US$10m. 'What?', he was told, 'Don't you know the economy's going down the tubes? We can let you have US$1m, but don't hang around, the country will be bust in a month!' Thus, at least most of the Romanovs were finally united with their ancestors – in a hurry, and on the cheap.   **Neil McGowan** (Russia)

Temporary exhibitions sometimes appear along the Nevskaya panorama roof walk. And if you take a walk around the outside of the fortress wall, you will spot intrepid locals sunbathing by the wall from March onwards and the local *morzhi* ('walruses') swimming in the Neva year-round. Join them if you dare.

Peter the Great's Log Cabin Домик Петра Великого   [Map 1]

A short stroll from the Peter and Paul fortress, this cabin (Petrovskaya naberezhnaya 6 Петровская Набережная 6, **M** Gorkovskaya, 11am-9pm closed Tue, adult/student R200/100), built in just two days in 1703, was Peter the Great's first residence in his new city. The only surviving original wooden building in St Petersburg, it's a surprisingly small and humble dwelling, given both the man's status and stature (Peter was said to have stood almost seven feet tall). Visitors can see the original furniture and tiled stove, some of Peter's collection of Dutch Masters, and even a boat built by the emperor himself.

Cruiser Aurora Крейсер Аврора   [Map 1]
Further along the Neva lies the battleship (Petrogradskaya nab Петроградская наб, **M** Gorkovskaya Горьковская, 11am-5.15pm Tue-Thur & Sat-Sun; admission R50; tour R300) famous for firing the shot that signalled the beginning of the 1917 revolution. Since the collapse of the Soviet Union, rumours have been circulating that this may be a replica. Either way, it's an impressive ship.

Rumyantsev Mansion Особняк Румянцева   [Map 1]
The first privately owned museum (Angliiskaya nab 44 Английская наб 44, **M** Sadovaya, 11am-6pm, until 5pm Tue, closed Wed, 🖥 www.spbmuseum.ru, adult/student R120/70) in Russia, this splendid neoclassical building was refurbished for the 200th anniversary of the city; several of its rooms reflect its former glory and feature the original belongings of its former owners. Other exhibitions focus on life in St Petersburg in the 1930s, while the most powerful display, 'Leningrad during the Great Patriotic War', focuses on the suffering of the city during the Siege of Leningrad during which 700,000 people perished. A particularly poignant exhibit is the siege diary kept by 11-year-old Tanya Savicheva, who continued going to school while her whole family died one by one; the display on bread rations shows just how critical the situation in the city was. Some displays are in English; there are very worthwhile temporary art and photography exhibitions as well.

★ Blockade Museum Музей Блокады Ленинграда   [Map 1]
Looking at St Petersburg today, a flourishing modern city, it's difficult to imagine its intense suffering during WWII, when the city was cut off by the Nazi forces and starved for 2½ years (872 days). This extremely moving museum (Solyanoy per 9, Соляной пер 9, **M** Chernyshevskaya, 10am-5pm closed Wed and last Thur of month, R200) chronicles the Blockade of Leningrad, focusing on the military and civilian aspects of it: the advance of the combined German-Finnish force and its eventual repulsion by the Red Army. A prominent fixture is the famine that ravaged the city in spite of the 'Road of Life' – the heroic Allied effort to get provisions across the frozen Lake Ladoga during the winter months, with 100,000 dying every month. There are stories of survivors here and a riveting exhibit detailing exactly what people were reduced to eating: leather belt soup, tree bark, bread made of flour that was 50% sawdust. Most of the exhibits were donated by survivors of the blockade.

Museum of Political History Музей Политической Истории России
[Map 1] An Art Nouveau mansion built for Matilda Kshesinskaya, a prima ballerina at the Mariinsky and Nicholas II's mistress, the museum building (ul

CITY GUIDES & PLANS

Kuibysheva 2-4 ул Куйбышева 2-4, **M** Gorkovskaya, 🖥 www.polithistory.ru, 10am-6pm, closed Thur and last Mon of month, adult/student R150/60) was also the Bolshevik headquarters during 1917; Lenin's office has been restored to its original state. The huge exhibition, spanning the whole of the Soviet period, is based on the original collection of artifacts collected by the key players in the Revolution, such as documents, posters and personal effects of Lenin, Gorbachev and others, and provides a fascinating insight into the period of collectivisation and the daily struggle for survival among others.

From the beginning of the 1990s, the displays of this former Museum of the Revolution were drastically reworked to reflect the museum's new goal: to dispassionately reveal the truth about the Soviet Union, including its most recent history. A particularly powerful display is dedicated to the GULAG prisoners, with its heartbreaking collection of items made by political prisoners. Contemporary exhibits include the camera used by Gorbachev to record his message to the nation in 1991, and a piece of the Berlin Wall.

Kunstkamera Кунсткамера   [Map 1]

Founded by Peter the Great in 1714 and known also as the **Peter the Great Museum of Anthropology and Ethnography** (Universitetskaya nab 3 Университетская наб 3, **M** Vasileostrovskaya, 🖥 www.kunstkamera.ru, 11am-6pm, closed Mon and last Tue of month, R200), the city's oldest museum is also the most bizarre. Exhibits comprise miscellaneous curios picked up by Peter during his travels and Peter's Anatomical Collection is usually crowded with spectators, looking in horrified fascination at the two-headed foetuses in jars, the 'cyclops' baby and other grotesquery.

The real treasure here, however, is the rich anthropological collection, divided by continent and featuring such items as samurai armour, Native American costume, some splendid Mongolian *morin khuur* (horse-head fiddles), an Iranian five-blade dagger, a Burman harp, elaborate jewellery from Arabia and an Indian ivory boot.

Railway museums

For Trans-Siberian railway and plain ol' train enthusiasts, the **Central Railway Museum Музей Железной Дороги** (Map 1; ul Sadovaya 50, ул Садовая 50, **M** Sadovaya/Sennaya Ploshchad, 11am-5.30pm Sun-Thur except last Thur of every month, R200) offers insight into the building of the railway and the trains that have served it. The exhibition charts the development of Russian railways from the first steam locomotive and includes incredibly detailed models and dioramas as well as a superb collection of scale locomotives going uphill and railway bridges, plus an original 1903 Trans-Siberian wagon you can climb into, fitted with a piano salon and bathtub. Labels in Russian only.

The open-air branch of the above, the **Locomotive Museum Паровозный Музей** (off Map 1; 11am-5pm Mon-Thur, admission R150) is a short suburban train ride from the city and includes 30 locomotives and 22 steam engines among other exhibits. To get there, take a suburban train from Vitebsky station to the Paravozny Muzey Паравозный Музей stop.

Contemporary art galleries

Besides boasting one of the world's richest collections of fine arts, St Petersburg also nurtures a thriving contemporary art scene.

★ **Erarta Эрарта** (off Map 1, 29-ya linya 2, Vasilyevsky Ostrov, 29-я линия 2, Васильевский Остров **M** Vasileostrovskaya, 🖵 www.erarta.com, 10am-8pm, closed Wed, adult/student R300/150) is Russia's biggest non-governmental contemporary museum. Housed in a spectacularly restored gallery, it features a monumental collection of Russian modern art from the last 60 years. Some of the installations are staggering due to their size alone and the curators regularly update the collection by travelling to the furthest reaches of Russia to seek out new and exciting work. You can now take part in one of four U-Space installations (R200 each) – private rooms whose interior ('Childhood', 'Origins') is designed to evoke certain feelings. Take tram 6 from **M** Vasileostrovskaya or trolleybus 10 or 11 from **M** Nevsky Prospekt to get here.

From its origins as a condemned apartment block that was taken over by artists in 1988, **Pushkinskaya 10 Пушкинская 10** (Map 2; entrance from Ligovsky pr 53 Лиговский пр 53, **M** Ploshchad Vosstaniya, 4-8pm Wed-Sun) has blossomed into a collection of small galleries, workshops and funky music clubs such as Fish Fabrique and Fish Fabrique Nouvelle (both on p165). It's a friendly scene and a good way to get to know local artists. On a wall on the ground floor you'll find a map directing you to various art spaces. Highlights include the 'big' and 'small' galleries of the **Museum of Non-conformist Art** (4th floor). The building is also home to Russia's best-known Beatles fan, Kolya Vasin, who opens the doors to his **Temple of Love, Peace and Music** some Friday evenings to share his John Lennon memorabilia with other Fab Four fans.

Loft Project Etazhi (Etagi) Лофт проект Этажи (Map 2; Ligovsky pr 74, Лиговский пр 74, **M** Ligovsky Prospekt, noon-10pm Mon-Fri, 10am-10pm Sat & Sun, 🖵 www.loftprojectetagi.ru) is a converted Smolinsky Bread Factory, its narrow corridors connecting two contemporary art galleries, four exhibition spaces, the popular Zelyonaya Komnata (Green Room) café, an industrial-chic Location Hostel (🖵 www.location-hostel.ru) for those who want to stay right on the premises, and a chill-out roof terrace. Art-wise, expect unusual photography and all manner of themed installations; check the website for the latest happenings.

★ **New Holland Новая Голландия** (Map 1; nab Kanala Kryukova, **M** Spasskaya, 🖵 www.newhollandsp.com) is difficult to pigeonhole. An island used as a ship-building complex during the reign of Peter the Great, the space consisted of old ship-building warehouses, a circular building that is the city's oldest prison and an impressive granite and brick arch designed by Jean-Baptiste Vallin de la Mothe in the late 18th century. Acquired in 2010 by Roman Abramovich and with the people behind Moscow's Garage (p178) on board, the space is in the process of being transformed and developed into a one-of-a-kind public space. At the moment the premises comprise a small contemporary art gallery (noon-8pm daily), a 'slow food' restaurant and a shashlyk terrace overlooking the water, a skater park, contemporary sculpture scattered outdoors, play area for children and Ecoworking (🖥 www.ecoworking.ru) where for R600/day you can rent a laptop, or an X-box and work in a tranquil space. By 2015, the prison is due to be converted into a boutique hotel and the warehouses are due to be restored, providing both extra gallery space and venues for boutique shops. Stop by the information office (11am-10pm Mon-Thur, to 11pm Fri-Sun) to find out what's new.

Literary Museums

St Petersburg has always been at the centre of events, so it's little surprise that it has been home to Russia's biggest literary figures. By and large, Russian literary museums tend to be of limited interest to anyone but hardcore fans, but there are a few exceptions.

Those interested in Dostoyevsky's turbulent life can stop by **Dostoyevsky House-Museum Дом-музей ФМ Достоевского** (Map 2; Kuznechny per 5/2 Кузнечный пер 5/2, **M** Vladimirskaya, 11am-6pm, closed Mon, 🖥 www.md.spb.ru, R160, audioguide R170). The displays in the author's well-worn apartment give you an insight into his arrest and exile and the inspiration behind his works, while the memorial space features his original belongings. An audioguide enhances the experience.

Heavy oak doors lead into a peaceful courtyard and **Pushkin House Дом Пушкина** (Map 1, nab Reki Moiki 12, наб Реки Мойки 12, **M** Nevsky Prospekt or Gostinny Dvor, Wed-Mon 10.30am-6pm, closed last Fri of month, 🖥 www.museumpushkin.ru, R250, audioguide R250), the apartment where the poet lived and later died from duel-inflicted wounds. Through the displays you can find out about his sources of inspiration; his death mask is a macabre crowning touch.

For an insight into the life and work of the man behind *Lolita*, stop by the **Nabokov Museum Музей Набокова** (Map 1, ul Bolshaya Morskaya 47, ул Большая Морская 47, **M** Admiralteyskaya, Tue-Fri 11am-6pm, Sat & Sun noon-5pm, 🖥 www.nabokovmuseum.org, free admission), where Nabokov lived before he and his family emigrated to Europe before finally settling in the USA.

Housed in **Fontanny Dom (Fountain House) Фонтанный Дом** (Map 1, Liteyny pr 53 Литейный пр 53), **Anna Akhmatova Museum Музей Анны Ахматовой** (**M** Mayakovskaya, Tue-Sun 10.30am-6.30pm, Wed noon-8pm, 🖥 www.akhmatova.spb.ru, R80, audioguide R100) traces the tragic life of Russia's most famous poetess through photographs, personal effects and letters from her imprisoned lover.

WHAT TO SEE AND DO AROUND ST PETERSBURG

Scorching heat and reeking rivers (the waterways doubled as open sewers) drove St Petersburg's aristocrats into the countryside in the summer, to residences no less grand than their *pied-à-terres* in town. Day-trips to these magnificent mansions make a rewarding change from yet another walk down Nevsky pr.

Peterhof Петергоф

Thirty kilometres west of the city lies Peterhof (🖥 www.peterhofmuseum.ru), built by Peter the Great as his Versailles-by-the-sea, with each subsequent ruler adding their own palace or fountain to the complex. Visiting the many attractions can also cost a king's ransom, so choose carefully. The vast, sculpted **grounds** (9am-8pm daily, adult/student R450/250) are bisected by waterways and studded with 147 gravity-powered **fountains** (10am-6pm), decorated with gilded figures – the most magnificent of which is the Grand Cascade at the end of the main Water Avenue – which are in themselves well worth the day trip out there. The centrepiece is the **Grand Palace** (10.30am-6pm, closed Mon & last Tue of month, adult/student R550/300), which became more grand when Empress Elizabeth had Rastrelli enlarge the original modest structure built for Peter the Great. Among the original furnishings and paintings, look out for the massive paintings depicting Russia's destruction of the Turkish fleet in the Chesme Hall. Also in the grounds you'll come across **Monplaisir** (10.30am-5pm Tue & Thur-Sun May-Sep, Sat & Sun Oct-Apr), a cheerful, wood-panelled villa that was Peter the Great's favourite spot to hold parties.

Getting there In summer the nicest way to arrive is by a Peterhof Express **hydrofoil** (10am-6pm May-Sep, every 30 mins, 🖳 www.peterhof-express.com, adult/student one way R650/450, return R1100/800, 30 mins), departing from Dvortsovaya nab 38 jetty outside the Hermitage's main entrance. Another river option is with Astra Marine Tours (see Tours p160). Alternatively, take a **suburban train** from Baltiisky station (**M** Baltiiskaya) or, alternatively, bus No 350, 351, 352, or 356, or marshrutka 404.

Pushkin and around Пушкин
Set in beautiful parklands (park 7am-9pm in summer, adult/student R100/50 May-Oct, free rest of year), at Pushkin (also known as Tsarskoye Selo, the 'royal village', 🖳 www.tzar.ru), 25km south of St Petersburg, is the vast **Catherine Palace Екатерининский Дворец** (10am-5pm Wed-Sun, to 8pm Mon, closed last Mon of month, adult/student R350/180), completed in 1756. The palace was looted by German soldiers in WWII, but the palace and the grounds underwent intensive restoration in time for the town's 300th birthday celebration in 2010. Its famous Amber Room (whose original amber panels disappeared during the German retreat and have never been found) has been called the largest piece of jewellery in the world.

The adjoining estate, 4km further south at **Pavlovsk Павловск** (🖳 www.pavlovskmuseum.ru, adult/student R150/80, park 8am-8pm, palace 10am-6pm, closed Fri & first Mon of the month, adult/student R450/250), was built by Catherine the Great for her son, 'mad' Tsar Paul I. Pavlovsk Palace, with its stunning neoclassical interior, is surrounded by an astounding 1500 acres of park, criss-crossed by streams and endless paths for strolling. Pavlovsk and Pushkin are joined by a country path and make a practical full-day's outing.

Getting there To get **to Pushkin**, take a suburban train from Vitebsky station (**M** Pushkinskaya), to Detskoye Selo Детское Село, from where you can either walk to the palace or take bus N371 or N382. Alternatively, take marshrutka 299, 287, 342, 347 or 545 from **M** Moskovskaya. To get **to Pavlovsk**, stay on that train until you get to Pavlovsk station (40 mins).

CITY GUIDES & PLANS

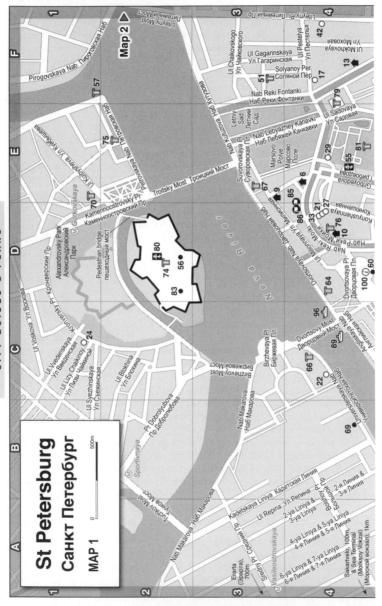

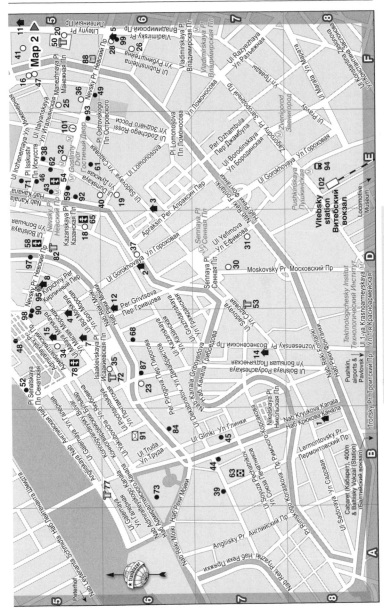

CITY GUIDES & PLANS

St Petersburg Map 1 Key

Санкт-Петербургская

WHERE TO STAY

1 [B8] Alexander House
2 [D6] Andrei and Sasha's Homestay
3 [E6] B&B Assembly
        Мини-отель Ассамблея1
4 [C5] Herzen House Герцен Хаус
5 [F6] Hostel Life
6 [E4] Hotel 3 Mosta
        Гостиница 3 Моста
7 [C5] Hotel Astoria Гостиница Астория
8 [D5] Nevsky Inn
9 [E3] Nevsky Inn
10 [D4] Pushka Inn Hotel
        Отель Пушка Инн
11 [F5] Red House Hostel
12 [D6] Soul Kitchen Junior
13 [F4] Swiss Star B&B
14 [C7] Underground Hall Hostel
15 [C5] W Hotel

WHERE TO EAT AND DRINK

16 [F5] Aragvi Арагви
17 [F4] Botanika Ботаника
18 [D5] Charlotte Café
19 [E6] Cherdak Khudozhnika
        Чердак Художника
20 [F5] Coyote Ugly

21 [D4] Daiquiri Bar
22 [C4] Grad Petrov Град Петров
23 [C6] Idiot Идиот
24 [C1] Mesto Место
25 [F5] Molly Shelter
26 [F6] Mops Мопс
27 [D4] Other Side, The
28 [F6] Palkin Палкинъ
29 [E4] Park Guiseppe
        Парк Джузеппе
30 [D7] Sennoi Market Сенной Рынок
31 [D7] Sumeta Сумета
32 [E5] Supermarket Passazh
        Пассаж
33 [D4] Stolle Café Кафе Штолле
34 [C5] Tandoor Тандур
35 [C6] Teplo Тепло
36 [F5] Yeliseyev Emporium Coffee
        Shop
        Магазин Купцов Елисеевых
37 [D6] ZooM Café

NIGHTLIFE & ENTERTAINMENT

38 [E5] Bolshoy Zal/St Petersburg
        Philharmonia Большой Зал/
        Санкт-Петербургская
        филармония
39 [B7] Concert Hall Концертный Зал
40 [E5/E6] Dacha Дача
41 [F5] Hat Bar, The

42 [F4] Jimi Hendrix Blues Club
43 [E5] Maly Zal Малый Зал
44 [B7] Mariinsky 2 Мариинский 2
45 [B7] Mariinsky Theatre
        Мариинский Театр
46 [E5] Mikhailovsky Theatre
        Михайловский Театр
47 [F5] Purga 1 Пурга 1

PLACES OF INTEREST

48 [C5] Admiralty Building
        Адмиралтейство
49 [F5] Anichkov Palace
        Аничков Дворец
50 [F5] Anna Akhmatova Museum
        (Fontanny Dom) Музей Анны
        Ахматовой (Фонтанный Дом)
51 [F3] Blockade Museum
        Музей Блокады Ленинграда
52 [C5] Bronze Horseman
        Медный Всадник
53 [D7] Central Railway Museum
        Музей Железной Дороги
54 [E5] Church of St Catherine
        Екатерининская Церковь
55 [E4] Church of the Resurrection
        Церковь Воскресения
        Христова
56 [D2] Commandant's House
        Комендантский Дом

PLACES OF INTEREST (cont'd)

57 [F1] Cruiser Aurora
Крейсер Аврора
58 [D5] Dutch Church
Голландская церковь
59 [E5] Former City Duma
Бывшая Городская Дума
60 [D4] Former General Staff Building
Бывшее Здание Главного
Штаба
61 [E5] Gostinny Dvor
Гостиный Двор
62 [E5] Grand Hotel Europe
Гранд Отель Европа
63 [B7] Great Choir Synagogue
Большая Хоральная Синагога
64 [D4] Hermitage/Winter Palace
Эрмитаж/Зимний Дворец
65 [D5] Kazan Cathedral
Казанский Собор
66 [C4] Kunstkamera   Кунсткамера
67 [E3] Marble Palace
Мраморный Дворец
68 [C6] Mariinsky Palace (now the City
Hall) Мариинский Дворец
69 [B4] Menshikov Palace
Меншиковский дворец
70 [E1] Museum of Political History
Музей Политический
Истории России
71 [E5] Mussorgsky (Maly) Theatre
Мусоргского (Малый) Театр

PLACES OF INTEREST (cont'd)

72 [C6] Nabokov Museum
Музей Набокова
73 [B6] New Holland Новая Голландия
74 [D2] Peter and Paul Fortress
Петропавловская Крепость
75 [E2] Peter the Great's Log Cabin
Домик Петра Великого
76 [D4] Pushkin House Дом Пушкина
77 [B6] Rumyantsev Mansion
Особняк Румянцева
78 [C5] St Isaac's Cathedral
Иссакиевский Собор
79 [F4] St Michael's Castle
Михайловский Замок
80 [D2] SS Peter and Paul Cathedral
Петропавловский Собор
81 [E4] State Russian Museum
Русский Государственный Музей
82 [D5] Stroganov Palace
Строгановский Дворец
83 [D2] Trubetskoy Bastion
Трубецкой Бастион
84 [B6] Yusupov Palace
Юсуповский Дворец

CONSULATES

85 [E4] Dutch Consulate
Консульство Нидерландов
86 [D4] French Consulate
Французское Консульство

OTHER

87 [C6] American Medical Clinic
88 [F5] Anglia Book Shop
Книжный магазин Англия
89 [C4] Astra Marine Tours
90 [D5] Central Air Ticket Office
Центральная Авиакасса
91 [B6] Central Post Office Почтамт
92 [E5] Central Train Ticket Office
Центральная
Железнодорожная Касса
93 [E5] City Bus Tour
94 [E8] Ecolines
95 [D5] Internet Café
96 [C4] Jetty (for hydrofoils) причал
97 [D5] Neptun (Boat Tour) Нептун
98 [C5] Nevsky Souvenir
99 [F6] Peter's Walking Tours
100 [D4] St Petersburg Tourist
Information Centre
Туристско-информационное
бюро Санкт-Петербурга
101 [E5] St Petersburg Tourist
Information Centre
Туристско-информационное
бюро Санкт-Петербурга
102 [E8] Vitebsky station
Витебский вокзал

CITY GUIDES & PLANS

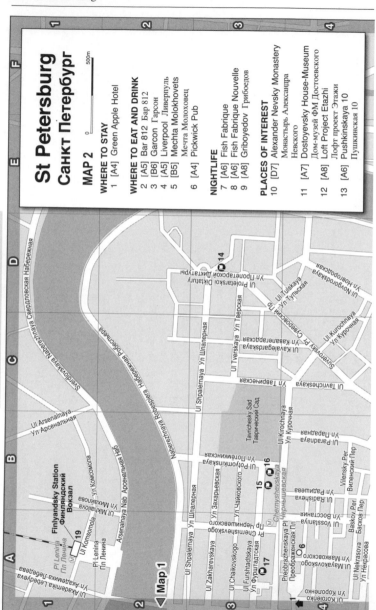

St Petersburg
Санкт Петербург

MAP 2

0 _____ 500m

WHERE TO STAY
1 [A4] Green Apple Hotel

WHERE TO EAT AND DRINK
2 [A5] Bar 812 Бар 812
3 [B6] Garcon Гарсон
4 [A5] Liverpool Ливерпуль
5 [B5] Mechta Molokhovets Мечта Молоховец
6 [A4] Pickwick Pub

NIGHTLIFE
7 [A6] Fish Fabrique
8 [A6] Fish Fabrique Nouvelle
9 [A8] Griboyedov Грибоедов

PLACES OF INTEREST
10 [D7] Alexander Nevsky Monastery Монастырь Александра Невского
11 [A7] Dostoyevsky House-Museum Дом-музей ФМ Достоевского
12 [A8] Loft Project Etazhi Лофт проект Этажи
13 [A6] Pushkinskaya 10 Пушкинская 10

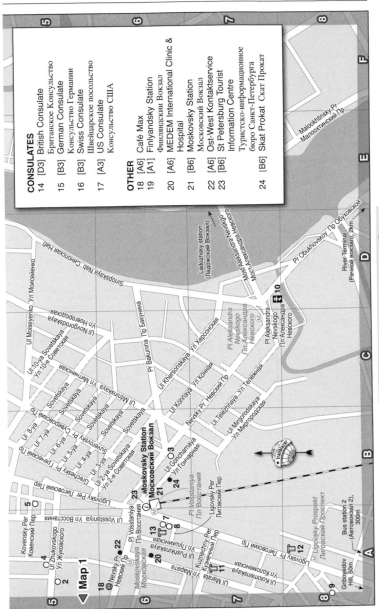

CONSULATES
14 [D3] British Consulate
     Британское Консульство
15 [B3] German Consulate
     Консульство Германии
16 [B3] Swiss Consulate
     Швейцарское посольство
17 [A3] US Consulate
     Консульство США

OTHER
18 [A6] Café Max
19 [A1] Finlyandsky Station
     Финляндский Вокзал
20 [A6] MEDEM International Clinic &
     Hospital
21 [B6] Moskovsky Station
     Московский Вокзал
22 [A6] Ost-West Kontaktservice
23 [B6] St Petersburg Tourist
     Information Centre
     Туристско-информационное
     бюро Санкт-Петербурга
24 [B6] Skat Prokat Скат Прокат

Комендантский Пр
Komendantsky Pr

Старая Деревня
Staraya Derevnya

Крестовский Остров
Krestovsky Ostrov

Чкаловская
Chkalovskaya

Спортивная
Sportivnaya

Адмиралтейская
Admiralteyskaya

Приморская
Primorskaya

Василеостровская
Vasileostrovskaya

Сенная Пл
Sennaya Pl

Театральная
Teatral'naya

Садовая
Sadovaya

Технологический Институт
Tekhnologichesky Institut

Балтийская Baltiiskaya
Валтийский вокзал
Baltiisky station

Нарвская
Narvskaya

Кировский Завод
Kirovsky Zavod

Автово
Avtovo

Ленинский Пр
Leninsky Pr

Пр Ветеранов
Pr Veteranov

Фрунзенская
Frunzenskaya

Электросила
Elektrosila

Парк Победы
Park Pobedy

Московская
Moskovskaya

Звёздная
Zvyozdnaya

Купчино
Kupchino

Парнас
Parnas

Пр Просвещения
Pr Prosveshcheniya

Озёрки
Ozyorki

Удельная
Udelnaya

Пионерская
Pionerskaya

Чёрная Речка
Chyornaya Rechka

Петроградская
Petrogradskaya

Горьковская
Gorkovskaya

Невский Пр
Nevsky Pr

Гостиный Двор
Gostinny Dvor

Спасская
Spasskaya

Достоевская
Dostoevskaya

Пушкинская
Pushkinskaya

Звенигорская
Zvenitogorskaya

Витебский вокзал
Vitebsky station

Московские Ворота
Moskovskie Vorota

Ломоносовская
Lomonosovskaya

Obvodny Kanal
Обводный Канал

Volkovskaya
Волковская

Bukharestskaya
Бухарестская

Mezhdunarodnaya
Международная

Пр Славы
Pr Slavy

Дунайская
Dunayskaya

Шушары Shushary

Девяткино
Devyatkino

Гражданский Пр
Grazhdansky Pr

Академическая
Akademicheskaya

Политехническая
Politekhnicheskaya

Пл Мужества
Pl Muzhestva

Лесная
Lesnaya

Выборгская
Vyborgskaya

Пл Ленина Pl Lenina
Финляндский вокзал
Finlyandsky station

Пл Восстания Pl Vosstaniya
Московский вокзал
Moskovsky station

Маяковская
Mayakovskaya

Владимирская
Vladimirskaya

Лиговский Пр
Ligovsky Pr

Пл Александра Невского
Pl Aleksandra Nevskogo

Новочеркасская
Novocherkasskaya

Ладожская Ladozhskaya
Ладожский вокзал
Ladozhsky station

Елизаровская
Yelizarovskaya

Пр Большевиков
Pr Bolshevikov

Ул Дыбенко
Ul Dybenko

Пролетарская
Proletarskaya

Обухово
Obukhovo

Рыбацкое
Rybatskoye

Чернышевская
Chernyshevskaya

——— Line 1
——— Line 2
——— Line 3
——— Line 4
——— Line 5

Метро Санкт Петербурга
St Petersburg Metro

PRACTICAL INFORMATION
Arriving in St Petersburg

By air St Petersburg has two airports, side by side, 18km south of the city. Both are short of facilities, though they do have tourist information kiosks as well as ATMs which may or may not work.

Pulkovo International Airport (aka Pulkovo-2, ▯ www.pulkovoairport.ru/eng) has daily flights to many major European cities, such as London, Berlin, Helsinki, Prague and Warsaw. Bus N13 and marshrutka N113 (R35) run every 15 minutes or so between **M** Moskovskaya and the airport (5.30am until the last flight). Less frequent marshrutkas N3 and N213 carry on to **M** Sennaya Ploshchad. Taxi drivers are notorious for overcharging, so agree on a price beforehand (at the time of writing, a reasonable price was around R800) or get a better deal by ordering a taxi in advance. Reputable taxi companies include Taxi Million (☎ 700 0000) and Ladybird (☎ 900 0504), a women-only taxi service (for both drivers or customers). Some accommodation options offer cheaper pickup.

Most domestic flights (and flights to Central Asia) use **Pulkovo-1**, a charmless Soviet heap 15 minutes further south. Hang on to your baggage-reclaim tag on domestic flights as you may have trouble retrieving your bag without it. Marshrutka N39 goes to **M** Moskovskaya (R35).

By train There are five railway stations in St Petersburg. Direct express trains from Helsinki arrive at **Finlyandsky station Финляндский Вокзал** (Map 2, pl Lenina 6 пл Ленина 6, **M** Ploshchad Lenina), while some Helsinki trains en route to Moscow arrive at **Ladozhsky station Ладожский Вокзал** (off Map 2, Zanevsky pr 75, Заневский пр 75, **M** Ladozhskaya, ▯ www .lvspb.ru).

The arrival point from almost anywhere in Eastern and Western Europe, including the Baltic States, Poland, Ukraine and Belarus, is **Vitebsky station Витебский вокзал** (Map 1, **M** Pushkinskaya).

Baltiisky station Балтийский вокзал (off Map 1) handles mostly domestic routes and suburban trains to Peterhof (see pp148-9), Krasnoye Selo and Gatchina.

Trains from Moscow and Siberia come into **Moskovsky station, Московский Вокзал** (Map 2), the grandest and most central, at Nevsky pr 85 (**M** Ploshchad Vosstaniya or Mayakovskaya, ▯ www.mo skovsky-vokzal.ru).

By bus All national and some international LuxExpress buses arrive at the city's only bus station (off Map 2, **Avtovokzal No 2 Автовокзал 2**, nab Obvodnogo Kanala 36, наб Обводного канала 36, **M** Obvodny Kanal, ▯ www.avokzal.ru). Lux Express buses (▯ www.luxexpress.eu) from Tallinn and Riga, also arrive at Baltiisky station (**M** Baltiiskaya), while **Ecolines** buses (Map 1, Podyezny per 3 Подъездный пер 3, **M** Pushkinskaya, ▯ www.ecolines.ru) from Riga, Tallinn, Kiev and Odessa arrive at Vitebsky station.

By boat Ocean-going cruisers anchor on the Neva, at Sea Terminal Morskoy vokzal (off Map 1, pl Morskoy Slavy 1 пл Морской Славы 1, ▯ www.portspb.ru) on Vasilyevsky Island.

River cruises use the river terminal Rechnoy vokzal (off Map 2, pr Obukhovskoy Oborony 195 пр Обуховской Обороны 195, **M** Proletarskaya, ▯ www .riverport.sp.ru).

Local transport
St Petersburg's **metro** is quick, cheap and efficient, and is open from 6am to just after midnight. A ticket to anywhere on the system costs R28; old-style tokens (zhetoni) are still used as well as magnetic cards (valid for 10, 20 or more rides). Unlike the 'Stalin-wedding-cake' style of Moscow's stations, many of those in St Petersburg, notably Mayakovskaya station, feature bold Soviet Constructivist designs.

But the metro network has great gaps where waterways prevent tunnelling (including vast swathes of the city centre); for these areas you must square up to the **buses, trams, trolley-buses** or **minibuses**. Buy your ticket from the conductor on board (R25 for any distance). Minibuses with the same numbers, on the same routes, provide a faster, more frequent service (R35). The city has now introduced the **Aquabus Аквабус** – four water bus (R100) routes that operate daily (in the summer months only) between 8am and 10pm, bypassing the rush-hour traffic on bridges; for sightseeing purposes the Central Центральная route is the most convenient one. For all transport route details, check out 🖳 www.transport.spb.ru. Pick up an Aquabus in front of the summer garden and Summer Palace (Dvortsovaya nab).

Orientation and services

St Petersburg stands at the mouth of the Neva, in a web of channels and islands (33 main ones and countless small ones) where the river meets the Baltic Sea's Gulf of Finland. The main axis is 4km-long Nevsky pr, with Dvortsovaya pl (Palace Sq) and the Hermitage at its north-western end. This square is the ceremonial centre, although the city's heart beats from the block of Nevsky pr between **M** Nevsky Prospekt and **M** Gostinny Dvor.

Across the Neva are the city's other main areas: Vasilevsky ostrov (St Basil's Island), Petrograd side (beyond Peter and Paul Fortress) and Vyborg side to the northeast.

Consulates British (Map 2, pl Proletarskoy Diktatury 5, **M** Chernyshevskaya, ☎ 320 3200); **Dutch** (Map 1, nab Reki Moiki 11, **M** Nevsky Prospekt, ☎ 334 0200); **French** (Map 1, nab Reki Moiki 15, **M** Nevsky Prospekt, ☎ 332 2270); **German** (Map 2, ul Furshtadskaya 39, **M** Chernyshevskaya, ☎ 320 2400); **Swiss** (Map 2, pr Chernyshevskogo 17, **M** Chernyshevskaya, ☎ 327 0817); **US** (Map 2, ul Furshtadtskaya 15, **M** Chernyshevskaya, ☎ 331 2600).

Internet The vast majority of accommodation options offer wi-fi; some offer internet access also. Internet cafés are not as prolific as they used to be, but those scattered around the city include **Café Max** (Map 2, Nevsky pr 90, Невский пр 90, **M**

Mayakovskaya, 24 hrs, 🖳 www.cafemax.ru) and **Internet Café** (Map 1, Nevsky pr 11, Невский пр 11, **M** Admiralteyskaya, 24 hours).

For those with their own laptops, pre-paid 3G and 4G modems can be purchased from most mobile phone stores.

Local publications You can find the following free English-language publications in bars, hotels, hostels and restaurants. *In Your Pocket* (🖳 www.inyourpocket.com/russia/st-petersburg) is an extremely useful bi-monthly listings booklet with irreverent reviews, useful practical info and short features. The slick and glossy colour monthly *Pulse* (🖳 www.pulse.ru) also has reviews and features. *The St Petersburg Times* (🖳 www.sptimes.ru) is a bi-weekly source for local news, with an excellent listings and arts review section on Fridays.

Medical For 24-hour medical, dental or emergency services, contact **American Medical Clinic** (Map 1, nab Reki Moiki 78, наб Реки Мойки 78, **M** Sadovaya, ☎ 740 2090, 🖳 www.amclinic.ru) or **MEDEM International Clinic & Hospital** (Map 2, ul Marata 6, ул Марата 6, **M** Mayakovskaya, ☎ 336 3333, 🖳 www.medem.ru).

Money Access to cash is not a problem in St Petersburg as ATMs and currency exchange spots are ubiquitous, with a particularly high concentration along the main tourist thoroughfares such as Nevsky pr.

Russian visas and visa registration St Petersburg is the one place where you can enter Russia visa-free for 72 hours. However, this is only available to those who arrive by cruise ship and who have prebooked a city tour with the likes of St Peter Line or Saimaa Travel (for details see Tours opposite). This option doesn't allow you to do your own thing, but can be a good way of seeing the city if your time is very limited and you only want to see St Petersburg.

Though visa registration regulations (see pp25-6) are not as strict as they used to be, you need to register your visa within seven days. Most accommodation options offer this service for an extra fee; otherwise drop off your immigration card at the offices of **Ost-West Kontaktservice** (Map 2, Ligovsky pr 10, 2nd floor, office 2133, Лиговский пр 10, **M** Ploshchad Vosstaniya, ☎ 327 3416, 💻 www.ostwest.com, 10am-6pm Mon-Fri) whose English-speaking staff can also book tickets and tours for you.

Telephone   Some hostels (see p160) allow free international calls. Otherwise, most travellers use the free Skype service to call abroad via the internet. It's inexpensive to purchase a SIM card for your mobile phone from any major provider, such as MTS, Megafon or Beeline – their shops abound in the city.

Otherwise, to make calls abroad from regular phones, you can purchase an IP phonecard *telefonnaya karta* (international phone card) available in shops, kiosks, post offices and metro ticket desks.

Post   The city's **central post office** Почтамт (Map 1, ul Pochtamtskaya 9 ул Почтамтская 9, **M** Nevsky Prospekt) was Russia's first! If you need a package sent abroad in a hurry, **DHL** (💻 www.dhl.com) has a couple of branches in the city.

Tourist information   St Petersburg Tourist Information Centre Туристско-информационное бюро Санкт-Петербурга (Map 1, ul Sadovaya 14/52 ул Садовая 14/52, **M** Nevsky Prospekt, ☎ 310 2822, 💻 www.ispb.info, 10am-7pm Mon-Fri, noon-6pm Sat) has English-speaking staff, city maps, brochures on attractions and tours on offer.

Other branches include: Dvortsovaya pl 12 Дворцовая пл 12 (Map 1), **M** Admiralteyskaya, 10am-7pm daily; and Pl

Vosstaniya Пл Восстания (Map 2), **M** Ploshchad Vosstaniya, 10am-7pm daily; there are also kiosks at both airports. In summer you'll find 'angels' wearing 'Can I help you?' t-shirts at Gostinny Dvor, Pl Vosstaniya, Nevsky pr 62 and 90; these multi-lingual young people help tourists.

Useful **websites** include 💻 www.saint petersburg.com which focuses on sights and current events, has a virtual city tour, and a message board used by other travellers. Run by the city tourist board, 💻 www.visitpetersburg.com is another comprehensive website, the downloadable walking tours being its best feature; 💻 www.inyourpocket.com/st-petersburg has comprehensive, offbeat listings, updated several times a year.

Tours   Peter's Walking Tours (💻 www .peterswalk.com) is highly recommended for its knowledgeable, innovative tours. Their daily Original Peter's Walking Tour (R650) starts at 10.30am at Hostel Life (see p160).

Another recommended operator is **VB Excursions** (💻 www.vb-excursions.com), offering themed tours such as Back in the USSR (R2300), Revolutionary St Petersburg (R1900) and Vodka Pub Crawl (R2400).

Cycling is a great way of exploring this completely flat city. Bike tours, such as White Nights Bike Tour and Sunday Morning Bike Tour are available, run jointly by **Skat Prokat** (Map 2, ul Goncharnaya 7 ул Гончарная 7, **M** Ploshchad Vosstaniya, 💻 www.skatprokat.ru) and Peter's Walking tours; you can also rent bikes at Skat Prokat (from R150/hr or R500/day).

The hop-on, hop-off **City Bus Tour** (R450) traces a route around the city's most popular sights and leaves every two hours from pl Ostrovskogo (Map 1), **M** Gostinny

CITY GUIDES & PLANS

❑ **Emergency numbers**
If you have been robbed, or hassled by the police, and you don't speak Russian, call the English-language Tourist Helpline: ☎ 300 3333.
Other useful numbers are: Fire ☎ 01; Police ☎ 02; Ambulance ☎ 03

Dvor, from 10am to 6pm daily year-round. Also consider St Peter Line (🖳 www .stpeterline.com) or Saimaa Travel (🖳 www.sai maatravel.fi).

Recommended boat tour operators include **Neptun** (🖳 neptun-boat.ru, adult/ student R600/500), which leaves from nab Reki Moiki 26 (Map 1), near the junction of Nevsky pr with the Moika Canal, several times in the afternoon and at 00.45 for the night tour in summer for the same price (book in advance in person or via ☎ 924 4451). You're provided with audioguides in several languages so you can enjoy the scenery without having to listen to the drone from the boat's speakers. Another recommended operator, **Astra Marine** (🖳 www.boattrip.ru, tours R300-800), leaves from nab Admiraltiyskaya 2, the 'Lion's Pier'. They specialise in daytime audioguide trips along the Neva and the Gulf of Finland, with some of their boats going as far as Peterhof (see pp148-9), but also do 90-minute canal tours of the city (R600).

For an ultra-cheap 'tour', hop on one of the **Aquabus services** (see p158) that take the Central route.

Where to stay
St Petersburg has a chronic shortage of accommodation at every level so you should make arrangements early, especially in the spring and summer.

Budget accommodation There are more and more state-of-the-art hostels with free internet access, wi-fi and even free phone calls abroad. Breakfast is not included (unless stated otherwise).

Utterly deserving of the 'Russia's Best Hostel' accolade, ★ *Soul Kitchen Junior* (Map 1, nab Reki Moiki 62/2, apt 2, наб Реки Мойки 62/2, кв 2, **M** Sadovaya/ Sennaya Ploshchad, ☎ 965 816 3470, 🖳 www.soulkitchenhostel.com, dorm/dbl from R650/2500, WI-FI), consists of a vast apartment inside a renovated 19th-century building right on the bank of Moika River.

Their en suite dorms are equipped with two-tiered double beds, each with a privacy curtain, reading light and plug sockets. There are communal dinners and organised activities, guests get free international calls and the staff couldn't be friendlier.

Another friendly hostel that really caters to the needs of backpackers, *Underground Hall Hostel* (Map 1, Voznesenky pr 41, Вознесенский пр 41, **M** Sennaya Pl, ☎ 243 1617, 🖳 hostel-undhall .ru, dorm/twn from R600/2100, WI-FI) is brightly painted and sparkling clean, central without being noisy, sociable without being a party hostel and the staff are always on hand to offer sightseeing tips.

Hostel Life (Map 1, Vladimirsky pr 1, Владимирский пр 1, **M** Mayakovskaya, ☎ 318 1808, 🖳 hostel-life.ru, dorm/sgl/dbl R1000/2850/4500, WI-FI) sports bright, individually decorated rooms, a psychedelic guest lounge and a warm atmosphere. Great location just off Nevsky pr and inexpensive airport pickup on offer.

Red House Hostel (Map 1, Liteyny pr 46, Литейный пр 46, **M** Ploshchad Vosstaniya, ☎ 444 8424, ☎ 380 7527, 🖳 redhousehostel.com, dorm/dbl R1100/ R4000, WI-FI) draws on inspiration from Jimi Hendrix for its décor and is a great place to meet fellow travellers if you're travelling solo, thanks to its large, busy guest lounge and social lubricant by way of cheap beer. Good central location, too.

Travellers are wonderfully well received at the home of a local couple – a doctor and photographer – Andrei and Sasha, *Andrei and Sasha's Homestay* (Map 1, nab Kanala Griboyedova 49 наб Канала Грибоедова 49, **M** Sadovaya/ Sennaya Pl, ☎ 315 3330, 🖳 asamatuga @mail.ru, sgl/dbl R2600/3000, WI-FI) – a beautiful, large apartment with exposed brick walls, hand-picked furnishings and huge mirrors in all the rooms. Your hosts have two more central apartments that they rent out and they may well welcome you with vodka and blini.

A great budget spot for those who don't want to stay in a hostel, *Green Apple Hotel* (Map 2, ul Korolenko 14, ул Короленко 14, **M** Chernyshevskaya, ☎ 272 1023, 💻 greenapplehotel.ru, sgl/dbl/semi-luxe from R2700/3200/4200, WI-FI) consists of 15 modern rooms decked out in placid creams, all within easy walking distance of the main attractions.

Homestays with a Russian family can be organised through Host Families Association (HOFA; 💻 www.hofa.ru).

Mid-range hotels

Tucked away down a historic street near the main attractions, 4th floor *Herzen House* **Герцен Хаус** (Map 1, ul Bolshaya Morskaya 25, ул Большая Морская 25, **M** Nevsky Prospekt; ☎ 315 5550, 💻 www.her zen-hotel.com, sgl/dbl from R6000/6800, WI-FI) is simple and stylish, its 29 rooms decorated in neutral tones and sporting plasma TVs. There's tea and coffee available around the clock and the English-speaking staff are very helpful.

If you want to stay in a historical building in a super-central location you can do little better than the delightful *Pushka Inn Hotel* **Отель Пушка Инн** (Map 1, наб Реки Мойки 14, nab Reki Moiki 14, **M** Nevsky Prospekt, ☎ 644 7120, 💻 www .pushka-inn.com, sgl/dbl/apt from R4000/ 6000/8900, WI-FI). Think spacious, individually decorated rooms with gleaming wooden floors, and three spacious apartments, presided over by professional staff.

An attractive, centrally located B&B, *Nevsky Inn* (Map 1, Kirpichny per 2 apt 19, code 19B, Кирпичный пер 2 кв 19 код 19В, **M** Nevsky Prospekt, ☎ 315 8836, ☎ 911 927 1166, 💻 www.nevskyinn.com, sgl/ twin €50-80/80-100, WI-FI) has seven light, bright en suite twin rooms. A good breakfast is included in the price and there's a guest kitchen. The **second branch**, ul Millionay 4/1 (Map 1), has four twin rooms plus shared kitchen for the same price, but with the additional bonus of air-conditioning.

Just a few minutes' walk from the Hermitage and in the region of three bridges over Griboyedov canal, boutique *Hotel 3 Mosta* **Гостиница 3 Моста** ('Hotel 3

Bridges', Map 1, nab Reki Moiki 3a, наб Реки Мойки 3a, ☎ 315 0200, 💻 3mosta.com, sgl/dbl from €91/159, WI-FI) has 26 elegant, comfortable rooms with large-screen plasma TVs and climate control; the double with 'superior view' overlooks the Church of the Saviour on the Blood.

Its modern rooms an ethereal white, the efficiently run *Swiss Star B&B* (Map 1, nab Reki Fontanki 26, 2nd flr, наб реки Фонтанки 26, 1-й этаж, **M** Sadovaya/ Sennaya Ploshchad, ☎ 911 929 2793, 💻 www.swissstar.ru, sgl/dbl €89/109, WI-FI) distinguishes itself with its convenient central location and warm welcome from its staff who can organise tours and arrange airport pickup. If you're a light sleeper, avoid the corner en suite room as it can be noisy. Economy rooms (sgl/dbl €69/85) share bathrooms.

★ *B&B Assembly* **Мини-отель Ассамблея** (Map 1, ul Sadovaya 32/1 apt 170, ул Садовая 32/1 кв 170, **M** Spasskaya, ☎ 911 966 9597, 💻 asmbl@mail.ru, 💻 assembly.spb@gmail.com, room with shared bathroom/en suite R1525/2070) has a homey atmosphere and four comfortable rooms, three of which share a bathroom. The effusive English-speaking owner, Natalia, can assist with your travel/sightseeing needs and the fully equipped guest kitchen is perfect for impromptu group dinners.

Upmarket hotels The rates quoted here are for the high season and include 18% VAT, but confirm this whenever you're quoted a price.

Anyone who was anyone in the 19th century stayed either at the Astoria or the Yevropeyskaya (now Grand Hotel Europe). The guestbook at the five-star Rocco Forte-owned *Hotel Astoria* **Гостиница Астория** (Map 1, ul Bolshaya Morskaya 39, ул Большая Морская 39, **M** Nevsky Prospekt, ☎ 494 5757, 💻 www.thehotelast oria.com, dbls/suites from R11,000/35,000, WI-FI) features writers, rock stars, artists and actors in endless streams of great names. All natural materials are used in the design of the fully equipped bedrooms, there is mosaic detail in the splendid bathrooms, facilities include a superb spa and the interior boasts stunning original marble work, such as images of the Winter Garden.

Subtlety is not the strongest suit at stylish five-star *W Hotel* (Map 1, Voznesensky pr 6, Вознесенский пр 6, **M** Admiralteyskaya, ☎ 610 6161, 💻 www .wstpetersburg.com, dbl/suite from R9000/ 38,000). Room names are preceded with adjectives such as 'wonderful' and 'spectacular', but the self-congratulations are well deserved, with nice touches such as Nespresso coffee makers, iPod docks and even TVs in bathrooms (so guests won't get bored). Décor includes Italian furniture and full-length windows. The snazzy Wow Suites on the top floor boast great views of the city, as well as Jacuzzis and fireplaces.

Almost like a country house in the middle of the city, ★ *Alexander House* (Map 1, nab Kryukova Kanala 27 наб Крюкова Канала 27, **M** Sennaya Ploshchad, ☎ 334 3540, 💻 www.a-house.ru, sgl/dbl/luxe R7565/8415/10,115, WI-FI) is a 19th-century historical building, each of its rooms lovingly designed to represent a far-flung (and not so far-flung) part of the world. Expect Thai prints in 'Bangkok', colourful frescoes in 'Mexico', cool Nordic chic in 'Stockholm' and bright textiles and African prints in 'Nairobi'. There's a wonderfully cosy guest lounge with fireplace and a stylish restaurant exclusively for guests.

Grand Hotel Europe Гранд Отель Европа (Map 1, ul Mikhailovskaya 1/7, ул Михайловская 1/7, **M** Nevsky Prospekt, ☎ 329 6000, 💻 www.grandhoteleurope.com; dbls/suites from R13,900/36,700, WI-FI) lives up to its name. Housed in a palatial building, this ultra-elegant hotel features original Art Deco detailing, extremely comfortable beds, and no fewer than five top-notch restaurants on the premises, including the bustling Caviar Bar. The guest list has included heads of state and the crowned heads of Europe; the service is flawless.

Where to eat and drink

St Petersburg boasts a dining scene to rival that of any cosmopolitan European city. Most restaurants are open 11.30am/noon-11.30pm/midnight daily.

Restaurants At the upper end of the spectrum for quality and price ★ *Palkin* Палкинъ (Map 1, Nevsky pr 47, Невский пр 47, **M** Gostinny Dvor, ☎ 703 5371, 💻 www.palkin.ru, mains R1500), puts a contemporary spin on the 'aristocratic cuisine' that melded French influences with traditional Russian recipes in the 18th and 19th centuries. Try the duck breast baked in maple syrup or the grilled wagyu beef with bone marrow sauce.

For upmarket 19th-century Russian cuisine head to ★ *Mechta Molokhovets* Мечта Молоховец (Map 2, ul Radisheva 10, ул Радишева 10, **M** Ploshchad Vosstaniya, ☎ 579 2247, 💻 mol okhovets.ru, mains from R1450, [V]), where baronial dishes are prepared according to Elena Molokhovets's famous cookbook. Only the freshest ingredients are used and the fish dishes, such as the sturgeon, are particularly superb. Well worth splurging on the tasting menu if you can (R3200 without wine).

Teplo Тепло (Map 1, ul Bolshaya Morskaya 45, ул Большая Морская 45, **M** Sennaya Ploshchad, 💻 www.v-teple.ru, mains R290-680, [V]) has a warm atmosphere to match its name (which means 'warmth'), leisurely service, and delicious pies, breads and meat dishes, best taken on the terrace in summer.

Named after the hero of Dostoyevsky's novel, *Idiot* Идиот (Map 1, nab Reki Moiki 82, наб Реки Мойки 82, **M** Sadovaya, 💻 idiot-spb.com, mains R410-880, [V]) serves a selection of vegetarian dishes such as stuffed aubergine, mushroom pelmeni and wild mushrooms baked with potato in a cosy, jokey Bohemian-intellectual basement with antique furniture. Pescatarians welcome: there are fish and seafood dishes aplenty.

For superb Georgian food go to homely ★ *Sakartvelo* Сакартвело (off Map 1, 12-ya Liniya 13, 12-я Линия 13, **M** Vasileostrovskaya, mains R280-500, [V]) where the shashlyk is perfectly grilled, there are 12 kinds of *khachapuri* (bread with cheese and other toppings), the homemade wine is served in bowls and there's live music in the evenings.

Also wonderful is *Aragvi* **Арагви** (Map 1, nab Reki Fontanki 9, наб Реки Фонтанки 9, **M** Gostinny Dvor, mains around R400, [V]), with its outstanding *lobio* (bean salad), tasty *satsivi* (chicken in walnut sauce), pork shashlyk and – for the more adventurous – sheep's brains braised with tomato and coriander.

Mops **Мопс** (Map 1, ul Rubinsteina 12, ул Рубинштейна 12, **M** Mayakovskaya, mains R450-650, [V]) is a decent-enough stab at Thai cooking, with good stir fries, well-spiced soups and curries. Avoid the sticky rice and mango dessert, though.

The heavenly smell of spices, combined with the warm décor and an excellent chef make *Tandoor* **Тандур** (Map 1, Voznesensky pr 2/10, Вознесенский пр 2/10, **M** Sadovaya, 🖳 www.tandoor-spb.ru, mains R450-950, [V]) the best place in town to sample northern Indian cuisine. Expect an extensive menu of dishes cooked in a tandoor, as well as a full range of curries, biriyanis and more.

The eclectic décor at *Mesto* **Место** (Map 1, Kronversky pr 59 Кронверский пр 59, **M** Gorkovskaya mains R300-450, [V]) is as appealing as its equally eclectic menu. Sink onto a dark wood padded bench and choose from the likes of beef Wellington, cold aubergine soup and saffron risotto with calamari.

Sumeta **Сумета** (Map 1, ul Yefimova 5, ул Ефимова 5, **M** Sennaya Ploshchad, mains R300-450) is a Dagestani joint in faux-cave surroundings. The grilled meats are excellent, as are the vegetable dishes such as grilled aubergine with walnut; *chudu* (pumpkin pancake) is unusual and very moreish.

Restrained Venice décor and a mostly Italian menu are the defining features of *Park Guiseppe* **Парк Джузеппе** (Map 1,

nab kanla Griboyedova 2b, наб канала Грибоедова 2в, **M** Gostinny Dvor, mains R430-630, [V]). Expect creamy wild mushroom risotto, porcini ravioli and salmon lasagne among its offerings.

Despite its not-so-central location, *Botanika* **Ботаника** (Map 1, ul Pestelya 7, ул Пестелья 7, **M** Chernishevskaya, 🖳 www.cafébotanika.ru, mains R290-450, [V]) is well worth seeking out for its great vegetarian food that spans the world: veggie Thai soup, pasta, curry and even veggie sushi are all present and correct.

Cafés and snacks With its Eurocentric menu and friendly English-speaking waitresses, ★ *ZooM Café* (Map 1, ul Gorokhovaya 22, ул Гороховая 22, **M** Sennaya Ploshchad, 🖳 www.cafezoom.ru, meal R100, [V], mains from R220) is a huge hit with both locals and visiting foreigners. Come here for the friendly atmosphere and stay for the porridge/salads/soups.

Yeliseyev Emporium Coffee Shop **Магазин Купцов Елисеевых** (Map 1, Nevsky pr 56, Невский пр 56, **M** Nevsky Prospekt) is a refined place where you can imbibe the wide selection of world teas and coffees and snack on fancy cream éclairs and cakes with fresh forest berries to the sounds of a tinkling piano.

Garcon **Гарсон** (Map 2, Nevsky pr 103, Невский пр 103, **M** Ploshchad Vosstaniya, 🖳 www.garcon.ru, [V]) is a delightful French-style bakery serving good coffee along with its sublime bread creations, quiches and sandwiches. The almond croissants are particularly good.

Cherdak Khudozhnika **Чердак Художника** (Map 1, Artist's Attic, ul Lomonosova 1/28, ул Ломлносова 1/28, **M** Nevsky Prospekt, 🖳 glassdesign.ru/cherdak, mains R280-980, [V]) is a minuscule roof

CITY GUIDES & PLANS

> ❏ **Don't drink the water!**
> Avoid St Petersburg's tap water at all costs (including ice in your drinks and for brushing your teeth) as it may be infected with *giardia*, a particularly nasty parasite which can cause stomach cramps, nausea and an unpleasant and persistent form of diarrhoea. Buy bottled water and stick to fresh fruit that you can peel.

terrace with funky furniture, particularly great for inventive salads, milkshakes and cocktails in summer, though its speciality is fondue – seven different types.

Particularly known for its sandwiches, *Charlotte Café* (Map 1, ul Kazanskaya 2, ул Казанская 2, **M** Nevsky Prospekt, 🖥 sharlotcafe.ru, sandwiches R350-430, [V]) is a chilled-out spot that doubles as a deli where you can enjoy the salads, cakes and more substantial dishes on the lovely covered terrace or get a takeaway.

With several branches around the city, *Stolle Café* Кафе Штолле (Map 1, Konyushenny per 1/6, Конюшенный пер 1/6, **M** Nevsky Prospekt, [V], half/whole pie R60/120, [V]) is justifiably popular for its pies, with fillings as varied as cherry, rabbit and mushroom, fish, meat and cabbage, as well as good coffee, served in a Viennese café ambience.

Self-catering Self-caterers should head to **Sennoi Market Сенной Рынок** (Map 1, Moskovsky pr 4a, Московский пр 4a, **M** Sennaya Ploshchad, 8am-8pm daily in summer) for fresh produce, where you can buy anything from fresh fruit to half a cow. More expensive, but well stocked, is the basement **Supermarket Passazh Пассаж** (Map 1, Nevsky pr 48, Невский пр 48, **M** Nevsky Prospekt, 10am-10pm daily), which stocks a lot of Western products and has an extensive alcohol section.

Bars and pubs Bars and pubs are generally open from noon till late. One of St Petersburg's liveliest places for drinking is **ul Dumskaya 9 ул Думская 9** (Map 1, E5) where you can find numerous hotspots under one roof.

The German food at *Grad Petrov* Град Петров (Map 1, Universitetskaya nab 5, Университетская наб 5, **M** Vasileostrovskaya, 🖥 www.die-kneipe.ru) is as good as its beer; it brews Hefe-Weizen, Dunkel, Lager and Pilsner in-house to classic Bavarian methods; it's even possible to arrange a tour with the brewmaster.

One of the best drinking venues in town, the English *Pickwick Pub* (Map 2, ul Ryleyeva 6, ул Рулеева 6, **M** Cherny-

shevskaya) draws the punters with its attractive, cosy interior with a fireplace, 20 beers on tap, premiership football on TV and friendly service.

A great place to linger over a drink is the welcoming American-owned *The Other Side* (Map 1, ul Bolshaya Konyushennaya 1, ул Большая Конюшенная 1, **M** Nevsky Prospekt, its menu offering a more exotic blend of Thai, Chinese and Mexican than your average bar menu.

With its inviting nooks and crannies, *Molly Shelter* (Map 1, ul Italyanskaya 29, ул Итальянская 29, **M** Gostinny Dvor) provides just that to those fond of Irish beers and a quiet corner to nurse them in.

If you like scantily-clad waitresses, dancing on the bar and being encouraged to get inebriated by a barmaid brandishing a bullhorn, you'll adore this branch of *Coyote Ugly* (Map 1, Liteyny pr 57 Литейный пр 57, **M** Mayakovskaya, 🖥 www.coyote ugly.ru). The drinks may be overpriced, but it's all good, raucous fun.

Join the well-heeled clientele at the upmarket *Sex and the City*-esque *Daiquiri Bar* Дайкири Бар (Map 1, ul Bolshaya Konyushennaya 1, ул Большая Конюшенная 1, **M** Nevsky Prospekt, 🖥 www.dbar.ru, 4pm-4am daily), where staff serve over 300 cocktails (the daiquiris are best), or else sip a cocktail at the quiet and friendly *Bar 812* Бар 812 (Map 2, ul Zhukovskogo 11 ул Жуковского 11, **M** Mayakovskaya).

Catering to Beatles' fans, *Liverpool* Ливерпуль (Map 2, ul Mayakovskogo 16, ул Маяковского 16, **M** Ploshchad Vosstaniya, 🖥 www.liverpool.ru) hosts

> ❏ **Face control**
> Though by no means an unknown concept in European and American nightclubs, this practice is particularly prevalent in Moscow and St Petersburg. 'Face control' means: 'If you're not dressed right and/or you're not good-looking enough, you're not coming in.'

nightly live bands, and the lively crowd of regulars adds to the atmosphere.

Nightlife
Nightclubs and live music *Dacha* Дача (Map 1, ul Dumskaya 9, ул Думская 9, **M** Gostinny Dvor, 6pm-6am daily) is a café by day and raucous,nightspot by night, with people dancing in the thimble-sized space.

The punk, ska and hardcore scene thrives at gritty *Fish Fabrique* (Map 2, Лиговский пер 53, Ligovsky per 53, **M** Ploshchad Vosstaniya, 🖥 www.fishfab rique.spb.ru, R100-500), while the branch next door, single-room *Fish Fabrique Nouvelle* (Map 2) that doubles as artists' centre, hosts rock and alternative concerts on Thursdays, Fridays and Saturdays.

Labyrinthine *Griboyedov* Грибоедов (Map 2, ul Voronezhskaya 2a, ул Воронежская 2a, **M** Ploshchad Vosstaniya, 🖥 www.griboyedovclub.ru, R300 after 8pm), a converted bomb shelter, plays electronica, drum'n'bass, house and alternative, and there is nightly live music at *Griboyedov Hill* (off Map 2), its café-bar extension with a lovely terrace.

Purga I Пурга 1 (Map 1, nab Reki Fontanki 11, наб Реки Фонтанки 11, **M** Mayakovskaya, 🖥 purga-club.ru) is kitsch fun, with the Soviet New Year celebrated nightly, complete with countdown and mock TV addresses by Soviet leaders.

Inside the former Soviet Culture Palace, *Cabaret* (off Map 1, nab Obvodnogo Kanala 181, наб Обводного Канала 181, **M** Baltiiskaya) is the city's oldest gay club; it is currently functioning as a risqué café.

The *Jimi Hendrix Blues Club* (Map 1, Liteyny pr 33, Литейный пр 33, **M** Mayakovskaya, 🖥 www.hendrix-club.ru, R250-350) is an intimate cellar bar that hosts excellent nightly blues by local musicians; it's well worth booking a table here to enjoy the freshly prepared Russian and Georgian dishes.

If you like whisky and you like jazz, you'll love *The Hat Bar* (Map 1, ul Belinskogo 9, ул Белинского 9, **M** Chernyshevskaya, 7pm-5am daily), an old-style American bar with nightly live music and over 30 types of whisky, not to mention the bourbon.

Cultural entertainment The classical season is from September until the end of June; in July and August all of St Petersburg's main companies go on holiday or on tour, though some performances are still staged by lesser ensembles.

Mariinsky Theatre Мариинский Театр (Map 1, Teatralnaya pl 1, Театральная пл 1, **M** Sadovaya, box office 11am-7pm daily, 🖥 www.mariinsky.ru), with its sublime interior, is where the world-famous Kirov Ballet and Opera company perform. The new **Mariinsky 2 Мариинский 2** (Map 1) has now opened as an additional venue at ul Dekabristov 34 ул Декабристов 34. You can purchase tickets on their website for performances here and at the new **concert hall концертный зал** (Map 1) on ul Dekabristov 37, ул Декабристов 37, known for its superb acoustics.

Opera and ballet performances at **Mikhailovsky Theatre Михайловский Театр** (Map 1, pl Isskusktv 1, пл Искусств 1, **M** Nevsky Prospekt, 🖥 www.mikhail ovsky.ru), a splendidly restored imperial theatre, rival those at the Mariinsky.

You can hear the renowned St Petersburg Philharmonia Санкт-Петербургская Филармония at the **Bolshoy Zal Большой Зал** (large concert hall) at (ul Mikhailovskaya 2, ул Михайловская 2, **M** Gostinny Dvor, 🖥 www.philharmonia.spb.ru), while the smaller **Maly Zal Малый Зал** (Map 1) – small concert hall – (Nevsky pr 30 Невский пр 30, **M** Nevsky Prospekt) not surprisingly hosts smaller ensembles.

Shopping
Try **Anglia Book Shop Книжный мага-зин Англия** (Map 1, nab Reki Fontanki 38 наб Реки Фонтанки 38, **M** Nevsky Prospekt) for the widest range of English-language books in the city, as well as five other European languages. It also stocks a variety of books on Russian history and culture.

For nifty souvenirs, head for **Nevsky Souvenir** (Map 1, Nevsky pr 3 Невский пр 3, **M** Nevsky Prospekt), where you can pick up Fabergé-style eggs, lacquered boxes, Russian string instruments and chess boards. English-speaking staff are happy to assist.

Moving on

By air To get to the international Pulkovo-2 airport, take bus N13 or marshrutka N113 (R35) from **M** Moskovskaya (4/hr, 5.30am until the last flight). Less-frequent marshrutkas (N3 and N213) run from **M** Sennaya Ploshchad via **M** Moskovskaya. To get to domestic Pulkovo-1, take marshrutka N39 from **M** Moskovskaya (R35).

Besides individual air companies' websites, tickets for most airlines can be purchased at the **Central Air Ticket Office Центральная Авиакасса** (Map 1, Nevsky pr 7/9 Невский пр 7/9, **M** Nevsky Prospekt, 8am-8pm Mon-Fri, to 6pm Sat & Sun), where you can also purchase train and international bus tickets.

By train If, for some reason, you haven't bought your ticket online at ▢ www.rzd .ru, tickets for same-day departure can only be purchased at the departure station, at the 'same-day' window (*sutochnaya* суточная).

Advance-purchase long-distance and international tickets can be bought from the departure station or from the **Central**

CITY GUIDES & PLANS

▢ TRAIN SERVICES FROM ST PETERSBURG

St Petersburg is an important train hub, serving a number of major Russian cities, allowing you to bypass Moscow en route to several major Trans-Siberian destinations. There are also connections to a number of cities in Eastern and Western Europe; below are some recommended routes.

● St Petersburg to other cities in Russia

Destination	Train name & No	Journey time	Dep time	Arr time	Frequency
From Ladozhsky station					
Novosibirsk	014	56hrs 35mins	15:24	23:59	every other day
Yaroslavl	045	11hrs 51mins	17:40	05:31	daily
Yekaterinburg	072	35hrs 17mins	17:07	04:24	daily

● International services from St Petersburg

Destination	Train name & No	Journey time	Dep time	Arr time	Frequency
From Finlyandsky station					
Helsinki	*Allegro* 151	3hrs 46mins	06:50	08:26	daily
Helsinki	*Allegro* 153	3hrs 46mins	11:25	13:01	daily
Helsinki	*Allegro* 155	3hrs 46mins	15:25	17:01	daily
Helsinki	*Allegro* 157	3hrs 46mins	20:25	22:01	daily
From Ladozhsky station					
Helsinki	*Lev Tolstoy* 032	7hrs 24mins	05:53	11:17	daily
From Vitebsky station					
Kyiv	053	22hrs 34mins	16:20	12:54	daily
Minsk	051	13hrs 01mins	19:13	07:14	daily
Prague	023	36hrs 48mins	23:59	09:47	Mon, Thur
Riga	037	14hrs 55mins	20:40	09:35	daily
Tallinn	809	6hrs 39mins	17:33	23:12	daily
Vilnius	091	13hrs 28mins	20:40	08:08	daily

Train Ticket Office Центральная Железнодорожная Касса (Map 1, nab Kanala Griboyedova 24 наб Канала Грибоедова 24, **M** Nevsky Prospekt, 8am-8pm Mon-Sat, to 4pm Sun); bring your passport. To avoid the crowds there is a little-used window in the Central Air Ticket Office (see By air opposite) that sells rail tickets.

By bus All national and some international Lux Express (🖥 www.luxexpress.eu) buses depart from **Avtovokzal No 2** (Bus Station No 2, off Map 2, nab Obvodnogo Kanala 36, наб Обводного канала 36, **M** Obvodny Kanal, 🖥 www.avokzal.ru); Lux

Express also leave from Baltiisky Station (off Map 1) **M** Baltiiskaya. **Ecolines** (Map 1, Podyezny per 3 Подъездный пер 3, **M** Pushkinskaya, 🖥 www.ecolines.ru) run daily buses to Riga, Tallinn, Kiev and Odessa from Vitebsky Station (Map 1).

Sample departures from Avtovokzal No 2 include: Moscow (4/day, 12hrs, R1200), Tallinn (15/day, 6½hrs, R1300), Helsinki (3/day, 8½hrs, R1800) and Riga (6/day, 10hrs, R1430). Tickets for all departures can be purchased from the Avtovokzal website, Avtovokzal itself or the Central Air Ticket Office (see By air opposite).

❑ TRAIN SERVICES BETWEEN ST PETERSBURG AND MOSCOW

The arrow-straight 650km railway between Moscow and St Petersburg is Russia's busiest and most prestigious line, and high standards are maintained in terms of both facilities and service. When it was opened in 1851 the average travel time was 25 hours, whereas now, the high-speed *Sapsan* (at least 6/day) takes around four hours.

There are about two dozen trains a day in each direction. Many travellers prefer an overnight journey as it saves accommodation costs and leaves more time for sightseeing, though the *Sapsan* is ideal for a quick daytime journey between the two cities. The firmenny *Smena A Bentakur* and *Ekspress* have an all-night restaurant service. First-class passengers get a packed lunch (daytime trains) or breakfast (overnight trains).

If you buy a ticket yourself for *Smena A Bentakur*, for example, a berth in a two-berth cabin (*SV*) on an overnight firmenny train costs R5222; in a four-berth cabin (*kupé*) it's R2937, and third class (*platzkartny*) is R1565. Non-firmenny train tickets cost a little less. *Sapsan* fares are typically from R2844 for a seat; prices go up on Fridays but are cheaper on Sundays.

See box p204 for services from Moscow to St Petersburg.

St Petersburg to Moscow

Train name	No	Journey time	Departure time	Arrival time
Arctica	015	8hrs 18min	23:10	07:28
Afanasiy Nikitich	037	7hrs 9min	22:15	05:24**
Ekspress	003	9hrs	23:30	08:30
Smena A Bentakur	025	8hrs 15mins	23:00	07:15
Krasnaya Strela	001	8hrs	23:55	07:55
Dve Stolitsy	063	6hrs 59mins	23:36	06:35
Nevsky Express	167	4hrs 10mins	14:30	18:40
Sapsan	151	3hrs 40mins	06:45	10:25
Sapsan	153	3hrs 50mins	07:00	10:50
Sapsan	157	4hrs 10mins	13:30	17:40
Sapsan	159	4hrs 10mins	13:45	17:55
Sapsan	161	3hrs 50mins	15:00	18:50
Sapsan	163	3hrs 49mins	19:25	23:14
Sapsan	165	3hrs 40mins	19:45	23:25

**= only offers platzkart and kupé; no lux option

CITY GUIDES & PLANS

Moscow
Москва

Just as all roads lead to Rome, all railroads lead to Moscow – the vast, cosmo-politan metropolis that is the pulsating heart of Russia. You can't really say that you've 'been to Russia' until you've walked the streets of its historical centre where so many key events played out that have shaped the world in the 20th century, or seen the iconic sights that embody the country in the popular imag-ination. A place of boundless energy, Moscow is continuously shifting and changing, yet at the same time it is perhaps more uncompromisingly Russian than any other city. If you're heading east, you might be exhausted by it after a few days, and relieved to be departing after getting your fill of the sights and sounds; if you're arriving from the east, you may well be drawn to the glitz, the food, the pulsing nightlife and the rich cultural life.

Moscow's historic sights alone make it a fascinating place to explore; bank on a minimum of three days to see the main attractions. Besides the revered his-torical locations, such as the Kremlin and the Tretyakov Gallery, Moscow boasts cutting-edge modern art galleries and other attractions that would have been inconceivable in Soviet times, such as the Gulag History Museum that sheds light on Russia's troubled 20th-century history.

Long gone are the queues for basic essentials and food staples; Moscow (population: 11,979,529) is now brimming with sushi bars, restaurants serving every cuisine imaginable and shopping malls stocked full of international goods – all for those who can afford it. At night, there are innumerable clubs, blues bars, arts cafés and drinking dives clamouring for your attention.

Take your time exploring Moscow, for Russia is famous for its rapid changes and you may not find the same city the next time you're here.

HISTORY

The archaeological record shows that the Moscow area has been inhabited since Neolithic times. However, the first written mention of the city was not until 1147, when Prince Yuri Dolgoruki founded the city by building a wooden fort beside the Moskva River, in the principality of Vladimir. The settlement, which grew up around the fort, soon developed into a major trading centre.

The Mongols

Disaster struck the Russian principalities in the early 13th century in the form of the Mongol invasion. Moscow was razed to the ground in 1238 and for the next 250 years was obliged to pay an annual tribute to the Mongol Khan. But in 1326 Moscow was made seat of the Russian Orthodox Church, a role carrying with it the title of capital of Russia. Prince Dmitry Donskoi strengthened the city's defences, built a stone wall around the Kremlin and in 1380 defeated a Mongol-Tatar army at Kulikovo. But it was not until 1476 that tributes to the Khan ceased.

The years of growth
The reign of Ivan III 'The Great' (1462-1505) was a period of intensive construction in the city. Italian architects were commissioned to redesign the Kremlin and many cathedrals and churches date from this period. Prosperity continued into the 16th century under Ivan IV 'The Terrible'; it was at this time that St Basil's Cathedral was built.

The early 17th century was a time of civil disorder, and a peasant uprising culminated in the invasion of Moscow by Polish and Lithuanian forces. When they were driven out in 1612 the city was again burnt to the ground. Rebuilt in stone, by the end of the 17th century Moscow had become Russia's most important trading city. It remained a major economic and cultural centre even after Peter the Great transferred the capital to St Petersburg in 1712.

The last sacking of the city occurred in 1812 when Napoleon invaded Russia. Muscovites, seeing the invasion as inevitable, torched their own city rather than let Napoleon have it (Tolstoy describes Count Bezukhkov being arrested as an arsonist in *War and Peace*, his semi-fictionalised account of the campaign). But recovery was swift and trade increased after the abolition of serfdom in 1861.

Revolution
Towards the end of the 19th century Moscow became a revolutionary centre, its factories hit by a series of strikes and riots. Michael Myres Shoemaker, who was here in 1903, wrote in *The Great Siberian Railway from St Petersburg to Peking*: 'Up to the present day the dissatisfaction has arisen from the middle classes especially the students, but now for the first time in Russia's history it is spreading downward to the peasants... but it will be a century at least before that vast inert mass awakens to life.' But in 1905 there was an armed uprising, and 12 years later 'that vast inert mass' stormed the Kremlin and established Soviet power in the city. The subsequent civil war saw terrible food shortages and great loss of life.

The capital once more
In March 1918 Lenin transferred the government back to Moscow. In the years between the two world wars the city embarked on an ambitious programme of industrial development; by 1939 the population had doubled to four million. During WWII many factories in the European part of the USSR were relocated across the Urals, a wise move in retrospect. By October 1941 the German army had advanced almost up to the city itself (getting as close as the present-day site of Sheremetyevo airport) but never further, as the Soviet defence effort deployed fresh forces from Siberia and reserve armies, halting the approach of the Nazis and pushing them back.

Moscow was rebuilt following the war, growing in size, grandeur and power right up to the disintegration of the Soviet Union in 1991. The several

CITY GUIDES & PLANS

years that followed saw a lot of lawlessness and a rise in crime in the capital as different branches of Russian mafia fought for control; public utilities were in a poor state while the major transitions were taking place.

Moscow today

The USSR has gone but the Soviet habit of centralised decision-making and financial control remains intact. This has made Moscow vastly wealthier than any other city in Russia, which is a source of resentment elsewhere in Russia, as the capital is seen to be benefitting from the country's natural resources much more than the regions that produce them. But even here remnants of the past coexist incongruously with the elegant shops, restaurants and shopping malls. Lenin's description of 19th-century London as 'two nations living in one city' has become true of Moscow itself.

The city's pugnacious former mayor, Yury Luzhkov, and his wife – Russia's wealthiest woman – reaped huge financial benefits from enormous infrastructure projects that have gone ahead with little help from the central government, changing the architectural face of the city in the process. On September 28, 2010, after 18 years in office, Luzhkov was finally sacked by Medvedev with Putin's blessing after Luzhkov had overstepped himself, repeatedly criticising Medvedev in print. He was then replaced by Sergei Sobyanin, a member of Putin's United Russia party who is lauded for halting the out-of-control construction projects of his predecessor but criticised for the banning of gay parades in the city. Sobyanin is currently serving his second term as mayor, having beaten his nearest rival, Aleksei Navalny – a prominent opponent of Putin's government who labelled United Russia 'a party of crooks and thieves' – in the September 2013 elections.

Moscow has been the centre of unwelcome international media attention after being rocked by a series of protests, unrest and mass demonstrations from December 2011 up until late 2013. First came clamours for fair elections as Putin was elected president once more, with crowds of protestors agitating against government corruption and the government funding pro-Putin counterdemonstrations. In February 2012, up to 120,000 people filled the city streets, and the police were criticised by international media for their heavy-handed approach to peaceful protestors. That same month, members of the punk band Pussy Riot caused a stir at the Christ the Saviour Cathedral, their subsequent trial and sentencing causing an international outcry. In October 2013, a violent nationalist mob went on the rampage in the Moscow suburb of Birulyovo after a Russian man was stabbed to death by a man allegedly of Caucasian origin. While racially motivated attacks on illegal migrants from the former Soviet republics are nothing new, this time the mob clashed violently with the police after overturning cars and smashing up businesses.

Occasional unrests aside, no other Russian city has as much to offer the visitor in terms of cultural heritage, entertainment, hotels, dining, nightlife and shopping. Love it or hate it, your visit to Moscow is likely to be a memorable one.

WHAT TO SEE AND DO

Around the Kremlin   [see map p173]
Red Square (Krasnaya ploshchad, Красная Площадь, M Ploshchad
Revolutsii or Okhotny Ryad) You're bound to feel a real sense of occasion
when you first set foot on this grand cobbled square, the heart of the city, fea-
turing the most Russian and the most recognisable of architectural landmarks:
St Basil's Cathedral (see p172). The square extends across the area beside the
north-eastern wall of the Kremlin and its name has nothing to do with
Communism or the colour 'red'; in old Russian, 'krasny' meant 'beautiful' and
it really is that, so much so that you stop in your tracks the first time you see it.
You're walking on history: these cobblestones have seen many executions
(Cossack rebel Stepan Razin in 1671, for one), countless military parades, festivals, protests and celebrations. On most days, you'll find Red Square teeming
with crowds of sightseers, trying to get that perfect snapshot of St Basil's
Cathedral, or on their way to Lenin's Mausoleum, the GUM shopping arcade or
the Kremlin with **Spasskaya Tower (Saviour Clock-Tower) Спасская Башня**
the most famous of the 20 towers.

Lenin's Mausoleum Мавзолей В И Ленина Built onto the side of the
Kremlin in 1930, the red granite mausoleum (**M** Ploshchad Revolutsii or
Okhotny Ryad, Tue-Thur, Sat & Sun 10am-1pm, 🖳 www.lenin.ru, free entry)
and its mummified occupant are the centre of a personality cult that flourished
for almost 70 years and still lingers on in some ways. Nowadays, the man who
shaped Russia's destiny in the early 20th century and his current resting place
continues to draw the crowds, with tourists queuing up to file past the compact
embalmed body, laid out in a dark suit and tie. The **body** is the real thing and

CITY GUIDES & PLANS

❏ **Mummification for the masses**
A few years ago the Centre for Biological Researches, responsible for the preservation of Lenin's body, announced the offer of full mummification services to anyone
for a mere US$300,000. Previous clients are a testimony to their skill. A few years
ago an independent team of embalmers inspected Lenin's corpse and declared it to be
in perfect condition.
    After Lenin's death from a massive stroke on 21 January 1924, at the age of 53,
an autopsy was carried out and a full report published in *Pravda*, treating the public
to the weights and measurements of their dead leader's internal organs. Then the
embalmers began their work. Boris Zbarsky, a biochemist, and Vladimir Vorobyov,
an anatomist, were given the task of preserving the Communist leader's body as a
sacred relic and they managed to find a way to stop the decaying process. The
embalming process was kept secret until the fall of Communism, when Zbarsky's
son, who took over from his father, admitted that the body is 'spruced up' every 18
months by being submerged in a tub of chemicals.
    Lenin's brain (1340g, far larger than average, of course) was removed and placed
in a specially founded Institute of Lenin's Brain, where scientists analysed deep-
frozen micro-slices in an attempt to discover the secret of his greatness. The Institute
was quietly closed in the 1960s and any discoveries it had made went unpublished.

not a waxwork, contrary to rumours. You descend into the sepulchral gloom in single file. Talking is not allowed and guards will move you along if you dawdle. And don't even think about taking photos! The one-way route also features the Tombs of Soviet Heroes in the Kremlin walls; the big names include Josef Stalin, Yuri Gagarin, Leonid Brezhnev, and Inessa Armand – rumoured to have been Lenin's lover.

The mausoleum was Stalin's idea; the deceased Stalin lay beside Lenin until his legacy was reassessed by Khrushchev. The tomb's design is the work of one AV Shchusev, who saw the cube, like the pyramid, as a symbol of eternity and envisaged every Soviet home having its own little cube to the memory of the dead leader.

The long queue moves along quickly, but make sure you leave your bags and cameras in the storage lockers provided before going through the metal detector.

St Basil's Cathedral Собор Василия Блаженного Also known as the Church of the Saviour (11am-5pm daily, R250), the colourful domes of St Basil's have become the unofficial symbol of Russia, and as much a symbol of Moscow as Tower Bridge is of London. It was commissioned by Ivan the Terrible to celebrate his victory over the Tatar Khan of Kazan and completed in 1561. So pleased was Ivan with the result that, according to legend, he had the architect's eyes put out so that he could never produce anything to equal or surpass it.

The cathedral is named after a holy hermit known as Basil the Simpleton, who dressed year-round in a loincloth, begging and sleeping in the street outside. Basil proved less of a simpleton when he denounced Tsar Boris Godunov as the murderer of the rightful ruler, Ivan the Terrible's weakling son Dmitry.

St Basil's is a quite incredible building, with its nine brightly painted, dissimilar domes, their paintwork dating back to the 18th century, and stonework decorated with intricate patterns more usually found on the wooden buildings of the time. Its painted interiors were burnt off when Napoleon used it as a stable and inside it's a labyrinthine warren of narrow corridors, tiny chapels and spiral staircases – a shock after seeing the grand open spaces of Russia's other cathedrals.

Outside the cathedral is a statue of Kuzma Minin and Prince Dmitry Pozharsky, who saved Russia from the Polish-Lithuanian invasion in the early 17th century.

GUM ГУМ The glass-roofed GUM shopping arcade (pronounced 'goom', an acronym for *Generalny Universalny Magazin*) was constructed in 1894 on the site of a covered market which was torn down as a health hazard. It was nationalised after the Revolution and turned into a huge department store, a monument to Soviet shortages, but now it's a shopping mall for the wealthy.

State History Museum Государственный Исторический Музей At the northern end of Red Square, this museum (10am-6pm Fri-Mon & Wed, 11am-9pm Thur, 🖳 www.shm.ru, adult/student R300/100, audioguide R300) traces Russia's long and turbulent history from the Stone Age to 1917. Extensive collections include relics from the Mongol invasions and personal items belonging

Moscow Kremlin
Московский Кремль

AROUND THE KREMLIN

1 [A3] Borovitskaya Tower Боровицкая Башня
2 [B1] Arsenal Tower Арсенальная Башня
3 [C1/D1] GUM ГУМ
4 [A2] Kutafya Tower Кутафья Башня
5 [C1] Lenin's Mausoleum
        Мавзолей В И Ленина
6 [D2] Minin & Pozharsky Memorial
        Памятник Минину и Пожарскому
7 [D1] Place of Executions Лобное Место
8 [C2] Spasskaya Tower Спасская Башня
9 [D2] St Basil's Cathedral
        Собор Василия Блаженного
10 [B1] State History Museum
        Государтвенный Исторический Музей
11 [A2] Ticket Office Кассы
12 [B1] Tomb of the Unknown Soldier
        Могила Неизвестного Солдата
13 [B2] Trinity Gate Tower Троицкая Башня
14 [A4] Water Tower Водяная Башня

THE KREMLIN

15 [B3] Annunciation Cathedral
        Благовещенский Собор
16 [A3] Armoury Chamber & Diamond Fund
        Оружейная Палата & Алмазный Фонд

17 [B2] Arsenal Арсенал
18 [B3] Assumption Cathedral
        Успенский Собор
19 [B3/C3] Bell Tower of Ivan the Great
        Колокольня Ивана Великого
20 [B3] Cathedral of the Archangel
        Michael Архангельский Собор
21 [B3] Church of the Deposition of
        the Robe Церковь Ризоположения
22 [B2] Church of the Twelve Apostles
        Церковь Двенадцати Апостолов
23 [B3] Facetted Chamber
        Грановитая Палата
24 [B3] Great Kremlin Palace
        Большой Кремлёвский Дворец
25 [C2] Lenin Memorial Памятник Ленину
26 [B2] Patriach's Palace
        Патриарший Дворец
27 [B2] Poteshny Palace Потешный Дворец
28 [B2] Senate Сенат
29 [C2] Supreme Soviet Верховный Совет
30 [B2] State Kremlin Palace
        Государственный Кремлёвский Дворец
31 [B3] Teremnoy Palace Теремной Дворец
32 [C3] Tsar Bell Царь Колокол
33 [B2] Tsar Cannon Царь Пушка

to Russia's rulers, and there's a grand portrait gallery educating you as to who is who in Russian aristocracy. The red palatial building, each of its rooms decorated in the style of a different period, is worth seeing in itself, but the best collections focus on medieval Rus and the landmark war of 1812.

Tomb of the Unknown Soldier Могила Неизвестного Солдата It is traditional for newlyweds to visit this monument in the Aleksandrovsky Gardens (the former Kremlin moat) to be photographed beside its eternal flame. Beneath the marble lies the body of one of the soldiers who helped to stop the German advance on Moscow in 1941, who died at Km41 of Leningradskoye Shosse, the closest the German army got to Moscow.

The blood-red marble caskets beside the flame contain soil from Soviet 'Hero-Cities' (those with the greatest number of WWII dead) and the inscription reads: 'Your name is unknown, your deeds immortal!' The honour guard which once stood watch at Lenin's Mausoleum now stands here, with a goose-stepping Changing of the Guard every hour.

★ The Kremlin Кремль   [see map p173]

The heart of Moscow, the seat of the Russian government, and formerly the centre of the Orthodox Church, the biggest single attraction that Moscow has to offer – the Kremlin (**M** Aleksandrovsky Sad, 🖥 www.kreml.ru, 10am-6pm May-Sep, until 5pm rest of the year, closed Thur) is a large walled citadel with the golden domes of the churches peeking from above the red brick walls. Our description doesn't really do it justice; the Russian poet Lermontov put it better in 1833: 'What can compare to the Kremlin which sits on a high hill like the crown of sovereignty on the brow of an awesome ruler. No, neither the Kremlin, nor the walls, nor its dark passages, nor the splendid palaces can be described. They must be seen, they must be seen!'

Although the site has been continuously occupied for at least eight centuries, the first fortress made of wood, the present walls and many of the cathedrals inside date from the 15th century. There are 20 towers, the most famous being Spasskaya Tower above Red Square, and assorted buildings ranging from Romanov imperial classicism to 1960s Soviet modernism in style. Though parts of the Kremlin are out of bounds for visitors, as they are part of the Government and Presidential estate – you'll see black Mercedes with darkened windows whisking government ministers in and out – the parts that you do see are some of the most impressive in Russia.

Around the Kremlin's **Cathedral Square Соборная Площадь** stand four main cathedrals and the **Bell Tower of Ivan the Great Колокольня Ивана Великого** (81m/263ft high; closed Thur) which Napoleon attempted to blow up in 1812 and which houses exhibitions on the ground level. You can also ascend the 137 steps of the tower (🖥 www.belltower.lagutin.ru, R200) for some great views, though only as part of a tour.

Beneath the tower stands the enormous **Tsar Bell Царь Колокол**, at 200 tons the heaviest in the world and too heavy to hang; the piece that stands beside it broke off during the fire of 1737. Nearby is **Tsar Cannon Царь Пушка**, the

❑ **Visiting the Kremlin**
At first glance, gaining entrance to Moscow's mighty fortress may seem as difficult as for those who tried to storm its walls back in the day. We'll try and simplify it for you.

The **main visitors' entrance and ticket office** for the Kremlin is in **Kutafya Tower Кутафья Башня** in Aleksandrovsky Park, on the opposite side from Red Square. You may not take large bags or rucksacks inside (there is a pay-per-item cloakroom in the basement of Kutafya Tower). If the State Kremlin Palace Государственный Кремлёвский Дворец is in use for a daytime concert or other function you may be redirected to the Borovitskaya Tower Боровицкая Башня entrance at the far end of Aleksandrovsky Gardens. The **exit** is under **Trinity Gate Tower Троицкая Башня**, the Kremlin's tallest (80m). The Kremlin may be partly or completely closed without warning if there are VIP visitors.

There are **five types of ticket**:
● The main grounds, Cathedral Square, five cathedral-museums, the Patriarch's Palace and exhibitions in the Assumption Belfry – but not in the Ivan the Great Bell Tower (adult/student R350/100)
● The Armoury Chamber* (adult/student R700/200)
● State Diamond Fund* – a priceless collection of state jewellery on display in the same building as the Armoury (adult/student R700/350)
● Bell Tower of Ivan the Great * (adult/student R500/250)
● Cathedral Square and its churches (adult/student R350/100)
● Exhibitions in the Assumption Belfry and Patriarch's Palace (R350).
So, if you wanted to see everything would it cost R2950.

* The Armoury, State Diamond Fund and Bell Tower of Ivan the Great may only be entered during timed sessions (the time is printed on your ticket), the tickets going on sale 45 minutes before the session is due to start. It's annoying, but you can't buy the tickets in advance, so time your queuing accordingly.

largest-calibre cannon in the world. The cannonballs don't fit the cannon, which never fired a shot. It's worth timing your visit so that you're in the main square on Saturday at noon (Apr-Oct) when the Presidential Regiment performs a ceremony on foot and horseback.

Assumption Cathedral Успенский собор, the work of Italian architect Aristotle Fiorovanti and his sons, was completed in 1479 and was the traditional place of coronation for Russia's tsars. The last coronation, on 26 May 1896, saw what many considered a bad omen: as Nicholas II climbed the steps to the altar the chain of the Order of St Anthony fell from his shoulders. The interior is one of the most richly decorated in Russia. There are three thrones; the wooden one, known as the Throne of Monomakh, to the right as you enter, belonged to Ivan the Terrible. Don't miss the splendid iconostasis.

Cathedral of the Archangel Michael Архангельский собор (1505-9) looks classically Russian from the outside but the hand of its Italian architect, Alevisio Novi, can be seen in the light interior. Forty-six tsars (including Ivan the Great and Ivan the Terrible) who ruled Rus between the 1320s and the 1690s are buried here, with the exception of Boris Godunov, interred at Sergiev Posad instead. The smaller **Annunciation Cathedral Благовещенский собор**

(1484-89), the tsars' private chapel, was the work of Russian architects and contains icons by the great master, Andrei Rublyov.

The **Church of the Deposition of the Robe Ризоположенская Церковь** (1484-5) was designed as a private chapel for the clergy and its walls feature some splendid frescoes. The Patriarch worshipped in the **Church of the Twelve Apostles Церковь Двенадцати Апостолов** next door to his residence, famous for its collection of 17th-century icons.

The **Armoury Chamber Оружейная Палата** (sessions daily 10am, noon, 2.30pm, 4.30pm, R700) is an incredible treasure house containing a dazzling display of tsars' jewellery and regalia, weapons and armour. Of special interest to Trans-Siberian passengers is the ornate Great Siberian Easter Egg (probably the finest of the 56 famous Imperial Easter Eggs made by Carl Fabergé), containing a tiny clockwork model of the train, complete with gold and platinum engine, five gold coaches and a church-car. Besides the ornate royal carriages, highlights include a huge collection of gold and silverware and the diamond-encrusted throne of Tsar Alexey Mikhailovich.

Speaking of diamonds, the collection of jewels in the adjoining **Diamond Fund Алмазный Фонд** (10am-1pm & 2-5pm Fri-Wed, 🖳 www.almazi.net, R500) is not to be missed. Peter the Great started the trend of jewellery collecting, specifying that his successors must each leave a number of jewels to the Russian state. Originally housed in St Petersburg's Winter Palace, the collection was hidden in the Kremlin's vaults during WWI and though two-thirds of it was sold off at Christie's in London in 1927 to raise funds for the Soviet Union's economy, the remains are vastly impressive, glittering in the atmospheric semi-gloom of the display halls. They include not just the world's largest sapphire but also the famous Orlov Diamond, thought to be the re-cut Great Mogul that was stolen from the Mogul treasury in the 17th century. The Orlov Diamond was presented to Catherine the Great as a gift by Count Gregory Orlov, who was trying to reignite a former flame. He was unsuccessful but Catherine the Great kept the diamond's original Indian rose cut. Incidentally, if you're talking too loudly, you might be hissed at (for upsetting the diamonds).

Other buildings in the Kremlin The **Great Kremlin Palace Большой Кремлёвский Дворец**, now a government building, is only open to guests of State and other VIPs. A total renovation, to restore the palace to its pre-Communist finery, was completed in 1999. 'Put it back as it was before', said Yeltsin, and they did, for a mere US$800 million. Also VIP-only is the sole secular building on Cathedral Square, the Italian-designed **Facetted Chamber Грановитая Палата**, so-called because of its façade of pointed stone blocks. **Teremnoy Palace Теремной Дворец**, closed to the public, has a striking red and white tiled roof.

The modern building facing the Kremlin's main entrance is the **State Kremlin Palace Государственный Кремлёвский Дворец**, formerly the seat of the Parliament of the USSR. It was designed also to do duty as a theatre in the evenings; now that Parliament meets elsewhere, this building is the full-time home of the Moscow Kremlin Ballet as well as hosting some big international

musicians, such as Leonard Cohen. Ticketholders get special entrance to the
Kremlin in the evenings, but you can't sightsee before the show.

Tretyakov Gallery Третьяковская Галерея   [see Map 3]

The best collection of Russian paintings, icons and sculpture is housed at the
Tretyakovka (Lavrushinsky per 10 Лаврушинский пер 10, **M** Tretyakovskaya,
🖥 www.tretyakovgallery.ru, 10am-7.30pm Tue-Sun, adult/student R300/180).
Highlights include: icons by Andrei Rublyov; two halls devoted to the great
Russian masters Ilya Repin and Vasily Surikov, including Repin's boozy,
vodka-stricken portrait of the composer Mussorgsky; *Christ's First Appearance
to the People* which took Alexander Ivanov 20 years to complete; and Ge's
Peter the Great Interrogates His Own Son and *Ivan the Terrible, Having
Murdered His Own Son*. Vasily Perov, the leader of the 1870s Peredvizhniki
movement, in which painting began to address social issues, has his own hall,
while Victor Vasnetsov is particularly good at his depictions of Russian folk
tales.

New Tretyakov Gallery Новая Третьяковская Галерея   [see Map 3]

The New Tretyakov Gallery (Krymsky Val 10 Крымский Вал 10, **M** Park
Kultury, 10am-7.30pm Tue-Sun, adult/student R300/180), 1km away from the
original, houses the best of **20th-century Soviet art**, the genres including
numerous socialist realism works as well as primitivism, cubism and more.
Artists to watch out for include Kazimir Malevich, Lyubov Popova, Vasily
Kandinsky, and Anatoly Komelin. The works are extremely well presented and
the visitor comes away with a real understanding of the complexities and different stages of the development of modern Russian art.

Next door is the **Central House of Artists Центральный Дом
Художника** (11am-8pm Tue-Sun, 🖥 www.cha.ru, adult/student R300/100),
featuring concerts, contemporary art exhibits and much more.

Muzeon Park Парк Музеон   [see Map 3]

Behind the museum you'll find this park (9am-9pm daily, R100), the final resting place of the many Soviet statues and sculptures which were torn from their
pedestals in the aftermath of the Soviet Union's collapse. Wander amongst the
Lenins, Red Army monuments and enormous hammer-and-sickles.
Overlooking the park is the **controversial nautical sculpture Скульптура
Петра Великого (Sculpture of Peter the Great)** by Zurab Tsereteli which
allegedly features Peter the Great, though the statue was originally supposed to
be Columbus; it was placed here when America wouldn't take him. On the
riverfront you'll find some scattered examples of modern sculpture.

★ Gorky Park Парк Горького   [see Map 3]

This venerable green space (**M** Park Kultury or Oktyabrskaya, 🖥 www.park-gor
kogo.com, WI-FI) in the centre of Moscow had a complete makeover in 2011,
with the old amusement park rides disposed of. Instead, the park has once again
reverted to an attractive public space, but with a few new twists. There's an ice
rink in winter, pedalos on the lakes in summer, free wi-fi throughout the park,

and numerous events, concerts, flea markets, open-air cinema and other goings-on at the weekend. If you get hungry, there are more than a dozen cafés and restaurants scattered throughout.

Gorky Park is now home to the superb **Garage (Centre for Contemporary Art) Гараж** (Krymsky Val 9, 11am-9pm Mon-Thur, to 10pm Fri-Sun, 💻 garageccc.com, adult/student R300/150), featuring temporary exhibitions by contemporary artists such as John Baldessi and holding lectures, workshops, cinema screenings and more.

Pushkin Museum of Fine Arts [see Map 4]
Музей Изобразительных Искусств имени А С Пушкина
This excellent museum of non-Russian art (ul Volkhonka 12 ул Волхонка 12, **M** Kropotkinskaya, 10am-7pm Tue-Wed & Fri-Sun, until 9pm Thur, 💻 www.artsmuseum.ru, adult/student R300/150, audioguide R200) boasts a large collection of European works, including numerous works from the 19th century, Greek and Roman sculptures in the Ancient Civilisation section, and also galleries of Egyptian antiquities and works by the Old Masters.

In a separate wing next door, at ul Volkhonka 14 (💻 www.newpaintart.ru, same opening days/hours, adult/student R300/150), you'll find a superb collection of Impressionist and post-Impressionist art, including works by Renoir, Pissarro, Monet, Manet, Picasso and Van Gogh. The Gaugin section is particularly splendid.

Museum of Private Collections Отдел Личных Коллекций [see Map 4]
Down the street at ul Volkhonka 10 this museum (10am-6pm Wed-Sun, 💻 www.artprivatecollections.ru, adult/student R200/100) displays the best of many works 'liberated' from wealthy Muscovites during the Revolution, the centrepiece being the collection of Ilya Silverstein.

Tsereteli Gallery Галерея Искусств Зураба Церетели [see Map 3]
(ul Prechistenka 19 ул Пречистенка 19, noon-7pm Tue-Sat, R200) is full of the Georgian artist Zurab Tsereteli's outlandish sculptures and bold paintings.

Novodevichy Convent Новодевичий Монастырь [see Map 3]
This beautiful convent (**M** Sportivnaya, 9am-5pm daily, R250), its 16th-century walls enclosing four cathedrals, has served as a fortress (holding out against a Polish siege in 1610) and a prison, as well as a house of God.

Peter the Great imprisoned his half-sister Sofia here for taking part in the Streltsy rebellion, in which the plotters intended to dethrone him and put Sofia in his place. Sofia's supporters were beheaded in Red Square (see p171). Many of the nuns here were daughters of noble families who had brought shame upon family honour in the days before contraception. Napoleon tried unsuccessfully to blow it up in 1812 but one brave nun rushed in and extinguished the fuses to the powder kegs at the last minute.

The white, imposing **Smolensky Cathedral Смоленский собор**, at the convent, is famous for its frescoes and highly ornate, multi-tiered iconostasis (the backdrop to the altar). The convent's private **cemetery** was a safe location for graves which might otherwise become unwanted shrines, including those of many Decembrist officers. Adjacent to the convent is a more **public cemetery** featuring a Who's Who of Russian dead. Famous 'residents' seeing out eternity here include Chekhov, Prokofiev, Khrushchev, Brezhnev, Yeltsin, Gogol and Einstein, the austerity of some memorials clashing with the more outlandish gravestones (one soldier lies under a model tank).

Cathedral of Christ the Saviour Храм Христа Спасителя [see Map 3]
Moscow's central cathedral was bulldozed by Stalin to make way for an ambitious Palace of the Soviets, planned as the world's largest building. But expert opinion concluded that the riverside location, directly opposite the Pushkin Museum, wouldn't support the weight and after an embarrassing hiatus a rather good swimming pool was built there instead. In 1997 a replica (ul Volkhonka 15 ул Волхонка 15, **M** Kropotkinskaya, 10am-5pm daily, services at 8am and 5pm Mon-Fri, 9am Sat, 10am Sun, 🖥 www.xxc.ru) of the original cathedral with an enormous golden dome, financed with public and corporate contributions of a paltry US$350 million, was opened by then Mayor Luzhkov. The view from the dome is worth the climb and much of the cathedral was designed by the industrious Georgian artist Zurab Tsereteli, whose work divides opinions.

Moscow Metro Museum Музей Московского Метрополитена
[see Map 3] This museum (ul Khamovnichesky Val 36, 2nd & 3rd floor, ул Хамовнический Вал 36, 2-й и 3-й этаж, 9am-4.30pm Tue-Fri, 10am-4.30pm Sat, free entry), attached to the southern exit of **M** Sportivnaya, answers questions that you may have never thought to ask: how is a metro built? How does an escalator work? Why is it warm in the metro in winter and cool in summer? There are maps, train models and documents about the history of Moscow's public transport system from the early 19th century; you can even sit in a full-size driver's cab and play with the equipment. The displays relating to the building of the first metro lines play up the role of Komsomol volunteers in their creation and downplay the role of forced labour used alongside.

❑ **A riot in the temple**
On February 21, 2012, three members of punk band Pussy Riot, known for performing in unusual venues in order to provoke a reaction, caused a bigger stir than any of them had anticipated. The three women made their way to the altar in the Cathedral of Christ the Saviour and sang 'Deliver us from Putin'. An enormous scandal, with thousands of Russians enraged at the blasphemy, was followed by a criminal trial, with two of the three young women sentenced to 'a lenient' two years in women's prisons. Their case has been taken up by Amnesty International, not least because freedom of speech is enshrined in the Russian constitution, and also because two of the three have young children and have been deliberately moved to detention facilities hundreds of miles from home to inconvenience family members wanting to visit. The two women were released in December 2013 as part of a general amnesty before the 2014 Winter Olympics in Sochi.

CITY GUIDES & PLANS

Sandunovskiye Baths Сандуновские Бани [see Map 4]

If you've just stepped off a Trans-Siberian train or even if you just fancy a bit of pampering, a traditional Russian bath in the oldest and most luxurious public *banya* in the city is an invigorating experience. Sandunovskiye (Sanduny) baths (ul Neglinnaya 14 ул Неглинная 14, **M** Chekhovskaya, 8am-midnight daily, 🖥 www.sanduny.ru, R1200-2000 for two hours' general admission, or else you can get a private cabin from R3500/hour) are beautifully decorated in classical style, with a colonnaded swimming pool, carved wooden dressing stalls and assistants on standby to give you a vigorous rubdown.

Ul Arbat ул Арбат [see Map 4]

Pedestrianised ul Arbat ([A5]; **M** Arbatskaya or Smolenskaya) is one of Moscow's most famous and well-loved streets. It teems with tourists, buskers, street artists and hawkers of everything from *matryoshka* dolls to McLenin T-shirts, but the 19th-century buildings which line it hint at former grandeur. Bargain hard and watch out for pickpockets. The best known of the 1960s singer-songwriter 'bards', **Bulat Okudjava**, lived here at Plotnikov per 43 – his

❏ Modern art explosion

Unimaginable during its Soviet past, the Russian contemporary art scene has exploded and Moscow got the lion's share of the venues – many of them created by converting old factories, showcasing the works of both home-grown and international artists.

Winzavod Винзавод (Map 2, 4-у Siromyatnichesky per 1/6, 4-й Сыромятнический пер 1/6, **M** Chkalovskaya, noon-8pm Tue-Sun, 🖥 www.winzavod.ru) is a former wine-bottling factory that's been converted into numerous prestigious art galleries, the entry to which is absolutely free. Outside there are murals by a local street artist crew, while inside you'll find sculpture, installations, painting, photography and a trendy café.

Red October Красный Октябрь (Map 3, Bersenevskaya nab, Берсеневская наб, **M** Kropotkinskaya, 🖥 www.redok.ru) A rather labyrinthine venue on the banks of the Moskva river, this massive red brick construction, opposite the Cathedral of Christ the Saviour, used to be a chocolate factory producing the famous Krasny Oktyabr chocolate. Now its various pockets have been converted into art spaces, the best one being the **Lumiere Brothers Photography Centre** (Map 3, noon-9pm Tue-Fri, from 11am Sat & Sun, 🖥 www.lumiere.ru, R300) that has recently featured a wonderful photographic exhibition of the best photos by National Geographic.

In a similar vein to Winzavod, **ArtPlay on Yauza** (Map 2, ul Nizhniya Siromyatnicheskaya 10, Ул Нижния Сыромятническая 10, **M** Chkalovskaya, noon-8pm daily, 🖥 www.artplay.ru) is found inside the former Manometer factory. Its exhibitions tend to focus on architectural design.

Finally, as part of the Luchshiy Gorod Zemli (Best City on Earth; 🖥 www.lgz-moscow.ru) summer festival in 2013, Moscow authorities have teamed up with street artists of both local and international renown to transform over 150 buildings, bridges and underpasses with enormous murals, the locations of which are found under Граффити (graffiti) on the website map. Not just that; if you own a building in Moscow and wish for it to be decorated with the help of local graffiti artists, you can send a request to that effect. The face of the city is changing very rapidly indeed!

statue stands on the corner – and wrote *Arbat*, his best-loved song. Banned from recording in Soviet times, his funeral drew 60,000 people. The 'Viktor we still love you' graffiti along Krivoarbatsky per refers to Viktor Tsoy, a cult-status underground rock star killed in a 1990 car crash. Spot the individually painted tiles that make up the **Wall of Peace** at Arbat's eastern end.

Patriarch's Ponds Патриаршие Пруды   [see Map 2]

Those who have read *The Master and Margarita* by Mikhail Bulgakov will recognise the large, peaceful pond as the spot where the devil made an appearance. Bulgakov and his wife lived in the area in the 1930s at what is now known as **Bulgakov House Дом Булгакова** at ul Bolshaya Sadovaya 10 ул Большая Садовая 10 (1-11pm Fri, to 1am Sat). There's an exhibition devoted to the writer as well as contemporary works by resident artists and a café featuring its very own Behemoth the cat.

White House Белый Дом   [see Map 2]

You may recognise the White House (Krasnopresnenskaya nab 2, Краснопресненская наб 2, **M** Krasnopresnenskaya) from two key episodes in recent Russian history. In front of that building Boris Yeltsin stood on a tank in 1991 in defiance of the hardline coup that tried to depose Gorbachev, rallying the civil opposition. Two years later, Yeltsin was the one to send tanks to storm the White House after a political standoff between himself and the parliament.

★ Jewish Museum & Tolerance Centre   [see Map 1]
Еврейский Музей и Центр Толерантности

This wonderfully engaging museum (ul Obraztsova 11/1a ул Образцова 11/1a, **M** Novoslobodskaya, noon-10pm Mon-Thur & Sun, to 3pm Fri, closed Sat, 🖥 www.jewish-museum.ru, R400), housed in a cutting-edge exhibition space that once used to be a bus depot, tells the complex story of Russian Jewry through personal testimony on large video screens, archival footage, and interactive displays. Jewish history is traced from the *shtetls* of medieval Europe to the role Jews played in public life in the Soviet Union, and while tragedy is recorded – the pogroms, the persecutions, the Holocaust (almost half of the victims were Soviet Jews), so are the triumphs and achievements. Visitors come away with a real appreciation of what it meant to be a 'Soviet Jew', as well as why so many left the USSR for other shores. Take tram No 19 from the metro.

Moscow Museum of Modern Art (MMOMA)   [see Map 4]
Московский Музей Современного Искусства (MMOMA)

With a collection of weird and wonderful metal sculptures in the garden, the main building of MMOMA (ul Petrovka 25/1 ул Петровка 25/1, **M** Checkhovskaya or Trubnaya, noon-8pm Mon-Wed & Fri-Sun, to 9pm Thur, 🖥 www.mmoma.ru, adult/student R250/100) is home to a collection of montages, paintings, sculpture, graphics and installations by contemporary Russian artists. The permanent collection features works by Kazimir Malevich, Marc Chagall, Natalia Goncharova and the like.

State Gulag History Museum [see Map 4]
Государственный Музей Истории ГУЛАГа
This museum (ul Petrovka 16 ул Петровка 16, **M** Kuznetsky Most, 11am-7pm
Tue-Wed & Fri-Sun, to 8pm Thur, R150) is a chilling eye-opener, shedding
light on the history of Russia's millions of 'repressed' persons. There are three
parts: a documentary on the persecution of various social groups; art by ex-
Gulag prisoners; and a reproduction of a punishment cell and Gulag barracks,
sealed off and accessed with a guide. Don't let the lack of Russian captioning
put you off.

All-Russia Exhibition Centre (VDNKh) [see Map 1]
Всероссийский Выставочный Центр (ВДНХ)
The initials stand for Vystavka Dostizheniy Narodnogo Khozyaystva SSSR –
USSR Economic Achievements Exhibition. This sprawling complex of pavilions and wide pedestrian avenues (pr Mira 119, **M** VDNKh, 9am-7pm daily),
often teeming with two-legged and two-wheeled traffic, was built in the 1930s
to showcase the triumph of the Soviet economic system. The pavilions – mighty
examples of Stalinist architecture – were formerly dedicated to the achievements of specific republics that made up the USSR as well as the fields of technology, science, agriculture, education and health, but nowadays they house a
motley collection of shops and second-rate museums. The main attraction for

❑ The Moscow metro and the secret metro [Metro map p530]
Construction of the metro began in the early 1930s and it was planned that the first
line would open on May Day 1935. In late April that year Stalin was invited to inspect
the system but his tour came to an unexpected 30-minute halt following a signal failure. Expecting imprisonment or worse, engineers nearly collapsed with relief when
Stalin suggested that it might be better to fix all the problems and delay the opening
until 15 May. The honour of driving the first train, which consisted of local copies of
1932 New York carriages, went to the alliteratively named Ivan Ivanovich Ivanov.

As well as transporting passengers, the metro served as a bomb shelter in 1941-
42. Male Muscovites slept on wooden platforms assembled every evening in the tunnels while women and children slept on camp stretchers on the platforms. During the
Cold War the metro was modified to contain fallout shelters. Evidence of both the
WWII and Cold War preparations can still be seen today; these include large recessed
blast doors at ground-level entrances, collapsible platform edges which become steps,
and large storerooms on the platforms for medical supplies.

A second 'secret' metro was finished in 1967 which would enable government
leaders to flee Moscow in the face of a nuclear attack. This 30km line runs from the
former Central Communist Headquarters building on Staraya pl (near **M** Kitay-
Gorod) via the government's underground bunker complex in the Ramenky region
(near **M** Universitet) to Vnukovo-2 airport. Closed to the public, the line is said to be
still operational.

New N5 metro carriages from Moscow's Mytishchi railway factory have been
phased in. They are significantly quieter, smoother and safer, with automatic fire
quenchers and extensive use of fireproof material.

lovers of socialist realism is wandering around the vast grounds and checking out the likes of the Friendship Fountain with its dancing maidens, each representing a Soviet Republic. If you get sore feet, there's a bus (R30), and several bike and Segway rental outfits in among the many fast-food stalls that line the avenues.

Just outside the entrance to VDNKh and backed by the 100m titanium obelisk celebrating the Soviet Union's race to the stars is the **Museum of Cosmonauts Музей Космонавтики** (10am-7pm daily, R200), a must for those with any interest in the history of space travel. Its collection includes a space flight simulator (R200), original Soviet and American space suits, satellite models, photos and documents relating to Yuri Gagarin and other famous astronauts, a moon buggy and the stuffed bodies of the first two dogs in space – Belka and Strelka. A wall of fame shows who's who of Soviet (and later Russian) astronauts and there's a separate exhibition dedicated to women in space.

Nearby, at pr Mira 123b пр Мира 123б, stands the iconic 24.5m **Rabochiy i Kolkhoznitsa ('The Worker and the Kolkhoz Woman') Рабочий и Колхозница** sculpture, 'the ideal and symbol of the Soviet epoch', created from stainless steel by Vera Mukhina to crown the Soviet pavilion at the 1937 World Fair in Paris. The statue is a powerful example of socialist realist art, the two figures holding aloft a hammer and a sickle in a display of unity.

Park Pobedy Парк Победы   [see Map 1]

This park was designed to celebrate Russia's victory in the Great Patriotic War, with its great promenade surrounded by fountains and the centrepiece 142m obelisk covered with representations of images from the war – each 10cm represents a day of war).

Behind the obelisk lies the **Museum of the Great Patriotic War Музей Великой Отечественной Войны** (M Park Pobedy, 10am-7pm Tue-Sun closed last Thur of month, R100), its exhibits including evocative dioramas of every major WWII battle with excellent English captioning. The Hall of Glory commemorates Soviet war heroes and contains weaponry, photos and other war memorabilia.

At the eastern end of the park, the **Memorial synagogue Мемориальная Синагога**, at Poklonnaya Mountain, stands next to an Orthodox church and a mosque – part of the outdoor museum dedicated to the Great Patriotic War victory.

Vorobyovy Gory Воробьёвы Горы   [see Map 1]

For an all-encompassing panoramic view of the capital, head to Vorobyovy Gory (Sparrow Hills M Vorobyovy Gory), formerly known as Leninskiye Gory (Lenin Hills). From the Moscow State University site, Moscow stretches out before you; the view cannot be described as beautiful, but it certainly gives you an appreciation of the capital's size.

Moscow Москва

MAP 1

0   3km

See map 2

See map 4

Sheremetyevo Airport (Аэропорт Шереметьево)

Leningradskoye Shosse Ленинградское Шоссе

Pokrovsko-Streshnevo Park, Лесопарк Покровско-Стрешнево

Vodny Stadion

Voykovskaya

Sokol

Aeroport

Dinamo Stadium Стадион Динамо

Dinamo

Stadium of Young Pioneers Стадион Юных Пионеров

Petrovskaya Razumovskaya

Timiryazev Academy Park Парк Академии имени Тимирязева

Timiryazevskaya

Ul. Milashenkova

Ul. Butyrskaya Ул Бутырская

Dmitrovskaya

Savyolovsky Station Савёловский Вокзал

Savelovskaya

Mendeleyevskaya

Novoslobodskaya

Belorusskaya

Belorussky Station Белорусский Вокзал

Vladykino

Botanical Garden Ботанический Сад

Ul Botanicheskaya Ул Ботаническая

Ostankino TV Tower Останкинская телебашня

Ostankinsky Park

VDNKh

Ul B. Galushkina

Ul Ak. Koroleva Ул Ак. Королёва

Alexeyevskaya

Rizhskaya

Rizhsky Station Рижский Вокзал

Maryina Roshcha

Leningradsky Station Ленинградский Вокзал

Yaroslavsky Station Ярославский Вокзал

Kazansky Station Казанский Вокзал

Komsomolskaya

Krasnoselskaya

Baumanskaya

Kursky Station Курский Вокзал

Kurskaya

Svibovo

U/S Eizenshteina

Ul Vilgelma Pika Ул Вильгельма Пика

Losiny Ostrov Park Парк Лосиный Остров

Botanicheskaya

Sokolniki Park Парк Сокольники

Sokolniki

Preobrazhenskaya Pl.

Semyonovskaya

Elektrozavodskaya

Cherkizovskaya

Shchyolkovskoye Shosse Щёлковское Шоссе

Ulitsa Podbelskogo

Ulitsa

Pervomayskaya

Izmailovsky Park Измайловский Парк

Izmailovsky Park

Partizanskaya

Shosse Entuziastov Шоссе Энтузиастов

Aviamotornaya

Pl'lyicha

Rimskaya

Volgogradsky Pr

Novogireyevo

Perovo

Kuskovo Park Парк Кусково

Markistskaya Taganskaya

Proletarskaya

Krestyanskaya Zastava

Varsh

Paveletsky Station Павелецкий Вокзал

Novoslobodskaya

Barrikadnaya

Krasnopresnenskaya

Ulitsa 1905 Goda

Ul Krasnopresnenskaya

Begovaya

Ulitsa 1905 Goda

Studencheskaya

Kievskaya

Kievsky Station Киевский Вокзал

Kutuzovskaya

Fili

Pionerskaya

Filyovsky Park Филёвский Парк

Filyovsky Park

Ul Bol Filyovskaya

Kutuzovsky Pr.

Bagrationovskaya

Park Pobedy Парк Победы

Polyezhayevskaya

Oktyabrskoye Polye

Polye

Shchukinskaya

Rt Mira Пр Мира

Pr. Mira Пр. Мира

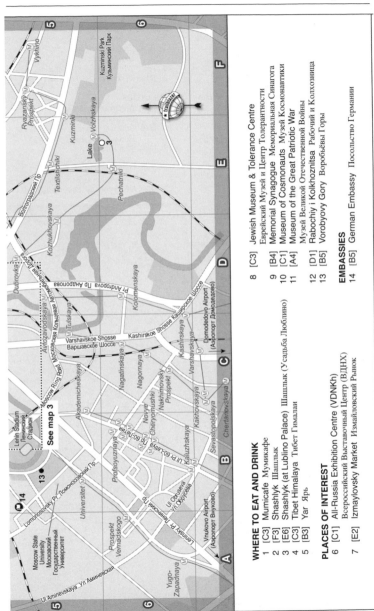

WHERE TO EAT AND DRINK

1 [C3] Mumicafe Мумикафе
2 [F3] Shashlyk Шашлык
3 [E6] Shashlyk (at Lublino Palace) Шашлык (Усадьба Люблино)
4 [C3] Tibet Himalaya Тибет Гималаи
5 [B3] Yar Ярь

PLACES OF INTEREST

6 [C1] All-Russia Exhibition Centre (VDNKh) Всероссийский Выставочный Центр (ВДНХ)
7 [E2] Izmaylovsky Market Измайловский Рынок
8 [C3] Jewish Museum & Tolerance Centre Еврейский Музей и Центр Толерантности
9 [B4] Memorial Synagogue Мемориальная Синагога
10 [C1] Museum of Cosmonauts Музей Космонавтики
11 [A4] Museum of the Great Patriotic War Музей Великой Отечественной Войны
12 [D1] Rabochiy i Kolkhoznitsa Рабочий и Колхозница
13 [B5] Vorobyov Gory Воробьёвы Горы

EMBASSIES

14 [B5] German Embassy Посольство Германии

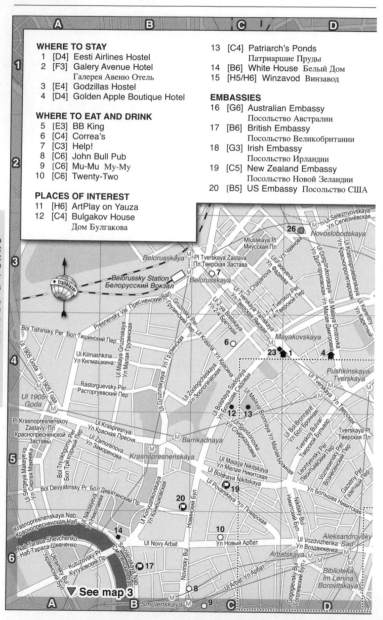

WHERE TO STAY
1   [D4]   Eesti Airlines Hostel
2   [F3]   Galery Avenue Hotel
            Галерея Авеню Отель
3   [E4]   Godzillas Hostel
4   [D4]   Golden Apple Boutique Hotel

WHERE TO EAT AND DRINK
5   [E3]   BB King
6   [C4]   Correa's
7   [C3]   Help!
8   [C6]   John Bull Pub
9   [C6]   Mu-Mu   My-My
10 [C6]   Twenty-Two

PLACES OF INTEREST
11 [H6]   ArtPlay on Yauza
12 [C4]   Bulgakov House
            Дом Булгакова
13 [C4]   Patriarch's Ponds
            Патриаршие Пруды
14 [B6]   White House Белый Дом
15 [H5/H6]   Winzavod Винзавод

EMBASSIES
16 [G6]   Australian Embassy
            Посольство Австралии
17 [B6]   British Embassy
            Посольство Великобритании
18 [G3]   Irish Embassy
            Посольство Ирландии
19 [C5]   New Zealand Embassy
            Посольство Новой Зеландии
20 [B5]   US Embassy Посольство США

▼ See map 3

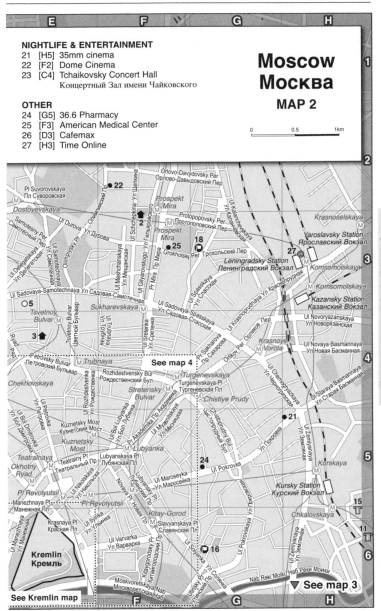

NIGHTLIFE & ENTERTAINMENT
21 [H5] 35mm cinema
22 [F2] Dome Cinema
23 [C4] Tchaikovsky Concert Hall
        Концертный Зал имени Чайковского

OTHER
24 [G5] 36.6 Pharmacy
25 [F3] American Medical Center
26 [D3] Cafemax
27 [H3] Time Online

Moscow
Москва

MAP 2

0   0.5   1km

CITY GUIDES & PLANS

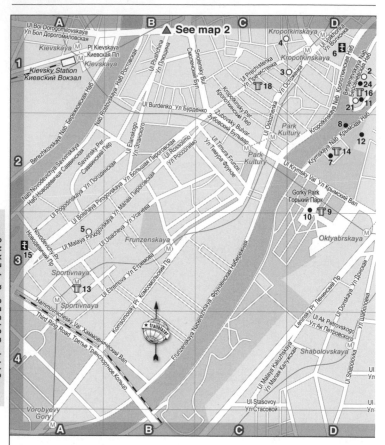

WHERE TO STAY

1 [F3] Ibis Paveletskaya
Ибис Павелецкая

WHERE TO EAT AND DRINK

2 [D1] Bar Strelka
3 [D1] Genatsvale Генацвале
4 [C1] Gogol Mogol Гоголь-Моголь
5 [A3] Stolle Штолле

PLACES OF INTEREST

6 [D1] Cathedral of Christ the Saviour
Храм Христа Спасителя

7 [D2] Central House of Artists
Центральный Дом Художника

8 [D2] Controversial nautical sculpture
(Sculpture of Peter the Great)
Скульптура Петра Великого

9 [D2/D3] Garage (Centre for
Contemporary Culture) Гараж

10 [D2] Gorky Park Парк Горького

11 [D1] Lumiere Brothers Photography
Centre Центр Фотографии им
Братьев Люмьер

12 [D2] Muzeon Park Парк Музеон

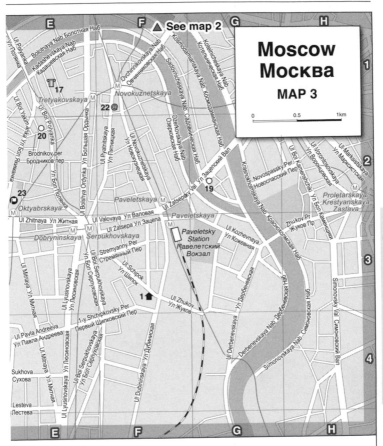

Moscow
Москва

MAP 3

0   0.5   1km

PLACES OF INTEREST (continued)
13 [A3] Moscow Metro Museum
         Музей Московского
         Метрополитена
14 [D2] New Tretyakov Gallery
         Новая Третьяковская Галерея
15 [A3] Novodevichy Convent
         Новодевичий Монастырь
16 [D1] Red October Красный Октябрь
17 [E1] Tretyakov Gallery
         Третьяковская Галерея
18 [C1] Tsereteli Gallery Галерея
         Искусств Зураба Церетели

NIGHTLIFE & ENTERTAINMENT
19 [G2] City Space
20 [E2] Garage Гараж
21 [D1] Gypsy

OTHER
22 [F1] Cafemax
23 [E2] French Embassy
         Французское Посольство
24 [D1] Russkaya Ulitsa Русская Улица

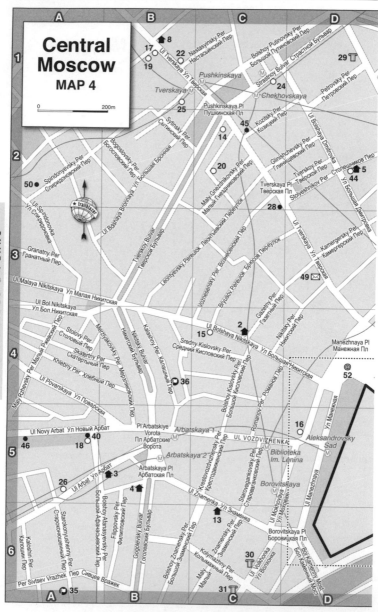

Central Moscow
MAP 4

0 _____ 200m

★ trailblazer

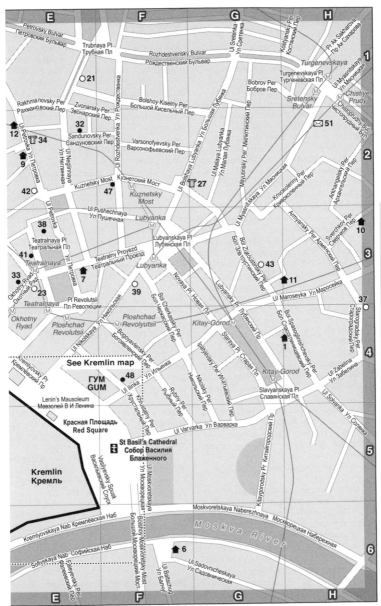

PRACTICAL INFORMATION
Arriving in Moscow

By air Moscow has five – count 'em! – airports, three of which handle international flights and are served by handy Aeroexpress (🖳 www.aeroexpress.ru; one-way/return R340/640 to any of the three airports) trains. If arriving out of hours, or if you have a lot of luggage, advance taxi bookings mean that you can get to Moscow city centre for a flat fee of around R1500-2000 from any of the three airports.

The largest and most commonly used international airport is **Domodedovo** Домодедово (DME, 🖳 www.domodedovo.ru), a rather chaotic facility 48km south of Moscow. Aeroexpress trains (2/hr, 6am-midnight) take 45 minutes to get to Paveletsky railway station (Map 1) and the adjacent **M** Paveletskaya.

Sheremetyevo 2 Шереметьево (SVO; 🖳 svo.aero), 30km north-west of the city centre, is the other main international airport. **Sheremetyevo 1**, across the runway from Sheremetyevo 2 and connected to it by free shuttle bus, receives some domestic flights as well as flights from Belarus, the Baltic states, and northern Europe. Aeroexpress trains (2/hr, 5.30am-12.30am) run to Belorussky station, right next to **M** Belorusskaya, in just 35 minutes.

Compact **Vnukovo Внуково** (VKO; 🖳 www.vnukovo.ru), 30km south-west of the city centre, receives numerous domestic flights, flights from Kaliningrad, the Caucasus and Moldova, as well as Transaero flights from many Western European cities such as Istanbul, Paris, London and Barcelona. Aeroexpress trains run hourly between 5.30am and 12.30am to Kievsky station (**M** Kievskaya), taking 35 minutes.

By train Moscow has eight main railway stations (*vokzal*; see Map 1 and p203), all of which are located in the city centre and with handy connections to the metro.

If you're arriving from Europe, you'll end up at either Kievsky, Belorussky or Rizhsky station; at Leningradsky station if you're coming from St Petersburg, or at either Yaroslavsky or Kazansky if you're coming from the east or the south.

Local transport

Metro The vast metro (🖳 www.mosmetro.ru) system (**see map p530**), some of its old, palatial stations a tourist attraction in themselves, is the most efficient way to travel around Moscow. The metro uses magnetic cards available in denominations of 1, 2, 5, 11 and 20 rides; it's worth buying a multiple-ride ticket to avoid queuing and to save a few roubles on the multi-ride cards. A single ride to anywhere on the system costs R30, while a 24-hour smartcard costs R200. Buy tickets inside the metro station building at windows marked касса or from ticket machines.

In 2013 a new type of ticket was introduced that allows you to ride any form of public transport for 90 minutes (with changeovers; R50 for a single); these are available as multiple-ride tickets as well.

The metro runs daily 6am-1am. During peak hours, trains arrive every one or two minutes and you're unlikely to wait more than five minutes even at midnight. Despite this peak-hour trains are *very* crowded. Metro stations are marked with **large red 'M' signs outside** and the stations' names are displayed in both Russian and English inside.

Useful Cyrillic signs to recognise are вход (entrance), выход (exit), переход (crossover between stations) and выход в город (way out or exit to street level).

Boat Boats are not considered to be public transport, strictly speaking, but a ride up the Moskva river is a great way to see the Kremlin and central Moscow.

Boats operated by the **Capital Shipping Company Столичная Судоходная Компания** (🖳 www.cck-ship.ru, 1½hrs; R450pp) stop at boat landings between Kievsky vokzal and Novospassky Most – the main route. The in-between stops include Vorobyovy Gory, Frunzenskaya, Gorky Park, Krymsky Most, Kamenny Most (opposite the Kremlin) and Ustinsky Most (by the Red Square).

Buses, trams and trolleybuses All of these function under the same ticketing

WHERE TO STAY
1 [H4] Apple Hostel
2 [C4] Assambleya Nikitskaya
        Ассамблея Никитская
3 [B5] Da! Hostel Да! Хостел
4 [B5] HM Hostel
5 [D2] Hotel Akvarel
        Гостиница Акварель
6 [F6] Hotel Baltschug-Kempinski
        Гостиница Балчуг-Кемпинскии
7 [E3] Hotel Metropol
        Гостиница Метрополь
8 [B1] Intercontinental Moscow
        Tverskaya Hotel
9 [E2] Marriott Moscow Royal Aurora
        Hotel
        Марриотт Москва Аврора
10 [H3] Mini-hotel Sverchkov 8
        Мини-Отель Сверчков 8
11 [H3] Napoleon Hostel
        Хостел Наполеон
12 [E2] Petrovka Loft Петровка Лофт
13 [C6] Z Hostel

WHERE TO EAT AND DRINK
14 [C2] Café Pushkin Кафе Пушкин
15 [C4] Coffeemania Кофемания
16 [D5] Eat & Talk
17 [B1] Filimonova & Yankel
        Филимонова & Янкель
18 [A5] Genatsvale Генацвале
19 [B1] Goodman Steak House
20 [C2] Hachapuri Хачапури
21 [E1] Kadril s Omarom
        Кадриль с Омаром
22 [B1] Pelman Пелмэн
23 [E3] Strana Kotoroi Net
        Страна Которой Нет
24 [C1] Venezia Венеция
25 [B1] VinoSyr ВиноСыр
26 [A5] Yolki-Palki Ёлки-Палки

PLACES OF INTEREST
27 [G2] KGB Museum Музей КГБ
28 [C2] Moscow Drama Theatre
        Московский Драматический
        Театр
29 [D1] Moscow Museum of Modern
        Art (MMOMA)
        Московский Музей
        Современного
        Искусства (ММОМА)

30 [C6] Museum of Private
        Collections
        Отдел Личных Коллекций
31 [C6] Pushkin Museum of Fine Arts
        Музей Изобразительных
        Искусств имени А С Пушкина
32 [E2] Sandunovskiye Baths
        Сандуновские Бани
33 [E3] State Duma House
        Государственная Дума
34 [E2] State Gulag History Museum
        Государственный Музей
        Истории ГУЛАГа

EMBASSIES
35 [A6] Canadian Embassy
        Канадское Посольство
36 [B4] Netherlands Embassy
        Посольство Нидерландов

NIGHTLIFE & ENTERTAINMENT
37 [H4] Art Garbage Запасник
38 [E3] Bolshoi Theatre & Bolshoi
        New Stage Большой Театр и
        Новая Сцена Большого Театра
39 [F3] Club Che Клуб Че
40 [A5] Helikon Opera Хеликон-опера
41 [E3] Molodejny Theatre
        Молодёжный Театр
42 [E2] My Bar
43 [G3] Propaganda Пропаганда
44 [D2] Simachev Shop & Bar
        Симачёв Бар & Бутик

SHOPPING
45 [C2] Yeliseyev Grocery Store
        Елисеевский магазин

OTHER
46 [A5] 36.6 Pharmacy
47 [F2] 36.6 Pharmacy
48 [F4] Capital Tours
49 [D3] Central Post Office
        Центральная Почта
50 [A2] European Medical Centre
        Европейский Медицинский
        Центр
51 [H2] Post office (main)
        Московский Главпочтамт
52 [D4] Time Online (Manezh
        Shopping Complex) Time
        Online (Манежная Площадь)

CITY GUIDES & PLANS

system. Services are comprehensive but can be overcrowded.

Tickets (R28) are sold by the driver or conductor and these services can be useful for some cross-town routes that are too circuitous by metro.

For information on the various routes see 🖳 www.mosgortrans.ru/en or 2Gis (see box p63).

Taxis The best way to get a taxi is to order one by phone or online.

Recommended taxi companies include **Welcome Taxi** (🖳 www.welcometaxi.ru) that you can only book online but they can provide English-speaking drivers, and **Taxi Martex** (☎ 739-52 25, 🖳 www.zz.ru).

Orientation and services

At the very centre of the city are the Kremlin, Red Square and St Basil's Cathedral. Moscow is not unlike a spider's web, with main roads branching out from the centre and consecutive circles of ring roads. The most conveniently placed (and generally more expensive) accommodation options are in this area.

The **Kremlin** (see pp174-7) in its original conception and the attached ceremonial square have been the heart of the city since the 12th century and comprise Moscow's most iconic sights.

Kitay-Gorod Китай-Город, while translated as 'Chinatown', is actually a reference to the palisades that supported the earthen ramparts surrounding the original Kremlin, from the word 'kita'. Ul Nikolskaya and ul Varvarka are the principal streets of the district, one of the city's oldest.

Zamoskvorechiye Замоскворечье, the neighbourhood 'beyond the Moskva river' inside the big river loop, opposite the Kremlin, features some of Moscow's most exciting art.

Khamovniki Хамовники is another art-rich district; it is surrounded on three sides by the Moskva river and is centred on two streets – ul Prechistenka and ul Ostozhenka – lined with historical mansions.

Presnya Пресня is the administrative heart of the city, featuring some of

Moscow's oldest neighbourhoods and its most famous street **ul Arbat ул Арбат** (see pp180-1).

Tverskoy district Тверской район is a trendy area which centres around the busy ul Tverskaya – a mixture of historic architecture and modern businesses. The side streets around it are dotted with fashionable eateries.

Ostankinsky district Останкинский район, immediately north of the city centre, features some of the best examples of Stalinist architecture and socialist realist art in Moscow, as well as the Ostankino TV tower (Map 1).

Ramenki district Раменки район lies south-west of the city centre and encompasses vast park areas as well as Moscow University.

Money Banks and **ATMs** are found along all main streets in the Moscow city centre.

US dollars, euros and pounds sterling can be exchanged at almost any bank or currency exchange; **currency exchanges** tend to change at least a dozen major currencies at competitive rates. Credit cards, Visa and MasterCard in particular, are widely accepted.

❏ STREET TERMINOLOGY

bulvar (bul)	boulevard
бульвар (бул)	
gostinny dvor	shopping
гостинный двор	arcade
most	bridge
мост	
naberezhnaya (nab)	embankment
набережная (наб)	
ploshchad (pl)	square
площадь (пл)	
prospekt (pr)	avenue
проспект (пр)	
pereulok (per)	lane/side street
переулок (пер)	
shosse	highway
шоссе	
ulitsa (ul)	street
улица (ул)	

Embassies Australian Map 2, Podkolokolny per 10A/2, **M** Kitay-Gorod, (☎ 495 956 6070, 🖳 www.russia.embassy .gov.au); **British** Map 2, Smolenskaya nab 10, **M** Smolenskaya (☎ 495 956 7200, 🖳 www.gov.uk/government/world/russia); **Canadian** Map 4, Starokonyushenny per 23, **M** Smolenskaya (☎ 495 956 6000, 🖳 www.russia.gc.ca); **French** Map 3, ul Bolshaya Yakimanka 35, **M** Oktyabyrskaya (☎ 495 937 1500, 🖳 www.ambafrance-ru .org); **German** Map 1; ul Mosfilmovskaya 56, **M** Universitet (☎ 495 937 9500, 🖳 www.germania.diplo.de); **Irish** Map 2, Grokholsky per 5, **M** Prospekt Mira (☎ 495 937 5900, 🖳 www.embassyofireland.ru); **Netherlands** Map 4, Kalashny per 6, **M** Arbatskaya (☎ 495 797 2900, 🖳 rusland.nl ambassade.org); **New Zealand** Map 2, ul Povarskaya 44, **M** Barrikadnaya (☎ 495 956 3579, 🖳 www.nzembassy.com/russia); **US** Map 2, Novinsky bul 19/23, **M** Smolenskaya (☎ 495 728 5000, 🖳 moscow .usembassy.gov).

Local publications English-language publications include *The Moscow Times* (🖳 www.themoscowtimes.com), whose week-end edition has good listings and travel sections, while *The Moscow News* (🖳 www .moscownews.ru) covers domestic and international politics.

Fun and foul-mouthed, *The eXile* (🖳 www.exile.ru) discards political correctness but is worth it for the ruthlessly honest listings. *element* (🖳 www.elementmoscow.ru) is a weekly featuring restaurant reviews and concert listings and art exhibits.

Finally, *In Your Pocket* guides (🖳 www .inyourpocket.com) update the *Moscow In Your Pocket* listings guide several times a year; the website features them all, plus up-to-date concert listings.

Medical The **European Medical Centre** **Европейский Медицинский Центр** (Map 4; Spiridonyevsky per 5/1, **M** Pushkinskaya, ☎ 495 933 6655, 🖳 www .emcmos.ru) offers 24-hour medical and dental services.

The **American Medical Center** **Американский Медицинский Центр** (Map 2; Grokholsky per 1 (**M** Prospekt Mira, ☎ 495 933 7700, 🖳 www.amcen ter.ru) also offers 24-hour emergency medical and dental services and has an on-site pharmacy with English-speaking staff.

Pharmacies are easy to come by: **36.6** is a good, reliable chain that's open 24 hours. Branches are located at ul Novy Arbat 15 (Map 4), **M** Arbatskaya; Kuznetsky Most 18/7 (Map 4), **M** Kuznetsky Most; and ul Pokrovka 1/13 (Map 2), **M** Kitay-Gorod/Lubyanka.

Russian visas At the time of writing, tourist visas had to be registered within seven days of staying in one city.

If heading west, bear in mind that many trains from Russia into Eastern Europe cross the border after midnight, so make sure your visa is still valid (see Russian visas, pp24-6).

Telecommunications The **main post office** Московский Главпочтамт (Map 4; ul Myasnitskaya 26, **M** Chistye Prudy) and the **Central Post Office** **Центральная Почта** (Map 4; ul Tverskaya 7, **M** Tverskaya) are both good places for all your postal needs. Rates are listed in English and there are some

CITY GUIDES & PLANS

❏ **Calling a Moscow phone**
Moscow has two **area codes**: ☎ 495 and 499. From outside Russia dial ☎ +7-495 or 499. Within the 495 area code, you dial the seven digits but not the area code itself. Within the 499 area code, you dial the code as well as the seven-digit number. To call between the two, dial 8 + the respective area code and seven-digit number.

The codes for **mobile phone numbers** begin with either 915, 916, or 926. Toll-**free numbers** begin with 800.

English-speaking staff. They also sell discount phonecards – their own Tsentel as well as rival brands – which offer much cheaper international calls from domestic or hotel telephones. For information on purchasing local SIM cards and making local and long-distance calls see pp67-8.

Most hotels and hostels cater to travellers, the vast majority of whom carry wi-fi enabled devices, by providing free or inexpensive **wi-fi**. Otherwise, there are a few **internet cafés** left, including Cafemax (Map 3, 24 hours; ul Pyatnintskaya 25/1, **M** Novokuznetskaya; also Map 2 ul Novoslobodskaya 3 **M** Novoslobodskaya). Time Online (Map 4; on the bottom level of the Manezh underground shopping complex, **M** Okhotny Ryad, and also at pl Komsomolskaya 3, Map 2, **M** Komsomolskaya) is also open 24 hours and has English-speaking staff.

Tours **Capital Tours** (Map 4; ul Ilyinka 4, entrance 6, office 21, **M** Kitay-Gorod, ☎ 495 232 2442, 🖳 www.capitaltours.ru) offer a walking tour of the Kremlin, a Moscow Metro/Secret Bunker tour, and 'Moscow All Around' – a bus tour that takes in the city's main sights. The bus doesn't run frequently enough to be a hop-on, hop-off bus, but it does give you around 20 minutes at each site to take photos.

Patriarshy Dom Tours (☎ 495 795 0927, 🖳 www.toursinrussia.com, 9am-6pm Mon-Fri) run highly rated English-language excursions – both obvious ones, such as tours of the Kremlin, and more specialised ones, such as Jewish Moscow and tours around famous literary neighbourhoods. Prices (US$12-80 per person) depend on the tour. It's worth enquiring about the KGB tour that they occasionally offer; this includes demonstrations of miniature cameras, micro-dots, bugging techniques and more at the Federal Counterintelligence Service (KGB) Museum, plus a great deal of whitewash about the darker side of the KGB's history. You cannot visit this museum except on a tour.

Moscow Mania (☎ 903 713 0583, 🖳 www.mosmania.com) is a team of young, energetic guides with a thorough knowledge of Moscow history who do all manner of themed walks, from classic Red Square/Kremlin jaunts to themed Soviet tours and 'Moscow mysteries' tours which titillate visitors with the more salacious tidbits from the city's history. Walking tours cost from around R450 per person.

Useful websites

● 🖳 **www.inyourpocket.com/russia/ Moscow** Extensive independent reviews of accommodation, clubs and restaurants, as well as a plethora of practical advice.

● 🖳 **www.redtape.ru** Expat forum where you can find answers to almost any question about the country.

● 🖳 **www.maps-moscow.com** Moscow Architecture Preservation Society focuses on historical buildings under threat in the capital.

● 🖳 **www.elementmoscow.ru** Weekly restaurant reviews, art exhibitions and concert listings.

● 🖳 **www.themoscowtimes.com** Russian and international news, entertainment and sports are featured in this excellent English-language daily.

Where to stay

All prices given below are for high season and include 18% VAT where applicable. In upmarket hotels you may be quoted a price without tax so it's worth checking.

Note that some places set their prices in US dollars or euros and then charge in roubles according to that day's rate or a rate set by the hostel or hotel.

Budget accommodation Moscow has numerous hostels, with more and more opening each year. They have English-speaking staff and facilities to satisfy most budget travellers.

In a historical building that's a stone's throw from the Kremlin, **Z Hostel** (Map 4; ul Znamenka 15, apt 16, ул Знаменка 15, кв 16, **M** Arbatskaya or Borovitskaya, ☎ 495 691 9844, 🖳 www.z-hostel.ru, dorm/dbl/trpl R690/2900/2400, WI-FI) gets Brownie points for its friendly, helpful staff and excellent location; there's also a cosy guest lounge for mingling.

Very well located in the historic Kitay-Gorod area, *Apple Hostel* (Map 4; Bolshoy Spasoglinishevsky per 6/1, Большой Спасоглинишевский пер 6/1, **M** Kitay-Gorod, ☎ 916 335 5333, 🖥 apple hostel.ru, dorm R600-700, WI-FI) is all green apple-themed décor and has the vibe of a student residence. There are computers in every room and the staff are wonderful.

Accommodating a mix of Russians and foreign backpackers, the large *Da! Hostel* Да! Хостел (Map 4; ul Arbat 11, ул Арбат 11, **M** Arbatskaya, ☎ 495 212 9383, 🖥 da-hostel.ru, dorm/trpl 690-850/2900, WI-FI) has a mixed ambiance, very bright wallpaper and a spacious guest lounge. There are two female-only dorms and the location is an absolute winner.

A great location in the historic heart of Moscow, lovely staff and an intimate feel are the key features of *HM Hostel* (Map 4; Gogolevsky bulvar 33/1, 4th floor, apt 14, Гоголевский бул 33/1, 4-й этаж, кв 14, **M** Arbatskaya, ☎ 495 778 8501, 🖥 www.hos tel-moscow.com, dorm R799-1199, WI-FI). There are only three individually decorated, spacious rooms, with options to stay in a same-sex dorm, a guest kitchen and decent bathrooms.

British-run ★ *Godzillas Hostel* (Map 2; Bolshoi Karetny per 6 apt 5 1st floor, Большой Каретный пер 6 1-й этаж кв 5, **M** Tsetnoy Bulvar, ☎ 495 699 4223, 🖥 godzillashostel.com, dorm/dbl/trpl US$16-32/75/105, WI-FI) is a large, lively hostel in a short distance from the centre in a quiet area. Perks include properly comfortable beds and bunks, human-sized towels, staff who actually know the city, two kitchens and free maps of the city. They also organise tours and book train tickets.

Napoleon Hostel Хостел Наполеон (Map 4; Maly Zlatoustinskiy per 2, 4th floor 6 Малый Златоустинский пер 2, 4-й этаж, **M** Kitay-Gorod, ☎ 495 628 6695, 🖥 www.napoleonhostel.com, dorms R549-799, WI-FI) is in a superb location only a

few minutes' walk from Red Square. It's a popular backpacker haunt with large bunk beds, a custom-built ventilation system, a female-only dorm and helpful staff. The comfy lounge has a plasma TV and there is a nightly happy hour at the on-site small bar. Two bathrooms for 47 guests, though, and rooms could be cleaner. Take the Maroseyka exit from **M** Kitay-Gorod.

On one of Moscow's most popular streets, *Eesti Airlines Hostel* (Map 2; ul Tverskaya 27/2 apt 83, ул Тверская 27/2 кв 83, **M** Tverskaya, ☎ 495 646 0005, 🖥 www.hostels.com – doesn't have own web-site, dorm/dbl R700/2000, WI-FI) is a compact hostel in a converted apartment. It does not have a common room, so all socialising is done in the dorms or in the small kitchen, but all rooms have air-con, which you'll appreciate in the summer. To reach the hostel, walk through the archway just before the blue Pepsi shop and take the first entrance on the left.

Homestays are possible from about R1500 per day. Contact Host Families Association (HOFA; see p161).

Mid-range accommodation *Petrovka Loft* Петровка Лофт (Map 4; ul Petrovka 17/2, ул Петровка 17/2, **M** Chekhovskaya, ☎ 495 626 2210, 🖥 petrovkalofthotel moscow.com, dbl from R3700, WI-FI), a few minutes' walk from the main attractions, is just that: a former communal apartment in a loft, divided into 10 attractive rooms with crisp white linens and exposed brick features. The rooms share bathrooms, but there's a good bathroom-to-guest ratio.

Galery Avenue Hotel Галерея Авеню Отель (Map 2; ul Shchepkina 32/1, ул Щепкина 32/1, **M** Prospekt Mira, ☎ 495 510 6737, 🖥 www.hotelgalery.ru, sgl/dbl R3900/6900, WI-FI) is an appealing boutique hotel, its rooms simple and stylish, with crimson accents. The décor is classical with Renaissance touches and a good buffet breakfast is included.

CITY GUIDES & PLANS

❏ **Abbreviations**

★ = Author's favourite; **sgl** = single; **dbl** = double; **twn** = twin; **trpl** = triple; **lux** = luxury room; **apt** = apartment; **pp** = per person; **[V]** = vegetarian.

The small, friendly *Hotel Akvarel* **Гостиница Акварель** (Map 4; Stoleshnikov per 12/3, Столешников пер 12/3, **M** Teatralnaya, ☎ 495 502 9430, ⌨ hotelakvarel.ru, sgl/dbl/suite R9250/11,000/14,350, WI-FI), located in a discreet courtyard, distinguishes itself by its excellent service and its rooms, where the beds are separated from the main room by an alcove, giving them a touch of personality. The décor features watercolours – a nod to the hotel's name; all rooms are non-smoking.

The beautiful boutique *Assambleya Nikitskaya* **Ассамблея Никитская** (Map 4; ul Bolshaya Nikitskaya 12/2, ул Большая Никитская 12/2, **M** Okhotny Ryad, ☎ 495 933 5001, ⌨ www.assambleya-hotels.ru, sgl/dbl/suite R9300/11,300/R15,300, WI-FI) should be particularly commended for its comfortable though small rooms, its excellent location and nice touches such as heated floors in the bathrooms. Order breakfast to your room if you don't want to fight for space in the small dining area.

A typically efficient representative of the Ibis chain, *Ibis Paveletskaya* **Ибис Павелецкая** (Map 3; ul Shchipok 22/1, ул Щипок 22/1, **M** Paveletskaya, ☎ 495 661 8500, ⌨ www.ibis.com, dbl from R3500, WI-FI), housed in a new building, features bright, fully equipped rooms, with the ones facing north being particularly spacious. Convenient for coming or going from Domodedovo airport. Breakfast costs extra. Disabled travellers welcome.

A 19th-century building down a quiet central street houses the characterful *Mini-hotel Sverchkov 8* **Мини-Отель Сверчков 8** (Map 4; Sverchkov per 8, Сверчков пер 8, **M** Chistye Prudy, ☎ 495 625 4978, ⌨ www.sverchkov-8.ru, sgl/dbl/half-luxe R5000/6000/8500, WI-FI), an appealing 11-room hotel. The rooms are homey and comfortable and the staff are extremely helpful.

Upmarket hotels These prices include 18% VAT, but it's always worth checking when you're quoted a price.

Marriott Moscow Royal Aurora Hotel **Марриотт Москва Аврора** (Map 4; ul Petrovka 11/20, ул Петровка 11/20, **M** Kuznetsky Most, ☎ 495 937 1000, ⌨ www.marriott.com, dbl/suite from R7600/35,000, WI-FI) is a bastion of refinement. Expect classically styled rooms, enormous, luxurious beds, marble bathrooms, well-trained butlers catering to your every need and white-gloved waiters serving you at the Polo Club Steakhouse, reminiscent of a British gentlemen's club.

In contrast, *Golden Apple Boutique Hotel* (Map 2; ul Malaya Dmitrovka 11, ул Малая Дмитровка 11, **M** Tverskaya, ☎ 495 980 7000, ⌨ www.goldenapple.ru, dbl/suite from R24,000/40,000, WI-FI) combines luxurious minimalism and quirky avant-garde features. Rooms are stylishly decorated with marble, stone and natural wood, the Apple Restaurant boasts skillfully prepared international dishes and, faithful to the hotel name, there are enough apples around to tempt any number of Eves – including the giant golden apple that you can sit in, in the lobby. Its central location is its main draw but the service is sometimes disorganised. Substantial online discounts available.

Centrally located on one of the best streets for eating out, *Intercontinental Moscow Tverskaya Hotel* (Map 4; ul Tverskaya 22, ул Тверская 22, **M** Tverskaya, ☎ 495 787 8887, ⌨ www.ihg.com, dbl/suite from R6300/24,500, WI-FI) is a large, contemporary hotel with sleek, modern rooms decorated in creams and browns, great views of Moscow from the balconies of the suites, and ultra-professional staff. The icing on the cake is the luxurious spa, and an excellent restaurant serving contemporary Russian cuisine.

As much an historic monument as a place to stay, it was at *Hotel Metropol* **Гостиница Метрополь** (Map 4; Teatralny proezd 2, Театральный проезд 2, **M** Teatralnaya, ☎ 499 501 7800, ⌨ www.metropol-moscow.ru, dbl/suite from R7500/22,500, WI-FI), close to Red Square, where Rasputin is said to have dined and Lenin to have made several speeches. Its beautiful Art Nouveau interior has remained unchanged since the 1917 revolution and it also featured in the film *Dr Zhivago*.

Besides the princely rooms, there is a sumptuous banquet hall, a large indoor swimming pool, and helpful staff to fuss over you.

It's difficult to get any closer to the Kremlin than in the *Hotel Baltschug Kempinski* **Гостиница Балчуг-Кемпинский** (Map 4; ul Baltschug 1, ул Балчуг 1, **M** Novokuznetskaya, ☎ 495 287 2000, ⌨ www.kempinski.com/ru/moscow, dbl/suite from R14,000/28,440, WI-FI). The service is impeccable and the riverside location affords superb views of the Kremlin. The facilities include marble bathtubs in the most incredible of bathrooms, and satellite telephones. Some of the rooms have even been designed by minor members of the British royal family.

On-site eating options include the highly recommended Baltchug and the Japanese restaurant Shogun. High-profile guests have included Helmut Kohl, Tina Turner and Sting.

Where to eat and drink

You can find just about anything you want to eat in Moscow and it is an immensely rewarding city for a diner with means.

Your budget will stretch furthest if you take advantage of the weekday 'business lunch' deals that numerous restaurants offer.

Ul Arbat (Map 4 and see pp180-1) is lined with restaurants largely aimed at tourists, so accordingly prices can be quite high. Other streets (see Map 4) with a fair number of reasonable eateries are **Myasnitskaya**, starting from **M** Lyubyanka, ul Tverskaya (**M** Tverskaya, see also Map 2) and **Maroseyka** (**M** Kitay-Gorod).

Cafés Wonderfully homey décor adds to the appeal of ★ *Mumicafe* **Мумикафе** (Map 1; ul Novoslobodskaya 46, ул Новослободская 46, **M** Chistye Prudy, ⌨ mumicafe.ru) where you can happily linger for hours over a *smorrebrod* (Danish sandwich), a plate of mini-tapas or papardelle with chanterelles, or just a coffee. It has a particular appeal to fans of the Moomins.

Gogol Mogol **Гоголь-Моголь** (Map 3; Gagarinsky per 6, Гагаринский пер 6, **M** Kropotkinskaya, ⌨ www.gogol-mogol.ru, [V]) is an attractive little café with a red silk interior, great coffee and a most tempting array of homemade desserts; try the *kasata* or the *alalia*. More substantial bites are also available.

Stolle **Штолле** (Map 3; ul Malaya Pirogovskaya 16, ул Малая Пироговская 16, **M** Sportivnaya, ⌨ msk.stolle.ru, [V]) serves pies and more pies – meat pies, fish pies and berry pies – and it executes them beyond reproach. Salads, soups and the likes of chicken Kiev play a supporting role.

Mu-Mu **Му-Му** (Map 2; ul Arbat 45/24, ул Арбат 45/24, **M** Smolenskaya, ⌨ www.cafémumu.ru, mains from R90, [V]) appeals to locals and visitors alike. Grab a tray and shuffle past the counters displaying an array of salads, soups, meat and fish dishes and desserts, pointing at what you want. Look for the gormless black-and-white plastic cow outside. There are 35 branches around the capital.

More kitschy than Mu-Mu, the *Yolki-Palki* **Ёлки-Палки** (Map 4; ul Arbat 16/2, ул Арбат 16/2, **M** Arbatskaya, ⌨ www.elki-palki.ru, mains from R250, [V]) rustic-style theme chain restaurant features an all-you-can-eat buffet and a wide selection of main courses and drinks. The name roughly translates as 'bleedin' 'ell!' Over a dozen locations.

★ *Correa's* (Map 2; Dukat Place II, ul Gasheka 7, Дукат Плейс II, ул Гашека 7, **M** Tverskaya, ⌨ www.correas.ru, mains from 250, [V]) dispels stereotypes of 'typical Russian' food by offering you some of the best light bites in town. Come here for perfectly poached eggs with spinach, bagels with smoked salmon, omelettes with fresh avocado and tomato salsa, fresh juices and more. Eight other locations around town.

In summer, some of the best *shashlyk* **шашлык** in the city is found in **Izmailovsky Park, Измайловский Парк** (Map 1; **M** Izmailovsky Park) though some people have been told one price upon ordering and a different price at the end. For even better shashlyk, look for the gazebo

CITY GUIDES & PLANS

run by the friendly Armenians at Lublino Palace Усадьба Люблино (Map 1).

On the west side of the Kremlin, *Eat & Talk* (Map 4; ul Mokhovaya 7, ул Моховая 7, **M** Aleksandrovsky Sad, 🖥 www.eat talk.ru, mains R300-780, [V], WI-FI) is perfect for just that. It's not the easiest place to find, being inside a nondescript building, but once you do, you can partake of their selection of coffees, smoothies, salads, pastas and more while simultaneously checking your email. They are open around the clock and even rent laptops by the hour!

Restaurants One of the hottest tables in town, ★ *Twenty-Two* (Map 2; ul Novy Arbat 22, ул Новый Арбат 22, **M** Arbatskaya, ☎ 495 776 8622, 🖥 twenty two22.ru, mains from R550, [V]), with its pan-Asian and European fusion cuisine, is the flagship restaurant of chef-on-the-rise Timur Abuzyarov. There's an open kitchen, a warm, stylish interior and immaculately presented dishes that don't fail to surprise. Reserve ahead.

Venerable *Genatsvale* Генацвале (Map 3; ul Ostozhenka 12/1, ул Остоженка 12/1, **M** Kropotkinskaya, 🖥 www.restoran-genatsvale.ru, mains from R500, [V]) serves wonderfully flavourful Georgian dishes in a refined setting. Don't miss the *satsivi* (chicken with walnut sauce), the ultra-cheesy khachapuri, the exquisite grilled meats, the *lobio* (bean paste with herbs), or the more adventurous *kuchmachi* (sizzling chicken giblet dish).

There's a more kitschy branch (Genatsvale na Arbate Генацвале На Арбате; Map 4) on ul Stary Arbat.

With its light interior and minimalist décor, *Hachapuri* Хачапури (Map 4; Bolshoy Gnezdnikovsky per 12, Большой Грездниковский пер 12, **M** Tverskaya, 🖥 www.hacha.ru, mains R380-790; [V]) offers a good selection of Georgian favourites, including nine types of the eponymous khachapuri, pork buvaki in sweet *tkemali* (plum) sauce, chicken *chakhokhbili* (slow-cooked chicken with vegetables) and aubergine stuffed with garlicky walnuts.

Goodman Steak House (Map 4; ul Tverskaya 23, ул Тверская 23, **M** Tverskaya, 🖥 www.goodman.ru, steaks R1780-2900) is particularly popular with the local business set. Chic interior, great service and expertly grilled steaks make this a good lunch or dinner spot. The business lunch (from R470) is a good deal.

In the same building as Goodman, *Filimonova & Yankel* Филимонова & Янкель (Map 4, ul Tverskaya 23, ул Тверская 23, **M** Tverskaya, 🖥 www.fish house.ru, mains R460-1750) is a busy spot specialising in excellent fish and seafood dishes. It's difficult to go wrong with the grilled dorado or Norwegian mussels, Provençale style. If you order the wine, watch your wallet.

For great Italian food, head to *Venezia* Венеция (Map 4; Strastnoy bul 4/3, bldg 3, Страстной бул 4/3, стр 3, **M** Tverskaya, 🖥 www.trattoria-venezia.ru, mains from R350, [V]), the cosiest branch of the four. Choose from the likes of black risotto with sepia ink, pizza di buffala, Milanese-style leg of veal and tiramisu, washed down with a wide range of Italian wines.

Worth going out of your way for, expat favourite *Tibet Himalaya* Тибет Гималаи (Map 1; Prospekt Mira 79, Проспект Мира 79, **M** Rizhskaya, 🖥 www.tibethimalaya .ru, mains R450, [V]) has a concise menu of Tibetan, Indian and, randomly, Kalmyk dishes. Try the aubergines stuffed with lamb, a Kalmyk bread plait, or steamed fish with ginger.

Adjacent to the Conservatoire, *Coffeemania* Кофеманиа (Map 4; ul Bolshaya Nikitskaya 14/2, ул Большая Никитская 14/2, **M** Okhotny Ryad, 🖥 cof feemania.ru, mains from R590, [V]) is an upscale restaurant serving imaginative dishes such as buckwheat noodles with prawns, papardelle with rabbit ragout, an array of lovely salads and great latte art.

If you feel like pushing the boat out for Moscow's top Russian food, ★ *Café Pushkin* Кафе Пушкин (Map 4; Tverskoy bul 26а, верской бул 26а, **M** Pushkinskaya, ☎ 495 739 0033, 🖥 www .café-pushkin.ru, mains R465-1785), is a favourite of government ministers and film stars alike.

The interior is in the style of a 19th-century gentleman's study, complete with globes, telescope and leather-bound books; you can feast on the likes of trout baked with crayfish, quail stuffed with duck, and roasted marrow bones with chilli sauce. Reservations essential.

***Kadril s Omarom* Кадриль с Омаром** (Map 4; ul Neglinnaya 18/1, ул Неглинная 18/1, **M** Trubnaya, mains from R350, [V]) serves flawless French cuisine in a surreal Alice-in-Wonderland setting. There are also three splurge-worthy taster menus (meat, fish and vegetarian) and sometimes meals are prepared by guest chefs.

Its menu largely drawing inspiration from the cuisines of the former Soviet republics, ***Strana Kotoroi Net* Страна Которой Нет** (Map 4; Okhotny Ryad 2, Охотный Ряд 2, **M** Okhotny Ryad) – Country Which Doesn't Exist – is all big mirrors, dark wood and the likes of authentic tom yum soup sitting on the menu side by side with dolma, golubtsi, shashlyk and pannacotta with acai berries. Strange, but it works.

With the slogan 'Dumplings of the world, unite!', it's little wonder that ***Pelman* Пелмэн** (Map 4; ul Tverskaya 20/1, ул Тверская 20/1, ⌨ pel-man.com, mains from R199; [V]) serves up all manner of pelmeni, ravioli, vareniki, dim sum and gyoza. Cheap, cheerful and very addictive.

Bars and pubs

Moscow has great nightlife. You can have as wild a time as in any Western city, or wilder, but be prepared to wake up with a throbbing head and an empty wallet.

VinoSyr (Map 4; Maliy Palashevskiy per 6, Малый Палашевский пер 6, **M** Pushkinskaya, 5pm-5am, ⌨ www.vinosyr .ru) is a great wine bar with an equally good selection of cheese to go with it.

Attached to the hip Red October art space (see box p180), ***Bar Strelka*** (Map 3; Bersenevskaya nab 14/5 Берсеневская наб 14/5, **M** Kropotkinskaya, ⌨ www.barstrel ka.com) is an equally hip drinking space with a sleek interior. Your outfit and face

will be scrutinised before you're allowed inside/on the dance floor.

John Bull Pub (Map 2; Karmanitsky per 9, Карманицкий пер 9, **M** Smolenskaya, ⌨ www.rmcom.ru/page-john-bull), part of the Europe-wide chain, is popular with locals and expats alike, thanks to its easy-going atmosphere, great range of imported beers and a Russian take on pub grub.

With its polished wooden floors and brick walls, the award-winning ***Help*** (Map 2; ul 1-ya Tverskaya-Yamskaya 27, ул 1-я Тверская-Ямская 27, **M** Belorusskaya, 24 hours, ⌨ www.helpbar.ru) is a cosy cocktail bar serving very affordable concoctions. Keep an eye out for the sign as you'll need to walk up the stairs.

Nightlife & entertainment

Nightclubs and live music In an area dominated by 'elitny' clubs where 'face control' (see box p164) is a feature of daily life, the expat-owned ***My Bar*** (Map 4; ul Kuznetsky Most 3/2, ул Кузнецкий Мост 3/2, **M** Teatralnaya) – which may well become your bar – is refreshingly down-to-earth, playing a selection of rock music while serving reasonably priced drinks into the wee hours.

On the 34th floor of Swissotel Krasniye Holmy, the chic ***City Space*** (Map 3; Kosmodamianskaya nab 52/6, Космодамьяиская наб 52/6, **M** Paveletskaya, ⌨ www.cityspacebar.com) offers unparalleled views of the city as well as an extensive cocktail menu with innovative twists; try the Trans-Siberian.

A boutique by day, ***Simachev Shop & Bar* Симачёв Бар & Бутик** (Map 4; Stoleshnikov per 12/2, Столешников пер 12/2, **M** Chekhovskaya, 24 hours), the brainchild of the designer of the same name, turns into a lively bar and club by night, attracting the city's beautiful people. It's a favourite post-clubbing stop on the Moscow party circuit.

As the name suggests. ***BB King*** (Map 2; ul Sadovaya-Samotechnaya 4/2, ул Садовая-Самотечная 4/2, **M** Tsvetnoy Bulvar, 11am-midnight, ⌨ www.bbking club.ru) plays the blues, with live performances at this dark cellar joint complemented by the Cajun dishes served by the kitchen. Get here before 8pm to catch a performance.

***Art Garbage* Запасник** (Map 4; Starogradsky per 5 Староградский пер 5, **M** Kitay-Gorod, noon-midnight Sun-Wed, to 6am Thur-Sat, 🖥 www.art-garbage.ru) has a great set-up, with an attractive terrace for outdoor drinks in summer, a bar, DJs spinning tunes in the basement club at the weekend and live music some evenings. Is it art or is it garbage? You decide.

Open 24 hours, ***Club Che* Клуб Че** (Map 4; ul Nikolskaya 10/2, ул Никольская 10/2, **M** Lubyanka, 🖥 www .clubche.ru) is an expat favourite – laidback, with salsa music enticing couples onto the dancefloor, and constantly packed at the weekend.

***Garage* Гараж** (Map 3, Brodnikov per 8, Бродников пер 8, **M** Polyanka, 24 hours, 🖥 www.garageclub.ru) is one of Moscow's longest-running clubs. Choose between chilling with a hookah and a cocktail on their summer terrace or showing off your moves during the Wed/Sun R'n'B nights.

For a raucous night on the town, head to *Gypsy* (Map 3; Bolotnaya nab 3/4, bldg 2, Болотная наб 3/4, дом 2, **M** Kropotkinskaya, 5.30pm-1am Mon-Thur, 2pm-6am Fri & Sat, 🖥 bargypsy.ru), with its myriad disco balls above the packed dance floor and the music veering between techno and international pop and alternative. Face control (see box p164) is strict, so dress nicely.

Still going strong after a decade and a half, the Thursday electronica night at

Propaganda **Пропаганда** (Map 4; Bolshoy Zlatoustinsky per 7, Большой Златоустинский пер 7, **M** Lubyanka/ Kitay-Gorod, noon-6am Mon-Fri, 3pm-6am Sat & Sun, 🖥 www.propaganda moscow.com) – 'Propka' to its friends – packs a crowd of lively student revellers.

Cultural entertainment The world-famous **Bolshoi Theatre Большой Театр** (Map 4; Teatralnaya pl 1 Театральная пл 1, **M** Teatralnaya, ☎ 495 455 5555, 🖥 www .bolshoi.ru), the sacred home of Russian opera and ballet, is now better than ever, having reopened after renovations in 2011.

Apart from the main stage, you can also catch performances by the world-famous ballet company at the adjacent **Bolshoi New Stage Новая Сцена Большого Театра**.

Tickets are easy to come by for around R300-2500, and can be purchased from the box office at either building or over the internet (to be collected from the box office before the performance).

For ballet or opera on a budget, there are equally good performances at **State Kremlin Palace Государственный Кремлёвский Дворец** (see map p173; 🖥 kremlinpalace.org, tickets R250-1400). Both venues close in the summer as the Bolshoi Ballet and Kremlin Ballet go on tour abroad but see box below.

Moscow is also home to the **Helikon Opera Геликон-Опера** (Map 4; ul Novy Arbat 11/2 ул Новый Арбат 11/2, **M** Arbatskaya, 🖥 www.helikon.ru) with extremely avant-garde productions.

❏ Summer ballet

Even though the Bolshoi and Kremlin ballet companies usually shut down from around July 1st to mid September, there is always a Summer Ballet season, held on the stage of **Molodejny Theatre Молодёжный Театр** (Map 4, Teatralnaya pl 2, adjacent to the Bolshoi; buy tickets at the box office – a cash window at the rear of the building on ul Bolshaya Dmitrovka). They do a rotating programme of classic ballets (*Swan Lake, Nutcracker, Sylphides, Bayadere, Spartacus* etc) in inoffensive classic productions.

Tickets cost R500-1500; the audience primarily consists of tourists, so expect some misbehaviour in the form of flash photography and mobile phones going off.

Splendid classical-music concerts can be heard at the **Tchaikovsky Concert Hall Консерватория имени Чайковского** (Map 2; Triumfalnaya pl 4/31, off ul Tverskaya, Триумфальная пл 4/31, **M** Mayakovskaya, 🖳 www.meloman.ru), while if you want to hear some Russian folk music and see some lively folk-dancing while enjoying some traditional Russian cuisine, head to **Yar Ярь** (Map 1; Leningradsky pr 32/2, Ленинградский пр 32/2, **M** Dinamo, 🖳 www.sovietsky.ru) at Sovietsky Hotel.

35mm cinema (Map 2; ul Pokrovka 47/24, ул Покровка 47/24 **M** Krasnye Vorota, 🖳 www.kino35 mm.ru) screens undubbed mainstream and art films in the original languages. For undubbed block-busters in English, check out **Dome Cinema** (Map 2; Olimpiysky pr 18/1 Олимпийский пр 18/1, **M** Prospekt Mira, 🖳 www.domecinema.ru).

Shopping

Moscow's main shopping street for kitsch (*matrioshkas*, ceramic boxes and furry hats) is ul Arbat (Map 4 [A6-B5]).

The best place for **Soviet souvenirs** is at the flea market at **Izmailovsky Market Измайловский Рынок** (Map 1; **M** Izmailovsky Park, 8am-8pm daily), where you may find everything from Soviet posters and badges to nesting dolls and lacquer boxes. From **M** Izmailovsky Park just follow the crowds to the market, a five-minute walk away. Get there early as some vendors leave around noon.

For home-grown fashion, head for **Russkaya Ulitsa Русская Улица** (Map 3; Bersenevskaya nab 8/1 Берсеневская наб 8 /1, **M** Kropotkinskaya), where you'll find boutiques stocked with clothes and accessories by over 60 Russian designers.

If you have plenty of money to spend on your nearest and dearest (or happen to adore caviar yourself), you can buy the 'black gold' at **Yeliseyev Grocery Store Елисеевский магазин** (Map 4; ul Tverskaya 14, ул Тверская 14, **M** Pushkinskaya), an upmarket deli inside the former mansion of merchant Yeliseyev.

Moving on

By air   The three airports that handle international and domestic flights – Domodedovo, Sheremetyevo-2 and Vnukovo – are connected to the Moscow city centre by frequent Aeroexpress trains (🖳 www.aeroexpress.ru, see p192).

Domodedovo serves the widest range of international destinations, and all three airports handle flights to all major Russian cities.

Arrive in plenty of time for your flight as queues are frequently long and chaotic and the inefficient bag drops take a long time, even if you've already checked in online.

By train

Moscow has eight main railway stations (*vokzal*; see Map 1), so whether you're beginning your trip or heading out of Russia, make sure you know which station you're leaving from: Trans-Siberian trains use Yaroslavsky and Kazansky stations. For timetables, see pp204-5 and pp507-12.
- **Belorussky vokzal Белорусский вок-зал** (**M** Belorusskaya, 🖳 www.belorusskiy .railclient.ru) Serves northern and central Europe: Berlin, Warsaw, Minsk, Vilnius, Kaliningrad and Prague, plus the Aeroexpress to Sheremetyevo-2 Airport.
- **Kazansky vokzal Казанский вокзал,** (**M** Komsomolskaya, 🖳 www.kazanskiy .railclient.ru) Covers southern and eastern Russia and Central Asia: trains to Kazan, Tashkent, Samara, Ulan-Ude, Yekaterinburg, Vladimir and Nizhny Novgorod.
- **Kievsky vokzal Киевский вокзал** (**M** Kievskaya, 🖳 www.kievskiy.railclient.ru) Trains to Kiev, Odessa, Belgrade, Sofia, Budapest and Bucharest, plus the Aeroexpress to Vnukovo Airport for mostly domestic flights.
- **Kursky vokzal Курский вокзал** (**M** Kurskaya, 🖳 www.kursky-vokzal.ru) Trains to northern and southern Russia, the Caucasus, Eastern Ukraine, Crimea. Some trains to St Petersburg, Vladimir, Nizhny Novgorod and Perm.
- **Leningradsky vokzal Ленинградский вокзал** (**M** Komsomolskaya, 🖳 www.lenin gradskiy.railclient.ru) Serves Helsinki, St

CITY GUIDES & PLANS

Petersburg, Tallinn, and the north of Russia.
● **Paveletsky vokzal Павелецкий вокзал**
(**M** Paveletskaya, 🖳 www.paveleckiy.rail
client.ru)   Aeroexpress to/from Domodedovo Airport. Also trains to southern Russia
and Azerbaijan.

❏ TRAIN SERVICES FROM MOSCOW

Moscow is Russia's biggest train hub, with numerous departures to all major cities,
both in Russia and abroad. The routes listed below are the best routes to each city in
question.

● **From Moscow to St Petersburg**

Train name	No	Journey time	Depart	Arrive
Afanasiy Nikitin	038	8hrs 4mins	00:44	08:48**
Ekspress	004	9hrs	23:30	08:30
Smena A Bentakur	026	7hrs 49min	22:50	06:39
Krasnaya Strela	002	8hrs	23:55	07:55
Dve Stolitsy	064	7hrs 50mins	22:10	06:00
Arctica	016	7hrs 45mins	01:00	08:45
Nevsky Express	168	4hrs 10mins	16:40	20:50
Sapsan	152	3hrs 40mins	06:45	10:25
Sapsan	154	3hrs 50mins	07:00	10:50*
Sapsan	158	4hrs 10mins	13:30	17:40
Sapsan	160	4hrs 10mins	13:45	17:55
Sapsan	162	3hrs 55mins	16:30	20:25
Sapsan	164	3hrs 49mins	19:25	23:14
Sapsan	166	3hrs 40mins	19:45	23:25

= alternate days only
***= only offers platzkart and kupé; no lux option*

See box p167 for services from St Petersburg to Moscow.

● **Moscow to other cities in Russia**

Destination	Train name & No	Journey time	Dep time	Arr time	Frequency
From Yaroslavsky station					
Irkutsk	*Rossiya* 002	74hrs 07mins	13:50	15:57	every other day
Novosibirsk	*Sibiryak* 026	47hrs 30mins	16:20	15:50	every other day
Krasnoyarsk	*Yenisey* 056	60hrs 28mins	16:20	04:48	every other day
Tomsk	*Tomich* 038	55hrs 10mins	22:50	06:00	every other day
Khabarovsk	044	149hrs 23mins	00:35	05:58	every other day
Vladivostok	*Rossiya* 002	143hrs 20mins	13:50	13:10	every other day
Nizhny Novgorod	*Sapsan* 172	3hrs 55mins	06:45	10:40	daily
From Kazansky station					
Ulan-Ude	082	88hrs 52mins	13:10	06:02	every other day
Yekaterinburg	*Ekaterinburg -Moskva* 016	25hrs 19mins	16:50	18:09	daily
From Kursky station					
Vladimir	176	1hr 45mins	14:15	16:00	daily

● **Rizhsky vokzal Рижский вокзал** (**M** Rizhskaya, 💻 www.rijskiy.railclient.ru) Serves Riga.

● **Yaroslavsky vokzal Ярославский вокзал** (**M** Komsomolskaya, 💻 yaroslavsky .dzvr.ru) The departure point for most Trans-Siberian trains serving Yaroslavl, destinations in Siberia, the Far East, Mongolia, China and North Korea. It's next to Leningradsky vokzal, so make sure you're at the correct railway station.

Also ensure you give yourself plenty of time before departure as finding your train may take longer than you think and

you mustn't underestimate the amount of time necessary to walk the length of a 20-carriage train!

The easiest way to **purchase tickets** for onward travel is using the RZD (Russian Railways) website (💻 www .rzd.ru). You can also buy tickets at a **service centre** at one of the stations: Yaroslavsky, Kazansky, Leningradsky, Belorussky (in the building across the tracks behind the station, at the end nearest the station), Paveletsky or Kievsky, though the latter requires you to pay a markup fee. For more on ticket purchase, see pp124-9.

CITY GUIDES & PLANS

● **International services from Moscow**

Destination	Train name & No	Journey time	Dep time	Arr time	Frequency
From Yaroslavsky station					
Beijing	*Vostok* 020	146 hrs 01mins	23:45	05:46	Saturdays
Beijing	043	131hrs 29mins	21:35	14:04	Tuesdays
Ulaanbaatar	006	101hrs 05mins	21:35	06:40	Wed, Thur
From Belorussky station					
Berlin	023	25hrs 09mins	08:43	06:53	Tue, Thur, Sun*
Nice	017	48hrs 10mins	12:40	09:50	Thursdays*
Paris	023	38hrs 48mins	08:43	20:31	Tue, Thur, Sun*
Basel	021	36hrs 46mins	23:44	10:30	daily
Prague	021	28hrs 04mins	08:43	09:47	daily
Vienna	021	28hrs 55min	08:23	10:30	daily
Vilnius	005	14hrs 05mins	18:55	07:00	daily
Minsk	001	9hrs 57mins	22:25	07:22	daily
Warsaw	009	18hrs 19mins	17:20	08:39	daily
From Kievsky station					
Belgrade	015	47hrs 20mins	00:30	20:50	daily
Bratislava	015	40hrs 35mins	00:30	14:05	daily
Budapest	015	37hrs 50mins	00:30	11:20	daily
Kyiv	001	8hrs 54mins	23:17	06:11	daily
Odessa	023	23hrs 02mins	21:25	18:27	daily
Sofia	059	50hrs 30mins	10:40	11:20	daily
From Leningradsky station					
Helsinki	*Lev Tolstoy*	14hrs 17mins	23:00	11:17	daily
Tallinn	034	15hrs 15min	18:05	08:20	daily
From Rizhsky station					
Riga	001	15hrs 37mins	20:08	09:45	daily

*=frequency of departure in peak season (June-Aug), less frequent at other times of year

Sergiev Posad
Сергиев Посад

[**Moscow Time; population: 108,490**] The former spiritual heart of Russia, Sergiev Posad is one of the holiest places of pilgrimage and a must even for those who are 'all churched out'. The town's big attraction is the Exalted Trinity Monastery of St Sergius; entering the white-walled monastery that is over six centuries old is like taking a step back into medieval Russia, with long-bearded monks in traditional black robes and tall *klobuki* hats, as well as continuous chanting emanating from lamp-lit, incense-filled churches.

HISTORY

The monastery was founded in 1340 by Sergius of Radonezh (1321-91), who was later to become Russia's patron saint. The power of his monastery grew quickly because he was closely allied to Moscow's princes, and actively worked for the unification of Russian lands by building a ring of 23 similar monastery-fortresses around Moscow. His friendship with Moscow's ruler, Grand Prince Dmitry Donskoi, was so strong that when Dmitry asked for the church's blessing in 1380 before leaving to fight the Tatar-Mongols at Kulikovo, Sergius himself delivered the service. While the resultant victory had already indicated to Sergius's followers that he had God's ear, 17 years after his death it became obvious that he also had divine protection: in 1408, after the Tatar-Mongols levelled the monastery, the only thing to survive unscathed was Sergius's corpse.

Between 1540 and 1550 the monastery was surrounded with a massive stone wall and 12 defensive towers. Never again was it to fall, even after an 18-month siege by 20,000 Poles against 1500 defenders in 1608. Both Ivan the Terrible and Peter the Great hid here after fleeing plotting princes in Moscow.

Besides its military function, the monastery was a great centre of learning. It became famous for its **Sergievsky**-style of manuscript illumination, with hand-copied pages adorned with gold and vermilion letters. Several of these manuscripts are on display at the museum inside the monastery. It is thought that Ivan Fedorov, Russia's first printer, studied here.

During the 18th century the monastery's spiritual power grew considerably. In 1744 it was elevated to a *lavra* or 'most exalted monastery'. At the time there were only four such monasteries in Russia, the other three being Kievo-Pechorskaya in Kiev, Aleksandro-Nevskaya in St Petersburg and Pochayevsko-Uspenskaya in Volyn. In 1749 a theological college was opened here and in 1814 an ecclesiastical academy.

Two years after the Communists came to power the monastery was closed down. It was reopened only in 1946 as part of a pact Stalin made with the Orthodox Church in return for the Church's support during WWII. Though the monastery is no longer the seat of the Patriarch of Russia (that was moved to Moscow's Danilovsky monastery in 1988), it is a place of enormous spiritual significance to believers, not to mention being a UNESCO World Heritage Site.

WHAT TO SEE AND DO

Exalted Trinity Monastery of St Sergius (Troitse-Sergiyeva Lavra) Троице-Сергиева Лавра

The monastery (🖥 www.stsl.ru, 10am-6pm daily, free) – studded with blue and gold onion domes and ringed by a whitewashed, 1km-long wall which is up to 15m thick – boasts a number of churches, many of which are open for services, but you may only enter them if appropriately dressed. If you have a camera but do not wish to take photos, you'll have to leave it at the kiosk near the entrance. The charge if you wish to take photos is R200.

Of its 12 defensive towers, note the **Duck Tower Утиная Башня**: the metal duck on its spire was put there for the young Peter the Great to use for archery practice.

You enter via the **Red Gate Красные Ворота** and the inner **Holy Gates Святые Ворота**. Above the latter is the **St John the Baptist Gate Church Надвратная Церковь Иоанна Предтечи**, paid for by the wealthy Stroganov family in 1693. The sky-blue and gold-starred, five-cupola **Assumption Cathedral Успенский Собор** is the heart of the complex. It was consecrated in 1585 in honour of Ivan the Terrible's victory over the Mongols near Astrakhan and Kazan, and is the cathedral in which many of the tsars were baptised. Outside the western door is the **tomb of Boris Godunov могила Бориса Годунова**, his wife and two of their children; Godunov is the only tsar not to be entombed in either the Moscow Kremlin or St Petersburg's Peter & Paul Cathedral.

The **Chapel over the Well Надкладезная Часовня** was built over a spring said to have appeared during the Polish siege of 1608. Here you'll find the longest queues of pilgrims waiting to fill their bottles with holy water. The baroque **Bell Tower Колокольня** (93m high) is the monastery's tallest building. Construction began in 1740 and took 30 years; it once featured 42 bells.

The **Refectory Трапезная Палата**, completed in 1693, served as a dining hall for pilgrims. You can't miss this red, blue, green and yellow chequered building with its carved columns. Outside it is the squat **Church of St Sergius Церковь Святого Сергия**, crowned with a single golden dome.

The **Descent of the Holy Spirit Church Духовная Церковь** contains the grave of the first Bishop of Russian Alaska.

Trinity Cathedral Троицкий Собор is the monastery's most sacred place, being the site of St Sergius's original wooden church. It contains Sergius's corpse in a dull silver

TRINITY CATHEDRAL

sarcophagus donated by Ivan the Terrible. Built in 1422 in honour of Sergius's canonisation, the cathedral contains 42 icons by Andrei Rublyov, Russia's most revered icon painter.

The **Church of Our Lady of Smolensk Смоленская Церковь** was built to house the icon of the same name in 1745. Decorated in baroque style, it resembles a rotunda. The **Tsar's Palace Царский Дворец** was built at the end of the 17th century to house Tsar Alexei and his entourage of over 500 people when they visited. It now houses the theological college and ecclesiastical academy.

MAP KEY

WHERE TO STAY
29 Hotel Russky Dvorik
   Гостиница Русский Дворик

WHERE TO EAT AND DRINK
16 Café Кафе
28 Restaurant Russky Dvorik
   Ресторан Русский Дворик

PLACES OF INTEREST
1 Duck Tower Утиная Башня
2 Konny Dvor Конный Двор
3 Pilgrim Gate Tower
   Каличья Воротная Башня
4 Bathhouse Баня
5 Tsar's Palace Царский Дворец
6 Church of Our Lady of Smolensk
   Смоленская Церковь
7 Bell Tower Колокольня
8 History Museum in Church of SS
   Zosima & Savvaty
   Исторический Музей и Церковь
   Зосимы и Савватия
9 Former Treasurer's Wing
   Казначейский Корпус
11 Former Hospital of the Trinity
   Monastery of St Sergei
   Больница-Богодельня
   Троице-Сергиевой Лавры
12 Museum of Ancient Russian Art
   (in vestry) Музей Древнерусского
   Прикладного Искусства (Ризница)
13 Trinity Cathedral Троицкий Собор
14 Chapel over the Well
   Надкладезная Часовня
15 Assumption Cathedral & Tomb of
   Boris Godunov
   Успенский Собор и могила Бориса
   Годунова

17 Red Gate, Holy Gates & John the
   Baptist Gate Church
   Красные Ворота, Святые Ворота и
   Надвратная Церковь Иоанна
   Предтечи
18 Descent of the Holy Spirit Church
   Духовная Церковь
19 St Micah's Church
   Михеевская Церковь
20 Refectory & Church of St Sergius
   Трапезная Палата и Церковь
   Святого Сергия
21 Metropolitan's Chambers
   Палаты Метрополитена
22 Water Gate/Tower
   Водяные Ворота/Башня
23 Elijah the Prophet's Church
   Ильинская Церковь
24 Church of St Paraskeva Pyatnitsa
   Пятницкая Церковь
25 Presentation of the Mother of God
   Church Веденская Церковь
26 Krasnogorskaya Chapel
   Красногорская Часовня
27 Lenin Bust Бюст Ленина
30 Pyatnitsa Well Chapel
   Часовня Пятницкого Колодца
31 War Memorial Памятник Великой
   Отечественной Войне
32 Toy Museum Музей Игрушек
33 Ascension Church
   Вознесенская Церковь
34 Dormition Church
   Успенская Церковь

OTHER
10 Museum Ticket Kiosk
   Музейная Касса
35 Bus Station Автовокзал
36 Railway Station
   Железнодорожный Вокзал

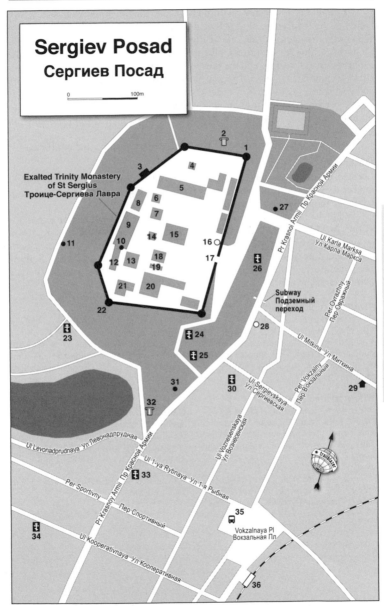

Sergiev Posad
Сергиев Посад

0 100m

Exalted Trinity Monastery
of St Sergius
Троице-Сергиева Лавра

2

1

3

4

5

27

8

6

7

9

11

14

15

16

10

17

12

13

18

19

26

21

20

23

22

24

25

Subway
Подземный
переход

28

31

30

Ul Sergievskaya
Ул Сергиевская

29

32

Ul Mitkina · Ул Миткина

Per Vokzalny · Пер Вокзальный

Per Ovrazhny · Пер Овражный

Ul Karla Marksa
Ул Карла Маркса

Pr Krasnoi Armii · Пр Красной Армии

Ul Voznesenskaya
Ул Вознесенская

Ul Levonadprudnaya · Ул Левонадпрудная

Per Sportivny
Пер Спортивный

Pr Krasnoi Armii · Пр Красной Армии

Ul 1-ya Rybnaya · Ул 1-я Рыбная

33

35

Vokzalnaya Pl
Вокзальная Пл.

34

Ul Kooperativnaya · Ул Кооперативная

36

The monastery's **vestry ризница** (*riznitsa*, 10am-5.30pm Wed-Sun, R200) contains the **Museum of Ancient Russian Art Музей Древнерусского Прикладного Искусства**, one of Russia's richest collections of ancient religious art (14th-17th centuries), plus gifts presented to the monastery over the centuries by the wealthy and the powerful – think solid gold receptacles, jewel-studded clothing and more. The gifts are displayed in the order they were given and it is interesting to see how tastes changed over the centuries. Tickets for this can be used only at the time printed on them; at peak times you may have to wait several hours so it's best to buy your ticket on arrival from the museum ticket kiosk.

English-language tours can be arranged at the respective ticket offices.

Other sights

Located by the monastery wall, **Konny Dvor Конный Двор** – the former monastery stables (ul Udarnoi Armii ул Ударной Армии, 10am-5pm Wed-Sun) are home to exhibitions on traditional crafts and history.

While the toys from around the world and from different historical periods at the **Toy Museum Музей Игрушек** (pr Krasnoi Armii 123 пр Красной Армии 123, 11am-5pm Wed-Sun) are largely of interest to little ones, the extensive collection of *matryoshkas* (nesting dolls) – many produced in Sergiev Posad before the revolution – are worth a look to anyone interested in Russia's quintessential symbol.

PRACTICAL INFORMATION
Orientation and services

The main street is pr Krasnoi Armii пр Красной Армии, while the bus and railway stations are located at the opposite corners of Vokzalnaya pl Вокзальная пл, east of the main street.

Where to stay and eat

The best overnight option is *Hotel Russky Dvorik* Гостиница Русский Дворик (ul Mitkina 14/2, ул Миткина 14/2, ☎ 096 547 5392, ☐ www.russky-dvorik.ru, sgl/dbl from R2700/3100, more expensive at weekends), a small hotel with views of the monastery's onion domes from some of its rooms. The nearby *Restaurant Russky Dvorik* Ресторан Русский Дворик serves well-prepared Russian classics – from soups to *pelmeni* to meat dishes – amidst kitschy rustic décor (mains R280-850), while a *café* in the monastery (Lavra) grounds serves tea, blinis, other light meals and bread that's freshly baked in the monastery itself.

Getting there

Around two trains per hour run to Sergiev Posad from suburban (*prigorodnie*, пригородные) platforms behind Moscow's Yaroslavsky station (1-1½hrs, R150); take any train bound for Sergiev Posad or Aleksandrov. The monastery is a 20-minute walk from the station.

Rostov-Velikiy (Rostov-Yaroslavskiy)
Ростов-Великий [Ростов-Ярославский]

[Moscow Time; population: 31,047] Rostov-Velikiy (to differentiate from Russia's other Rostov – Rostov-na-Donu), 225km north-east of Moscow, is one of the most attractive Golden Ring cities to visit and a worthy detour from the main Trans-Siberian route. It's a village-like town in a beautiful location beside scenic Lake Nero with a wonderfully sleepy atmosphere, crowing roosters in the mornings, and the added attraction of being able to spend the night inside the Kremlin itself, when the streets are eerily quiet and deserted. The town's coat-of-arms is a stag with golden horns against a crimson field.

Founded in 862, Rostov played a major role in the formation of Russia and at one time was as big as the mighty capitals of Kiev and Novgorod. Yuri Dolgoruky, who founded Moscow in 1147, gave Rostov the honourable and rare title of *velikiy*, meaning 'great'.

Rostov-Velikiy soon became an independent principality. Rebuilt after the Tatar-Mongol sacking, it continued to have political importance for two more centuries until the local prince sold the remainder of his hereditary domain to Moscow's Grand Prince Ivan III in 1474. The city remained an important ecclesiastical centre as it was the religious capital of northern Russia and home to the senior religious leader called the Metropolitan.

In the 17th century, however, the Metropolitan was moved to the larger city of Yaroslavl and Rostov dwindled into genteel decay. Don't let the drab, modern part put you off, though: the historical centre is as pleasant as they come.

WHAT TO SEE AND DO

The Rostov Kremlin Ростовский Кремль

The Rostov Kremlin (10am-5pm daily, grounds R50, exhibitions R30-80 each, all-inclusive ticket R500), situated picturesquely on the bank of Lake Nero, is one of the most photogenic in the country. Its solid whitewashed walls, tinged with pink and studded with eleven towers, enclose six churches – a profusion of blue, silver and elaborate wooden onion domes – and a handful of museums, hidden among the various other buildings on its territory. The Kremlin was founded in 1162 by Prince Andrei Bogolybusky, son of Yuri Dolgoruky, though all traces of the original buildings disappeared in the 17th century when the Kremlin was rebuilt.

Despite its mighty 12m high and 2m thick walls and towers, this reconstructed Kremlin is actually an imitation fortress. All the elements of real fortifications are missing. The ambitious 17th-century Metropolitan, Ioan Sisoyevich, wanted a residence to reflect his importance but after the 17th century, when the Metropolitan was moved to nearby Yaroslavl, the Kremlin became derelict.

Today most of the buildings have been restored to their 16th- and 17th-century condition, though restoration continues inside the cathedral and the churches. Access to **Cathedral Square Соборная Площадь** is free; to enter the rest of the grounds you have to pay the R50 fee; the combined ticket for R500 is only worth getting if you're planning on visiting every single attraction inside the Kremlin; otherwise it's cheaper to pick and choose which exhibitions you see. Also in Cathedral Square, the **cathedral bell-tower соборная звонница** that you can ascend for R60 contains superb examples of 17th-century Russian bells, the largest, Sysoi, weighing 32 tons. There are 15 in all and most of them have their own names; they're rung every day from Wednesday to Sunday and can be heard up to 20km away. To attend one of the fantastic bell-ringing concerts (R1500), contact the ticket office.

Just off Cathedral Square in the northern part of the Kremlin is the star of the show – the **Cathedral of the Assumption Успенский Собор**, an impressive 16th-century, 60m-high, five-domed building with white stone friezes decorating the outside and the almost living tendrils of grapevines encircling the columns in the dimly lit interior. The cathedral contains the tomb of the canonised Bishop Leontius who was martyred by Rostov's pagans in 1071 during his Christianity drive and the Metropolitan Ioan is also buried here. Those of a female persuasion are obliged to put on the wrap-around skirts and headkerchiefs provided before entering as God is watching for signs of immodesty.

CATHEDRAL OF THE
ASSUMPTION

The Kremlin's **main entrance** and ticket office is on its western side through the **St John the Divine Gateway Church Церковь Иоана Богослова**, built in 1683, which has a richly decorated façade. The entrance to the Kremlin's northern part from the central part is through the **Resurrection of Christ Gate Church Церковь Воскресения** built in 1670. This church has a stone iconostasis instead of the traditional wooden one.

The **Transfiguration of the Saviour above the Cellars Church Церковь Спаса на Сенях**, the tallest in the Kremlin, was the private church of the Metropolitan. It is quite austere from the outside but its interior is lavish. The **White Chamber Белая Палата** next door was designed as a sumptuous dining hall; it now houses the Museum of Church Antiquities. The large yellow building in the heart of the Kremlin, **Samuilov block Самуилов корпус** is home to the thorough **Museum of Ancient Russian Art Музей Древне-Русского Искусства** (R60) – 16th-century church icons through to an image of St Christopher depicted with a dog's head.

North of Samuilov block, to the east of the gate between the north and central parts of the Kremlin, is the very worthwhile **Museum of Finift Музей Финифти** (R70); you may spot heavy Bibles with enamelled designs, 18th-century crowns inlaid with pearls and *finift* (see box opposite), finift depictions of saints, and finift portraits of Stalin, Kalinin and Voroshilov produced during the Soviet era.

For unparalleled 360° views of the Kremlin and Lake Nero ascend the stairs of the **Water Tower Водяная Башня** (R60), just east of the Samuilov block. Also worthwhile are the walkways along the **Kremlin walls переходы** (R80) that give you a glimpse of the well-tended **Metropolitan's Garden Митрополичий Сад**, as well as the central part of the Kremlin from different angles.

The **Church of the Virgin Hodegitria Ценрковь Одигитрии**, in the north-west corner of the central section, was erected 20 years after the death of Metropolitan Ioan and has a Moscow baroque interior. It now contains an exhibition of church vestments and the exterior is in dire need of a coat of paint.

The building housing the **Prince's Chambers Иерашие Палаты**, currently undergoing renovation, is the oldest here, dating from the 16th century. It's claustrophobic with small dark passages, narrow doors and slit windows filled with slivers of mica. This is a good place to get an impression of the daily life of 16th-century Russian nobility.

The white-washed, misleadingly named **Red Chamber Красная Палата**, just south of the main entrance, was originally built as a residence for visiting tsars and their large retinue. The servants' quarters – now a popular guesthouse (see Where to Stay p214) were in the modest red building just to the north-east of the Samuilov block.

Other places of interest

In front of the eastern entrance of the Kremlin is the **Church of the Saviour on the Market Place Церковь Спаса на Торгу**. It was built in the late 1600s and is now a library. The name comes from the rows of shops and stalls around the church that have stood there for centuries. Beside the church is the Arcade built in the 1830s and on the opposite side of the street is the Traders' Row.

CITY GUIDES & PLANS

❏ **Finift**

Rostov-Velikiy's most famous handicraft is *finift*, multi-coloured enamel work. This craft originated in Byzantium: the name derives from the Greek *fingitis* meaning colourful and shiny. Finift was used to decorate icons, sacred utensils and bible covers, as well as in portraits of people. The enamel's greatest advantages are that it cannot be damaged by water and does not fade with time.

The process of making the enamel is extremely complex and involves oxidising various metals to produce different colours. Iron produces yellow, orange-red and brown, copper produces green and blue, tin produces a non-transparent white, and gold with tin produces a cold ruby red.

Finift has been produced here since the 12th century and the Rostov Finift Factory has been operating since the 18th century. You can see unusual, contemporary works of art involving enamel in combination with wood, metal and stone at **Khors House of Art Хорс** (see p216; ul Podozyorka 31 ул Подозёрка 31, ⌨ www.khors.org, noon-8pm), a small gallery between the Kremlin and the lake, in the home of artist Mikhail Selishchev.

The neoclassical **St Nicholas in the Field Church Церковь Святово Николая** (on ul Gogolya ул Гоголя) was built in 1813 and has been well restored. It has a golden iconostasis with finift enamel decorations and icons from the 15th to 19th centuries. This was one of two main churches in Rostov that conducted services during the Communist era (the other was the **Church of the Tolg Virgin Церковь Толгской Богоматери**), on ul Malaya Zarovskaya ул Малая Заровская.

The single-domed **Church of St Isidore the Blessed Церковь Исидора Блаженного** (ul Karla Marksa ул Карла Маркса) dates from the 16th century and was originally called Ascension Church. It is hidden partly by the old Kremlin walls.

It's worth walking the 1500m to **St Jacob Monastery Яковлевский Монастырь**. Although it seems almost deserted, it is still functioning and you might glimpse a monk walking silently between the buildings.

PRACTICAL INFORMATION

You can hire rowing boats at the **river station** from near Khors House of Art. Hotel Podozyorka organise boat excursions on the lake.

There is an **ATM** at the railway station and wi-fi is available in the hotels.

Where to stay

For a small place, Rostov has a good selection of inexpensive accommodation. Book ahead, as places tend to fill up, particularly on weekends.

For atmosphere, the most appealing place is ***Dom na Pogrebakh* Дом на Погребах** (☎ 61244, 💻 www.domnapogrebah.ru, sgl/dbl/trpl/lux with shared bath R700/900/1500, lux R2800-3000), the former servants' quarters of the Rostov Kremlin set amidst grounds that are eerily quiet and dark at night. All the rooms have

MAP KEY

WHERE TO STAY
5 Hotel Russkoye Podvorie
Гостиница Русское Подворье
13 Dom na Pogrebakh
Дом на Погребах
14 Khors House of Art Хорс
15 Hotel Podozyorka
Гостиница Подозёрка

WHERE TO EAT AND DRINK
6 Restaurant Russkoye Podvorie
Ресторан Русское Подворье
7 Alyosha Popovich Алёша Попович
17 Restaurant Slavyansky
Ресторан Славянскии

PLACES OF INTEREST
2 St Nicholas in the Field Church
Церковь Святово Николая
3 Lenin statue Памятник Ленину

4 Church of St Isidore the Blessed
Церковь Исидора Блаженного
8 Church of the Tolg Virgin
Церковь Толгской Богоматери
9 Church of the Saviour on the Market Place
Церковь Спаса на Торгу
10 Museum of Finift Музей Финифти
11 Cathedral of the Assumption
Успенский Собор
12 Cathedral Square
Соборная Площадь
13 Red Chamber Красная Палата
14 Khors House of Art Хорс
18 Church of the Virgin Birth
Церковь Рождества Богородицы

OTHER
1 Railway Station & ATM, Bus Station
Железнодорожный Вокзал, Автовокзал
16 River Station Причал

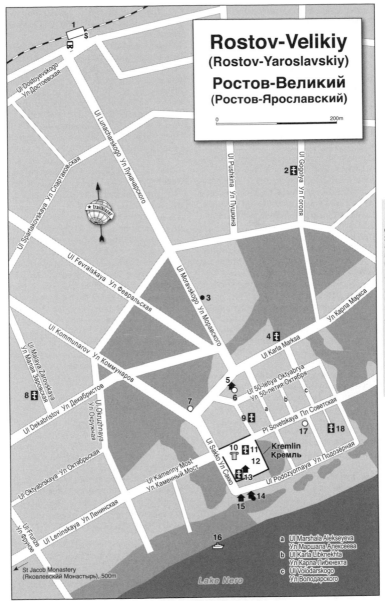

Rostov-Velikiy
(Rostov-Yaroslavskiy)
Ростов-Великий
(Ростов-Ярославский)

0   200m

1 $

Ul Dostoyevskogo
Ул Достоевская

Ul Lunacharskogo Ул Луначарского

Ul Spartakovskaya Ул Спартаковская

★ trailblazer

Ul Fevralskaya Ул Февральская

Ul Pushkina Ул Пушкина

Ul Gogolya Ул Гоголя

2

Ul Moravskogo Ул Моравского

● 3

Ul Karla Marksa Ул Карла Маркса

Ul Kommunarov Ул Коммунаров

4

Ul Karla Marksa

Ul Malaya Zarovskaya
Ул Малая Заровская

Ul Dekabristov Ул Декабристов

Ul Okruzhnaya
Ул Окружная

8

5

6

Ul 50-letiya Oktyabrya
Ул 50-летия Октября

7

9

a   b   c

Pl Sovetskaya Пл Советская

17   18

10 11

Kremlin
Кремль

12

Ul Oktyabrskaya Ул Октябрьская

Ul Savko Ул Савко

13

Ul Kamenny Most
Ул. Каменный Мост

Ul Podozyornaya Ул Подозёрная

14

15

Ul Leninskaya Ул Ленинская

Ul Frunze
Ул Фрунзе

16

St Jacob Monastery
(Яковлевский Монастырь), 500m

Lake Nero

a Ul Marshala Alekseyeva
   Ул Маршала Алексеева
b Ul Karla Libknekhta
   Ул Карла Либкнехта
c Ul Volodarskogo
   Ул Володарского

large, comfortable beds and heavy medieval wooden doors; the cheapest share facilities. If you arrive after 5pm, ring the bell at the door just to the left of the main entrance.

Originally intended to be a bohemian retreat for visiting artists, *Khors House of Art* Хорс (see box p213; ул Подозёрка 31, ul Podozerka 31, ☎ 624 83 or ☎ 962 209 0605, 🖳 www.khors.org, sgl/dbl/quad R500/700/1500, internet access), is the home of a friendly couple: Mikhail Selishchev, who does wonderful things with finift, and his wife. The small summer guesthouse, set in an orchard next to Mikhail's workshop, has compact, cosy rooms that share facilities but is open May-September only. There's a guest kitchen, a rowing boat you can borrow and the views from the terrace of the lake and the Kremlin are just wonderful. To get here, take the dirt path that skirts the west side of the Kremlin.

Hotel Russkoye Podvorie Гостиница Русское Подворье (ул Маршала Алексеева 9, ul Marshala Alekseeva 9, ☎ 64255, 🖳 www.russkoye-podvorie.ru, sgl/dbl/lux from R1000/2200/3500, WI-FI) offers comfortable, if nondescript, rooms in an 18th-century building. The compact singles share facilities, but the location is great, the service friendly and a good cooked breakfast is included. Prices go down on weekdays.

In an appealing, traditional wooden house right by the lake, *Hotel Podozyorka* Гостиница Подозёрка (ул Подозёрка 33, ul Podozyorka 33, ☎ 917 553 75 55, ☎ 985 643 3084, 🖳 www.podozerka.ru, dbl R2500) offers homey wood-panelled rooms with iron bedsteads. You can also pay to use the Russian *banya* – if you're particularly brave! – in conjunction with a dip in the lake in winter. A room with lake view costs R500 extra.

Where to eat and drink
Rostov's eating scene is rather limited. Besides a *café* inside the Kremlin, there are few decent eating options.

The best of the lot is *Restaurant Russkoye Podvorie* Ресторан Русское Подворье (ул Маршала Алексеева 9, ul Marshala Alekseeva 9, mains R280-460), decked out as a peasant's log cabin, complete with imitation tile stove. Here you can feast like a medieval noble on traditional dishes such as pike poached in milk, beef roasted with potatoes and wild mushrooms, and more exotic fare such as veal brains, as well as *blini* (R95) and superb *solyanka* and other soups. Wash it down with a tankard of honey mead.

In the same vein, *Restaurant Slavyansky* Ресторан Славянский (пл Советская 8, pl Sovetskaya 8, mains R300-550, WI-FI) is locally famous for its inventive Russian dishes such as stuffed pike, goose baked with apples and soup made of fresh porcini mushrooms. The portions are not overly generous, but everything is well prepared.

Named after a mythical folk hero said to have been born in Rostov, *Alyosha Popovich* Алёша Попович (ул Карла Маркса 1, ul Karla Marksa 1, 9am-6pm daily, mains R60-140, WI-FI) is a cheap and cheerful wood-panelled café serving sweet and savoury blini, salads and more substantial mains to a mostly young local clientele. You won't find any alcohol stronger than honey mead (медовуха) here.

Getting there
Long-distance trains stop daily stop at Rostov on their way from Moscow (8/day, 2¾-3½hrs), the fastest being the 104 and the 106 in the afternoons. If you're coming here from Sergiev Posad, you have to change at Aleksandrov; from Aleksandrov there are elektrichkas (3/day; 2-2¼hrs).

To get from the railway station or from the main bus station to the Kremlin, take bus No 6. Marshrutka No 7 runs along ul Lenina, stopping a block away from St Jacob Monastery.

The Rostov-Velikiy area code is ☎ 48536. From outside Russia dial ☎ +7-48536.

Yaroslavl
Ярославль

[**Moscow Time; population: 599,169**] With its proliferation of golden-domed churches, lining the Volga promenade, and an enviable location, flanked by two rivers, Yaroslavl's old central section and the tree-lined streets and squares make this one of the most attractive cities in Russia. In many ways the architectural treasures in this old section surpass those of Moscow as they have not suffered as much from the ravages of war and rapid industrialisation. It's well worth adding Yaroslavl to your itinerary, easily reachable from the main Trans-Siberian route, which now runs through Vladimir.

Yaroslavl is the Volga River's oldest city, founded in 1010 by Grand Prince Yaroslav the Wise to protect the north-eastern border of Kievan Rus and originally known as Medvezhy Ugol (Bears' Corner), partly due to the Finno-Ugric inhabitants of the area who worshipped the brown bear and whom the prince forced into Christianity, adopting the halberd-bearing bear emblem for the city's coat of arms. With the expansion of river trade from the 16th century, Yaroslavl became the second most populous city after Moscow. Until the opening of the Moscow–Volga River Canal in 1937, which gave Moscow direct access to the Volga, Yaroslavl was Moscow's main port. Today, Yaroslavl is a lively city of culture, featuring one of Russia's most illustrious universities.

WHAT TO SEE AND DO

Transfiguration of Our Saviour Monastery
Спасо-Преображенский Монастырь
This attractive monastery (Bogoyavlenskaya pl 25 Богоявленская пр 25, 🖥 www.yarmp.yar.ru, exhibits 10am-5pm Tue-Sun, grounds 8.30am-8pm daily, exhibits R40-60 each, grounds R25, all-inclusive ticket R550 but this is only worth it if you're planning to see every museum/exhibition), encircled by white stone walls on the bank of the Kotorosl river, was founded in the 12th century. The oldest building to be seen today, however, dates from 1516 when the wooden walls were replaced with stone and brick. As it was considered impregnable, part of the tsar's treasury was stored here, protected by a garrison.

Transfiguration of Our Saviour Cathedral Преображенский Собор occupies central place in the monastery. This three-domed cathedral was built in 1516 after the original building was destroyed in a fire in 1501. Sixteenth-century frescoes include depictions of John the Baptist on the eastern wall, Christ Pantokrator on the cupola in the central dome, and the Last Judgement on the western wall.

The **Refectory** was built in the 16th century. On the second floor a single mighty pillar supports the vaults, creating a large open dining area. You can scramble up to the **bell tower звонница** for a panoramic view of the city (R120). There are four flights of stairs, each getting narrower and more claustrophobia-inducing, and you'll end up standing on the wooden roof. Directly above you is the main bell which was cast in 1738. The bell-tower's clock was installed in 1624 after being brought from the Saviour (Spassky) Tower in the Moscow Kremlin.

The **Monks' Cell Block** consists of four buildings and was built at the end of the 17th century. It now contains a large museum of Old Russia which includes icons, handicrafts, weapons, armour and books, and there are other museums and exhibits scattered throughout the Kremlin buildings.

One not to miss is the **Treasures of Yaroslavl Сокровища Ярославля** exhibition (R120), featuring such priceless artefacts as a setting of Mother of God icon inlaid with pearls and sapphires, wonderfully ornate episcopal *croziers* (staffs), vast Bibles weighed down by covers of solid gold, and carved silver bowls for holy water storage.

EPIPHANY CHURCH TOWER

Around the monastery

Directly opposite the monastery on Moskovskoye Shosse (Moscow Highway) is the **Epiphany Church Церковь Богоявления**. The five-domed church was completed in 1693 and has nine large windows which make the interior extraordinarily light. It is an excellent example of the Yaroslavl school of architecture (see box opposite) with its glazed tiles and festive decorations.

The **Church of St Nicholas on the Waters Церковь Николы Мокрого** (ul Tchaikovskogo 1 ул Чайковского 1) was built from 1665 to 1672 in red brick and has marvellous glazed bands around the altar windows. The five green onion-domes complement the red brick and make for an impressive sight.

The white **Church of the Tikhvin Virgin Церковь Тихвинской Богоматери** (7am-7pm), next door, is a small church dwarfed by its neighbour but specially designed for winter worship as it can be heated. It has extensive glazed tilework on its exterior.

Volga River Embankment

A stroll down the landscaped high right bank of the Volga River from the river station to Strelka Park is an enjoyable way of exploring this area. At the end of Volzhskaya nab is the **river station**: one section is for long-distance hydrofoils and, slightly downstream, there's another for local passenger ferries.

Half a block south of the river station, at Volzhskaya nab 33a Волжская наб 33a is the wonderful **Music & Time Музыка и Время** (10am-7pm daily, R160), in a wooden house surrounded by trees festooned with bells. This gives you a taster for what's inside: namely, things that make music and tell the time – rows of bells, walls lined with grandfather clocks, old music boxes, gramophones, and even a piano-like instrument operated by bellows that sounds like an accordion. Guided tours (English tours can be organised most days) make a real show of all these noisemakers, as well as curiosities such an English fuel-powered steam iron.

The tent-roofed **Church of the Nativity Церковь Рождества Христова** (ul Kedrova 1 Ул Кедрова 1), built over nine years starting in 1635, is famous as being the first church to use glazed tiles for external decoration. This practice was soon adopted everywhere and led to the development of the Yaroslavl architecture style. The names of those involved in the building of the church have been inscribed on the tiles and, if you look closely, you can still see them.

The **Art Museum Художественный Музей** (Volzhskaya nab 23 Волжская наб 23, ☐ artmuseum.yar.ru, 10am-5.30pm Tue-Sun, exhibitions R60-110 each) is housed in the former governor's residence and it consists of permanent exhibits of Russian 18th- to 20th-century art, an outdoor sculpture garden and changing contemporary art exhibitions. The 20th-century art, with its whacky *House from the Inside* and homoerotic *Water Station* is particularly entertaining. The museum's other branch, the **Metropolitan's Chamber Метрополичьи Палаты** (Volzhskaya nab 1 Волжская наб 1, 10am-5pm, closed Fri, R60) was built in the 1680s for the Metropolitan of the nearby city of Rostov-Velikiy and is now one of the country's richest museums of old Russian Art; particularly interesting are the 13th- and 14th-century Mongolian icons.

The worthwhile **Yaroslavl History Museum Музей Истории Ярославля** (Volzhskaya nab 17 Волжская наб 17, ☐ museum.city-yar.ru, 10am-5pm, closed Tue, R64) traces the city's thousand-year history in a series of well-presented exhibits.

Volga Tower Волжская Башня, also known as the Arsenal Tower, sits on the river bank at Volzhskaya nab 7 Волжская наб 7. It is one of two towers which remain from the former Yaroslavl Kremlin. This citadel consisted of earth ramparts with wooden fortress walls and stone towers. This tower was finished in 1668 and is now a naval club. *(continued on p222)*

❏ **Yaroslavl style**
The Yaroslavl school of architecture dates from the second half of the 16th century and is epitomised by tall, pointed tent roofs, free-standing bell-towers, large airy churches with side chapels, external glazed tiles, and large interior frescoes and mosaics. Yaroslavl has many buildings in this style as its evolution coincided with a massive reconstruction drive after the great fire in 1658. The city had developed a rich merchant class which commissioned churches to its own taste. As this style also appealed to hereditary nobles and peasants, it became widespread throughout Russia, much to the chagrin of the conservative clergy.

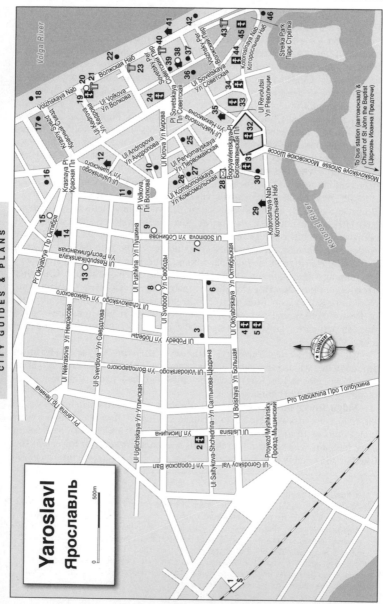

Yaroslavl
Ярославль

0 ___ 500m

Volga River

Volzhskaya Nab Волжская Наб

Krasnaya Pl Красная Пл

Strelka Park Парк Стрелка

Kotoroslnaya Nab Которосльная Наб

Kotorosl River

To bus station (автовокзал) &
Church of St John the Baptist
(Церковь Иоанна Предтечи)

Moskovskoye Shosse Московское шоссе

Pro Tolbukhina Про Толбухина

22 Provincial Governor's Rotunda-Pavilion Павильон
23 Art Museum Художественный Музей
24 Church of St Elijah the Prophet Церковь Ильи Пророка
26 Znamenskaya Tower Знаменская Башня
27 Gostinny Dvor (Traders' Arcade) Гостиный Двор
30 Descent of Holy Spirit Consistorium
   Духовная Консистория
31 Epiphany Church Церковь Богоявления
32 Transfiguration of Our Saviour Monastery
   Спасо-Преображенский Монастырь
33 Church of St Michael the Archangel
   Церковь Михаила Архангела
34 Church of Saviour in the Town Спасская Церковь
36 Chelyuskintsev Park Парк Челюскинцев
37 House of the Vakhrameyevs Дом Вахрамеевых
39 House of Matreev Дом Матреева
40 Yaroslavl History Museum Музей Истории Ярославля
42 Volga Tower Волжская Башня
43 Metropolitan's Chamber Палаты Метрополита
44 Church of St Nicholas in Log Town Церковь Святого Николы
45 Annunciation Cathedral Успенский Кафедральный Собор
46 Memorial Park Мемориальный Парк

OTHER
1 Yaroslavl-Glavny (main railway station) & ATM
   Вокзал Ярославль-Главный & ATM
16 University Унтверситет
18 River Station Речной Вокзал
25 Market Рынок
28 Central Post Office Почтамт

WHERE TO STAY
12 Hotel Ibis Отель Ибис
14 Hostel Good Luck Хостел 'Good Luck'
29 Hotel Yubileynaya Гостиница Юбилейная
35 Ioann Vasilyevich Иоанн Васильевич
38 Hotel Paradnaya Гостиница Парадная
41 Volzhskaya Zhemchuzhina Волжская Жемчужина

WHERE TO EAT AND DRINK
7 Café No 1 Кафе No 1
8 Traveler's Coffee
9 Dudki Дудки
13 Pirosmani Пиросмани
15 Traveler's Coffee
20 Sobraniye Собрание
38 Café Boulevard Кафе Бульвар

PLACES OF INTEREST
2 Church of Vladimir Mother of God
   Церковь Владимирской Богоматери
3 Bell-tower of St Nicholas Колокольня Святого Николы
4 Church of St Nicholas on the Waters
   Церковь Николы Мокрого
5 Church of the Tikhvin Virgin
   Церковь Тихвинской Богоматери
6 Seminary Духовная Семинария
10 Philharmonic Hall Филармония
11 Volkov Drama Theatre
   Драматический Театр имени Волкова
17 Nekrasov Monument Памятник Некрасову
19 Church of the Nativity Церковь Рождества Христова
21 Music & Time Музыка и Время

CITY GUIDES & PLANS

(Continued from p219) Further along at Kotoroslnaya nab 2a Которосльная наб 2a is the extremely photogenic, golden-domed **Annunciation Cathedral Успенский Кафедральный Собор** (7am-7pm daily), rebuilt in 2010 in place of the one blown up by the Bolsheviks in 1937 just in time for Yaroslavl's 1000th birthday celebrations; a stone memorial in front of the cathedral marks the spot where the city was allegedly founded. Just south of the cathedral is the attractively landscaped **memorial park Мемориальный Парк**, created on the sliver of land between the Volga and the Kotorosl rivers also for said millennial celebrations.

Yaroslavl centre

One of the city's main squares is Soviet Square (pl Sovetskaya пл Советская). On the north side of the square is a government office building of circa 1780, while the east side is graced by the imposing **Church of St Elijah the Prophet Церковь Ильи Пророка** (10am-1pm & 2-6pm, closed Wed), which stands out in a city full of beautiful churches due to its superb 17th-century frescoes, still in excellent condition. The church was commissioned by one of the richest and most influential Russian merchant dynasties, the Shripins. **Znamenskaya Tower Знаменская Башня** (ul Pervomaiskaya 2a ул Первомайская 2a) is the second of the two towers that remain from Yaroslavl's original Kremlin.

Standing proud on the main square – ploschad Volkova площадь Волкова – is the national **Volkov Drama Theatre Драматический Театр имени Волкова**, built in 1911 and named after Fedor Volkov (1729-63) who is considered the founder of Russian national theatre. He inherited his stepfather's factories in Yaroslavl which enabled him to organise his own private theatre company before moving on to bigger and better things. Amongst his claims to fame was that he organised the first staging of *Hamlet* in Russia.

Church of St John the Baptist Церковь Иоанна Предтечи

In the Tolchkovski district, once famous for its leather work, this impressive 15-domed church (Zakotoroslnaya 2-ya nab 69 Закоторосльная 2-я наб 69, 7am-7pm), built between 1671 and 1687, is considered the architectural pinnacle of Yaroslavl. From a distance it looks as if it is trimmed in lace and carved of wood but this deception is created by carved and patterned bricks. It consists of two side chapels, unusual in that they are practically as tall as the church and each is crowned with five domes. Inside is a mass of frescoes – reputedly more than in any other church in Russia.

You can see this church from the train as you cross over the Kotorosl River, though don't be put off by its grim industrial surroundings from visiting the church proper.

PRACTICAL INFORMATION
Orientation and services
Yaroslavl-Glavny railway station Вокзал Ярославль-Главный (Yaroslavl-Main), serves the vast majority of destinations. Only trains travelling along the east and west line (such as from St Petersburg) go through **Yaroslavl-Moskovski**; it is on the southern side of the river.

The main thoroughfare is **ul Svobody ул Свободы**. Most attractions are found either along or near the Volga embankment, while numerous places to stay and eat are found within easy walking distance of pl Volkova, the main square, reachable by trolleybus No 1 (R16) from the railway station. Bus 8 runs up and down ul Svobody.

There are several **ATMs** inside the railway station, including the reliable TransCredit Bank.

The **market** sells produce.

In the summer there are various **river trips** leaving from the river station; take your pick from hourly jaunts or multi-day cruises down the Volga.

Where to stay

Guarded by lifesize statues with *halberds*, each of the 29 rooms at ★ *Ioann Vasilyevich* **Иоанн Васильевич** (ул Революционная 34 ul Revolyutsionnaya 34, ☎ 670 760, 🖳 www.ivyar.ru, sgl/dbl/lux from R2300/3600/4200, wi-fi) has its own movie-based theme reflected in the eclectic décor. The on-site feasting hall serves beautifully presented Russian classics.

If you don't mind sleeping under the watchful eye of Putin, Dali, Einstein, Marilyn Monroe and other Pop Art-y heroes, then the small and colourful *Hostel Good Luck* (пр Октября 11, pr Oktyabrya 11, ☎ 920 651 1999, 🖳 goodluck-hostel .com, dorms/twn from R450/795pp; wi-fi) is for you. There's a compact kitchen that doubles as a common area; you may have to queue for the only bathroom, but the location's great, and so are the helpful staff.

For those wishing to be lulled to sleep by the waves of the mighty Volga, the hotel-boat *Volzhskaya Zhemchuzhina* **Волжская Жемчужина** (Волжская наб, Volzhskaya nab, ☎ 731 273, 🖳 www.river hotel-vp.ru, sgl/dbl/suite from R2500/3600/ 5500, wi-fi) offers compact, bright rooms with air-con. The boat itself has a sauna and the on-board restaurant.

On a quiet street in an enviable central location, brand-new *Hotel Ibis* **Отель**

Ибис (Pervomaysky per 2a Первомайский пер 2a, ☎ 592 900, 🖳 www.accorhotels .com, sgl/dbl/lux R2500/4300/6900, wi-fi) offers well-appointed rooms decked out in placid creams, all with flat-screen TVs and air-con; there is a 24-hour restaurant on-site for night owls.

Rooms at the revamped Soviet throwback *Hotel Yubileynaya* **Гостиница Юбилейная** (наб Которосльная 26, nab Kotorosolnaya 26, ☎ 726 565, 🖳 www .yubil.yar.ru, sgl/dbl/lux R3000/3650/ 4800, wi-fi) range from compact singles and doubles to grand apartments with parquet floors. Buffet breakfast included.

Where to eat and drink

Decked out like a rustic pub, *Pirosmani* **Пиросмани** (ul Respublikanskaya 48 ул Республиканская 48, mains R140-360) is the city's top spot for flavourful, aromatic Georgian dishes. You can't go wrong with the *pkhali* selection (cold vegetable starters) or the grilled meats (including the more exotic chicken giblets cooked in a *ketsi* (clay dish). Don't skip the excellent selection of Georgian wines – from Saperavi to Khvanchkara (R100-120/ glass).

Trendy *Dudki* **Дудки** bar (ул Собинова 33 ul Sobinova 33, ☎ 330 933) packs the locals into the lively small bar downstairs and a larger one upstairs. Since this place also serves great international food, don't even think about getting a table on a weekend night without a reservation.

Sobraniye **Собрание** (Volzhskaya nab 33 Волжская наб 33, 🖳 sobranierf.ru, mains R230-450) thrills locals and visitors alike with its traditional Russian cuisine. Go for the dishes cooked in a traditional stone oven, such as the lamb with aubergine, pelmeni baked with mushroom sauce, or the millet porridge with pumpkin and honey.

Inside Hotel Paradnaya, ★ *Café Boulevard* **Кафе Бульвар** (pl Chelyuskintsev 14 пл Челюскинцев 14,

The Yaroslavl area code is ☎ 4852. From outside Russia dial ☎ +7-4852.

mains R320-740) gets rave reviews for its beautifully presented fusion dishes, such as noisette of lamb with aubergine sauce and duck with caramelised peaches. Also a great breakfast spot, with rice and buckwheat porridge, eggs any way you like and *syrniki* (cottage cheese fritters) on offer.

Café No 1 Кафе No 1 (ul Sobinova 54 ул Собинова 54) may be tooting its own horn, but that's largely justified by a menu of innovative Italian and Japanese dishes. Seasonal specials such slow-cooked venison soup and venison steak are on offer; skip the sushi, but don't scrimp on the wonderful tea-and-fruit specials. The downside is the lack of a non-smoking section.

California-chain *Traveler's Coffee* (pr Oktyabrya 21, пр Октября 21, WI-FI) is now firmly planted in Yaroslavl, meaning that you benefit from their large selection of global teas and coffees, cheesecakes, muffins, shakes, fresh juice and something more substantial for those who've got the munchies. Another branch at ul Svobody 32a ул Свободы 32a.

Moving on

There are departures from Yaroslavl-Glavny **railway station** to Moscow (13/day, 3½-4½hrs, from R400), the fastest being the two express trains, No 101 and 105, leaving at 7.44am and 1.44pm respectively).

The **bus station Автовокзал** is about 2km south of the city on Moskovsky pr Московский пр. There are buses to Vladimir (2/day, R556, 5¼hrs) and to Moscow's Shchyolkovskaya station (6/day, R640, 6hrs), most of which stop at Sergiev Posad and Rostov-Velikiy.

Vladimir
Владимир

[Moscow Time; population: 347,930] Vladimir, 180km from Moscow, is a rewarding town to visit as a day trip, thanks to the introduction of the high-speed Sapsan trains between the capital and Nizhny Novgorod, or even as a Trans-Siberian stopover. One of Russia's oldest cities, and part of the Golden Ring (the cities that shaped early Russian history), Vladimir boasts some splendid churches and other architectural gems; most are found along the easily walkable ul Bolshaya Moskovskaya. Eleven kilometres from Vladimir, Bogolyubovo (see pp229-30) was formerly the site of the palace of Prince Andrei Bogolyubsky but is now famous for the beautiful Church of the Intercession on the Nerl.

HISTORY

Vladimir was officially founded in 1108, although there was a village here as early as 500BC. During the great migration of Slavs from the disintegrating Kievian Rus empire in the late 10th and early 11th centuries the Vladimir region was settled and its ancient inhabitants evicted.

In 1108 Grand Prince Vladimir Monomakh of Kiev, after whom the town is named, built a fortress here to protect his eastern lands. Vladimir's grandson, Andrei Bogolyubsky, stormed and pillaged Kiev in 1157 and took its master craftsmen away to build a new Russian capital at Vladimir. By the time of Andrei's murder at Bogolyubovo in 1174, Vladimir surpassed Kiev in grandeur and had become the centre of a powerful principality. Unfortunately Andrei's brother and successor, Vsevolod III, was unable to hold the principality together and it was soon divided amongst family members.

Despite its defeat by Tatar-Mongols in 1238 the town remained the political centre of north-eastern Russia. It became the religious centre of the entire country in 1300 when the seat of the Metropolitan of All Rus was moved here from Kiev, but this power disappeared too when the seat was shifted to Moscow 20 years later. Vladimir's glory came to an end in 1392 with its absorption into the Moscow Principality. It rapidly became a backwater and by 1668 its population numbered just 990, though it has since bounced back as an industrial centre.

WHAT TO SEE AND DO

The Golden Gate Золотые Ворота
Vladimir was once ringed by several kilometres of earth ramparts topped with oaken walls. Traditionally, a city Kremlin consisted of a small, heavily fortified citadel with an unprotected settlement beyond its walls. With a defensive wall around the entire city, the town's population swelled as settlers arrived seeking security. The only surviving remnant of these defences is the so-called Golden Gate – a formidable white creation that sits on the busy roundabout at the western end of ul Bolshaya Moskovskaya. Built by Andrei Bogolyubsky in 1158, it was modelled on that of Kiev, which, in turn, was based on the Golden Gates of Constantinople. To emphasise further Vladimir's inherited majesty, the heavy oaken outer doors were covered in gilded copper. Adorning the gate is a copy of the Byzantine icon of Our Lady of Vladimir (the original went to Moscow when the Metropolitan's seat was moved there in 1320). In 1785 two ornamental towers were added as buttresses and most earth ramparts removed to make way for increased traffic. Remnants of the earthen walls can be seen across the street from the gate.

Around the Golden Gate
Above the Golden Gate is the golden-domed Gate-Church of the Deposition of the Robe. Climb the ultra-steep steps to the entertaining **Military Museum Военный Музей** (10am-6pm, closed Tue and last Fri of month, R50), centred on a diorama of the storming of Vladimir by the Tatar-Mongols in 1238 and 1293, complete with sound and light effects. The rest of the exhibits are a quick romp through several major military campaigns, up to the Patriotic War of 1812, complemented by displays of period weaponry. The 'Heroes of the Soviet Union' exhibition features photos of the local fallen and the space suit of Valeri Kubasov.

Just west of the Golden Gate is the **Crystal, Lacquer Miniatures & Embroidery Museum Музей Хрусталя, Лаковой Миниатюры и Вышивки** (ul Dvoryanskaya 2, 11am-7pm, closed Tue and last Wed of month, R65), featuring crafts from nearby towns and villages, the most famous being the brightly coloured crystal flowers, vases and more from Gus-Khrustalny. Tacky or beautiful? You decide. The red-brick building it is housed in was formerly the Old Believers' Trinity Church, built in 1913.

CITY GUIDES & PLANS

South of the gate is the **Exhibition of 'Old Vladimir' Выставка 'Старый Владимир'** (ul Kozlov Val 14, 10am-5pm Tue & Fri-Sun, Wed & Thur 10am-4pm, closed last Wed of month, R60) housed in a 19th-century **Water Tower Водяная Башня**. On the top floor is an observation deck offering panoramic views of Vladimir.

Assumption Cathedral Успенский Собор

The city is justifiably proud of its centrepiece – the gleaming white, golden-domed cathedral (Sobornaya pl, 7am-8pm Tue-Sun, accessible to non-worshippers 1.30-4.45pm Tue-Sun, R80) built by Andrei Bogolyubsky in 1160 to rival Kiev's St Sophia Cathedral. At the time this was the tallest building in all of Russia. Following a fire in 1185 it was enlarged to hold 4000 worshippers. All of Russia's rulers from Andrei Bogolyubsky to Ivan III (the Great) were crowned here. This served in turn as the 15th-century model for its namesake in Moscow's Kremlin. The cathedral's 25m-high iconostasis contains 100 icons. These once included works by Andrei Rublyov, now held in Moscow's Tretyakov Gallery and St Petersburg's State Russian Museum. But Rublyov's work can still be seen in the form of the splendid Last Judgement frescoes, done in 1408 and found in the inner south isle and the central nave. The marble coffin of Alexander Nevsky, 13th-century Grand Prince of Vladimir, particularly famous for the victorious Neva battle of 1240 against the Swedes, is also found here; Nevsky was buried inside the Nativity Monastery (see p228).

During visitor hours, you can wander through the candle-lit semi-gloom, rubbing shoulders with the devout. Tours (R150) in several languages are available.

Adjacent to the cathedral are the **Chapel of St George**, a 'winter church' (meaning it could be heated) built in 1862, and a three-storey **bell tower** built in 1810 after the original tent-roofed tower was destroyed by lightning.

History Museum Исторический Музей

The exhibits at this well-lit, well-presented museum (ul Bolshaya Moskovskaya 64, Tue-Sun 10am-5pm, until 4pm Wed & Thur, closed last Thur of month, R50) cover regional history from the Stone Age to the revolution of 1917, with a particular focus on ornamentation from the city's two cathedrals, such as the Vladimir Mother of God icon, attributed to Andrei Rublyov. Amidst a profusion of maps, period objects and photographs you may also spot mammoth bone jewellery, a model of 7th-century Vladimir, ornate antique Bibles, and a display dedicated to 19th-century explorer Mikhail Lazarev.

Cathedral of St Demetrius of Salonica Дмитриевский Собор

The unusual, single-domed, square Cathedral of St Demetrius of Salonica (ul Bolshaya Moskovskaya

CATHEDRAL OF ST DEMETRIUS OF SALONICA

Vladimir Владимир

WHERE TO STAY
15 Hotel Vladimir
Гостиница Владимир

WHERE TO EAT & DRINK
4 Traktir Трактир
7 Traveler's Coffee
16 Shesh-Besh Шеш-Беш

PLACES OF INTEREST
1 Crystal, Lacquer Miniatures & Embroidery Museum
Музей Хрусталя, Лаковой Миниатюры и Вышивки
2 Military Museum
Военный Музей
3 Golden Gate Золотые Ворота
5 Exhibition of 'Old Vladimir' in Water Tower Выставка 'Старый Владимир' и Водяная Башня
6 Water Tower Водяная Башня
8 House of Officers
Дом Офицеров

9 Monument to 850th Anniversary of Vladimir
Монумент в честь 850-летия города Владимир
10 Assumption Cathedral
Успенский Собор
11 Oblast Arts Centre
Областной Центр Живописи
12 Cathedral of St Demetrius of Salonica Дмитриевский Собор
13 History Museum
Исторический Музей
14 Nativity Monastery
Богородице-Рождественский Монастырь

OTHER
7 Traveler's Coffee
17 Bus Station Автовокзал
18 Railway Station & ATM
Железнодорожный вокзал & АТМ

CITY GUIDES & PLANS

60, 9am-6pm daily, R50) nearby was completed in 1197 as Vsevolod III's court church. It is built from white limestone blocks and its exterior walls have over 1300 bas-relief carvings showing an incredible range of people, events, animals and plants. Highlights include the labours of Hercules on the west wall, David playing his secret chord to the birds and the animals along the top centre of the west, south and north walls, and Prince Vsevolod, responsible for the building of this cathedral, depicted in the top left section of the north wall, surrounded by his offspring.

Other attractions

Oblast Art Centre Областной Центр Живописи (ul Bolshaya Moskovskaya 58; Tue-Sun 10am-5pm, until 4pm Wed & Thur; R150) is the city art gallery, its offerings running the gamut from wonderful 18th-century depictions of the Golden Ring towns to present-day painting and sculpture. It's also a good place to pick up regional souvenirs, such as crystal creations, birch bark items, embroidery and wood carvings.

The **House of Officers Дом Офицеров**, formerly the Noblemen's Assembly Club, was built in 1826. The building, opposite the Assumption Cathedral, played an interesting role in the anti-religion campaign of the 1970s and 1980s. Every time a major service was held in the cathedral, loudspeakers in the House of Officers blared out (rarely heard) Western rock music. The decision to use decadent music to destroy insidious religion must have been full of anguish for the local Soviet leadership.

The **Monument to the 850th Anniversary of Vladimir Монумент в честь 850-летия города Владимир**, unveiled in 1958, symbolises, with its bronze figures of an architect, a soldier and a worker, the Communist theory that ordinary people are the makers of history.

The **Nativity Monastery Богородице-Рождественский Монастырь** (ul Bolshaya Moskovskaya 68) was completed in 1196 and was the city's most important monastery until the end of the 16th century. Alexander Nevsky was buried here in 1262, until Peter the Great had him reinterred in St Petersburg in 1724.

Frunze Monument (Памятник Фрунзе; 600m to the east) honours Communist hero Mikhail Frunze, who carried out revolutionary work in this region. Just 300m away is the maximum-security prison where Frunze was incarcerated in 1907. The walls around this part of the city followed the Lybed River which now flows through large pipes under the road.

PRACTICAL INFORMATION
Orientation and services

The long-distance **bus station** and the **railway station** are opposite one another on ul Vokzalnaya. The handy trolleybus No 5 runs from the railway station to the Golden Gate along ul Bolshaya Moskovskaya (R15).

Free **wi-fi** is becoming a feature of Vladimir life with hotspots available at Traveler's Coffee (see Where to eat). For more information on the city visit 🖥 www .vladimir-russia.info.

There's a TransCreditBank **ATM** inside the railway station.

If you're here in late August, you may catch the **regional fair** that takes place on Sobornaya Ploshchad, with live music, national costume, food and handicrafts from neighbouring villages.

The Vladimir area code is ☎ 4922. From outside Russia dial ☎ +7-4922.

Where to stay

Vladimir's congenial hostel, *Hostel Piligrim* Хостел **Пилигрим** (ул Токарева 8a, ul Tokareva 8a, ☎ 900 474 9594, 🖳 www.piligrimhostel.ru, dorm/dbl R500/1200, WI-FI), is a little out of the centre (see website for directions) but really caters to backpackers' needs, with reading lights by every bed in the dorm, a fully equipped guest kitchen, book exchange and tons of useful information on the city (and nearby Suzdal).

The closest hotel to the station is *Hotel Vladimir* **Гостиница Владимир** (ул Большая Московская 74, ul Bolshaya Moskovskaya 74, ☎ 324 447, 🖳 www.hotel-vladimir.ru, twn/suite R2100/4300; WI-FI), with renovated, comfortable en suite rooms that retain Soviet interior design. The cheapest rooms are rather compact. Free wi-fi is available for anyone eating at the restaurant.

Also with some English-speaking staff, beautifully located north-west of the railway station overlooking the river valley, the Art Nouveau *Voznesenskaya Sloboda* **Вознесенская Слобода** (ул Вознесенская 4-16, ul Voznesenskaya 4-16, ☎ 322 787, 🖳 www.vsloboda.ru, dbl R4800) offers stylish rooms either in European or 'classic Russian' style, the latter with wood-panelled walls. Guests have access to a small swimming pool and Finnish sauna.

Where to eat and drink

There are numerous places to eat at along ul Bolshaya Moskovskaya, ул Большая Московская. *Shesh-Besh* **Шеш-Беш** at No 78, specialises in Central Asian dishes

such as *kharcho* (spicy mutton soup) and aubergine with walnut sauce, as well as over a dozen different types of shashlyk (R200-340). The weekday set lunch (R180) is excellent value. *Traveler's Coffee* at No 10 (🖳 www.travelerscoffee.ru, 8am-midnight daily) is an ever-reliable chain that draws you in with the tantalising scents of the aromatic brew from all over the world, as well as red velvet cake, muffins, wraps, sandwiches and more.

Traktir **Трактир** (ул Летнеперевозинская 19, ul Letneperevozinskaya 19), in a cute wooden cottage, serves an assortment of Russian soups, salads and meaty mains; its summer terrace is a good spot for *shashlyk* (R200-260) and beer, though the service can be glacial in both demeanour and efficiency.

At Voznesenskaya Sloboda Вознесенская Слобода (see Where to stay) there is a steakhouse, popular restaurant *Krucha* **(Круча)**, a café and a summer barbecue area for self-caterers that overlooks Old Vladimir.

Moving on

There are both local and long-distance **rail services** from Vladimir to Moscow (20-21/day, 1¾-3¼hrs), the fastest and the most expensive being the two high-speed Sapsan trains (8.52am and 4.52pm), and to Nizhny Novgorod (16/day, 2¼-3¼hrs), with the fastest again being the Sapsan (8.32am and 9.17pm).

From the bus station opposite the railway station, **buses** to Suzdal run every half an hour or so between 6.30am and 9.40pm (R65; 50 mins).

SIDE TRIP TO BOGOLYUBOVO (Боголюбово)

Eleven kilometres from Vladimir, this ancient town was the site of the royal palace of Prince Andrei Bogolyubsky, who developed Vladimir into the capital of Rus after – as legend has it – he stopped in Bogolyubovo in 1150 and his horses refused to go any further. He chose this site rather than Vladimir because of its strategic position at the junction of the Klyazma River, which runs through Vladimir, and the Nerl River, which runs through the rival city of Suzdal.

CITY GUIDES & PLANS

This quickly became Vladimir's real power centre but, following Andrei's murder here in 1174, the whole lot was turned over to **Bogolyubovo Monastery Боголюбовский Монастырь**. Andrei's assassins, powerful *boyars* from Suzdal, wounded him in his bedchamber before stabbing him to death on a staircase.

Today only one tower and a covered archway date from Andrei's time, the rest from 19th-century renovations. Major buildings still standing include the Holy Gates, a bell tower from 1841 and the huge five-domed Bogolyubovo Cathedral of the Icon of the Mother of God, built in 1866 and open for services.

Walk along Vokzalanaya ul to the east of the monastery, go over the railway tracks and carry on along the cobbled path across a field to reach Bogolyubovo's treasure: the **Church of the Intercession on the Nerl Церковь Покрова на Нерли** (10am-6pm Tue-Sun, May-Sep). Situated on the bank of the river Nerl and largely unadorned by Russian standards, this church sports delicate carvings of King David who is charming the wild beasts with his music. This church was allegedly built by Andrei to honour his son Izyaslav, who perished in the offensive against the Bulgars. (See also p431.)

Getting there To get to Bogolyubovo, take trolleybus 1 from Vladimir railway station to the first stop and then switch to marshrutka 18 or 53 (15 mins).

Suzdal
Суздаль

[**Moscow Time; population: 10,240**] Of all the Golden Ring towns, Suzdal is the true gem. It must hold the record for the largest number of churches per capita in Russia: incredibly, at one time there was a church for every 12 of its citizens, along with 15 monasteries (more than any other Russian city except Moscow) and over 100 major architectural monuments, all in the space of just 8 square kilometres.

Aside from its historic draw, Suzdal delights visitors by presenting an idyllic picture of Russian village life without even trying. It's the sort of town where goats and chickens roam the streets, cattle graze in the meadows, and children fish in the slow-moving waters from wooden bridges. Wander the rutted streets along the river in the afternoon, or watch the mist rise to shroud the placid River Kamenka at night; you'll find yourself wanting to stay long after you've seen the sights.

Over 40 old religious buildings survive in Suzdal. The explanation for this is that in medieval times just about every street in every town had its own small, invariably wooden, church – it also means several churches have the same name so be careful you know which one you want to go to. This tradition was effectively sustained as a result of Suzdal's shrinking population, even as it was forgotten elsewhere, and taken a step further with the gradual replacement of wooden churches with durable stone ones. Two other events contributed to this unprecedented degree of historical preservation. In 1788 a new town plan limiting building heights to two storeys forced urban growth outwards instead of upwards, leaving many older, central buildings still standing instead of being replaced. Then in 1862 the railway from Moscow to Nizhny Novgorod bypassed Suzdal by 30km, reducing the town to an underdeveloped backwater until its renaissance in the last years of the Communist era – as a tourist attraction.

HISTORY

The first recorded mention of Suzdal was in 1024 when many townsfolk were put to the sword by the local prince after a peasant rebellion. By the end of that century the town's first major fortification had been built and in 1152 Yuri Dolgoruky, son of Prince Vladimir Monomakh, transferred the seat of princely power here. Within a few years Suzdal had more people than London at that time.

Despite the shift of power by Dolgoruky's son, Andrei Bogolyubsky, to Vladimir, Suzdal continued to grow until 1238, when it was devastated by the Tatar-Mongols. The town tried to rebuild itself as a trading and political centre but its dreams were shattered after another rebellion was put down by Moscow in the mid 15th century. Although most of its people eventually moved elsewhere, Suzdal remained a strong religious centre; at one point there were seven churches and cathedrals in the Kremlin, 14 within the city ramparts and 27 more scattered around various local monasteries.

In 1573 the town had just 400 households; disasters over the next few centuries ensured that the number didn't rise much. Between 1608 and 1610 the town was raided several times by Polish and Lithuanian forces: in 1634 it was devastated by Crimean Tatars; in 1644 most of its wooden buildings were burnt down; in 1654 the plague wiped out almost half the population; and in a huge fire in 1719 every remaining wooden building in the centre was destroyed.

WHAT TO SEE AND DO

Kremlin Кремль

The Suzdal Kremlin (10am-6pm daily, closed last Fri of month, individual exhibits R40-70, all-inclusive ticket R400) of the 11th century was ringed by 1400m of earth embankments topped with log walls and towers. These fortifications survived until the 18th century but the only sections left today are the small earth walls dotted around the city.

The enormous **Cathedral of the Birth of the Mother of God Собор Рождества Богородицы**, its five blue onion domes dotted with golden stars and containing stunning 13th- to 17th-century frescoes, is the most striking building within the Kremlin and one of the oldest cathedrals in Russia. It was begun in 1222 and completed in just two years; the upper tier was rebuilt in 1530. The octagonal **bell tower**, added in 1635, was once fitted with bells that chimed not only hourly but on the minute. Attached to the bell tower by a gallery is the 15th- to 18th-century Archbishop's Chambers, which now houses

Suzdal History Museum Суздальский Исторический Музей. The museum
traces the history of the town through Iron Age artefacts, medieval costumes
and weaponry and exhibits dealing with the Soviet destruction of Suzdal's
wealth and its subsequent restoration. Nearby is the Cross Chamber, a vast ceremonial reception hall built in the 18th century.

Also within the old walls are two **churches** dedicated to **St Nicholas**: a
stone one to the south-east, completed in 1739 and considered one of Suzdal's
finest 18th-century buildings, and a wooden one to the south-west, brought here
from the nearby village of Glotovo. (Note: there is also a Church of St Nicholas
near the Convent of the Intercession.)

Torgovaya ploshchad Торговая площадь

On the western side of Torgovaya pl (Market Sq) are the pillared **Torgoviye
Ryady (Trading Arcades) Торговые Ряды** built at the turn of the 19th century, now containing shops, bars and restaurants. Locals sell fresh produce just
outside the Trading Arcades, so here's your chance to stock up on excellent
homemade jams and dried mushrooms as well as fresh fruit and vegetables.
Originally there was a second arcade facing the Kamenka River.

Nearby are several more 18th-century churches, including the
Resurrection Church Воскресенская Церковь, with its faded frescoes.
Climb the musty spiral staircase of the belltower (R50) for a sweeping view of
Suzdal's rooftops. (Note there is another Resurrection Church on ul Tolstogo.)

On the square and along the adjoining ul Kremlyovskaya ул
Кремлёвская, you'll usually find a number of stalls selling *medovukha*, the
traditional mead made by mixing distilled honey and water together. It ranges
from mildly giggle-inducing to potent and you can choose your poison at the
Mead-Tasting Hall (see p236) inside the Trading Arcades.

Monastery of the Saviour and St Euthimius
Спасо-Евфимеевский Монастырь

This fortified monastery (10am-6pm, closed Mon and last Thur of month, R70
to access the attractive grounds and R70 per museum, or R350 all-inclusive,
camera R100) was founded in the mid 14th century to protect Suzdal's northern
approaches, and greatly expanded during its heyday in the 16th and 17th centuries, thanks to patronage by Ivan the Terrible, among others. Its various buildings are home to several museums.

You enter the monastery via a 22m-high tower gate and beneath the **Gate-
Church of the Annunciation**. In the church is an exhibition on a local prince,
Dmitry Pozharsky, who raised the volunteer army which liberated Moscow
from Polish-Lithuanian forces in 1612 with the help of Kuzma Minin, a village
elder in Nizhny Novgorod.

Pozharsky's grave is by the eastern wall of the **Cathedral of the
Transfiguration of the Saviour**. The 17th-century frescoes here are particularly impressive. Some mornings a choir gives a short but beautiful recital in the
cathedral and you can hear the bells being rung on the hour, every hour. In a side
chapel is the grave of St Euthimius, who founded the monastery in 1352.

Beside the 17th-century Church of St Nicholas is the **Infirmary**, where a museum called the **Golden Treasury** features Russian decorative art of the 13th-20th centuries.

The long, single-storey building nearby was the monastery **prison**, used between 1766 and 1905 for those who had committed crimes against the faith. Now it's become the **Convicts of the Monastery Prison Museum**. In Stalinist times, political prisoners were kept here before being sent to Siberia; exhibits include heartbreaking letters to their loved ones and personal effects. The same prison was used to house Italian and German prisoners of war after WWII; a separate exhibit, 'Interweaving of Fates', tells their story. Incidentally, foreign visitors to Suzdal have included many Italians – first, the ex-liberated prisoners, then their descendants.

The **Monks' Cells** now house a thorough exhibition showing the history of the town's convents and monasteries and 'Defeating Time' charts their restoration. The only drawback is the lack of labelling in English.

Convent of the Intercession Покровский Монастырь

This convent (9.30am-4.30pm Thur-Mon, free), founded in 1364, offers an insight into the patriarchal nature of traditional Russian society. Euphemistically referred to as a retreat for high-spirited women, it was in fact a place of banishment for infertile wives, victims of dynastic squabbles and women who broke any of the harsh customs of medieval society.

First to use it in this way, in 1525, was Moscow's Grand Prince Vasily, whose wife Solomonia Saburova bore him no heirs. Solomonia, whose revenge was to outlive Vasily and his second wife, is buried in the **Intercession Cathedral**, completed in 1518. Legend has it that she then gave birth to a baby boy and, fearing for his life as a rival of Vasily's second wife's son – Ivan the Terrible – she pretended that he'd died, giving him up for adoption instead. The absence of any body in the small crypt next to her own, and the presence of a shirt stuffed to resemble a baby, discovered by historians in 1934, lends credibility to the story. Other famous women forced into the habit here were: Praskovya Solovaya, second wife of Ivan the Great; Anna Vasilchikova, Ivan the Terrible's fourth wife; and Evdokya Lopukhina, Peter the Great's first wife.

The three-domed **Gateway Church of the Annunciation** sits above the Holy Gates. The two-storey **Refectory Church of the Conception of St Anna** was built in 1551 on the orders of Ivan the Great. This is a working convent and not a museum, so many of the buildings, including the simple log cabins that house the convent's residents, are off limits, but that doesn't detract from the pleasure of wandering through the grounds which are particularly attractive in the summer when the flowers are in full bloom.

Museum of Wooden Architecture Музей Деревянного Зодчества

This open-air museum (ul Pushkarskaya, May-Oct Wed-Mon 9.30am-7pm, until 4pm Nov-Apr, closed last Wed of month, all-inclusive ticket R160) comprises around 20 examples of a vanishing regional wooden architecture, including churches, peasant houses, windmills, barns and granaries. Among the most striking buildings are the **Church of the Transfiguration**, erected in 1756, and the **Church of the Resurrection**, built in 1776. Though you may only enter three of the above buildings you can imagine what life was like for Russian peasants, thanks to museum staff in traditional costumes who can demonstrate the workings of a weaving loom and other equipment.

Monastery of the Deposition of the Robe
Ризоположенский Монастырь

Founded in 1207, this is Suzdal's oldest monastery, although only a few of its original buildings remain: the asymmetrical, double-arched **Holy Gates** (1688), topped with tiny onion domes; the plain **Cathedral of the Deposition of the Robe**, dating from the first half of the 16th century; and a 72m-high **bell tower** visible from all over town and thought to have been erected in honour of Napoleon's defeat in 1812.

MAP KEY

WHERE TO STAY
1 Surikov home Дом Суриковых
6 Stromynka 2 Стромынка 2
8 Best Western Art Hotel Nikolaevsky Posad Гостиница Покровская
11 Godzillas Suzdal
27 Kremlyovsky Hotel
   Кремлёвский Отель
29 Pushkarskaya Sloboda
   Пушкарская Слобода

WHERE TO EAT AND DRINK
13 Kharchevnya Харчевня
15 Mead-Tasting Hall
   Дегустационный зал
17 Losos I Kofe Лосось и Кофе
18 Chaynaya Чайная
21 Restaurant Trapeznaya (in the Kremlin) Ресторан Трапезная

PLACES OF INTEREST
2 Monastery of the Saviour & St Euthimius
   Спасо-Евфимеевский Монастырь
3 Convent of the Intercession
   Покровский Монастырь
4 Church of SS Peter & Paul
   Петропавловская Церковь
5 Church of St Nicholas
   Никольская Церковь

7 St Aleksandr Nevsky Monastery
   Александровский Монастырь
10 Monastery of the Deposition of the Robe
   Ризоположенский Монастырь
14 Torgoviye Ryady (Trading Arcades)
   Торговые Ряды
16 Resurrection Church
   Воскресенская Церковь
19 Cathedral of the Birth of the Mother of God
   Собор Рождества Богородицы
20 Suzdal History Museum
   Суздальский Исторический Музей
22 Church of St Nicholas
   Никольская Церковь
23 Wooden church of St Nicholas
   Церковь Святого Николы
25 Church of the Transfiguration
   Преображенская Церковь
26 Resurrection Church
   Воскресенская Церковь
28 Museum of Wooden Architecture
   Музей Деревянного Зодчества
30 Church of the Deposition of the Robe
   Ризоположенская церковь

OTHER
9 Post Office Почта
12 Sberbank Сбербанк
24 Dva Kolesa Два Колеса

The Suzdal area code is ☎ 49231. From outside Russia dial ☎ +7-49231.

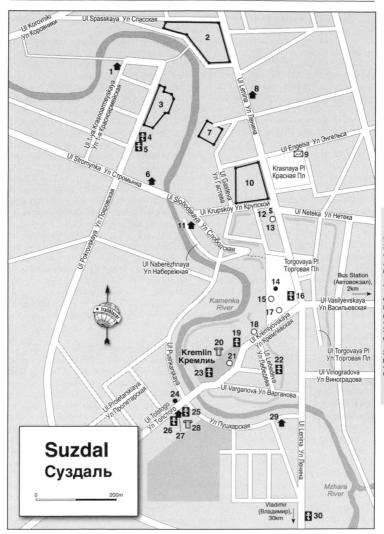

Ul Korovniki Ул Коровники
Ul.Spasskaya Ул Спасская
2
1
Ul.1-ya Krasnoarmeyskaya Ул 1-я Красноармейская
3
8
Ul Lenina Ул Ленина
4
5
7
Ul Stromynka Ул Стромынка
Ul Engelsa Ул Энгельса
9
6
Ul Gasteva Ул Гастева
Krasnaya Pl Красная Пл
10
Ul Slobodskaya Ул Слободская
Ul Pokrovskaya Ул Покровская
Ul Krupskoy Ул Крупской
Ul Neteka Ул Нетека
12 $
11
13
Ul Naberezhnaya Ул Набережная
Torgovaya Pl Торговая Пл
14
Bus Station (Автовокзал), 2km
Kamenka River
15
16
Ul Vasilyevskaya Ул Васильевская
17
18
Ul Kremlyovskaya Ул Кремлёвская
19
Ul Pushkarskaya Ул Пушкарская
20
Kremlin Кремлиь
Ul Lebedeva Ул Лебедева
21
Ul Torgovaya Pl Ул Торговая Пл
22
23
UI Vinogradova Ул Виноградова
Ul Varganova Ул Варганова
24
Ul Proletarskaya Ул Пролетарская
UI Tolstogo Ул Толстого
25
Ул Пушкарская
29
26
27
28
UI Lenina Ул Ленина

Suzdal
Суздаль

0   200m

Mzhara River

Vladimir (Владимир), 30km
30

PRACTICAL INFORMATION
Orientation and services
Ul Lenina ул Ленина is the town's main street, running north–south. Virtually everything to see is within walking distance, though if you prefer to get about on two wheels, you can **rent bicycles** from Dva Kolesa (Two Wheels) Два Колеса (☎ 910-182 0252) at ul Tolstogo 5.

There's a **post office почта** (8am-8pm Mon-Sat) on Krasnaya pl. There is no internet café and very few accommodation options offer internet or wi-fi.

To get to and from the **bus station автовокзал** (see Moving on), either take one of the frequent buses along ul Vasilyevskaya ул Васильевская (or pay the driver an additional R13 if coming from out of town to get you to the centre of Suzdal), or walk for around 20 minutes.

Where to stay

For a small place, popular Suzdal has a wide range of accommodation to suit all budgets.

Backpackers make straight for the busy and popular *Godzillas Suzdal* (ул Набережная 32, ul Naberezhnaya 32, ☎ 25146, 💻 www.godzillashostel.com, dorm bed R650-750; WI-FI) by the river. This branch of the popular Moscow hostel is a large, well-furnished wooden house with spacious en suite dorms, comfortable bunks with reading lights and plenty of common spaces. The friendly woman who runs it doesn't speak much English, but she goes out of her way to make you feel welcome; the bath towels provided are human-sized rather than Hobbit-sized – a rarity in Russia.

The well-located *Best Western Art Hotel Nikolaevsky Posad* **Гостиница Покровская** (ул Ленина 138 ul Lenina 138, ☎ 252 52, 💻 www.bestwestern.com, dbl R3650-6150, WI-FI) consists of modern, comfortable rooms with satellite TV surrounded by plusher 'cottages' with Jacuzzis. The (mostly) bilingual service is helpful, but eating at one of the three on-site restaurants does not come cheap; use of the swimming pool costs extra.

Elena Surikova and her artist husband, Vladimir, have converted their house (*Surikov Home*, **Дом Суриковых**, ул Красноармейская 53, ul Krasnoarmeyskaya 53, ☎ 215 68, 💻 www .surikovs.ru, dbl/trpl/quad R2500/3500/4000) into a small hotel with bright rooms decked out in soothing creams. Breakfast is included.

Also central, *Pushkarskaya Sloboda* **Пушкарская Слобода** (ул Ленина 45, ul

Lenina 45, ☎ 233 03, 💻 www.sloboda-gk .ru, dbl/lux from R3200-4100/8800-10,900) is a family-friendly holiday complex with something for everyone – from romantic honeymoon suites to 'Russkoye Podvorye' pine log cabins. There's also a swimming pool, Turkish bath, Russian banya and a fondue bar, besides the okayish on-site restaurants, but you may be sharing the hotel with several wedding parties.

Smelling like the forest, the spacious en suite rooms at the log cabin hotel *Stromynka 2* **Стромынка 2** (ул Стромынка 2, ul Stromynka 2, ☎ 251 55, ☎ 235 69, 💻 www.stromynka2.ru, dbl/lux R2800-3600/5200-6000) have untreated wooden walls that give them their wonderful scent. Deduct R400 from double room prices for single occupancy.

If you want to wake up with the Kremlin's towers outside your window, the subtly lit, contemporary rooms at *Kremlyovsky Hotel* **Кремлёвский Отель** (ул Толстого 5, ul Tolstogo 5, ☎ 234 80, 250 55, 💻 www.kremlinhotel.ru, sgl/dbl/lux from R2700/2900/5000) offer great views of Suzdal's star attraction across the river.

Where to eat and drink

There are several eateries inside Torgoviye Ryady. In the vaulted *Mead-Tasting Hall* **Дегустационный Зал** you can sample seven different versions of *medovukha* (the main one ranging from 'mildly tipsy' to 'strong'; R20-25 per sample). Bizarrely, though the restaurant in the room next door has medovukha on the menu, you may only order it in the 'tasting hall'. In the southeastern corner there's *Losos I Kofe* **Лосось и Кофе** ([V], mains from R200), a trendy café serving (true to its name – 'Salmon and Coffee') well-prepared salmon dishes and good coffee, as well as sushi, Japanese noodle bento boxes, blini, salads and other light mains.

Your best bet for good Russian food that won't hurt the wallet is *Chaynaya* **Чайная** (ул Кремлёвская 10, ul Kremlyovskaya 10), decorated like a pre-revolutionary teahouse and overlooking the river. All the favourites are on offer: superb blini, hearty *solyanka* and borsch, pelmeni, mushroom julienne and more. Wash it all down with a selection of *mors* drinks, ranging from cranberry to hawthorn berry.

Along the main street, friendly, dimly lit *Kharchevnya* Харчевня (ul Lenina 73, ул Ленина 73, [V]) is also a good spot for inexpensive soups and fish and meat dishes.

Though *Restaurant Trapeznaya* Ресторан Трапезная inside the Kremlin (mains from R350) is a favourite with tour groups, don't let this put you off the upmarket Russian dishes, which are imaginative and well prepared. Try the stuffed karp baked in foil, the tender-baked rabbit, the salmon shashlyk, or the 'monastery-style' meat.

Moving on
Buses leave every half an hour or so to Vladimir between 7.20am and 10.30pm (R65, 50 mins).

Suzdal's bus station is just under 2km east of the centre of the town.

Nizhny Novgorod
Нижний Новгород

[**Moscow Time, population: 1,259,921**] The fifth largest city in Russia, Nizhny (as it's locally known) takes pride in its attractive riverside location and hilltop Kremlin, with locals promenading till late at night along the embankment and on the pedestrianised ul Bolshaya Pokrovskaya.

Nizhny Novgorod was founded in 1221 by Prince Vladimir Monomakh at the junction of the Oka and Volga rivers. This strategic location on two central shipping routes virtually guaranteed its growth and prosperity, and in 1612, the army rallied by merchant Kuzma Minin and Count Dmitri Pozharsky (see p232) fought off the Polish forces that had designs on the city. Nizhny's importance as a major trading centre was consolidated with the opening in 1817 of the Nizhny Novgorod Fair. By the 1870s this fair had a turnover of some 300 million gold roubles. To put this into perspective, the entire Trans-Siberian railway cost about 1000 million roubles to build.

In the 1930s Nizhny was turned into a major Soviet military-industrial centre, closed to foreigners and renamed Gorky, after the Russian novelist and playwright Maxim Gorky (1868-1936), who was born here. In the 1980s it was best known outside the USSR as a place of internal exile for dissidents, most famously the nuclear physicist and Nobel Peace Prize winner Andrei Sakharov.

Following the collapse of communism the city was reopened in 1991 and given back its old name, and its fair was reborn in the fabulously renovated 1800s Empire-style Fair Building. Nizhny Novgorod's history as a proud part of the old Rus, its attractive old centre with ramshackle old wooden buildings, killer views of the Volga, and a laidback atmosphere have turned it into a popular destination.

Additional places of interest are Gorodets (see p243), known for its folk crafts, and Makariev (see p244) whose main attraction is its monastery.

WHAT TO SEE AND DO

Kremlin Кремль

The well-preserved Kremlin (🖥 www.ngiamz.ru), with its 13 impressive towers, dating back to the 16th century, sits on a hill dominating the area. The sweeping views of the Volga and Oka rivers from the memorial park more than justify the steep walk up inside the Kremlin and there's another attractive walk around its 12m-high walls. Inside are the City Hall, the appealing 17th-century **Cathedral of the Archangel Michael Собор Михаила Архангела**, and an eternal flame dedicated to the memory of the unknown soldier next to the **Monument to Heroes of WWII Памятник героем Великой Отечественной войны**.

Also on-site is the main building of the excellent **Nizhegorodsky State Art Museum Нижегородский Государственный Художественный Музей** (11am-6pm Wed-Mon, until 8pm Thur, 🖥 www.artmuseumnn.ru, R120), in the former Governor's House, its exhibitions tracing the history of Russian art from 16th-century icons and Russian masters such as Nikolai Rerikh, Vasily Surikov and Ilya Repin to Soviet art. The former **Arsenal**, just to the right of the main gate, is home to the **National Centre of Contemporary Art Государственный Центр Современного Искусства** (noon-8pm Tue-Sun, 🖥 www.ncca.ru, R120) which doubles as a workspace for artists and an art gallery with temporary exhibitions by home-grown talent and international artists.

Three of the Kremlin's towers (combined ticket R150), **Dmitry Tower Дмитриевская Башня** (10am-4.30pm Tue-Sun, R50), **Ivanov Tower Ивановская Башня** (10am-5pm Tue-Sun, R35) and **Zachatskaya Tower Зачатская Башня** (10am-8pm daily May-Oct, R100) feature changing local history exhibits. Dmitry Tower is also the starting point for the Kremlin wall walk (10am-8pm daily May-Oct, free).

Old Nizhny Novgorod

The old town has two interesting pedestrian-only streets. The one-kilometre long **ul Bolshaya Pokrovskaya Ул Большая Покровскаяruns** runs from pl Gorkogo to pl Minina i Pozharskogo (in front of the Kremlin), past the Drama Theatre, the impressive Art Nouveau State Bank building and the Duma parliamentary building. Typical of Russian cobbled streets of the late 18th century is **ul Rozhdestvenskaya Ул Рождественская**, the most appealing section of which is from the river station to the northern gate of the Kremlin.

The **Ostrog Острог**, currently under renovation, is where prisoners exiled to

SS PETER & PAUL CHURCH

Siberia were kept overnight on their forced march to the east. Its most famous prisoner was the USSR's first prime minister, Mikhail Sverdlov.

A short walk from the Kremlin, in **Sirotkin House Дом Сироткина** at Verkhne-Volzhskaya nab 3 (Верхне-Волжская наб 3), is the second branch of the Nizhnegorodsky State Art Museum (same opening times, R120), comprising a collection of lesser-known European artists, as well as a separate exhibition devoted to the dramatic landmark painting by K Makovsky, *Minin's Appeal* (R50). A couple of doors down at Verkhne-Volzhskaya nab 7 (Верхне-Волжская наб 7) and well-worth visiting is **Rukavishnikov House Дом Рукавишниковых** (10am-5pm Tue-Thur, to 7pm Fri-Sun, tours R350), a splendid 19th-century mansion belonging to the family of merchant Rukavishnikov. Tours in Russian and English leave every 90 minutes and last around 40 minutes.

Other sights

The dissident nuclear physicist Andrei Sakharov was exiled to Gorky from January 1981 to December 1986. His old flat at pr Gagarina 214 (пр Гагарина 214) has been turned into the **Andrei Sakharov Apartment-Museum Квартира-Музей Андрея Сахарова** (10am-5pm, closed Fri, R55); the exhibition includes the telephone which Gorbachev called to tell Sakharov that he was free. It's 3km south of the centre; take bus No 1 from pl Minina i Pozharskogo or marshrutka No 19 from the railway station.

The **Museum of Volga People's Architecture and Culture Музей Архитектуры и Быта Народов Нижнегородского Поволжья** (ul Gorbatovskaya 41 ул Горбатовская 41; 10am-4pm Sat-Thur, R60, 🖥 www.ngiamz.ru) is set in the park area known as Shcholokovsky Khutor, south-east of the city centre and at the end of bus route No 28, which passes along ul Belinskogo, a block from M Gorkogo. There's an entertaining collection of traditional Russian and Mordovan wooden buildings, including an Old Believers' Church; if you're lucky, you'll catch one of five annual festivals celebrated here.

The walled **Assumption Pechorskiy Monastery Печёрский Вознесенский монастырь** (Privolzhskaya Sloboda 108 Приволжская Слобода 108, 7.30am-6.30pm daily, 🖥 www.percherskiy.nne.ru), built in the 17th century, boasts attractive grounds and green onion-domed churches.

Take a peek into the **Museum of the History of the Diocese Музей Истории Епархии** (10am-5pm daily, R30), with archaeological displays, icons and other church art and an exhibition devoted to the repressions against the Church during the Soviet years. Take any bus or marshrutka from pl Minina i Pozharskogo to the nearby Sennaya pl (Сенная Площадь).

The even more beautiful, golden-domed **Annunciation Monastery Вознесенский монастырь** (8am-7pm daily, 🖥 www.blagovmm.ru), on Melnichny per 7a (Мельничный пер 7a), dates back to 1221, which makes it one of Nizhny's oldest original buildings. Take marshrutka No 51 from pl Minina i Pozharskogo or bus No 5 along Nizhne-Volzhskaya nab.

Maxim Gorky, born here in 1868, wrote of the cruelty and injustice of rural Tsarist Russia, making his books compulsory reading for Soviet children. Gorky historical sites include: his **birthplace Место Рождения Горького** (ul

CITY GUIDES & PLANS

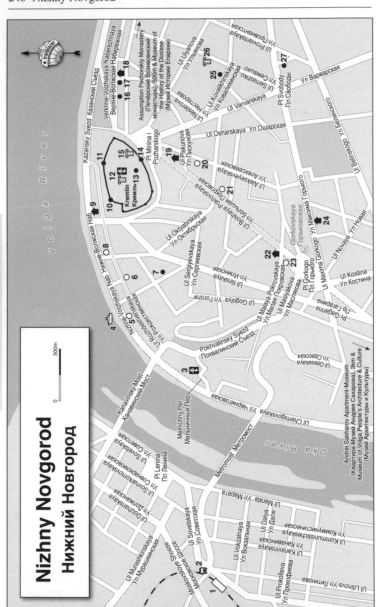

Nizhny Novgorod
Нижний Новгород

Volga River
Volga River

Oka River

Kazansky Syezd Казанский Съезд
Verkhne-Volzhskaya Naberezhnaya
Верхне-Волжская Набережная

Assumption Pechorsky Monastery
(Печерский Вознесенский
монастырь), 500m & Museum of
the History of the Diocese
(Музей Истории Епархии)

Ul Ulyanova Ул Ульянова
Ul Kovalikhinskaya Ул Ковалихинская
Ul Semashko Ул Семашко
Ul Nesterova Ул Нестерова
Ul Varvarskaya Ул Варварская
Pl Svobody Пл Свободы
Ul Varvarskaya Ул Варварская

Ul Osharskaya Ул Ошарская

Pl Minina i
Pozharskogo
Pl Minina i Pozharskogo

Kazansky Syezd Казанский Съезд

Ul Piskunova Ул Пискунова
Ul Aleksseyevskaya Ул Алексеевская
Ul Bolshaya Pokrovskaya Ул Большая Покровская
Ul Alekseyevskaya

Kremlin
Кремль

Ul Oktyabrskaya Ул Октябрьская
Ul Sergiyevskaya Ул Сергиевская
Ul Ilinskaya Ул Ильинская
Ul Gogolya Ул Гоголя
Ul Malaya Pokrovskaya Ул Малая Покровская
Ul Maslyakova Ул Маслякова

Nizhne-Volzhskaya Nab Нижне-Волжская Наб
Ul Rozhdestvenskaya Ул Рождественская

Ul Gorkogo Ул Максима Горького
Pl Gorkogo Пл Горького
Ul Novaya Ул Новая
Ul Kostina Ул Костина
Pr Gagarina Пр Гагарина

Ul Belinskogo Ул Белинского
Ul Proletarskaya Ул Пролетарская

Pokhvalinsky Syezd
Похвалинский Съезд

Kanavinsky Most
Канавинский Мост
Melnichny Per
Мельничный Пер

Ul Chernigovskaya Ул Черниговская
Ul Odesskaya Ул Одесская

Metromost Метромост

Andrei Sakharov Apartment-Museum
(Квартира-Музей Андрея Сахарова), 3km &
Museum of Volga People's Architecture & Culture
(Музей Архитектуры и Культуры)

Ul Murashkinskaya Ул Мурашкинская
Ul Sovetskaya Ул Советская
Ul Lenina Пл Ленина
Ul Sverdlovskaya Ул Свердловская
Ul Sovetskaya Ул Советская

Ul Marata Ул Марата
Ul Vokzalnaya Ул Вокзальная
Ul Dalya Ул Даля
Ul Chavainskaya Ул Чавайнская
Ul Kanavinskaya Ул Канавинская
Ul Kommunisticheskaya Ул Коммунистическая

Ul Litinova Ул Литинова
Ul Prokofieva Ул Прокофьева

500m
0

N trailblazer

Kovalikhinskaya 33); **Domik Kashirina**, his grandfather's house on Pochtovy syezd, where he and his mother moved in 1870; and **Gorky Apartment-Museum Музей Горького** (ul Semashko 19) where he lived from 1902 to 1904. However, these are of limited interest to anyone other than Russian-speaking Gorky fans. There's also a **statue** commemorating the man on pl Gorkogo.

Another well-known regional son is air pioneer Valery Chkalov; his fame comes from circumnavigating the USSR in June 1936 and flying non-stop from Moscow via the North Pole to Vancouver in June 1937. Chkalov's **statue** stands by the Aleksandrovsky Gardens.

PRACTICAL INFORMATION
Orientation and services

The central part of Nizhny Novgorod and the Kremlin lie at the junction of the Volga and Oka rivers. There are three main focal points: the railway station, aka Moscow Station, Железнодорожный Вокзал (or Московский вокзал) is across the river from the centre; pl Minina i Pozharskogo is directly in front of the Kremlin, and pedestrianised ul Bolshaya Pokrovskaya ул

MAP KEY

WHERE TO STAY
9 Hostel Naberezhnaya Хостел Набережная
18 Hotel Oktyabrskaya Гостиница Октябрьская
19 Smile Hostel
22 Hotel Jouk Jacque Гостиница Жук-Жак
24 Hotel Ibis Отель Ибис

WHERE TO EAT & DRINK
5 Tyubiteyka Тюбетейка
6 Papasha Billy Папаша Билли
8 Restoryatsiya Pyatkin Реторація Пяткинъ
20 Moloko Молоко
21 Traveler's Coffee
23 Angliyskoye Posol'stvo Английское Посольство

PLACES OF INTEREST
3 Annunciation Monastery Вознесенский монастырь
7 Domik Kashirina Домик Каширина
10 Ivanov Tower Ивановская Башня
11 Zachatskaya Tower Зачатская Башня
12 Kremlin Кремль
12 Cathedral of the Archangel Michael Собор Михаила Архангела
12 Nizhegorodsky State Art Museum Нижегородский Художественный Музей
13 Monument to Heroes of WWII Памятник Героям Великой Отечественной Войны
14 Dmitry Tower Дмитриевская Башня
15 National Centre of Contemporary Art in former Arsenal Государственный Центр Современного Искусства и Арсенал
16 Sirotkin House Дом Сироткина
17 Rukavishnikov House Дом Рукавишниковых
25 Gorky's Birthplace Место Рождения Горького
26 Gorky Apartment-Museum Музей Горького
27 Ostrog Острог

OTHER
1 Railway Station Железнодорожный Вокзал
2 Bus Station Автовокзал
4 River Station Речной Вокзал

Большая Покровская is the main shopping street, which links it with pl Gorkogo.

Wi-fi is available at the station and at most of the accommodation options.

Local transport
Nizhny Novgorod's **metro** has now opened: the handy Gorkovskaya station (**M** Горьковская) a block away from the southern end of ul Bolshaya Pokrovskaya, handy for visiting all the central attractions and just a stop away from **M** Moskovskaya, just in front of the railway station. There's a comprehensive network of **trams** and **buses**; to go to the Kremlin, take any with пл Минина и Пожарского (pl Minina i Pozharskogo) as its destination. To return to the railway station, catch buses and marshrutkas on the Kremlin side. Pick up a city map with transport routes at a kiosk across the road from the railway station.

You can reach both Gorodets and Makariev (see opposite) by boat from the **River station**.

Where to stay
Out of several hostels that have opened in Nizhny, the best is ★ *Smile Hostel* (ул Большая Покровская 4, ul Bolshaya Pokrovskaya 4, ☎ 216 0222, 🖥 www.smile hostel.net, dorm/dbl R590-690/1700, WI-FI), right on the main pedestrianised street. Street art greets you on the stairs, there's an open-plan kitchen/lounge strewn with bean bags, with an extra chillout space in the loft; each bunk bed is hidden behind brightly patterned curtains for privacy and the reception staff are very helpful.

Hostel Naberezhnaya **Хостел Набережная** (Нижне-Волжская наб 7/2 Nizhne-Volzhskaya nab 7/2, ☎ 831 230 1315, 🖥 www.bereg-hostel.ru, dorm/dbl from R350/990, WI-FI) features rather spartan rooms with high ceilings and utilitarian shared facilities (including guest kitchen); its advantage is its location right below the Kremlin.

Hotel Ibis **Отель Ибис** (ул Максима Горького 115, ul Maksima Gorkogo 115, ☎ 233 1100, 🖥 www.ibishotel.com, rooms from R3500, WI-FI), well located near a metro stop, is an efficient mid-range place aimed largely at business travellers.

The décor at the post-Soviet *Hotel Oktyabrskaya* **Гостиница Октябрьская** (наб Верхне-Волжская 9a, nab Verkhne-Volzhskaya 9a, ☎ 432 8080, 🖥 www.oktya brskaya.ru, sgl/dbl/lux from R3400/5000/8000, WI-FI) is unlikely to wow you and the staff are unlikely to win prizes for congeniality, but it does overlook the mighty Volga and its rooms are mostly spacious, renovated affairs. Buffet breakfast included.

The small boutique *Hotel Jouk Jacque* **Гостиница Жук-Жак** (ул Большая Покровская 57, ul Bolshaya Pokrovskaya 57, ☎ 433 4194, 🖥 www.jak-hotel.ru, sgl/dbl/lux from R3750/6825/9375, WI-FI) gets Brownie points for the great central location, equally great breakfast and helpful English-speaking staff. However, the cheapest rooms are small and local drunks may relieve themselves in the alleyway outside your window.

Where to eat and drink
There's a good range of inexpensive cafés and eateries along the pedestrianised ul Bolshaya Pokrovskaya (ул Большая Покровская), while ul Rozhdestvenskaya (ул Рождественская) is home to more upmarket restaurants. A useful website to look at is 🖥 www.pir.nnov.ru.

The menu at trendy *Moloko* **Молоко** (ул Алексеевская 15, ul Alekseevskaya 15, mains from R250, noon-2am daily, 🖥 www.molokocafe.ru, WI-FI) serves the three things Russians love the most: shashlyk, sushi and pasta, but it's all very nicely done; there's even a 'milk' page in homage to the restaurant's name, featuring rice porridge, *syrniki* (cottage cheese fritters), pancakes and other delights that involve the white stuff.

The Nizhny Novgorod area code is ☎ 831. From outside Russia dial ☎ +7-831.

A reliable stop for a caffeine hit, *Traveler's Coffee* (ул Большая Покровская 20б, ul Bolshaya Pokrovskaya 20b, 🖥 www.travelerscoffee.ru, 8am to midnight daily, WI-FI) may also tempt you with its array of cakes, shakes, and things that don't end in -akes, such as salads and light pasta dishes. A favourite with young, iPad-toting locals.

Restoryatsiya Pyatkin **Ресторація Пяткинъ** (ул Рождественская 23, ul Rozhdestvenskaya 23, mains from R300), with its aristocratic setting, lets you pretend that you're a wealthy merchant from days of old by serving you the likes of pike cutlets, beef stroganoff and veal kidneys, washed down with homemade, tangy white apple kvas; a 3-course business lunch is only R275.

The décor at the cowboy saloon-like *Papasha Billy* **Папаша Билли** (ул Рождественская 22, ul Rozhdestvenskaya 22, daily 24 hours, mains from R365, steaks from R1395) may be as clichéd as a saloon bar fight with tumbleweed rolling down the street, but locals flock here in droves for the sizzling steaks, the passable Mexican enchiladas, quesadillas and nachos, and solidly Russian business lunch classics.

If the combination of colourful rugs on walls, brightly tiled entrance and tinkling fountain don't transport you into some Eastern fantasy, at *Tyubiteyka* **Тюбетейка** (ул Рождественская 45б, ul Rozhdestvenskaya 45b, noon-2am daily, mains R500, WI-FI) the Uzbek cuisine just might. It's hard to go wrong with aubergine stuffed with walnuts, tender veal shashlyk, *manti* (giant meat dumplings) and *chebureki* (spiced meat pastries). The service? Meh. Good business lunch for R300.

Though you'd only normally go to *Angliyskoye Posol'stvo* **Английское Посольство** (ул Звездинка 12 ul Zvezdinka 12, **M** Gorkovskaya, open daily, mains from R395) if you lose your passport, here you can make an exception. The menu at the 'English Consulate' is a mélange of Russian, European and 'British' dishes and the atmosphere is what Russians believe a British pub is like; the end result is, actually, rather great.

Moving on

By air There are daily flights to and from Moscow, St Petersburg and other major Russian cities from Nizhny Novgorod International Airport (☎ 256 74 36, 🖥 www.nnov-airport.ru), as well as direct flights from Frankfurt with Lufthansa (5/weekly) and Ural Airlines flights to Prague (4/weekly).

By rail Westbound: There are 17 trains a day between Nizhny Novgorod and Moscow (4-7½hrs), the fastest being the high-speed Sapsan (6.45am and 2.45pm, 4hrs); all trains stop at Vladimir (2-3½hrs, via Vladimir 15/day 41/2245.

Eastbound: Perm (7/day, 13½-15½hrs), the most convenient being the overnight No 92, leaving at 7.28pm; Yekaterinburg (6/day, 20-20hrs) and Irkutsk (002 leaves on alternate days at 8.03pm, 68hrs).

SIDE TRIPS TO GORODETS AND MAKARIEV

Gorodets Городец

The village of Gorodets, home of folk artists, is famous for its hand-painted toys. You can see them being made at the Gorodetskaya Rospis handicraft factory (closed weekends). It's also known for *pryaniki* (the hard honey cakes that Russians eat with tea).

Ferries travel regularly between Nizhny Novgorod (River Station) and Gorodets. On the way you pass **Gorkovsky hydro-electric station** with its 15km-long dam.

CITY GUIDES & PLANS

Makariev Макарьев

A small, quiet village (population: around 200) 60km east along the Volga. The main attraction is **Makariev Monastery Макарьевский Монастырь** (8am-6pm, daily, free), whose walls and domes loom over the town. The monastery was founded in the 15th century and the town grew up around it as a river trading post. Today there's a small museum in the village schoolhouse and several rustic wooden homes. Locals come to take a dip or sunbathe on the sandy beach. Bring your own food as there are few shops here. Boats leave from Nizhny Novgorod's river station (🖳 www.vftour.ru) several times daily in summer.

Perm
Пермь

[Moscow Time +4; population: 1,013,887]   The city of Perm, Pasternak's Yuryatin in *Dr Zhivago*, is the gateway to Siberia. Lying in the foothills of the Ural Mountains, it's a large industrial city with a lively arts scene that includes one of Russia's top ballet schools.

Perm dates back to 1723 and the construction of the Yegoshikhinsky copper foundry, established by VN Tatichev, a close associate of Peter the Great. Its location on two major trading rivers ensured that it grew as both an industrial and a trading city. Salt caravans arrived along the Kama River while wheat, honey and metal products from the Urals travelled along the Chusovoy River. The arrival of the railway in 1878, the discovery of oil in the region and the transfer of factories from European Russia during WWII all boosted the local economy further. The city's most familiar product is the seemingly indestructible Kama bicycle which, while rarely seen on the streets of Russian cities, is still widely used in the country. Perm's most specialised products are the first-stage engines for Proton Heavy-Lift rockets. Despite its industrial history Perm has a tradition of culture and scholarship, thanks largely to the revolutionaries, intellectuals and political prisoners exiled here in the 19th century. Perm had the Urals' first university, whose most famous student was Alexander Popov (1859-1905), a local boy (born in nearby Krasnoturinsk) and, according to Russian historians, the inventor of the wireless. Popov is said to have demonstrated his invention in 1895, the same year that Marconi proved his concept. From 1940 to 1957 Perm was called Molotov, after the subsequently disgraced Soviet Foreign Minister who signed the 1939 Ribbentrop-Molotov Pact, dividing up Poland with the Nazis.

See pp249-51 for details about Kungur Ice Cave, Perm-36 (a gulag-museum) and Khokhlovka, an open-air Museum of Architecture and Ethnography.

WHAT TO SEE AND DO

The most interesting part of town is the old quarter around Perm 1 railway station. Old churches here include the baroque **Cathedral of SS Peter and Paul**

Петропавловский Монастырь (1757-65, with a 19th-century belfry) and the Empire-style **Cathedral of the Saviour Спасский Монастырь**, part of the **Transfiguration Monastery Преображенский Монастырь** (1798-1832). There are also numerous examples of eclectic and Art Nouveau architectural styles, of which the old building of Perm 2 station is one.

★ Museum of Contemporary Art PERMM
Музей Современного Искусства ПЕРММ

The former river station by the Kama river has been transformed into a cutting-edge modern art venue, PERMM (ул Монастырская 2, ul Monastyrskaya 2, noon-9pm Tue-Sun, 💻 www.permm.ru, R120), largely through the efforts of Marat Gelman, gallery owner and sometime political activist. The museum is instantly recognisable by a Batmobile-like car by the entrance.

The changing exhibitions have caused strong reactions; recent ones have included 'Best of Russia' photography, contemporary art of France and Kazakhstan, and 'The Motherland'. Take bus No 3 or trolleybus No 1 or 3 to 'Станция Пермь-1' stop.

Perm Art Gallery **Пермская Галерея Изобразительных Искусст**

The vast former Cathedral of Christ Transfiguration houses one of the largest art galleries in Russia (Комсомольский пр 4, Komsomolsky pr 4, Tue, Wed, Fri & Sat 10am-6pm, Thur noon-9pm, Sun 11am-6pm, 💻 www.permartmuseum .com, R120), complete with interactive elements. Standout exhibits include a collection of wooden sculptures carved by the native Finno-Ugric population following their conversion to Christianity; these include a figure of Jesus with Mongolian features and saints with the blood of sacrificial animals on their faces as a nod back to the ancient Finno-Ugric deities. There are also plenty of landscape and still-life paintings by Russian artists, an expressionist section, decorative art and even a small gallery dedicated to Flemish and Italian Masters.

Take bus No 3 or trolleybus No 1 to 'Художественная Галерея' stop.

Museum of Local Studies **Краеведческий Музей**

Inside the splendid **Meshkov Mansion Дом Мешкова**, this thorough museum (ул Монастырская 11, ul Monastyrskaya 11, 10am-7pm Tue-Sun, 💻 www.mu seumperm.ru, R120) has well-presented exhibits charting the region's history from the earliest human settlement to the 20th century, including weaponry and

---

❏ Follow the arrows

An excellent recent initiative is the treasure hunt-like Green Line (💻 www .lines.perm.ru) that numbers and links all the key historical buildings and sights of interest in the city centre, with detailed info in front of each sight in Russian and English. For a do-it-yourself walking tour, all you have to do is follow the green arrows along the pavement. Your path may also cross the Red Line that links 20 dramatic love stories connected with famous Russian writers, noblemen and others, that have taken place at various central locations. The walk will take from two to eight hours depending on how much you stop to visit museums etc.

CITY GUIDES & PLANS

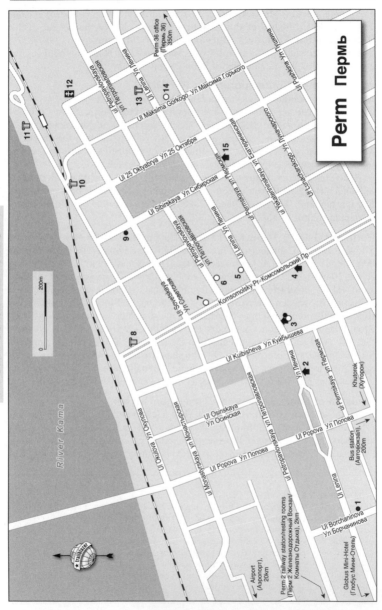

Perm Пермь

Perm 36 office (Пермь 36) 350m

ul Petropavlovskaya Ул Петропавловская

Ул Ленина Ul Lenina

Ul Maksima Gorkogo Ул Максима Горького

13

14

Ul 25 Oktyabrya Ул 25 Октября

Ul Pushkina Ул Пушкина

Ul Sibirskaya Ул Сибирская

ul Lunacharskogo Ул Луначарского

ul Ekaterininskaya Ул Екатерининская

ul Permskaya Ул Пермская

ul Petropavlovskaya Ул Петропавловская

Ul Lenina Ул Ленина

Komsomolsky Pr Комсомольский Пр

Ul Sovetskaya Ул Советская

ul Osinskaya Ул Осинская

Ul Kuibysheva Ул Куйбышева

Ul Lenina Ул Ленина

ul Monastyrskaya Ул Монастырская

ul Petropavlovskaya Ул Петропавловская

Ul Osinskaya Ул Осинская

Ul Popova Ул Попова

Ul Okulova Ул Окулова

Ul Popova Ул Попова

River Kama

200m

0

Ul Lenina Ул Ленина

ul Permskaya Ул Пермская

ul Remzaka Ул Ремзака

Khutorok (Хуторок)

Bus station (Автовокзал), 200m

Ul Borchaninova Ул Борчанинова

Globus Mini-Hotel (Глобус Мини-Отель)

Airport, (Аэропорт), 20km

Perm 2 railway station/resting rooms (Пермь 2 Железнодорожный Вокзал/ Комнаты Отдыха), 2km

1
2
3
4
5
6
7
8
9
10
11
12
15

everyday objects. Of particular interest are the metal castings of the 'Perm animal style', as practised by the ancient Finno-Ugric tribes, as well as the exhibit dedicated to the impact of the civil war and WWII on the Perm area. Other exhibits include the fauna and flora of the region and a section dedicated to prominent manufacturer families in Siberia.

Other sights

Other sights include **Gribushin House Дом Грибушина** (ul Lenina 13 ул Ленина 13) on which Dr Zhivago's 'house with figures' was based. At ul Osinskaya 5 ул Осипская 5 you'll find an attractive mosque, while those with an interest in macabre facts may wish to wander past **Hotel Tsentralnaya Гостиница Центральная** (ul Sibirskaya 5 ул Сибирская 5), where the man next in line for the throne after the demise of the Romanov family, Grand Prince Mikhail, stayed on his last night before the Bolsheviks dispatched him.

PRACTICAL INFORMATION
Orientation and services

The town is spread along the Kama River with its centre just south of the old Perm-1 station, on the left (eastern) bank. At the southern end of Perm, also on the left bank, is Perm-2 station where Trans-Siberian trains stop. Perm-2, around 2km from the city centre, is connected to the centre by tram Nos 4, 5 and 7 (R16).

Perm has a bad habit of frequently renaming its streets. **Street names** were correct at the time of writing, but don't be surprised if they change more than once during the lifetime of this edition.

Krasnov Tourism Краснов Туризм (ул Борчанинова 4, ul Borchaninova 4, ☎ 238 3520, ☎ 236 0707, 🖥 www.uraltourism .com, 10am-6pm Mon-Fri) is recommended

CITY GUIDES & PLANS

WHERE TO STAY
2 Hostel P Хостел П
3 Hotel Ural Гостиница Урал
4 Hotel Prikamiye Гостиница Прикамье
15 Hotel Tsvety Гостиница Цветы

WHERE TO EAT & DRINK
3 Stroganovskaya Votchina Строгановская Вотчина
5 Zhivago & Café Pasternak Живаго & Кафе Пастернак
6 Crêperie Française Крепери Франсез
7 Cup by Cup
14 Grill Tavern Montenegro Гриль-Таверна Монтенегро

PLACES OF INTEREST
8 Perm Art Gallery Пермская Галерея Изобразительных Искусств
9 Hotel Tsentralnaya Гостиница Центральная
10 Museum of Local Studies, Meshkov Mansion Краеведческий Музей Дом Мешкова
11 Museum of Contemporary Art PERMM Музей Современного Искусства ПЕРММ
12 Cathedral of SS Peter & Paul & Cathedral of the Saviour (part of the Transfiguration Monastery) Петропавловская Собор & Спасская Собор
13 Gribushin House Дом Грибушина

OTHER
1 Krasnov Tourism Краснов Туризм
3 Permtourist Пермьтурист

and arranges all manner of tours, ranging from multi-day wilderness excursions and river cruises to Perm city tours and trips to Kungur Ice Cave (see opposite).

Helpful **Permtourist Пермьтурист** (☎ 218 6999, 🖳 www.permtourist.ru) inside Hotel Ural, 2nd Fl, can arrange boat trips along the Kama and Chusovoy rivers and also does day trips to Kungur Ice Cave. They also issue a Russian-language booklet on the attractions along the Green Line, with detailed information on each sight.

Where to stay

The wonderful *Globus Mini-Hotel* Глобус **Мини-Отель** (ул Кронштадтская 4, ul Kronshtadtskaya 4, ☎ 238 4222, 🖳 www .globus-hotel.com, dbl R1950-2500, WI-FI) consists of just four bright, sweet en suite rooms in a good location. The English-speaking staff get rave reviews for their helpfulness and attentiveness to guests' needs and price includes a continental breakfast. To get there take tram 4 or 5 from Perm 2 to the ul Petroparbuskaya stop, then walk south along ul Plekanova until it crosses ul Kronshtodtskaya.

Backpackers rejoice: a bona fide hostel has opened in Perm and its name is *Hostel P* Хостел П (ул Ленина 62, ul Lenina 62, ☎ 214 7847, 🖳 www.permhostel.ru, dorm/dbl R400-600/1500, WI-FI). Not only are its beds equipped with orthopaedic mattresses, but the English- and German-speaking staff are very helpful and the amazing showers (you'll see!) do everything but bake cookies and call your mother. Take trolleybus 5 to Плеханово (Plekhanovo), then walk a couple of blocks.

The monolithic ex-Soviet *Hotel Ural* Гостиница Урал (ул Ленина 58, ul Lenina 58, ☎ 218 6262, 🖳 www.hotel-ural .com, sgl/dbl/lux from R3150/4000/7000, WI-FI) consists of a whopping 415 rooms, some of which fail to live up the expectations raised by the glamorous lobby, though they are perfectly modern and comfortable. There's also a fitness hall,

sauna, Permtourist travel agency (see column opposite), and a restaurant (see Where to eat below). To get there take tram No 3, 4, 7 or 11 to Сквер Уральских Добровольцев (Skver Ural'skikh Dobrovoltsev).

Hotel Prikamiye Гостиница **Прикамье** (Комсомольский пр 27, Komsomolsky pr 27, ☎ 237 7607, 🖳 www .prikamie-hotel.ru, sgl/dbl/lux from R2300/3000/4600, WI-FI) is a good mid-range option, each of its en suite rooms equipped with TV and fridge. Wi-fi costs extra. Take tram No 3, 4, 7 or 11 to the 'ЦУМ (Tsum) stop.

Inside a high-rise building in a super-central location, *Hotel Tsvety* Отель **Цветы** (ул Пермская 56, ul Permskaya 56, ☎ 240 3888, 🖳 www.отельцветы.рф, dbl /lux from R2000/4000 for 24hrs, WI-FI), offers modern, bright, comfortable rooms – both overnight and also for 12-hour day slots and 2-hour slots, making one wonder whether it's used for illicit trysts. Handy if you want to rest in between trains leaving at odd times, though. Take tram 3, 4, 5 or 7 to Плеханово (Plekhanovo) stop.

The *resting rooms* комнаты отдыха (komnaty otdykha) at Perm-2 (sgl/twin/5-person room R2000/1500/900 for 24 hours) are basic but perfectly adequate for a night's stay.

Where to eat and drink

A slice of France in the heart of Perm, *Crêperie Française* Крепери Франсез (ул Петропавловская 40, ul Petropavlovskaya 40, crêpes from R165, [V], 8am-11pm Mon-Sat, noon-11pm Sun) does excellent crêpes with imaginative savoury and sweet fillings, with more substantial French dishes for those with a hearty appetite.

A feast for carnivores, *Grill Tavern Montenegro* Гриль-Таверна Монтенегро (ул Горького 28, ul Gorkogo 28, 🖳 www.vkusnoest.ru, open daily, mains R294-784, WI-FI) specialises in beautifully grilled

The Perm area code is ☎ 342. From outside Russia dial ☎ +7-342.

meats (but not steak). The Kalmyk lamb shashlyk melts in your mouth, the veal with nutmeg sauce is inspired and if your other half loves meat as much as you do, order the 2-person 'assortment'. To get there follow ul Lenina east and turn right onto ul Gorkogo.

Zhivago Живаго (ул Ленина 37, ul Lenina 37, 🖥 www.permrest.ru, open daily, mains R340-680) is a dress-smartly kind of restaurant serving some wonderfully experimental meat and seafood medleys, such as beetroot ravioli with smoked duck and fish skewers with lemongrass – all very reasonably priced given the quality. On the ground floor of the same building, *Café Pasternak* Кафе Пастернак has a similar menu as they share the same chef, but here the emphasis is more on light meals – imaginative salads, light dishes such as spinach pelmeni with pike, courgette lasagne, and sushi.

In Hotel Ural *Stroganovskaya Votchina* Строгановская Вотчина serves European and Russian dishes that would have been enjoyed by the nobility in days of old.

This particular branch of the popular Ukrainian restaurant chain, *Khutorok* Хуторок (ул Крисанова 24 ul Krisanova 24, mains from R250) has an over-the-top kitschy summer terrace with jolly wooden figures, waiters in traditional costume and all the moreish, calorie-laden delights you expect from a good Ukrainian joint: *vareniki*, *salo* (lard), *draniki* (potato fritters),

shashlyk, etc. Large portions, too. To reach this branch follow ul Yekaterininskaya west; the restaurant is at the crossroads with ul Krisanova.

Walking past *Cup by Cup* (Комсомольский пр 16, Komsomolsky pr 16, 8am-midnight Mon-Fri, 10am-midnight Sat & Sun), you'll be drawn in by the aroma of freshly roasted coffee. This thimble-sized café offers quite a number of varieties, with cakes and juice for those wishing to forego the caffeine jolt.

Moving on

The city's main **airport**, Bolshoye Savino, is located 20km to the west of the city. You can buy tickets for destinations such as Moscow (several daily, 2hrs) and Frankfurt (Lufthansa 4/week, 6hrs) from the ticket office in the lobby of Hotel Ural.

Westbound departures from **Perm 2 railway station** include Moscow (11/day, 20-25½hrs), most via Nizhny Novgorod (13-15½hrs) and Vladimir (17½-19½hrs). Eastbound departures include Novosibirsk (8/day, 27-30½hrs) and Yekaterinburg (12/day, 5½-12hrs). See below for details of trains to Kungur.

From the **bus station** автовокзал at ul Revolutsii 68 ул Революции 68, there are numerous departures to or via Kungur (at least once hourly between 8.20am and 7.45pm, 2hrs, R190) and to Khokhlovka (4/day, 1hr 20 mins).

SIDE TRIPS FROM PERM

Kungur Ice Cave Кунгурская Ледяная Пещера

About 100km from Perm and 6km from the town of Kungur is the impressive Kungur Ice Cave (☎ 34271 62 610; 🖥 www.kungurcave.ru), among the biggest in the Urals and an estimated 10,000-12,000 years old. It is 5.7km long including 48 grottos, underground lakes and hundreds of stalactites and stalagmites. Only some 1.5km of the cave is open to the public and fitted with electric lights. Most of the year, the tour takes place along the central route, whereas in spring, you might have to take the shorter route as sections of the main route are prone to flooding. March is the best time for visits, since the frozen waterfalls and other ice formations are in place, though it's entertaining year-round.

Highlights include the **Diamond Cave**, the snow and ice crystals glittering like precious stones, ice sculptures such as **The Bat**, the **Underwater Cave**, its rock formations reminiscent of coral formations, two underwater lakes (where people are baptised in winter), and a series of uneven rock steps called '**Ladies' Tears**'. When two female members of the British royal family went on a tour of the cave in the 1930s, they were inappropriately dressed in long dresses and high heels, and naturally tripped and fell on the steps. They both married princes afterwards and local lore suggests that if you're an unmarried woman who happens to trip and fall in the same place, you may marry royalty.

All tours are guided (in Russian) and take place at set times: 10am, noon, 2pm and 4pm – up to 20 people at a time (R500pp). There are also laser shows inside the cave at 11am, 1pm and 3pm (request in advance; R600pp). Dress warmly, as even in summer the temperature inside the cave can be down to -5° Celsius.

Tours to Kungur Ice Cave from Perm are far pricier than doing it solo, though if you book it with Permtourist (see p248), they can arrange an invaluable interpreter, as well as transport there and back. If you want to go independently there are several direct trains a day from Perm to Kungur, both suburban (2hrs) and long-distance (1hr 40 mins). To get to the cave, you either take bus No 9 that runs past the station to Hotel Stalagmit or take a taxi: Troika (☎ 342 713 33 33) or Taksi-Ekspress (☎ 342 713 30 30).

You can stay at the friendly *Hotel Stalagmit* **Гостиница Сталагмит** (☎ 34271 62 610, 🖳 www.hotel.kungurcave.ru, sgl/twin from R800/1400; advance booking requires paying an extra 25% of room cost) with clean, basic rooms and a restaurant serving uninspired, hit-and-miss Russian dishes. The *café* next to the Ice Cave ticket booth serves canteen-style soups and salads.

Perm-36 Пермь-36

Located in the village of **Kuchino Кучино**, around 125km from Perm is this unique Gulag-turned-museum (🖳 www.perm36.ru, 10am-5pm Tue-Sun, R100, excursions R500). It is unique because it's the only one of its kind with the original buildings remaining, restored to recreate the conditions under which scores of inmates lived and toiled between 1946 and 1988. The camp was originally geared up towards logging – hard labour that 90% of the inmates typically did not survive due to unrealistic quotas of production, atrocious living conditions and measly food rations that were reduced further as punishment if quotas were not fulfilled – and dissidents who passed through it ranged from criminals and political prisoners to corrupt servants of the law, those accused of espionage and 'nationalists' who fought for the secession of their respective republic from the Soviet Union.

At Perm-36 you can check out the photo exhibition on how the inmates used to live, peer into the dank isolation cells in the punishment block and check out the remaining work quarters, barracks, water tower and infirmary. Getting here under your own steam is tricky and can take hours: take a bus heading for Lysva Лысьва or Chusovoy Чусовой (2hrs), get off at Tyomnaya Тёмная stop, walk back to the Kuchino Кучино turnoff, from where it's another 30 minutes' walk to the village and museum. Alternatively, contact the museum office in Perm (ul Gagarina 10, off 122, ул Гагарина 10 оф 122, ☎ 217 0714) to see if they can organise a taxi there and back, as well as an interpreter.

Khokhlovka Хохловка
About 45km out of town near the village of Khokhlovka is a year-round, open-air **Museum of Architecture and Ethnography Этнографическо-Архитектурный Музей** (10am-6pm May-Oct, 9am-5pm rest of year, 🖥 www .museum.perm.ru, R120) with a collection of 16th- to 20th-century buildings, including a traditional *izba* (peasant dwelling), two attractive 18th-century wooden churches, and a firehouse. Check the website for special annual celebrations. To get here, catch one of the four daily buses from Perm's bus station at 6.15am, 9.55am, 3pm and 6.20pm (1hr 20 mins; R92); return journeys at 7.35am, 11.15am, 4.20pm and 7.40pm.

Yekaterinburg
Екатеринбург

[**Moscow Time +3; population: 1,396,074**] Yekaterinburg's role in shaping Russian history has been both immense and paradoxical: ushering in the Socialist era in 1918 with the murder of the Romanov family, providing the setting for the 1960s 'U2 Affair' (effectively a caricature of the Cold War itself) and giving the country Boris Yeltsin, who played a key role in dismantling the Soviet myth.

Its historical significance alone justifies a visit and the wealth of pre-Stalinist architecture makes a change from other Siberian cities, harking back to the days before the Revolution when Yekaterinburg was already the centre of a rich mining region. This is the heart of a region that gave rise to tales of the supernatural, such as the *Queen of Copper Mountain* and *Malachite Casket*, inspired by the folk tales of the Ural miners and put on paper by one of Yekaterinburg's most famous sons, writer Pavel Petrovich Bazhov (see box, p254).

Known as Sverdlovsk from 1924 to 1992, Yekaterinburg is a very pleasant, eminently walkable city with an attractive riverside promenade, a cluster of excellent museums and a lively dining and nightlife scene.

See pp261-2 for details about visiting the Monastery of the Holy Martyrs, Ganina-Yama, and the Europe-Asia marker.

HISTORY

The earliest settlers in the area were 'Old Believers', religious dissidents fleeing the reforms of the Russian Orthodox Church in 1672. They created the **Shartash** township here and were the first to discover that the area was rich in iron ore. This discovery was the key to later development: Peter the Great, embroiled in the Great Northern War against Sweden, gave instructions for new sources of iron to be sought; the first ironworks were established here just as the war ended in 1721. A fortress was built a year later and in 1723 the town of Yekaterinburg was founded, in honour of Peter's new wife, Catherine. The railway arrived in 1888, bringing foreign travellers on their way to Siberia.

The murder of the Romanovs

The Romanov family was moved from Tobolsk to Yekaterinburg in April 1918 and imprisoned in a house belonging to a rich merchant named Ipatyev. Here they spent the last 78 days of their lives being tormented by the guards, who openly referred to Nicholas as the 'Blood Drinker' and scrawled lewd pictures on the walls depicting the Tsarina with Rasputin.

Several attempts were made to save the royal family and eventually the Bolshevik government, deciding that the Tsar was too great a threat to its security, ordered his elimination. Shortly before midnight on 16 July, Nicholas, Alexandra, their four daughters and their haemophiliac son Alexis, were taken to the cellar where they were shot and bayoneted to death by four Bolsheviks and seven Hungarian soldiers – prisoners of war. The bodies were then taken to the Four Brothers' Mine, 40km outside the city, where guards spent three days destroying the evidence. The corpses were dismembered, doused with petrol and burned.

A week later the White Army took Yekaterinburg and their suspicions were immediately aroused by the sight of the cellar's blood-spattered walls. In the garden they found the Tsarevich's spaniel, Joy, neglected and half starved. However, it was not until the following January that investigators were led to the mineshaft, where they found fragments of bone and pieces of jewellery that had once belonged to members of the Imperial Family. They also found the

---

❑ The road to Romanov sainthood

The story behind the discovery of the Romanov remains is almost as bizarre as that of their 'disappearance'. In July 1991 it was announced that parts of nine bodies had been found and that these were almost certainly those of the Imperial Family. Perhaps the most intriguing aspect of the discovery was that three of the skulls, including that of the Tsar himself, had been placed in a wooden box. In fact the bodies had been discovered some 20 years before by a local detective-novel writer named Geli Ryabov. He deduced from the skulls' immaculate dental work that these were indeed the bodies of the Royal Family, but reburied them for fear of persecution by the secret police. In December 1992, DNA testing at the Forensic Science Service laboratory in Aldermaston (UK) matched samples from the bodies with those from a blood sample provided by Prince Philip, Duke of Edinburgh (Tsarina Alexandra's sister was Philip's maternal grandmother).

The state burial of the royal remains was delayed for several years following a disagreement between the government, which favoured burial of the bones in St Petersburg, and surviving members of the Romanov family who wanted them returned to Yekaterinburg as a memorial to the millions killed by the Communists. On 19 August 1998 the remains were finally interred in the Romanov vault in St Petersburg's Peter and Paul Cathedral. At the service, then President Boris Yeltsin made the first official apology: 'The massacre of the Tsar was one of the most shameful pages of our history ... We are all guilty. It is impossible to lie to ourselves by justifying the senseless cruelty on political grounds'.

On 20 August 2000, at a special ceremony in Moscow's Cathedral of Christ the Saviour, Patriarch Alexi II canonised the Tsar, the royal family and hundreds of priests who died as 'zealots of faith and piety' during the Communist era.

body of Jimmy, Anastasia's dog, which the murderers had callously flung down the mineshaft without bothering to kill it first. All the evidence was identified by the Tsarevich's tutor, Pierre Gilliard. At first the Bolsheviks would not admit to more than the 'execution' of Nicholas, accusing a group of counter-revolutionaries of the murders of his family. Five of them were tried, 'found guilty' and executed. However, in 1919 after the death of Party official Yacob Sverdlov, it was acknowledged that it was in fact he who had arranged the massacre. In his honour the town was renamed Sverdlovsk.

The U2 Affair
The next time the town became the focus of world attention was in May 1960 when the American U2 pilot, Gary Powers, was shot down in this area (see box p440). He survived the crash, parachuting into the arms of the Soviets and confirming that he had been spying. The ensuing confrontation led to the collapse of the Summit conference in Paris.

The city today
Yekaterinburg is Russia's fourth-largest city (after Moscow, St Petersburg and Novosibirsk), a major transportation hub and one of the country's most important industrial centres, ever since hundreds of factories were relocated here during WWII. The city once specialised in armaments research and production but munitions factories, including the vast 'Pentagon' building in the eastern part of town, have closed down. Because of its strategic importance, the city was off-limits to foreigners until 1990. In 1991, Sverdlovsk became Yekaterinburg. The city's most famous son is, of course, Boris Yeltsin: coup-buster, economic reformer, referendum winner, dissolver of parliament and former Russian President.

Today, Yekaterinburg is a modern, lively city, but was no doubt disappointed to be unsuccessful in its bid to host the 2020 World Expo, losing out to Dubai.

WHAT TO SEE AND DO

Church on the Blood Храм на Крови
The golden-domed, Byzantine-style Church on the Blood (7.30am-11pm daily), dominating the city centre at ul Tolmachyova 34 (ул Толмачёва 34), forms an expensive memorial to the 'Tsar martyrs', as the Romanovs were declared when they were canonised by the Russian Orthodox Church. Rumour has it that the icon inside the church is the most expensive ever to be commissioned. In 1976, Yeltsin ordered the demolition of the engineer's house (Ipatyev House Бывший Дом Ипатьева) in the basement of which the Imperial family was murdered, concerned that it would make a focal point for monarchist sympathisers. The church was built in its place after the collapse of the Soviet Union.

Not everyone reveres the Romanovs; many believe that sainthood is incompatible with virulent anti-Semitism and poor military leadership – two prominent qualities displayed by Tsar Nicholas II. It seems that the Russian Orthodox Church is trying to instil a sense of guilt in the population over the royal deaths, much more so than over the deaths of any others who were executed in far more horrific fashion during Communist times.

CITY GUIDES & PLANS

The church contains several monuments to the Romanovs, including icons of the royal family and memorabilia from their last days in Yekaterinburg. Upstairs, the main sanctuary is a soaring and brightly lit affair. Above the main entrance there are dramatic metal sculptures of the Romanovs, with Nicholas II holding his son in his arms, while sellers do a brisk trade in Romanov-related souvenirs opposite.

Chapel of the Revered Martyr Princess Yelizaveta Fyodorovna
Часовня Великомученицы Княгини Елизаветы Фёдоровны

Next to the Church on the Blood is this humble and far more attractive wooden chapel (9am-5pm daily) with an intricately carved cupola, built in the late 1980s and repeatedly burnt down by anti-monarchists. It's dedicated to St Elizabeth (Grand Princess Yelizaveta Fyodorovna), Alexander II's sister-in-law and great-aunt to Nicholas II, who, following the Romanov murders, was thrown down a mineshaft and left to die. Local villagers claimed to have heard her miserable wailings for two days as she prayed for the souls of her attackers who, when they realised that she was still alive, piped poisonous gas into the well and filled the hole with earth. When they came to collect her body, it was allegedly found in a sitting position, looking as though she were merely asleep, with no signs of decomposition. She and her faithful maidservant have since been canonised as well.

★ Urals Museum of Stone Уральский Музей Камня

If anything is guaranteed to awaken your inner geologist, it's this incredible private collection of crystals, minerals and semi-precious stones belonging to Vladimir Pelepenko – the perfect introduction to the mineral wealth of the Urals.

The subtly lit displays showcase unrefined minerals – fungus-like formations, spiky quartz crystals, remarkable cube-like pyrite (fool's gold), mammoth-sized chunks of amethyst – and fossil prints of crayfish, tiny lizards, fish. The highlights here, however, are the man-made creations of semi-precious stone: spheres of pink-with-black-streaks rhodonite; caskets and jewellery made of vivid purple charoite, endemic to Siberia; goblets made of jasper, its colour

---

❑ **The Malachite Casket and other tales from the Urals**

Though one of the most famous local sons, Pavel Petrovich Bazhov, was not originally from Yekaterinburg, this Urals-born author spent a significant-enough period of his life in the city, first studying at a religious school and then working variously as a Russian teacher and one of the editors of the *Krestianka* ('*Peasant Woman*') newspaper. In the early 1920s he also travelled around the region, collecting local folklore and creatively adapting it into what was to become *The Malachite Casket* – a collection of miners' tales from the Ural Mountains – an area particularly rich in precious stones, as well as gold and copper ore. In these tales, malachite in particular is endowed with certain mythical powers and has special significance for those who seek it and work with it. *The Malachite Casket* was followed up with *The Mistress of Copper Mountain and other Tales*; the Mistress, occasionally appearing in the guise of a lizard, is a capricious supernatural being who protects the gems and stones and who only shares the wealth of the land with those who please her.

variations resembling a restless crimson sea, and more. The pride of place goes to figures and caskets made of deep-green malachite, its endless circle and swirl patterns underlining the stone's mythical significance in many Russian folk tales (see box opposite).

The museum (10am-6pm Mon-Fri, 10am-5pm Sat & Sun, R100) is located in Bolshoy Ural Hotel (see p257). The semi-precious items at the gift shop don't come cheap, but the quality of craftsmanship is excellent.

Museum of Fine Arts Музей Изобразительных Искусст
Housed in two separate buildings (ul Voyevodina 5 ул Воеводина 5 and ul Vaynera 11 ул Вайнера 11, 11am-7pm Tue-Sun, until 8pm Wed & Thur, 🖳 www .emii.ru, R150 entry to each branch), this is one of the most important museums in the area. In the former you'll find a fine collection of 19th-century iron sculpture, a gallery of Russian paintings including works by Ivanov and Tarakanova, a portrait of PA Stroganov (of beef Stroganoff fame) and a famous painting of Christ by Polenov. Pride of place goes to the iron pavilion, which won first prize in the Paris Exhibition in 1900 and which is now a UNESCO treasure. The second branch on ul Vaynera is particularly good for thought-provoking temporary exhibitions, such as the recent 'Best of Russia' photography.

Metenkov House/Photography Museum
Дом Метенкова/Фотографический Музей
Housed in the former 19th-century studio of famous local photographer Veniamin Metenkov, this excellent museum (ul Karla Libknekhta 36 ул Карла Либкнехта 36, 🖳 www.metenkov.narod.ru, Mon-Fri 10am-6pm, Sat & Sun 11am-6pm; R150) features evocative early 20th-century photos of Yekaterinburg and its inhabitants as well as 19th-century cameras. Superb changing photography exhibits have recently included the works of award-winning Vladimir Vyatkin (Владимир Вяткин), his 'Faces of Moscow in the 2010s' capturing the intensity and the mood of different demonstrations.

Military History Museum Музей «Боевая Слава Урала»
There is a small exhibit on the U2 incident (see p253 and box p440) in the Military History Museum at the **House of Officers** Доме Офицеров (Dom Ofitserov, ul Pervomayskaya 27 ул Первомайская 27, 10am-6pm daily, R100). On display upstairs are a few pieces of the aircraft, photos of the wreckage and of Gary Powers in court, plus items from his survival kit. The House of Officers is easily recognisable by the massive armoury outside; around the back is a collection of Soviet military hardware.

Other attractions
The **Museum of Local History Краеведческий Музей** (ul Malysheva 46 ул Малышева 46, 11am-7pm Wed-Sun, R80) has interesting displays on 19th-century Yekaterinburg, the Revolution, the murder of the Romanovs and the discovery of their remains.

Sverdlovsk Railway History Museum Музей Истории Свердловской Железной Дороги (ul Chelyuskintsev ул Челюскинцев, in the old railway station building with chequered roof, opposite **M** Uralskaya, 10am-6pm Tue-Sat, R100) traces the history of the railroad in the region and features railbikes, models of locomotives, rail controllers' apparatus, adorable model railway and more.

Inside Urals Mining University, **Urals Geology Museum Уральский Геологический Музей** (ul Kuibysheva 39 ул Куйбышева 39, 11am-5.30pm Tue-Sat, R100) comprises an extensive, meticulously catalogued mineral collection from all over the region, as well as meteorites, spread out over four floors. Keep an eye out for the rhodonite and malachite vases, dinosaur remains and chunks of the meteorite that landed in Chelyabinsk in February 2013.

The quiet streets of the Literary Quarter north of skver Popova are home to several literary museums dedicated to famous local writers such as Pavel Bazhov (see box p254), found inside several of the restored wooden houses.

There are also some interesting buildings in the city including the classical-style **Mining Office** and the **former Rastorguiev-Kharitonov Estate Бывшая Усадьба Расторгуева-Харитонова** (1794-1824); both are at ul Karla Libknehkta 44 ул Карла Либкнехта 44 north of the Romanov memorial. At the western end of pr Lenina is the **Urals Polytechnic Institute Уральский Политехнический Институт** (UPI), an impressive building which often features on postcards (it is in fact a university but the old name has stuck). The building beside it with cannons outside is the city's military college.

The **Opera and Ballet Theatre Театр Оперы и Балета** (pr Lenina 46а пр Ленина 46а) is Russia's third most important such theatre after those in Moscow and St Petersburg.

In the square opposite the House of Officers is a powerful **Afghan War Memorial Памятник Войне в Афганистане**. The pose of the soldier, very different from most such memorials around Russia, offers an interesting insight into how people feel about the war.

PRACTICAL INFORMATION
Orientation and services

The main street, pr Lenina пр Ленина, runs east–west through the city. The city centre is more or less between pr Lenina and ul Malysheva; most of the hotels, restaurants and sights are within walking distance of here. The **railway station** is around 2km north of the city centre, and easily reachable by public transport.

Tour agents include the experienced and recommended **Ekaterinburg Guide Centre Екатеринбургский Центр Гидов** (pr Lenina 52/1, office 12, ☎ 384 0048, 🖳 www.ekaterinburgguide.com). They can arrange tours of the city and surrounding sites, including trekking and rafting in the Urals, as well as cheap accommodation in the city.

There are numerous **ATMs** around the city centre as well as the reliable TransCreditBank ATM at the railway station. The **Central Post Office Почтамт** is at pr Lenina 51 пр Ленина 51. **Internet access** is available here.

THE MODERNIST CENTRAL POST OFFICE

Consulates

Diplomatic representation includes a **British Consulate** (ul Gogolya 15a, ☎ 379 4931, 🖳 ukinrussia.fco.gov.uk), a **US Consulate** (ul Gogolya 15, ☎ 379 3001, 🖳 yekaterinburg.usconsulate.gov) and a **German consulate** (ul Kuibysheva 44, ☎ 351 1300 🖳 www.germania.diplo.de).

Local transport

Yekaterinburg has a good bus, tram and trolleybus system and a limited metro system. Tram Nos 2, 3, 8, 14, 21, 22, 25, 26, 27 and 32 run south from the railway station along ul Lunacharskogo, with Nos 3, 21, 27 and 32 passing by the railway station and 32 doing a handy loop that takes in ul Chelyuskintsev and ul Kuibysheva. Ul Karla Libknekhta is served by numerous buses, with Nos 1, 20 and 23 stopping by the railway station, as do trolleybus Nos 1, 5, 9, 11 and 17.

To get to the city centre you can also take the metro from **M** Uralskaya Уральская in front of the railway station to **M** Ploshchad 1905 Goda Площадь 1905 Года, followed by the handy **M** Geologicheskaya Геологическая. Tram Nos 13, 15, 18, and 26 run the entire length of Pr Lenina while ul Malysheva is covered in its entirety by trolleybus No 17 and bus No 61, with a few others running part of the way. Public transport costs R23 per ride.

Where to stay

Over the last couple of years, Yekaterinburg has seen an explosion of hostels. The pick of the bunch is **Omnomnom Hostel** (ул Вайнера 60, кв 26, ul Vaynera 60, apt 26, ☎ 912 047 4331, 🖳 omnomnomhostel @gmail.com, 🖳 www.hostelworld.com, dorm R600, dbl R1700, WI-FI; **M** Geologicheskaya Геологическая), high up in a centrally located new multi-storey residential building and run by knowledgeable, helpful English-speaking Tanya. The apartment is spacious, there's a good ratio of bathrooms to travellers and the large

guest kitchen is a sociable place in the evenings.

Another good bet is **Art Hostel** (ул Красноармейская 4, п.2, No 11, ul Krasnoarmeyskaya 4, entr. 2, No 11, ☎ 343 346 8050, 🖳 arthostels.ru, dorm R499, dbl R1400), with brightly painted rooms and nice little touches such as orthopaedic mattresses, reading lights by each dorm bed and laptops for guest use. However, you'll have to join the queue for the only bathroom and the hostel can be difficult to find, so ask for precise directions in advance. There's another branch (ул Ленина 62/2, п.4, No 56, ul Lenina 62/2, entr. 4, No 56, ☎ 343 346 3908) with similar facilities and prices.

Bolshoy Ural Hotel Гостиница **Большой Урал** (ул Красноармейская ul Krasnoarmeyskaya 1a, ☎ 384 0143, 🖳 www.b-ural.ru, sgl/dbl R1100-3500/1400-5550, WI-FI) is a Soviet-era monolith with an enviable central location and rooms ranging from modernised to well-worn cheapies with shared facilities (queues for the shower inevitable). Buffet breakfast included; wi-fi only works in the lobby.

Small and centrally located, boutique **Hotel Chekhov** Гостиница **Чеховъ** (ул 8-Марта 32, ul 8-Marta 32, ☎ 282 9737, 🖳 www.chekhov-hotel.ru, sgl/dbl from R4400/4900, WI-FI) charms visitors with its original décor, friendly English-speaking staff and cosy rooms. Breakfast buffet is included; you may well need the nourishment after carrying your luggage up to the 4th floor (there's no lift).

Part of the Radisson stable, the bright rooms at the centrally located **Hotel Park Inn** Отель Парк Инн (ул Мамина-Сибиряка 98, ul Mamina-Sibiryaka 98, ☎ 216 6000, 🖳 www.parkinn.com/hotel-eka terinburg, sgl/dbl R5500/6300, WI-FI) come equipped with satellite TV, the breakfast spread is generous, and the on-site Magellan Restaurant serves a good variety of Russian and European dishes. On the downside, the climate control doesn't work

The Yekaterinburg area code is ☎ 343. From outside Russia dial ☎ +7-343.

very well and the windows are sealed, so in summer you may be in for a sweltering stay.

In a historical Art Nouveau building, *Hotel Ekaterinburg-Tsentralny* Отель Екатеринбург-Центральный (ул Малышева 74, ul Malysheva 74, ☎ 350 0505, 💻 www.hotelcentr.ru, sgl/dbl/lux R3600/4500/6300, WI-FI), has luxurious rooms and efficient, English-speaking staff.

MAP KEY

WHERE TO STAY
23 Hotel Chekhov Гостиница Чеховъ
24 Omnomnom Hostel
30 Hotel Onegin Отель Онегин
33 Hotel Ekaterinburg-Tsentralny
    Отель Екатеринбург-Центральныи
34 Hotel Park Inn Отель Парк Инн
35 Bolshoy Ural Hotel
    Гостиница Большой Урал
36 Art Hostel

WHERE TO EAT & DRINK
3   Nigora Нигора
13 Pashtet Паштет
14 Paul Bakery Поль Бейкери
16 The Rosy Jane
18 Pozharka Пожарка
20 Paul Bakery Поль Бейкери
22 Doctor Scotch Pub
    Паб Доктор Скотч
26 Nigora Нигора
28 Ben Hall
33 Restaurant Savoy
39 Pozharka Пожарка
40 Uralskiye Pelmeni
    Уральские Пельмени
41 Khmeli-Suneli Хмели-Сунели

PLACES OF INTEREST
1   Sverdlovsk Railway History
    Museum Музей Истории
    Свердловской Железной Дороги
4   Mining Office and former
    Rastorguiev-Kharitonov Estate
    Бывшая Усадьба Расторгуева-
    Харитонова
5   Church on the Blood
    Храм на Крови
6   Chapel of the Revered Martyr
    Princess Yelizaveta Fyodorovna
    Часовня Великомученицы
    Княгини Елизаветы Фёдоровны

7   Romanov Memorial (former
    Ipatyev House)
    Памятник Романовым (Бывший
    Дом Ипатьева)
8   Monument to Urals Young
    Communists
    Памятник Комсомолу Урала
9   Ascension Cathedral
    Церковь Вознесения
10 Military History Museum
    (in the House of Officers)
    Музей «Боевая Слава Урала»
    (в Доме Офицеров)
11 Afghan War Memorial
    Памятник Войне в Афганистане
12 Metenkov House / Photography
    Museum
    Дом Метенькова / Музей
    Фотографии
17 Museum of Fine Arts Музей
    Изобразительных Искусств
19 Museum of Fine Arts Музей
    Изобразительных Искусств
21 Museum of Local History
    Краеведческий Музеи
25 Urals Geology Museum
    Уральский Геологический Музеи
35 Urals Museum of Stone
    Уральский Музей Камня
37 Opera & Ballet Theatre
    Театр Оперы и Балета
38 Sverdlov Statue
    Памятник Свердлову

OTHER
2   Railway Station & ATM
    Железнодорожный Вокзал & ATM
15 Central Post Office & Internet
    Почтамт и Интернет
27 Pyatachok Пятачок
29 German Consulate
    Консульство Германии
31 US Consulate Консульство США
32 British Consulate
    Британское Консульство

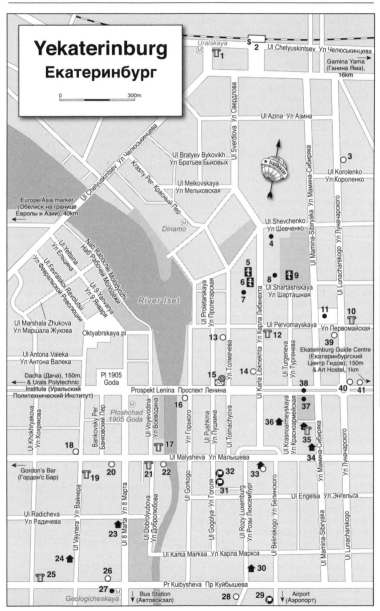

While the rooms at the efficient *Hotel Onegin* Отель Онегин (ул Розы Люксембург 49, ul Rozy Luxemburg 49, ☎ 253 5678, 🖳 www.hotelonegin.com, dbl/lux from R4700/8500, wɪ-ғɪ) may be geared towards business travellers, all guests benefit from the bright, stylish rooms with a host of creature comforts. Many staff speak English and the breakfast spread is excellent.

Where to eat

Uralskiye Pelmeni Уральские Пельмени (пр Ленина 69/1, pr Lenina 69/1, meals R300, wɪ-ғɪ) celebrates the 'ear dough' so dear to the Russian stomach: varieties include rabbit with horseradish sauce, beef, lamb, veal and chicken, with Ukrainian vareniki with sweet and savoury fillings making an appearance. If the dumplings don't float your boat, there's a large variety of salads, soups, meat dishes, and shashlyk as well. Open until 2am at weekends.

Decked out like a fire station, popular *Pozharka* Пожарка (ул Луначарского 128, ul Lunacharskogo 128, mains from R295) attracts locals and visitors alike with its large helpings of Russian dishes such as beef stroganoff, pork medallions, hearty soups, salads, pelmeni and their very own Pozharka beer (R90) to wash it down with. Another, subtler-looking location is at ул Малышева 44 ul Malysheva 44 with the downstairs self-serve canteen open for lunch; dinner from 4pm upstairs.

The *Paul Bakery* Поль Бейкери (ул Малышева 36, ul Malysheva 36, 🖳 www.paulbakery.ru, daily 9am-10pm [V]) chain is a good one-stop shop for baked goodies, mini-quiches, wraps, milkshakes, teas, decent coffee and light meals. Another location is at ул Карла Либкнехта 23, ul Karla Libknekhta 23.

Restaurant Savoy, at Hotel Ekaterinburg-Tsentralny, once entertained the likes of Fidel Castro and poet Osip Mandelshtam; it now serves imaginative fusion dishes as well as Russian standards and has an extensive wine list.

Pashtet Паштет (ул Толмачёва 23, ul Tolmachyova 23, mains R350-1350) is a firm favourite with locals due to its ultra-cosy home-style décor, well-presented Italian dishes as well as shashlyk and resident cat, Pashka, to fuss over. Service occasionally lives on Zen time.

Its atmospheric two-tier dining area decked out with colourful weavings, ★ *Khmeli-Suneli* Хмели-Сунели (ул Ленина 69/10, ul Lenina 69/10, 🖳 www.hmeli.ru, mains R310-650; [V]) is a temple to the aromatic, flavourful Georgian food. While the weekday business lunch (mains R130-210) will give you a taste, only by ordering à la carte delights such as aubergine rolls with walnut sauce, meat dishes cooked in a *ketsi* (кеци) – traditional shallow clay or stone pot, and tender, succulent shashlyk will you truly appreciate why this Caucasian cuisine is so loved in Russia.

With its cellar-like interior, decorated with colourful tiles and carpets, *Nigohra* Нигора (ул Куйбышева 55, ul Kuibysheva 55, mains R155-420) dishes up genuine Uzbek food. The service is friendly and you can feast yourself on the likes of lamb shashlyk, grilled salmon with pomegranate sauce, *manty* (giant steamed dumplings), *lagman* (hearty beef noodle soup) and *chuchvara* (Uzbek pelmeni). Another location at ул Луначарского 31 ul Lunachharskogo 31.

Dacha Дача (пр Ленина 20а, pr Lenina 20а, ☎ 379 3569) specialises in fine Russian cuisine, each of its rooms decorated as if it's part of a wealthy merchant's house. Reservations recommended at weekends. The three-course business lunch on weekdays (R340) is a bargain.

Bars and nightlife

Right near the river, *Doctor Scotch Pub* Паб Доктор Скотч (ул Малышева 56а, ul Malysheva 56а, 🖳 www.doctorscotch.ru) attracts a good mix of locals and expats. Its offshoot, *Gordon's Bar* Гордон'с Бар (ул Крылова 27 ul Krylova 27) is the place for Scotch whiskies. Take tram 3 or 7 to Institut Svyazi Институт Связи and walk north up Krylova.

East of the river, *The Rosy Jane* (пр Ленина 34, pr Lenina 34, 🖳 www.rosyjane.ru, 7am-6am Mon-Thur, 9am-7am Fri-Sun,

WI-FI) is a lively British-style pub serving Russian and English dishes, English ales and stouts and quite a selection of Scotch whiskies amidst clouds of aromatic cigar smoke.

For local rock music, check out **Ben Hall** (ул Народной Воли 65, ul Narodnoi Voli 65, 🖳 www.benhall.ru) at the weekend.

Shopping
For some unusual local souvenirs, such as caskets made of malachite and busts of Lenin, head to **Pyatachok Пятачок**, the local outdoor market on the corner of ul Kuibysheva and ul 8 Marta, open at the weekend (10am-5pm) – as good for its atmosphere as it is for the shopping.

Moving on
By rail Yekaterinburg is a major train hub. **Westbound**: Moscow (13-14/day, 25-31hrs, the fastest and most comfortable being the firmenny 015), with all Moscow-bound trains stopping at Perm (5½-6hrs), Nizhny Novgorod (19-21hrs) and Vladimir (22-24hrs). There are also trains to Kazan (2/day, 15hrs, the most convenient being the overnight No 377) and St Petersburg (2/day, 36hrs, both services leaving in the evening). **Eastbound**: Tobolsk (7/day, 9½-10½hrs,

the most convenient being the overnight 342, 012 and the firmenny 060 departures), Omsk (11/day, 13-15½hrs, the best overnighters being the 080, 082 and the firmenny 026), Novosibirsk (10/day, 22-24½hrs, the swiftest being the firmenny 026), and Irkutsk (3-4/day, 48½-56½hrs, the fastest being the firmenny 002 on alternate days or the weekly firmenny 006 to Ulaanbaatar on Fridays).

If you are waiting for a train, or arrive late at night, there is a comfortable **VIP hall** with soft seats, toilets and a bar. The entrance is to the left of the main station entrance and it costs R150/hour, with showers an extra R200.

By air Airport Koltsovo (☎ 226 8582, 🖳 www.koltsovo.ru), the largest airport in the Urals, is 16km south of the city and served by Czech Airlines, Air China, Lufthansa, Finnair and Turkish Airlines, as well as Aeroflot, Vladivostok Avia, S7 and Transaero, among others. There are frequent flights to Moscow, St Petersburg, Irkutsk, Krasnoyarsk, Khabarovsk, Yakutsk and Vladivostok, as well as Prague, Frankfurt, Almaty and Beijing. Catch bus No 1 from the railway station (1hr) every half hour 6am-10pm or hourly thereafter.

CITY GUIDES & PLANS

SIDE TRIPS FROM YEKATERINBURG

Ganina Yama Ганина Яма
Located in a lovely wooded area 16km north-east of Yekaterinburg is the **Monastery of the Holy Martyrs Монастырь Святых Царственных Страстотерпцев** (daily 6am-9pm, 🖳 www.ganinayama.ru), built around the spot where the Romanovs' bodies were originally disposed of in an abandoned mine.

The monastery consists of several attractive wooden churches, a holy pool (the premises of which you may enter only if previously blessed), and a horseshoe-shaped covered walk that skirts the remnants of the pit where the bodies were dumped. Holy relics include the icon depicting the Romanov family. The covered walk is decorated with endearing family photographs of the royal family, though the Tsarevich looks perpetually unhappy in the photos, with a scowl and weak chin. The monastery is considered sacred ground by the Russian Orthodox Church, even though the royal bodies have now been reburied in St Petersburg (see box p144), so women have to don headscarves and wraparound skirts; these are provided at the entrance.

To get here, you can take marshrutka No 223 (6/day) from the bus stop to the left of the railway station entrance along the main street, getting off at the final Monastyr/'Монастырь' stop, but unless you speak Russian, you won't be able to ask one of the priests for a guided tour. To get the most out of a visit, your best bet is to join an English-speaking tour organised by Ekaterinburg Guide Centre (see p256) from R1295 per person.

Europe/Asia marker Обелиск на границе Европы и Азии
About 40km to the west along the main road to Moscow (Novy Moscovsky Trakt) is the point which the German scientists Humboldt and Roze designated as the border between Europe and Asia while doing barometric surveys in 1829. The original marker was destroyed in the 1920s and replaced with a concrete obelisk faced with granite. Trips (R1295 per person for a group of five) can be arranged through Ekaterinburg Guide Centre (see p256). There's another marker beside the railway line, 36km west of Yekaterinburg at Vershina (Вершина).

Tyumen
Тюмень

[**Moscow Time +2; population: 634,171**] Tyumen is the booming oil capital of Western Siberia and certainly feels more affluent than many other Siberian cities. Local pride is visible in the 'best city in the world' banners around the city; even if you think that's a bit over the top, it's a pleasant-enough place. Its tree-lined streets and pedestrianised City Park make for enjoyable strolling in good weather.

Founded in 1586, Tyumen's location on a major trading river, the Tura, made it an important transit point for goods between Siberia and China, not to mention the first proper Russian settlement in Siberia. It was also a major transit point for settlers and convicts destined for Siberia and the Russian Far East. By 1900 over a million convicts had tramped through the town.

During WWII, many of European Russia's people, treasures and factories were relocated to Siberia. The greatest treasure to be transferred from Moscow to Tyumen during this time was Lenin's corpse. For years he rested secretly in a building of the Agricultural Institute, tended by a team of specialists.

Prior to the drilling of the region's first oil well in 1960, Tyumen was just a dusty backwater of 150,000 inhabitants, though its population has exploded since then and the region's oil wealth has turned it into the go-ahead business centre with a youthful vibe that it is today.

WHAT TO SEE AND DO

Tyumen's sights are sufficient to entertain you for a day or so. The museums generally leave something to be desired, but one exception is the **Fine Arts Museum Музей Изобразительных Искусств** (ul Ordzhonikidze 47,

10am-6pm Tue-Sun, exhibitions R50-150). Besides the small but excellent permanent collection of 18th-, 19th- and 20th-century Russian art, including a lone Kandinsky, the museum hosts a variety of other exhibitions. Recent ones have included 'The Temptation of Pablo Picasso', 'The Romanovs in Siberia' and a superb photographic display consisting of intimate portraits of ordinary Siberians. Outside the museum, on nearby Tsentralnaya pl, you'll find a large **Lenin statue**.

In the city centre, along ul Pervomayskaya between ul Lenina and ul Respubliki, you'll come across the **Siberian Cats park Парк Сибирских Кошек** featuring 12 golden-plated sculptures of frolicking cats and kittens. This is a monument to the 238 cats rounded up in February 1944 in Tyumen and around 5000 in Siberia overall; the cats were then sent in comfortable kitty carriages to St Petersburg (then Leningrad) to save the Hermitage treasures from rodents and to establish a new cat population after the famine caused by the Leningrad Blockade.

Architecturally, the most interesting sites are just north of the city centre at Kommunisticheskaya 10, where you'll find several fine religious buildings including the **Church of SS Peter and Paul Петропавловская Церковь**, with its bright, mural-covered interior, and the 'Ukrainian baroque' **Cathedral of Trinity Monastery Троицкий Собор** inside the walls of the **Trinity Monastery Свято-Троицкий Монастырь**, founded in 1616 and visible from far away due to its cluster of gold-and-black onion domes. Admission to the grounds (7am-7pm daily) is free. You can reach the monastery by taking bus No 14 or 30 along ul Respubliki from the city centre; both stop a block and a half away.

If you walk here, you'll pass the **Bridge of Love Мост Любви** across the River Tura; it's an obligatory stop of local wedding parties, with couples swearing undying love for each other by locking a padlock with their names to the bridge's railings.

In the city centre, the **City Park Парк**, with its fairground rides, kvas and candy floss stalls, and segway riders darting in and out of the crowd, is good for a stroll in sunny weather. The covered **Central Market Центральный рынок** (7am-5pm, daily) at its eastern end is the best place for fresh produce. Further east, along ul Melnikaite, there is a giant candle-shaped **war memorial Мемориал Великой Отечественной Войны**.

Near the railway station, along ul Pervomayskaya, you'll spy an **FD-class locomotive** through the greenery.

PRACTICAL INFORMATION
Orientation and services
The railway station is 1.5km south of the city centre. From there all buses and trolleybuses take you up ul Pervomayskaya either to ul Lenina or ul Respubliki.

Most of the accommodation options listed offer free internet access and/or wi-fi; otherwise there's **internet access** at the main **post office Почтамт** (ул Республики 56, ul Respubliki 56).

The railway station has a reliable TransCredit Bank **ATM** and there are several more ATMs in the centre, particularly along ul Respubliki.

CITY GUIDES & PLANS

Where to stay

If all you're looking for is a cheap, basic place to lay your head try the railway station's *resting rooms* комнаты отдыха (☎ 523 073; *komnaty otdykha;* sgl/dbl from R1500/2500, quad from R800pp per 12 hours) on the 8th floor. The entrance is to the left of the main station entrance.

The brand-new hostel ★ *Vse Prosto!* Всё Просто! (ul Pervomayskaya 40, kr 1, ул Первомайская 40, кр 1, ☎ 3452 441 072, 🖳 www.hostelvseprosto.ru, dorm/twin R590/990 per person; WI-FI) is a far, far better budget option. The friendly owners offer huge rooms, a lime-green guest kitchen, lounge sofa so deep you can really sink into it, giant plasma-screen TV and game consoles, mountain bikes for rent and free breakfast – just a few perks shared by a mixed Russian and international clientele. Some English spoken.

Hotel Spasskaya Гостиница Спасская (ul Lenina 2a, ул Ленина 2a, ☎ 550 008, 🖳 www.hotel-spasskaya.ru, sgl/dbl from R4500/4900; WI-FI) is an efficient, stylish cog in the Best Western machinery. Expect plaid-heavy décor, orthopaedic mattresses, hypoallergenic bed linen, modern bathrooms, guest gym and English-speaking staff. Only downside is that the air-con doesn't always work as well as it should.

Monolithic, ex-Soviet *Hotel Vostok* Отель Восток (ul Respubliki 159, ул Республики 159, ☎ 686 111, 🖳 vostok.tmn .ru, sgl/dbl from R2500/3200, WI-FI) is one of the few central, inexpensive options. The rooms are compact and the walls thin so you may feel as if you're in bed with your neighbours. The buffet breakfast is good, but the wi-fi doesn't work too well on the top couple of floors. Get a room overlooking the little square if possible. Take marshrutka No 35 from the railway station or bus No 15, 86 or 96 along ul Lenina from the corner of ul Prosoyuznaya and get off at 'Гостиница Восток' ('Gostinitsa Vostok').

The 230-room *Hotel Tyumen* Гостиница Тюмень (ul Ordzhonikidze 46, ул Орджоникидзе 46, ☎ 3452 494 040, 🖳 www.hoteltyumen.ru, sgl/dbl/lux from R6500/8700/12,600, WI-FI) is a typical Russian four-star hotel, meaning that the rooms are not terribly memorable, but comfortable, with satellite TV. There are English-speaking receptionists, the price includes a buffet breakfast and there's a good Russian restaurant on-site.

Where to eat and drink

In Da USA Ин Да ЮСА (ul Cheliuskintsev 10, ул Челюскинцев 10, 🖳 www.indausa.ru; daily noon-6am; WI-FI [V]) has won a loyal local following, thanks to the efforts of the ultra-helpful waitresses and its Tex-Mex menu (mains from R260) of fajitas, burritos, nachos, steaks and burgers. Live music most nights. The weekday business lunch is a bargain at R190-290.

Faux-rustic décor and a full stable of Ukrainian favourites distinguishes *Shinok Telega* Шинок Телега (ul Melnikayte 100, ул Мельникайте 100, mains R300-525, [V]). Feast yourself on *vareniki* (sweet and savoury dumplings), pork baked in kvass, *golubtsy* (meat and rice baked in cabbage leaf), *draniki* (potato fritters), blini with caviar and more, so much more. Prepare for a leisurely meal.

With an emphasis on fresh, seasonal ingredients, ★ *Potaskuy* Потаскуй (ul Khokhryakova 53a, ул Хохрякова 53a, 🖳 www.potaskuy.com; WI-FI) has understated grey and charcoal décor and serves refined, beautifully flavoured dishes such as pike cutlets with wild mushroom sauce, braised veal cheek in red wine and spring vegetable salad with mango. Business lunch means 20% off the main menu and the vodka bar gets lively in the evenings.

People's Bar & Grill (ul Lenina 57, ул Ленина 57, 🖳 www.peoples72.ru, daily noon-2am) is a carnivore's delight: the grilled meats, shashlyk and steaks (R378-1150) are melt-in-your-mouth tender and expertly cooked. There are also lighter options in the form of tom yum soup, Greek salad and more. Business lunch salads (R75) and mains (R139) are great value.

Popular with young, iPad-toting locals, *Malina Bar* Малина Бар (ul Pervomayskaya 18, ул Первомайская 18, WI-FI; daily 24 hours) is a one-stop shop for all those things dear to the Russian stomach:

WHERE TO STAY
4   Hotel Spasskaya Гостиница Спасская
22 Hotel Tyumen Гостиница Тюмень
25 Hotel Vostok Гостиница Восток

WHERE TO EAT AND DRINK
9   In Da USA Ин Да ЮСА
11 People's Bar & Grill
12 Malina Bar Малина Бар
19 Potaskuy Потаскуй
21 Central Market Центральный рынок

PLACES OF INTEREST
1   SS Peter & Paul Church &
    Cathedral of Trinity Monastery
    Петропавловская Церковь и Троицкий
    Собор (Свято-Троицкий Монастырь)
2   Elevation of the Cross Church
    Крестовоздвиженская Церковь
3   Remains of the Kremlin Walls
    Остатки Земляных Валов
    бывшего Кремля
5   Bridge of Love Мост Любви
6   Church of Mikhaila Maleina
    Церковь Михаила Малеина
7   Cathedral of the Holy Cross
    Знаменский Собор
8   Church of the Saviour
    Спасская Церковь
10 Philharmonic Hall Филармония
13 Drama Theatre Драматический Театр
14 City Park Парк
15 Siberian Cats park
    Парк Сибирских Кошек
17 Soviet House Дом Советов
23 Fine Arts Museum
    Музей Изобразительных Искусств
24 WWII War Memorial
    Мемориал Великои Отечественной Войны

OTHER
16 Central Stadium Центральный Стадион
18 Central Square Центральная Площадь
20 Central Post Office & Internet
    Почтамт и Интернет

The Tyumen area code is ☎ 3452.
From outside Russia dial ☎ +7-3452.

sushi, pasta, shashlyk, blini and more. Perfect for night owls, since it's open around the clock, and you can smoke a hookah après-dinner.

The **central market** (see p263) should meet all the fresh produce needs of the self-caterers.

Moving on
Tyumen is about halfway between Moscow and Irkutsk, with numerous trains to all Trans-Siberian destinations. Departures include Kazan (2/day, 20¾-22hrs), Omsk (11-12/day, 7½-9¼hrs) – the most convenient being the 082, 093 and the 138 overnight trains, Yekaterinburg (19-20/day, 4¾-5¾hrs) and Tobolsk (11/day, 3½-4½hrs).

Tobolsk
Тобольск

[Moscow Time +3; population: 98,169] Though it's 250km from Tyumen and the Trans-Siberian line, the old Siberian capital of Tobolsk boasts a splendid, golden-domed Kremlin and a crumbling, atmospheric Old Town – both well worth a detour from the main railway line. Poverty and monolithic Soviet housing blocks have a strong grip here, but locals take pride in the city's once-great history and in the skill of its craftsmen, who have specialised in intricate bone carvings since the 19th century.

Lying at the confluence of the Tobol and Irtysh rivers, Tobolsk is famed as the site where Yermak Timofeevich and his Cossack forces defeated a Tatar army in 1582. Though the Russian victors were soon driven out, they declared their 'conquest' of Siberia and a fort was founded here in 1587. The outpost grew into the administrative, financial and religious centre of the region; home of Siberia's first bishopric and seat of the governor-general, who ruled from the Urals to the Far East.

The city was sidestepped by the Great Siberian Trakt road, which cut further south, and later by the Trans-Siberian Railway. Its influence waned, but Tobolsk remained a cultural centre until the end of the 19th century, aided by the arrival of educated Decembrist exiles, who founded a school for women and treated the sick free of charge. Dostoyevsky was jailed here for a short time in 1850 on his way to exile in Omsk, and Tobolsk was the Romanovs' last stop before their fatal visit to Yekaterinburg in 1918.

WHAT TO SEE AND DO

The Kremlin Кремль
Most of the main attractions are centred around the handsome white Kremlin with a cluster of golden domes, perched on a hill above the plain where Yermak won his victory. Originally the site of a wooden fort, its stone walls were built starting in 1700. The perimeter wall is 620 metres long and contains nine towers — don't miss the view from the bottom of the hill.

Inside the Kremlin is the large **Cathedral of St Sophia Собор Святой Софии**, with a splendid ceiling mural inside. Built between 1686 and 1700, before the defensive walls, it's the oldest original stone building in Siberia. Just south is the 75-metre-tall **bell tower**, built in 1799 – once home to the Uglich bell. When Ivan the Terrible's youngest son, Dmitry, was found dead under mysterious circumstances in 1581, the bell was rung to signal the death and some Uglich citizens fell upon the tsarevich's suspected murderers and killed them. Upon the orders of the tsar's advisor and future usurper of the throne, Boris Godunov, who himself fell under suspicion of murder but was later cleared, the bell that rang the news of the boy's death was detongued, publicly whipped 12 times and 'exiled' to Tobolsk until the end of the 19th century, when it was returned to Uglich and hung in the Church of Dmitry on the Blood.

Next to the bell tower, the small **Cathedral of the Intercession Покровский Собор** (1746), where services are held in the evenings, boasts some lovely ceiling murals. The Kremlin also contains **Arkhereisky Dom**, formerly the bishop's residence.

Outside the Kremlin

Just outside the Kremlin is the **Deputy's Palace Дворец Наместника**, home to the worthwhile **history museum Исторический Музей** (10am-6pm Tue-Sun, R200). It features maps of Siberia made by the first Russian settlers, weaponry from the 16th to 18th centuries, such period objects as a knife with mammoth-bone sheath and whip used to punish criminals as well as an exhibition on the chemist **Mendeleyev**, one of the city's famous sons. The museum also contains a replica of the **Uglich bell** (see above). Until sometime in 2014 there is a separate exhibit dedicated to the Romanov family (R100), featuring some original furniture, photos and personal effects, since the small museum in the Old Town is under restoration. Tsar Nicholas II and his family spent eight months in Tobolsk following his abdication and their lifestyle became progressively more restrictive, until they were no longer allowed to attend church.

Just north-west of the Kremlin is a **former prison Тюремный Замок** (Krasnaya pl 5, 10am-5pm Tue-Sun, R120) where tsarist exiles were held while awaiting their final place of banishment. Built in 1855 and closed in 1989, it's now open to visitors, who can wander through its dark halls and peer into the small, depressing cells.

On the southern side of the Kremlin, a cobbled ramp leads to 189 wooden steps descending to the Old Town. This was originally just a muddy slope where merchants dragged their wares from the town up to Gostinny Dvor. Looming over the path is the **Swedish House Шведский Дом**, built by Swedish exiles and formerly home to the government treasury.

Governor's Museum Губернский Музей

This entertaining museum (ul Oktyabrskaya 1 ул Октябрьская 1, 10am-6pm Tue-Sun, R120) gives you the history and culture of the region in a nutshell (with some English captioning). Proceed from fossils and mammoth teeth to a display on Aleksandr Dunin-Gorkavich – 19th-century explorer of eastern Siberia – followed by the natural history section encompassing a mammoth

> ❏ **Written in bone**
>
> The art of bone carving in Siberia dates far, far back, with samples of amulets and weapons made from mammoth, reindeer and elk bone by the indigenous Khanty and Mansy people dating back to the 10th century, and the elaborate carvings that Tobolsk became known for in the mid 19th century. The tradition continues to this day, with artists such as Tatar master Minsalim (☎ 922-481 3188) drawing inspiration from Russian folk tales. His depictions of characters from the said tales, hunting scenes and more can be found at his workshop at ul Oktyabrskaya 4 (look for the Palitra Палитра sign), across from Hotel Sibir, where visitors can see how an antler is turned into an intricate bone carving. His carvings are also sold in the shop attached to the café in the grounds of the Deputy's Palace, but the most extensive collection of carvings for sale, by Minsalim and other artists, is found inside Hotel Slavyanskaya (see p270).

skeleton, and another on the indigenous Khanty people, complete with shaman wear and tambourine as well as assorted fishing equipment. The highlight, however, is the exhibit dedicated to Tobolsk's celebrated bone-carving craft (see box above), the tiny mammoth bone and reindeer antler creations including a delicate pin with leaf, animal scenes and egg and spoon.

The Old Town Старинный Тобольск

The Old Town's many churches and wooden homes are mostly in a rundown condition and its streets are largely devoid of people, creating an atmosphere of genteel decay – this is particularly the case along the stretch of ul Mira leading towards ul Bazarnaya pl. The **Church of Michael Archangel Церковь Михаила Архангела** (1745-54), on ul Lenina 24, has been restored, but the larger **Church of Zacharias and Elizabeth Церковь Захария и Елизаветы**, on ul Bazarnaya pl, has been left to crumble. Also worth a glimpse are the **Catholic Church of the Holy Trinity Церковь Святой Троицы**, built by Polish exiles on ul Roza Luxemburg, and a small **mosque мечеть** on ul Pushkina, still used by a handful of local Tatars.

The contents of the preserved office of Tsar Nicholas II, inside the large administrative building on ul Kirova, have been temporarily transferred to the Deputy's Palace (see p267). Across the street from the administrative building, at ul Mira 9, is **Mendeleyev House Дом Менделеева**, the former home of the famous chemist.

PRACTICAL INFORMATION
Orientation and services

The city centre is divided into two parts: the dilapidated wooden Old Town to the south on the plain below, and a giant 1970s Soviet housing complex above it to the north. Between them is a cluster of older apartment blocks and the Kremlin.

The **railway station** is inconveniently located 10km north-east of the city centre. Bus No 4 runs from the railway station to the Kremlin (every half an hour; 30 mins, R15), as does marshrutka No 20 (R20), which continues down to Old Town. Bus Nos 1, 3 and 10 connect Old Town with ul Remezova, north of the Kremlin; bus 10 makes a convenient loop around Old Town.

There is a handy TransCredit Bank **ATM** inside the railway station, and other ATMs inside the respective lobbies of Hotel Slavyanskaya and in Hotel Sibir.

Tobolsk Тобольск

WHERE TO STAY
- 2 Hotel Slavyanskaya
  Гостиница Славянская
- 5 Hotel Georgievskaya
  Гостиница Георгиевская
- 7 Hotel Sibir
  Гостиница Сибирь

WHERE TO EAT & DRINK
- 2 Romanov, Anastacia &
  Café Maria Романов,
  Анастасия & Кафе Мария
- 5 Restaurant Yekaterina
  Ресторан Екатерина
- 6 Restaurant Ladeyny
  Ресторан Ладейный
- 12 Café Кафе

PLACES OF INTEREST
- 4 Peter & Paul Church
- 8 Art Salon
- 9 Governor's Museum Музей
  Изобразительных Искусств
- 10 Gostinny Dvor
  Гостинный Двор
- 11 Former Prison
  Тюремный Замок
- 13 History museum in Deputy's
  Palace Исторический Музей и
  Дворец Наместника
- 14 Cathedral of the Intercession
  Покровский Собор
- 15 Cathedral of St Sophia
  Собор Святой Софии
- 16 Swedish House Шведский Дом

PLACES OF INTEREST *(cont'd)*
- 17 Catholic Church of the Holy
  Trinity Церковь Святой Троицы
- 18 Church of Zacharias &
  Elizabeth Церковь Захария и
  Елизаветы
- 19 Museum of Tsar Nicholas II
  Кабинет-Музей Императора
  Николая II
- 20 Mendeleyev House
  Дом Менделеева
- 21 Church of Michael Archangel
  Церковь Михаила Архангела
- 22 Mosque Мечеть

OTHER
- 1 Bus Station Автовокзал
- 2 ATM (Hotel Slavyanskaya)
- 3 Post Office Почта
- 7 ATM (in Hotel Sibir)

Railway station, resting rooms,
ATM & café (Ж Д Вокзал, комнаты
отдыха, ATM & кафе), 10km

Pr Mendeleyeva Пр Менделеева

Ul Semyona Remezova Ул Семена Ремезова

Komsomolsky Pr Комсомольский Пр

Ul Severnaya Ул Северная

Ul Znamenskogo Ул Знаменского

Ul Oktyabrskaya Ул Октябрьская

Ul Sverdlova Ул Свердлова

Kremlin Кремль

Ul Rozy Luxemburg Ул Розы Люксембург

Ul Mira Ул Мира

Ul Kirova Ул Кирова

OLD TOWN

Ul Dekabristov Ул Декабристов

Ul Yershova Ул Ершова

Ul Semakova Ул Семакова

Ul Kooperativnaya Ул Кооперативная

Ul Novaya Ул Новая

Ul Lenina Ул Ленина

Ul Slesarskaya Ул Слесарская

Irtysh River

trailblazer

0 250 500m

CITY GUIDES & PLANS

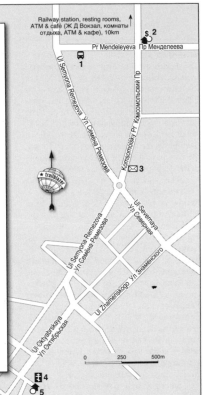

The Tobolsk area code is ☎ 3456. From outside Russia dial ☎ +7-3456.

Where to stay

The refurbished *resting rooms* комнаты отдыха (*komnaty otdykha*; ☎ 362 551) at the railway station (place in sgl/dbl/quad for 12hrs R800/600/470) are spartan but spotless but available for 3/6/12/24 hours. The hot water is temperamental. It's worth booking ahead if you're arriving in the middle of the night as the rooms tend to fill up. To pay, the receptionist might send you downstairs to the dezhurnaya дежурная window.

The location of *Hotel Sibir* Гостиница Сибирь (Ремизова пл 1, Remizova pl 1, ☎ 251 353, sgl/dbl from R1400/2800) is a winner – it's across the road from the Kremlin. The deliberately old-fashioned décor (think iron bedsteads, heavy curtains and period photography) in the cosy rooms is belied by the modern bathrooms (the cheapest rooms share one bathroom between two rooms). A plusher choice is *Hotel Georgievskaya* Гостиница Георгиевская (ул Ленская 35, ul Lenskaya 35, ☎ 220 909, 🖳 www.hotel-georgievskaya.ru, sgl/dbl from R2800/3800, lux from R6300; WI-FI), a stylish, modern hotel a short walk from the Kremlin. The well-appointed rooms are spacious and warm, the young staff are helpful.

Siberia's first five-star hotel, *Hotel Slavyanskaya* Гостиница Славянская (пр Менделеева и Комсомольский пр, corner of pr Mendeleeva and Komsomolsky pr, ☎ 399 101, 🖳 www.slavjanskaja.ru, sgl/dbl/lux from R3600/4800/8600; WI-FI), 3km north of the Kremlin, is not near the attractions but it is right on Bus No 4's route. The grand complex hosted former president Medvedev during his 2010 visit. Note that the cheapest rooms are located under the nightclub.

Where to eat and drink

Tobolsk railway station has an on-site *café* and along the platform there are numerous **stalls** selling smoked fish, berries, salted cucumbers and other homemade food.

The excellent *Restaurant Yekaterina* Ресторан Екатерина at Hotel Georgievskaya serves all manner of Russian classics. Hotel Slavyanskaya boasts two good **restaurants** – *Romanov* Романов and *Anastacia* Анастасия, as well as *Café Maria* Кафе Мария for light meals, and a full-size swimming pool and spa. The Romanov in particular is worth a visit for the cheesy fresco of the royal family on the ceiling and a full stable of Russian classics, as well as more imaginative salmon with raspberry sauce, and rabbit baked in clay pot (mains R650-1000).

Restaurant Ladeyny Ресторан Ладейный (mains R200-350) – the kitschy gingerbread castle near the Kremlin (ul Revolutsionnaya 2 ул Революционная 2) is good for a lunch stop, with soups, meats and salads served to the accompaniment of relentless Russian pop.

Moving on

By rail From Tobolsk there are no particularly convenient departures for Omsk; the 363 leaves on alternate days at 10.21am local time but arrives at 11.50pm local time (13½hrs), while the 195 arrives in Omsk at a reasonable 3.28pm local time but departs Tobolsk at an ungodly 3.26am on alternate days (13hrs).

Other departures include Yekaterinburg (7-8/day, 9½-11½hrs, the most convenient being the 59 and 109 overnighters) and Tyumen (11/day, 3½-5hrs).

❏ **Abbreviations**
★ = Author's favourite; **sgl** = single; **dbl** = double; **twn** = twin; **trpl** = triple; **lux** = luxury room; **apt** = apartment; **pp** = per person; **[V]** = vegetarian.
Street names: see box p80.

CITY GUIDES & PLANS

Omsk
Омск

[**Moscow Time +3; population: 1,160,670**]   With a laid-back atmosphere accentuated by a wealth of parks and public sculptures, Omsk, Siberia's second-largest city, is a pleasant and slightly offbeat place to break your Trans-Siberian trip though its sights are decidedly modest.

The city was founded in 1719 as a small fortress on the west bank of the River Om, to be used as the military headquarters of the Cossack regiments in Siberia. It had been considerably enlarged and included a large *ostrog* (prison) by the time Fyodor Dostoyevsky arrived in 1849 to begin four years of hard labour for political crimes. His unenviable experiences were recorded in *Buried Alive in Siberia*. He was twice flogged, once for complaining about a lump of dirt in his soup; the second time he saved the life of a drowning prisoner, ignoring a guard who ordered that the man be left to drown. Dostoyevsky received so severe a flogging for this charitable act that he almost died and had to spend six weeks in the hospital.

During the Civil War Omsk was the capital of the White Russian government of Admiral Kolchak, until November 1919 when the Red Army entered and took the city. During WWII, Omsk suffered incredible losses: half the men who went to the front did not return at all; out of the rest, many came back crippled. Today, Omsk makes its living in textiles, food, agricultural machinery and timber industries.

WHAT TO SEE AND DO

Inside the grand former Siberian governor's palace, **Vrubel Fine Arts Museum Художественный Музей имени Врубеля** (ul Lenina 23 ул Ленина 23, 🖳 vrubel.ru, 10am-6pm Tue-Sun, R150) is home to decorative arts by Russian and Western artists from the 16th to the early 20th century. The building itself has an interesting history as it was the home of White Army Admiral Kolchak between 1918 and 1919 before the Red Army overran the city. There's a separate wing of the museum at ul Lenina 3 (same opening times, R150) showcasing an extensive collection of Russian art from the 18th to the 20th centuries, as well as icons and a smaller collection of Western art.

Next door, **Omsk State Museum of History and Regional Studies Омский Государственный Историческо-Краеведческий Музей** (ul Lenina 23a ул Ленина 23а, 11am-6pm Tue-Sun, exhibitions R60-80 each) consists of separately priced exhibitions on a plethora of subjects – from 'Asian Russia' and 'Hunter's Trophies' to 'Mysteries of Ancient History'. The latter charts the first human settlement in the area through archaeological remains and tells the story of eastern Siberia and how it came to be linked to the Russian

CITY GUIDES & PLANS

empire. The ethnographic displays show traditional dwellings of the peoples who've populated Siberia, and the national costumes of Tatars, Cossacks, Russians and Ukrainians are colourful and varied.

In front of the museum a **WWII memorial Мемориал Великой Отечественной Войне** states: 'We sing our praise to the madness of the brave,' and there's a small **Lenin statue памятник Ленину** nearby.

On pl Lenina there's a long overdue **memorial to the victims of Stalinist repression памятник Жертвам Сталинских Репрессий**.

You'll recognise the **Military Museum Военный Музей** (ul Taube 7 ул Таубе 7, 10am-6pm Tue-Sun, R100) by the bristling of tanks and other military apparel in the fenced-off area outside it. Inside there are displays on WWI, the Afghan and Chechnya conflicts and a particularly extensive WWII section, created in time for the 65th anniversary of the end of the war.

Near the junction of the Om and Irtysh rivers are the ramparts and **Tobolsk Gate Тобольские Ворота** of the old Omsk fortress.

By the Om River is the distinctive **Serafimo-Aleksievskaya Chapel Серафимо-Алексиевская часовня**, built to commemorate the birth of the Tsarevich Alexis in 1904 and restored in the 1990s.

On the northern part of ul Lenina you'll find a **Slacker Workman statue Памятник Рабочему**, consisting of the jolly upper body of a man sticking out of a manhole.

SERAFIMO-ALEKSIEVSKAYA
CHAPEL

PRACTICAL INFORMATION
Orientation and services
The attractions are in the city centre which is about 6km north of the station, around the junction of the Om and Irtysh rivers.

Several buses and trolleybuses run the length of pr Karla Marksa to the centre, the most handy being trolleybus No 4 (R17) that takes you from the railway station to the central pl Lenina ('пл Ленина') stop.

Where to stay
The railway station has cosy but basic *resting rooms* комнаты отдыха (*komnaty otdykha*; sgl/twin/quad R2500/900/700pp per 12hrs) on the left as you exit the station.

Ultra-central *Hotel Ibis Sibir* Отель Ибис Сибирь (ul Lenina 22, ул Ленина 22, ☎ 311 551, 🖥 www.ibis.com, dbl from R3700, WI-FI) is a quality business hotel. Its rooms are decorated in creams and browns; ask for one not facing ul Lenina.

★ *Hotel Polyot* Отель Полёт (ul 7 Liniya 180, ул 7 Линия 180, ☎ 906 809, 🖥 polet-omsk.ru, dbl R2400, WI-FI) is a friendly mini-hotel, consisting of just eight rooms, that comes heartily recommended for the warm welcome of its owners, attention to detail (orthopaedic beds, power showers), and good breakfasts. Take trolleybus No 3 or 11 from the railway station to Лизы Чайкиной 'Lizy Chaikinoi' stop, walk south one block, turn into ul Ippodromnaya ул Ипподромная, then take the first left.

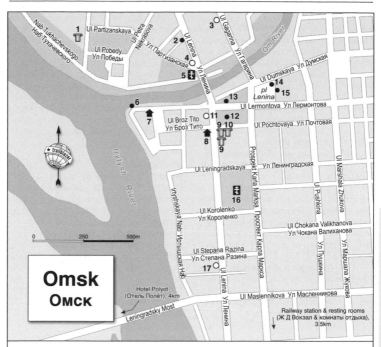

WHERE TO STAY
7 Hotel Mayak Гостиница Маяк
8 Hotel Ibis Sibir Omsk

WHERE TO EAT AND DRINK
3 Tamada Тамада
4 Pertsy Перцы
11 Café Berlin Кафе Берлин
17 ГраForman

PLACES OF INTEREST
1 Military Museum Военный Музеи
2 Slacker Workman statue
Памятник Рабочему
5 Serafimo-Aleksievskaya Chapel
Серафимо-Алексиевская часовня
6 Tobolsk Gate Тобольские Ворота

9 Vrubel Fine Arts Museum
Художественный Музей имени
Врубеля
10 Omsk State Museum of History
and Regional Studies
Государственный Историческо-
Краеведческий Музеи
12 WWII Memorial Памятник
Великой Отечественной Войне
13 Lenin Statue Памятник Ленину
14 Memorial to Victims of Stalinist
Repression Памятник Жертвам
Сталинских Репрессии
15 Musical Theatre
Музыкальный Театр
16 St Nicholas Cathedral
Никольский Собор

The Omsk area code is ☎ 3812. From outside Russia dial ☎ +7-3812.

Overlooking the river, the nautically themed four-star *Hotel Mayak* **Гостиница Маяк** (ul Lermontova 2, ул Лермонтова 2, ☎ 330 303, 💻 www.hotel-mayak.ru, sgl/dbl/suite from R3250/3800/4800, wi-fi) has smart, stylish rooms with excellent modern bathrooms. Dining choices on the premises consist of a sushi bar, pub, and restaurant serving Russian and European dishes and the staff are friendly and helpful.

Where to eat and drink
Somewhat hidden, just off the main strip, the vast basement restaurant ★ *Tamada* **Тамада** (ul Gagarina 3 ул Гагарина 3, mains R200-360) serves Georgian dishes inside what is essentially a dimly lit cavern festooned with grapevines and with its own water feature. *Kuchmachi* (chicken giblets cooked with herbs and spices) is a standout dish, but it's hard to go wrong with any of the grilled meats.

Café Berlin **Кафе Берлин** (ul Lenina 20 ул Ленина 20, wi-fi) is good for a quick refuelling stop if you want to munch on a sandwich or salad with your coffee while updating your Facebook status.

The place to go for inexpensive pasta dishes and good thin-and-crispy pizzas is *Pertsy* **Перцы** (corner of ul Partizanskaya and ul Lenina, ул Партизанская и ул Ленина, mains R280-380, [V]).

Having replaced a venerable restaurant that paid homage to the newsman's trade, new munchery *ГраForman* (ul Lenina 34 ул Ленина 34, mains R250-350) is your 24-hour pit stop for steaks, sushi, tea, coffee, bliny and other items from a mishmash Russian/European menu.

Moving on
By rail Destinations include Novosibirsk (14/day, 7-9hrs, the most convenient overnighter being the firmenny 088), Tobolsk (1-2/day, 12-13hrs, with the 195 on alternate days arriving inconveniently at 3.24am local time and the 363 also on alternate days but arriving at a more sensible 11.05pm), Tomsk (1/day, 14hrs, 038 on alternate days and 120 also on alternate days – both convenient overnighters), and Yekaterinburg (12/day, 11-18hrs, the 001, 023, 025 and 067 being convenient overnighters).

Novosibirsk
Новосибирск

[Moscow Time +3; population: 1,523,801] Novosibirsk thinks big. Siberia's largest city and Russia's third most populous city after Moscow and St Petersburg feels the need to stretch its limbs, so everything here is oversized – the massive railway station, Russia's largest opera house, vast squares, straight, wide streets that go on for miles…

Compared to many other Trans-Siberian cities, Novosibirsk is a relatively young city with few remaining historical buildings, but instead a lively vibe, a large student population and an excellent dining scene. Its attractions include a smattering of good museums (including an excellent railway museum in the nearby town of Seyatel, see p281), impressive Communist-era statues on the enormous main square and a slice of Soviet-era nostalgia in the form of the nearby town of Akademgorodok (see box p282), the 'City of Scientists' where researchers live in a purpose-built, lakeside town. Novosibirsk is the terminus of the Turksib railway (see pp110-11) and travellers can also catch a train from here to Almaty in Kazakhstan and then continue east into China.

HISTORY

Novosibirsk didn't exist before the Trans-Siberian was built. Its spectacular growth in the 20th century is largely due to the railway. In 1891 it was decided that a railway bridge over the Ob should be built here and two years later a small settlement sprang up on the river bank to house the bridge builders. The town was named Novo-Nikolayevsk in honour of the accession of the new Tsar.

By 1900 over 15,000 people lived here and the numbers grew as railway and water-borne trade developed. As far as tourists were concerned there was only one reason to get off the Trans-Siberian here, as Baedeker's 1914 *Guide to Russia* points out: 'It is a favourite starting point for sportsmen in pursuit of the wapiti, mountain sheep, ibex and other big game on the north slopes of the Altai'.

The town suffered badly during the Civil War when 30,000 people lost their lives. During the first four months of 1920 a further 60,000 died of typhus. In 1925 Novo-Nikolayevsk was re-christened Novosibirsk ('New Siberia').

Between 1926 and 1939 the population mushroomed as smelting furnaces were built and fed with coal from the nearby Kuznetsk Basin and iron ore from the Urals. The early 1930s saw the laying of the final sections of the Turksib Railway (a project begun in the years just before WWI), completing a 2600km line from Novosibirsk across Kazakhstan via Semey (Semipalatinsk) and Almaty to Arys in the fertile valley of the Syr-Darya river in Central Asia. Grain from the lands around Novosibirsk could now be exchanged for cotton, which grew best in Central Asia.

During WWII many civilians and complete factories were shifted to Novosibirsk from European Russia; the city has been growing ever since. It's now the area's busiest river port and Siberia's major industrial centre, with many people employed in engineering and metallurgy factories.

WHAT TO SEE AND DO

Lenin Square Площадь Ленина

Ploshchad Lenina (Lenin Sq) is the heart of the city. It's dominated by the vast **Opera and Ballet Theatre Театр Оперы и Балета** (see p281), one of the largest in the world, with its silver dome, gigantic portico and splendid interior. The theatre was completed in 1945 after most able-bodied young men had been sent off to war. The effort was seen as all the more heroic in that many of the city's women and children helped the few builders who remained behind.

In the middle of the square is the most dramatic-looking **statue of Lenin** along the Trans-Siberian railway, his coat blowing behind him in the cold Siberian wind. He is flanked by three partisans on his right and by two 'Peace' figures on his left – a man and a woman – who look as if they are directing the traffic that flows around the great square with their stalk of wheat and torch. In the winter there are troika rides here and people build ice-sculptures. Come summer, the square and the adjacent park are the venue for a thriving local promenade scene.

The low building above **M** Ploshchad Lenina is the oldest stone structure in the city.

Museum of Local Studies Краеведческий Музей

The Museum of Local Studies (🖥 www.museum.nsk.ru) consists of **four sections** in three locations: the History Museum, the Natural History Museum which shares the building with the Siberian Centre of Modern Art, and Kirov House-Museum.

The **History Museum Исторический Музей** (Krasny pr 23 Красный пр 23) traces the history of the region from its earliest settlement through to Soviet Siberia and the Novosibirsk area's participation in WWII. Ethnographic displays covering the Altai, Evenk, Yakut, Siberian Tatar and other native people of Siberia are particularly interesting, featuring traditional dress, tools and ceremonial objects. It was closed for renovation at the time of research and won't reopen till late 2014 at the earliest. The revamped, partly interactive **Natural History Museum Музей Природы** (Vokzalnaya Magistral 11 Вокзальная Магистраль 11, daily 10am-8pm, R60) contains an extensive display of Siberian flora and fauna including some of the 50 species of mammals, 30 species of fish, and 30 species of birds that are found only in Novosibirsk Oblast, including such rareties as black stork and white pelican. There's also a collection of Siberian flora, the skeleton of a mammoth and a geological display; look out for the charoite here – reportedly discovered in the 1940s, it is a rare stone that's purple in colour. First described in 1978, it's named after the Chara River and is endemic to the Sakha Republic, Siberia. English captioning is available. Its neighbour, **Siberian Centre of Contemporary Art Сибирский Центр Современного Искусства** (daily 10am-8pm, 🖥 www .artcentresibir.ru) hosts innovative temporary exhibitions by Russian artists and photographers. **Kirov House-Museum Дом-Музей Кирова** (ul Lenina 23 ул Ленина 23, Mon-Fri 10am-6pm, free entry) is devoted to Sergey Kirov, a rising Communist Party leader who was assassinated in 1934 on Stalin's orders and who lived here for a relatively short while in 1908. It's an abandoned-looking log cabin (though it should be open in theory) containing original furnishings.

History Museum of the Western Siberian Railway
Музей Истории Западно-Сибирской Железной Дороги

Near the main railway station, this thorough museum (ul Shamshurina 39 ул Шамшурина 39, 8am-7pm Mon-Fri, 11am-5pm Sat & Sun; free entry) covers the history of the Western Siberian railway, starting with its conception along the Siberian Trakt and spanning the Revolution and the two world wars up to the present day. The series of railway-related artefacts, such as the photos of the immense bridges spanning the mighty Siberian rivers, bring across what a monumental effort this was. Exhibits include uniforms through the ages, train furniture, and scale models of freight and passenger locomotives (you'll learn the difference between ИС, ФД, Р, СУ, П-36 and СО) as well as a delightful model railway (though unfortunately, visitors are not allowed to play with it).

NOVOSIBIRSK RAILWAY STATION – SIBERIA'S LARGEST

State Art Museum Государственный Художествнный Музей
Besides a rich collection of church art and a respectable one of Italian, French and Dutch masters, this museum (Krasny pr 5 Красный пр 5, 10am-6pm Tue, Wed & Fri, 11am-7pm Thur, Sat & Sun, 🖵 www.nsartmuseum.ru, adult/student R200/120) features Russian art from the 18th to the 21st century, including a vibrant Soviet section. The temporary art and photography exhibitions by local and international artists provide the icing on the cake.

Other sights
The restored 1898 red-brick **Aleksander Nevsky Cathedral Собор Александра Невского** (at the southern end of Krasny pr Красный пр near the river) features colourful new murals. Just south of pl Lenina is the tiny **Chapel of St Nicholas Часовня Святителя Николая**, in the middle of the road and reached from beneath via the pedestrian subway. It was built on the spot said to mark the geographic centre of Russia and opened during the city's centenary celebrations in 1993. The original church here was destroyed after the Revolution.

On ul Sovetskaya ул Советская, the blue-domed **Cathedral of the Ascension Вознесенский Собор** was built in 1914 and surprises you with its particularly appealing interior.

PRACTICAL INFORMATION
Orientation and services
Novosibirsk was designed on a grand scale. Krasny prospect Красный проспект, its main street, extends for over 10km. The mighty River Ob bisects the city, leaving the main hotels, sights and railway station on the east bank.

You can buy **city maps** from the many newspaper kiosks outside the main railway station; just ask for a '*karta gohroda*'. You can access the **internet** at the **central post office почтамт** (ul Lenina 5, 8am-9pm Mon-Fri, to 7pm Sat & Sun) and there's free wi-fi at all accommodation options reviewed.

There are several **ATMs** at the railway station, including the reliable Trans-CreditBank, and more ATMs along Krasny pr.

Local transport
On foot, the central pl Lenina пл Ленина is about 20 minutes from the railway station, straight down Vokzalnaya Magistral Вокзальная Магистраль. Novosibirsk has a limited **metro** system (including some stations panelled in Siberian marble; R21

per ride). To reach pl Lenina from the railway station (**M** Ploshchad Garina-Mikhailovs-kogo Площадь Гарина-Михаиловского), go one stop to **M** Sibirskaya/Krasny Prospekt Сибирская/Красный Проспект, change to the Studencheskaya Студенческая line and go one stop to **M** Ploshchad Lenina Площадь Ленина.

Near **M** Rechnoy Vokzal Речной Вокзал (meaning 'river station') is the **long-distance bus station**.

There's plenty of public transport going up and down Krasny pr, including trolleybus Nos 5, 13 and 29 and bus Nos 13, 28 and 97 (R16).

Novosibirsk has two **airports**: the international Tolmachyovo airport (Аэропорт Толмачёво), 23km from the city centre on the western bank, and the domestic Severny airport (Северный Аэропорт), 6km to the north of the centre. Bus No 111 and marshrutka No 312 run to Tolmachyovo from the railway station and the bus station, while trolleybus No 2 connects Severny to the railway station.

Where to stay

The railway station has spacious *resting rooms* комнаты отдыха (*komnaty otdykha*, ☎ 229 2376, sgl/twin/quad R2000/1200/850pp per 12 hours), but price-wise, they are not terribly good value. Book ahead, as they are often full; you must show a ticket for onward travel to stay here.

Novosibirsk's original *Hostel Dostoyevsky* (ul Shchetinkina 49, apt 14, ул Щетинкина 49, кв 14, ☎ 913 759 9182, 🖳 hosteldostoevsky.com, dorms/twn R450/1700, WI-FI) now has an ultra-convenient location right in the city centre. Expect brightly decorated dorms, friendly young staff, and a good guest kitchen – all for the cheapest prices in town.

Just across from the railway station,

Hotel Novosibirsk Гостиница Новосибирск (Vokzalnaya magistral 1, Вокзальная магистраль 1, ☎ 364 0101, 🖳 www.hotel-novosibirsk.ru, sgl/twn/lux R3010/3290/6230, WI-FI) is a hideous Soviet tower on the outside, but a revamped, modern hotel on the inside, featuring spacious, carpeted rooms. They throw in a good breakfast and one of the Beermen restaurant branches is located downstairs.

Hidden in a quiet, green corner in the centre (yes, such things do exist!), mini-hotel ★ *Avenue* Авеню (ul Sovetskaya 57 ул Советская 57, ☎ 227 0543, 🖳 www.avenu.vipngs.ru, sgl/dbl from R3400/3800, WI-FI) is all about spacious rooms with individual décor, tiled bathrooms as well as guest access to Jacuzzi and two saunas. 'Optima'

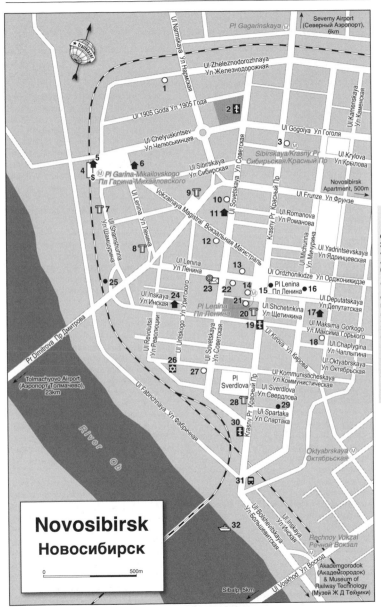

Novosibirsk
Новосибирск

0   500m

The Novosibirsk area code is ☎ 383. From outside Russia dial ☎ +7-383.

economy rooms have been introduced (sgl/twn R1500/2400) and there are discounts for staying for 12 rather than 24 hours, making this a great central bet.

***Zokol Hostel* Хостел Цоколь** (ul Inskaya 39, ул Инская 39, ☎ 906 996 4206, 🖳 www.hostelzokol.ru, dorm/twn R600/800-1000pp, WI-FI), in a you-can't-get-more-central-than-this location, is a homey hostel with bilingual staff, a thick folder full of eating/drinking listings to help you, and two compact kitchen/lounge areas that encourage mingling. Downside: only the superior twin has a window.

Where to eat and drink

Need your morning caffeine fix? Then look no further than Californian transplant ***Traveler's Coffee*** (Krasny pr 86, Красный пр 86, 9am-midnight daily), its aromatic brews spanning the world, with a supporting cast of teas, cheesecakes, smoothies, shakes and more.

***Murakami* Мураками** (Krasny pr 25, Красный пр 25, meals R400-600) is a stylish Japanese restaurant with oriental décor, private booths and very good sushi sets. Directly opposite (also in the same building), ***Perchini* Перчини** (Krasny pr 25, Красный пр 25, mains R260-380, [V], WI-FI) serves veal carpaccio alongside imaginatively topped thin-and-crispy pizzas (pear and Dor Blu cheese, anyone?) and homemade pasta dishes to Novosibirsk's mostly young, smartphone-and-iPad-toting clientele. There's an extensive cocktail list, too, and a good business lunch deal.

Just around the corner (but also in the same building), ***Pechki-Lavochki* Печки-Лавочки** (Krasny pr 25, Красный пр 25, mains R200-300) is a kitschy, friendly place specialising in inexpensive Russian dishes.

For steaks, head for the muted lighting and dark wood of stylish ***Goodman Steakhouse* Гудман Стейкхаус** (ul Sovetskaya 5, ул Советская 5, 🖳 nsk.good man.ru, steaks R1480-2170), already popular in Moscow.

For more carnivorous delights, hit ***People's Bar & Grill*** (Vokzalnaya magistral 16 Вокзальная магистраль 16) where different types of shashlyk (R385-630) – or else the likes of Salmon Pulp Fish'on, if meat's not your thing – are brought to your booth by helpful staff. Sometimes the kitchen has trouble getting your main and your side dish to you at the same time.

For a very Siberian splurge, look no further than ★ ***Ekspeditsiya* Экспедиция** (ul Zheleznodorozhnaya 12/1, ул Железнодорожная 12/1, 🖳 expedicia-nsk.ru, mains R850-1500), with its expedition/hunting décor (including an orange helicopter) and a menu full of Siberia's wildlife. Your options include a hunting platter of wild birds, marinated bear steak with taiga herbs, elk shashlyk, baked taimen and other Siberian fish; even the soups feature wild mushrooms or wild duck, served in sturdy tin dishes. You won't find anything like this at home!

You can probably guess the speciality at ***Beerman & Pelmeni*** (ul Kamenskaya 7, ул Каменская 7, 🖳 beermanpelmen.ru, meals R300), with own beer on tap, as well as Belgian, Czech, German and Irish bottled brew, and the widest selection of the beloved pelmeni (19 types, to be precise) in the Urals, including squid ink, scallop and chicken and courgette. There's another branch at Vokzalnaya Magistral 1, Вокзальная Магистраль 1.

***Tiflis* Тифлис** (Sovetskaya 65 ул, Советская 65, 🖳 www.tiflisnsk.ru, mains R290-420, [V]), down in the basement, titillates your tastebuds with Georgian dishes such as Georgian hotpot, a selection of shashlyks, the signature dish that involves some of the best offal you'll ever taste, plus melt-in-your-mouth *khachapuri* and a full assortment of fantastic vegetable dishes.

Good places for a drink and live music in the evening are ***Shultz* Шульц** (Krasny pr 66, Красный пр 66), a German-style beer house with Blagbacher, Kellers and Bierbach on tap, among others, accompanied by meaty German dishes.

Entertainment

Novosibirsk boasts the grand **Opera and Ballet Theatre Театр Оперы и Балета** (Krasny pr 36, Красный пр 36, ☎ 209 0006, 💻 www.opera-novosibirsk.ru), which opera and ballet devotees shouldn't miss, as its sumptuous interior and excellent acoustics make for a wonderful experience. You can get tickets from the kiosk on the left side of the theatre. The cheapest performances are in the morning, with seats costing as little as R170; if the theatre isn't full you can move to the more expensive seats for free.

The **Philharmonia Филармония** (ул Спартака 11, ul Spartaka 11, ☎ 4302, 💻 www.philharmonia-nsk.ru) is the prime venue for classical symphony concerts.

Moving on

By rail Novosibirsk is a major train hub with numerous departures east, west and south.

Westbound departures include Moscow via Omsk, Yekaterinburg and other major cities (7-9/day, 47½-54½hrs, the fastest being the firmenny 055 on alternate days). For Omsk (up to 15/day, 7-8¾hrs), the 087 and 069 are convenient over-nighters. For Yekaterinburg (10/day, 20-22hrs).

Eastbound departures include Krasnoyarsk (9/day, 12-13hrs, the 134, 080 and 078 being convenient overnighters), Irkutsk (6/day, 28½-31½hrs, the most convenient being the 078 and the 210 – the latter originating in Novosibirsk – with their convenient morning arrival) and Vladivostok (1-3/day, 97½-105¾hrs, the fastest being the firmenny 002 on alternate days, and the equally fast 008 also on alternate days). To Tomsk, there is the overnight 038 on alternate days (5½hrs), leaving at an ungodly 3.24am local time.

On the **Turksib railway**, there are departures to Almaty, Kazakhstan (1-2/day, 38-40hrs) and Tashkent, Uzbekistan (Sun & Thur 1.51pm local time, 63hrs).

By air Most international and long-distance domestic flights use **Tolmachyovo Airport** (💻 www.tolmachevo.ru has a timetable). There are several daily flights to Moscow (4hrs) with Transaero and Siberian Airlines. Other well-served destinations include St Petersburg, Vladivostok, Yekaterinburg, Beijing, Amsterdam and Tashkent.

The much-smaller **Severny airport** handles a decreasing amount of domestic air traffic.

SIDE TRIP FROM NOVOSIBIRSK

Museum of Railway Technology Музей Железнодорожной Техники

This large open-air **museum** (11am-5pm Tue-Sun, entry R250, camera R100) contains an impressive display of locomotives, most of which have worked on the Western Siberian railway, and carriages, including some of the first used on the Trans-Siberian Railway. This is one of just three such museums in Russia (the other two being in St Petersburg and Rostov-na-Donu) and there are over 100 exhibits, including 12 locomotives, sitting there, spruced up and proud. You can take a peek inside some of the exhibits, though most can only be viewed from the outside.

The museum is at **Seyatel Сеятель**, 25km from Novosibirsk on the road to Akademgorodok; take any Akademgorodok-bound bus (No 36, 38, 52, 65, 121) or marshrutka (No 6, 15, 20) and get off at the Klinika Meshalkina (Клиника Мешалкина) stop; you can't miss the museum on your left.

❏ Demise of a dream: Akademgorodok

Akademgorodok Академгородок, 30km from Novosibirsk, was established in the 1950s as a university and research centre for scientists at Khrushchev's bidding, who dreamed that this concentration of Russia's greatest minds would work (scientific) miracles and push the Soviet Union to the forefront of the scientific world.

Soon after its foundation it grew into an élite township of over 40,000 of the Soviet Union's top intellectuals and their families. In this pleasant sylvan setting researchers and students grappled with scientific problems with a two-fold aim: to push ahead of the West in the arms race and to harness the wealth of Siberia for the good of the USSR. Some of the ideas they considered turning into reality were the creation of a Siberian town under a dome, with its own artificially maintained micro-climate, and fuelling power stations with steam from Kamchatka's volcanoes, though little had come to pass. As with its Olympic athletes, the Soviet Union believed in training its academics from a very early age, spiriting them away from home to attend special boarding schools for the gifted in Akademgorodok. Compared to the ordinary citizen they were well looked after, the shops stocked with little luxuries hard to find elsewhere. As government funding slowed to a trickle in the early 1990s, the utopian dream ended and the brightest scientific minds were either lured abroad or into the private sector, where they could actually earn a decent wage; government-funded scientists barely subsisted on the breadline.

While Akademgorodok still functions as a centre for Russia's software and IT sector it seems that as far as grandiose scientific achievements are concerned the dream is well and truly over. In 2013, the Russian Duma voted into law an act opposed by academics everywhere; whereas before, RAN (Rossiyskaya Akademia Nauk – Russian Academy of Sciences) controlled the scientific community's finances for projects, the majority of funds will now pass into the hands of bureaucrats without scientific training and funds for projects will have to be solicited from them, which paints a truly bleak picture – not just for Akademgorodok, but for science in Russia as a whole.

The forested, lakeside setting offers a relaxing opportunity to get away from Novosibirsk, and the town, with its badly maintained buildings and rather melancholic atmosphere, is a Soviet relic which hints at the old Soviet utopian dream. South of Akademgorodok through the birch forest and over the railway track lie the man-made **beaches** of the **Obskoye Morye** ('Ob Sea'), the vast reservoir created by the construction of the Novosibirskaya power station, Siberia's first large hydroelectric project.

Should you wish to visit either, many Akademgorodok-bound buses run from the main bus station (Avtovokzal Автовокзал) or from **M** Rechnoy Vokzal. Alternatively, up to 10 suburban trains per day stop at 'Obskoye Morye' Обское Море.

Tomsk
Томск

[Moscow Time +3; population: 547,989] A university town with some finely preserved wooden 'lace' architecture, Tomsk is 270km north-east of Novosibirsk and easily reached by overnight trains from Omsk and Krasnoyarsk from the main Trans-Siberian line.

Founded in 1604 on the River Tom, Tomsk developed into a large administrative, trading and gold-smelting centre on the Great Siberian Post Road. For a time it was the most important place in Siberia, visited by almost every 19th-century traveller. The city was an important exile centre and had a large forwarding prison. Having almost succumbed to the stench from the overcrowded cells in 1887, Kennan wrote: 'If you visit the prison my advice to you is to breakfast heartily before starting, and to keep out of the hospital wards.'

Tomsk was bypassed by the original Trans-Siberian railway and began to lose out to stations along the main line. But it underwent a renaissance in the 1960s, when various artistic types – writers, film directors, thespians – responded to the invitation to move there. Today Tomsk remains a lively city with an intellectual and open atmosphere that's hard to find elsewhere in Siberia, as well as an excellent dining and nightlife scene.

WHAT TO SEE AND DO

Wooden 'Lace' Houses
It's rewarding to simply wander and check out the fine old wooden homes that still survive, especially along ul Krasnoarmeyskaya, though many are buckling and in dire need of restoration. At No 71 is the vivid blue **Russian-German House Российско-Немецкий Дом**, with elaborate white ornamentation featuring snowflake motifs.

Down the street at No 68 is **Dragon House Дом Дракона**, with a stylised dragon head over the door and more sprouting from the roof. At No 67a is the most beautiful and best restored of them all – **Peacock House Дом Павлина**, with a red roof topped with mini-turrets and white 'lace' peacocks and intricate white 'lace' under the eaves.

There are also some **stately homes** along ul Gagarina and ul Tatarskaya, as well as **Shushkin House Дом Шушкина** at ul Shishkova 10.

Tomsk Memorial Museum Томский Мемориальный Музей
This cellar museum (10am-6pm Fri-Wed, noon-9pm Thur, 🖥 www.sledturmn kvd.info, R50), housed in a former KGB office at pr Lenina 44 пр Ленина 44 (enter around the side), is dedicated to the victims of the Communist regime. The displays in the five cells include maps of the Gulag system, personal belongings of those sentenced to a brutal existence, letters to their parents from children of 'enemies of the people' who were forcibly separated from their families and put into orphanages as well as many photos of haunted-looking men and women, only some of whom survived the repression. Unfortunately there's little English captioning and tours are in Russian only, but you certainly get the general idea. There are also temporary exhibitions, such as a recent one on Vasily Grossman's 'Life and Fate.'

By the museum you'll find two **Monuments to Victims of Stalinist Repressions Памятник Жертвам Сталинских Репрессий** – the larger one to local victims and the smaller one to Poles.

❑ Tomsk's memorable monuments

If you check out some of Tomsk's monuments, you'll get the impression that during the time of the tsars and the subsequent Communist era, sculptors were exiled to Tomsk primarily for their sense of humour.

Some of the gems include a **statue of Anton Chekhov Памятник Антону Чехову**, as seen through the eyes of a drunk – with oversized feet and exaggerated features (pl Lenina 10). Near Hotel Tomsk (ul Kirova 65), you'll find a **sculpture of a pair of slippers Памятник тапочкам** – perhaps to suggest that guests make themselves at home. In Russian folk tales, babies are not brought by the stork, but rather found in the cabbage patch; to commemorate this, there's a **giant cabbage and baby Памятник младенцу в капусте** opposite the city's maternity ward at pr Lenina 65. When walking around town keep an eye out for a fat man wearing nothing but enormous underpants hanging from a windowsill – that's the **monument of the lover**, making a daring escape to avoid being caught by the furious husband; it doesn't have a permanent location because Casanova keeps moving around the city.

Opposite Troitsky skver, just off pr Lenina, you find the **world's largest rouble coin Памятник рублю** made of wood.

Finally, football fans will be familiar with the expression on the face of the **bronze football fan Памятник болельщику** who sits on a bench in the 4th section of the Tomsk Trud stadium (ul Belinskogo 13) – perhaps he's upset because Tom Tomsk FC slipped back into the 2nd division in 2012-13.

Other sights

The city's **World War II Memorial Памятник Великой Отечественной Войне**, in the peaceful **Lagerny Gardens Лагерный Сад**, at the southern end of pr Lenina, consists of imposing socialist statues of a mother and her armed fighter son, with piped music erupting from endless rows of eerie beech trees.

Walking up pr Lenina from Lagerny Gardens you pass the **University Университет**, with a handsome white colonnaded building as its centrepiece.

Just up from Troitsky skver, **Atashev Palace & Regional Museum Дворец Аташева & Краеведческий Музей** (pr Lenina 75, 10am-6pm Fri-Tue, noon-9pm Thur, R50-100 per exhibition) is dedicated almost entirely to temporary exhibitions such as trade along the Siberian Trakt, which are only of modest interest to non-Russian visitors.

Further north along pr Lenina, at per Nakhanovicha 5 пер Нахановича 5, is the smartphone-enabled **Tomsk Regional Art Museum Томский Областной Художественный Музей** (10am-6pm Fri-Wed, noon-9pm Thur, 🖥 www.artmuseum.tomsk.ru, permanent collection R100), featuring such evocative works by Russian artists as *On the Volga*, *The Village Beauty* and *The Crimean Landscape*, as well as a small collection by Dutch and Italian masters.

The messy, shapeless pl Lenina, presided over by a **Lenin statue** that seems to be directing the traffic from its vantage point on the roundabout, is partially saved by the pink, golden-domed apparition that is the **Epiphany Cathedral Богоявленский Кафедральный Собор** looming above it. Just to the west of the cathedral, police tend to lie in wait for unsuspecting jaywalkers (such as this author), so watch where you cross the street.

A couple of blocks from pr Lenina, **Tomsk History Museum Томский Исторический Музей** (ul Bakunina 3 ул Бакунина 3, 10am-7pm Tue-Sun, 🖳 www.muzeum.tomsk.ru, R43) is reachable by heading uphill. It has some fairly interesting local history exhibits, but actually the view of the city from the top of the wooden tower alone is worth the price of admission.

PRACTICAL INFORMATION
Orientation and services
Tomsk's railway and bus stations are next to each other about 2km south-east of the centre. Running north–south near the Tom River, pr Lenina is the city's main artery. Buy a city map with bus/trolleybus/tram routes marked on it from the kiosk in front of the station. To get to pr Lenina from the railway station, take trolleybus No 4, or bus No 119 or 442, or marshrutka No 2 or 4.

There's **internet access** at the **post office почта** (9am-7.30pm Mon-Fri, 8am-5pm Sat, 9am-5pm Sun) at pr Lenina 95 in the centre of town. There is a TransCredit bank **ATM** at the railway station, and more ATMs along pr Lenina, including in most hotels and banks.

Tours of the city in English, German and French are available from **Tomsktourist Томсктурист** (pr Lenina 59, ☎ 531 723, 🖳 www.tomskturist.ru).

Where to stay
Several hostels have now opened in Tomsk. Best of the bunch is ★ *Domino Hostel* **Хостел Домино** (ул Карла Маркса 3, кв 2, ul Karla Marksa 3, apt 2, ☎ 505 958, 🖳 www.domino-hostel.ru, dorm/dbl R450/1200, WI-FI), in two large, modern flats in a brand new apartment block. Expect parquet floors, fully equipped guest kitchen, genuinely comfortable beds and friendly, helpful bilingual staff (when you can find them, that is).

The railway station *resting rooms* **комнаты отдыха** (*komnaty otdykha*, R550/660/900 for a place in a 4-bed/2-bed/single room for 12 hours, WI-FI) are spotless and share facilities. There is a curfew between 1am and 5am.

Modern *Hotel Toyan* **Гостиница Тоян** (ул Обруб 2, ul Obrub 2, ☎ 510 151, 🖳 www.toyan.ru, sgl/dbl/suite from R4200/5400/8800, WI-FI) certainly gets points for style and comfort, with its slate, glass and steel décor and fantastic showers. If you don't mind living in sepulchral gloom like a vampire, that is.

Well-located *Hotel Sputnik* **Гостиница Спутник** (ул Белинского 15, ul Belinskogo 15, ☎ 526 660, 🖳 sputnik.tomskturist.ru, sgl/dbl/lux R1100-3200/1500-3900/4150, WI-FI) offers two types of accommodation: business traveller-style rooms and budget cheapies with shared bathrooms.

The staff at the centrally located *Hotel Sibir* **Гостиница Сибирь** (пр Ленина 91, pr Lenina 91, ☎ 527 225, 🖳 www.hotelsibir.tomsk.ru, dbl/lux R3300/5800, WI-FI) are particularly attentive and the rooms have classic décor; incidentally it's possible to turn down the heat in the steamy rooms. Amenities include a sauna and swimming pool. Light sleepers should ask for a room away from the street.

A splendid choice is the no-smoking, four-star *Magistrat Hotel* **Гостиница Магистрат** (пл Ленина 15, pl Lenina 15, ☎ 511 111, 🖳 www.magistrathotel.com, sgl/dbl/suite R5800/6600/9700, internet access), in a fully renovated early 19th century neo-classical building featuring one of the city's top restaurants, the Italian-themed *Restaurant Parmesan* **Ресторан Пармезан**. The professional staff are bilingual and the spacious, stylish rooms come with cable TV.

The Tomsk area code is ☎ 3822. From outside Russia dial ☎ +7-3822.

Where to eat and drink

A particularly reliable bet for carnivores, ***People's Bar & Grill*** (ul Krasnoarmeyskaya 31, ул Красноармейская 31, 🖳 www.bar peoples.ru, mains R300-550) offers several different types of shashlyk, steak and other meat dishes. A few fish and vegetable dishes make sure that pescetarians and vegetarians don't feel alienated.

Tsekh No 10 **Цех No 10** (proyezd Vershinina 10/2, проезд Вершинина 10/2, 🖳 tseh10.ru) is a former-lorry-garage-cum-grill-and-wine-bar that attracts a lively crowd of Tomsk students. Besides the thematic music evenings and live music by local musicians, the food is inexpensive and mostly good. Take bus No 3 or marshrutka No 3 or 4 from along pr Lenina пр Ленина to the Obshchezhitiye No 7 ('Общежитие No 7') stop.

Pelmeni Project **Пельмени Project** (pr Lenina 81/1, пр Ленина 81/1, daily 24 hours) specialises in everyone's favourite 'ear dough', with squid ink pelmeni with scallops sitting alongside the more conventional Siberian ones. Pelmeni aside, you can expect a full roster of soups, salads and a selection of breakfast porridge, blini and syrniki, as well as the Ukrainian take on dumplings: vareniki. Another 24-hour branch at ul Uchebnaya 46 ул Учебная 46 is also good for night owls.

Vechny Zov **Вечный Зов** (ul Novosobornaya 2, ул Новособорная 2, 🖳 www.vechzov.tomsk.ru, mains R266-1488) serves a vast spread of imaginative Russian dishes in splendid cellar surroundings to a loyal local clientele. Apart from soups, salads, shashlyk and blini, the menu is also representative of local wildlife, with elk

MAP KEY

WHERE TO STAY
1 Domino Hostel Хостел Домино
3 Magistrat Hotel
   Гостиница Магистрат
4 Hotel Toyan Гостиница Тоян
11 Hotel Sibir Гостиница Сибирь
23 Hotel Sputnik Гостиница Спутник

WHERE TO EAT AND DRINK
3 Restaurant Parmesan
   Ресторан Пармезан
8 Bulanzhe Буланже
12 Perchini Перчини
13 Pelmeni Project Пельмени Project
15 Jazz Café Underground
   Джаз Кафе Underground
19 Vechny Zov Вечный Зов
25 People's Bar & Grill
29 Pelmeni Project
   Пельмени Project

PLACES OF INTEREST
2 Epiphany Cathedral
   Богоявленский Собор
5 Tomsk History Museum
   Томский Исторический Музей
6 Shushkin House
   Дом Шушкина

7 Statue of Anton Chekhov
   Памятник Антону Чехову
9 Tomsk Regional Art Museum
   Томский Областной
   Художественный Музей
14 Atashev Palace & Regional
   Museum Дворец Аташева &
   Краеведческий Музей
16 Tomsk Memorial Museum
   Томский Мемориальный Музей
17 Monuments to Victims of Stalinist
   Repressions Памятник Жертвам
   Сталинских Репрессии
18 Giant rouble coin
   Памятник рублю
20 Giant cabbage and baby
   Памятник младенцу в капусте
21 University Университет
24 Bronze football fan
   Памятник болельщику
26 Dragon House Дом Дракона
27 Peacock House Дом Павлина
28 Russian-German House
   Российско-Немецкий Дом
30 World War II Memorial/Lagerny
   Gardens Памятник/Лагерный Сад

OTHER
10 Post Office/internet Почта/Интернет
22 Tomsktourist Томсктурист

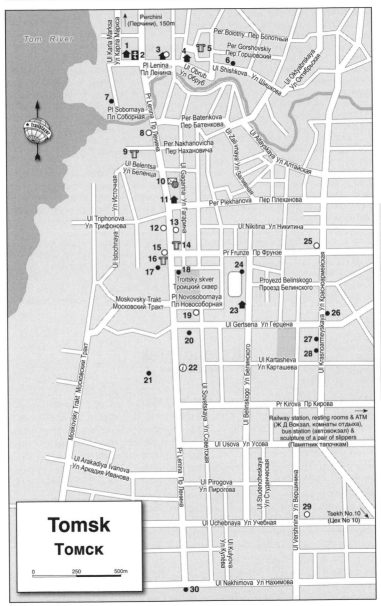

Perchini
(Перчини), 150m

Per Bolotny Пер Болотный

Per Gorshovskiy
Пер Горшовский

Ul Karla Marksa
Ул Карла Маркса

1
2   3   4   5

Ul Obrub
Ул Обруб

Ul Shishkova Ул Шишкова

Ul Oktyabrskaya
Ул Октябрьская

Pl Lenina
Пл Ленина

6

7

Pl Sobornaya
Пл Соборная

Pr Lenina Пр Ленина

Per Batenkova
Пер Батенкова

8

Per Nakhanovicha
Пер Нахановича

Ul Zalivnaya Ул Заливная

Ul Altayskaya Ул Алтайская

9

Ul Belentsa
Ул Беленца

Ul Istochnaya Ул Источная

10

11

Ul Gagarina Ул Гагарина

Per Plekhanova Пер Плеханова

Ul Triphonova
Ул Трифонова

12   13

Ul Nikitina Ул Никитина

15   14

25

16

17

Pr Frunze Пр Фрунзе

24

18

Troitsky skver
Троицкий сквер

Proyezd Belinskogo
Проезд Белинского

Moskovsky Trakt
Московский Тракт

Pl Novosobornaya
Пл Новособорная

23

26

19

Ul Gertsena Ул Герцена

Ul Krasnoarmeyskaya Ул Красноармейская

20

27
28

Ul Kartasheva
Ул Карташева

22

21

Ul Sovetskaya Ул Советская

Ul Belinskogo Ул Белинского

Pr Kirova Пр Кирова

Railway station, resting rooms & ATM
(Ж Д Вокзал, комнаты отдыха),
bus station (автовокзал) &
sculpture of a pair of slippers
(Памятник тапочкам)

Ul Usova Ул Усова

Pr Lenina Пр Ленина

Ul Arakadiya Ivanova
Ул Аркадия Иванова

Ul Pirogova
Ул Пирогова

Ul Studencheskaya Ул Студенческая

Ul Vershinina Ул Вершинина

29

Tsekh No.10
(Цех No 10)

Ul Uchebnaya Ул Учебная

Ul Kulyova Ул Кулёва

Tomsk
Томск

0   250   500m

Ul Nakhimova Ул Нахимова

30

with honey-pomegranate marinade, venison steak, and occasionally even bear making a guest appearance.

Perchini Перчини (pr Lenina 77a, пр Ленина 77a, 🖥 www.perchini.ru; mains R229-239, [V]) attracts a mostly young and trendy clientele with its selection of delicious pizza and pasta. Everything is nicely presented and the service is efficient. Another branch is at ul Karla Marksa 23a ул Карла Маркса 23a.

Jazz Café Underground Джаз Кафе **Underground** (пр Ленина 46, pr Lenina 46, 🖥 www.jazz-cafe.tomsk.ru) is a stylish underground venue with good live music – both by home-grown and international jazz artists, mute black-and-white films and excellent service. There's an extensive food and drink menu, too.

Ever-popular *Bulanzhe* Буланже (pr Lenina 80, пр Ленина 80, 🖥 bulange .tomsk.ru, daily 8.30am-9pm) is an excellent spot for coffee and cakes, with a great quality/price ratio and friendly and efficient service. There's a wide selection of sweet and savoury blini (from R75), porridge and omelettes for breakfast and a handful of substantial mains.

Moving on
By rail   There are departures to Moscow (firmenny 037 *Tomich*, alternate days only, departing at 11.30am local time, 56hrs), Novosibirsk (1-2/day, 5½-9½hrs), with the slow 647 (twice weekly) making a convenient overnight journey and continuing on to Krasnoyarsk (12hrs), the 037 arriving at Omsk (14½hrs) in the wee hours of the morning on alternate days.

By bus   There are numerous buses to Novosibirsk (5½hrs); they are a more flexible option than the train as they leave every hour. Minibuses also ply the same route (3½-4hrs).

By air   There are 4-5 daily flights from Tomsk to Moscow, one on Mondays to Irkutsk, Monday departures for St Petersburg, daily flights to Novosibirsk and Saturday flights to Krasnoyarsk from Tomsk's airport (🖥 www.airport.tomsk.ru).

Krasnoyarsk
Красноярск

[Moscow Time +4; population: 1,016,385] Nestled among commanding hills and cliffs along the Yenisey River, Krasnoyarsk is certainly more pleasantly located than many Siberian cities. While its architecture isn't its distinguishing feature (with the odd exception of a historical wooden mansion), the city does boast some of the best cultural life in the region as well as the status of Siberia's oldest town. That, and the nearby attractions of the Stolby Nature Reserve (see pp295-6) and Yenisey Hydroelectric Dam (see p296), near Divnogorsk, make Krasnoyarsk an excellent place for a stopover.

Russian settlement dates back to the construction of the wooden Krasny Yar fort on a hill overlooking the River Yenisey in 1628, predating the Sibirsky Trakt; that fort, and others north along the river, was reachable either by water or on foot. The Krasny Yar fort was founded by some Cossacks with Andrei Dubenskyas their leader, and built to protect those Siberians who swore loyalty to the Russian tsar in exchange for *yasak* – fur tribute – from the marauding Yenisei Kyrgyz who lived south along the Yenisei. The region, with Yeniseisk as its capital, was at the time sparsely populated by a mixture of Russian settlers and the indigenous Kitó people, whose language has turned out to be identical to that of the Denet Native Americans, further cementing the theory that North America was populated by Siberian tribes who crossed the Bering Strait.

By 1900 Krasnoyarsk's population was 27,000 and the town boasted 20 churches and two cathedrals, a synagogue, 26 schools, a railway technical college and a botanical garden reputed to be the finest in Siberia.

RL Jefferson (see pp95-6) visited Krasnoyarsk in 1897: 'Its situation cannot fail to elicit admiration – the tall mountains rear up around it.' Most of the townsfolk he met here were ex-convicts. So used were they to their own kind that they were particularly suspicious of anyone who lacked a criminal record. He was told of a certain merchant in the city who found it difficult to do business, never having been behind bars. To remedy the situation this merchant is said to have travelled back to St Petersburg and deliberately committed a crime punishable by exile to Siberia. After a short sentence in Irkutsk he returned to his business in Krasnoyarsk and 'got on famously' thereafter.

During WWII, Krasnoyarsk became an important munitions centre, with workers often working as the arms factories were built around them. After the war, munitions manufacturing continued, and Russia's largest aluminium factory was built here in the 1970s, powered by the Divnogorsk dam. Krasnoyarsk was closed to foreigners until 1989 and heavy industry remains a big employer.

WHAT TO SEE AND DO

Regional Museum Краеведческий Музей
Housed rather oddly in a fake Egyptian temple, this riverside museum (ul Dubrovinskogo 84 ул Дубровинского 84, 🖳 www.kkkm.ru, Tue-Sun 10am-6pm, until 7pm in summer, R150) is a must-see for its excellent ethnographic exhibits, with shamanic ritual dress and objects. Also here are interactive displays of Siberian fauna, where you can press a button by each one to listen to the distinctive bird calls and animal cries. Other displays include Christian and Buddhist relics and a full-size replica of a Cossack riverboat. There are also several multi-lingual interactive points within the museum where you can learn more about the history and culture of the region.

★ Krasnoyarsk Museum Centre Красноярский Музейный Центр
By the waterfront, this excellent museum (pl Mira 1, 🖳 www.mira1.ru, 11am-7pm Tue-Sun, R150) is dedicated largely to contemporary art. The building formerly housed the Lenin Museum, its exhibits now compressed into the 'Red Room' – with busts of Comrade Lenin and other members of the Communist pantheon, an adorable dolls' house-sized model of Lenin's study in the Kremlin, and *Farewell*, depicting the beloved leader's death. Another permanent exhibit, 'The War Diaries', focuses on the involvement of Russian troops in the Afghan and Chechen conflicts and leads you through an 'Afghan pass' tunnel, full of sounds of explosions and vivid cartoon figures of the mujahadeen. Temporary contemporary art runs the gamut from video installation and gritty cityscape photography to chalkboard paintings and totem poles made of recyclable rubbish.

CITY GUIDES & PLANS

❏ **The 10-rouble sights**
The 10-rouble note is being phased out and will probably be completely replaced with R10 coins in this book's lifetime, so if you get an R10 note hold onto it as it makes an excellent souvenir of Krasnoyarsk. Why? Because it features three prominent landmarks: the Yenisey Dam (see p296) near Divnogorsk; the Kommunalny bridge that you cross if going to Stolby Nature Reserve or Divnogorsk; and the Chapel of St Paraskeva Pyatnitsa (see below) that sits high above the city. Want to see all three in one day? SibTourGuide (see opposite) offer just such a tour.

In front of the museum, moored on the Yenisey, is *SS Nikolay* Пароход «Св Николай» (11am-9pm daily, R50), the steamship (now also a museum) on which Lenin sailed to exile in Shushenkoye on 30 April 1897, and on which Tsar Nicholas II – the only Russian ruler to have seen his entire dominion – sailed in 1891. You can descend the neck-breakingly steep stairs to see his surprisingly modest quarters and try to figure out how the steamship's main room could have allegedly carried 150 passengers.

Surikov sights

Born in Krasnoyarsk, Vasily Surikov (1848-1916) is the best-known painter of grand Russian historical subjects (such as the *Conquest of Siberia by Yermak*, now in St Petersburg), as well as portraits of ordinary local people. **Surikov Estate Museum** Музей Сурикова (Wed-Sun 10am-6pm, R100) is located in the 19th-century wooden house at ul Lenina 98 alongside a peaceful garden; exhibits upstairs trace the artist's career, from early watercolours to the later oils, while downstairs, some original furniture and numerous photographs of the family indicate how they had lived.

The worthwhile **Krasnoyarsk VI Surikov Art Museum** Красноярский Художественый Музей имени В И Сурикова has two branches: one at ul Karla Marksa 36 ул Карла Маркса 36 (10am-6pm Tue-Sun, R120), where you can see Surikov's works, and the other at pr Mira 12 пр Мира 12 (10am-6pm Tue-Sun, R100), with changing exhibitions by 20th-century artists.

Other sights

The restored **Annunciation Cathedral** Благовещенский Собор, on ul Lenina, is a good example of Siberian Baroque architecture. The old **Catholic Church** Католическая Церковь, which contains an organ, is near the Central Park.

The tiny **Chapel of Paraskeva Pyatnitsa** Часовня Параскевы Пятницы (see box above) stands above the city at ul Stepana Razina 51 ул Степана Разина 51; there are good views from the little park, but to get there, it's a convoluted walk. Bus No 32 along ul Lenina drops you off a block away if you alight at 'Kakhovskaya' ('Каховская') stop.

The Krasnoyarsk area code is ☎ 391. From outside Russia dial ☎ +7-391.

PRACTICAL INFORMATION
Orientation and services
Krasnoyarsk has two parts, separated by the Yenisey River. The northern bank is a mass of terraces and is bounded on the north by a steep hill known as Karaulnaya Mountain and on the west by the forested Gremyachinskaya Ridge. The railway station, museums and hotels are on this side. Just south of the station is the academic area (another Akademgorodok). The southern bank is relatively flat and is mostly factories and multi-storey apartment blocks.

Going strong since 2003, **SibTourGuide** (☎ 251 2654, 💻 www.sib tourguide.com, see also below) is run by the knowledgeable, energetic, English-speaking Anatoliy Brewhanov. It's warmly recommended by travellers for its '10-Rouble Tour' (see box opposite), half- and full-day trips to Stolby (see pp295-6), visits to the Yenisey hydroelectric dam and rural stays at Anatoliy's dacha.

There are **ATMs** in Hotel Krasnoyarsk (see Where to stay), along ul Karla Marksa, and at the railway station.

Local transport
There's one-way traffic along the main streets of ul Karla Marksa (west to east) and ul Lenina (east to west), so the numerous buses and trolleybuses that run into the city centre from the railway station along the former tend to come back along the latter. The easiest way into town is to take trolley-bus No 7 from the railway station (R16).

Where to stay
★ *SibTourGuide Hostel* (pr Mira 85, apt 72, пр Мира 85, кв 72; ☎ 251 2654, 💻 www.sibtourguide.com, dorm/sgl R700/900; internet access, WI-FI) have now opened a spotless little hostel right in the centre of town. Apart from the kitchen and book exchange, guests have access to the collective wisdom of Anatoliy (SibTourGuide himself) and Aleksandr, who know the area and its attractions in intimate detail. They also operate a 'Coffee House' (see Where to eat).

Attracting a young, mixed Russian and foreign crowd, *Titmouse House* (pr Mira 120-35a, 5th entrance, 4th fl, пр Мира 120-35a, 5-й подъезд, 4-й этаж, ☎ 913 527 2283, 💻 www.tithouse.ru, dorm/twn R600/1600, WI-FI) is a large, airy flat with a compact communal kitchen and lounge, occasional queue for the only bathroom and helpful English-speaking staff (when they're on-site, that is). If you'll be arriving after office hours, give them advance warning.

The most modern in town, ★ *Dom Hotel* Дом Отель (ul Krasnoi Armii 16a, ул Красной Армии 16a, ☎ 290 6666, 💻 www.dom-hotel24.ru, sgl/dbl/lux from R4300/6000/7900, WI-FI) is a small hotel that combines modern rooms with orthopaedic mattresses and cable TV with a 'home away from home' ambience and excellent service. The on-site gastropub is an excellent dining option; the buffet breakfast costs extra.

Centrally located *Hotel Krasnoyarsk* Гостиница Красноярск (ul Uritskogo 94, ул Уритского 94, ☎ 274 9403, 💻 www .hotelkrs.ru, sgl/dbl/suite from R4300/5780/7380, WI-FI) may not immediately sway you with the Soviet charm of its exterior, but all the rooms are fully renovated and come with all mod cons, though only the priciest have air-con. The sauna and swimming pool are nice bonuses.

The most luxurious hotel in the city centre, *Hotel Metelitsa* Гостиница Метелица (pr Mira 14/1, pr Mira 14/1, ☎ 227 6060, 💻 www.hotel-metelica.ru, sgl/dbl/suite from R4300/5300/7950, WI-FI) is all avant-garde suites and bright, carpeted, tastefully decorated rooms with plasma satellite TV and daily fresh fruit. Price includes breakfast and there's an on-site restaurant.

The classic décor and consistently good service at the three-star *Hotel Oktyabrskaya* Гостиница Октябрьская (pr Mira 15, pr Mira 15, ☎ 227 3780, 💻 www.hotelocto ber.ru, sgl/dbl/lux from R4600/5600/6100, WI-FI), as well as somewhat bland rooms with satellite TV, make this a solid central choice. Some English spoken.

Central cheapie *Hotel Ogni Yeniseya* Гостиница Огни Енисея (ул

CITY GUIDES & PLANS

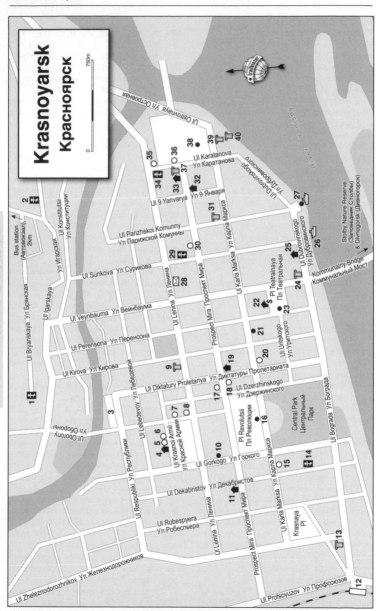

Krasnoyarsk
Красноярск

0   750m

Bus station
(Автовокзал)
2km

Ul Ostrovnaya Ул Островная

Ul Konstitutsii Ул Конституции

Ul Itarskaya Ул Итарская

Ul Igarskaya

Ul Bryanskaya Ул Брянская

Ul Oborony Ул Обороны

Ul Surikova Ул Сурикова

Ul Veynbauma Ул Вейнбаума

Ul Perensona Ул Перенсона

Ul Kirova Ул Кирова

Ul Diktatury Proletariya Ул Диктатуры Пролетариата

Ul Respubliki Ул Республики

Ul Lebedevoy Ул Лебедевой

Ul Krasnoi Armii Ул Красной Армии

Ul Gorkogo Ул Горкого

Ul Dekabristov Ул Декабристов

Ul Robespyera Ул Робеспьера

Ul Lenina Ул Ленина

Ul Zheleznodorozhnikov Ул Железнодорожников

Ul Profsoyuzov Ул Профсоюзов

Prospect Mira Проспект Мира

Ul Karla Marksa Ул Карла Маркса

Krasnaya Pl

Central Park Центральный Парк

Ul Bograda Ул Бограда

Pl Revolutsii Пл Революции

Ul Dzerzhinskogo Ул Дзержинского

Ul Uritskogo Ул Уритского

Pl Teatralnaya Пл Театральная

Ul Dubrovinskogo Ул Дубровинского

Kommunalny Bridge Коммунальный Мост

River Yenisey

Stolby Nature Reserve (Заповедник Столбы) & Divnogorsk (Дивногорск)

Ul Parizhskoi Komunny Ул Парижской Комунны

Ul 9 Yanvarya Ул 9 Января

Ul Karatanova Ул Каратанова

Дубровинского 80, ul Dubrovinskogo 80, ☎ 227 5262, 💻 www.oe-hotel.ru, sgl/dbl/studio from R1200/2400/4500, WI-FI) is the only one that commands river views from its location near the city museum. Choose between cheapo singles and doubles with shared bathrooms or opt for an 'improved' version or a swankier studio.

Where to eat and drink

Self-caterers can pick up fresh produce at the large **central market Центральный Рынок** (7.30am-5pm daily). **Krasny Yar**

Красный Яр supermarkets are scattered around the city; ul Karla Marksa 133 and ul Gorkogo 10 are two of the locations.

★ *English School Coffee House* (ul Lenina 116, ул Ленина 116, mains R150-300, 💻 www.esc24.ru), the brainchild of the SibTourGuide folks, is a medieval-style lair complete with suit of armour, friendly service and an extensive menu of fresh juices, salads, soups, meaty mains, the best syrniki in town, and even peach crumble on the dessert list. Their teas and coffees span the world, their business lunch

---

WHERE TO STAY
4 Dom Hotel Дом Отель
11 Titmouse House
19 SibTourGuide Hostel
22 Hotel Krasnoyarsk Гостиница Красноярск
25 Hotel Ogni Yeniseya Гостиница Огни Енисея
32 Hotel Oktyabrskaya Гостиница Октябрьская
33 Hotel Metelitsa Отель Метелица

WHERE TO EAT AND DRINK
3 Central Market Центральный Рынок
5 Svinya i Biser ('Swine and Pearl') Свинья и Бисер
6 Syem Slona Съем Слона
7 Chemodan Чемодан
8 English School Coffee House
10 Krasny Yar (supermarket) Красный Яр
15 James Shark Pub
17 Shkvarok Шкварок
18 Telyonok Tabaka Телёнок Табака
20 Traveler's Coffee
21 Krasny Yar (supermarket) Красный Яр
30 Traveler's Coffee
35 Pertsy Перцы
36 Krem Крем

PLACES OF INTEREST
1 Chapel of St Paraskeva Pyatnitsa Часовня Параскевы Пятницы
2 Trinity Church Троицкая Церковь
9 Surikov Estate Museum Музей Сурикова
13 Palace of Culture of the Combine Harvester Builders Дворец Культуры Комбайностроителей
14 Catholic Church Католическая Церковь
16 Lenin Statue Памятник Ленину
23 Opera & Ballet Theatre Театр Оперы и Балета
24 Regional Museum Краеведческий Музей
29 Intercession Church Покровская Церковь
31 Krasnoyarsk V I Surikov Art Museum Красноярский Художественный Музей имени В И Сурикова
34 Annunciation Cathedral Благовещенский Собор
37 Krasnoyarsk V I Surikov Art Museum Красноярский Художественный Музей имени В И Сурикова
38 Main Concert Hall Большой Концертный Зал
39 Krasnoyarsk Museum Centre Красноярский Музейный Центр
40 SS Nikolay Пароход «Св. Николай»

OTHER
12 Railway Station Железнодорожный Вокзал
22 ATM (in Hotel Krasnoyarsk)
26 Hydrofoils to Divnogorsk
27 River Station Речной Вокзал
28 Central Post Office Почтамт

CITY GUIDES & PLANS

(R120) is a steal and customers get to make a 5-minute phone call anywhere in the world for free.

Around the clock service, stylish décor and attentive personnel are just a couple of the perks at *Krem* **Крем** (pr Mira 10, пр Мира 10, mains R250). The salads are delicious, there's a fantastic array of teas and coffees (including Blue Mountain), and there's a great little summer terrace as well.

Pertsy **Перцы** (pr Mira 10, пр Мира 10, mains R280-380) serves good thin-and-crispy pizza and homemade pasta dishes in a stylish setting.

Syem Slona **Съем Слона** ('I Could Eat an Elephant'; ul Krasnoi Armii 14, ул Красной Армии 14, mains R45-70) is a cafeteria-type chain with brash orange tables, and a large array of inexpensive Russian dishes. Those with a pachyderm-sized appetite at odd hours can head to the 24-hour branch on ul Karla Marksa 95.

At *Traveler's Coffee* (ul Karla Marksa 135, ул Карла Маркса 135), expect light, comfortable surroundings, good cakes, coffee varieties that span the world, and slow, relaxed service. There's another branch at pr Mira 54.

Who'd have thought that in Russia you could get a decent steak for R350? Yet the popular ★ *Telyonok Tabaka* **Телёнок Табака** (pr Mira 91, пр Мира 91) steakhouse does just that; place yourself in one of their comfortable basement booths and order one of six steaks on offer (R350-780); each comes with a sauce/fresh salsa of your choice and side dish. The service is swift and friendly and there's a good selection of Georgian reds to complement your meat, along with wines from around the world.

At *Svinya i Biser ('Swine and Pearl')* **Свинья и Бисер** (ul Krasnoi Armii 16a, ул Красной Армии 16a, mains R229-659) you'll certainly find the former on the menu, along with veal medallions, beef stroganoff, steak, sausages and other carnivorous delights. The meaty stars have a supporting cast of blini, soups and salads – all consumed in what appears to be a 19th-century British pub setting.

The faux-rustic cellar that is *Shkvarok* **Шкварок** (пр Мира 102, pr Mira 102, mains R220-600; daily 11am-1am) – think giant sunflowers and brightly painted wooden folk art – serves you solid Ukrainian flavours: *vareniki* (dumplings with sweet and savoury fillings), *golubtsy* (cabbage leaves stuffed with meat and rice), expertly grilled shashlyk and meaty mains such as baked rabbit with mushrooms. Still hungry? Try the *salo v schokolade* (chocolate-covered lard).

Chemodan **Чемодан** (ul Lenina 116, ул Ленина 116, mains from R600) is part-classy watering hole, serving Guinness and other Irish brews, as well as a dark Czech beer, part upmarket restaurant with a 1940s atmosphere and a menu featuring 'aristocratic Siberian cuisine' (think smoked venison, bear steak, fish dishes featuring local fish…). A very worthy splurge.

James Shark Pub (ul Karla Marksa 155a, ул Карла Маркса 155a) aspires to be an English pub, what with Premiership scarves and other Brit-friendly décor (no English menu, though!). It has three types of its own brew on tap, an extensive whisky and liqueur list and an imaginative menu.

Moving on
By rail Krasnoyarsk is served by all major Trans-Siberian and China-bound trains.

Westbound departures include Novosibirsk (12/day, 11¼-13¾hrs, the 083, 085 and 173 being good overnight options, all originating in Krasnoyarsk), Omsk (12/day, 19½-21½hrs, the 137 and 129 are good options originating in Krasnoyarsk), Yekaterinburg (4-5/day, 32½-36hrs) and Moscow (6/day, 58½-68hrs, the quickest option is the firmenny 001, though it's also the most expensive by far). For Tomsk, there are a couple of direct long-distance trains per week (13-14hrs), but otherwise your best bet is to take any westbound train to Taiga and then catch either a suburban or long-distance train up to Tomsk from there (several daily, 2½hrs).

Eastbound departures include Severobaikalsk (1-2/day, 27½-34½hrs), Tynda (2/day, 55½-65½hrs), Irkutsk (6/day, 17-18½hrs) and Ulan-Ude (6/day, 24-26½hrs).

STALINIST-GOTHIC RIVER STATION

By river Yenisey River is a major communications link and passenger ferries sail nearly 2000km along it from Krasnoyarsk. For three months in the summer boats go north to Dudinka or on to Dickson on the Arctic Ocean, a four- or five-day trip northbound and about a week coming back. However, at the time of writing, foreigners could only go as far as Igarka. Tickets are available on the ground floor of the **river station Речной Вокзал** (8am-7pm); SibTourGuide (see p291) can also help arrange tickets. It's not usually necessary to book more than a few days in advance if you don't mind which class you travel in.

Hydrofoils operate to Divnogorsk (see p296).

By air Krasnoyarsk's Yemelyanovo airport is 40km north of the city; catch bus No 501 from the **bus station автовокзал** (R80) or take a taxi (R2000). There are daily flights to Moscow (4hrs) and several flights a week to Novosibirsk, Yekaterinburg, Khabarovsk and Yakutsk, among other major Russian cities.

SIDE TRIPS AROUND KRASNOYARSK

Stolby Nature Reserve Заповедник Столбы

Krasnoyarsk is particularly well known for its vast 17,000-hectare recreational area, covered in forest and dotted with giant boulder formations known as **stolby** (pillars). There are over 100 formations in total, some of them up to 100m high, but the most popular walking route is the loop that takes in the 1st Stolb, Babka (Grandma), Ded (Grandpa), Perya (Feathers), Lviniye Vorota (Lion's Gates) and 4th Stolb formations. The park is very popular with locals who come here to picnic, stroll and go rock-climbing on the rock formations.

To get to the main part of the park it's a 7km gentle uphill walk from the main road; you can't miss it thanks to all the locals who are heading there. Halfway up the trail is an information booth where you can purchase a map of the park; it's a good idea unless you're here with knowledgeable locals as the park is criss-crossed with many (largely unmarked) trails and it's easy to get lost unless you stick to the main ones.

Take bus 50 or marshrutka 106a to the Turbaza (Турбаза) stop from the Opera and Ballet Theatre (Театр Оперы и Балета) stop in central Krasnoyarsk; the turn-off is on the left, 100m down the road. Cars are no longer allowed on the 7km access road to the Stolby (though some exceptions are made for tour agencies such as SibTourGuide) so you still have to pay extra to be driven all the way up.

Alternatively, if you don't want to do all that walking and still wish to see some of the Stolby, you can take bus No 37 to **Bobrovy Log Funpark Фанпарк Бобровый Лог** (🖥 www.bobrovylog.ru) which is a ski and snowboard resort in

CITY GUIDES & PLANS

winter and a centre for zorbing and other extreme sports in summer. From here you can take the year-round chairlift (R200, Tue-Sun 10am-5pm) up to a viewpoint which gives you an expansive view of the rock formations. From the viewpoint, it's a 40-minute walk along the trail to the impressive cluster of Takmak formations, from which you can continue to the main group of stolby. People have been known to get lost in the park, so if you approach it from the chairlift, make sure you have a good map. Another excellent option is to take a tour with SibTourGuide (see p291).

Yenisey Hydroelectric Dam Енисейская ГЭС

About 30km away, past Stolby Nature Reserve, is the town of **Divnogorsk** **Дивногорск**; another 6km or so along is Yenisey Hydroelectric Dam. Built between 1968 and 1972, the hydroelectric dam was the second largest in the world at the time, though since then it's been surpassed by the following: Three Gorges (China), Itaipu (Brazil/Paraguay), Guri (Venezuela), Grand Coulee (USA) and Sayana-Shushenskaya (also along the Yenisey). The 100m-high dam has 12 turbines, nine of which are always working, and seven sluices, only five of which are used at most to get rid of the extra spring meltwater; when the sluices are open (typically for several days in June), spectators gather to witness the powerful spectacle of mighty waterfalls gushing through.

The dam's unique feature, however, is a huge 'escalator', with a kind of mobile basin mounted on a cog railway to lift boats right over the dam; it's the only one of its kind in the world to lift a boat up along with the water it sits in. The whole operation is relatively swift, taking around 40 minutes. While entry to the turbine rooms is forbidden, you can view the dam in its entirety by walking across the bridge in front of it. It's possible to drive up to a closer viewpoint for a more intimate view of the dam, the boat lift and the cranes that sit on top of the dam that look remarkably like the AT-AT Walkers from *Star Wars: The Empire Strikes Back*; in fact, there's a theory that George Lucas was inspired by them and that the evil Empire encased in snow is none other than the Soviet Union.

Hydrofoils travel between Krasnoyarsk's river station and Divnogorsk (technically May-Sep, but only at weekends, 5/day, 45mins, R350), which makes for a picturesque trip. However, it's not a terribly reliable mode of transport as trips are cancelled in the events of bad weather or if there are not enough passengers. It's a 5km cab ride from the jetty to the dam itself.

To get to Divnogorsk proper, you can take marshrutka No 106 from pl Teatralnaya – it drops you off at Divnogorsk bus station (автовокзал), a bit higher up than the suburban train stop. There are only two inconveniently timed suburban trains to Divnogorsk (Дивногорск) station and you then still have to find a taxi to take you to the dam. To get the most out of the visit, it pays to go with SibTourGuide (see p291).

Irkutsk
Иркутск

[**Moscow Time +5; population: 606,137**] Irkutsk is one of the most popular stops for Trans-Siberian travellers due to its proximity to Lake Baikal. Though dubbing the city the 'Paris of Siberia' may have been a little over the top, the exiled Decembrists did bring with them a welcome bit of European culture in the 19th century. Though a fairly large city, central Irkutsk still retains some 19th-century wooden houses, their eaves and windows decorated with intricate fretwork, typical of the Siberian style of domestic architecture and only surviving in a few Siberian cities.

Some 64km from Irkutsk is the incredible natural phenomenon of Lake Baikal, set within some of the world's most beautiful countryside. Trekking, camping, boat excursions, diving and riding are just a few of the pursuits available in what we unselfconsciously describe as an 'outdoor paradise'.

HISTORY
Military outpost
Irkutsk was founded as a military outpost in 1652 by Ivan Pakhobov, a tax collector who had come to encourage the local Buryat tribesmen to pay their fur tribute. By 1686 a church had been built and a small town established on the banks of the Angara. Tea caravans from China passed through Irkutsk, fur-traders sold their pelts here and the town quickly developed into a centre for trade in Siberia.

By the beginning of the 19th century Irkutsk was recognised as Siberia's administrative capital. The Governor, who lived in the elegant white building that still stands by the river (opposite the statue of Alexander III), presided over an area 20 times the size of France. Being the capital it was the destination of many exiled nobles from Western Russia. The most celebrated exiles were the Decembrists, who had attempted a coup against the tsar in St Petersburg in 1825 and who arrived in Irkutsk in 1826. These highly educated men and women brought with them their knowledge of mathematics, natural sciences, French and music, having a profound influence on the development of local society and benefitting it in other ways: starting a school for children, teaching peasants to read and practising medicine.

Boom town
With the discovery of gold in the area in the early 19th century, 'Gold Fever' hit Irkutsk. Fortunes were made in a day and lost overnight in its gambling dens. In spite of a great fire in 1879 which destroyed 75% of its houses, by the end of the century the city had become the financial and cultural centre of Siberia. Its cosmopolitan population included fur traders, tea merchants, gold prospectors,

exiles and ex-convicts. A few lucky prospectors became exceedingly rich, amassing personal fortunes equivalent to £70-80 million (US$105-120 million) today. Often no more than illiterate adventurers, they spent their money on lavish houses, French tutors for their children and Parisian clothes for their wives.

By far the most exciting occasion in the Irkutskian social calendar for 1891 was the visit of the Tsarevich (later Nicholas II), who stayed only a day but had time to visit the museum, a gold-smelting laboratory and the monastery, to consecrate and open a pontoon bridge over the Angara (replaced only in 1936), to review the troops and to attend a ball.

The first rail travellers arrive

On 16 August 1898 Irkutsk was linked by rail to Europe with the arrival of the first Trans-Siberian train. The railway brought more European tourists than had dared venture into Siberia in the days when travelling meant weeks of discomfort bumping along the Trakt (the Post Road) in a wooden *tarantass* (carriage).

Their guidebooks warned them of the dangers awaiting them in Irkutsk. Bradshaw's *Through Routes to the Capitals of the World* (1903) had this to say: 'The streets are not paved or lighted; the sidewalks are merely boards on crosspieces over the open sewers. In summer it is almost impassable owing to the mud, or unbearable owing to the dust. The police are few, escaped criminals and ticket-of-leave criminals many. In Irkutsk and all towns east of it, the stranger should not walk after dark; if a carriage cannot be got as is often the case, the only way is to walk noisily along the planked walk; be careful in making crossings, and do not stop, or the immense mongrel mastiffs turned loose into the streets as guards will attack. To walk in the middle of the road is to court attack from the garrotters with which Siberian towns abound.' The dangers that Bradshaw warned his travellers against were no exaggeration for at the time the average number of reported murders per year in Irkutsk was over 400, out of a population of barely 50,000.

❏ How to get on in society

Travelling along the Trans-Siberian at the end of the 19th century, John Foster Fraser spent several days in Irkutsk. Recording his observations on the city's social order he wrote, 'To do things in the proper way and be correct and Western is, of course, the ambition of Irkutsk. So there is quite a social code. The old millionaires, who for forty years found Irkutsk society – such as it was before the coming of the railway – quite satisfied with a red shirt and a pair of greased top boots, are now 'out of it'. A millionaire only becomes a gentleman when he tucks in his shirt and wears his trousers outside and not inside his boots. It is etiquette to put on a black coat between the hours of ten in the morning and noon. No matter how sultry the evening is, if you go for the usual promenade and do not wear a black overcoat you proclaim you are unacquainted with the ways of good society. As to wealth, there is but one standard in Irkutsk. A man is known by his furs, and his wife by her furs and pearls'.

In Irkutsk Fraser was unimpressed by the standards of hygiene exhibited by all classes of society and declared that 'certainly the Russian is as sparing with water as though it were holy oil from Jerusalem'.

John Foster Fraser, *The Real Siberia* (1902)

❏ Shamanism

Shamanism is a religion centred around the shaman, a medium and healer. Although the concept of the shaman is fairly common throughout the world, the word itself comes from the language of the Tungus tribes of Siberia.

Wearing spectacular robes, the shaman beats a drum and goes into a trance in order to communicate with the spirits. From them the shaman discovers the cause of an illness, the reason for the failure of the crops, a warning of some approaching disaster. Commonly, spirits are thought to select their shamans before they are born and brand them with distinguishing features: an extra finger or toe or a large birthmark. During their adolescence they may be 'tortured' by the spirits with an illness of some kind until they agree to act as shaman. Some shamans may be physically weak, epileptic, mentally disordered, but through their spiritual power they gain authority and perform rituals.

'Shamanism played an extremely negative role in the history of the Siberian peoples... In status, activity and interests, the shamans were hand in glove with the ruling cliques of the indigenous populations', wrote the Marxist anthropologists MG Levin and LP Potapov in *The Peoples of Siberia*. Other anthropologists have been less severe, noting that shamanism gave those with mental and physical disorders a place in society at a time when most other societies shunned the handicapped.

In the spirit of freedom of religious expression in Russia today shamanism is undergoing something of a revival, though it is difficult to find a high-ranking shaman, as they had all been executed during Stalinist times. The Republic of Tuva, west of Irkutsk, is the modern centre of Shamanism.

WHAT TO SEE AND DO

Regional Museum Краеведческий Музей

This museum (ul Karla Marksa 2 ул Карла Маркса 2, 10am-6pm Tue-Sun, 💻 www.museum.irkutsk.ru, R200) is in the late 19th-century Siberian Geographical Society building – an explorers' club. It focuses on local history and features a 'local achievements' gallery including a model of part of the BAM railway. Above the stairs is a panorama showing the Great Irkutsk Fire of 1879.

Ethnographic galleries downstairs include flints and bones from an archaeological site at nearby Malta, where evidence of human habitation has been found dating back 24,000 years: the inside of an early 20th-century settler's house with a carved wooden sideboard; a shaman's robes, antlers and drum; old photographs; and a most peculiar article of clothing – a suit made completely of fish skins, standard summer attire of the Goldi tribe who lived in the Far Eastern Territories.

Art Museum Художественный Музей

Comprising works by 18th- and 19th-century Russian, German, Flemish, French, Italian and English painters, this collection (ul Lenina 5 ул Ленина 5, 10am-6pm, closed Tue, R200) was begun by Vladimir Sukachev in the 1870s and 'donated' to the city after the Revolution. There are dimly lit Mongolian *thangkas* (Buddhist scroll paintings), modern Soviet masterpieces, such as AA Plastov's *Supper of Tractor Operators* and AV Moravov's *Calculation of Working Days*, as well as Siberian landscapes and peasant themes. Oddly moving are the likes of

CITY GUIDES & PLANS

DG Zhukov's *Lonely* – an old woman with long-suffering face, clutching a rosary, and IE Repin's *Poor* – a girl in threadbare clothes, fishing. The gallery devoted to 19th-century local scenes is particularly interesting; in the gallery of Western Art (15th-19th centuries) you'll find a small canvas labelled 'Landsir 1802-73' which is *The Family of Dogs* by Sir Edwin Landseer, who designed the lions in Trafalgar Square. Temporary exhibitions have recently included brand-new works by Zurad Tsereteli in bold blues, yellows and red.

The **extension gallery of the Art Museum** (ul Karla Marksa 23 ул Карла Маркса 23, 10am-6pm Tue-Sun, R150) has an interesting collection of 17th-century icons as well as Siberian landscapes.

Volkonsky House-Museum Музей-усадьба Волконского

The large, attractive house of this famous Decembrist, whose wife Maria followed him into Siberian exile, is open to the public (per Volkonskogo 10 пер Волконского 10, 10am-6pm Tue-Sun, R110). If you've read Caroline Sutherland's *The Princess of Siberia* you must visit the house, with the servants' quarters, a barn and stables outside. In the 1840s and the first half of the 1850s, this mansion threw parties for the likes of the governor of Eastern Siberia and other Decembrists, thus giving Irkutsk their 'window to Europe'. Displays include Maria's clothes, letters and furniture, beadwork, church robes of the 18th and 19th centuries and a very unusual, pyramid-like piano.

Trubetskoy House-Museum Музей-усадьба Трубецкого

The wooden house (ul Dzerzhinskogo 64 ул Дзержинского 64, R200) once occupied by Sergey Trubetskoy and Yekaterina Trubetskaya and other nobles involved in the unsuccessful coup of 1825 was preserved as a museum, kept as it was when the exiles lived here. Finally renovated by 2011, after sitting closed for four years, it gives you a good insight into what the Decembrists' aims were, their failed coup against the tsar, and charts their fates, from being sentenced to hard labour and imprisonment in Chita to life beyond exile. There's a cute black-and-white video, some interactive displays and some original artefacts.

Trans-Siberian Builders' Monument
Памятник Строителям Транссибирской Магистрали

In 1900 the city duma commissioned a monument to commemorate the construction of the Trans-Siberian Railway. Designed by PP Bakh, it was made of Finnish red granite, topped by a statue of Tsar Alexander III, and included Yermak and Count Muravyev-Amursky on its sides and the double-headed Imperial eagle on the railings surrounding it.

In 1920 the statue of the tsar was removed and destroyed and it was not until 1964 that his replacement, a drab obelisk, was installed. In 2004, however, a reconstruction of the statue was returned to the plinth. Alexander looks north in the direction of the great railway line he founded in 1886.

Znamensky Monastery Знаменский Монастырь

This monastery, also known as Monastery of the Apparition of the Virgin, with its turquoise domes, lies north-east of the city. The frescoes inside are impressive and the interior is home to the casket containing the body of **St Innokent**, a Siberian missionary who died here in 1731 and was returned to Irkutsk in the 1990s. It is said that his body is incorruptible and has been the source of many miracles.

Beside the church are the graves of Yekaterina Trubetskaya (see opposite) and Gregory Shelekhov who founded the colony of Alaska in 1784 (sold to the USA in 1868). Shelekhov's grave is marked by an obelisk decorated with cartographic instruments. By the gate stands a controversial statue commemorating the White Russian Admiral Kolchak, erected in 2004 near the spot where he was executed by the Bolsheviks; its plinth is deliberately high to deter dyed-in-the-wool Communist vandals. To get here, take trolley-bus No 3 from the south end of pl Kirova to the Remeslennoye Uchilishche Ремесленное Училище stop.

Church of our Saviour and around

In 1900 Irkutsk had two cathedrals: the splendid Cathedral of Our Lady of Kazan, bigger than Kazan Cathedral in St Petersburg, was damaged during the Civil War. It was demolished and the ugly bulk of the **Central Government Headquarters Дом Правительства** now stands in its place, opposite the **WWII Memorial**. Behind it, however, the 1706 boat-shaped **Church of our Saviour Спасская Церковь** features some interesting exterior frescoes which depict, from left to right, Buryats being baptised, Christ being baptised and the local bishop, Innokent, being canonised.

CHURCH OF OUR SAVIOUR

Opposite the Church of Our Saviour is a **Polish Catholic Church Польский Костёл**, a church with a tall steeple. It is Siberia's only neo-Gothic church, built in 1883 by exiled Poles; services are held on Sundays for their descendants. During summer there are usually organ concerts on Sundays and Wednesdays, starting at around 7.30pm.

Near the riverfront across the road, the restored **Cathedral of the Epiphany Богоявленский Собор** (1724) with its attractive green, white and pink towers is much more colourful by comparison. In the great fire of 1879 it was badly damaged and the heat was so intense that it melted one of the 12-ton bells. It served for a time as a museum of icons but is now a practising church again; the icons have been relocated to the Art Museum.

It's also interesting to visit the old **synagogue синагога**, a large blue building at ul Karla Libknekhta 23, the lower storey of which has been converted into a factory. Enter through the door on the left with the three stars above it.

Angara icebreaker / Angara Dam Ледоход «Ангара» / Ангарская ГЭС

Moored near the Raketa hydrofoil terminal, 6km south-east of the centre, the

Angara (daily 10am-8pm, R45) commissioned in 1899, was partially assembled in Newcastle-upon-Tyne (UK) and then sent to Irkutsk in pieces by train. Until the completion of the Circumbaikal line she ferried rail passengers across the lake together with her bigger sister, the *Baikal*. Following the line's completion in 1904 the *Angara* performed a series of menial tasks before being abandoned, partially submerged, in 1958. She was later restored as a Museum of Nautical Navigation. Nearby, the 2km-long **Angara Dam**, constructed in 1956, wreaked havoc with Lake Baikal ecology; the lake's waters, raised by one metre, destroyed the so-called singing sands on the eastern shore of the lake.

To get here, take trolleybus No 1, 3 or 5 to the Zhukova Prospekt Жукова Проспект stop.

River cruises

Rivers are navigable from mid-May to September and services operate from the river station. For details of hydrofoil services and boats to Lake Baikal see p307.

PRACTICAL INFORMATION
Orientation and services

Irkutsk railway station is on the west bank of the river; the city centre and tourist hotels are on the east. The city centre is along two intersecting arteries, ul Lenina and the shopping and museum street, ul Karla Marksa; ul Lenina runs north-west from the administrative and public transport centre of pl Kirova.

You can get good **maps** of Irkutsk and the Baikal region from Hotel Baikal, or from **Knigomir bookshop** (ul Karla Marksa 28), where they also sell wall maps of Lake Baikal.

The **Mongolian Consulate** (ul Lapina 11 ул Лапина 11, ☎ 342 145, 9.30am-noon & 2.30-5pm Mon, Tue, Thur & Fri) issues both transit visas and 30-day visas; turnaround time is two business days. Bring a passport photo and your ticket out of Mongolia.

There's an actual **tourist information office** (daily 9am-5pm) on the premises of Trubetskoy House Museum (see p300). It's not terribly well signposted but the staff really do their best to help and there are a few brochures on the city's attractions.

The **Central Post Office** is in the same block as Knigomir at ul Karla Marksa 28.

There are several **ATMs** inside the railway station, including the ever-reliable TransCreditBank, and numerous ATMs in the city centre, particularly along ul Karla Marksa, ul Stepana Razina and bulvar Gagarina. There are also several **currency-exchange places**; one is next to Lenin Coffee.

Local transport

Most sights, restaurants and shops are easily reachable on foot. However, *marshrutka* No 20 runs between the railway station and the airport down ul Lenina.

Tram Nos 1, 2 and 4a go from the station over the bridge and into the centre of town along ul Lenina and ul Timiryazeva. **Trolleybus** No 4 goes out to the airport from Skver im Kirova. Tickets cost R17 per journey regardless of the distance.

Travel agents and tours

The travel agents listed here run city tours, day trips and **adventure tours** such as hiking, skiing and trekking. They also offer trips along the **Circumbaikal Railway Line** (see box p311) and excursions to **Olkhon Island**. Also on offer are **scuba-diving** and **horse-riding**.

Baikaler (☎ 336 240, 🖥 www.baikaler.com), run by bilingual Yevgeny 'Jack' Sheremetoff, is an excellent choice for budget travellers. Imaginative group and personalised tours abound; the hostel (see Where to stay) can organise your onward travel as well. **Baikal Complex** (☎ 461 557, 🖥 www.baikalcomplex.com), run by the friendly Yuri Nemirovsky, organises homestays and excursions into the surrounding area. Call ahead for directions to the office (it's not in the town centre) or for a visit by staff.

Another helpful tour operator is Andrey Berenovsky whose company, **AquaEco** (ul Karla Libknekhta 12, ул Карла Либкнехта 12, ☎ 334 290, 🖳 www .aquaeco.eu.org), specialises in diving and sailing on Baikal.

Green Express (ul Dekabrskikh Sobytiy 24, ул Декбрьских Событий 24, ☎ 734 400, 🖳 www.greenexpress.ru) is an outfit that runs a hotel in Listvyanka and organises a range of outdoor activities.

Where to stay

If you arrive in the middle of the night, the *railway station resting rooms* комнаты отдыха (*komnaty otdykha*, ☎ 632 006, R110pp/hour) are a good choice as you can pay you for the time you need. Showers cost R140 extra.

Baikal Explorer Hostel (ul 5-Armii 71, apt 6, ул 5-й Армии 71, кв 6, ☎ 950 089 0255, 🖳 explorerhostel.ru, dorm/twn R500/700pp, WI-FI) is a central apartment hostel with room for 6-10 people and a guest kitchen; free pickup is available. The owners can arrange tours of Lake Baikal as well as stays at their rustic hostel in the tiny Baklan village along the Circumbaikal Railway.

Nerpa Backpackers Hostel (Sportivny per 5a, apt 1, Спортивный пер 5a, кв 1, dorm/twn R600/750pp, WI-FI) is ideal for those arriving or leaving early, as it's right near the railway station: to reach it walk north from the station, turn left into ul Mayakorskogo, then first right into Sportivny per. The staff get rave reviews, and the hostel – with its kitchenette and lounge – is comfortable enough. Let them know when you're arriving, though, as the staff have a tendency to disappear.

Highly rated by backpackers, German-run *Baikal Hostel* (ul Lermontova 136 apt

1, ул Лермонтова 136 кв 1, ☎ 525 742, 🖳 www.baikalhostels.com, dorm/dbl R650/ 1600, WI-FI) is a good place for travellers interested in Lake Baikal's ecology, as Irkutsk's first hostel has played a big part in the creation of the Great Baikal Trail (see box p308). It's not in the centre; take either marshrutka No 72 from the railway station, or bus No 1, 3, 7, 10, 24 or 84, or trolleybus No 1 from the centre; get off at the 'Institut Microchirurgii Glaza Институт Микрохирургии Глаза' stop. Free breakfast and transfers are offered; the staff speak English and German.

★ *Baikaler* Байкалер (ul Lenina 9 apt 11 ул Ленина 9 кв 11, ☎ 3952 336 240, Jack: 929 686, 🖳 www.baikaler.com, dorm/twn R600/750pp, WI-FI) is centrally located and extremely popular so you must book in advance.

The cheerful apartment has a guest kitchen and very helpful staff. 'Jack' Sheremetoff, the owner, is a bilingual treasure trove of local knowledge and can arrange all manner of tours in the area (see Travel agents). Jack now has a superb hostel in Listvyanka, too (see p314).

The central location of the brownstone and glass *Hotel Viktoria* Гостиница Виктория (ul Bogdana Khmelnitskogo 1 ул Богдана Хмельницкого 1, ☎ 792 879, 🖳 www.victoryhotel.ru, sgl/dbl/studio from R3300/3800/6500, WI-FI) makes it a good mid-range choice; your own bathtub might be very welcome after days of riding the rails and the staff are efficient and helpful.

Sleek and resembling an Alpine chalet, *Hotel Zvezda* Гостиница Звезда (ul Yadrintseva 1, ул Ядринцева 1, ☎ 540 000, 🖳 www.zvezdahotel.ru, dbl/suite R4400/ 14,000, WI-FI) offers a full range of services, stylish, spacious rooms (the suite comes with its own Jacuzzi), a sauna and swimming pool with waterfalls and two fine restaurants – one specialising in game and fish and another in Chinese dishes.

To get there take bus no 20 from the railway station. Get off at Shkola No 23

The Irkutsk area code is ☎ 3952. From outside Russia dial ☎ +7-3952.

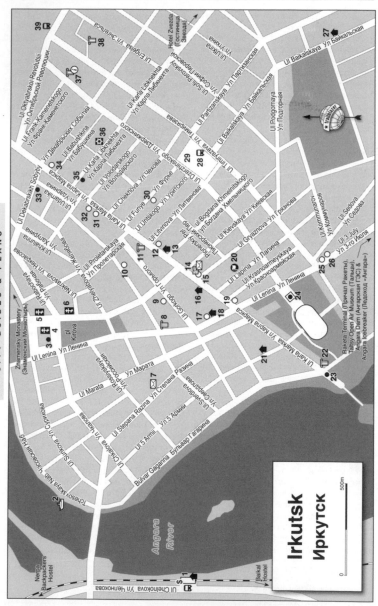

Irkutsk
Иркутск

Школа No 23 and turn right into ul Yadrintseva ул Ядринцева.

A good four-star choice just out of the centre, **Hotel Yevropa Гостиница Европа** (ul Baiklaskaya 69 ул Байкальская 69, ☎ 291 515, 💻 www.europehotel.ru, sgl/dbl/ studio from R31900/3960/6900, WI-FI) offers comfortable, spotless rooms, an excellent buffet breakfast, and helpful, English-speaking staff. The studio comes with its own infra-red sauna and fireplace and guests have use of the hotel gym.

Japanese-designed ★ **Sayen International Hotel** (ул Карла Маркса 136, ul Karla Marksa 136, ☎ 3952 500 000, 💻 www.sayen.ru, dbl/lux from R8600/15,500, WI-FI) distinguishes itself with its minimalist design, friendly English-speaking service and the ultimate in creature comforts (at least in Irkutsk). All rooms have balconies, climate control and plasma TVs; the Japanese-style spa offers numerous relaxation options and the hotel sports three excellent restaurants – including the Japanese 'Kyoto', as well as a genuine Irish pub.

WHERE TO STAY
1 Resting Rooms Ул Дзержинского
13 Hotel Viktoria Гостиница Виктория
16 Sayen International Hotel Гостиница Саен
18 Baikaler Байкалер
21 Baikal Explorer Hostel
27 Hotel Yevropa Гостиница Европа

WHERE TO EAT AND DRINK
9 Kochevnik Кочевник
10 Liverpool Ливерпуль
12 Café Snezhinka Кафе Снежинка
15 Bier Haus
17 Lenin Street Coffee
19 Figaro Фигаро
25 Chento Ченто
26 Rassolnik Рассольник
29 Central Market Центральный Рынок
30 Govinda Говинда
31 Belaya Vorona Coffee Shop Кафе Белая Ворона
32 Mamochka Мамочка
34 U Shveyka У Швейка

ENTERTAINMENT
24 Philharmonic Hall Филармония

PLACES OF INTEREST
3 Central Government Headquarters Дом Правительства
4 Church of Our Saviour Спасская Церковь

5 Cathedral of the Epiphany Богоявленский Собор
6 Polish Catholic Church Польский Костёл
8 Art Museum Художественный Музей
11 Art Museum Художественный Музей
22 Regional Museum Краеведческий Музей
23 Trans-Siberian Builders' Monument Памятник Строителям Транссибирской Магистрали
36 Synagogue Синагога
37 Trubetskoy House-Museum Музей-усадьба Трубецкого
38 Volkonsky House-Museum Музей-усадьба Волконского

OTHER
1 Railway Station & ATM Железнодорожный Вокзал
1 Minibuses to Ulan-Ude
2 River Station Речной Вокзал
7 Post Office Почтамт
14 Knigomir (bookshop) Книгомир & Central Post Office Почтамт
20 Mongolian Consulate Консульство Монголии
28 Minibus stop for Olkhon Island
33 Green Express
35 AquaEco АкваЭко
37 Tourist information office
39 Bus Station Автовокзал

Where to eat and drink

One local delicacy worth looking out for on menus and at the **central market** is smoked *omul*, a delicious fish native to Lake Baikal.

Irkutsk's Communist-themed answer to Starbucks, *Lenin Street Coffee* (ul Lenina 9 ул Ленина 9, coffee R150, daily 8.30am-9pm, WI-FI) greets you with a selection of coffees, teas, smoothies, a few cakes/muffins and a spot to plug in your laptop/tablet/iPad.

Nostalgia is the theme of our basement favourite, ★ *Rassolnik* **Рассольник** (ul 3 July 3 ул 3-го Июля 3, 🖥 www.rassolnik.su, mains R250-500, daily 10am-midnight), the vast cellar dining room decorated with old cassette tapes, vintage cameras and abacuses, with vintage films on the screen. The fine Russian dishes are beautifully prepared, whether you opt for beef stroganoff, solyanka, *draniki* (potato fritters) or the signature rassolnik – hearty meat and wild mushroom soup, served in a bread bowl.

Govinda **Говинда** (ul Furiye 4, 2 fl, ул Фурье 4, 2-й эатж, 🖥 govinda.su, mains R150) answers your question as to whether there is good vegetarian food in Siberia. There is, and it includes veggie goulash, soya-veggie cutlets, stuffed bell peppers, Bengal-style veggies, five types of soup and salad as well as creative desserts.

Belaya Vorona Coffee Shop **Кафе Белая Ворона** (ul Karla Marksa 37 ул Карла Маркса 37, coffee R150, WI-FI, daily 9am-10pm) is a cosy, caffeine-serving nook right on the main street. Linger here with a laptop or borrow one of the books from the mini-library. Some of the best coffee and tea in town, and the odd musical evening, too.

A *stolovaya* with a kitschy Soviet theme, *Mamochka* **Мамочка** (ul Karla Marksa 41 ул Карла Маркса 41, meals R120) is the place for simple, hearty fare, be it salted herring salad, fried pelmeni, or meat cutlets 'just like Mama used to make'. Wash it down with *kefir* (a yogurt-like drink), or a selection of German or Czech beers.

At *Café Snezhinka* **Кафе Снежинка** (ul Litvinova 2 ул Литвинова 2, mains R170-380, 9am-midnight daily) – Irkutsk's oldest café, dating back to 1957, you can imagine you're in Paris, or 'the Paris of Siberia' at the very least. Its understated 'old world' décor, punctuated by sepia photos of 'ye olde Irkutsk', adds atmosphere to such dishes as steak in truffle sauce with risotto, mushroom julienne and summer gazpacho. Efficient, English-speaking service, too.

Though the menu at *Chento* **Ченто** (ul 3 July 3 ул 3-го Июля 3, mains R350-750) seems to be a bit of a mishmash of everything Russians enjoy – pasta, pizza, sushi and steak – it's all very nicely prepared, the meats grilled to your exact specifications, and helped along by a nice selection of imported (and expensive) wines.

For Italian cuisine head to upmarket (but surprisingly not expensive) ★ *Figaro* **Фигаро** (ul Karla Marksa 22 ул Карла Маркса 22, 🖥 www.figaro-resto.com, mains R250-360). The chef is some kind of mad genius: who else would conceive of lasagne with smoked salmon flambéed in vodka, chocolate tagliatelle with speck sauce, and pork with coconut sauce. Even the salads – try Hell's salad (halibut, pears, Gorgonzola sauce) are wonderfully creative and it's well worth going for the fish or meat degustation menu (R900/1000).

If you're heading towards Mongolia, the nomadically titled *Kochevnik* **Кочевник** (ul Gorkogo 19, ул Горького 19, mains R270-700) can help get you in the mood. Feast on enormous portions of grilled meats, *buuzy* (steamed dumplings), made-to-share salads (something you're less likely to find in Mongolia) and tureens of hearty soup.

Liverpool **Ливерпуль** (ul Sverdlova 28 ул Свердлова 28) is a semi-grungy basement Beatles-themed pub, plastered with photos of the Fab Four, and with a beer menu that spans the world. Frequent live music courtesy of local cover bands.

U Shveyka **У Швейка** (ul Karla Marksa 34, ул Карла Маркса 34) brews Czech Pilsner Urquell, and that, along with its wonderful summer terrace, is enough to make it one of the most popular watering holes in the city (during the warmer months, at least).

At the mock-Bavarian *Bier Haus* (ul Gryaznova 1, ул Грязнова 1, enter from ul Karla Marksa) with its hefty dark wood furniture, jolly barmaids in Alpine dress present you with excellent German beers and platters of sausages.

Entertainment
Concerts are given at the **Philharmonic Hall Филармония** (ul Dzerzhinskogo 2, ул Дзержинского 2, 💻 www.filarmoniya .irk.ru).

Moving on
By rail Heading **west**, departures include Moscow (4/day, 75-86½hrs) and all the major cities in between.

Heading **east**, there are departures to Vladivostok (2-3/day, 69-73½hrs) on alternate days with the 002 (69hrs) and the 008 (69hrs) via Khabarovsk. The Trans-Mongolian 004 to Beijing (58hrs) passes through early on Saturday mornings, while the fast 006 to Ulaanbaatar passes through on Sundays and Mondays (26½hrs), as does the daily 362 (32hrs).

By bus From the **bus station**, buses and minibuses depart for Listvyanka (at least hourly in summer, 50 mins), Olkhon Island (around 4/day in summer, all departing before noon, 5½-7hrs).

Buses for Bratsk (8pm, 11hrs) depart from the ticket booth opposite the bus station, while minibuses to Ulan-Ude (around 4/day in summer, departures before noon, 7hrs) leave from the railway station forecourt. Minibuses bound for Olkhon Island leave at around 10am daily in summer from next to the Central Market; alternatively, your hostel can arrange for you to be picked up.

By river Boats for **Lake Baikal** depart from Raketa Terminal above Angara Dam;

the dam is 5km upstream (south) of Irkutsk; for up-to-date timetables, check 💻 www .vsrp.ru. Bus No 16 (but not the 16M or 16K) runs to the terminal from the railway station via pl Kirova (20mins; get off at the Raketa (Ракета) stop.

From Raketa Terminal there are hydrofoils to **Listvyanka** (1hr, R380) and **Bolshiye Koty** (1½hrs, R650) between late June and late August (3/day Tue, Wed, Fri, Sat & Sun). These boats fill up, so book two days in advance at the river station or through your accommodation.

Services to **Nizhneangarsk** (12¼hrs, R4600) and **Severobaikalsk** (12hrs, R4600) via Olkhon Island (6hrs, R3200) and Port Baikal go on Tuesday and Friday mornings at 8.50am, arriving at Nizhneangarsk at 9.10pm, and departing Nizhneangarsk on Wednesday and Saturday at 7.50am.

Hydrofoils for **Bratsk** (12hrs, R1430) via **Angarsk** depart from the River Station, near the bridge from the railway station, on Tuesday and Saturday (early June to late Sep). Buy your ticket two days in advance from the river station.

All hydrofoil services are subject to weather-induced delays and cancellations.

By air There are direct **international flights** from Irkutsk airport (💻 www.ikt port.ru) to Beijing (4/week, 4hrs), Seoul (2/week Tue & Sat, 3hrs), Harbin (1/week on Mon, 4hrs) and Tashkent (1/week on Sun, 7½hrs).

Domestic flights include Moscow (at least 2/day, 5hrs), as well as flights to Vladivostok (2/week, 3hrs), Khabarovsk (3/week, 2½hrs), Novosibirsk (2/week, 2hrs), Yekaterinburg (3/week, 2½hrs), Krasnoyarsk (1/week, 1hr), Ulan-Ude (4/week, 1hr), Nizhneangarsk (3/week, 2hrs) and Yakutsk (2/week, 3½hrs).

CITY GUIDES & PLANS

❏ **Abbreviations**
★ = Author's favourite; **sgl** = single; **dbl** = double; **twn** = twin; **trpl** = triple; **lux** = luxury room; **apt** = apartment; **pp** = per person; **[V]** = vegetarian.
Street names: Russia see box p80.

Lake Baikal
Озеро Байкал

The world's deepest lake

Lake Baikal, 64km (40 miles) south-east of Irkutsk, is 1637m (5371ft) deep and estimated to contain more than 20,000 cubic kilometres of water, roughly 20% of the world's freshwater supplies. If all the rest of the world's drinking water ran out tomorrow, Lake Baikal could supply the entire population of the planet for the next 40 years. It also contains more water than all of America's Great Lakes combined.

Known as the 'Blue Eye of Siberia,' it is the world's oldest lake, formed almost 50 million years ago. It is also among the planet's largest lakes; about 400 miles long and between 20 and 40 miles wide.

The water is incredibly clear and, except around Baikalsk and the Selenga delta, completely safe to drink, owing to the filtering action of numerous types of sponge which live in its depths, along with hundreds of other species found nowhere else on earth. Superlatives do not do this lake justice: Baikal has to be seen to be believed.

'Holy Sea'

Russian colonists called Baikal the 'Holy Sea' since there were so many local myths and legends surrounding it. The Buryats believed that the evil spirit Begdozi lived on Olkhon Island in the middle of the lake, though Evenki shamans

> ❏ **The Great Baikal Trail (Bolshaya Baikalskaya Tropa)**
>
> In 2002 some enthusiastic locals began work on a sustainable tourism initiative, grandly entitled the Great Baikal Trail (GBT), or Bolshaya Baikalskaya Tropa. The original plan was to create a continuous hiking trail that may eventually encircle Lake Baikal, not unlike the Tahoe Rim Trail in California, though that goal seems quite far-fetched at the moment. This trail is the first of its kind in Russia. In 2008 the GBT gained international prominence when it was nominated as a finalist in National Geographic's Geotourism Challenge and in 2012 they held 10 summer projects revolving around building trails to celebrate the 10th anniversary of the project.
>
> For the moment, efforts are being made to improve on ancient trails that have been used by the indigenous tribes in the area before Baikal was 'civilised' by the Soviets. Every year volunteers come from all over the world to take part in trail construction, helping with building footbridges, clearing and marking existing trails, or even planting trees or acting as interpreters for other volunteers who don't speak Russian. Current trail sections include Listvyanka to Bolshoye Golustnoye via Bolshiye Koty, two trails along the Holy Nose on the eastern side of Lake Baikal, accessed from Ust-Barguzin and the Mount Poroshisty climb.
>
> For further information on the trails, or if you wish to volunteer, visit 💻 www .greatbaikaltrail.org.

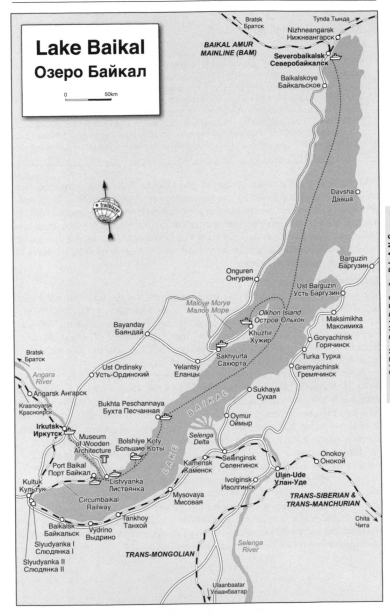

> ## ❑ Lake Baikal wildlife
> Over 80% of the species in Lake Baikal cannot be found anywhere else in the world.
> These include 1085 types of algae, 250 mosses, 450 lichens, 1500 vascular plants,
> 255 small crustaceans, 83 gastropods, 86 worms and 52 fish.
>
> Exceptionally high oxygen levels in the lake create an ideal environment for
> many creatures which have become, or are becoming, extinct elsewhere. These
> include *nerpas* – freshwater seals, until recently threatened with extinction by the
> Buryats who turned them into overcoats. They are now a protected species, listed in
> the *Red Book of Endangered Species* and currently numbering an estimated 80,000.
>
> A unique Baikal fish is the tiny *golomyanka*, which lives at depths up to 1.5km and
> is made up of 35% fat. Surprisingly, it gives birth to its young alive and fully formed.

held that this was the home of the sea god Dianda. It is hardly surprising that
these tribes were impressed by the strange power of the lake for at times sudden violent storms spring up, lashing the coast with waves two metres high or
more. It freezes to a depth of three metres for four months of the year, from late
December. The Angara is the only river that flows **out** of the lake. Since a dam
and hydroelectric power station were built on the Angara in 1959 the level of
the lake has been slowly rising.

Environmental threats
The lake's remoteness kept it safe from environmental damage until the building of the Trans-Siberian railway at the end of the 19th century. The risk of damage has further increased with the construction of new towns on the northern
shores for the construction of the BAM line, and because of industrial waste
from Ulan-Ude (the Selenga River flows past this city into the lake via one of
the world's last large wetlands, the Selenga delta).

The most famous campaigner for the protection of the lake is author
Valentin Rasputin. Demonstrations in Irkutsk in 1987 resulted in filtration
equipment being installed in the wood pulp mill at Baikalsk on the edge of the
lake but reports suggest it is inefficient and that pollution is continuing. A
coastal protection zone was established around the entire lake in 1987 but cam-
paigners bemoan the fact that government anti-pollution laws have no teeth.

Baikal became a UNESCO World Heritage Site in 1996 and is ringed by
nature reserves, but this hasn't stopped environmental threats to the lake. Today
the main concerns stem from numerous gas and oil pipelines – some proposed
but some already built – that pass near the shore on their way to China and the
Sea of Japan. Activists worry that a pipeline rupture in this earthquake-prone
region might not be noticed for days, allowing millions of gallons to seep into
the lake. For more on environmental issues related to Lake Baikal see 🖥 www
.greenpeace.org/russia/en/campaigns/lake-baikal.

CITY GUIDES & PLANS

AROUND LAKE BAIKAL

Museum of Wooden Architecture, Taltsy [see map p309]
Архитектурно-этнографический Музей Тальцы

This open-air museum (9am-6pm Mon-Fri, R200, 🖳 www.talci.ru), on the road between Irkutsk and Listvyanka, has a collection of reconstructed traditional wooden houses, some around 300 years old, which gives the visitor insight into the lives of the first Siberian settlers. There is a large farmhouse, a bathroom with a vast wooden tub, a water-mill and a post-house, complete with Imperial crest on its roof-top. When the only way to cross Siberia was by road and river, fresh horses and simple accommodation were available from post-houses such as this. The museum also hosts seasonal celebrations with staff dressing up in traditional costume. Taltsy is located at the km47 marker from Irkutsk or the km23 marker from Listvyanka; ask the bus driver for 'moo-*zey*' музей.

LISTVYANKA Листвянка [see map p313]

Listvyanka, an attractive village of wooden houses beside Lake Baikal, 60km or so from Irkutsk, is the most popular tourist destination on the lake, though not necessarily the most attractive one, due to the seemingly uncontrolled

---

❏ **Riding the Circumbaikal Railway**

Rail enthusiasts and anyone seeking extended views of the lake can hop on a train running twice a week along the old Circumbaikal Railway (see p460), from Irkutsk to Port Baikal via Slyudyanka. You have two options. You can take the train the locals use, the matanya, which is slow, but very cheap. You might also be able to persuade the train driver to let you ride up front for an added fee so that you can take photos. Alternatively, you can opt for the far more comfortable tourist train package; it is considerably more expensive but includes scenic stops and a bilingual guide who'll describe to you what you are seeing (though some travellers don't feel that the guides add much to the experience) and which can easily be arranged with the travel agents listed on pp302-3.

To catch the **matanya**, you have to take the suburban train (see 🖳 kbzd.tran ssib.ru for timetables) from Irkutsk to Slyudyanka II (not Slyudyanka station), departing at 8.35am and arriving at 12.10pm. The matanya leaves Slyudyanka II at 1.41pm on Mondays, Thursdays, Fridays and Sundays, arriving in Port Baikal at 7.40pm, too late for the ferry to Listvyanka, so you have to arrange accommodation in Port Baikal in advance. Going the other way, the matanya leaves Port Baikal at an anti-social 2.25am, arriving at Slyudyanka II at 8.05am. A trip on the matanya costs around R250.

The **tourist train** – the Circumbaikal Express, bookable through Krugobaikalsky Ekspress (☎ 202 973, 🖳 www.krugobaikalka.ru) – departs from Irkutsk on Wednesdays and Fridays at 8.20am, arriving in Port Baikal at 7.10pm (5pm on Fridays), followed by a boat crossing to the mainland and a bus back to Irkutsk. On Thursdays, Saturdays and Sundays, the tour package involves being taken by bus and boat to Port Baikal at 8.30am, then the train ride from Port Baikal to Slyudyanka between 10.40am and 6.35pm, followed by a return to Irkutsk. The tourist train package costs R2100 for 2nd class and R2500 for 1st class; meals cost extra and have to be ordered three days in advance.

development, reckless weekend drivers, and litter on the beaches. The village comprises three valleys and is spread out along the shore for 6km or so. The main part of the village is set back from the lake in a valley, with more and more guesthouses popping up continuously.

The busiest part of the village is around the hydrofoil quay where you'll find a tourist information centre, bus stop and a cluster of hotels. Further east is the **Nerpinarium Нерпинарий**, where you can see performances by Lake Baikal's famous freshwater seals. Beyond the Nerpinarium, the **market Рынок** sells produce and souvenirs; most of the offerings are touristy tat, but you can also buy wooden images of 'Grandpa Baikal', carved from 'singing' cedar by local woodcarver Kezer, and pick up jewellery made of charoite, a vivid purple semi-precious stone that is endemic to Siberia (see p276). Baikal Museum (see below) and Hotel Baikal, above it, are at the western end of the village on the road from Irkutsk. Behind the hotel is a **hilltop lookout point** with a fine view over the water to the Khamar-Daban Mountains. The half-hour hike up is well worth it. At the top there's a little shelter and an *obo* – a tree decorated with ribbons that people have tied to it for good luck, which is an old Siberian custom.

What to see and do

Baikal Museum Музей Вайкала This thorough museum (ул Академическая 1, ul Akademicheskaya 1, 9am-7pm daily, R250) features fascinating displays on the unique marine life and animals in the Baikal area, though most of the captioning is in Russian. It also contains a model of the *Angara* and a collection of the sponges which keep the water so clean. Colonists' wives discovered that they were also very useful for polishing the samovar. The best parts of the museum are the aquarium tanks featuring numerous species of fish from Lake Baikal, as well as the tiny crayfish-like creatures that are unique to the lake. There are also two large tanks housing two adorable nerpas (Baikal seals), who are zeppelin-like and unwieldy on land, but extremely fast and graceful in the water. An extra attraction (R15) – the **submarine room** – simulates submersion into Baikal's depths in a special Mir submarine. You look at fish and wildlife swimming past the 'portholes' as the guide explains which creatures you get to see at different depths (in Russian only).

St Nicholas Church Церковь Святого Николая A pleasant 10-minute walk up the main valley – Krestovka – takes you to the tiny Svyato-Nikolskaya church, built in 1846 and originally situated in the nearby Nikola village, though it had to be relocated when the Angara Dam raised the water levels.

Retro Park Ретропарк A short walk back along the Krestovka stream brings you to this sculpture park resembling a scrap yard, where the different works of art are made from parts of old Soviet cars.

Lake Baikal activities Besides sunning yourself on a pebble beach beside the lake, you can also visit Listvyanka for a host of winter activities, which include dog sledding, hovercraft rides on the frozen lake, snowmobiling and even ice-cycling on the lake involving bikes fitted with special ice tyres.

CITY GUIDES & PLANS

'Jack' Sheremetoff (see Baikaler Hostel, p303) can help arrange all the above and you can contact **Baikal Dog Sledding centre Байкальский Центр Ездового Спорта** (ul Kulikova 136a, Krestovka valley, ☎ 908 660 5098 (Oleg), 🖳 www.baikalsled.ru – in Russian) to arrange dogsled runs through

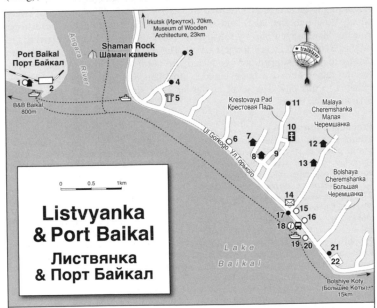

PORT BAIKAL
1 Yakhont Яхонт
2 Railway Station
   Железнодорожная Станция

LISTVYANKA
Where to stay
7 Derevenka Деревенька
8 Krestovaya Pad Hotel
   Гостиница Крестовая Падь
12 Baikaler Eco Hostel
13 Baikal Dream

Where to eat and drink
6 Proshliy Vek Прошлый Век
15 Café Podlemore Кафе Подлеморе
16 Pyaty Okean Пятый Океан
20 Shury Mury Шуры-Муры
22 Market Рынок

Places of interest (Listvyanka)
3 Hilltop Lookout Point
5 Baikal Museum Музей Байкала
9 Retro Park Ретропарк
10 St Nicholas Church
   Церковь Святого Николая
17 War memorial Памятник Великой
   Отечественной Войне
21 Nerpinarium Нерпинарии
22 Market Рынок

Other
4 Hotel Baikal Гостиница Вайкал
11 Baikal Dog Sledding Centre
   Байкальский Центр Ездового Спорта
14 Post Office Почта
18 Tourist Information Centre/Bus stop
   Туристическая Информация/
   Автобусная остановка
19 Hydrofoil Quay Причал

CITY GUIDES & PLANS

the winter forest – an unforgettable experience (run by Oleg and Natalia whose sons speak English).

Shaman Rock Камень-Шаман

In the stretch of water between Baikal Museum and Port Baikal it's possible to discern a rock sticking out of the water. According to local legend, Old Man Baikal had 336 sons (the number of rivers which flow into the lake) and one daughter, the beautiful but headstrong Angara. She enraged him by refusing to marry the feeble Irkut, preferring the mighty Yenisey (Russia's longest river). The old man chained her up but one stormy night she slipped her bonds and fled north to her lover. As she ran her furious father hurled a huge boulder after her. She got away but the rock remains to this day. The level of the lake has since risen and very little of Shaman Rock is now visible.

Practical information

Where to stay Listvyanka has no shortage of places to stay and new places are springing up every year, though book in advance if coming in July and August.

★ *Baikaler Eco Hostel* (ul Chapaeva 77а, ул Чапаева 77а, along the central Malaya Cheremshanka Малая Черемшанка, ☎ 924 839 6520 ▯ www.bai kaler.com/eco-hostel, dorm/twn R600/750pp) is what every guesthouse in Listvyanka should strive for: sustainable (solar-heated showers, basalt-foam insulation), comfortable (hand-made timber beds rather than bunks, guest banya, guest kitchen, even a yoga deck!), and with a friendly atmosphere, courtesy of its hard-working staff. Reservations essential.

Baikal Dream (ul Chapaeva 69, Malaya Cheremshanka, ул Чапаева 69, Малая Черемшанка, ☎ 3952 496 758, dbl from R1700) is a brick guesthouse with spartan but comfortable rooms, a cosy common room and guest kitchen. Nikolai, the effusive owner, offers pickup from the bus stop and can cook delicious meals on request. There's an excellent banya for guest use.

Dereven'ka Деревенька (ul Gornaya 1, ул Горная 1, ☎ 914 877 5599, ▯ www .baikal-derevenka.ru, sgl/dbl R2000/3000) consists of a family-run log cabin complex, each compact cabin equipped with toilet; in the summer you can use the shared shower cabin, whereas in the winter the banya is your only means of getting clean. The price includes breakfast; the owners can organise

dog sledding, snowmobiling and diving in the Baikal. In the summer, backpackers can put up their own tents (R180/tent) and pay to make use of the showers (R100).

The light and bright *Krestovaya Pad Hotel* Гостиница Крестовая Падь (ul Gornaya 14а, ул Горная 14а, ☎ 3952 496 863, ▯ www.krestovayapad.ru, dbl R3000-5500) consists of two modern curvy buildings featuring spacious, wood-panelled rooms, and two VIP cottages. The **restaurant** serves a mélange of Russian and European dishes; the summer terrace is perfect for shashlyk. The rooms come equipped with air-con.

Where to eat and drink Freshly smoked (though expensive) omul and fresh produce are sold at the (outdoor) **market рынок** that's surrounded by a cluster of eateries serving *shashlyk* (grilled meat skewers) and *plov* (Central Asian-style rice).

Café Podlemore Кафе Подлеморе (ul Gorkogo 31, ул Горького 31) serves inexpensive Russian dishes, including warming porridge and pastries. *Shury Mury* Шуры-Муры, by the tourist information centre, has a lively summer terrace, but is pricey for what it is, while *Pyaty Okean* Пятый Океан (ul Gorkogo 59а, ул Горького 59а) and *Proshliy Vek* Прошлый Век (ul Lazlo 1, ул Лазло 1) both specialise in fish dishes, many of which involve omul.

Getting there and moving on In summer, scheduled buses run at least once an hour between Irkutsk's bus station and Listvyanka's hydrofoil quay, also stopping to pick up passengers in front of Baikal Museum. There are also numerous *marshrutkas* (minibuses) travelling that route. If heading to Irkutsk towards the end of the day, you're more likely to get a seat if you board at the hydrofoil quay; Russian speakers can buy tickets in advance and ask to be picked up in front of the museum. For the scheduled buses, buy tickets at the tourist information centre, whereas with the rest of the minibuses, you can just pile in according to seat availability.

Hydrofoils operate from Irkutsk in summer (Tue & Wed, Fri-Sun 3/day, R380, 1hr) if there are enough passengers; if you want to go to Irkutsk by river, buy your ticket in the city, as seats are often taken up by daytrippers who make a return trip.

PORT BAIKAL Порт Байкал

Across the water from Listvyanka is the spread-out village of Port Baikal (🖳 www.portbaikal.com), which you reach by walking through a nautical graveyard of rusted ship hulks. You are likely to stay here if you catch the local train along the Circumbaikal railway, which arrives from Slyudyanka too late for you to take the last ferry across to Listvyanka on the mainland, or if you hike the Circumbaikal railway. Since the village is relatively isolated, this may be the place to come if you wish to avoid the Listvyanka crowds and to enjoy the sight of the Baikal from the village's viewpoints.

Prior to 1904 Trans-Siberian passengers had to stop here and cross the lake by steamer to Mysovaya, from where the trains continued. The largest steamer was a 90m ice-breaker, the *Baikal*, which transported train carriages on her deck. She was built by the British firm of Sir WG Armstrong, Whitworth and Co in Newcastle, UK, and delivered in sections by train. She was sunk in 1919 during the Civil War. Her smaller sister ship, the *Angara*, supplied by the same firm, survived (see pp301-2).

Practical information
Where to stay and eat Several home-stays operate here now, though some are quite a hike from the ferry quay, up the valley.

B&B Baikal (ul Baikalskaya 11, ул Байкальская 11, ☎ 3952 607 450, R1200pp), a 10-minute walk from the pier, was under reconstruction (being enlarged) at the time of writing. It has plain, homely rooms, a pool table, small, spotless bathrooms and a banya. The hostess cooks delicious homemade food if you ask her in advance.

There is also the underused *Yakhont* Яхонт (ul Naberezhnaya 3, ул Набережная 3, ☎ 3952 250 496, ☎ 908 669 9888, 🖳 www.baikalrest.ru, dbl from R2600), an attractive timber-and-stone guesthouse by the ferry quay, with a locomotive on a plinth nearby. The wood-panelled rooms are comfortable, guests have use of the lakeside terrace and banya and there's even a *restaurant* on the premises – the only one in the village – though you have to order meals in advance.

You can buy basic groceries from a couple of little **stores** near the railway station.

Getting there and moving on Three **ferries** a day run between Port Baikal and Listvyanka from May to December. Departures from Port Baikal at the time of writing were at 6.40am, 3.50pm and 5.15pm, while departures from Listvyanka were at 8.15am, 4.15pm and 6.15pm; check 🖳 www.vsrp.ru for timetables.

CITY GUIDES & PLANS

BOLSHIYE KOTY Большие Коты

Bolshiye Koty is a small village north of Listvyanka. Its main attraction is the peace and quiet and the picturesque 18km hiking trail that runs between the village and Listvyanka. Irkutsk University's Limnological Institute is here; it's where students do their practical work. Given that it's now home to fewer than 50 people, it's hard to believe that in the late 19th century, the village was the epicentre of a gold rush. Gold used to be extracted from the Bolshiye Koty River and the rusting dredges can still be seen 1km beyond the village.

Practical information

Where to stay and eat Baikal Complex (see pp302-3) organises trips here and you can stay at *Lesnaya 7 Hostel* (ul Lesnaya 7, ул Лесная 7, ☎ 904 118 7275, 🖳 www .lesnaya7.com, R700pp) during both the summer season (June-Oct) and winter season (Feb-April); it's a traditional wooden cottage with electric heating and hot showers (showers in summer only).

There are several other accommodation options, which you can book through 🖳 www.baikalnature.com.

Getting there and moving on In summer there are **hydrofoils** between Bolshiye Koty and Irkutsk's Raketa Terminal (late June to late Aug; Tue, Wed, Fri, Sat & Sun, 3/day, 1½hrs, R650) via Listvyanka; check 🖳 www.vsrp.ru for up-to-date timetables.

During the winter (Nov-Mar) the village is accessible only by skis or snowmobiles.

HIKES AROUND LAKE BAIKAL

Surrounded by spectacular mountain chains and rugged coastline, Lake Baikal presents possibilities for outdoor adventure that are virtually unlimited. Camping gear is available for rent in Irkutsk, and travel agents there are prepared to help, supplying guides or simply organising transportation. Two treks that are easy to arrange independently, and are popular with Russians and foreigners alike, include a hike along the Circumbaikal Railway and camping on beautiful Olkhon Island.

Hiking the Circumbaikal Railway

Stretching along the shore between Port Baikal and Slyudyanka, the Circumbaikal Railway automatically defeats one problem often encountered by hikers in Russia: the lack of marked trails. There's a good path along the tracks for much of the way, and when it fades out, you simply walk the ties. Drinking water and a cold bath are always available from the lake, and there's no lack of camping spots on either the shore or in the woods; many of them are used (and abused) by local fishermen.

The 95km from Slyudyanka to Port Baikal, or vice versa, is an easy five- to seven-day hike over flat ground; or simply walk as far as you want and then head back. Each kilometre is marked, starting at km72 in Port Baikal (or km166 at Slyudyanka), so it's easy to tell where you are. Good topographical maps of the route are available at Hotel Baikal in Irkutsk.

There are 53 tunnels along the track; bring a torch. Along the way you pass through five villages as well as some smaller settlements: Shuminka is at km102, Ponamarevka at km107, Polovinniy at km110, Marituy at km120, and Kultuk is just before Slyudyanka at km156. Food and other supplies are available for purchase in basic grocery stores in the villages, though it's best to bring what you need with you.

OLKHON ISLAND

Set midway up Lake Baikal's western shore, Olkhon has a dry climate and the same banana shape as the lake itself; the island is some 70km long and 15km at its widest point. Inhabited since the 5th century AD by Turkic Kurystan tribes, which were absorbed into Buryat culture in the 12th and 13th centuries, when the latter arrived at the height of Genghis Khan's empire, the island was finally colonised by Russians in the early 20th century. During the Soviet years, Olkhon was the setting for a fish-processing factory, as well as one of the country's nicer (one imagines) gulags. The largest island on Lake Baikal, Olkhon offers hikers a chance to roam across grassy steppe or dense taiga, making camp on sandy beaches or on majestic clifftops over the water. Sparsely inhabited by native Buryats and Russians, the island celebrated getting its first electric power lines in summer 2005. Though tourism has certainly made inroads here, Olkhon gives you ample opportunity to lose yourself amidst its graceful hills and deserted bays, and provides you with the most beautiful setting from which to witness the world's most impressive lake.

Khuzhir and around

There are several settlements on the island, the largest being the centrally located village of **Khuzhir**, a spread-out collection of wooden houses and wide dirt roads on the lake's western shore, which is where you are likely to base yourself. There are beautiful views of the lake from the steep cliffs behind Nikita's Homestead (see p318) and if you walk further north along the coast, you will come to the distinctive Shaman Rock sticking out into the lake – two boulder mountains which are a sacred site to the shamanism-practising Buryat. You'll often see people trying to scramble to the top for the views.

Even further north, beyond the impressive collection of *obo* (tree trunks covered in multicoloured ribbons, with offerings strewn on the ground next to them), a long, wide crescent of golden sand stretches into the distance and makes for good sunbathing. There's a smaller, more sheltered beach near Shaman Rock; both are visited by the banya-on-wheels trucks which can be rented by the hour, thus combining a lakefront steamroom session with exhilarating dips in the lake's frigid waters.

The stretch of water between Olkhon's north-western shore and the mainland is known as **Maloye Morye** ('Small Sea'); it is the shallower part of the lake that becomes relatively warm in the summer; it's also the part that freezes over the quickest in winter, enabling vehicles to cross over to the island on the ice. Legend has it that swimming in the Baikal adds five years to your life; see how long you can tolerate the cold – even in the height of summer, the lake can be a cool 9°C.

CITY GUIDES & PLANS

Exploring the island

Tours of the island tend to focus on either the northern half or the southern half, the **northern half** being the more popular one. On a typical day trip you would be picked up from your guesthouse in a Soviet off-road vehicle and driven on the island's dirt road along the north-west coast, which takes in the splendid sandy **Long Beach**, the **'Crocodile' rock formation**, the **remains of the fish factory and the gulag**, and various cliff formations until you reach **Khoboy Peninsula** – the most sacred part of the island for Buryats with an impressive *obo* at the tip of it with offerings scattered around. There is a 'window' in the rock along the southern part of the peninsula; if you're lucky, you might see nerpas sunbathing on the rocky beach far below. Your driver/guide fixes up a picnic which involves cooking *ukha* (fish soup) and you then return to Khuzhir via the village of **Uzury** – the only east coast settlement – where all the houses have only solar power. On the way back, you pass **Mount Zhima (1274m)** on your left – the highest point on the island, taboo to the Buryat, who consider it sacred. Occasionally, Nikita's Homestead organises a return trip from Uzury by boat, which takes around four hours and gives you a unique view of the coastline; pack lots of layers as it gets very cold out on the lake.

The **southern half** of the island is more popular with hikers and mountain bikers than off-road vehicle tours, though it's possible to arrange trips to **Shara-Nuur (Yellow Lake)**. Its water is said to have medicinal properties and to turn your skin red if you bathe too long. You can also visit the remnants of the earliest human settlements on the island.

If guided tours do not appeal, you can lose yourself for days on the island, camping on deserted beaches and eating by a campfire. Since there is an absence of marked trails, it's best to **head north-east from Khuzhir along the coast**. The route passes one scenic bay and clifftop promontory after another, along beaches and open hills where trails aren't needed to find your way. There are plenty of places to camp on beaches or hilltops (though firewood can be hard to find). Russian families park along the shore and set up camp for days, often bringing noise and litter, but they can be avoided.

It's possible to follow this route for 40km (3-4 days) to the Khoboy peninsula, a stunning clifftop at the far northern tip of the island. Access to the lake ends about two-thirds of the way, with steep cliffs dropping to the shore from there onward. **Bring food with you**, as only Khuzhir has grocery stores, and stock up on water at your last opportunity – at the end of the long, forested Nyurdanskaya Guba Bay. From Khoboy you can catch a ride back to Khuzhir from the many jeeps that run there. If hiking independently, make sure you're armed with a good map of the island.

Practical information

Where to stay, eat & drink More and more guesthouses are springing up in Khuzhir and around, but the most popular place to stay on the island is still *Nikita's Homestead* Усадьба Никиты Бенчарова (ul Kirpichnaya 8, ул Кирпичная 8, ☎ 914 895 7865, 💻 www.olkhon.info, rooms R900-1500pp inc full board), a complex consisting of log cabins, timber houses and yurts, with its own café-bar and restaurant on-site (most guests opt for full board), as well as two banyas and showers. Nikita Bencharov is almost singlehandedly responsible for making the island so accessible to visitors; the staff are multilingual and the Homestead runs a reliable variety of tours. If they are full (as they frequently are in summer), they might still be able to put you up in basic accommodation at a separate house run by their neighbours and you can still partake of the communal meals.

More upmarket than Nikita's but far less lively is *Hotel Olkhon* **Гостиница Ольхон** (ul Baikalskaya 64, ул Байкальская 64, ☎ 3952 708 885, 💻 www .alphatour.ru, huts from R1500, sgl/dbl from R1700/1900), a brick hotel off Khuzhir's main square, with en suite rooms and flushing loos for those not keen on the rustic latrines popular at Nikita's and elsewhere. The rooms have lake views.

Another place to try in Khuzhir is *Solnechnaya* **Солнечная** (ул Солнечная 14, ul Solnechnaya 14, ☎ 3952 683 216, 💻 www.olkhon.com) with accommodation in small chalets (from R1200 for a twin), also offering full board, with meals served in a yurt. A variety of tours are arranged daily. They also have a new mini-hotel a stone's throw from Baikal's shores; doubles start from R3200.

Locals often rent spare **rooms** in summer; look for 'сдаются комнаты' signs.

Nikita's and other places offer **full board**; menus tend to be fish-heavy, with omul being prepared in a variety of ways. In summer, informal **cafés** spring up along the main ul Baikalskaya, where you can have shashlyk, *buuzy*, grilled fish and beer; there are also a couple of well-stocked **supermarkets**.

Moving on In summer, there are around four minibuses per day from Olkhon to Irkutsk and vice versa, all departing before noon (5-7hrs, R600 one way); pickup is arranged by various accommodation options in Irkutsk, or else you can stop by the central market before 10am to see if there's a free spot. Nikita's Homestead runs additional minibuses; book your passage in advance. The ticket price includes the short ferry ride.

There are also daily hydrofoils from Irkutsk from mid July to late August, departing from the Raketa terminal at 8.50am and arriving on Olkhon Island near the ferry terminal, from where you could hitch a lift to Khuzhir, at 1.50pm (R2700).

Ulan-Ude
Улан-Удэ

[**Moscow Time +5; population: 416,079**] Ulan-Ude, the capital of the Buryat Republic, is a relaxed and pleasant city with quite a few traditional Siberian wooden buildings still standing in the midst of the usual concrete monstrosities, an attractive pedestrianised section, friendly and hospitable people and the world's largest Lenin head overlooking the main square. The city feels quite Asian, given that the Buryats make up roughly half the population, and it makes a particularly worthwhile stopover if you visit **Ivolginsky Datsan** (see pp326-7), a spectacular temple complex and the centre of Buddhism in Russia.

HISTORY

In 1668 a military outpost was founded here, in a valley between the Khamar-Daban and Tsaga-Daban ranges. Strategically located beside the Selenga and

Ude rivers, it was named Verkhneudinsk. A cathedral was built in 1745 and the town became a key centre on the route of tea caravans from China. The railway reached the town in 1900 and in 1949 the branch line to Mongolia was opened.

Buildings here require firm foundations since the city is in an earthquake zone. The most recent major tremor, measuring 9.5 on the Richter scale, was in 1959 but because its epicentre was directly beneath Lake Baikal there were no fatalities in Ulan-Ude. Military bases in the area meant that Ulan-Ude was off-limits to foreigners until the thaw in East–West relations. In 1990 Britain's Princess Anne led the tourists in with the first royal visit to Russia since the Tsar's execution. A local official declared that her visit was probably the most exciting thing to have happened since Chinggis Khan swept through on his way to Moscow in 1239.

Ulan-Ude seems to be going through a spiritual regeneration process, with its Buryat residents demonstrating pride in their national origins through artwork and music and reconnecting with their Buddhist roots, which were harshly suppressed under communism. This has been actively encouraged by the Dalai Lama, who has made five trips to the region since the fall of the Soviet Union.

WHAT TO SEE AND DO

Ploshchad Sovetov Площадь Советов

Ploshchad Sovetov – the main square – is dominated by the bulk of the world's biggest **Lenin head памятник Ленину**, 7.7 metres tall and weighing a whopping 42 tonnes. Standing in front of it you feel a bit like Dorothy meeting the Wizard of Oz. Local Buryats believe it was put there as revenge after they resisted Sovietisation; but they say they got the last laugh. If you look closely, Lenin's eyes seem curiously Asian. Across the road from the square is the **Opera and Ballet Theatre Театр Оперы и Балета**, revamped in 2011 and featuring splendid socialist-realist paintings and murals inside. The theatre was built by some of the 18,000 Japanese prisoners of war interned in Buryatia between 1945 and 1948. On summer evenings, locals gather in the little square in front of it for the entertaining sound-and-light show with the soaring and dropping waters of the fountain as its centrepiece.

★ National Museum of the Buryat Republic
Национальный Музей Республики Бурятия

This excellent museum (ul Profsoyuznaya 29 ул Профсоюзная 29, 11am-7pm Tue-Sun, R200) includes a fantastic collection of items relating to Lamaism (Tibetan Buddhism) and the spiritual culture of the Buryats. Assembled from monasteries closed after the Revolution, the collection includes Buddha figures; the robes of a Buryat shaman; musical instruments (conches and horns and a beautiful guitar with a carved horse's head); a large collection of masks used in Buddhist mystery plays; and a valuable collection of Tibetan *thangkas* (devotional paintings). In addition to thangkas used by monks practising traditional medicine, there's a unique *Atlas of Tibetan Medicine*. The history of Buryatiya is also covered, from the migration of Buryats into this area, to shamanism, the arrival of the Circumbaikal Railway, and national costume and jewelry. There is also a section dedicated to Old Believers and Buddhist ceremonial costume and temporary exhibitions have recently included one on wolf imagery in various cultures of the world.

Open-Air Ethnographic Museum
Этнографический Музей Народов Забайкалья

One of Ulan-Ude's most popular attractions, this large open-air museum (9am-5pm Tue-Sun, R110), located around 7km north of Ulan-Ude, consists of pleasant wooded grounds, dotted with reconstructed dwellings of the people from the Baikal area – from Evenki shaman's dwelling and *chooms* (teepees) made of bark (for summer) and covered with reindeer skins (for winter), both with birch-bark containers and other traditional utensils on display, to reconstructed Kazakh and Cossack dwellings and a humble wooden chapel belonging to the Old Believers (see box below). The Buryat area contains *gers* (yurts) of felt and wood and a log cabin stocked with day-to-day items, and there's a giant ger-like wooden structure with displays on Uzbeks, Kyrgyzy, Lithuanians, Poles and Germans, who also settled near Lake Baikal. The downside is the dreadful little on-site zoo, with bears, wolves, tigers and birds of prey kept in inadequate conditions; (the more people who complain to the guides about this the better).

There's a good *café* near the entrance, selling shashlyk and other inexpensive Russian staples. Marshrutka No 37 leaves from the main square for the Verkhnyaya Berezovka area; tell the driver in advance that you want the 'moozey' (музей) and he'll take a short detour from the T-junction up to the museum. Otherwise, it's a 10-minute walk from the main road.

CITY GUIDES & PLANS

❑ Old Believers

Tarbagai, a village 50km north of Ulan-Ude, as well as other villages in Siberia and the Russian Far East, is inhabited by Old Believers (старове́ры or старообря́дцы starovery or starohobryadtsy) – a branch that split away from the Russian Orthodox Church in 1666 in protest against the reforms introduced by the Patriarch Nikon between 1652 and 1666 that were meant to align the rites and texts of the Russian Orthodox Church with those of the Greek Orthodox Church.

Those who remained loyal to the old rites became known as raskol'niki (раскольники) and became subject to severe persecution from the late 17th century to the early 20th century, which ranged from double taxation under Peter the Great (including a separate tax for wearing a beard) to torture and execution. The period between 1905 and 1917 – the signing of the Act of Religious Freedom by Nicholas II and the Revolution – is seen as the Golden Age of the Old Faith; after the Revolution they were subjected to persecution once more by the Communists and many fled abroad, forming Old Believer communities in locations as diverse as Brazil, Australia and Minnesota, USA. The Old Believers are by no means a single entity (there are many different denominations – some have no sacraments, no priests and no churches; others deliberately cut off one of their fingers so as not to be forced to make the sign of the cross with three fingers rather than two, as practised by the reformed Orthodox Church. However, the one thing they do have in common is leading simple, spartan lives, with all the men sporting beards, as they believe it's a sin to go without one.

Other sights

It's worth spending some time wandering around the town as there are quite a few interesting buildings. These include several handsome **mansions** built by pre-Revolutionary merchants along ul Lenina and an early 20th-century home with statues near ul Kalandarishvili. **Virgin Hodegetria Cathedral Одегитриевский Собор**, at the southern end of the attractive, partially pedestrianised ul Lenina, built between 1745 and 1785, has been fully renovated. The streets around the cathedral are lined with picturesque old wooden buildings, some now being restored. The attractive **Trinity Church Церковь Святой Троицы**, built in 1798, was closed during the Communist era but has now been reopened. As at many Russian churches, begging babushkas station themselves next to the entrance.

The **Fine Arts Museum Музей Художественного Искусства** (ul Kyibysheva 29, ул Куйбышева 29, Tue-Sun 11am-7pm, R200-250) features excellent changing exhibitions of Buryat painting and sculpture. Recent exhibitions have included works by Mark Chagall and 'Memoria' – an exploration of Buryat wood and bronze sculpture in the 20th and 21st centuries.

CITY GUIDES & PLANS

MAP KEY

WHERE TO STAY
1 Hostel House
4 Hotel Sagaan Morin
   Отель Сагаан Морин
6 Travellers House Hostel
14 Baikal Plaza Hotel
   Гостиница Байкал Плаза
15 Hotel Buryatia
   Гостиница Бурятия
16 Hotel Sibir Гостиница Сибирь

WHERE TO EAT AND DRINK
3 Sagaan Marin Market
   Рынок Сагаан Морин
5 Market Рынок
10 Modern Nomads
17 Bochka Бочка
18 Marco Polo Марко Поло
19 Supermarket Sputnik
   Супермаркет Спутник
24 Traveler's Coffee

PLACES OF INTEREST
8 Giant Head of Lenin
   Памятник Ленину
9 Opera and Ballet Theatre
   Театр Оперы и Балета

13 Triumphal Arch
   Триумфальная Арка
20 National Museum of the Buryat
   Republic Национальный Музей
   Республики Бурятия
21 Shopping Arcade
   Гостиный Двор
23 Virgin Hodegetria Cathedral
   Одегитриевский Собор
25 Fine Arts Museum Музей
   Художественного Искусства
26 T-34 Tank Monument
   Памятник-монумент «Танк Т-34»
27 Trinity Church
   Церковь Святой Троицы
28 Buryat Drama Theatre
   Бурятский Драматический Театр

OTHER
2 Railway Station & ATM
   Железнодорожный Вокзал & ATM
7 Central Post Office Почтамт
11 Selenga Central Bus Station
   Автовокзал Селенга
12 Mongolian Consulate
   Кунсульство Монголии
22 Banzarova Bus Station
   Автовокзал Банзарова

PRACTICAL INFORMATION
Orientation and services

To reach the town centre from the railway station cross the lines via the pedestrian bridge. It takes about 10 minutes to walk to the main pl Sovetov along ul Borsoyeva. There's a **Mongolian Consulate** (ul Profsoyuznaya 6, ул

Профсоюзная 6, ☎ 220 499); for information on Mongolian visas see pp26-8.

There is a useful TransCredit Bank **ATM** inside the railway station, with others along ul Lenina, inside Supermarket Sputnik (see p325) and also in Hotel Buryatia. You can change money at most banks.

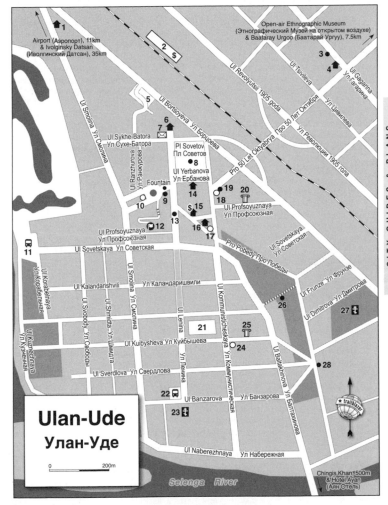

Local transport
Most places, except the Datsan complex and the Open-Air Museum, are within walking distance. **Marshrutkas** No 55 and 77 run from pl Sovetov to the airport. Marshrutka No 4 runs from the railway station past pl Sovetov and Baikal Plaza Hotel. Marshrutkas No 29 and 30 run past pl Sovetov to **Selenga central bus station Автовокзал Селенга**.

Taxis congregate by the railway and bus stations, and by pl Sovetov.

Where to stay
Several hostels have sprung up in Ulan-Ude. The one closest to the railway station, reachable by the pedestrian bridge, is *Hostel House* **ul** Smolina 54a, ул Смолина 54a, ☎ 902 562 0888, ☐ www .hostelhouse.ru, room/dorm R600pp; WI-FI), which consists of an apartment with dorms and a spacious guest kitchen in the main building, with helpful English-speaking staff, and two plush, fully equipped apartments across the road with private rooms; the 3-bedder apartment has no window.

★ *Travellers House Hostel* (ul Lenina 63, apt 18, ул Ленина 63, кв 18, ☎ 950 391 63 25 ☐ uuhostel.com, dorm R650; WI-FI), right off the main square, gets rave reviews from travellers thanks to hospitable English-speaking owner, Denis, who is full of good travel advice and who's always up for a strum on his guitar. The Russian- and Buryat-themed dorms are roomy and there's even a light breakfast thrown in.

Looming above the city centre, the megalithic Soviet *Hotel Buryatia* **Гостиница Бурятия** (ul Kommunisticheskaya 47a, ул Коммунистическая 47a, ☎ 214 888, sgl/ dbl/lux from R1950/2700/ 6000, WI-FI) offers rooms of wildly different sizes and standards, though most have been renovated by now. Some of the pluses include ATMs, an internet centre, an excellent tour company and even its own Buddhist temple.

The six-storey *Hotel Ayan* **Отель Аян** (ul Babushkina 164, ул Бабушкина 164, ☎ 415 222, ☎ 415 141, ☐ www.ayanhotel.ru, sgl/twn/lux from R1500/1800/4000, WI-FI) may be a 20-minute walk south of the cen-

tre, but the high standard of its modern rooms makes up for it. The pricier rooms have air-con and there's a small café; however, you'll have to haul your luggage upstairs without the aid of a lift.

The super-central location of *Baikal Plaza Hotel* **Гостиница Байкал Плаза** (ul Yerbanova 12, ул Ербанова 12, ☎ 800 500 6920, ☎ 210 070, ☐ www.baikalplaza .com, sgl/dbl/suite R3500/3900/7000) is its best selling point; its rooms, while perfectly comfortable, are overpriced for what they are and wi-fi is at the café only.

Decorated in stylish creams and browns, the modern, spacious rooms at the 17-storey 'White Horse', *Hotel Sagaan Morin* **Отель Сагаан Морин** (ul Gagarina 25, ул Гагарина 25, ☎ 444 019, ☎ 447 052, ☐ www.sagaan-morin.ru, sgl/dbl/ lux R3500/4700/6000, WI-FI) feature plasma-screen TVs, great bathrooms and a top floor restaurant/bar that overlooks the city.

Aimed largely at business travellers, the efficient, cube-like *Hotel Sibir* **Гостиница Сибирь** (ul Pochtamtskaya 1, ул Почтамтская 1, ☎ 297 257, ☐ www .hoteltrk.ru, sgl/dbl/suite R3000/6500/ 8000, WI-FI) has large (with the exception of the cheapest singles), modern rooms, fitness hall for that time away from the computer, room service and staff who can order onward travel tickets.

Where to eat and drink
It's difficult to miss *Bochka* **Бочка** ('Barrel', ul Pochtamtskaya 1, ул Почтамтская 1, mains R200-450), housed inside a giant barrel. They specialise in grilled meats and what they do best is shashlyk accompanied by fries and Blonder beer (R150-180).

Baataray Urgöö **Баатарай Ургоо** (Bargyzinsky Trakt, Verkhnyaya Beryozovka, Баргузинский Тракт, Верхняя Берёзовка, mains R300) is justifiably considered to be one of the best restaurants in town. It serves Buryat cuisine – *buuzy* (large steamed dumplings), *bukhuler* (meat soup) – in a delightful setting consisting of several interconnected yurts, lavishly decorated with Buryat national costume and rugs. This is a place for a leisurely meal that's located further along the highway than the Open-air Ethnographic Museum (see p321); take marshrutka No 37 from pl Sovetov, get off at 'pos Lenina' ('пос Ленина') stop and walk along the main road for five minutes.

A worthy splurge, *Chingis Khan* **Чингисхан** (Sun Tower, bul Karla Marksa 25а, Солнечная Башня, бульвар Карла Маркса 25а, mains from R600) also specialises in Buryat cuisine; in addition they serve delicious Russian and Chinese dishes – all in an atmospheric setting. It's around 4km south of the Uda river, so take tram 1, 2 or 4 running south along ul Baltakhinova and get off at Russky Dramaticheskiy Teatr Русский Драматический Театр stop, then walk a block south along bul Karla Marksa.

Having spread beyond its country's border, excellent Mongolian-chain *Modern Nomads* (ul Randzhurova 1ул Ранжурова 1, mains R100-1250) boasts a meat-heavy menu of Mongolian and Buryat dishes, as well as tasty salads – something you're less likely to find in Mongolia proper.

Traveler's Coffee (ул Куйбышева, ul Kuibysheva; wi-fi; daily 8am-10pm) serves an extensive range of coffees (R150), spanning the world from Colombia to Java, an equally thorough range of black, green and white teas, milkshakes, fresh fruit juices (R170), a good range of cakes (R80-150) and more substantial offerings of pasta, sandwiches and soups.

Another good place for coffee is *Marco Polo* **Марко Поло** (ul Kommunisticheskaya 51, ул Коммунистическая 51, wi-fi, [V], mains from R200), with its random décor, bare brick walls and unhurried, friendly staff. Vegetarians are catered for, with a selection of meatless salads, pastas and soup; desserts include a cracking apple strudel with pine nuts.

Self-caterers can head to the large indoor **market** (ул Балтахинова, ul Baltakhinova) for fresh produce and the 24-hour *Sputnik supermarket* **Спутник Супермаркет** (ул Коммунистическая 48,

ul Kommunisticheskaya 48) for a good but pricey array of local and imported groceries.

Moving on
By rail Ulan-Ude has frequent departures to all points along the Trans-Siberian, as well as Mongolia and China. **Westbound departures** include Irkutsk (7-8/day, 6¼-9hrs), the handiest being the 001 overnighter (alternate days) or the 361 (alternate days), while **eastbound departures** include Chita (6/day, 9-12hrs), the 070 (alternate days) and 080 (alternate days) being handy overnighters, and Vladivostok (2-3/day, 62-67hrs).

Heading **south**, there are daily trains to Ulaanbaatar (18-22¾hrs) in summer (fewer services outside peak season), the firmenny 006 on Mondays, the 043 on Saturdays and the slowest being the 362 on Tuesdays; tickets for the first two need to be booked well in advance as they originate in Moscow. There are two trains a week to Beijing – the 020 (63¼hrs) on Wednesdays and the 043 (50hrs) on Saturdays; book well in advance in summer.

By air From Ulan-Ude's upgraded airport (🖳 www.airportbaikal.ru) there are connections to Moscow (up to 3/day, 6hrs), Irkutsk (1/day, 1hr), Novosibirsk (3½hrs), Krasnoyarsk (2½hrs), Yakutsk (Tue & Thur, 5hrs) and Nizhneangarsk (near Severobaikalsk, Tue, Fri & Sun, 1½hrs). There are also international flights to Beijing (Sat, 1¾hrs).

By bus If you can't get hold of a train ticket to Ulaanbaatar (or don't wish to spend 24 hours getting there), you can take one of the Vostok Trans (Восток Транс) buses that depart daily from the car park by the Opera House at 7.30am and take only 10-12 hours to reach Mongolia's capital. Tickets can be purchased inside Hotel Baikal Plaza or organised by your hostel or hotel.

CITY GUIDES & PLANS

The Ulan-Ude area code is ☎ 3012. From outside Russia dial ☎ +7-3012.

SIDE TRIP TO IVOLGINSKY DATSAN Иволгинский Датсан

This Tibetan Buddhist monastery, the centre of Russian Buddhism, stands on a wide plain 35km outside the city, and is a fascinating place to visit. Before the Revolution there were hundreds of similar monasteries in the area with the largest and most important at Selenginsk. Almost all were closed and the monks sent to the Gulags in the 1930s. In 1945, amazingly, Stalin gave permission for Ivolginsky Datsan to be constructed here as a mark of gratitude for Buryatiya's help during WWII; the monastery was completed in 1946 and now teems with both Buddhist pilgrims and daytrippers from Ulan-Ude.

Visiting the Datsan

As you stroll around the Datsan, walk clockwise around objects of Buddhist veneration (prayer wheels, temples and stupas), remove your hat inside the temples, don't cross your arms, and never turn your back on the deities – which does mean having to shuffle out backwards. Be sure, also, to make a donation.

The largest building in the complex is the elaborately designed and brilliantly coloured **Temple of Khambo Lama Itigilov Храм Хамбо Ламы Итигэлова**. Itigilov was the 12th Khambo Lama and just before he died in 1927 he stipulated that his body should be buried in the position in which he died, and that it should be exhumed 30 years later. He died in the lotus position and was buried in a pine chest; when monks dug him up in 1955 they were amazed to discover his body miraculously preserved. In 2002 his body was exhumed again, still looking as if he'd only recently died. He has been declared a sacred object of Buddhism and his mortal remains are brought out during special festivals; touching them allegedly heals the sick.

The **central temple**, a three-storey building constructed in 1971, burnt down four months after completion with the loss of numerous valuable *thangkas*. It was rebuilt in just seven months. Its joyous technicolour interior features golden dragons sliding down the 16 wooden columns supporting the upper galleries (where there is a library of Tantric texts), and hundreds of incarnations of the Buddha line one wall. Easy to recognise is Manla, the Buddha of Tibetan medicine, with the dark blue face. The largest thangka hanging above the incarnations is of the founder of the Gelugpa (Yellow Hat) sect of Tibetan Buddhism. Juniper wood is burnt and food and money offered to the incarnations.

Beside this is a smaller stupa, and the **green temple** behind it is the oldest building in the complex, constructed in 1946. The octagonal white building houses a model of **Paradise** (*Devashin*) and a library of several hundred Tibetan and Mongolian texts, each wrapped in silk. In the big **white stupa** nearby are the ashes of the most famous of the Datsan's head lamas, Sherapov, who died in 1961. There is even a **Bo tree** (sacred fig tree) growing very successfully in its own greenhouse from seeds brought in 1956 from Delhi. Students now come from all over the region to study Buddhism here. Don't miss the incredible **mandala** inside the Tantric temple, at the far right side as you enter the complex, or a prayer session with the monks in their maroon robes chanting hypnotically in Tibetan amidst incense smoke and a crescendo of clashing cymbals.

You might be surprised at the number of non-Buryat worshippers here, but in Ulan-Ude it's fairly common for people to attend Buddhist temples, Orthodox churches *and* Shamanist ceremonies. Given the hardship and uncertainty of Russian life, some Russians come here for the peaceful atmosphere and to throw in their lot with another deity, just in case.

In summer, the temple grounds are alive with young animal life – kittens, puppies and domesticated baby deer.

Getting there Marshrutka No 125 (R45) runs frequently from Banzarova bus station Автовокзал Банзарова and along ul Smolina to the village of Ivolga. In Ivolga you have to change to another marshrutka (R30), waiting to take you the last few kilometres to the Datsan.

Chita
Чита

[**Moscow Time +6; population: 331,346**] At the junction of the Trans-Siberian and Trans-Manchurian railway lines, Chita was closed to foreigners until the late 1980s, as it was the army headquarters for Eastern Siberia.

Founded in 1653, Chita became a *sloboda* (tax-exempt settlement) in 1690, populated by Cossacks and trappers. It was famous in the 19th century as a place of exile for many revolutionary Decembrists; more than 80 of them arrived here in 1827 and settled in wooden cottages along what is now the tail end of ul Stolyarova ул Столярова, though sadly none is truly intact. George Kennan was here in 1887 and wrote: 'Among the exiles of Chita were some of the brightest, most cultivated, most sympathetic men and women we had met in Eastern Siberia.'

By 1900 more than 11,000 people lived here. There were nine churches, a cathedral, a nunnery, a synagogue, thirteen schools and even a telephone system. Soviet power was established in the city on 16 February 1918 but on 26 August the city was captured by the White Army. On 22 October, however, it was firmly back in Soviet hands.

Though Chita, Eastern Siberia's major industrial and cultural centre, is still dominated by a large military presence, trade with China has really taken off. There's just about enough to keep you occupied for a day here; those who've just run the Irkutsk/Lake Baikal tourist gauntlet may find it refreshing to be the only tourist in town.

WHAT TO SEE AND DO

Decembrists' Museum Музей Декабристов

This small museum (ul Dekabristov 3b, ул Декабристов 3б, 10am-6pm Tue-Sun, R100) is housed in the former Archangel Michael Church, a 20-minute walk from the railway station. This log church was the gathering point for those

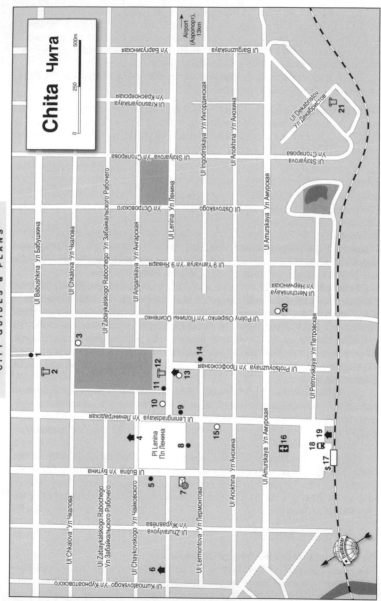

Chita Чита

0   250   500m

Airport (Аэропорт), 13km

Ul Barguzinskaya Ул Баргузинская

Ul Krasnoyarskaya Ул Красноярская

Ul Babushkina Ул Бабушкина

Ul Chkalova Ул Чкалова

Ul Zabaykalskogo Rabochego Ул Забайкальского Рабочего

Ul Angarskaya Ул Ангарская

Ul Stolyarova Ул Столярова

Ul Ingodinskaya Ул Ингодинская

Ul Anokhina Ул Анохина

Ul Dekabristov Ул Декабристов

Ul Stolyarova Ул Столярова

Ul Lenina Ул Ленина

Ul Ostrovskogo Ул Островского

Ul 9 Yanvarya Ул 9 Января

Ul Amurskaya Ул Амурская

Ul Nerchinskaya Ул Нерчинская

Ul Poliny Osipenko Ул Полины Осипенко

Ul Leningradskaya Ул Ленинградская

Ul Protsoyuznaya Ул Профсоюзная

Ul Petrovskaya Ул Петровская

Pl Lenina Пл Ленина

Ul Butina Ул Бутина

Ul Amurskaya Ул Амурская

Ul Anokhina Ул Анохина

Ul Zhuravleva Ул Журавлёва

Ul Zhuravleva Ул Журавлёва

Ul Chaykovskogo Ул Чайковского

Ul Lermontova Ул Лермонтова

Ul Chkalova Ул Чкалова

Ul Zabaykalskogo Rabochego Ул Забайкальского Рабочего

Ul Kumzalovskogo Ул Кумзаловского

1
2
3
4
5
6
7
8
9
10
11
12
13
14
15
16
17 $
18
19
20
21

sent into exile – for prayer, for weddings (Annekov and his French mistress Pauline), and for funerals (the Volkonskys' daughter Sofia). The Decembrists' names and post-exile fates are on display here, along with the original imperial order sentencing them to forced labour in the Nerchinsk silver mines, while displays upstairs focus on their womenfolk who followed their men into exile; these courageous women not only had to scrape together enough money to get themselves to Siberia in style (it cost the modern equivalent of around US$10,000 to get from St Petersburg to Irkutsk in 1827), but they are also largely credited with bringing gentility and 'European standards of behaviour' to a rough, largely untamed region. They also kept their men alive by supplementing their meagre rations.

Kuznetsov Museum of Regional Studies
Краеведческий Музей имени Кузнецова

In this surprisingly engrossing museum of its kind (ul Babushkina 113 ул Бабушкина 113, 10am-6pm Tue-Sun, R120), besides its contribution to the demise of endangered species in the shape of the stuffed snow leopard in the thorough Natural History section, there are also some wonderful landscape photos that are so varied, it's hard to believe they're part of the same country.

CITY GUIDES & PLANS

WHERE TO STAY
4 Hotel Montblanc
   Отель Монгблан
6 Hotel Arcadia
   Гостиница Аркадия
13 Hotel Visit
   Гостиница Визит
19 Resting rooms
   комнаты отдыха

WHERE TO EAT AND DRINK
3 Café Traktir
   Кафе Трактир
10 Shokoladnitsa
   Шоколадница
13 Privoz Привоз
15 Poznaya Altergana
   Позная Алтаргана
20 Khmelnaya Korchma
   Хмельная Корчма

PLACES OF INTEREST
1 Tank Monument
2 Kuznetsov Museum of Regional Studies
   Краеведческий Музей имени Кузнецова
5 City Administration Building Дом Советов
8 Siberian Military District Headquarters Штаб
   Сибирского Военного Округа
9 Post-Baikal Railway Management Office
   Управление Забайкальской Железной Дороги
11 Army Officers' Club
   Дом Офицеров
12 Military Museum
   Музей Истории Воиск СибВО
14 Drama Theatre
   Драматический Театр
16 Church of the Icon of the Kazan Madonna Церковь
   Казанской Божьей Матери
21 Decembrists' Museum
   Музей Декабристов

OTHER
7 Central Post Office & internet
   Почтамт и Интернет
17 Chita 2 Railway Station & ATM Железнодорожный
   Вокзал Чита 2 & ATM
18 Long-distance bus station
   Автовокзал

OLD HOUSE, CHITA

Upstairs, behold the weaponry section (Buryat knives in intricate sheaths, Indian daggers, Kossack sabres), displays on Buryats (national costume, the anatomy of a yurt) and the Evenki reindeer herders, with plenty of fascinating everyday tools, shamanic dress and ritual objects. The WWII section, with its graphic war propaganda posters and photos of local heroes, is also well worth a look.

Other sights

Across from the railway station is the enormous blue and gold **Church of the Icon of the Kazan Madonna Церковь Казанской Божьей Матери**, rebuilt in 2004 after being destroyed in the 1930s. If you're just stepping off the train, you'll involuntarily do a double take, unprepared for such an unexpected vision of beauty amidst Chita's industrial setting.

On Chita's main square, **pl Lenina пл Ленина**, the requisite statue of the former leader is overshadowed by the vast scale of the square itself and several of its buildings. To the east is the **Post-Baikal Railway Management Office Управление Забайкальской Железной Дороги**, which controls lucrative cross-border trade, including oil shipments. To the south is the massive yellow **Siberian Military District Headquarters Штаб Сибирского Военного Округа**, commanding troops from Omsk to Chita. And to the west is the aquamarine **City Administration Building Дом Советов**. Around the corner is the **Army Officers' Club Дом Офицеров** (ul Lenina 80).

The **Military Museum Музей Истории Воиск СибВО** (ul Lenina 86 ул Ленина 86, 9am-1pm & 2-6pm daily, R100) is next door to the Club and instantly noticeable thanks to the golden soldier statues flanking the entrance. It consists of six floors dedicated to the art of war, or, more specifically, to exhibits on the Soviet military operation in Afghanistan, Beketov's Cossacks, Communist-era repressions, and more rocket launchers and guns than you can shake a very big stick at. Captions in Russian only. Out at the back is a collection of tanks and artillery.

PRACTICAL INFORMATION
Orientation and services

The main **railway station**, Chita 2, is three blocks south-west of pl Lenina, a short walk from the centre of the town and most hotels. There are **ATMs** in the station. The **long-distance bus station** is in front of the railway station.

There is **internet access** at the **post office** on ul Lenina 2 ул Ленина 2 (8am-8pm Mon-Fri, until 7pm Sat, until 6pm Sun).

Where to stay

Budget accommodation is difficult to come by, as it's mostly taken up by soldiers and Chinese traders, so it's a really good idea to book ahead.

In the building just to the left of the bus station entrance, the *resting rooms* **комнаты отдыха** (☎ 225 128, sgl/quad from R797/393pp for 6 hours; then R75 by the hour) are basic but very clean; you can have a nice hot shower for R135.

Interior designers are unlikely to win prizes for the décor at *Hotel Arcadia* **Гостиница Аркадия** (ul Lenina 120 ул Ленина 120, ☎ 352 636, 🖳 www.arkadia .chita.ru, sgl/twn/lux from R1800/2500/ 4500), but the rooms are spic-and-span and there's a decent breakfast.

Monolithic *Hotel Montblanc* **Отель Монтбланк** (ul Kostyushko Grigotovicha 5 ул Костюшко Григорьевича 5, ☎ 357 272, 🖳 montblanc.eldonet.ru, sgl/dbl/lux from R3450/4250/7650, wi-fi), a stone's throw from the main square, caters mostly to businessmen, with suitably modern and comfortable rooms. Buffet breakfast is included.

One of the plushest places in town is *Hotel Visit* Гостиница Визит (ул Ленина 93, ul Lenina 93, ☎ 356 945, 🖳 chitahotel vizit.ru, sgl/twin/lux R3400/5200/7400, wi-fi), with comfortable, air-conditioned rooms on the 5th floor of a modern glass tower, and accommodating, English-speaking staff. If there is availability you can stay for 6-12 hours for half the price.

Where to eat and drink

Due to the abundance of trade with China, you'll find a lot of places serving (or at least claiming to serve) good Chinese food.

Good quick eats include *Poznaya Altergana* Позная Алтаргана (ul Leningradskaya 5 ул Ленинградская 5, daily 10am-10pm), where you can get big servings of *pozy* (large, steamed, meat-filled dumplings, Buryat style) from mid-morning to midnight.

Inside the same glass tower as Hotel Visit (see above), *Privoz* Привозъ (daily 11.30am-10pm) consists of a smart restaurant on the 2nd floor, serving good Russian dishes and a business lunch for R300, while downstairs is the self-serve cafeteria section where you can load your tray with inexpensive salads, soup of the day and a choice of several meaty mains.

Shokoladnitsa Шоколадница (ul Leningradskaya 36, ул Ленинградская 36, 9am-midnight daily) is a reliable chain where you can get an omelette for breakfast, signature hot chocolate, a range of coffees, teas and smoothies, sweet and savoury blini and a limited choice of pastas and soups, as well as the likes of grilled salmon and Greek salad. Efficient, friendly service, but smoky, soporific atmosphere.

Khmelnaya Korchma Хмельная Корчма (ul Amurskaya 69, ул Амурская 69, mains R180-450, daily 11.30am-10pm),

decked out in chirpy folksy style, is a great local favourite for hearty Ukrainian dishes, accompanied by live music in the evenings. The borsch, *golubtsy* (cabbage leaves stuffed with meat and rice) and *vareniki* (sour cherry dumplings) are all a stomach-fillingly safe bet. The business lunch for R180 is a good deal.

For good Russian food, head for *Café Traktir* Кафе Трактир (ul Chkalova 93, ул Чкалова 93, mains R260-480, daily 11.30am-10pm), an attractive wooden lace cottage serving a good range of soups, salads and grilled meat and fish dishes. In summer, there's a popular beer tent outside where you can get some great shashlyk.

Moving on

By rail The 001 stops in Chita on the way to Moscow (92½-106hrs) on alternate days; other good and cheaper options include the 043 (alternate days) and 099 (alternate days). Other **westbound** departures include Ulan-Ude (6/day, 9-11hrs), with the 079 (alternate days) and the 069 (alternate days) being convenient overnighters; Irkutsk (5/day, 16-19hrs) and Krasnoyarsk (5/day, 34-37¾hrs). **Eastbound**, the 002 heads to Vladivostok (52¾-54hrs) on alternate days, while a good option is the 008 or the 100, also leaving on alternate days. The Beijing-bound 020 passes through at 3.10am local time on Wednesdays; if there are no tickets for that, you may consider taking the 650 in the evening to Zabaikalsk (11hrs) on the border and then catching a bus into China from there.

By air Marshrutka No 14 (R24) runs between the railway/bus station and the airport, which is 15km away. The airport stop, 'Аэропорт', in front of an ugly 5-storey building in the middle of nowhere (the airport is a 2-minute walk from here), is not very obvious; if you make it as far as the end stop in a squat mining town consisting of wooden cabins with corrugated iron roofs, you've gone too far.

CITY GUIDES & PLANS

The Chita area code is ☎ 3022. From outside Russia dial ☎ +7-3022.

Birobidzhan
Биробиджан

[**Moscow Time +7; population: 75,542**] Sedate Birobidzhan is the capital of the so-called Jewish Autonomous Region, a remote site selected in 1928 as a 'homeland' for Soviet Jews. An effective propaganda campaign, as well as starvation in Eastern Europe, encouraged 43,000 Jews from the Soviet Union, and even as far away as the USA, Belarus and Ukraine, to move here in the 1930s. Jewish schools and synagogues were established and a considerable effort was made to give the city a Jewish feel. This included Hebrew street signs, designation of Hebrew as the region's official language and the founding of Russia's only Hebrew-language newspaper, *Birobidzhaner Stern*.

It soon became obvious, however, that 'Stalin's Zion' was no Promised Land. Conditions were extremely harsh with winter lows of minus 40°C and vicious mosquitoes in summer; things were made worse in 1937 by a resurgence of anti-Semitism, including closure of the synagogues and the banning of Hebrew and Yiddish. By 1938 60% of the Jewish population had left.

In the 1950s the town developed into an agricultural and industrial centre. Birobidzhan's most famous export was rice combine harvesters from the Dalselmash factory on the western outskirts of town. Though by 1991, the Jewish population grew again to around 22,000, since the breakup of the Soviet Union in 1991, many Jews have moved to Israel and today less than 6% (around 3000-4000) of the population has Jewish ancestry.

WHAT TO SEE AND DO

Note the giant **menorah Менора** in front of the railway station building and the Hebrew characters inscribed on its façade. The square in front of the railway station commemorates the first Jewish settlers in statue form; you'll find a **statue of Sholom Aleikhem памятник Шолому-Алейхему**, a writer whose stories inspired *Fiddler on the Roof*, along the pedestrian stretch of ul Sholom-Aleikhema.

The **Museum of Regional Studies Краеведческий Музей** (ul Lenina 24 ул Ленина 24, 10am-6pm Wed & Thur, 9am-5pm Fri-Sun, R130) has a particularly good exhibit on the local branch of the Jewish Diaspora, and a gory diorama of the Volochaevska Civil War battle, as well as the ubiquitous stuffed animals.

Off ul Sholom-Aleykhema, attractive **Park Pobedy Парк Победы** has a modern art sculpture in the centre. At ul Lenina 19 ул Ленина 19 you'll find **Freid Фрейд** (10am-5pm Mon-Fri), Birobidzhan's Jewish cultural centre with semi-helpful staff. Next door is the working **synagogue синагога** with a small Jewish museum (by appointment only).

The **beach** on River Bira is packed on summer weekends; walk down ul Gorkogo to the river and you'll see it on the left beside **Park Kultury Парк**

Культуры. There's also an attractive promenade along the river, abloom with flowers in spring and summer.

PRACTICAL INFORMATION
Orientation and services
Everything is within walking distance of the railway and bus stations. The main streets are ul Lenina and the partially pedestrianised ul Sholom-Aleykhema.

Where to stay and eat
The standard *Hotel Vostok* **Гостиница Восток** (ul Sholom-Aleykhema 1 ул Шолом-Алейхема 1, ☎ 42622 65 330, 🖳 hotel79.ru, sgl/dbl/lux R2200/3500/5500,

WHERE TO STAY, EAT & DRINK
7 Resting rooms
  Комнаты Отдыха
13 Café Kakadu Кафе Какаду
14 Market Рынок
15 Hotel & Restaurant Vostok
  Гостиница и Ресторан Восток
16 Teatralny Café
  Театральное Кафе

PLACES OF INTEREST
1 Museum of Regional Studies
  Краеведческий Музей
2 Park Pobedy Парк Победы

3 Statue of Sholom Aleikhem
  памятник Шолому-Алейхему
4 Freid Фрейд
5 Synagogue Синагога
6 Menorah Менора
9 Lenin Statue Памятник Ленину
11 Beach Пляж
12 Philharmonic Hall Филармония
17 Park Kultury Парк Культуры

OTHER
7 Railway Station
  Железнодорожный Вокзал
8 Bus Station Автовокзал
10 Post Office Почтамт

WI-FI) is still the only hotel in town. Its stuffy restaurant with unhurried staff is one of the few places to eat out but there's a 10% booking charge.

For another sleeping option try the *resting rooms* комнаты отдыха at the railway station (☎ 42622 91 605, sgl/twin/trpl R1850/800/600pp per 12 hours; shower R100).

Busy *Café Kakadu* Кафе Какаду near Hotel Vostok serves *draniki* (potato fritters), blini, pelmeni and hot dogs in a cafeteria setting, while *Teatralny Café* **Театральный Кафе** (pr 60 let SSSR 14 пр 60 лет СССР 14) doubles as both a Chinese restaurant and a summer shashlyk joint.

There's a produce **market** near Hotel Vostok.

Moving on
All Trans-Siberian **trains** pass through Birobidzhan and there are also two local trains daily to Khabarovsk (2-2½hrs), so you could do this as a day trip, hopping off at Birobidzhan in the morning, storing your luggage at the railway station, and then catching another train to Khabarovsk when you've finished sightseeing.

Another option to Khabarovsk is to take a local **marshrutka** (3hrs), leaving hourly from the bus station beside the railway station.

Khabarovsk
Хабаровск

[Moscow Time +7; population: 593,636] Khabarovsk is a relaxed provincial city, picturesquely situated on three hills above the junction of the Amur River and its tributary, the Ussuri, and previous winner of the 'most comfortable city in Russia' title. In summer, holiday crowds flock to the sandy river bank and landscaped park, giving the place the atmosphere of a friendly seaside resort. It's bitterly cold in winter, allowing locals to fill pl Lenina with ice sculptures; when the river freezes, people drive their cars onto it and fish through holes chopped in the half-metre-thick ice. In summer, the mighty Amur is a source of both transport and entertainment (see pp326-7).

HISTORY

In 1858 a military settlement was founded here by Count Muravyov-Amursky, the Governor-General of East Siberia who did much to advance Russia's interests in the Far East by kicking out the Manchus. It was named Khabarovka, in honour of the Cossack explorer Yerofey Khabarov, who conquered the Amur region in the 17th century, and whose statue now stands in the square in front of the railway station.

By 1883 the town was known as Khabarovsk and until the first train arrived from Vladivostok on September 3, 1897, via the Ussuri Railway built between 1893 and 1897, the town was just a trading and military post, and a junction for passengers arriving by steamer along the Shilka and Amur rivers from Western Siberia. Here they would transfer to another ship for the voyage down the Amur and Ussuri to Vladivostok.

Early visitors

As more sections of the Trans-Siberian Railway were built, greater numbers of foreign travellers arrived in Khabarovsk. The *1900 Guide to the Great Siberian Railway* did not encourage them to stay long, reporting that: 'The conditions of life in Khabarovsk are not attractive, on account of the absence of comfortable dwellings, and the expensiveness of some products and of most necessary articles ... Imported colonial goods are sold at a high price and only fish is very cheap.' Tourists were also advised against trying Mr Khlebnikov's locally produced wine, made from the area's wild vines, because 'it is of inferior quality and without any flavour'.

Recommended sights included the wooden triumphal arch (now demolished) erected in commemoration of the visit of Tsarevich Nicholas in 1891, and the bronze statue of Count Muravyov-Amursky on the promontory above the river. After the Revolution the Count was traded in for an image from the Lenin Statue Factory, but he has since reappeared.

The city today

The railway brought more trade than tourists, and though it suffered during the Civil War, the town quickly grew into the modern city it is today. Few of its old wooden cabins remain but there are some attractive stone buildings from Imperial times. It is the capital of Khabarovsk Territory, surrounded by some of the richest mineral deposits in Russia, and a major industrial centre involved in engineering, petroleum refining and timber-working, as well as trading with South Korea and Japan.

WHAT TO SEE AND DO

Museum of Regional Studies Краеведческий Музей

This excellent, partially interactive museum (ul Shevchenko 11 ул Шевченко 11, 10am-6pm Tue-Sun, R350), based on the extensive collection of Baron Korff, a former governor-general of the Amur region, was opened in 1894 and is housed in two attractive buildings next to each other. With donations from hunters and explorers over the last century, the collection has grown into an impressive display of local history, flora and fauna.

Among the stuffed animals in the ground-floor galleries are four Amur tigers. Also known as the Siberian or Manchurian tiger (*Felis/Panthera tigris altaica*), this is the largest member of the cat family and can weigh up to 350kg, about twice the average weight of an African lion. In the same gallery are various fur-bearing animals including the large sea-otter or Kamchatka beaver (*Enhydra lutris*) from which come the highest-priced pelts in the world. Before this animal came under official protection in the early 20th century, its pelts were selling for over US$2000 each and its population had dwindled to 750 individuals in its Russian habitat of the Kuril Islands and Kamchatka; the species have now bounced back and number around 27,000 in Russia alone. There is a small aquarium section, acquainting visitors with the scaled denizens of the Amur river.

The upper galleries feature superb ethnography exhibitions. The area was inhabited by several tribes at the time of the Revolution; the Goldi and Orochi lived near the mouth of the Ussuri, and Olchi and Giliak beside the Amur. Each tribe had its *shaman*, and some of their beribboned robes and ritual objects – check out the wooden receptacle made to hold the hearts of ritually killed bears – are on display as well as a suit made entirely of fish-skins (the skin of a common fish, the *keta*, was used not only for clothing but also for tents, sails and boots). You may spot an Evenki birchbark cradle with bone charms, Even *chums* – winter and summer dwellings – and an Udegei carving of a crafty-looking old man. There's also a display of early settlers' furniture, samovars and other utensils, including some bread baked by the original colonists.

Also look out for the panoramic painting of the Russian Civil War, see p476.

Far Eastern Art Museum Дальневосточный Художественный Музей
At ul Shevchenko 7 ул Шевченко 7, this art museum (10am-6pm Tue-Sun, R260) was partly under restoration at the time of writing. The first floor featured a captivating temporary exhibition of the best of nature photography from across Russia. The permanent collection on the top floor is divided into Russian art, which includes a selection of 17th- and 18th-century religious icons and also some wonderful landscapes, such as *In the Caucasus* and *Venice*, as well as a dramatic piece by ES Sorokin of a young man holding back an enraged bull, and portraiture and landscapes by German, Italian, French and Dutch works, the standout being *Arab holding head of dead man* by Venet Horace. Don't miss the graphic WWII propaganda posters in the corridor.

Military Museum Музей Истории Краснознаменного Дальневосточного Военного Округа (ДВО)
This worthwhile museum (ul Shevchenko 20 ул Шевченко 20, 10am-5pm Tue-Sun, R150) provides a record of military activity here since the city was founded. There are numerous pictures of Russian soldiers as well as photographs of British, French, Italians and Americans in Vladivostok in 1918. The walls are decorated with medals and old weapons, including a weather-beaten Winchester rifle and a few Smith & Wesson pistols. A small display on Mongolia includes a photo of Lenin and prominent Mongolian Communist leader Sukhe Bator sharing a joke. Upstairs you'll find WWII memorabilia and an interesting display on the war in Afghanistan, as well as an extensive collection of WWII propaganda posters. Behind the building there's a row of armoured vehicles including a tiny MC-1 two-man tank, as well as a MiG fighter plane and a train carriage (usually locked) once used by the commander of the Russian Far East military forces.

Other sights and things to do
The **Amur River** река Амур is a focus of interest in winter or summer. In winter when it freezes, locals drill holes through the ice and set up little tents from which they fish. In summer the banks and the landscaped riverside park are crowded with sun-worshippers and swimmers; there are a couple of shashlyk tents in the summer also. Swimming is not advisable as the summer floods of 2013 (see box opposite) wreaked havoc with the sewage systems of a number of

❑ The Amur rages

Between July and September 2013, the Russian Far East was hit with the worst flooding in recorded history, caused by particularly heavy snowfall the winter before and unusually heavy rainfall over the months of July and August which, in turn, swelled the waters of the mighty Amur River that flows through the Amur Oblast, the Jewish Autonomous Oblast and Khabarovsk Krai. One hundred and twenty-six towns were affected, with isolated villages suffering the most due to difficulty of access and the damage to property and infrastructure; over 120,000 people were evacuated and the damage to agriculture alone was to the tune of 10 billion roubles. The worst-hit cities included: Blagoveshchensk; Khabarovsk, with the water levels reaching a record 784cm (the previous record in 1897 standing at 642cm and 600cm considered critical level); and Komsomolsk-na-Amure, where the waters reached a record high of 902cm, beating the previous flood record on 1959 by over two metres. Unlike nearby China, which was also badly affected by the floods, in Russia there were practically no casualties. Russians handled the situation very pragmatically, many choosing to stay in their partially flooded homes to prevent looting, getting about by boat and fishing from their rooftops. Rescue efforts were undertaken by the army, along with over 30,000 volunteers, whose tasks included anything from laying down sandbags to try to hold back the river to getting around the half-abandoned villages to feed the cats and dogs left behind.

flooded villages and towns. One way to enjoy the Amur is to take one of the hour-long party boat cruises (R250-350) that leave regularly from the river station in summer, or to walk along the attractive riverfront promenade, popular with locals strolling or skating.

Looming over the riverbank, on Komsomolskaya pl Комсомольская пл, is the new **Assumption Cathedral Успенский Собор**, rebuilt in 2001 after being torn down in the 1930s.

It's worth the walk up ul Turgeneva ул Тургенева to view **Glory Square Площадь Победы**, including a **Victory Monument Монумент Победы** commemorating local soldiers fallen in WWII, and the very photogenic **Church of the Transfiguration Преображенская Церковь** with its five golden domes. There are also fine views of the river, especially at sunset.

PRACTICAL INFORMATION
Orientation and services

Khabarovsk is a spread-out city: the railway station and the waterfront, where many of the attractions are found, are almost 3km apart, a half-hour walk.

The main street, ul Karla Marksa, is to the east of the city's central square, pl Lenina, and its continuation, ul Muravyeva-Amurskogo, is to the west of it.

Knizhny Mir Книжный Мир (ul Karla Marksa 37, 9am-7pm daily) bookshop has an excellent range of maps of Khabarovsk and surrounding oblasts and cities. There are reliable TransCredit Bank **ATMs** in the railway station and several others in the more upmarket hotels and along ul Muravyeva-Amurskogo.

There's **internet access** (8am-9pm daily, R100/hour) in the **central post office** at ul Muravyova-Amurskogo 28.

The **Chinese Consulate** (Lenin Stadium 1 Стадион Ленина 1, ☎ 302 590) is open for visa appointments, but see p28 for details about Chinese visas.

CITY GUIDES & PLANS

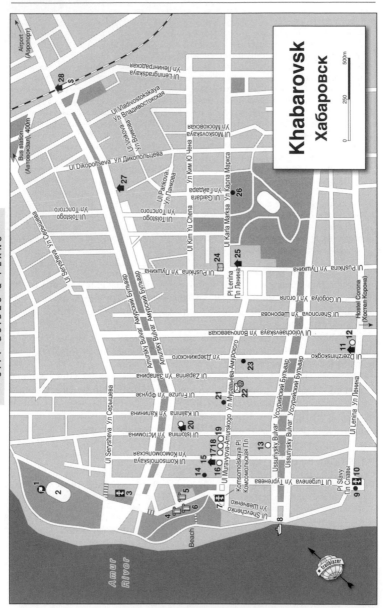

Khabarovsk
Хабаровск

0   250   500m

Airport (Аэропорт)

Ул Ленинградская
Ul Leningradskaya

Ul Vladivostokskaya
Ул Владивостокская

Ul Voikova
Ул Воикова

Bus station (Автовокзал), 400m

Ul Dikopoltseva Ул Дикопольцева

Ul Serysheva Ул Серышева

Ul Serysheva Ул Серышева

Ul Tolstogo
Ул Толстого

Ul Pankova
Ул Панкова

Ul Kim Yu Chena
Ул Ким Ю Чена

Ul Tolstogo
Ул Толстого

Ul Kim Yu Chena
Ул Ким Ю Чена

Ul Moskovskaya
Ул Московская

Ul Gaidara
Ул Гайдара

Ul Karla Marksa Ул Карла Маркса

Ul Pushkina Ул Пушкина

Ul Pushkina Ул Пушкина

Pl Lenina
Пл Ленина

Ul Shelgonova Ул Шелгонова

Ul Gogolya Ул Гоголя

Ul Sheronova Ул Шеронова

Hostel Corona
(Хостел Корона)

Amursky Bulvar Амурский Бульвар

Amursky Bulvar Амурский Бульвар

Ul Dzerzhinskogo
Ул Дзержинского

Ul Voloчaevskaya Ул Волочаевская

Ul Dzerzhinskogo
Ул Дзержинского

Ul Zaparina Ул Запарина

Ul Frunze Ул Фрунзе

Ul Muravyeva-Amurskogo Ул Муравьёва-Амурского

Ul Kalinina Ул Калинина

Ul Istomina Ул Истомина

Ul Komsomolskaya Ул Комсомольская

Ul Serysheva Ул Серышева

Ussuriysky Bulvar Уссурийский Бульвар

Ussuriysky Bulvar Уссурийский Бульвар

Ul Lenina Ул Ленина

Komsomolskaya Pl
Комсомольская Пл

Ul Shevchenko
Ул Шевченко

Ul Turgeneva Ул Тургенева

Pl Slavy
Пл Славы

Beach

Amur River

trailblazer

Travel agents Dalgeo (ul Turgeneva 78 ул Тургенева 78, ☎ 318 829, 🖥 www.dalgeo.com), with English-speaking staff, offer a wide range of tours, including a visit to the local Nanai village, and another to the zoo featuring the mammals of the Far East, multi-day trips to Komsomolsk-na-Amure and winter crossings of the Amur River.

Local transport
There are regular **bus**, **trolleybus** and **tram**

services (R15). From the railway station, trams No 1 and 2 run to near pl Lenina, buses No 4 and 34 run to pl Komsomolskaya, while bus No 1 runs down along ul Lenina, passing near the Cathedral of Transfiguration before looping back to the railway station along ul Serysheva.

To get to the airport, take trolleybus No 1 from pl Komsomolskaya or bus No 35 from the railway station.

THE MEMORIAL OF GLORY, KHABAROVSK

CITY GUIDES & PLANS

WHERE TO STAY
11 Amur Hotel Гостиница Амур
15 Hotel Sapporo Гостиница Саппоро
20 Boutique Hotel Khabarovsk City Бутик-отель Хабаровск-Сити
25 Hotel Tsentralnaya Гостиница Центральная
27 Versailles Версаль
28 Resting rooms Комнаты Отдыха

WHERE TO EAT AND DRINK
12 Amur Café and Restaurant Ресторан Амур
13 Russky Restaurant Русский Ресторан
16 BeerHaus
17 Harley-Davidson Bar
18 Blin! Блин!
19 Pepperone Пеппероне
20 Tsvety Цветы

PLACES OF INTEREST
3 Church of St Innokent Церковь Святого Иннокентия
4 Museum of Regional Studies Краеведческий Музей
5 Military Museum Музей Истории Краснознаменного Дальневосточного Военного Округа (ДВО)
6 Far Eastern Art Museum Дальневосточный Художественный Музей
7 Assumption Cathedral Успенский Собор
9 Victory Monument (Glory Square) Монумент Победы (Площадь Победы)

10 Church of the Transfiguration Преображенская Церковь
23 Drama Theatre Театр Драмы
26 Musical Comedy Theatre Театр музыкальной комедии

SHOPPING
21 Tayny Remesla Art Store Магазин Тайны Ремесла
24 Knizhny Mir Bookshop Книжный Мир

OTHER
1 Chinese Consulate Китайское Консульство
2 Lenin Stadium Стадион Ленина
8 River Station Речной Вокзал
14 Dalgeo Tours Далгео Тур
22 Central Post Office & internet Почтамт и интернет
24 Knizhny Mir Bookshop Книжный Мир
28 Railway Station & ATM Железнодорожный Вокзал & АТМ

Where to stay

Inexpensive accommodation options are thin on the ground; hotels are generally of good quality but overpriced for what they are.

The *resting rooms* комнаты отдыха (*komnaty otdykha*) on the top floor of the railway station (for 12hrs: sgl/twn R1000/1130, or quad R720/1050pp for 12/24 hours; cheaper rates during daytime) are clean and tidy, and the single room even has a desk and a TV. Toilets are shared and hot showers are free, though there's only one shower.

Overlooking pl Lenina, the mildly revamped Soviet standard *Hotel Tsentralnaya* Гостиница Центральная (ul Pushkina 52 ул Пушкина 52, ☎ 324 759, sgl/dbl/lux from R2321/2767/3568; 25% booking fee applies), offers unremarkable, air-conditioned rooms. Its main claim to fame is that Paul Theroux stayed here while researching *The Great Railway Bazaar*.

The cream-coloured rooms with classic décor at *Amur Hotel* Гостиница Амур (ul Lenina 29 ул Ленина 29, ☎ 221 223, 🖥 www.amurhotel.ru, sgl/dbl from R2550/2850) come with plasma screen TV, fridge and kettle, with an excellent banya downstairs (R1500/hour) and tropical showers in the suites. The staff are friendly and helpful, though little English is spoken; the price includes a good buffet breakfast and you'll also find one of the city's best restaurants (see opposite) on the premises.

Close to the railway station, *Versailles* Версаль (Amursky bul 46а Амурский бульвар 46а, ☎ 910 150, 🖥 versal-hotel.net, sgl/dbl R3500/5800, WI-FI) offers cheerful rooms with all mod-cons. Staff are friendly and speak English, the buffet breakfast is good and guests can use the gym/sauna/pool.

Essentially a mid-range option but at top end prices, central *Hotel Sapporo* Гостиница Саппоро (ul Komsomolskaya 79, ul Komsomolskaya 79, ☎ 800 200 4418 (free), 🖥 www.sapporo-hotel.ru, sgl/dbl/

lux R3900/5000/7700, WI-FI) is particularly popular with Japanese businessmen, which is reflected in its semi-Japanese décor. The air-conditioned, simple, but comfortable rooms come with reliable internet/WI-FI access and breakfast is included.

An excellent top-end option, justifiably commended by Conde Nast *Traveler* magazine, ★ *Boutique Hotel Khabarovsk City* Бутик-отель Хабаровск-Сити (ul Istomina 64 ул Истомина 64, ☎ 767 676, 🖥 www.boutique-hotel.ru, sgl/dbl/lux R4600/5500/10,000, WI-FI) pleases with its light, bright, spacious rooms with tiled bathrooms and assortment of mod-cons, while the colour-themed suites come with iPod/iPad docking stations, Jacuzzi and heated floors. Too pricey? Then you can opt for one of the six rooms at the adjoining mini-hotel (R3500).

The only hostel in town, *Hostel Corona* Хостел Корона (ul Volochayevskaya 87 ул Волочаевская 87, ☎ 914 772 4270, 🖥 www.hostelworld.com, no website of its own, dorm R700, WI-FI) consists of an apartment with a few comfortable bunk beds in a large room, a rather congested common area and an owner who communicates reasonably well in English and tries hard to please. Take tram No 1 from the railway station to Ussuriyskaya 'Уссурийская'.

Where to eat and drink

In the summer, you'll find inexpensive shashlyk and beer tents by the river; expect to spend around R250 on shashlyk and under R100 for beer.

As you might expect, *BeerHaus* (ul Komsomolskaya and ul Muravyova-Amurskogo ул Комсомольская и ул Муравьёва-Амурского) is an establishment dedicated to bringing you German (and non-German) beer, sausage platters (big enough for two) and, occasionally, Uzbek food when it does a guest slot. Mains from R600.

The Khabarovsk area code is ☎ 4212. From outside Russia dial ☎ +7-4212.

Russky Restaurant Русский Ресторан (Ussuriysky bul 9 Уссурийский бульвар 9, mains R480-1250) has an established fan base, thanks to its imaginative Russian dishes such as lamb baked with aubergine and courgette, chicken cutlets in wild mushroom sauce, homemade pelmeni and savoury vareniki. Expect mid-sized portions and friendly, efficient service.

In the basement of the **Lotus Shopping Centre** on the corner of ul Volochayevskaya and ul Muravyova-Amurskogo (ул Волочаевская и ул Мурвьёва-Амурского, R60), *Blin!* Блин! serves just that – blini and more blini with numerous sweet and savoury fillings. Cheap and cheerful.

In the basement next door (ул Волочаевская и ул Мурвьёва-Амурского, mains from R150) is arguably Khabarovsk's best pizza place, *Pepperone* Пеппероне; besides the thin and crispy pizza you can help yourself to some inexpensive pasta dishes and coffee.

The dishes at ★ *Amur Café and Restaurant* Ресторан Амур (ul Lenina 29 ул Ленина 29, mains R460-1500) will forever make you eat your words if you've ever referred to Russian food as unimaginative; expect halibut smoked in green tea with mango sauce, seared scallops on black rice, and venison in chocolate sauce. Not enough? Try the strawberry gazpacho with meringue, or another sweet creation.

In Boutique Hotel and winning fans with its concise menu of European dishes, *Tsvety* Цветы (see Where to stay, mains R480-1400) offers the likes of seafood lasagne, lamb noisette with couscous and Caesar salad. One of the best places for breakfast, too, with three types of porridge (R150), omelettes any which way and blini. Portion sizes will appeal to those watching their weight. Would it kill them to provide pepper grinders?

With some of the clientele actually wearing cowboy hats in a non-ironic manner, the *Harley-Davidson Bar* (ul Komsomolskaya 88 ул Комсомольская 88, 6pm-6am daily) is a bloke's bar, with 10 beers on tap, live rock music most nights and parties till dawn on the weekends.

Shopping

Interesting local products include ginseng and a special blend of vodka and herbs known as *aralyevaya vodka*. The best souvenir shop is **Tayny Remesla Тайны Ремесла**, ul Muravyova-Amurskogo 17.

Hit **Knizhny Mir Книжный Мир** at ul Karla Marksa 37 for maps and books.

Moving on

By rail From Khabarovsk, half of the services **south** to Vladivostok run overnight (11-15¼hrs); the firmenny 002 and 006 tend to be significantly more expensive than the rest.

Heading **west**, Moscow-bound trains stop in Chita (6/day, 37-42½hrs), Irkutsk (5/day, 56-61hrs) and other major cities before reaching Moscow (1-2/day, 133-146¼hrs); the fastest is the firmenny 001 (alternate days), while slower and cheaper alternatives are the 043 (alternate days), originating in Khabarovsk, and the 099 (alternate days). Heading **north**, there are also daily links to Tynda with the 325 (29hrs), to Komsomolsk-na-Amure (1-2/day, 10hrs) and daily services to Vanino/SovGavan on the 351 (25hrs), handy if you're catching a ferry to Sakhalin Island.

By bus Buses and marshrutkas leave frequently from the bus station for Birobidzhan (3hrs).

By boat Boats operate along the Amur River from late May to late October. Local ferries and long-distance hydrofoils all depart from the **river station** at ul Shevchenko 1. However, the disastrous flooding along the Amur (see box p337) has affected boat timetables and, indeed, the hydrofoil/boat destinations mentioned below, so it remains to be seen in what form the services will resume. Before the flooding, hydrofoils ran between Khabarovsk and Nikolayevsk-na-Amure via Komsomolsk-na-Amure five times per week (7am, 19hrs to Nikolayevsk-na-Amure and 6hrs to Komsomolsk-na-Amure).

There were also several daily boats from Khabarovsk to Fuyuan in China, departing around 8am and returning around

10pm (around R900 return, 1½hrs). Customs procedures are straightforward. Tickets are sold from kiosks prominently signposted 'Fuyuan', near the river station. You must show a Chinese visa to buy a boat ticket. From Fuyuan it's a 15-hour bus ride on to Harbin, or a shorter one to Jiamusi from where there are trains to Harbin.

By air Khabarovsk Novy Airport (💻 air khv.ru) – the largest airport in Russia's Far East – is 7km east of the city centre and served by S7, Vladivostok Air, Korean Air, Yakutia Airlines, China Southern and Aeroflot, among other airlines. Domestic flights include: Moscow (several daily, 8½hrs), Vladivostok (daily, 1¾hrs), Irkutsk (daily, 3hrs), Yakutsk (twice weekly, 1½hrs), and Yekaterinburg via Novosibirsk (4/week, 5hrs and 4hrs, respectively), among other major cities. International departures include Beijing (1/week, 2hrs), Harbin (3/week, 1½hrs), Seoul (daily, 2hrs) and Tokyo (2/week, 1¾hrs).

Vladivostok
Владивосток

[Moscow Time +7; population: 600,378] Sometimes described as 'Russia's San Francisco due to its steep streets, Golden Gate-esque Golden Horn Bridge and strategic location on the ocean, Vladivostok is the eastern terminus of the Trans-Siberian line and home of Russia's Pacific Fleet, its port a hub of activity. Whether you're heading east or west, it's well worth stopping off to explore one of the country's biggest Cold War secrets and to enjoy the seaside town atmosphere.

Until 1990 Vladivostok was off-limits to all visitors because of its military and strategic importance as one of Russia's key naval ports. Even Soviet citizens needed special permits, and foreigners, with a few notable exceptions (such as US President Gerald Ford in 1975), required nothing short of divine intervention. Now ferries link Vladivostok with ports in Japan and Korea, and although the city saw major infrastructure development (the Golden Horn Bridge, for one) in time for the 2012 Asia-Pacific Economic Cooperation summit, and new hotels are still springing up, this has not impacted negatively on the attractive historic streets of the city centre. The revamping of the city has led to great improvements in Vladivostok's dining scene, much to the delight of its locals and visitors.

HISTORY

This region has been occupied for many thousands of years, certainly back at least to the 2nd millennium BC; but inhabitants were largely nomadic so few relics remain. Eastern chronicles reveal that this was considered part of the Chinese empire at a very early stage but also that it was so remote and conditions so harsh that it was left well alone.

The Russians arrive

In the mid 19th century the Russians were concentrating on expanding their territory eastwards at China's expense. At the head of the exploratory missions was

Count Muravyov-Amursky, who from his steamer, the *Amerika*, chose this site for a harbour in 1859. A year later a party of 40 soldiers landed to secure the region. The port was named Vladivostok ('Rule the East').

In 1861 more soldiers arrived to protect Russia's new eastern frontier, with settlers not far behind. It soon became apparent just how important a find this settlement was: Vladivostok's harbour, one of the few deep-water ports on the east coast, remains unfrozen for longer than any other in Siberia, being inaccessible for an average of just 72 days per year, compared with Nakhodka's 98. This and Vladivostok's strategic location resulted in the shift to here of Russia's eastern naval base in 1872 from Nikolaevsk-na-Amure (frozen for an inconvenient 190 days per year).

Conflict in the east

In 1904 the Russo-Japanese war broke out. Vladivostok was heavily bombarded and trade virtually ceased but while large parts of the port were destroyed, the war was ultimately to prove beneficial: peace settlements with Japan left Vladivostok as Russia's prime east coast port although Japan gained Port Arthur and parts of Sakhalin Island.

During WWI the city served as the chief entry point for supplies and ammunition from the USA, and British, Japanese, American, Canadian and Italian troops streamed in to support the White Russians' struggle against the Bolsheviks. The most notorious foreign 'visitors' were Czech legions who had fought their way east all the way from the Ukraine in a desperate bid for freedom (see p107). The graves of many of them, and of other foreigners, can still be found in the cemetery here.

As it became clear that the Bolsheviks were gaining the upper hand, many White Russians fled abroad, and the foreign forces departed. Most had left by 1920 although some Japanese stayed on until October 1922. Finally, on 25 October, the city was 'liberated' and Soviet power established, prompting Lenin's famous comment about Vladivostok: 'It's a long way away. But it's ours'.

The Soviet period

The Soviet period meant considerable investment in the city's development. Money poured in, along with orders to develop the port and build more ships. In the last days of WWII Vladivostok assumed a key role as the centre of operations for the fight against the Japanese in Manchuria. In the space of four years 25 ships were sunk here and some 30,000 sailors perished. During the Stalin years, the port lost much of its cosmopolitan character as most of the city's foreign population were shot or deported.

As the Cold War set in, the city was sealed off from the outside world and the Pacific Fleet expanded fast. The West heard little more of this protected port until 1986 when Gorbachev made his 'Vladivostok Initiative' speech, highlighting a grand new plan for Soviet economic and military commitments in the Far East. Echoing Peter the Great, he announced that Vladivostok was to become 'a wide open window to the East'.

CITY GUIDES & PLANS

WHAT TO SEE AND DO

Orlinoye Gnezdo (Eagle's Nest lookout point) Орлиное Гнездо

For the best panoramic view of this large, gritty port city and the Golden Horn Bay, studded with vast naval ships and straddled by Vladivostok's answer to the Golden Gate Bridge – the Golden Horn Bridge – you have to head high. The city's favourite lookout spot is Orlinoye Gnezdo, on a hill overlooking the port, and itself overlooked by a **statue of St Cyril and St Methodius Памятник Святому Кириллу и Святому Мефодию** – inventors of the Cyrillic alphabet. To get to the top, take one of the frequent rides up the short but sweet **funicular railway фуникулёр** (R8; 7.30am-8pm daily) from ul Pushkinskaya, go through the underpass under ul Sukhanova and then climb up to your left.

I M Arsenyev Regional Museum Краеведческий Музей И М Арсенева

Newly revamped, this is the biggest and best of Vladivostok's museums (ul Svetlanskaya 20 ул Светланская 20, 10am-6pm Tue-Sun; R150), recalling the history of the city and the region, and named after a local writer. The impressive wildlife display has labels in English: local sea life, an Ussuri leopard, a large Amur tiger and a couple of moose locking antlers. Rarer specimens include a *goral* (a small goat-like antelope), a Steller's albatross, an Amursky leopard and a Chinese soft-shelled turtle. Also on the bottom floor, partially interactive displays focus on settlement of the area in the 19th century, the contribution of various merchants to the economic life of the city (a shelf per merchant), and the story of 'Millionka' (see box opposite), the lawless slum populated by the Chinese who'd moved to the city in the 1850s and '60s; check out the gambling equipment on display.

The well-labelled archaeology exhibition stampedes from the Stone Age up to the Jurchan settlement in the 10th century, with pottery and Jin dynasty weapons on display. Ethnographic exhibits on the Far East's and Siberia's indigenous peoples are very good, featuring Nanai, Udegei and Orochi items; you may spot the Udegei iziubr caller made of birch bark and shaman's belt, an Udegei crib, and an Orochi seven (a wooden talisman, typically in the shape of an animal, designed to protect against illness).

Primorskaya Art Gallery Приморская Картинная Галерея

The **original building** housing the gallery (ul Aleutskaya 12 ул Алеутская 12 10am-6pm Tue-Sun, R150) has finally been renovated and currently hosts worthwhile temporary exhibitions. Recent ones have included the colourful, joyful, almost childlike drawings of Korean artist Su An, and Siberian landscapes and portraiture by Vasily Doromin.

The **other gallery site** (Partizansky pr 12 пр Партизанский 12, 9am-6pm Tue-Sun R150) has had much of its west wing art donated by the Tretyakov Gallery in Moscow. The east wing hosts temporary exhibitions by local artists, while the west wing features 19th- and 20th-century oil paintings. To get there, take bus No 17, 23, 40 or 41 from the bus stop on pl Semyonovskaya пл Семёновская two stops to the 'Kartinnaya Galereya' 'Картинная Галерея' stop.

❑ Millionka

Modern Vladivostok has not avoided the racism prevalent in Russia and local ultra-nationalists tend to focus on what they term the 'Chinese threat' – a fear that there's a rapidly growing Chinese population that will overtake the Russian one in numbers, even if in reality that is rather far-fetched.

Chinese migrants have been living in Vladivostok since the mid 19th century, their numbers reaching 3909 people by 1884, and 5580 in 1897. Though the Chinese were forbidden to own property in Vladivostok and even though there were plans to relocate them en masse to another part of the city, they mostly settled in the area near modern-day Sportivnaya Gavan, where there was a Chinese market and since Chinese junks would dock there. By the end of the 19th century, the streets near Sportivnaya Gavan were built up with houses built specifically for renting to the Chinese who were prepared to live in overcrowded, highly unsanitary conditions. By 1910, the Millionka quarter comprised parts of ul Svetlanskaya, ul Admirala Fokina, ul Batareynaya, ul Aleutskaya, and ul Utkinskaya; with a population of around 50,000, it became a 'city within a city', which the city authorities left alone and where prostitution, contraband smuggling, opium dens and gambling prevailed. Other minorities – Jews, Koreans, people of the Caucasus region – found refuge there: you could spend years in the quarter without venturing out, as everything you needed was available and its myriad dank alleyways and wooden walkways overhead could be used to evade capture.

Millionka went into decline in the mid 1920s, when the local authorities pointedly stopped using foreign labour and by the mid 1930s, a Politburo decision was made regarding the liquidation of the quarter as it 'served as a refuge for all the criminal and undocumented elements in the city', as well as alleged Japanese spies. In December 1936, Millionka ceased to exist, its legal residents given living space elsewhere and its vast illegal population forced to flee abroad, with the exception of those executed for alleged espionage.

Submarine Museum   Мемориальный Комплекс «Боевая Слава Краснознаменного Тихоокеанского Флота»

On the waterfront, next to the eternal flame and the WWII memorial inscribed with the names of local soldiers who perished, is an old S56 submarine (9am-8pm daily, R100), housing a display on the history of submarines in Vladivostok. There are early uniforms, ships' instruments, pictures of the earliest submarine (1865) and the first flotillas (1906). The old photographs are of limited interest; the fun part is scrambling through circular openings into the bowels of the submarine. Here you can check out the control room, peer through the telescope and see the living quarters of the crew, which consisted of two tiers of short bunks suspended above the floor. No English captioning.

Krasny Vympel «Красный Вымпел»

The Soviet Pacific Fleet's first ship, launched on 24 January 1923, is moored just opposite the Submarine Museum. Displays include photographs of early crew members, medals, uniforms and other salty memorabilia, and some of the machinery is preserved down below. However, at the time of writing, the museum was closed indefinitely for 'repairs.'

Vladivostok Fortress Museum Музей Владивостоская Крепость

Up on the hill, reached via some stairs from the seafront promenade, this museum (10am-6pm daily, R150) consists of a unique fortress and outdoor spaces, dotted with anti-aircraft guns, sea mines, torpedoes, supersonic missiles, the odd tank and other military hardware. The bunker-like rooms inside the fortress proper, used from 1882 to 1923, contain exhibits with English captioning that show the region's many fortresses, including scale models, some of the history of the Russian-Japanese struggle for control of the Kurile Islands and an entertaining collection of items confiscated by the Frunzensky police division that includes knuckledusters, a plethora of knives, a small sabre and some nunchuks.

The fortress itself is one of 16 that encircle the city, some of which are linked to underground tunnels.

Antique Automobile Museum Музей Автомотостарины

This museum (ul Sakhalinskaya 2a, ул Сахалинская 2a, 10am-6pm daily, 🖳 www.automotomuseum.vl.ru, R100) is a must if you're an enthusiast of all things motorised. The exhibits are not restricted just to beautiful antique ZILs and other lovingly preserved and restored Soviet cars; there are also the Soviet Union's earliest motorcycles, German and Japanese motorcycles captured during WWII and Russian military vehicles from WWII, including the legendary Katyusha (anti-tank vehicle). A recent display focuses on the Primorsky sport of motorbiking on ice.

Further afield

Russky Island Русский Остров Of the several islands that lie offshore in Zolotoy Rog (Golden Horn) Bay, Russky Island is the most important, having been of strategic military importance for over 150 years. It has only been open to foreigners since 2000 and is now connected to the mainland by the landmark Golden Horn Bridge, the longest cable-stayed bridge in the world, completed in 2012 in time for the 24th summit of Asia-Pacific Economic Cooperation (APEC).

The island is still served by frequent boats from the smaller Local Ferry terminal, 100m north of the main Marine Terminal; the boats drop you at **Podnozhye village Подножье**, famous for its monastery. Buses are timed to meet the boats and they whisk passengers off either west to Rynda, with the beaches, or east to DOF (Dom Ofitsera Flota), from where you can do the easy 5km walk along a paved road to the island's main sight – **Voroshilov Battery Ворошиловка Батарея** (9am-5pm Wed-Sun, R100). The battery is a military museum; you can explore its tunnels, admire its three massive cannon, and check out the ocean views. Unless you come here as part of a tour (see opposite), you'll have to walk or hitch a ride back to the DOF and catch a bus to the ferry from there.

The Vladivostok area code is ☎ 4232. From outside Russia dial ☎ +7-4232.

PRACTICAL INFORMATION
Orientation and services
Vladivostok is built along the Muravyov Peninsula, which stretches south-west into the Sea of Japan. Scattered around it is a series of islands, of which Russky Island (Russky Ostrov) remains the most important. The city's focal point is **Zolotoy Rog ('Golden Horn') Bay**, so called because of its resemblance to Istanbul's Golden Horn. It's here that most ferries, warships and fishing boats dock.

The **railway station** is conveniently located on the waterfront, connected to the **marine terminal** (*morskoy vokzal*) by a pedestrian bridge. Next to the main railway station building is the Aeroexpress building, where you can buy tickets for the trains to the airport. All attractions in the centre are within walking distance of one another, though Vladivostok is a hilly place so distances can seem longer. Ul Pogranichnaya, ul Admirala Fokina, ul Svetlanskaya and ul Sukhanova are particularly good for restaurants.

Note that the **Central Bus Station** (the long-distance bus station) is not at all central, being near Vtoraya Rechka Вторая Речка suburban railway station.

There are **ATMs** at a business centre in the same building as the post office and at major banks, as well as at the railway station. The **central post office** is on ul Aleutskaya opposite the railway station. **Internet access** is available here.

Tours and travel agents
Helpful **Pyat' Zvyozd (Five Stars) Пять Звёзд** (ul Admirala Fokina 5 ул Адмирала

VLADIVOSTOK RAILWAY STATION

Фокина 5, ☎ 222 8090, 🖳 www.fivestars .vl.ru) offers an excellent range of city tours, from walking tours of the historical centre to day trips to Fort No 7, Russky Island, Popov Island and multi-day trips to the zoological centre for Himalayan black bears and the 350,000-hectare Sikhote-Alin Nature Reserve, centre of a Russian-American effort to save the Amur tiger.

Consulates
Australian (pr Krasnogo Znameni 42, пр Красного Знамени 42, ☎ 244 6782, 🖳 www.russia.embassy.gov.au); **British** (ul Svetlanskaya 9, ул Светланская 9, ☎ 241 4872); **Chinese** (Hotel Gavan, ul Krygina 3, Отель Гавань, ул Крыгина 3, ☎ 249 7204), visa applications 9am-12.30pm on Mon, Wed and Fri; **US** (ul Pushkinskaya 32, ул Пушкинская 32, ☎ 230 0070, 🖳 vladivostok.usconsulate.gov).

Local transport
The **airport** is 40km outside Vladivostok. The quickest and easiest way is to take the Aeroexpress (R200 one-way), with trains running daily almost every hour between 8am and 8pm (48 mins), or else take bus No 107 (R100, 1½hrs, hourly between 6.40am and 5.45pm) from in front of the railway station.

Vladivostok is served by an extensive network of **buses**, **trolleybuses** and **trams**; buy a transport route map from one of the kiosks.

There are a few daily ferries in summer from the **local ferry terminal** near the Marine Terminal. Destinations include the popular swimming spots of Russky Island, Popov Island (known for its beaches), Reyniky Island and Cape Peshanaya.

Where to stay
Vladivostok has a shortage of beds in summer and budget accommodation is thin on the ground.

See You Hostel (ул Крыгина 42а, кв 133 ul Krygina 42a, apt 133, ☎ 487 779, 🖳 www.seeyouhostel.com, dorm R500, WI-FI) is the original hostel here but it's a short bus ride from the centre. It consists of an apartment with guest lounge and kitchen;

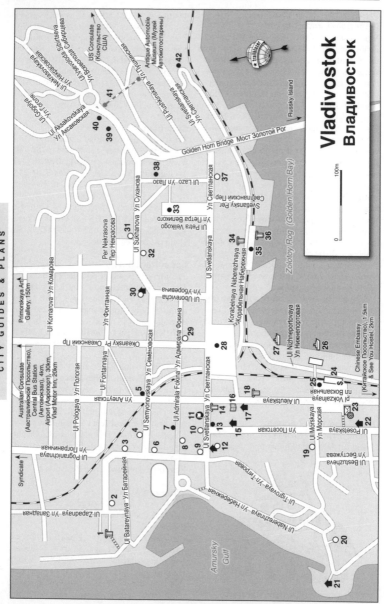

Vladivostok
Владивосток

Zolotoy Rog (Golden Horn Bay)

Russky Island

Golden Horn Bridge Мост Золотой Рог

Amursky Gulf

0   100m

US Consulate (Консульство США)

Antique Automobile Museum (Музей Автомотостарины)

Primorskaya Art Gallery, 150m

Central Bus Station (Автовокзал), 4km, Airport (Аэропорт), 30km, Vlad Motor Inn, 20km

Australian Consulate (Австралийское Посольство), 1km

Syndicate

Chinese Embassy (Китайское Посольство), 1.5km & See You Hostel, 2km

Svetlansky Pier Светланский Пер

Ул Светланская
Ul Svetlanskaya

Ul Pushkinskaya Ул Пушкинская
Ul Svetlanskaya Ул Светланская

Ul Aksakovskaya Ул Аксаковская

Ул Некрасовская Ul Nekrasovskaya
Ul Vsevoloda Sibirtseva Ул Всеволода Сибирцева
Ul Prborezhnaya
Ul Gogolya Ул Гоголя
Ul Sukhanova Ул Суханова
Ul Lazo Ул Лазо

Per Nekrasova Пер Некрасова
Ul Sukhanova Ул Суханова
Ul Petra Velikogo Ул Петра Великого

Ul Komarova Ул Комарова

Ul Fontannaya Ул Фонтанная

Oceansky Pr Океанский Пр

Ul Uborevicha Ул Уборевича

Korabelnaya Naberezhnaya Корабельная Набережная

Ul Pologaya Ул Пологая
Ul Semyonovskaya Ул Семёновская
Ul Admirala Fokina Ул Адмирала Фокина
Ul Svetlanskaya Ул Светланская

Ul Aleutskaya Ул Алеутская
pl Vokzalnaya пл Вокзальная

Ul Nizhneportovaya Ул Нижнепортовая

Ul Pogranichnaya Ул Пограничная
Ul Aleutskaya Ул Алеутская
Ul Batareynaya Ул Батарейная

Ul Ploestkaya Ул Плоестская

Ul Posetskaya Ул Посетская

Ul Morskaya Ул Морская

Ul Zapadnaya Ул Западная

Ul Tigrovaya Ул Тигровая
Ul Naberezhnaya Ул Набережная

Ul Bestuzheva Ул Бестужева
Ul Bezuzheva

trailblazer

Aleksei, the well-travelled owner, is happy to give sightseeing tips. Take bus No 59, 60, 61 or 62 from the railway station to Yaltinskaya (Ялтинская) stop.

In an enviable central location just two minutes' walk from the railway station is

Optimum Hostel (ul Aleutskaya 17, ул Алеутская 17, ☎ 272 9111, 🖳 www.hostel-optimum.ru, dorm/trpl/twn R700/2100/1700, WI-FI). Frequented by a mix of Russian and foreign travellers, the spacious flat is brightly decorated, the dorm has

WHERE TO STAY
12 Hotel Versailles
   Гостиница Версаль
15 Hotel Moryak
   Гостиница Моряк
17 Optimum Hostel
21 Hyatt Burny Vladivostok
   Гостиница Ренесанс
22 Hotel Primorye
   Гостиница Приморье
30 Hotel Hyundai
   Гостиница Хундаи

WHERE TO EAT
3 Kitchen
4 Korea House
   Корейский Дом
5 Supermarket in Clover Leaf
8 Sitiy Gorinich Сытый Горыныч
9 Stolovaya No 1 Столовая No 1
19 Café Nostalgia
   Кафе Ностальги
29 Edem Эдем
31 Palau Fish Restaurant
32 Moloko i Myod Молоко и Мёд
37 La Trattoria Ла Траттория

BARS AND CLUBS
2 Zima Зима
6 Mumiy Troll Music Bar
   Мумий Троль Music Bar
10 Rock's Cocktail Bar

20 Zabriskie Point
   Забриский Поинт
30 Sky Bar

PLACES OF INTEREST
1 Vladivostok Fortress Museum
   Музей Владивостокская
   Крепость
14 I M Arsenyev Regional
   Museum Краеведческий
   Музей И М Арсенева
18 Primorskaya Art Gallery
   Приморская Картинная Галерея
28 Victory of Soviet Power
   Monument Памятник
   «Борцам за Власть Советов»
33 Drama Theatre
   Драматический Театр
34 Submarine Museum
   Комплекс «Боевая Слава
   Краснознаменного
   Тихоокеанского Флота»
35 125th Anniversary of
   Vladivostok Monument
   Обелиск в честь 125-летия
   Основания Города
   Владивостока
36 Krasny Vympel
   «Красный Вымпел»
38 Statue of Nikolai Muravyov-
   Amurski Памятник Николай
   Муравьёв-Амурский

39 Statue of St Cyril and St
   Methodius Памятник Святому
   Кириллу и Святому Мефодию
40 Eagle's Nest Орлиное Гнездо
41 Funicular Railway Фуникулёр
42 Admiral Nevelsky Monument
   Памятник Адмиралу
   Невельскому

SHOPPING
13 Flotsky Univermag
   Флотский Универмаг
16 Dom Knigi Bookshop
   Дом Книги

OTHER
7 Pyat' Zvyozd (Five Stars)
   Пять Звёзд
11 British Consulate
   Консульство Британии
23 Central Post Office & internet
   Почтамт и интернет
24 Railway Station & ATM
   Железнодорожный Вокзал
   & ATM
25 Aeroexpress ticket office
   Аэроэкспресс
26 Marine Terminal
   Морской Вокзал
27 Local Ferry Terminal
   Морской Вокзал Прибрежных
   Сообщении

CITY GUIDES & PLANS

some of the most comfortable bunks we've ever come across, and you can even do laundry – something rarely offered in budget accommodation.

Hyatt Burny Vladivostok **Гостиница Ренесанс** (ul Sukhanova 3, ул Суханова 3, ☎ 406 865, 🖳 www.vladivostok.burny .hyatt.com), a new luxury hotel, is due to open sometime in 2014 but at the time of writing details were not available.

Very popular with Chinese visitors and one of the few inexpensive central options, ***Hotel Moryak*** **Гостиница Моряк** (ul Posteskaya 38, ул Посетская 38, ☎ 249 9499, 🖳 hotelm.ru, sgl/dbl/lux from R1700 /2100/4000, WI-FI) may not look like much from the outside, but the compact rooms are comfy and en suite, and there's a good café on the 2nd floor. Wi-fi doesn't work too well on floor 0.

Near the station, ***Hotel Primorye*** **Гостиница Приморье** (ul Posetskaya 20, ул Посетская 20, ☎ 241 1422, 🖳 www.ho telprimorye.ru, sgl/dbl/lux from R3900/ 4100/7700, WI-FI), popular with Korean and Japanese tourists, has friendly English-speaking staff, sauna, and attractive, spotless rooms, the pricier ones with views of the Golden Horn Bay.

In an attractive 1907 historical building, ***Hotel Versailles*** **Гостиница Версаль** (ul Svetlanskaya 10, ул Светланская 10, ☎ 226 4201, 🖳 www.versailles.vl.ru, sgl/dbl from R6500/7500, WI-FI) has luxurious rooms, along with a gym and *Eurocentric Restaurant Versailles*.

Popular with Asian tour groups, the monolithic ***Hotel Hyundai*** **Гостиница Хёндэ** (ul Semyonovskaya 29, ул Семёновская 29, ☎ 240 2233, 🖳 www .hotelhyundai.ru, dbl/suite R9000/from 17,000, WI-FI) is central and sumptuous. Services includes a health club, swimming-pool, sauna and two very good restaurants – European cuisine at the *Pacific*, and Korean dishes at *Khekimgang*.

Far from the hustle and bustle of Vladivostok, in a pretty forested area near the sea, ***Vlad Motor Inn*** (ul 8-ya 35, Sanatornaya, ул 8-я 35, Санаторная, ☎ 238 8888, 🖳 www.vlad-inn.ru, dbl/lux from R5500/6500, WI-FI) is an attractive retreat popular with expats. Rooms are spacious and light, the restaurant dishes are a mix of European and American, and staff speak English. Take a suburban train to Sanatornaya.

Where to eat
Down by the popular beach at Sportivnaya there are several **cafés** serving drinks and snacks all day.

A restaurant that evokes nostalgia for the tsarist era, ***Café Nostalgia*** **Кафе Ностальгия** (ul Morskaya 6/25, ул Морская 6/25, mains R400-650) serves genuinely good coffee and a smattering of hearty, well-prepared Russian dishes. Good gift shop attached.

Syndicate (ul Komsomolskaya 11 ул Комсомольская 11, 🖳 www.club-syndi cate.ru, steaks R800-2200) is the kind of place you imagine 1930s American gangsters coming to for steak. Because that's the highlight here – from the classic T-bone to the 'Syndicate' house special. An order of perfectly grilled meat just might be the ideal way to end (or start) a Trans-Sib trip, but if you order the wine, watch your wallet.

Stolovaya No 1 **Столовая No 1** (ul Svetlanskaya 1, ул Светланская 1, meals R200) is just that: the top self-serve canteen in the city, in a prime location and featuring an inexpensive range of salads, soups, and meaty mains, with plenty of Russian beers, *kvas* and *mors* to wash it down.

In a similar vein but in a faux-rustic setting, ***Sitiy Gorinich*** **Сытый Горыныч** (ul Admirala Fokina 4, ул Адмирала Фокина 4, meals R180) is the place to fill up on inexpensive Russian dishes until you feel like a contented Zmei Gorinich (mythical three-headed dragon from Russian fairy tales).

Specialising largely in Neptune's subjects (though there's the odd lamb/veal on the bone dish) stylish ***Palau Fish Restaurant*** (ul Sukhanova 1, ул Суханова 1, mains R400-1500) is good for a splurge when it comes to unadorned, beautiful scallops, Kamchatka king crab and other seafood grilled by weight (at least R350/100g) or the likes of flounder baked in bamboo leaf; the rest is pretty poor value for money.

With what looks like Leonardo da Vinci's flying machine strapped to the ceiling, the cosy cellar *La Trattoria* **Ла Траттория** (ul Svetlanskaya 52, ул Светланская 52 [V], mains R400-850) serves a full range of pastas, lasagne, bruschettas and antipasti, accompanied by a full list of fine Italian wines.

All white leather, exposed brick and mirrors, ★ *Moloko i Myod* **Молоко и Мёд** (ul Sukhanova 6a ул Суханова 6a, mains R200-420) is a sleek café with an excellent selection of loose-leaf teas, salads, fresh juices and other light bites; go for the thin and crispy pizza if you want something more substantial. The staff are particularly friendly and efficient.

Open the sliding door into *Korea House* **Корейский Дом** (ul Semyonovskaya 7b ул Семёновская 7б, mains R460-980) and you're presented with understated Korean décor (including traditional masks) and an extensive menu of the likes of spicy pork with kimchi, seafood dumplings, sizzling squid and a numerous sushi sets. The authentic spice is there, as are the accompanying side dishes, and the staff couldn't be more attentive.

At ★ *Kitchen* (ul Pogranichnaya 12, ул Пограничная 12, mains from R300) the name doesn't give much away, but we can tell you that it's a harmonious marriage of stylish décor and beautifully presented, innovative, Eurocentric dishes. The chef prepares such delights as delicate seafood risotto, fresh fig and goat's cheese salad and expertly grilled steak, and there's usually a daily special or two chalked up on the menu outside.

For excellent sushi, try *Edem* **Эдем** (ul Admirala Fokina 22, ул Адмирала Фокина 22, sushi/sashimi combos from R1500, sets from R350), a venerated cellar restaurant with cosy nooks. Discounts on sushi sets between 11am and 5pm.

Other options are the restaurants at the hotels (see Where to stay) and Zima (see Bars and entertainment).

Self-caterers can head for **Clover Leaf** on the corner of ul Aleutskaya and ul Semenovskaya – a shopping mall with a **24-hour supermarket**.

Bars and clubs

It's difficult to say whether ★ *Zima* **Зима** (ul Fintannaya 2 ул Фонтанная 2) is a trendy bar that also does great food, or a great restaurant that's also one of the city's most enjoyable watering holes, but we love it regardless. Place your order on the iPad provided and go for the Leffe beer on tap if you suspect that imbibing all those wonderful cocktails will make you drift into insolvency.

Founded by and named after Vladivostok's most famous band, *Mumiy Troll Music Bar* **Мумий Троль Music Bar** (ul Pogranichnaya 6, ул Пограничная 6, ⌨ www.mumiytrollbar.com) features nightly live acts, great cocktails and Neanderthals at the door who implement 'face control' (see box p164).

Peopled by a young and lively clientele, *Rock's Cocktail Bar* (ul Svetlanskaya 7, ул Светланская 7, ⌨ rocksbar.ru) hosts varied live music, from ska to jazz to rock to hip hop. To enjoy the best night (and day) views of the city while sipping your expensive cocktail among the most moneyed of Vladivostok's business visitors and some high class 'ladies of the night', go to *Sky Bar* (Hotel Hyundai, see opposite).

Zabriskie Point **Забриский Поинт** (ul Naberezhnaya 9a ул Набережная 9a, ⌨ www.zabriskie-point.com), behind Hotel Amursky, plays rock and jazz nightly.

Shopping

Some good souvenirs are sold at **Café Nostalgia Art Shop** (ul Pervaya Morskaya 6/25); take your pick from intricate wooden boat models, paintings of Vladivostok and Asian art. **Flotsky Univermag Флотский Универмаг** (ul Svetlanskaya 11) stocks all sorts of navy-related goodies. **Dom Knigi** bookshop (ul Aleutskaya 23) stocks a few classics, plus Stephen King, in English.

Moving on

By rail From Vladivostok, the fastest (and most expensive) train to Moscow is the firmenny 001 *Rossiya* (alternate days only, 145½hrs). It stops at all the major cities along the Trans-Sib. The only other direct train to Moscow is the slower and considerably

---

❑ **Ferries from Vladivostok to Japan and South Korea**
There is an *Eastern Dream* ferry run by DBS Ferries (Marine Terminal, office No 124, ☎ 230 2664, 🖥 en.go-to-japan.jp/daisenguide/dbscruiseferry) operating between Vladivostok and Sakaiminato, **Japan**, via Donghae, **South Korea**, departing on Wednesdays at 2pm, arriving in Donghae on Thursday morning at 11am, departing at 6pm, and arriving in Sakaiminato at 9am the next day. The ferry then departs for Vladivostok at 7pm on Saturday evening.

Dong Chun Ferry (Marine Terminal, office No 129, ☎ 302 660, 🖥 www.dong chunferry.co.kr – in Russian/Korean) goes to Sokcho, **South Korea,** three times a week in summer, departing from Vladivostok at 11am on Mondays, arriving at Sokcho at 8am on Tuesdays, departing Sokcho at 1pm on Tuesdays, arriving at Zarubino (5hrs' drive from Vladivostok) on Wednesdays at 11am. From Zarubino, the ferry departs again for Sokcho on Thursdays at 4pm, arriving at 11am on Fridays, then leaving for Vladivostok at 4pm the same day and returning to Vladivostok at 5pm on Saturdays.

---

cheaper 099 (alternate days only, 160hrs). The most comfortable train to Khabarovsk (5/day, 11-14¼hrs) is the overnight firmenny 005, though the 107 and 351 are cheaper. The daily 351 continues to Komsomlsk-na-Amure (25¼hrs) and Vanino/Sovetskaya Gavan (40½hrs). The 652 runs to North Korea's Pyongyang (Пхеньян in Russian) on Tuesdays from Ussuriysk (44½hrs), a short train ride from Vladivostok.

By bus The bus station автовокзал (ul Russkaya ул Русская) is 4km north of the centre (see Orientation and services). If you're heading into China, you can take a bus or share a taxi to the border at Grodekovo, four hours from Vladivostok. On the other side you catch a local bus or taxi to Suifenhe (5km), where buses to Harbin run twice a day and trains three times a day. There are two buses to Harbin (daily except Sunday, 8hrs, R3000), departing at 8.20am and 8.50am.

By air The revamped Vladivistok airport (🖥 vvo.aero) is served by several major airlines, including Aeroflot, Transaero, Korean Air, S7 and Vladivostok Air (🖥 www.vladivostokavia.ru).

Domestic departures include: Moscow (1-2 daily, 8hrs), Irkutsk (1-2/day except Tue & Thur, 4hrs), Yekaterinburg (1/day, Wed, Fri & Sun, 7hrs), Khabarovsk (up to 5/day, 1¼hrs), Novosibirsk (2-3/day, 6hrs), St Petersburg (daily except Wed and Sun, 9hrs), Petropavlovsk-Kamchatsky (2-4/day, 3hrs), Yuzhno-Sakhalinsk (up to 5/day, 2hrs), Yakutsk (1-2/day Tue, Wed, Fri & Sat, 2hrs), and Magadan (2-3/day, 2½hrs).

International destinations include Beijing (up to 3/day, 2½hrs), Hong Kong (1-2/day except Tue, 3hrs), Tokyo (2/day on Mon, Wed, Fri & Sat), Pyongyang (2/day on Wed, 3hrs), and Seoul (up to 4/day, 4½hrs).

Ulaanbaatar
Улаанбаатар

[GMT +8; population: 1,144,954] The world's coldest capital is a fascinating place to visit even if it is, at first sight, a misshapen jumble of Soviet-style concrete apartment blocks, ancient Buddhist temples, old palaces and Dubai-style curved glass buildings jostling each other for space amidst chaotic traffic snarls. Things are changing fast here and the capital is filled with fascinating incongruities. Nomadic herders from the countryside have filled the city's outskirts with their *ger* tents and today they share the sidewalks of downtown Ulaanbaatar with young, professional urbanites.

Mongolia is a haven for adventure-seeking backpackers, with Ulaanbaatar's guesthouses serving as their base. The relatively free and democratic political system, compared with other nations in the region, has made Mongolia a darling of the international donor community. In bars and restaurants you'll likely run into UN officials, US Peace Corps volunteers or staffers from international NGOs, who make up much of the city's expat community.

Home to just under half the country's 2.8 million population, Ulaanbaatar sits in a basin surrounded by four mountains: Bogd Uul, Songino Khairkhan, Chingeltei and Bayanzurkh, all part of the beautiful Khentii range, the southernmost boundary of the great Siberian taiga. The city experiences great climatic extremes; the temperature ranges from -49°C (-46°F) in winter to 38°C (93°F) in summer. Ulaanbaatar is 1350m above sea level.

The busiest time to visit Ulaanbaatar is during the **Naadam Festival**, held between 11 and 13 July (book well in advance, as demand for accommodation and Trans-Mongolian train tickets outstrips supply). The festival involves the three traditional Mongolian sports of horse-riding, wrestling and archery as well as anklebone shooting (see box pp358-9).

See pp373-6 for information about other places to visit in Mongolia.

HISTORY

Home of the Living Buddha

For much of its 350-year existence the town was little more than a semi-nomadic settlement. From 1639 to 1778 it moved some 30 times, like a migrating *ger* (yurt) city. Da Khure Lamasery, built here in 1639, was the abode of one of the three most important lines of 'Living Buddhas', the others being the Dalai Lama in Tibet and the Panchen Lama in Peking. The one at Da Khure was usually a child who had died, or rather was murdered, shortly before reaching puberty, since it was believed that the soul of a deity could dwell only in the body of a child. Between 1639 and 1706 the town was known as Örgöö, from the Mongolian word for 'palace'. From 1706 to 1911 it was Ikh Khuree or Da Khure to Mongolians, or Urga to foreigners.

Independence

When Mongolia declared itself independent of China in 1911 the city was renamed Niislel Khurehe. By this time it had become a large trading centre on the route between China and Russia. There were, in fact, three separate cities here: the Chinese, the Russian and the Mongolian. The Chinese and Russian cities were engaged in the tea and silk trades but the Mongolian city's concern was the salvation (or rather the liberation) of souls. There was a population of some 30,000 Buddhist monks in the lamaseries here.

Soviet Mongolia

After the Communist Party came to power in 1921 the capital was renamed Ulaanbaatar, meaning 'Red Hero'. With considerable help from the USSR, the city was redesigned; the architectural origins of its austere tower blocks and municipal buildings are recognisably Soviet. Besides the hideous multi-storey buildings, close ties to the Communist giant led to the destruction of private enterprise, redistribution of wealth, and the creation of cooperatives which led to famine, just as it had done in the Soviet Union. Political repressions and persecution of religious figures led to the deaths and disappearances of 27,000 people in 1937 alone, almost two-thirds of whom were monks. When Sino-Soviet relations soured in the 1960s, Mongolia sided with the latter, resulting in a disastrous loss of trade with China and increased economic dependence on the Soviet Union.

From totalitarianism to democracy

When the Soviet Union fell apart, the resulting shockwaves led to hunger strikes and pro-democracy protests. In May 1990, an amendment to the constitution allowed multi-party elections and the resulting coalition government included the old Communists rather than expelling them completely, with the Mongolian People's Revolutionary Party (renamed the Mongolian People's Party in 2010) continuing to lead the country until 1996 – a clean continuous run since 1921. The first few post-communism years were a difficult time for the Mongolian economy as it collapsed without the Soviet subsidies. Nevertheless, the country recovered by building relationships with European countries, Japan, South Korea and the United States. In the mid 1990s the city experienced a private-sector boom, with new buildings springing up everywhere and shops and restaurants opening. As in Russia, most of the money for this came from Communist-era power brokers who quickly took control of privatised state assets. In 1999-2000 Mongolia was hit by severe weather conditions: a serious drought followed by an extremely cold winter. Massive loss of livestock caused food shortages and forced many nomadic herders to flee to the city, though the Communist era's social-support system no longer existed to help them. In 2003, Mongolia embarked on the world's biggest mining project – that of the Oyu Tolgoi copper mine in the south Gobi desert, the copper mine becoming responsible for 30% of the country's GDP. Since 2010 the Chinese have engaged in major oil drilling in Eastern Mongolia, the venture also bringing the Mongolian government much-needed revenue but prompting fears of imminent ecological disasters.

WHAT TO SEE AND DO

Chinggis Khan Square Чингис Хаан талбай (formerly Sühbaatariin Talbai, Sükhbaatar Square Сухбаатарын Талбай)

At the heart of the city is this large square, the scene of the pro-democracy demonstrations in 1990 that led to the first free elections. Today it's the site of patriotic celebrations and a popular meeting place. At the centre is a mounted statue of the Mongolian revolutionary leader Damdinii Sühbaatar in heroic pose on a horse; newlyweds queue up to have their photos taken here.

The square is dominated by **Parliament House** on the north side, with a massive bronze statue of the seated Chinggis Khan in front of it, flanked by equally large statues of his son, Ögedei (west) and grandson Kublai (east), while the entrance is guarded by two legendary warriors, Boruchu and Mukhlai. There is a large ceremonial *ger* inside the courtyard of Parliament House which is used for receiving visiting dignitaries.

On the north-east side of the square is the modernistic Cultural Palace, housing the **Mongolian National Modern Art Gallery Монголын Уран Зургийн Үзэсгэлэн** (🖳 www.art-gallery.mn, 10am-6pm daily, T3500), which features fascinating depictions of Mongolian nomadic life through painting and sculpture (enter from the courtyard, accessed from Amaryn Gudamj).

The salmon-coloured building in the south-east corner of the square is the **Opera and Ballet Theatre**, while the red building to the south-west is the **Mongolian Stock Exchange**, opened in 1992.

The excellent ★ **National Museum of Mongolia Монголын Үндэсний Музей** (🖳 www.nationalmuseum.mn, 9.30am-6pm daily mid May to Aug, rest of the year 9.30am-5.30pm Tue-Sat, adult/student T5000/2800) is found in the concrete structure on the north-west side of the square. The well-presented exhibits (with English captioning) trace the history of the country from the Stone Age and Bronze Age (think petroglyphs, deer stones, steles, Uighur- and Hun-era burial sites) to the post-1990 transition from communism to democracy.

Highlights include the haul of gold treasure, discovered by archaeologists in 2001, a superb section featuring national costume from different parts of the country – including the elaborate silver jewellery once made by the Dariganga and the heavy bling worn by the Khalkh (some up to 25kg of silver at a time) – as well as traditional musical instruments (keep an eye out for a wind instrument made from a human thigh bone and some splendid *morin khuur* – horse-head fiddles), and a collection of ornate snuff boxes.

Mongol Horde fans shouldn't miss the outstanding collection on the third floor which includes 12th-century armour and weaponry, correspondence in Latin and Persian between Pope Innocent IV and Guyuk Khaan with the khan's own seal, and a huge scale model of ancient Karakorum.

Finally, the section on Mongolian culture features a traditionally furnished ger, multicoloured sheep's anklebone set, horse tackle and more, while the 20th-century section tackles Mongolia's Socialist Era, as the Communist period is known; check out Sükhbaatar's hollow whip, used to smuggle a secret letter from the Bogd Khan to the Russians, requesting the Red Army's help.

CITY GUIDES & PLANS

❏ **Snapping that pricey photo**

You'll find that most museums charge up to five times as much as the entry fee for the privilege of taking photos or shooting a video. Expect to pay T6000-10,000 for photos and T12,000 for video, though Bogd Khan Winter Palace has taken it all to a new level, charging T50,000 for photos and T70,000 for video. They really don't want you to take photos.

★ **Gandan Khiid (Gandantegchenlin Khiid)** Гандантэгчэнлин Хийд
This **monastery** complex (8.30am-7pm daily, T5000) at the northern end of
Zanabazaryn Gudamj, the name of which translates as 'the great place of complete joy', is home to the spiritual head of Mongolia, the Khamba Lama, and is
one of the largest and most important monasteries in the country. Mongolia
once had 700 monasteries but virtually all were destroyed in the Communist
crackdown at the end of the 1930s. Between 14,000 and 18,000 monks were
killed and tens of thousands forced to give up their vows. Following the pro-
democracy movement in 1990, restrictions were eased allowing some monasteries to reopen and Gandan began operating as something more than a tourist
showpiece.

GANDAN KHIID (MONASTERY)

The original monastery on this site was
built in 1785. The first group of new buildings
was put up in 1938; along with the main temple
there are stupas, a library and accommodation
for the monks – today the monastery is home to
over 600. Powdered juniper, to be thrown into
the big burner outside the temple as an offering,
is dispensed in a side building.

From the main entrance, the path leads to
the right to two temples: the most significant
ceremonies are held in the one to the north-east,
Ochidara Temple; the statue inside the glass is Tsongkhapa, responsible for
founding the Gelugpa sect. The main path from the entrance leads to the splendid white main temple, Migjid Janraisig Süm, where you can marvel at the
26.5m tall Buddha statue, made of copper and covered in gold. The original
statue, commissioned by the 8th Bogd Khan in 1911 to restore his eyesight after
a bout of syphillis, was taken by the Russians in 1937 and rumour has it that it
was melted down to make weaponry. The current statue dates back to 1996, paid
for by donations from Japan and Nepal, its hollow interior filled with 334
sutras, 2 million mantra bundles, 27 tonnes of medicinal herbs and a ger complete with furniture.

It's best to visit the monastery during morning prayers around 9am to
observe the intricate ceremony at Vajradhara Temple.

Bogd Khan Winter Palace Богд Хааны Өвлийн Ордон
The winter palace of the last Bogd Khan ('holy king') of Mongolia (Chingisiin
Örgön Chölöö, 9am-5.30pm daily May-Sep, until 4.30pm and Fri-Tue Oct-Apr,
T5000) is a wonderful old place, full of ghosts and resembling Beijing's
Forbidden City on a much smaller scale and in need of a coat of paint.

Entered through a gateway guarded by four fierce-looking incarnations, the
palace – the home of Mongolia's last king and eighth Living Buddha, Jebtzun
Damba Hutagt VIII (aka the Bogd Khan) for 20 years – comprises two courtyards with small pavilions on each side, miraculously left intact by the
Russians. Inside the six temples – their design showing heavy Manchu influence right up to the pagoda-style roofs and roof guardian figures – there are

extensively labelled exhibits of *thangkas* (Buddhist devotional paintings), musical instruments and Buddha figures wearing expressions of both tranquility and rage, as well as a collection of musical instruments used in religious ceremonies, a bronze Zanabazar and an ebony model of the Heaven Palace.

Bogd Khan Winter Palace is the white building on the right as you pass through the main gate. Inside, the museum's exhibits include Bogd Khan's throne, ebony and marble bed, his seat with 25 cushions, making him a real-life 'princess and the pea' (in this classic story the princess could feel a single dried pea through many layers of bedding); there is also his contribution to the demise of endangered species, including a fur robe made of 816 sables, and his luxurious ger (the exterior covered with the skins of 150 snow leopards, and containing a stove and portable altar). Don't miss the finely detailed paintings of the winter and summer palaces, complete with copulating camels and tiny people engaging in brawls and all sorts of other activities.

To get here, take bus No 7 heading south along Chingisiin Örgön Chölöö and get off after you've crossed the overpass.

Choijin Lama Temple Museum Чойжин Ламын Хийд-Музей

Preserved under communism as a museum of religion, this temple complex (9am-7pm daily mid May-Sep, 10am-4pm daily Oct-mid May, T5000), which hasn't been in operation since 1938, was the former home of Luvsan Haidav Choijin Lama, the brother of the 8th Bogdo Gegen (Bogd Khan). They were both born Tibetans.

The five brightly coloured wooden temple buildings house some beautiful and fascinating exhibits, including a large collection of *tsam* (ornate masks for Buddhist mystery plays) and graphic depictions of suffering in the underworld. In the main temple, featuring statues of Choijin Lama and Sakayamuni (historic Buddha), take a close look at the golden seated figure of Baltung Choimba (spiritual teacher of the Bogd Khan), not a statue but the mummified body of a lama, encased in gold. In the northern pavilion you may also want to check out the statues, which depict Tantric sexual positions, while Yadam Süm is home to bronze and wooden depictions of various deities, some made by the famous Mongolian sculptor Zanabazar. There's a self-portrait of the man himself inside the Amgalan Süm.

★ Zanabazar Fine Arts Museum Занабазарын Уран Зургийн Музей

This fascinating art museum (Juulchin Gudamj, 10am-6pm daily May-Sep, to 5pm rest of year, T5000) includes a comprehensive display of thangkas, the wonderfully detailed Kalachakra mandala, as well as other religious exhibits, such as fine Buddha statues, and mural paintings from temples. There's also elaborate silver jewellery worn by Buriat, Barga and Khalkha women, knife and chopstick sets worn by men, ceremonial costume and masks of fearsome multi-eyed, fanged deities from Buddhist Tsan dances. You also find a number of Mongol zurag paintings, depicting traditional nomad life, with animals, archery and airag feasts featuring heavily in the fine detail reminiscent of *Where's Wally?* books; carvings and sculptures, including numerous works by

Mongolia's most-celebrated sculptor and artist after whom the museum is named, and woodblock prints. The Red Ger Gallery on the 1st floor features some fine examples of contemporary Mongolian art.

International Intellectual Museum

By far the most original exhibition in the city, the Intellectual Museum (10am-6pm Mon-Sat, T3000), on a tiny side street off Ikh Toiruu near its junction with Peace Ave, displays the life work of Tumen-Ulzii Zandraa, a genius who from the age of 11 has been designing and building incredibly complex, three-dimensional Mongolian wood puzzles. Boggling to the mind and dazzling to the eye with their ornate workmanship, these come in endless shapes and sizes,

❑ NAADAM FESTIVAL

Naadam is the biggest and most important Mongolian festival and is held in Ulaanbaatar and most other Mongolian towns between 11 and 13 July; some are held later on in the month. In the ethnically Mongolian region of Tuva, in southern Siberia, the Tuvans of Russia celebrate the similar Naadym on 15 August.

In Mongolia, even though since between the 1921 revolution and the fall of communism the festival was organised in honour of the Mongolian People's Revolutionary Party, its roots go back several thousand years and it comprises three manly games: wrestling, archery and horse-racing – skills considered essential in ancient times.

In the capital, the festival kicks off with parades and carnivals and an opening ceremony at the **Naadam stadium** (see map p361), which lasts for around two hours on the morning of the first day. Check out the events programme in the English-language newspapers and in hotels and hostels to find out what events are taking place during and even in the lead-up to the festival.

While admission to the events themselves is free, you need tickets for the opening and closing ceremonies, as well as the final round of wrestling. You can purchase tickets from tour operators and hotels, with the best seats in the stadium (protected from the elements and with the best view of the action) going for as much as T50,000. You can pick up cheap but marked-up tickets for as little as T5000 from the scalpers who hang around the stadium, though that way you're not guaranteed a seat.

Smaller Naadams take place all over the country and can be a better way of getting really close to the action (or even participating in it!).

Wrestling

The national sport begins with either 512 or 1024 wrestlers competing in a single-elimination tournament that lasts nine rounds; the event is held in the Wrestling Stadium. The final round, which takes place before the closing ceremony, is the most exciting. Rounds are untimed and a wrestler only loses if he touches the ground with any part of his body except hands and feet. Competitors wear traditional boots, *zodog* (open-chest vest) and *shuudag* (tight-fitting shorts).

The style of a wrestler's movements depends on which bird he is representing, be it a falcon or a hawk, and before each faceoff, the two wrestlers will slap their thighs twice, meaning: 'Whether I win or lose, I will have no complaints.' The loser will untie his *zodog* as a mark of respect to the winner and all contestants perform the 'eagle dance' before the start of the tournament, imitating the bird's flight.

from cubes to animals to copies of world-famous buildings to puzzle chess sets, decorated with gemstones (check out the tiny chess set and the one featuring an evolution of gers), to metal puzzles. The largest wooden puzzle in the collection consists of 673 pieces and requires 56,831 moves to take it apart. You're led around by an English-speaking guide and visitors are challenged to try their hand at the simpler puzzles. The cash prize of US$100,000 for dismantling and reassembling a silver turtle in under 10 minutes, requiring 108 moves, is yet to be claimed. The little gift shop stocks plenty of puzzles for purchase and the ambitious owner's dream is to turn the entire building into something resembling a giant puzzle.

Horse-racing

Mongolian horse-racing, unlike Western horse-racing, is a cross-county race of between 15km and 30km, which takes place on the open steppe and is divided into six categories in accordance with the horse's age: the two-year olds do 15km, while the six-year olds and the stallions do 30km; the rest fall in between. The jockeys are children, some of them as young as five years old.

The winning horse of each race is given the title 'The Winner of Ten Thousand', while the last horse is given the title of 'Complete Happiness'. It is the herders' tradition to praise the last horse rather than blame it to encourage it and its young rider to win the next race. The winning riders are given *airag* to drink and are then anointed with it, along with their steeds. It's believed that a winning horse's sweat brings luck, so don't be surprised if you see a crowd of spectators chase the winning horse after it crosses the finishing line to scrape the horse's sides and anoint their faces with its sweat. The races kick off at Hui Doloon Kutag, 28km west of the city; you can either take a bus or minivan there from outside Naadam stadium, or grab a taxi. Go early as the late morning traffic is murder.

Archery

The nomadic tribes have been using a bow and arrow for over 3000 years, first for hunting and then in battle and as a sport. The Huns had a multitude of different arrows for different purposes and used archery contests to test their warriors' strength, eyesight and ability to shoot. There are all kinds of traditional archery competitions, ranging from shooting a sheep's skin from a distance of 40 bows or shooting at balls made of hide while galloping on a horse. The Naadam event, however, consists of shooting 40 arrows at targets that are walls of leather rings, 4m long and 50cm high, from a distance of either 75m (men) or 60m (women). Women only shoot 20 arrows. The judges emit one of three kinds of calls (*uukhai*) after each shot, indicating its quality, and the person to hit the targets the most times is proclaimed the best *mergen*. This competition is held in an open (archery) stadium next to the main stadium. The composite bows are sightless and made of layered horn, wood and bark, while the arrows are made from young willow branches and vulture feathers.

Anklebone shooting

This lesser event takes place in a smaller tent next to the archery stadium and consists of flicking a sheep's anklebone at a target (also made of anklebones), around 3m away, amidst much excited shouting and yodelling.

CITY GUIDES & PLANS

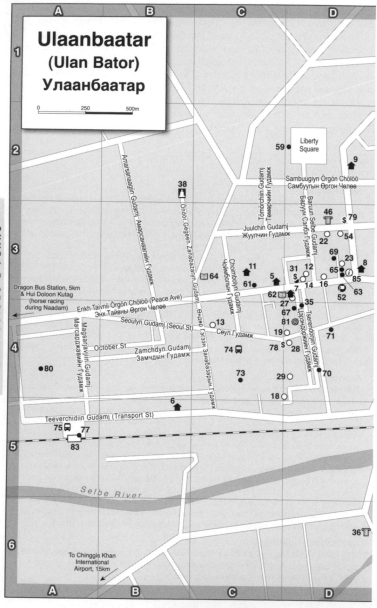

Ulaanbaatar
(Ulan Bator)
Улаанбаатар

0   250   500m

Liberty Square

59

9

Sambuugiyn Örgön Chölöö
Самбуугын Өргөн Чөлөө

Amarsanaagiin Gudamj · Амарсанаагийн Гудамж

Öndör Gegeen Zanabazaryn Gudamj

Tömörchin Gudamj
Төмөрчин Гудамж

Juulchin Gudamj
Жуулчин Гудамж

Chombolyn Gudamj · Чойболын Гудамж

38

46   79
54
22
69   23   8
31   12   65   85
5    $ 63
11   7   52
64   61   62   14   16
27   35
81   @
13   19   67   71
Séoulyn Gudamj (Seoul St)   28   70
74   78 $
73   29
18
6

Baruun Selbe Gudamj · Баруун Сэлбэ Гудамж

Tserendorjiin Gudamj · Цэрэндоржийн Гудамж

Enkh Taivnii Örgön Chölöö (Peace Ave)
Энх Тайвны Өргөн Чөлөө

Dragon Bus Station, 5km
& Hui Doloon Kutag
(horse racing
during Naadam)

Öndör Gazan Zanabazaryn Gudamj

Magsarjaviin Gudamj · Магсаржавийн Гудамж

October St

Zamchdyn Gudamj
Замчдын Гудамж

Séul Gudamj

80

Teeverchidiin Gudamj (Transport St)

75   77
83

Selbe River

36

To Chinggis Khan
International
Airport, 15km

Ikh Toiruu
Ikh Surguuliin Gudamj
Их Сургуулийн Гудамж

(Big Ring Rd) Их Тойруу

Sühbaatarin Gudamj Сүхбаатарын Гудамж

Baga Toiruu
Бага Тойруу

Erkhuugiin Gudamj
Эрхүүгийн Гудамж

Tokyo Gudamj Токио Гудамж

Namaste, 1km

Baga Toiruu Бага Тойруу

Zaluuchuudiin Örgön Chölöö
Залуучуудын Өргөн Чөлөө

Tokyo Gudamj – Токио Гудамж

Chinggis
Khan Talbai
Чингис Хаан
талбаи

Enkh Taivnii

Örgön Chölöö

Ikh Toiruu (Big Ring Rd) Их Тойруу

Jamyan Guunii Gudamj
Жамян Гуний Гудамж

Choidog Gudamj
Чойдог Гудамж

Erkhuugiin Gudamj
Эрхүүгийн Гудамж

Foreign Embassy
St

Nairamdal
Park

Chingislin Örgön Chölöö Чингисийн Өргөн Чөлөө

Olimpin Gudamj (Olympic St) Олимпийн Гудамж

Tuul River

43

66

Zaisan
Memorial, 1km

1 2 3 4 5 6

E F G H

55 53 84 26 51 49 25 2 21 72 44 10 40 58 41 4 30 3 15 47 48 42 45 20 39 76 56 50 68 1 57 32 17 24 37 60 82 34 33

MAP KEY – WHERE TO STAY
1 [E3] Blue Sky Hotel & Tower
2 [G2] Chinggis Khaan Hotel
3 [E3] Hotel Örgöö
4 [H3] Kempinski Hotel Khan Palace
5 [C3] Khonghor Guesthouse
6 [B5] LG Guesthouse A
7 [D3] LG Guesthouse B
8 [D3] Nassan's Guesthouse
9 [D2] Sunpath Mongolia
10 [E3/F3] Tuushin Hotel
11 [C3] Zaya's Hostel

WHERE TO EAT AND DRINK
12 [D3] American Burgers and Fries
13 [C4] BD's Mongolian Barbeque &
Detroit (American Bar)
14 [D3] Beer tent
15 [E3] Biwon (in Central Tower Food
Court)
16 [D3] Café Amsterdam
17 [E4] Chinggis Khan Irish Pub
18 [D4] Dalai Eej Market &
Merkuri Market
19 [D4] Dublin
20 [G3] Hazara Indian Restaurant
21 [E2] Le Bistro Français
22 [D3] Luna Blanca
23 [D3] Michele's French Bakery
24 [E4] Millie's Café

25 [G2] Namaste
26 [E2] Namaste
27 [D3] Revolution
28 [D4] Ristorante Marco Polo
29 [D4] Sacher Coffee
30 [H3] Sakura
31 [D3] State Department Store
Supermarket
32 [E4] Veranda

PLACES OF INTEREST
33 [E6] Anklebone Shooting Area
34 [E6] Archery Stadium
35 [D4] Beatles' monument, The
36 [D6] Bogd Khan Winter Palace
Богд Хааны хвлийн Ордон
37 [E4] Choijin Lama Temple
Museum
Чойжин Ламын Хийд-Музей
38 [B2] Gandan Khiid
(Gandantegchenling Khiid)
Гандантэгчэнлин Хиид
39 [H3] International Intellectual
Museum
40 [E3] National Museum of Mongolia
Монголын Үндэсний Музеи
41 [F3] Mongolian National Modern
Art Gallery
42 [E3] Mongolian Stock Exchange
43 [E6] Naadam Stadium

Zaisan Memorial Зайсан
Perched atop a hill at the southern edge of town is the remarkable Zaisan Memorial, built by the Soviets, with panoramic views of the city. The colourful murals and gigantic statue of a soldier celebrate Russian-Mongolian cooperation in WWII and the Soviet space programme.

Nearby is a large golden Buddha statue, erected in 2005. To get there take bus No 7 along Chingisiin Örgön Chölöö and get off at the end-stop, 'Zaisan' (Зайсан).

PRACTICAL INFORMATION
Orientation and services
The city's main thoroughfare is Enkh Taivnii Örgön Chölöö (Peace Ave), lined with eateries, businesses, travel agencies and hotels; it stretches for around 10km and is perpetually clogged with traffic. The heart of the city is Chinggis Khan Square

Чингис Хаан талбай (formerly called Sühbaatariin Talbai, Sukhe Bator Sq), while another major landmark is the centrally located State Department Store, with most attractions, embassies, restaurants and hotels located within walking distance of either of them.

PLACES OF INTEREST *(cont'd)*
44 [E2] Parliament House
45 [G3] Wrestling Stadium
46 [D3] Zanabazar Fine Arts Museum
     Занабазарын Уран Зургийн
     Музей

EMBASSIES AND CONSULATES
47 [G3] British Embassy
48 [E3] Canadian Consulate
49 [F2] Chinese Embassy
50 [E3] French Embassy
51 [E2] German Embassy
52 [D3] Russian Embassy
53 [F1] US Embassy

NIGHTLIFE & ENTERTAINMENT
54 [D3] Face Club
55 [F1] Hollywood
56 [F3] Metropolis
57 [E4] National Academic Drama
     Theatre
58 [E3] Opera and Ballet Theatre
59 [D2] Tengis (cinema)
60 [E4] Tumen Ekh Song & Dance
     Ensemble

SHOPPING
61 [C3] Antique & Art Gallery
62 [C3] Books in English

63 [D3] Gobi Cashmere Shop
64 [C3] Map Shop
65 [D3] Mary & Martha Mongolia
66 [H4] Narantuul Market
67 [D4] Tsagaan Alt Wool Shop

TOUR OPERATORS
68 [E3] Blue Bandana Expeditions
69 [D3] Ger to Ger
70 [D4] Karakorum Expeditions
71 [D4] Legend Tour
72 [E2] Nomadic Journeys
73 [C4] Wind of Mongolia

OTHER
74 [C4] Bus station
75 [A5] Buses to Ulan-Ude
76 [E3] Central Post Office
77 [A5] Domestic ticket-booking office
78 [C4] Golomt Bank
79 [D3] Golomt Bank
80 [A4] International railway ticket
     booking office
81 [D4] Internet Center
82 [E4] Office of Immigration,
     Naturalization & Foreign
     Citizens
83 [A5] Railway station
84 [G1] SOS Medica Mongolia Clinic
85 [D3] Tourist information centre

CITY GUIDES & PLANS

From Ulaanbaatar railway station to Chinggis Khan Square is about 2km. Trolleybus No 4 runs from the station to the square every half-hour, or else it's a 20-minute walk to Peace Ave.

Most long-distance buses depart from the 'Dragon' bus station, on Peace Ave, about 8km west of the centre. Taxis there cost around T5000, or take bus No 26, 27 or 32 heading west along Peace Ave.

Street addresses and building numbers are rarely used, making many places hard to locate. To complicate matters further, many buildings are set back in no-man's land between streets, entrances to guest-houses are usually in the back of the building, and many businesses, especially travel offices, have no signs!

Information There's a private **tourist information centre** at the corner of Baga Toiruu and Peace Ave that's actually a tour agency but nevertheless offers useful info about the city.

The **central post office** (see p364) sells maps of Mongolia, including topographical ones, and the Ulaanbaatar City Map, all updated annually. The best place for detailed maps for other parts of Mongolia is the **Map Shop** (Ikh Toiruu, 9am-1pm & 2-6pm Mon-Fri, 10am-4pm Sat). There is also an **information booth** at the airport that opens for arriving flights.

English-language weeklies include the *Mongol Messenger* (💻 www.mongolia-web.com), available from Ulaanbaatar Hotel among other places. There's also the *UB Post* (💻 ubpost.mongolnews.mn), and the free *UB Guide*, containing local news and entertainment info. The Arts Council of Mongolia (🖳 www.artscouncil.mn) produces a monthly calendar that covers events, exhibitions and goings-on at most museums, galleries and theatres.

Mongolia's tourism department website is 🖳 www.mongoliatourism.gov.mn.

Money and banks The *tugrik* or togrog (MNT) is the Mongolian unit of currency; it comes in notes of 1, 5, 10, 20, 50, 100, 500, 1000, 5000, 10,000 and 20,000. Mongolian currency is almost impossible to find or change outside the country, so get rid of it before you leave Mongolia, either in Ulaanbaatar or with the help of the unofficial money changers who await you on platforms of border towns. Many hotels and banks will exchange hard currency for tugriks, and buy tugriks.

ATMs are found on the 5th floor of the ever-helpful State Department Store, in the more upmarket hotels, and also the bigger banks; note that they tend to be located inside the banks and 24-hour ATMs are thin on the ground.

You can change your money for a decent rate on the ground floor of the State Department Store (Peace Ave 44). **Golomt Bank** (several branches around town including Seoul St and the corner of Juulchin Gudamj & Baga Toiruu) has 24-hour ATMs.

❏ **Exchange rates**

To get the latest rates of exchange see 🖳 www.xe.com

	Tugrik
Aus$1	T1645
Can$1	T1607
China Y10	T2851
Euro€1	T2449
Japan ¥100	T1740
NZ$1	T1528
Sing$1	T1416
S Africa R10	T1672
UK£1	T2974
US$1	T1772

Post and telecommunications The **Central Post Office** (8am-9pm Mon-Fri, 9am-8pm Sat & Sun) is on the corner of Peace Ave and Chinggis Khan Square. The postal service is reasonably reliable but can be slow, so allow a couple of weeks for a postcard to reach Europe or the US.

These days **International telephone calls** can be made for free or very cheaply via Skype at an internet café or via your own wi-fi enabled device at any wi-fi hotspot. Otherwise you can make reasonably inexpensive calls abroad from central Telecom offices in any Mongolian town. If you have an unlocked mobile phone and are planning on spending a while in Mongolia, it's a good idea to get a local pay-as-you-go SIM card from Mobicom or G-Mobile outlet.

There are some **internet cafés** in town (look for интэрнэт кафэ signs), though connection can be slow and they are becoming obsolete, thanks to the proliferation of wi-fi. One of the largest is **Internet Center** (Tserendorjiin Gudamj 65, 9am-2am daily). Numerous **free wi-fi** hotspots are scattered about town, plus you can get online in the vast majority of hotels and hostels.

Embassies and consulates **British Embassy** (Enkh Taivnii Örgön Chölöö 30, ☎ 458 133); **Canadian Consulate** (Central Tower, suites 603-607, Chinggis Khan Square, ☎ 332 500, 🖳 www.mongolia.gc .ca); **Chinese Embassy** (5 Zaluuchuudiin Örgön Chölöö, ☎ 323 940, visa section: 9.30am-noon Mon, Wed & Fri); **French Embassy** (Enkh Taivnii Örgön Chölöö 3, ☎ 324 519); **German Embassy** (Baga Toiruu 2, Negdsen Undestnii Gudamj, ☎ 323 325, 🖳 www.ulan-bator.diplo.de); **Russian Embassy** (Enkh Taivnii Örgön Chölöö 6a, ☎ 326 037, 2-3pm Mon-Fri for visa applications); **US Embassy** (Ikh Toiruu 59, ☎ 329 095, 🖳 mongolia.usembassy.gov).

Visa extensions and registration It's possible to **extend** your visa for up to 30 extra days at the Office for Immigration, Naturalisation and Foreign Citizens (9am-1pm & 2-5pm Mon-Fri, 9am–1pm Wed, ☎ 011-313616), which is at 11 Chinggis Ave,

❑ **Visas for onward travel**

Getting a **Chinese visa** is fairly straightforward, though it's best to get it in your home country if possible. The Chinese embassy issues transit visas (US$35, valid for seven days from date of entry) and single-/double-entry tourist visas (US$35/70, valid for 30 days). Visas take four working days to process or you can pay US$20/30 extra to get it done in 2-3 days/same day. US citizens pay US$150 for all visas. You must provide your passport, a passport photo, proof of departure from China (ie plane ticket), proof of booked accommodation for at least three nights and a printout of a recent bank statement; visas must be paid for in US$ cash. Passports can be dropped off between 9am and noon on Mondays, Wednesdays and Fridays; pickup is between 4 and 5pm on the same days. Trying to get a visa in August or early September can be difficult as Mongolian students queue up from 6am and it's a case of first come, first served. For up-to-date information, see ☐ mn.china-embassy.org.

Obtaining a **Russian visa** is a far more tricky process because, in addition to a passport-sized photo, the antiquated Soviet rules require you to have an 'invitation' in order to get your 21-day visa (costs vary depending on your nationality but tend to be between US$30 and US$200). The visa itself can be issued in a day or two, depending on how much you're willing to pay, but can take 2-3 weeks. Tourist visas are issued to American, French, Dutch and Australian citizens, while citizens of the UK, Germany and New Zealand cannot get tourist visas here, but they can get transit visas of up to 7 days – enough time to reach Moscow by train. To obtain a transit visa, you must show the consul your onward travel tickets so that he knows exactly when you are due to leave Russia. Transit visas can take up to 4 days to process.

Legend Tour (Seoul St, Sant Asar Trading Centre, ☎ 315 158, ☐ www.legend tour.ru, 9am-1pm & 2-6pm Mon-Fri) can provide visa support.

on the loop road that runs off Chinggis Ave, inside the Department of Transport Building, on the west side of the Peace Bridge, opposite Naran Plaza. To extend a visa, you'll need your passport, a passport-sized photo and an application form (T1000). The processing fee is about US$5 and visa extensions cost US$15 for the first seven days, after which you pay US$2 per day for up to 23 additional days. You may not extend a transit visa. Some guesthouses may be able to do the visa extension for you for an additional fee and it's less time-consuming to let them do it. The extension is done on the same day.

If you intend to stay in Mongolia for more than 30 days, regardless of whether you need a visa or not, you must **register** within seven days of arrival at the same office. The process is free, but you'll need a passport-sized photo and about US$0.90 for the application form. It's best to go in the morning.

Medical SOS Medica Mongolia Clinic (4a Bldg, Ikh Toiruu, ☎ 464 325, 9am-6pm Mon-Fri, mobile number for 24-hour on-call doctors ☎ 9911 0335), staffed by Western doctors, is the best place for an emergency, though its rates are high and it pays to have proper travel insurance.

Local transport

It is not necessary to use local transport in the city centre because most places of interest can be reached on foot and since the introduction of traffic lights for pedestrians, you no longer have to defy every time you cross a street (see box p366).

To get to outlying attractions, you can use the extensive **bus** (T350) and **trolleybus**

❑ **Emergency numbers**
Medical emergency ☎ 103
Police ☎ 102

CITY GUIDES & PLANS

(T200) system that covers the city, with bus route maps displayed at most bus stops. Bus 22 stops near Tengis cinema stop around 500m away from Chinggis Khan International Airport (2/hr, 30mins, T600), while a taxi should cost around T18,000.

Official taxis cost T450 per kilometre, though rigged meters can be a problem. Expect to pay about T3500 for a ride from the railway station, though it may be cheaper if you hail a taxi a little way down the street and not directly at the station.

Where to stay

Most of the prices in this section are listed in US$, since many guesthouses and hotels set their rates in dollars and then collect the equivalent in *tugriks*.

Budget accommodation

The city's hostels and guesthouses have international standards in terms of cleanliness etc and are good places to arrange trips to the countryside (see box pp372-3). Most also provide visa services, sell rail tickets and offer free railway station pickup.

Sunpath Mongolia (Baga Toiruu 37-56, door code 13, ☎ 326 323, 🖳 www.sunpath-mongolia.com, dorm/dbl US$6/20-25, WI-FI) is a welcoming family-run hostel that consists of two apartments on the 2nd floor of a residential buildings. Good facilities, including guest kitchens, and their tours come highly recommended, though some travellers have mentioned that the welcome gets less warm if you're just looking for a place to stay without doing a tour.

❏ Street names

Finding your way around Ulaanbaatar is tricky: street names are now written in Mongolian Cyrillic, which has a few more characters than Russian Cyrillic. There is no single accepted way for names to be transliterated into Latin letters: Ulaanbaatar, for example, is often written Ulan Bator.

The Mongolian word for 'street' is *gudamj*, 'avenue' is *örgön chölöö* (meaning 'wide space') and 'square' is *talbai*.

Some examples:

Chinggis Khan Talbai	Chinggis Khan Sq
Olimpiin Örgön Chölöö	Olympic Ave
Chinggis Khaan Örgön Chölöö	Chinggis Khan Ave
Enkh Taivnii Örgön Chölöö	Peace Ave
Ikh Toiruu	Big Ring Rd
Baga Toiruu	Small Ring Rd
Zaluuchuudiin Örgön Chölöö	Youth Ave

A five-minute walk from the railway station, behind Panorama Hotel, *LG Guesthouse A* (Teeverchidiin Gudamj Building No 7, ☎ 976 998 584 19, ☎ 7011 8243, 🖳 www.lghostel.com, dorm/dbl US$8-10/30, WI-FI) is one of the largest in

---

❏ Crime and danger in Ulaanbaatar

Petty theft and **bag slitting** is a persistent problem, particularly during Naadam time, and also at the railway station, on buses and in the market. There have been some reports of foreigners being mugged late at night, but if you don't get drunk and stray into dodgy areas in the wee hours of the morning, it's unlikely to happen to you.

The biggest danger you're likely to face as a visitor to UB is the **traffic**. Most drivers obey traffic signals and stop at red lights, but some don't. Crossing the street used to involve defying death every time, with pedestrian crossings being particularly dangerous places as foreigners actually expected drivers to stop, whereas the Mongolian way is to speed up and beep the horn. Now that pedestrian traffic lights have been installed in crucial places (in front of the State Department Store, for instance), it's considerably safer to cross, but be on your guard at all times.

town, highly recommended by readers for its friendly and accommodating staff, and the spacious, clean, warm rooms with good beds and little touches like reading lights. There's a restaurant on the premises serving Mongolian hotpot and a guest kitchen for self-caterers. *LG Guesthouse B* is on Peace Ave, almost opposite the State Department Store – very central but with fewer facilities.

Nassan's Guesthouse (Baga Toiruu West, ☎ 321 078, 💻 www.nassantours .com, dorm/sgl/dbl US$8/25/30, WI-FI) has been going strong for over 20 years now. Besides large, bright rooms, Nassan offers a slew of services and recommended tours. Enter from Baga Toiruu by going around the back of the second building up from Peace Ave. It's building A4, second entrance, third floor.

Right near the State Department Store, ★ *Khonghor Guesthouse* (Peace Ave 15, Apt 6, ☎ 316 415, 💻 www.khongor-expedi tion.com, dorm/sgl/dbl US$8/15/18, WI-FI) may have rather compact rooms and bathrooms, but it's always busy and the welcoming staff, including owners Toroo and Degi, are brilliant at arranging anything from day trips into the nearby countryside to multi-week adventures all over Mongolia.

Perfectly quiet even though it's in a central location, just off Peace Ave, ★ *Zaya's Hostel* (Peace Ave Building 25/4, 3rd floor, apt 5, ☎ 331 575, 💻 www.zayahostel.com, sgl/dbl/trpl US$30/40/50, WI-FI) consists of a quiet, spacious apartment with large, comfortable rooms, some en suite. In spite of being constantly full, it never seems crowded, and the super-helpful Amar who runs the show is happy to give advice or help out with travel arrangements.

Mid-range and upmarket hotels
Breakfast is included in the rate unless stated otherwise.

Taken over by the Best Western chain, the ultra-central, multi-storey *Tuushin Hotel* (Amaryn Gudamj 2, ☎ 323 162, 💻 www.bestwesternmongolia.mn, dbl from

US$175, WI-FI) has risen like a 21st-century phoenix from its Soviet ashes. Its rooms are decked out in stylish creams and browns and all come with hot tubs, air-con and plasma screen TV.

Stylish and subtly decorated, the boutique ★ *Hotel Örgöö* (Juulchin Gudamj, M100 bldg, ☎ 313 772, 💻 www.urgoohotel .com, sgl/dbl from US$50/80, rooms with shared bath US$35/60) has wonderfully comfortable beds and each room comes equipped with a bath as well as shower (or rain shower, in the case of de luxe rooms). It's a stone's throw from the National Museum, too.

Looming over the main square, the curved glass of the *Blue Sky Hotel & Tower* (Peace Ave, ☎ 7010 0505, 💻 www.hotel bluesky.mn, dbl/ste from US$208/ 325, WI-FI) is impossible to miss. The location is great and the large-ish rooms of this brand-new business hotel are flooded with light, thanks to the floor-to-ceiling windows. Guests have access to a sauna, gym and pool and the Blue Sky Lounge on the top two floors offers superb views of the city. The downside is that the climate control doesn't always work too well and when we visited there were some teething troubles with staff.

One of the smartest places to stay, *Chinggis Khaan Hotel* (Tokyo Gudamj 5, ☎ 313 380, 💻 www.chinggis-hotel.com, sgl/dbl/suite from US$100/130/225, WI-FI) offers top-class air-conditioned rooms with classic, understated décor; even the singles feature king-size beds. Hotel amenities include two restaurants – a Mongolian and a Chinese/Korean – an indoor swimming pool, sauna and spa, and a fitness centre.

The luxurious *Kempinski Hotel Khan Palace* (Ikh Toiruu, ☎ 463 463, 💻 www .kempinski.com, dbl/suite from US$146/ 302, WI-FI) is a little way east of the centre, but its facilities more than make up for the inconvenience. The English-speaking staff are helpful, the classically decorated rooms have luxurious bathrooms, extras in the suites include iPod docking stations, the

CITY GUIDES & PLANS

fitness centre boats a Japanese-style hot tub, and there's an excellent Japanese restaurant, Sakura (see opposite), on site.

Where to eat and drink

Ubiquitous *buuz* (see box below) joints are also found all over the city; you can't go more Mongolian than that! Look out for the **Khaan Buuz Хаан Бууз** and **Zochin Buuz Зочин Бууз** branches, though if we're honest, if you spend time in the Mongolian countryside, you'll be mighty glad that Ulaanbaatar has some excellent international restaurants when you return to the capital.

Unless specified restaurants are generally open daily from 11.30am/noon to 10.30/11.30pm.

Restaurants The best pizza in town is at *Ristorante Marco Polo* (Seoulyn Gudamj, [V]), with pizzas for T8000-11,000 and decent pasta dishes for around T10,000.

One of the best restaurants in UB is *Hazara Indian Restaurant* (16 Enkh Taivnii Örgön Chölöö behind the Wrestling Stadium, meals around T25,000, [V]), with large portions of delicious North Indian cuisine served under colourful hangings. The garlic naan and the mango lassi are absolutely superb.

Its only competition is *Namaste* (Baga Toiruu, mains T10,000-16,000, [V]); their fish dishes particularly packed with flavour and their curries and *saag aloo* just begging to be mopped up with tandoori roti and wonderful naan. The other location, out of

---

❏ Eating and drinking the Mongolian way

You may have heard horror stories about Mongolian food: namely, that it all involves boiled mutton. While mutton does indeed feature on nearly every menu, there is more to Mongolian cuisine than that. You are likely to encounter delicious **dairy products**, such as *süü* (cow, goat, sheep or yak milk), *öröm* or *üürag* (sweet clotted cream made from cow's milk), *tarag* (yogurt), *aarts* (soft fermented cheese) and *aaruul* (dried milk curds).

Meat comes in many guises; some is either preserved for the winter through smoking or drying, such as *bortz* (dried beef), or cooked using stones preheated in the fire, a technique perfected over the centuries. One such dish is *boodog*, where the hot stones are placed inside the animal, cooking it from the inside, while the fur is singed off in a fire or with a blowtorch. Another dish is *khorkhog*, with meat and vegetables placed in a container alongside the hot stones, with some water or *airag* (see below) added; the container is then sealed. Other meaty delights include *kazy* (salted horse-meat sausages), boiled sheep's head and *khavchaakai* (slices of meat seasoned with salt and onion, put between two thin stones and placed on hot ashes). In towns you're likely to come across *buuz* (steamed mutton dumplings) and *khuushuur* (fried mutton-filled pastries and pancakes). Another common dish is *shölte khuul* (hearty soup with meat, pasta and potato).

Vegetables are not widely eaten; Mongolians have never thought much of vegetarians, as some identify vegetable-eating with Chinese culture, while others are convinced that eating vegetables is just not healthy, though wild herbs, aromatic roots and onion-like greens are widely used for seasoning, as is yogurt, sour milk and dried curds. However, vegetarianism is getting a tentative foothold in the capital, as demonstrated by the highly successful Luna Blanca (see opposite).

Talkh (**bread**) or *bortzig* (unleavened bread) form part of most meals.

Since **milk** is such an integral part of the Mongolian diet, you are likely to come across *süütei tsai* (salty, milky tea) and *airag* (a clear spirit with a milky smell, made of fermented mare's milk).

Mongolian **beer** is strong and quite good: Khanbraü is brewed in Ulaanbaatar under a German licence. Another local brand is Chinggis Khan.

the centre at Zaluuchuudin Örgön Chölöö, has wonderfully comfortable seats, ideal for a leisurely meal.

Biwon is one of the best spots in town for Korean food. Mains (T11,500-25,000) such as grilled spicy squid and vegetarian *bibimbap* are accompanied by almost a dozen small side dishes; the service is friendly and efficient. It is part of the **Central Tower Food Court** (off Chinggis Khan Sq) which also features a good ramen joint and a café that also does fresh fruit juices and smoothies.

Mongolia may be the last place in the world where you'd expect to find good vegan food; nevertheless, *Luna Blanca* (Juulchin Gudamj, mains T4000-5000, [V]) is popular with locals as well as travellers, thanks to its flavourful, imaginative dishes such as chilli tofu with rice, noodle salad, lentil cutlets and soya meat 'day special'. Skip dessert, though.

Upstairs from the Silk Road Bar & Grill (Jamiyan Gumii Gudamj) is *Veranda* (mains from T8000) where you can enjoy views of Choijin Lama Temple while feasting on excellent pasta and other Italian dishes; their spicy ragout is particularly good.

You won't find Mongolian barbecue like the barbecue at *BD's Mongolian Barbeque* (Seoul St, meals from T9000, [V]) anywhere else in Mongolia, but that doesn't make this Americanised joint any less fun. Choose your own ingredients and watch the chefs cook your food and throw it up in the air before dispensing it onto your plate. The all-you-can-eat buffet is particularly great after days on the train. It is above *Detroit* (see Bars).

Though it's out of the centre, *Sakura* (mains T15,000-25,000) is worth seeking out for the excellent Japanese food prepared by the resident chef at Kempinski Hotel Khan Palace (see p367). The sushi sets are expertly prepared and beautifully presented, the tempura is done just right and desserts feature the strange and wonderful green tea jelly with sweet red beans.

Beautifully grilled steak and offal in a rich cream sauce do not come cheap, but *Le Bistro Français* (Ikh Surguuliin Gudamj 2, mains T18,000-35,000) makes a worthy splurge if you're in the mood for classic French cooking. Their profiterole dessert is superb.

Cafés and light meals In summer, a **beer tent** pops up next to the State Department Store. All it offers is beer, pizza and particularly delicious beef, pork or chicken skewers, grilled in front of you.

Millie's Café (Marco Polo Bldg, WI-FI) is a bustling café opposite Choijin Lama Temple, specialising in a mix of Mongolian and European dishes and expensive imported coffee.

Homesick and craving a full English breakfast, baked beans and everything? Go to *Café Amsterdam* (8am-10pm daily, mains T2500-5000) on Peace Ave right near the State Department Store; it is decked out with dramatic photos of Mongolian wilderness and also offers muesli, sandwiches, tea and coffee and soup. The terrace here is a great place for people-watching in summer.

Sacher Coffee (9am-6pm daily, sandwiches T10,000, WI-FI), diagonally across from Metro Express, off a side street that's off Seoul St, lures you in with the titillating scent of coffee, freshly ground and brewed on the premises. Choose your brew, or else a fresh juice combo or tea, grab a muffin or sandwich (their roast beef is particularly good) and settle into one of their comfy chairs with your laptop/iPad.

Michele's French Bakery (8am-6pm daily [V]) is a particular favourite of the expat community and rightly so: you can enjoy their fabulous chocolate croissants (T1500) and apple strudel, as well as the paninis (T4000) and crêpes with a multitude of fillings, while chilling out to mellow music.

Just round the side of the State Department Store, *American Burgers and Fries* (mains T8000-17,000) is a consistent hit with a youthful clientele, thanks to the delicious, enormous burgers that you can't bite without half the contents slithering out. Get a bib and tuck in.

Self-caterers can pick up a wide range of groceries at the supermarkets on the

CITY GUIDES & PLANS

ground floor of the **State Department Store** (Peace Ave) or at **Dalai Eej Market** (otherwise known as Minii Delguur), off Tserendorjiin Gudamj and next to Merkuri Market.

Bars *Revolution*, near the rather cool monument to The Beatles' on Tserendorjiin Gudamj, also does okay-ish lasagne and other Eurocentric dishes, but most people come for a beer and the congenial atmosphere at this expat-friendly bar.

An American-themed bar, *Detroit* (Seoul St, beneath BD's Mongolian Barbecue) is decked out with sports paraphernalia and serves good ol' burgers to go with your beer. Live music a couple of nights a week.

If you're not expecting authentic Irishness you won't be disappointed by the popular *Chinggis Khan Irish Pub* (Seoul St), which draws a large and lively crowd of expats and locals alike and serves up Guinness and pub grub.

Another expat favourite, *Dublin* (Seoul St) serves Irish coffee as well as beer and the pub grub is surprisingly decent.

Nightlife & entertainment
Check the English-language publications (see Information) for weekly listings.

Clubs Ulaanbaatar has a lively club scene pretty much every night of the week. **Metropolis** (in Sky Shopping Centre, T7000) is the most stylish of them all, with the DJ playing an eclectic mix of salsa, rock, disco, techno and pop.

Centrally located **Face Club** (opposite Zanabazar Fine Arts Museum, T5000) is a small, lively joint with a Tahiti theme and live band, so dig out your grass skirt, while the DJ sets at **Hollywood** (Academich Sodnomyn Gudamj) are particularly popular with the students from the nearby university.

Traditional music and dance Not to be missed is a nightly summer performance of traditional song, dance and *khöömii* (throat

singing) by **Tumen Ekh Song & Dance Ensemble** (State Youth & Children's Theatre, Naraimdal Park, T15,000).

The Mongolian National Song & Dance Ensemble performs several times a week at the **National Academic Drama Theatre** (corner of Seoul St & Chingisiin Örgön Chölöö, T9000) in summer.

More traditional pursuits include ballet or opera at the **Opera and Ballet Theatre** (Chinggis Khan Square, T7000-10,000, closed in Aug), which stages opera performances on Saturday and Sunday evenings in June and July, as well as occasional plays in English.

Cinema Tengis (Liberty Square, 🖳 www .tengis.mn) has screenings of Hollywood blockbusters in English with Mongolian subtitles.

Shopping
Things to buy include cashmere shawls and sweaters, sheepskin, woollen goods, leather goods, bags of sheeps' anklebones (for those traditional Mongolian games in the countryside), *moriin khuur* (horsehead fiddles), traditional bows and arrows, brightly embroidered traditional clothing, antiques, and representations of Mongolian deities, the latter sold in some museums.

Though Mongolia is known for its dinosaur remains, it is forbidden to purchase fossils; trying to take them out of the country will cost you a decade of repentance in a Mongolian jail.

Mongolia is also known for its wonderfully bizarre, oversized **postage stamps** with naïve representations of cars and trains; you can pick those up at the Central Post Office. Many shops sell 'art' and 'antiques', but most of it is tat, made in China. However, we can highly recommend the following places:

The **State Department Store** (daily 9am-9pm) sells high-quality cashmere, leather and suede clothing, and on the top floor, around the corner from the food court, is the vast souvenir section where you can pick up traditional bows (with a hefty price tag), *moriin khuur*, Mongolian toys and traditional wooden pizzles, traditional clothing and not-so-traditional T-shirts, some artwork, a wagonload of leather goods – handbags, boots, felt slippers, genuine fur coats, bags of sheeps' anklebones and more, so much more.

The fascinating **Narantuul Market** (Naaran Tuul Zakh, 10am-7pm daily), formerly known as the 'black market', at the corner of Ikh Toiruu and Teeverchidiin Gudamj, is a good spot for anything from counterfeit clothing to food to horse tackle and saddles to ger furniture. It's a bit of a sprawl but particularly worth the trip because you never know what you'll find. Amidst the Buddha statuettes, Communist memorabilia, sheeps' anklebones, traditional coats and boots, horse saddles and the technically-banned gazelle-foot whips (don't buy them as the gazelles are a protected species!), you may unexpectedly come across a brass bust of Hitler or Stalin.

To get there, take bus No 4 heading east from the southern side of Chinggis Khan Square and then walk along the main road south to the corner of Ikh Toiruu and Teeverchidiin Gudamj. At the market watch out for bag-slitters and pickpockets.

High-quality cashmere goods are sold at **Gobi Cashmere Shop** (Peace Ave, opposite the Russian embassy).

For all sorts of felt and woollen goodies, such as hats and quality clothing, check out **Tsagaan Alt Wool Shop** (⌨ www.mongolianwoolcraft.com), Tserendorjiin Gudamj, opposite the State Department Store. It's a Fairtrade store that supports craftsmen who come from disadvantaged backgrounds.

Mary & Martha Mongolia (⌨ www.mmmongolia.com), at their new location near Michele's French Bakery, is another excellent place for woollen ponchos, shawls and scarves, felt slippers and silk goods and, like Tsagaan Alt Wool Shop, supports traditional Mongolian crafts by paying local artisans a fair wage.

You can stock up on reading material for the train trip at **Books in English** (Peace Ave). They have a collection of secondhand classics and a few good contemporary novels.

Antique & Art Gallery (Peace Ave) is a reputable antiques store dealing mainly in brassware, art and jewellery.

Moving on
By rail Tickets for rail travel within Mongolia can be booked at the **Domestic ticket-booking office** on the east side of the railway station, though no English is spoken.

Tickets for trains to Beijing, Irkutsk and Moscow can be booked at the yellow **International Railway Ticket Booking Office** 200m north-west of the station on Zamchdyn Gudamj (8am-8pm Mon-Fri). Some English is spoken at the foreigners' booking office upstairs in Room 212. For a few dollars extra just about any guesthouse or tourist agency will do the legwork for you. You cannot buy tickets for the Moscow–Beijing trains more than a day in advance because the station ticket staff don't know how many free seats there are. Instead you might want to consider taking a train originating in Ulaanbaatar, or book through a travel agent. Tickets to Moscow and Beijing need to be booked well in advance in summer, but it's easy enough to get tickets to Irkutsk and Ulan-Ude.

Going **north**, in summer there are nightly departures of train 361 from Ulaanbaatar to Irkutsk via Ulan-Ude (daily, 33hrs); only kupé berths are available. For Russian travel beyond Irkutsk take the 005 Ulaanbaatar–Moscow (Tue 1.50pm, mid May to mid Nov, less frequently the rest of the year, 101hrs to Moscow), or get aboard the once-weekly Trans-Mongolian 003 from Beijing to Moscow (Thur 1.20pm).

If northbound tickets are sold out or you're in a hurry, take a bus to Ulan-Ude instead (see By bus p372).

Heading **south**, the 004 Moscow–Beijing departs Ulaanbaatar (Sun at 7.15am, 30hrs). Unless you booked your ticket weeks in advance, it's almost impossible to get seats on the direct Moscow–Beijing train in peak season, so you can also take the somewhat cheaper 024 Ulaanbaatar–Beijing (Thur 7.15am).

If you happen to be in Ulaanbaatar during Naadam when all tickets for direct trains to Beijing tend to be sold out, it's possible to take the Ulaanbaatar to Hohhot 034 train (Mon & Fri 8pm), booking your ticket as far as Jining on the main line and switching there to a nightly train to Beijing.

By air Ulaanbaatar's **Chinggis Khan International Airport** is located around 18km south-west of the city; its facilities include ATMs and internet access.

Many guesthouses offer free or discounted pickup if you book several days' accommodation. Taxis generally try to overcharge tourists, so agree on a price before setting off (some drivers have been known to ask up to US$50) and keep your luggage with you if you can so that they don't hold it hostage in the boot while demanding more money.

Mongolian Airlines (MIAT, 💻 www .miat.com) flies to Beijing, Tokyo, Osaka, Seoul, Moscow, Irkutsk and Berlin. **Air China** (💻 www.airchina.com) has frequent flights to Beijing. **Aeroflot** (💻 www.aero flot.ru) has flights to Moscow, Irkutsk and Ulan-Ude. **Korean Air** (💻 www.korean air.com) has several flights a week to Seoul.

Together, MIAT, Ez Niz and AeroMongolia offer flights to major Mongolian cities.

By bus If you don't wish to do the Ulaanbaatar to Ulan-Ude segment by rail in 24 hours, daily buses leave from the railway station car park at around 7.30am, costing far less and taking half the time (10-12 hours, T45,000). Ask your hotel/guesthouse/hostel to book a ticket for you.

💻 Mongolia – individual travel vs package tours

If you're visiting only Ulaanbaatar you can get by fine on your own, but it's not so easy outside the capital. If you wish to see a particular part of the country and you're bound by time/finance constraints, it's well worth hooking up with a tour agency that specialises in tours of that particular region, as they will provide knowledgeable English-speaking guides and iron out any problems with food, accommodation and transport; allow at least US$100 per day for two people.

On top of that, pretty much every guesthouse in UB offers tours of the countryside and they can add single travellers to existing groups; guesthouse tours tend to be cheaper, as little as US$50 per day, but they may use Mongolian students on their summer break rather than knowledgeable guides, so it pays to do your homework before you sign up for a trip.

If you've only got a few days to spare but want to get a feel for the vast Mongolian countryside, a standard three-day, two-night tour that includes accommodation in a *ger*, all meals and transportation, camel and horse riding as well as an opportunity to see the Przewalsky horses costs around US$230 per person.

Recommended tour operators

● **Nomadic Journeys** (Sühbaatariin Gudamj 1, ☎ 328 737, 💻 www.nomadicjour neys.com) This Swedish-Mongolian outfit is the company of choice for the eco-conscious traveller; it is also one of the few locally based consolidators for train tickets. On offer are horse-riding, sports fishing, popular *ger* (yurt) camp stays and longer horseback expeditions. Camps are low-impact and quiet, with wind and solar power instead of generators. See Eco Tour Production, p33.

● **Wind of Mongolia** (5th micro district, Bldg 7, apt 15, ☎ 328 754, ☎ 9909 0593, 💻 www.windofmongolia.mn) is a French outfit that does both summer and winter multi-day trips, as well as rock climbing and dog-sledding adventures. The best way to reach their office is by taxi.

SIDE TRIPS FROM ULAANBAATAR

Mongolia's real draw is its countryside – vast grass plains stretching as far as the eye can see, with tiny *ger* encampments dwarfed by the enormous craggy mountains and sand dunes. This is a nomadic land, where many people still lead traditional lives, herding cattle and hunting with eagles. There's no better antidote to the polluted capital than a night or two camping in a ger and a few days trekking or riding.

If you're going to use the services of a **travel agency** (see box below), or if you're looking to sign up for a guesthouse tour, make absolutely sure what the tour will entail. Ask travellers who've just been on excursions for the latest recommendations.

Entry to all **national parks** in Mongolia tends to be more expensive for foreigners than locals and there is also a charge per vehicle.

Terelj Тэрэлж
One of the most popular places for travellers is **Gorkhi-Terelj National Park** (T5000), only 80km from Ulaanbaatar. You can sleep out under the stars, drink mare's milk for breakfast and sit around campfires lulled by the sound of

- **Karakorum Expeditions** (Gandariin Gurav Bldg, at the southern end of Tserendonjiin Gudamj, ☎ 315 655, 🖳 www.gomongolia.com) specialises in hiking and biking tours in western Mongolia as well as wildlife tours and snow leopard research tours.
- **Ger to Ger** An innovative and socially conscious tour company (Arizona Plaza, Baruun Selbe Gudamj 5/3, ☎ 313 336, 🖳 www.gertoger.org) aims to introduce travellers to traditional Mongolian culture while supporting local communities in a constructive way. Ger to Ger specialises in multi-day trips, which take travellers through different parts of the country; you decide on either steppe, mountains or desert, as well as the duration and difficulty of the journey and stay with a different nomadic family each night. During the day, the families lead you to the next destination either on horseback or by ox and yak carts. Accommodation is in tents, which you provide yourself, pitched outside the gers. A basic breakfast and dinner is provided by each family. You can take part in the nomads' daily routine, learn skills such as archery and horse-riding, and so witness what may soon be a vanished way of life. The project is funded by the Swiss government and a Mongolian NGO; more than half the proceeds go directly to the communities.
- **Blue Bandana Expeditions** (in The Seven Summits outdoor shop opposite the Central Post Office, ☎ 329 456, 🖳 www.activemongolia.com) organises individual and group hiking, biking, horse-riding and jeep tours off the beaten track in the far west and north of Mongolia. Their multi-day horse treks around Lake Khuvsgul and expeditions into the Gobi come recommended.
- **Panoramic Journeys** A UK-based company (☎ +44 1608-676821, 🖳 www.panoramicjourneys.com) that specialises in tailor-made journeys and small group tours around Mongolia – from winter dog-sled tours to visits to the eagle hunters in Western Mongolia and staying with the Tsaatan reindeer herders on the Mongolia–Russia border. The only tour operator to work directly with the Tsaatan.

CITY GUIDES & PLANS

gently sizzling mutton kebabs. The scenery is spectacularly alpine, with icy streams crisscrossing forested mountainous terrain that's perfect for biking, but the one downside is the sheer number of tourist ger camps in the park; during peak season, it may feel more like summer camp than a retreat into the wild. Many guesthouses and tour agencies do Terelj as a day trip, which includes horse-riding, a traditional meal and a hike up to the appropriately named Turtle Rock, from where you can do an hour's climb to the Aryapala Buddhist meditation retreat to admire the view of the valley below.

Most companies make a stop at the 40-metre tall metal **statue of Chinggis Khan** on horseback in the southern part of Terelj. Tickets (T15,000) include entry to the excellent archaeological museum in the basement and views of the valley from the horse's head; to reach this you must go up in the lift to Chinggis's crotch.

If travelling on your own and planning on staying overnight, a daily bus (T3000) for Terelj leaves at 11am and 4pm from Peace Ave, opposite Narantuul Hotel, returning at 8am and 7pm. There are two types of accommodation here: *ger camps* and *hotels*. Ger camps are more rustic; you get to sleep in a ger and there may or may not be hot showers. Most are linked to a single travel agency in Ulaanbaatar, through which you must book (see box pp372-3): **Jalnan Meadows/Khan Khentii Ger Camp** (Nomadic Journeys) is one such place; you can rent horses from locals here.

Bogd Khan Uul Nature Reserve Богдхан Уул

This unique mountain region directly south of Ulaanbaatar was proclaimed a protected area back in 1778, although conservation of Bogd Uul (which means 'Holy Mountain') actually began in the 12th century when Khan Turil declared the mountains sacred and prohibited logging and hunting in them.

A total of 65,000 hectares of Bogd Uul is a biosphere reserve. The area contains 116 species of birds, including 20 identified as endangered. Other animals

---

❏ A stay at the Khot Ail camp

Some travellers who come to stay in *ger* camps around the country are disappointed to find that modern life has not left the nomadic communities untouched; they may find that their ger has an electric generator, solar panels or even a television. Khot Ail camp, 60km south-east of the capital, located on the banks of the Tuul River, still maintains a traditional way of life. Here, when your guide picks you up at the railway station, you get to choose whether you'd like a car or a horse. At the camp, you stay with Sara's welcoming family, and partake in daily activities, such as milking cows, learning to cook traditional Mongolian dishes, being taught Mongolian songs and how to shoot a bow and arrow. Horse and camel riding are also included, as is the opportunity to try on Mongolian dress.

Yes, most ger stays are now touristy, but this one is up there with the very best, and the family goes out of their way to make you feel included. A two-day, three-night stay costs around US$260 per person.

Tireless Sara can also arrange tours of Ulaanbaatar for you, which take in traditional dance and throat singing. Contact her on ☎ 9822 9832 or ☎ 8885 1035 or email her at ✉ mmunxzul@yahoo.com.sg.

in the area include musk deer, ibex, roe-deer, hare and native sable. Most of the trees are larch. Rolling, hilly, steppe grasslands stretch to the south. Clouds hang over the mountains in summer and there are frequent thunderstorms. Snow is abundant in winter.

Bogdhan Uul's highest peak is **Tsetsee Gun (2268m)**. It is possible to hike over the ridge to the ruins of the ancient **Manzshir Monastery Мандшир Хийд** and the museum (T6000) on the southern slope of Bogd Uul, overlooking a forested valley studded with boulders. The monastery complex was constructed in 1733 and was once home to 350 monks. The complex was destroyed in 1937 during the Communist crackdown, though the main temple has since been rebuilt. A German photographer visited in 1926 and took some amazing photos of the monastery which are now on display in the museum. Spot the Buddhist rock paintings along the rocks behind the main temple. Most hostels and hotels run day trips to the monastery that usually include horse-riding.

EXCURSIONS AROUND MONGOLIA

Hustain Nuruu National Park Хустайн Нуруу
About 110km west of Ulaanbaatar is this reserve dedicated to the reintroduction and preservation of the last truly wild horse, known in the West as Przewalski's horse and in Mongolia as the *takhi*. Desertification, hunting, cross breeding and competition with domestic livestock resulted in its extinction in the wild by 1969. At that time the world population was down to 161 animals in zoos. A carefully monitored breeding programme has resulted in the wild population increasing to several hundred. Accommodation is in guest gers. Most travel agencies and guesthouses can arrange trips to the reserve.

Karakorum (Harhorin) Каракорум (Хархорин)
This ruined city, now scattered round the modern town of Harhorin, 370km from Ulaanbaatar, was the capital of the Mongolian Empire in the 13th century. Today its centrepiece is **Erdene Zuu Monastery Эрдэнэ Зуу Хийд**, which was built in 1586 and was the first Buddhist centre in Mongolia. At its height the monastery housed about 1000 monks in 100 temples. During the Stalinist purges of the 1930s the monastery was badly damaged but it is once again functioning and open to visitors. The monastery is not actually in the unattractive modern city; it's to the north of it, and while you can easily catch a daily bus to Harhorin from Dragon bus station, getting out to the ger camps near the monastery is more problematic; a taxi is possible but the best option is to join a tour.

Lake Khuvsgul Хөвсгөл Нуур
In the north of the country, by the Russian border, lies Mongolia's answer to Lake Baikal – a smaller (only 136km in length) but almost equally dramatic lake surrounded by Alpine-looking mountains. At its southern end you'll find numerous ger camps, varying in luxury and eco-sustainability; you can also stay in the town of Khatkhal, from where it's possible to arrange multi-day horse-trekking adventures around the lake. Khatkhal is reachable from the gateway town of Mörön, a short flight from Ulaanbaatar. Beyond the north edge of

the lake, by the Russian border, live two groups of nomadic Tsaatan reindeer herders – a fragile way of life that's under threat from irresponsible tourism. It's possible to visit them, which often requires many hours on horseback, and it's best to go through Panoramic Journeys (see box p373).

The Gobi

The Gobi stretches for almost 4000km along the border between Mongolia and China. It's said to contain some 33 different ecosystems as well as gazelles, the rare Argali sheep, Asiatic wild ass, wild Bactrian camel, snow leopard and ibex. The site of an ancient inland sea, the Gobi is also a treasure-chest of fossilised dinosaur bones and eggs. Only about 3% of the Gobi is true desert, so if you're expecting to see massive sand dunes everywhere, you might be disappointed. Much of the Gobi is made up of rolling steppe, though if it is dunes you want, **Khongoryn Els Хонгорын Элс** in the eastern part of **Gurvan Saikhan National Park Гурван Сайхан** are the largest in Mongolia, up to 300m high and perfect for organising camel rides. Nestled between the beautiful peaks of the **Gurvan Saikhan (Three Beauties) Mountains**, which tower 3km above the surrounding steppe, is **Yol Am Valley**. The canyon shelters glaciers which remain frozen in its shadow even through the hottest summers. Camping is not allowed in the national park but there are plenty of tourist ger camps nearby. Most travel companies organise three-day trips to the Gobi from Ulaanbaatar.

Harbin
哈尔滨

[GMT +8; population: 4,596,313] Harbin straddles two worlds. Though it's a thriving Chinese city, Harbin prides itself on its European flair, thanks to the stately architecture of its early Russian builders. With a relaxed and affluent air along the riverfront and on pedestrianised Zhongyang Dajie, Harbin makes an ideal transition point on your way into or out of China.

Lying on the Songhua River, over 1000km north-east of Beijing, this was just another small Manchurian fishing village until the construction of the East Chinese Railway in 1897-1901. The new Russian-built railway passed through Harbin; this was also the junction for the southern spur to Port Arthur. The former village grew rapidly into a major trading centre, albeit with a wild reputation. The Hon Maurice Baring visited in 1904, expecting to find a modern industrial metropolis, but he was not impressed: 'Harbin is now called the Chicago of the East. This is not a compliment to Chicago'. Harbin continued to grow under Japanese control during the Russo-Japanese War as it served as a supply base for Japanese troops. A great many White Russian refugees settled here following the 1917 Revolution, preceded by an influx of Russian Jews, and the Russian influence remained strong, despite the Japanese presence, until after WWII when Manchuria was officially handed over to the Kuomintang.

After the reform of the late 1970s, Harbin, along with the rest of China, experienced enormous growth and economic progress. The city became a major river port and has hosted eight international trade fairs and the 1996 Asian Winter Games.

In 1996, the government incorporated the Songhua River region into Harbin, tripling the city's population and making it the largest city in north-east China. The goal now is to make Harbin the major international economic and trade centre of north-east China. The area hit the international news in late 2005 when a major chemical accident led to vast quantities of benzene escaping into the Songhua River, poisoning the city's water supplies.

Most foreign visitors to the city nowadays are Russians on shopping trips, though in January and February the frozen city puts on the **Ice Lantern Festival** (see box p379) in Zhaolin Park, with a large collection of beautifully illuminated ice sculptures that draws visitors from all over the world.

WHAT TO SEE AND DO

It's particularly rewarding to stroll around the **Daoliqu** area – the historical heart of the city where you are likely to be staying – especially along the pedestrianised, cobbled Zhongyang Dajie. Here you will see good examples of Imperial Russian architecture, with its turrets and cupolas, and pass lively food markets – the more adventurous places to eat.

Church of St Sophia 圣索菲亚大教堂
& Harbin Architecture Centre

Built in 1907, the Russian Orthodox **Church of St Sophia** (corner of Zhaolin Jie & Toulong Jie) faces a square with snack stalls, a popular place for locals to sit and relax. The church's exterior has been heavily restored since being damaged during the Cultural Revolution; it looks particularly beautiful when lit up at night. Inside you can see original murals and a huge, ornate chandelier. The church is also the home of **Harbin Architecture Centre** (8.30am-5.30pm daily, adult/student Y40/20), which consists mainly of photographs of the city dating back to the turn of the 20th century

CHURCH OF ST SOPHIA

and some architectural models. In a passage at the back of the church is a selection of religious icons. With your ticket you can also visit what appears to be a nearby annexe of the museum: walk around to a courtyard at the back of the church, where you will see steps leading underground. Down here are more Harbin photographs, including some of its annual Ice Festival, but the main attraction is an enormous and impressive scale model of the city.

Seven-Tiered Pagoda & Temple of Bliss

At 15 Dongdazhi Jie 东大直街15号, south-east of the railway station, stands a large temple complex (8.30am-4pm daily; Y15 for entry to both temples) built in 1924, with a **seven-tiered pagoda** 七级浮屠塔 and an enormous statue of the Buddha. Next door is the **Temple of Bliss** 极乐寺 with active attendance by a large Buddhist contingent and an impressive collection of statues that includes Maitreya, the Buddha-still-to-come.

Sun Island Park 太阳岛公园

This park, on an island in the middle of the Songhua River, is a pleasant and (except at weekends) quiet place for a stroll. There are boating lakes, mini-forests, small galleries, water slides and other amusements. Entry is free, though some attractions, such as the Russian Village and the Scenic Gardens, charge admission. To get there you can take a **boat** (daily and reasonably frequent, Y15) from below the Flood Control Monument, or a **cable car** (8.30am-6.30pm daily, one way/round trip Y60/120) a few hundred metres to the west.

Other parks

One of the most popular places to relax in is **Stalin Park** 斯大林公园 at the northern end of Zhongyang Dajie; people stroll here, fly kites and sit on giant stairways leading down to the river and it's lit up with neon colours at night. There are ice-cream stands and a café in the historic **Russian wooden chalet**, which sits halfway between the cable car that runs to Sun Island Park and the 1958 **Flood Control Monument** 防洪胜利纪念塔 that commemorates the victims of floods up to that point in time.

The **Children's Park** 儿童公园 (9am-7pm daily, adult/child Y5/3), on the corner of Guogeli Dajie and Hegou Dajie, south-east of the city centre, has a small railway with a miniature diesel train; it is run by children dressed as engineers and ticket collectors but is big enough to carry adults around the park (Y10). There is also table tennis in the middle of the park if you fancy challenging anyone from the world's greatest ping-pong-playing nation. To get here, take bus No 8 from the southern end of Zhongyang Dajie.

CITY GUIDES & PLANS

❏ Jews in Harbin

From the early 20th century, Harbin played host to a lively Russian Jewish community that numbered 20,000 during its 1920s heyday, who'd fled the pogroms in Russia, and whose lives centred around Tongjiang Jie. This is where you'll find the 1909 **Main Synagogue** 犹太就会堂 (82 Tongjiang Jie 通江街82号), formerly housing a hostel but being restored to be turned into a Jewish museum at the time of writing.

Nearby, at 162 Jingwei Jie 经纬街162号, is the restored **Harbin New Synagogue** 哈尔滨犹太新会堂 (8.30am-5pm daily; Y30), the 1st floor featuring an art gallery with evocative photographs of Old Harbin. The exhibits on the 2nd and 3rd floors trace the history of Harbin's Jews. The museum can also advise as to the former locations of kosher butchers, Jewish businesses and more.

Finally, there's **Huangshan Jewish Cemetery** – the largest of its kind in the Far East – in the eastern part of Harbin, with over 600 graves in good shape. A taxi there from central Harbin costs around Y55-60 one way.

❏ **Ice Lantern Festival** 冰灯节

The bleak midwinter is the liveliest time to be in Harbin because it coincides with an absolutely magical spectacle. The festival takes place in Zhaolin Park (enter from the Flood Control Monument), Sun Island Park and along the banks of the Songhua River, with incredible snow and ice sculptures springing up, ranging from icy recreations of the Forbidden City to fantastical creatures from legends. They are created either using modern technology (lasers) or traditional ice lanterns and when lit up from inside at night, take your breath away (though the cold might do that anyway!).

The festival also includes a number of winter sports, including ice-skating shows, and the frozen Songhua River becomes a hive of activity, with people tobogganing, ice sailing and even swimming in the frigid water using specially cut holes in the ice. The festival officially lasts between January 5 and mid-February, though if weather conditions are right, it runs into March. Entry to the main sculpture area costs Y220.

Zhaolin Park 兆麟公园, a block east of Zhongyang Dajie, is good for a bit of peace and quiet. If you're here early enough in the morning you can watch groups of locals go through their Tai Chi exercises. See also box above.

Around Harbin
Siberian Tiger Park 东北虎林园 Fifteen kilometres north of Harbin is the Siberian Tiger Park (8am-4.30pm daily, Y75), a breeding centre for the Amur/Siberian/Manchurian tiger (see box p479), whose goal is allegedly to prepare and then release the tigers into the wild, thus saving them from extinction.

The park is home to around 500 tigers; visitors will see some of them during the 'safari' experience, along with white tigers, lions, leopards, jaguars and pumas. You're taken around in minibuses protected with wire mesh and visitors may purchase live chickens, ducks and even cows which are let loose among the tigers who then hunt them, though it is unclear how that's preparing the tigers for independent existence. Still, you're guaranteed a sighting of these magnificent creatures, only 50 of which are left in the wild.

To get here, take bus No 67 from its stop along Hongzhuan Jie, just past Gaoyi Jie, and get off at the Gonglu Da Qiao stop, just before the bus crosses the bridge over the Songhua River. From here, take bus no 54 to the park entrance (marked with a tiger statue). Taxis to the park cost around Y50 one-way.

Unit 731 Japanese Germ Warfare Base 侵华日军第731部队遗址 To experience the full horror of Japanese military activity during WWII, take a trip to the germ warfare base (9-11am & 1-3.30pm Tue-Sun), run by Unit 731. The Japanese military captured Harbin in 1932 and conducted experiments on prisoners-of-war here between 1939 and 1945, to test the endurance of the human body. Over 4000 prisoners, mostly Chinese but also Soviet, Korean, British and Mongolian, were killed in the most horrific ways: frozen to death, roasted alive, injected with syphilis and infected with the bubonic plague. Just before Harbin was retaken by the Soviets in 1945, the Japanese tried to cover their tracks by blowing up the base; the story did not come to light until the 1980s, when a Japanese journalist published his findings. Little is left of the base, but the main building contains a two-room museum featuring the equipment used by the Japanese, as well as photos and some sculptures, all with extensive captioning in English.

The base is south of Harbin. Take bus No 343 from the railway station, get off at the Xin Jiang Da Jie (新疆大街) stop (45-60 mins) and walk for five minutes. If you get lost, ask locals to show you the way to '731' or 'Qi San Yi'.

PRACTICAL INFORMATION
Orientation and services

The area around Zhongyang Dajie, 2km north of the city centre, has most of the city's attractions in and around it, and its historical streets also have the most character. This is also where most hotels and shopping malls are.

The main **railway station** 火车站 is located in the centre of the city, with the **long-distance bus station** 公共汽车站 opposite it.

The **airport** 机场 is 46km from the city centre, reachable by shuttle bus (Y25) from the railway station; a taxi costs around Y130 and takes an hour.

The main shopping streets, Dongdazhi Jie and Guogeli Dajie, lie several blocks east-south-east of the railway station.

There's a convenient **post office** 邮局 (8.30am-5pm daily) on Tielu Jie by the railway station. **Internet access** is available at the railway station as well as at an Internet Bar 网吧 (24hrs; Y4/hour) on Xiliu Dajie, off Zhongyang Dajie, and at a couple more places along Songhuajiang Jie, near the railway station.

WHERE TO STAY
11 Modern Hotel 马迭尔宾馆
15 Kazy International Youth Hostel
    卡兹国际青年旅社
16 Zhong Da Hotel 中大大酒店
19 Ibis Harbin Shangzhi
    宜必思哈尔滨索菲亚教堂酒店

WHERE TO EAT AND DRINK
 6 Bi Feng Tang 避风塘
 9 Food market 市场
10 Portman 波特曼西餐厅
12 Food market 市场
18 Dongfang Jiaozi Wang 东方饺子王
21 California Beef Noodle King USA
22 Ding Ding Xiang 鼎鼎香
29 California Beef Noodle King USA
31 Dongfang Jiaozi Wang 东方饺子王

PLACES OF INTEREST
 1 Cable Car (to Sun Island Park)
    缆车 (太阳岛公园)
 2 Stalin Park 斯大林公园
 3 Boats (to Sun Island Park)
    轮渡 (太阳岛公园)
 4 Flood Control Monument
    防洪胜利纪念塔
 7 Zhaolin Park 兆麟公园

14 Main Synagogue
17 Harbin New Synagogue
    哈尔滨犹太新会堂
20 Church of St Sophia
    圣索菲亚大教堂 &
    Harbin Architecture Centre
32 Seven-Tiered Pagoda
    七级浮屠塔
33 Temple of Bliss 极乐寺
34 Children's Park 儿童公园

OTHER
 5 Bank of China/ATM 自动取款机
 8 Internet Bar 网吧
13 Bus stop for bus No 67 (for
    Siberian Tiger Park)
23 Railway Station 火车站
24 Internet Café 网吧
25 Post Office 邮局
26 China Telecom 中国电信
27 Harbin Railway International Travel
    Service (in Kunlun Hotel)
    哈尔滨铁道国际旅行社
    (黑龙江昆仑大酒店)
28 Long-distance Bus Station
    公共汽车站
30 ATM

You can find reliable 24-hour **ATMs** in the Bank of China 自动取款机, with a handy branch at 37 Zhaolin Jie, off Zhongyang Dajie, and another at 19 Hongjun Jie. International phone calls can be made from the **China Telecom** 中国电信 office on the 2nd floor of the railway station.

Harbin Railway International Travel Service 哈尔滨铁道国际旅行社 (☎ 5361 6717), in Kunlun Hotel 黑龙江昆仑大酒店 at 8 Tielu Jie 黑龙江省哈尔滨市南岗区铁路街8号, can assist with booking train tickets to Russia.

Taxis start at Y10 flagfall, with most trips around town under Y15. Watch the meter: some of them are fixed and will run up very quickly. To get to the **Daoliqu area** from the railway or bus station, catch **bus No 13 (Y1)** from the bus stop across the square from the railway station, where Guogeli Dajie meets Chunshen Jie; it runs towards Stalin Park along Tongjiang Jie; alternatively, bus Nos 101 and 103 drop you at the northern end of Zhongyang Dajie.

Where to stay

Prices go up by at least 20% during the Ice Lantern Festival and places get booked up so book in advance.

Kazy International Youth Hostel 卡兹国际青年旅社 (27 Tongjiang Jie, 通江街27,

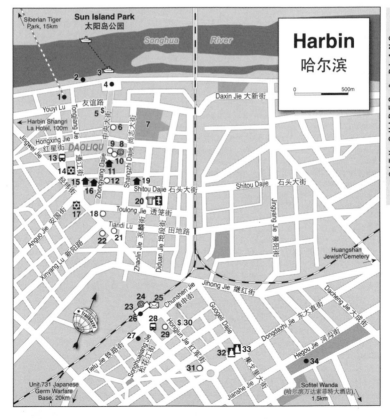

☎ 8765 4211, 🖳 www.yhachina.com, dorm/room from Y50/170, WI-FI), housed inside a heritage building, is one of the more atmospheric cheapies. The rambling hostel, popular with Chinese and international students, has basic dorms and rooms with shared facilities. Staff are friendly and helpful.

A luxurious central option, *Sofitel Wanda* 哈尔滨万达索菲特大酒店 (赣水路 68号 香坊区黑龙江省 68 Ganshui Jie, Xiangfang, ☎ 8233 6888, 🖳 www.sofitel .com, dbl/ste from US$218/367, WI-FI), has English-speaking staff, spotless international-standard rooms decorated in creams and browns. There are perks in the form of a spa and swimming pool. The best way to reach the Sofitel is by taxi.

Close to central attractions, *Ibis Harbin Shangzhi* 宜必思哈尔滨索菲亚教堂酒店 (兆麟街 92 号 道里区 92 Zhaolin Jie, Daoli, ☎ 8785 2222, 🖳 www.ibis.com, dbl from US$31, WI-FI) is an efficient business hotel with unmemorable but clean rooms, some English-speaking staff and modern facilities.

A few blocks away from the action, *Harbin Shangri-La Hotel* 哈尔滨香格里拉大饭店 (555 Yuyui Lu, 友谊路555号, ☎ 8485 8888, 🖳 www.shangri-la.com, dbl/ste from Y1588/3188, WI-FI) is one of the most attractive hotels in town, with a swimming pool and non-smoking rooms – a rarity in China. In the winter, there are great views of the Ice Lantern Festival.

One of the cheapest places to stay in the nicest part of town is *Zhong Da Hotel* 中大大酒店 (Zhongyang Dajie 32, 中央大街32号, ☎ 8463 8888), where the large and bright en suite rooms with attached bath start at Y270. Internet access and Chinese breakfast are included.

The misnamed *Modern Hotel* 马迭尔宾馆 (89 Zhongyang Dajie, 中央大街89号, ☎ 8488 4099, 🖳 hotel.hrbmodern.com, dbl/ste from Y970/1450), in a fully renovated 1906 building, retains some of the original Art Nouveau and marble. The pastel-shaded rooms all have internet access and the restaurants serve a combination of fine Chinese cuisine along with European and Russian dishes.

Where to eat and drink

You'll find numerous restaurants and bakeries along and off Zhongyang Dajie and plenty of cheap eateries around the railway station. There's also a huge variety of inexpensive eats at the two covered **food markets** along Zhongyang Dajie. The stalls along the sides serve fine noodles, dumplings, rice dishes, fried meat, lamb & squid kebabs, and desserts, as well as nuts, pastries, and candy. The more adventurous offerings include black armoured grubs, fried grasshoppers and centipedes. Open daily in summer 8.30am-8pm.

California Beef Noodle King USA is a popular chain serving heaped bowls of noodles for Y15. There are two branches here: one is across from the railway station and the other is along Tiandi Lu.

Bi Feng Tang 避风塘 (185 Zhongyang Dajie 中央大街185号), a Shanghai restaurant that's always packed with locals, serves myriad kinds of steamed dumplings as well as noodle and rice dishes. The pork belly is excellent and the picture menus have English translations. Mains from Y15.

During the sub-zero winter cold, nothing warms you up like a hotpot, as evidenced by the patrons who pack into *Ding Ding Xiang* 鼎鼎香 (Hotpot Heaven, 58 Jingwei Jie 经纬街58号, hotpots from Y20) in the colder months. Pick your own ingredients and a special sauce, but be careful what you order, as some of the elements are quite pricey.

Portman 波特曼西餐厅 (Xi 7 Dao Jie 53 南岗区西大直街53), also just off Zhongyang Dajie, serves Russian-style food for Y60-120, fried rice dishes for Y40 and American steaks for Y220. The dining room is elegant but comfortable.

The Harbin area code is ☎ 0451. From outside China dial ☎ +86-451.

The popular ***Dongfang Jiaozi Wang*** 东方饺子王 chain (Kingdom of Eastern Dumplings, 35 Zhongyang Dajie 中央大街 35号 and Hongjun Jie, next to the Overseas Chinese Hotel, [V]) has an English menu and is the place to fill up on cheap *jiaozi* (dumplings), including many vegetarian ones. Plates of jiaozi from Y5.

Moving on

By rail The Trans-Manchurian *Vostok* 019/020 passes through on Thursday on the way to Beijing and Moscow-bound on Sunday. There are 13 trains a day to Beijing (8-15hrs); the most comfortable is the Z15/16 overnighter (soft sleeper only, from Y520), while the fastest is the D-class train (from Y400/seat).

There are two weekly trains (9hrs) to Suifenhe on the China–Russia border, from where buses run to Vladivostok.

You can buy your own ticket at the station if you don't mind the queues or the confusion of the massive railway station, or alternatively get it through your hotel for about Y50 commission. For Trans-Siberian tickets contact Harbin Railway International Travel Service on the 7th floor of Kunlun Hotel (see p381).

You wait for the train in the assigned waiting room, not on the platform.

By bus If travelling in peak times, such as late August, when students are heading back to their respective universities and there's a shortage of train tickets to and from Beijing, you can take a daily overnight bus instead (12-16hrs). There are also daily buses to Vladivostok; ask at the long-distance bus station for details.

By air There are flights from Harbin's airport to Beijing (several daily, 2hrs), and other domestic destinations, as well as to Khabarovsk (weekly, 1½hrs) and Vladivostok (2/week, 1¼hrs).

Beijing
北京

[GMT+8; population: 16,446,857] Stepping off the Trans-Siberian at Beijing's futuristic railway station feels like stepping into a new world – a world of neon, pollution, incredible crowds of people, convoys of bicycles and silent scooters at every traffic light and strange but delicious smells. The city was transformed as a result of hosting the 2008 Olympic Games, making it greener and more visitor-friendly. Beijing feels like an affluent international city, with streets and subway stations signposted in English (as well as Mandarin, of course), slick shopping malls and gleaming skyscrapers everywhere, and world-class eating, shopping and nightlife. At the same time it maintains its heritage and has world-class historical attractions, such as the Forbidden City and the nearby Great Wall of China, as well as a multitude of parks and traditional neighbourhoods consisting of *hutong* (narrow alleyways; see box p390) – the best places to observe daily life with all its quirks.

Both the Trans-Manchurian and Trans-Mongolian routes, by far the most popular with travellers crossing Siberia, start or finish in Beijing, so you may wish to set a few days aside to see as much as you can of what China's bustling, vibrant capital has to offer.

CITY GUIDES & PLANS

HISTORY

Early history

Remains of China's oldest known inhabitant, Peking Man, were unearthed some 50km south of present-day Beijing in 1921, proving that life in this region dates back at least to 500,000BC. Chinese records go back only as far as the Zhou dynasty (12th century BC to 771BC) but indicate that by this period this region was acknowledged as the country's capital.

The city and its environs were to remain at the heart of Chinese culture and politics, although the role of capital was often lost to other cities, including Xi'an (where the 'Terracotta Army' now draws the tourists) and Luoyang. Beijing's strength, however, lay in its proximity to China's northern frontiers: by ruling from here emperors could keep a close eye on military developments to the north, where 'barbarians' were constantly threatening invasion. Despite the construction of the Great Wall (a continuous process dating from the 2nd century BC) Chinggis Khan marched through in 1215, sacked the city and then proceeded to rebuild it as his capital; the Mongols called this Khanbalik (City of the Khan). It was at this stage that the first Westerners visited, including Marco Polo, who liked the place so much that he stayed for 17 years.

The Mongol collapse and further developments

The Mongol empire fell in 1368 and the Chinese shifted their capital to Nanjing. Following a coup led by the son of the first Ming emperor, the government was moved back here and the city renamed Beijing (Northern Capital). The Manchurian invasion in 1644 established the final Chinese dynasty, the Qing, which was to rule from here until the abdication of Pu Yi, the 'Last Emperor', in 1912. Although the early years of Qing dynasty rule were successful, corruption, opium and foreign intervention soon undermined Chinese authority, and there were major rebellions in the city in the late 19th century.

From the Civil War to the present day

Under Chiang Kai-Shek the Kuomintang relocated China's capital to Nanjing in 1928, although following the Communist victory in 1949 it was moved back to Beijing. The People's Liberation Army (PLA) took over the city in January 1949, and in October, Chairman Mao declared the foundation of the People's Republic of China in Beijing. As the emperors had done before them, the Communists reshaped Beijing's architecture to further their own ends, knocking down the city's outer walls to make room for motor traffic. The city has hardly been quiet since then: every major movement in the country has had its roots here, notably the mass conventions of the Cultural Revolution and the democracy rallies (culminating in the Tiananmen Square Incident of 1989, when over 2000 civilians were killed). During the 2008 Olympic Games Beijing revealed itself to be a visitor-friendly city with world-class art and culture and dining scenes. As China roars through the second decade of the 21st century, the economy is booming, the country is changing fast and ever-growing, transforming Beijing is the face that China wants to present to the world. The down side of all this development is the terrible air quality in the city.

WHAT TO SEE AND DO

★ Tiananmen Square 天安门广场

Lying at the centre of the city, Tiananmen Square (**D** Tiananmen West/Tiananmen East/Qianmen) is the world's biggest square (40,000 sq metres) – three times the size of Moscow's Red Square. A political focal point since 1919 and notorious for the violence of 1989, when tanks were used against dissidents, it is the major focal point for visitors; you'll find it teeming with people most of the time. Unless specified all sights are open daily.

At the centre of the square is **Chairman Mao's Mausoleum** 毛主席纪念堂 (8am-noon Tue-Sun, free) where, after joining a long but surprisingly fast-moving queue, you can catch a brief glimpse of Mao's mummified body. The official party line now is that 'Mao was 70% right', but he is still revered by the enormous crowds who come to pay their respects to him. Before you enter you must leave your bags and cameras at one of the nearby kiosks (storage Y2-10).

North of the mausoleum, the 10,000-tonne, 36m-tall marble and granite obelisk is the **Monument to the People's Heroes** 人民英雄纪念碑. It was erected in 1958 and depicts the people's revolts against oppressors and the 1949 'liberation' by the PLA. It's lit up at night.

Tiananmen means 'Gate of Heaven', and at the northern end of the square is the gate for which the square is named, guarded by a pair of stone lions. The **Gate of Heavenly Peace** 天安门 (8.30am-4.30pm, Y15), built in the 15th century and restored in the 17th is these days used by the political elite to watch the parades in the square. It's adorned with an enormous portrait of Mao on the outside, and historical photos of the gate on the inside, and is one of the best places from which to observe the square. The **ticket office** 售票处 for the gate is at its northern side; don't confuse it with the ticket booths for the Forbidden City, which are further into the complex.

The southern end of the square is defined by the Ming-dynasty front gate (8.30am-4pm), consisting of the **Arrow Tower** 箭楼 to the south and **Zhengyang Gate** 正阳门 to the north. It dates back to the 15th century, when a wall was in place to guard the Inner City, and was the largest of the nine gates that separated the inner city from

CITY GUIDES & PLANS

Tiananmen Square
天安门广场

❏ **Beijing Museum Pass**
This pass (🖳 www.bowuguan.com.cn) is a great deal if you're planning extensive sight-seeing in Beijing as, for Y120, you are entitled to free, or discounted, entry (typically 50% off) to 110 attractions (including temples) of which 65 are museums; you only have to visit a few to get your money's worth. Only a limited number of passes are issued (between late December and the end of January), so they are more likely to be available early in the year; they are valid for the entire calendar year. You can pick up a pass at participating sights, which include Confucius Temple and the Ancient Observatory.

the outer, flanked as it was by temples which have disappeared along with the wall. You can ascend Zhengyang Gate (9am-4pm Tue-Sun, Y20) to check out the fascinating historical photographs of the area when the wall was still intact.

On the west side of the square is the **Great Hall of the People** 人民大会堂 (8.30am-3pm, Y30), used for meetings of the National People's Congress and featuring an impressive 10,000-seat auditorium. It's open for tours whenever the Congress isn't in session; you get to see its 29 rooms, named after provinces of the Chinese universe.

To the east of Tiananmen Square is the **National Museum of China** 中国国家博物馆 (D Tiananmen East, 9am-5pm Tue-Sun; free admission; 🖳 www.chnmuseum.cn) which became the largest of its kind in the world after the massive expansion effort was completed in March 2011. This immense and rather austere building boast 620,000 priceless relics from every period of China's history, including much about the post-WWII period, all with English labels, but it is missing the greatest of the imperial-era treasures, which were moved to Taiwan before the Cultural Revolution and thus survived. Beijing can't ask for the relics back as Taiwan is officially part of China.

There are exhibitions on everything from calligraphy and Tang dynasty pottery to modern art in the many rooms on its many floors (some of the galleries are due to open in years to come). The History of China wing is particularly interesting because it takes liberties with events; one diorama shows the Chinese successfully fighting off modern Japanese ships with cannons (which didn't happen), and the period of the Cultural Revolution is conspicuous by its utter absence, while the Japanese brutalities during the invasion of Nanking are described in great detail, with photographs to illustrate. Don't miss the basement exhibition on Ancient China: standout exhibits include Qing dynasty artefacts and a jade burial suit that's over 2000 years old, made for the Western Han Dynasty king Liu Xiu. Pick up your free ticket at the ticket office by the West Gate by showing photo ID.

★ **Forbidden City (Imperial Palace)** 紫禁城   [see map pp392-3]
To the north of Tiananmen Square is the incomparable Imperial Palace (daily 8.30am-4pm Apr-Oct, 8.30am-3.30pm Nov-Mar, adult/student Y60/20, 🖳 www.dpm.org.cn), better known as the Forbidden City, entered through the **front gate**, not to be confused with the Gate of Heavenly Peace.

The palace, which is the largest and best-preserved surviving complex of ancient buildings in China, took 14 years to complete. It was erected by the Ming emperor, Yong Le, in the early 15th century and was thereafter the home of 24 more emperors, up until the overthrow of the Qing dynasty in 1911, although following his abdication Emperor Pu Yi remained in the inner courts until 1924. The palace was off-limits to everyone except the emperors and their servants, and the emperors rarely ventured out of this enormous complex, comprising over 70 hectares and more than 8700 rooms. The sheer size and opulence of its many buildings was designed to dwarf and humble the mere humans who stepped inside. The grandiose main palace buildings are located along the centre of the palace complex, with the more intimate living quarters of the emperor and his family, consisting of smaller palaces and gardens, found at the northern end.

It's difficult to see all of the palace's attractions in one go, but do set time aside for the vast palace **museum collections**, found in exhibition rooms alongside the main buildings, with exhibits on calligraphy, emperors' weddings and other subjects. Likewise, the **Gallery of Treasures** (Y10) in the north-eastern corner of the palace features jewelry, statuettes made of precious stones, and gives you access to the splendid **Nine Dragon Screen**.

Don't miss the **Clock Exhibition Hall** (Y10), part of the **Hall of Ancestral Worship**, and home to an incredible array of fine timepieces from Britain, America, Switzerland and Japan, many of which were given to the Qing emperors as gifts. See if you can spot the Gilt Copper Clock with a robot that writes Chinese characters with a brush.

It's worthwhile getting an audioguide (Y40), and have everything explained to you by Roger Moore, or else get to the palace early and see the main attractions before the crowds arrive, before making a beeline for the more secluded parts of the palace which you'll have largely to yourself.

Jingshan Park 景山公园 [see map pp392-3]

Rising directly to the north of the Forbidden City, the park (**D** Tiananmen West, 6am-9pm daily, Y5) comprises sculpted gardens and a hill created in 1420 using the dirt from the moat, which serves the purpose of sheltering the palace from the bitter northern winds and spring dust storms. The last emperor of the Ming dynasty allegedly hanged himself here while the Manchu troops stormed the city and the last thing he would have seen was an incredible panoramic view of the Forbidden City below. You can enjoy that same view (the viewing platform becomes particularly crowded at sunset) or come here in the early morning to observe groups of Beijingers do their Tai-Chi exercises or walk their caged birds.

★ Tian Tan (Temple of Heaven) 天坛 [see map pp392-3]

Set inside the enormous, 267-hectare park, the Temple of Heaven (Tiantan Donglu 天坛东路, **D** Tiantandongmen, daily park 6am-9pm, sights 8am-4.30pm, entry to park Y15, entry to all sights Y35) is the site from which China's emperors conducted the country's most important religious rituals, upon which depended the well-being of the population. Natural disasters such as poor harvests were seen as a sign of the emperor losing Heaven's favour, so the Son of Heaven would come here three times a year to fulfill his spiritual duty.

The emperor would have entered the park through the **west entrance** (which is far more attractive than the east one, which teems with tourists) and spent the night inside the **Hall of Abstinence**, which is by the West Celestial Gate, east of the entrance. The most striking building in the park is the circular **Hall of Prayer for Good Harvest**, where the emperor came on the tenth day of the first lunar month. It was built entirely without the use of glue or nails, with a triple roof tiled in cobalt blue, which symbolises heaven, and decorated with dragon motifs.

TIAN TAN
(TEMPLE OF HEAVEN)

To the south lies the **Imperial Vault of Heaven**, where ancestral tablets were stored, surrounded by **Echo Wall** (where a whisper towards the surface on one side is perfectly audible around the opposite side – though you'd have to get here early to put it to the test without competing with other tourists). Even further south you'll find the **Round Altar**, where great attention is paid to the heavenly number nine and its multiples – nine altar steps, nine rings of stone, and so on. Here the emperor communicated with the heavens and an entire bullock was burnt as an offering.

The park is at its best early in the morning, when you get to witness the more bizarre of the Beijing morning rituals and have the attractions to yourself for an hour or so before the hordes arrive.

Lama Temple (Yonghegong) 雍和宫 [see map pp392-3]

The huge and superbly colourful Lama Temple (12 Yonghegong Dajie 雍和宫大街12号, **D** Yonghegong, 9am-4.30pm daily, Y25, audioguide Y20 with Y200 deposit) – the most important Tibetan Buddhist temple outside Tibet – is usually teeming with monks, tourists and worshippers, and awash with the scent and smoke of burning incense, which makes for an incredible spectacle.

This was originally the home of Qing dynasty Prince Yong before he became Emperor Yongzheng and moved to the Forbidden City. Many of the temples and halls were completed in 1694, though it wasn't a lamasery for Tibetan monks until 1744 and the entire temple survived the Cultural Revolution unharmed, some say due to direct orders from Zhou Enlai (the first Premier of the People's Republic of China).

The worshippers crowd around the incense burners, which are centuries old, and the buildings are brightly painted both inside and out, with lots of dragon motifs, all leading you to the centrepiece, a stunning 18m statue of the Buddha carved from a single piece of sandalwood. It looks slightly shorter than its actual height because part of it is underground to prevent it from falling over.

The most exciting time to be here is the Spring Festival and the last day of the lunar month when the monks perform 'Devil Dances' dressed in huge masks made to look like animal heads.

Confucius Temple 孔庙 [see map pp392-3]

Near Lama Temple, the peaceful Confucius Temple (13 Guozijian Jie 国子监街 13号, **D** Yonghegong, 8.30am-5.30pm daily, adult/student Y30/15) provides respite from the bustle and clamour of the city. In warmer months you'll find art students sketching the attractive grounds, or reading on benches in tranquil corners. In the main courtyard, beside the statue of the great man himself, there are 198 stone tablets with the names of *jinshi* scholars who passed a civil service examination during the Qing, Ming and Yuan dynasties. It is also here that Beijing writer Lao She was dragged in 1966, beaten and made to confess his anti-revolutionary crimes; he drowned himself the following day.

Just west of the temple, **Guozijian Imperial College** (国子监) is where China's brightest students were educated in Confucianism for centuries.

Ancient Observatory 古观象台 [see map pp392-3]

If the weather is good you can easily spend an hour or so looking at the huge array of bizarre astronomical instruments, designed by Jesuit missionaries in the 17th and 18th centuries, and a reproduction of a Ming dynasty star map, in the largely open-air Ancient Observatory (2 Dongbiaobeng Hutong, **D** Jianguomen, Tue-Sun 9.30am-4.30pm, adult/student Y20/10). It's hard to figure out what most of them were for but they are fantastic pieces of engineering and artistry which wouldn't look out of place in a Harry Potter film. The observatory is located in a watchtower which was part of the Ming city wall, its predecessors having stood just north of the present spot since Yuan dynasty.

Drum Tower 鼓楼 and Bell Tower 钟楼 [see map pp392-3]

Rebuilt in 1800 on the same spot where similar towers have stood for over 700 years, the **Drum Tower** (off Gulou Dongdajie, **D** Guloudajie, 9am-5pm daily, adult/student Y20/10; combined admission with the bell Tower Y30/15) has always been used for timekeeping: from the Song dynasty clepsydras (water clocks) to the convoluted system of the Qing dynasty, which involved beating the drum 13 times at 7pm and then once every two hours afterwards. Today it's home to 25 drums that are beaten for visitors at 9.30am, 10.30am, 11.30am, 1.30pm, 2.30pm, 3.30pm and 4.45pm. Besides the impressive drum performances, it's worth climbing 69 incredibly steep steps for the view over some of Beijing's most picturesque *hutong* (see box p390).

The nearby **Bell Tower** (Dianmen Dajie 地安门大街, 9am-5pm daily, adult/student Y20/10) also dates back to the Yuan dynasty (though the current one is only 300 years old) and is named after the bells used by Beijing's official timekeepers during the Yuan, Ming and Qing dynasties. These bells don't have clappers; they are struck with poles. Behold the 500-year-old bronze bell that weighs 63 tonnes; visitors can ring that bell for a princely sum of Y100 during the Spring Festival.

★ **Summer Palace** 故宫

This palace (8km north-west of the city, Yiheyuan Lu 颐和园路, **D** Xiyuan/
Beigongmen, 8.30am-5pm daily, entry to the park adult/student Y20, entry to
all sections Y50/30), the summer retreat of the Imperial family since 1750, covers an area about four times the size of the Forbidden City, and is dominated by
Kunming Lake, a Yuan dynasty reservoir. The entire area was razed by the
British and French in 1860 as retribution for the Opium Wars, and then again in
1900 after the Boxer Rebellion, and rebuilt by Empress Dowager Cixi.

The Summer Palace is a great place to explore slowly: highlights include
the **Long Corridor**, with its 10,000 different painted scenes, Empress Cixi's
personal three-level **Peking opera theatre** in the **Garden of Harmonious
Virtue**, and, of course, **Kunming Lake** with its stunning marble footbridges.
On the north shore you'll find a **marble boat** – the Empress's tribute to the
Chinese navy, though the navy may have preferred a real boat, having been decimated by the Japanese in 1894. You can get away from the crowds either by
strolling along the west side of the lake or by renting a boat near the North
Palace Gate.

CITY GUIDES & PLANS

❏ **A stroll through the *hutong*** 胡同
An integral part of the city's history, the historical *hutong* neigbourhoods originally
came into being during the Zhou Dynasty (1027-526BC), when Beijing was divided
into residential areas according to one's social class. During the Ming Dynasty (early
15th century), the heart of the city became the Imperial Palace (the Forbidden City),
with those of higher social standing permitted to live closer to the centre. Hutong are
narrow alleyways, lined with *siheyuan* (traditional residences centered around a
courtyard), with gates traditionally facing south for more light and in accordance with
feng shui principles; hence most hutong run east to west, connected by tiny north–
south alleys. The siheyuan belonging to nobility and wealthy merchants were particularly spacious and grand, whereas the hutong further away from the centre tended to
be simpler and narrower. A typical siheyuan will have a pair of grand red doors,
guarded by a pair of stone lions.

Between 1911 and 1948, the hutong became overcrowded, as residences previously belonging to a single family suddenly had to be subdivided to accommodate
four, while in the second half of the 20th century, many traditional neighbourhoods
were demolished to make way for wide streets and high-rise buildings. Numerous
ancient hutong still survive and give Beijing a character that other Chinese cities lack,
but their days are nevertheless numbered; a street near the Drum and Bell towers has
recently undergone demolition in spite of residents' protests; the former residents
have been relocated to anonymous suburbs way on the city's outskirts.

Though pedicab (rickshaw) tours of the hutong are widely offered, it can actually be more rewarding to explore them on foot by yourself, the best-preserved neighbourhoods being around the Drum Tower and Bell Tower area. You may find that
some of your fondest memories of Beijing revolve around getting lost in the alleyways, accompanied by the delicious and unfamiliar smells of a multitude of food
stalls, peering into courtyards and observing the bizarre daily life. The streets really
come to life in the evening with residents playing *mah jong*, eating, bursting into
impromptu musical recitals, having their hair cut, or simply strolling to the communal bathrooms at the end of the street in their pyjamas.

❏ Beijing's Olympic legacy

Hosting the planet's biggest sporting event in 2008 has left Beijing with the **world's largest airport**, designed by Lord Norman Foster, world-class sporting facilities and daring architecture that has forever altered the city's skyline.

Affectionately known as the **'Bird's Nest'** 鸟巢, the Swiss-designed **National Stadium** 北京国家体育场 (9am-5pm, adult/student Y50/25) is the largest steel structure in the world, accommodating 91,000 people and now hosting concerts and international football games. It looks spectacular when lit up at night.

Next door, the curvy, LED-lit bubble-wrapped exterior of the energy-efficient **National Aquatic Centre** 北京国家游泳中心 (9am-5.30pm Nov-Feb, to 6.30pm rest of year, adult/student Y30/15) or **'Water Cube'** 水立方 contrasts with the stadium's rigid lines. No fewer than 25 world records were set here, and the main pool remains intact, while the rest of the venue now hosts the Happy Magic Water Park. Both the Bird's Nest and the Water Cube are at **D** Olympic Green, where you can stroll the wide pedestrian avenue lined with snack stalls and immensely tall streetlights.

Just west of Tiananmen Square, the 6500-seat **National Centre for Performing Arts** 国家大剧院 (2 Xichangan Jie 北京, 西长安街2号, **D** Tiananmen West, 💻 www .chncpa.org, 9am-5pm, Y30), otherwise known as **'The Egg'** for its distinctive golden titanium-and-glass dome, and designed by French architect Paul Andreu, has won great praise for its excellent acoustics as well as its futuristic appearance. The entrance lies through the tunnel under the moat.

Perhaps the strangest of them all is the **CCTV Headquarters** 中央电视台总部 大楼 (32 Dongsanhuan Zhonglu 东三环中路32号, **D** Jintaixizhao), created by Rem Koolhaas, which has acquired the bizarre moniker of **'big underpants'**, though **'twisted doughnut'** would be a more accurate description of the two skyscrapers melded together in a kind of incredible angular loop.

Yuanmingyuan, the **Old Summer Palace** 圆明园 which lies a short taxi ride to the north-east of the Summer Palace, was less fortunate: the Anglo-French forces wilfully destroyed the largest collection of Chinese artistic and architectural treasures outside the Forbidden City and it still lies in ruins.

798 Art District 798 艺术新区

The best of Beijing's contemporary art is found at this incredible collection of galleries (Jiuxianqiao Beilu and Jiuxianqiao Lu), housed in abandoned factory spaces 4km north-east of the city centre. While several years ago this became an artists' enclave, it is now government sponsored but no less worthwhile. Wander through the narrow alleys, stop at the little cafés and check out the highlights, which include the **798 Photo Gallery** (4 Jiuxianqiao Lu, 💻 www.798photo gallery.cn, 10am-6pm) with interesting photographic exhibitions by Chinese and international photographers, **Beijing Art Now Gallery** (BANG, Red Yard No 1, 💻 www.beijingartnow.com, noon-6pm), dedicated to quality exhibitions by some of the best local contemporary artists, and **Beijing Tokyo Art Projects** (4 Jiuxianqiao Lu, 💻 www.tokyo-gallery.com, 10.30am-6.30pm), featuring consistently cutting-edge work by Japanese and other international artists.

To get here, take bus 909 (Y2, 25 mins) from Exit C of Dongzhimen subway station along the Airport Expressway until you see the huge 798 sign.

CITY GUIDES & PLANS

Beijing 北京

0   0.5   1km

Pure Lotus 净心莲, 1km
798 Art District
798艺术新区, 4km &
Beijing Capital
International Airport

Muse 妙
World of
Suzie Wong
苏西黄, 700m

Agricultural
Exhibition
Centre

Tuanjiehu Park
团结湖南路

Dongsanhuan Beilu 东三环北路

Sanlitun Lu

Sanlitun Beixiaojie
三里屯北小街

Gongti Donglu

Sanlitun Beilu

Workers'
Stadium

Gongrentiyuchang Beilu 工人体育场北路

Chunxiu Lu

Gongrentiyuchang Nanlu 工人体育场南路

Gongrenmenwai Dajie 朝阳门外大街

Chaoyangmennei Dajie 朝阳门内大街
Chaoyangmen

Xiangheyuan Xielu 香河园斜路

Xingdong Lu

Xindong Lu 新东路

Dongzhimenwai Dajie

Dongzhimen

Happiness Lounge 乐满堂,
National Stadium
北京国家体育场,
National Aquatic Centre
北京国家游泳中心, 3km

Bei Zhan (Beijing
North Railway Station)
北站

Hepinglibeijie

Hepingli Xijie

Gui Jie
簋街 (Ghost St)

Dongzhimen Beixiaojie
东直门北小街

Dongzhimen Nanixiaojie
东直门南小街

Chaoyangmen Beixiaojie
朝阳门北小街

Chaoyangmen

Dongzhimen Beidajie

Dongzhimennei Dajie

Zhangzizhonglu

Dongsishitiao

Summer Palace &
Old Summer Palace, 8km

Deshengmen Dongdajie

Yonghegong Dajie

Andingmen Dongdajie 安定门东大街

Andingmen Qiao

Andingmen 安定门

Yonghegong
雍和宫大街

Dongsi Beidajie 东四北大街

Beixinqiao

Dibei

Dongsi
Dongsi Xidajie

Beiheyan Dajie
北河沿大街

Dongsi Xidajie

Andingmen Xidajie 安定门西大街

Jiaodaokou Dajie
交道口大街

Beixinqiao Dongdajie
北新桥东大街

Jiaodaokou
交道口大街

Gulou Xidajie 鼓楼西大街

Jiugulou Dajie
旧鼓楼大街

HUTONG 胡同

Beiluogu Xiang
北锣鼓巷

Beluoguxiang Dongdajie
北锣鼓巷东大街

Nanluogu Xiang
南锣鼓巷

HUTONG 胡同

Gulou Dongdajie 鼓楼东大街

HUTONG 胡同

Di'anmen Dongdajie
地安门东大街

Nanluoguxiang

Di'anmennei Dajie

Jingshan Park
景山公园

Jingshan Houjie
景山后街

Jingshan Qianjie 景山前街

HUTONG 胡同

Gulou Xidajie 鼓楼西大街

Di'anmen Xidajie 地安门西大街

Di'anmenwai Dajie
地安门外大街

Di'anmen Xidajie
地安门西大街

Houhai
Lake
后海

Yandai Xiejie
烟袋斜街

Red Lantern House

Red Lantern East Yard
仿古园, 500m

Red Lantern West Yard
红灯笼家院西院, 900m

Qianhai
Lake

Shichahai
什刹海

Beihai Park
北海公园

Beihai
North
北海北

Wenjin Jie 文津街

Beihai 北海公园

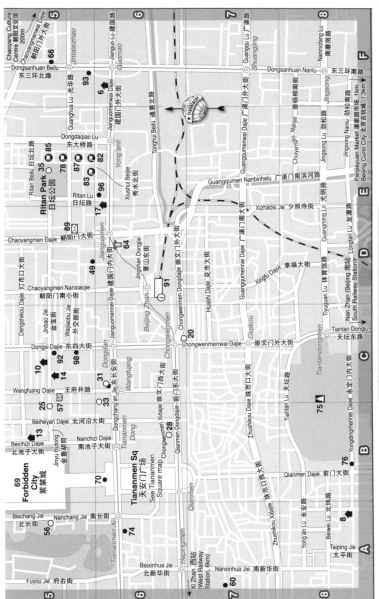

Beijing map key 北京

WHERE TO STAY

1 [B2] 3 plus 1 精品酒店
2 [C3] 4 Banqiao 板桥胡同4号
3 [A2] Bamboo Garden Hotel 竹园宾馆
4 [B3] Downtown Backpackers 东堂客栈
5 [C4] Beijing Double Happiness Courtyard Hotel 北京阅微庄精品宾馆
6 [F6] China World Hotel 中国大饭店
7 [A2/B2] Drum Tower Youth Hostel 古韵青年酒店
8 [A8] Home Inn 如家快捷酒店
9 [C4] Hotel Côté Cour S L 演乐酒店
10 [C5] Novotel Peace Hotel 诺福特和平宾馆
11 [E3] Opposite House, The 瑜舍
12 [B2] Orchid Hotel, The 兰花宾馆
13 [B5] Peking International Youth Hostel 北平国际青年旅社
14 [C5] Peninsula Beijing 王府饭店
15 [E3] Sanlitun Youth Hostel 三里屯青年旅社
16 [B4] Sitting On The City Walls Courtyard House 城墙旅舍
17 [E6] St Regis Beijing 北京国际俱乐部饭店

WHERE TO EAT

18 [E2] April Gourmet 绿叶子食品店
19 [F3] Beijing Da Dong Roast Duck Restaurant 便宜坊北京烤鸭
20 [C6] Bian Yi Fang Roast Duck Restaurant 便宜坊北京烤鸭
21 [B3] Black Sesame Kitchen
22 [F3] Bookworm 书虫
23 [B2] Café Sambal
24 [E3] Crepanini 可百尼尼
25 [B5] Donghuamen Night Market 东华门夜市
26 [E3] Feiteng Yuxiang 沸腾鱼乡
27 [C2] Jin Ding Xuan 金鼎轩
28 [B6] Lost Heaven 华马天堂
29 [F2] Lufthansa Center Youyi Shopping City 燕莎友谊商城
30 [B4] Oasis Café
31 [C6] Oriental Plaza 东方广场
32 [E3] Super 24
33 [C6] Wangfujing Snack Street 王府井小吃街
34 [E3] Xiao Wang's Home Restaurant 小王府
35 [E5] Xiao Wang's Home Restaurant 小王府
36 [B3] Xiongdi Chuancai 兄弟川菜
37 [C2] Xu Xiang Zhai Vegetarian Restaurant 叙香斋
38 [B2] Yunnan Restaurant 凤凰竹

WHERE TO DRINK

39 [B2] Bed 床吧
40 [B2] Contempio
41 [E4] Drei Kronen 1308 Brauhaus 皇冠自酿啤酒坊
42 [B3] Drum and Bell, The 鼓钟咖啡馆
43 [B3] Great Leap Brewing 大跃啤酒
44 [E3] Paddy O'Shea's 爱尔兰酒吧
45 [C3] Salud 老伍
46 [E3] Tree 隐藏的树
47 [B2] Za Jia 杂家

NIGHTLIFE & ENTERTAINMENT

48 [F4] Beijing Chaoyang Theatre 北京朝阳剧场
49 [D5] Chang An Grand Theatre 长安大戏院
50 [E4] Destination 目的地
51 [B3] Mao Livehouse 光芒酒吧
52 [E3] Mix 密克斯俱乐部
53 [F4] Salsa Caribe 卡利庚拉丁舞俱乐部
54 [D3] Tiandi Theatre 天地剧院
55 [E3] Vics 威克斯
56 [A5] What? Bar 什么酒吧

SHOPPING

57 [C5] Foreign Languages Bookstore 外文书店
58 [E4] Hong Ying 红英
59 [B3] In
60 [A7] Liulichang Lu 琉璃厂路
61 [B3] Plastered T-shirts

PRACTICAL INFORMATION
Arriving in Beijing

By train Trans-Siberian trains arrive at the central railway station, **Beijing Zhan** 北京站, 3km south-east of the Forbidden City and handily located next to the subway station on Line 2. Many other trains, including those serving Xi'an, Kowloon (Hong Kong) and Hanoi in Vietnam, as well as the high-speed Z-series trains, arrive and depart from Beijing's smart West (**Xi Zhan** 西站) station, accessible by Subway Line 9. The ultra-modern Beijing South Railway station (**Nan Zhan** 南站), said to be the biggest in Asia and accessible by Subway Line 4 (and Line 14), is a massive transportation hub which serves the high-speed 'bullet' trains to destinations such as Shanghai. Beijing North station (**Bei Zhan** 北站) is accessible by Subway lines 2 and 13 and is served by trains from Hohhot and Badaling.

By air The futuristic **Beijing Capital International Airport** 北京首都国际机场 (⌨ en.bcia.com.cn) is 27km north-east of the city centre. A convenient **light rail line** links Terminals 2 and 3 to Sanyuanqiao (Line 10) and Dongzhimen (Lines 2 & 13) subway stations. From Terminal 3 trains run every 15 minutes or so between 6.21am

---

SHOPPING (*continued*)
62 [C2] SQY-T
63 [B3] Yandai Xiejie 烟袋斜街

PLACES OF INTEREST
64 [D6] Ancient Observatory 古观象台
65 [B2] Bell Tower 钟楼
66 [F5] CCTV Headquarters 中央电视台总部大楼
67 [C2] Confucius Temple 孔庙
68 [B2] Drum Tower 鼓楼
69 [B5] Forbidden City (Imperial Palace) 紫禁城
70 [B6] Front Gate
71 [C2] Guozijian Imperial College 国子监
72 [B4] Jingshan Park 景山公园
73 [C2] Lama Temple (Yonghegong) 雍和宫
74 [A6] National Centre for Performing Arts 国家大剧院
75 [C8] Tian Tan (Temple of Heaven) 天坛
76 [B8] West entrance of Tian Tan (Temple of Heaven)

EMBASSIES
77 [E3] Australian Embassy 澳大利亚大使馆
78 [E5] British Embassy 英国大使馆
79 [E3] Canadian Embassy 加拿大大使馆
80 [F3] French Embassy 法国大使馆
81 [E3] German Embassy 德国大使馆
82 [E5] Irish Embassy 爱尔兰大使馆
83 [E5] Mongolian Embassy 蒙古大使馆
84 [F2] Netherlands Embassy 荷兰大使馆
85 [E5] New Zealand Embassy 新西兰大使馆
86 [D2] Russian Embassy 俄罗斯大使馆
87 [E5] US Embassy 美国大使馆

OTHER
88 [E3] Beijing International Post Office 北京国际邮电局
89 [D5] Beijing International Post Office 北京国际邮电局
90 [E2] Beijing International SOS Clinic 北京国际救援中心
91 [D6] Beijing Zhan (central railway station) 北京站
92 [C5] China International Travel Service (CITS) 中国国际旅行社
93 [F5] China World Trade Center 中国国际贸易中心
94 [D2] Dongzhimen Long-distance Bus Station 东直门长途汽车站
95 [F4] Internet Café
96 [E6] Mongolian Airlines 蒙古航空
97 [C5] Monkey Business
98 [C5] Peking Union Medical College Hospital 北京协和医院
99 [D2] Public Security Bureau (PSB) 公安局

CITY GUIDES & PLANS

and 10.51pm; from Terminal 2 it's between 6.35am and 11.10pm, while from Dongzhimen trains run between 6am and 10.30pm. Tickets cost Y25 one-way.

The cheapest way into town is by **express shuttle bus** (40-90 mins depending on traffic between 5am and midnight; Y16); there are ten lines, the most popular with travellers being Line 3 that runs to and from Beijing Zhan Railway Station (7am-midnight from the airport, 5.30am-9pm from the railway station) via Dongzhimen.

Taxis cost around Y100 (including Y15 road toll); grab one from the taxi ranks and ignore approaches from drivers as scams are common; have the name and address of your accommodation written in Mandarin as very few drivers read or speak English.

By bus If you come by bus (from Harbin) you will arrive at Dongzhimen Long Distance Bus Station.

Local transport
[see p531 for Beijing subway plan]
The **subway system** (🖥 www.exploremetro .com/static/pdf/en/beijing.pdf), consisting of fourteen lines with five more to be constructed by 2015, is the best and quickest way of getting around much of the city. Stations are marked with a blue 'D' sign outside and station names are in English. Trains are frequent and cheap (Y2 per ride, 6am-11pm daily); however, single ride cards purchased at stations are valid only from that station on the same day; if you don't wish to queue every time, get an **IC smartcard** (see box below; refundable deposit Y20) that can be topped up from any major subway station.

Many travellers end up joining the rest of the city's population on two wheels: there are many places that rent out **bicycles**, particularly hostels and budget hotels. Cycling is a great way of covering distances between attractions that are not comfortably walkable, and cycling around the *hutong* (see box p390) is positively enjoyable. However, it might be daunting at first to join the city's cycling hordes as you'll be sharing the road space with scores of silent scooters that creep up on you, motorised carts and other two-wheeled, three-wheeled and four-wheeled modes of transport; most obey the traffic lights, but some don't.

Taxis are easy to flag down anywhere and are inexpensive. They're metered: Y10 flagfall (Y11 at night) plus Y2/km and are great value when shared. A taxi from Beijing Zhan railway station to Sanlitun in the north of the city is about Y25. If you can't speak Chinese, get your destination written down in Chinese script and show it to the driver.

Orientation and services
Orientation The biggest problem Beijing poses for visitors is its sheer size – about the same as a small European country. A walking tour, taking in three or more sights in one day, is difficult. You'll mainly find yourself hitting one major sight (such as the Forbidden City or Summer Palace) each day, with lots of time spent on public transport.

Fortunately, most streets are laid out in a neat grid with the Forbidden City and Tiananmen Square at the centre and five ring roads circling the city centre, so it's difficult to get lost.

❏ **The IC smartcard** 一卡通
The IC card, or the Yikatong (one card pass), is a multi-purpose travel card that can be topped up. Though primarily used to pay subway and bus fares, it can also be used with some taxi companies, restaurants and supermarkets, saving you from queuing up and also saving you money due to discounted fares on buses. You will most likely be using it for transport only; if staying in Beijing for a few days, it's a good idea to get an IC card valid for 3, 7 or 15 days (these cannot be topped up).

IC cards can be purchased at most central subway stations. To get your Y20 deposit back, return your card to any of the stations that issues them.

You will have to get used to the crowded streets and packed underground, though.

China visa extensions Visa extensions are done at the Foreign Affairs branch of the **Public Security Bureau** 北京公安局出入境管理处(PSB; 2 Andingmendong Dajie 安定门东大街2号, Dongcheng **D** Yonghegong, ☎ 8402 0101, 8.30am-4.30pm Mon-Sat), on the north-east corner of the second ring road in a huge building by the flyover; go up to the 2nd floor.

It's relatively straightforward to extend a tourist visa by 30 days (this takes 4-5 working days to process), but it's more difficult to obtain more than one extension. The price for an extension depends on your nationality and is subject to change at short notice. The penalty for overstaying your Chinese visa is Y500 per day.

Embassies Embassies are located in two main areas: Sanlitun and Jianguomenwai. Standard opening hours are 9am-noon and 1.30-4/5pm, though consular sections tend to open only in the morning. If you can't find the embassy you need on the lists here, try 🖳 www.travelchinaguide.com/embassy /foreign/beijing.
● **Embassies in the Sanlitun area:**
Australian (21 Dongzhimenwai Dajie, ☎ 5140 4111); **Canadian** (19 Dongzhimenwai Dajie, ☎ 5139 4000); **French** (3 Sanlitun Dongsanjie, ☎ 8532 8080); **German** (17 Dongzhimenwai Dajie, ☎ 8532 9000); **Netherlands** (4 Liangmahe Nanlu, ☎ 8532 0200); **Russian** (4 Dongzhimen Beizhongjie, consular department ☎ 010-6532 1267, 🖳 www.russia.org .cn); open for applications 2-6pm Monday to Friday.
● **Embassies in the Jianguomenwai area:**
British (1 Guanghua Lu, ☎ 8529 6600); **Irish** (3 Ritan Donglu, ☎ 6532 2691); **Mongolian** (2 Xiushui Beijie, ☎ 6532 1203, 🖳 www.mongolianconsulate.com .au); the consular section is open for applications 9-11am Monday to Friday. Visa issue time is typically four working days; **New Zealand** (1 Ritan Dong Erjie, ☎ 6532 7000); **US** (55 Anjialou Lu, entrance on Tianze Lu, ☎ 8531 3000).

❏ **Chinese street names**

jie / dajie	街 / 大街	avenue / street
lu / xiang	路 / 巷	road / lane
hutong	胡同	narrow alleyway

Information The **Beijing Tourist Information Centre** 北京旅游咨询服务中心 outlets, including those at the airport (9am-5pm) and at Beijing Zhan railway station, have a plethora of leaflets about the city and the staff speak very basic English. You can also buy detailed maps of the city (Y15) in the underpass as you come off the train at Beijing Zhan station.

Free English-language **listings magazines**, the monthly *Beijinger* (🖳 www.the beijinger.com) and the bi-weekly *City Weekend* (🖳 www.cityweekend.com.cn) and *Agenda* (🖳 www.agendabeijing.com), are found in expat bars and restaurants, particularly in Sanlitun and also in the Qianhai Lake area.

You can find information on the city's attractions, hotel and restaurant listings and travel bargains on 🖳 www.beijing-visitor .com which is a good catch-all site, while 🖳 www.tour-beijing.com offers all manner of city tours, including themed ones.

Sections of the Great Wall (see pp407-9) are more easily reached if you take a tour (rather than going independently) – most hotels and hostels offer them and can also book tickets for performances of Chinese acrobatics, kung fu and Beijing opera (see Nightlife).

Medical Beijing has excellent medical facilities.

The leading hospital is **Peking Union Medical College Hospital** 协和医院 (53 Dongdan Beidajie 东单北大街53号, **D**

❏ **Emergency numbers**
Ambulance ☎ 120
Ambulance Beijing ☎ 999
Fire ☎ 119   **Police** ☎ 110

CITY GUIDES & PLANS

Dengshikou or Dongdan, emergency ☎ 6529 5284, 24-hour emergency service), which covers medical and dental emergency treatment. Most doctors speak good English and there's a large foreigners' wing south of the inpatient building.

There's also **Beijing International SOS Clinic** 国际SOS医务诊所 (Suite 105, Wing 1, Kunsha Building, 16 Xinyanli, Ⓓ Lingmahe, 9am-6pm Mon-Fri, emergencies ☎ 6462 9100, 🖳 www.internationalsos .com), offering all manner of medical services, with multi-lingual staff.

Money The unit of currency is the *yuan* (Y; also called *renminbi* or RMB), which is divided into 10 *jiao* or 100 *fen* and comes in denominations of 1, 2, 5, 10, 20, 50 and 100 yuan.

ATMs are easy to find particularly along the main shopping streets, inside shopping malls and international hotels. Good places to change foreign currency are the Industrial and Commercial Bank of China (ICBC) branches and the Bank of China; you'll find a branch in the Arrival Hall at the airport as well as at Oriental Plaza (see Shopping p405).

Post and telecommunications
Beijing International Post Office 国际邮 电局 is on Chaoyangmen Dajie, Ⓓ Jianguomen, with another branch on Gongretiyuchang Beilu (aka Gong Ti Beilu), opposite the Workers' Stadium. Post

offices tend to be open daily between 9am and 5pm and you can send letters and postcards from most hotels, though packages need to be sent from post office branches. Don't seal the packages because they'll need to be inspected.

There are fewer **internet cafés** now that most hotels and hostels offer free internet and/or wi-fi. If the place where you're staying by some chance doesn't have access, you'll find a 24-hour internet café (Y5/hour) just east of Bookworm (see p405), on the 2nd floor, or keep an eye out for a *wangba* 网吧 sign. **Free wi-fi** spots dot the city now; many cafés and restaurants in trendy parts of town will give you a password along with your coffee.

The cheapest way to make international calls is via Skype, made easier by the proliferation of wi-fi hotspots. Otherwise, to make phone calls you can use a **prepaid IP card** for long-distance and international calls from either a landline or mobile. You can buy both at China Telecom offices, newsstands and kiosks; you should never pay the face value for an IP card, as a Y100 card typically sells for around Y40. Different IP cards have different long-distance rates and some may only be used locally, while others can be used throughout the country.

China Mobile and China Unicom **SIM cards** are relatively inexpensive, setting you back Y60-100, and coming with Y50 worth of credit, which can be topped up using a credit-charging card of Y50 or Y100. Calls to local numbers are cheap, but to call abroad, dial 17951, follow the instructions and add 00 before dialling your country code for the Y4.80/minute rate.

Travel agencies These agencies can help you organise your onward travel.

Trans-Siberian specialist **Monkey Business** (Room 202, Bldg 2, 27 Beisanli Community, East Courtyard, Chaoyang, Ⓓ Tuanjiehu, ☎ 6591 6519, 🖳 www.monkeyshrine.com, 10am-6pm Mon-Sat) can help you book your Trans-Siberian train tickets, including stopovers in Russia and Mongolia, as well as providing visa support and arranging tailor-made trips.

❏ Exchange rates
To get the latest rates of exchange see 🖳 www.xe.com

	Yuan
Aus$1	Y5.82
Can$1	Y5.65
Euro€1	Y8.59
Japan ¥100	Y6.08
Mong T100	Y0.35
NZ$1	Y5.34
Sing$1	Y4.97
S Africa R10	Y5.94
UK£1	Y10.47
US$1	Y6.24

CITY GUIDES & PLANS

China International Travel Service (**CITS**; Room 1212, CITS Bldg, 1 Dongdan Beidajie, Dongcheng, **D** Dongsi, ☎ 8511 8522, 🖳 www.cits.com.cn, 9am-7pm daily) also sells Trans-Siberian tickets.

Where to stay
Beijing has plenty of accommodation to suit every budget.

Budget accommodation Beijing's hostels tend to be of a very good quality and the ones listed here, unless stated otherwise, have kitchen facilities or on-site cafés, laundry, lockers, free internet and/or wi-fi as well as air-conditioning which is essential in summer. Many are in the *hutong* (see box p390).

Peking International Youth Hostel 北平国际青年旅社 (5 Beichizi Ertiao, Beichizi Dajie, 东城区北池子二条5号, **D** Tiananmen Dong, ☎ 6526 8855, 🖳 www .peking.hostel.com, dorm/dbl Y120/ 450), located in a traditional *siheyuan* residence with an attractive flowering courtyard and very popular with backpackers, comes highly recommended for its trips to the Great Wall, the tasty café food, excellent showers and book exchange. The staff can also help you get tickets to acrobatics and kung fu shows.

Conveniently located on one of the most popular hutong streets, the perpetually full *Downtown Backpackers* 东堂客栈 (85 Nanluogu Xiang, 东城区南锣鼓巷85号, **D** Andingmen, ☎ 8400 2429, 🖳 www.back packingchina.com, dorm/dbl from Y75/ 160) is an established backpacker favourite.

Great Wall trips, an excellent restaurant and bar, private bathrooms in all rooms, handy bike rental and proximity to great nightlife make this one of the top budget choices.

★ *Sitting On The City Walls Courtyard House* 城墙旅舍 (57 Nianzi Hutong, 碾子胡同57号, Jingshanhoujie, Dongcheng, **D** Nanluoguxiang, ☎ 6402 7805, 🖳 www.beijingcitywalls.com, dorm/ sgl/dbl Y100/220/380) is a secluded, traditionally decorated courtyard house that attracts a sociable crowd without being a party hostel. The staff are very knowledgeable and can help you plan your China adventure.

A Sanlitun favourite, the large *Sanlitun Youth Hostel* 三里屯青年旅社 (1 Chunxiu Lu, off Gongti Beilu, 朝阳区春秀路1号, **D** Gongtibeilu, ☎ 5190 9288, 🖳 www.sanlitun.hostel.com, dorm/sgl/dbl Y60-80/260/280) stands out thanks to the efforts of its warm and helpful staff. The dorms are spacious and clean and the bar is a great place to mingle with fellow travellers looking to hit the night scene.

Drum Tower Youth Hostel 古韵青年酒店 (51 Jiugulou Dajie, 西城区旧鼓楼大街51号, **D** Guloudajie, ☎ 6403 7702, 🖳 www .drumtowerhostel.com, dorm/sgl/dbl Y40-60/ 160/320) offers superb views of the nearby *hutong* and the Drum Tower from its rooftop bar and patio, and if that weren't enough, the street it's on is teeming with bars and eateries. On-site perks include a lounge with big-screen TV and the staff can help you book your train tickets as well as organising Great Wall trips and lively nights out.

★ Tucked back in a *hutong* near the hopping Houhai-area nightlife, *Red Lantern House* 仿古园 (500m west of map, 5 Zhengjue Hutong, 西城区正觉胡同5号, **D** Xinjekou, ☎ 6611 5771, 🖳 www.redlan ternhouse.com, dorm/dbl from Y85/220), has a high-ceilinged lobby done up like an old Beijing alley, which doubles as a canteen and bar. Staff are very friendly and speak excellent English and there's a travel desk for all your ticket needs as well as trips to the Great Wall. If the main Red Lantern House is full the staff can find a place for you at the nearby (a 5-min walk) courtyard residence of *Red Lantern West Yard* 红灯笼客栈西院 (111 Xinjekou Nandajie, 西城区新街口南大街111号, **D** Ping'anli); it has an attractive covered common area with a tiny bridge over a carp pond. However, at the time of writing West

CITY GUIDES & PLANS

Yard was closed for renovation so check before you go.

Just around the corner from the main Red Lantern, its new **Red Lantern East Yard** (仿古元; contact details as above) sports attractive en suite rooms (sgl/dbl/trpl Y340/450/580).

If you're after efficient, no-frills rooms, **Home Inn** 如家快捷酒店 (2A Xinzhong Jie, 东城区新中街甲2号, **D** Dongsishitiao, freephone ☎ 400 820 3333, 🖥 www.homeinns.com, dbl from Y399) fits the bill perfectly. This branch is one of over 70 around the city.

Mid-range hotels The most attractive of the mid-range options are those in *hutong* neighbourhoods (see box p390). At midrange and top hotels it's always worth asking what discounted rates (*zhekou* 折扣) they do outside the holiday seasons. Unless stated otherwise wi-fi is available though not always free.

Shiny, efficient and within walking distance of the Forbidden City, **Novotel Peace Hotel** 诺福特和平宾馆 (3 Jinyu Hutong, 东城区金鱼胡同3号, **D** Dengshikou, ☎ 6512 8833, 🖥 www.novotel.com, dbl/suite from US$73/145) has large, light rooms with satellite TV, wi-fi that you pay for and 24-hour room service.

With an enviable hutong location in the Drum and Bell Tower area, the delightful sanctuary that is ★ **The Orchid Hotel** 兰 花 宾 馆 (65 Baochao Hutong, Gouloudong, 宝抄胡同65号 **D** Guloudajie, ☎ 8404 4818, 🖥 www.theorchidbeijing .com, dbl Y700-1200) has just 10 rooms, all wonderfully comfortable, with crisp white linen, exposed wooden beams and air purifiers. Some of the rooms face the flowering courtyard, while one looks out over the towers themselves, and the most luxurious options boast private gardens.

Hiding behind a silver sliding industrial door, **3 Plus 1** 精品酒店 is a tiny boutique hotel (17 Zhangwang Hutong, Jiugulou Dajie, 东城区旧鼓楼大街张旺胡同17, **D** Gulou-dajie, ☎ 6404 7030, 🖥 www.3plus1bedrooms.com, rooms from US$189) consisting of just four luxurious rooms each with custom-designed furniture

and its own private courtyard. You can make use of the library and TV room, the afternoon fruit and tea is a nice touch and the ladies in charge are wonderfully helpful. Why not '4 bedrooms'? Because the Chinese word for 'four' is very similar to the Chinese word for 'death'.

The former home of the Qing scholar and dignitary Ji Xiaolan, ★ **Beijing Double Happiness Courtyard Hotel** 北京阅微庄宾馆 (37 Dongsi Sitiao, 东城区东四四条37号, **D** Dongsi Sitiao, ☎ 6400 7762, 🖥 www.hotel37.com, sgl/dbl/family room Y900/1680/2400) is beautifully situated around two shaded courtyards inside a hutong, with rooms featuring traditional ornate wooden furniture as well as modern touches such as flat screen TVs. The staff are extremely well informed and go out of their way to help you.

Hidden behind large doors is another hutong gem. A mix of traditional and contemporary, **4 Banqiao** 板桥胡同4号 (4 Banqiao Hutong, 东城区北新桥板桥胡同4号, **D** Beixingqiao, ☎ 8403 0968, 🖥 www .4banqiao.com, sgl/dbl/suite Y518/768/1238) has attractive rooms around a pleasant courtyard, with free internet in the guest lounge. The rooftop patio is a great spot to retreat to after sight-seeing all day.

One of the best traditional courtyard hotels is **Bamboo Garden Hotel** 竹园宾馆 (24 Xiaoshiqiao Hutong, Jiugulou Dajie, 西城区旧鼓楼大街小石桥胡同24号, **D** Guloudajie, ☎ 5852 0088, 🖥 www.bbgh .com.cn, sgl/twin/dbl/suite Y520/640/700/1600); its former owners include Empress Cixi's head eunuch and Kang Sheng, one of the masterminds behind the Cultural Revolution. The rooms are decorated with reproduction Ming furniture, the bamboo grove and the pavilions are a delight and the restaurant serves elaborate Chinese dishes fit for aristocracy.

Upmarket hotels The rates quoted at upmarket hotels don't tend to include a 15% tax though it will be added to your bill. It's common for some five-star places to set their rates in US$, but collect in yuan.

Japanese-designed, minimalist ★ **The Opposite House** 瑜舍 (11 Sanlitun Lu, 朝阳

区三里屯路11号院1号楼, **D** Gongtibeilu, ☎ 6417 6688, 🖳 www.theoppositehouse .com, studio from Y1935, suite Y25,000) is all wood and light; the sumptuous spa-style bathrooms have rain showers and there's a swimming pool. The on-site restaurants serve imaginative Mediterranean and North Asian cuisine and by night you can relax in the Mesh cocktail lounge or check out the international DJs in the basement Punk club.

Hotel Côté Cour S L 演乐酒店 (70 Yanyue Hutong, 东城区演乐胡同70号, **D** Dongsi, ☎ 6512 8020, 🖳 www.hotelcote courbj.com, dbl/suite from Y1268/2168) is a luxurious boutique hotel with all the charm of a 500-year-old *hutong* residence. There's incredible attention to detail in its 14 rooms, from the emerald mosaic tiles in the bathroom to the handmade Chinese silk beds, and the suites have views of the tranquil garden. A nice touch is a reading lounge stocked with English books.

All marble and wood, *St Regis Beijing* 北京国际俱乐部饭店 (21 Jianguomenwai Dajie, 朝阳区建国门外大街21号, **D** Jianguomen, ☎ 6460 6688, 🖳 www.stregis .com/beijing, dbl/ste from Y1670/2420) is one of the city's most luxurious hotels. Your personal butler and professional masseurs are available around the clock, there's a spa to pamper you and a swimming pool so that you can stay in shape after dining at the on-site Astor Grill.

Also excellent is the award-winning *Peninsula Beijing* 王府饭店 (8 Jinyu Hutong, 东城区王府井金鱼胡同8号, **D** Wangfujing, ☎ 8516 2888, 🖳 www.penin sula.com, dbl/suite from Y3150/4500), its elegant rooms furnished with Chinese rugs and big-screen plasma TVs. You can feast on fusion cuisine at the Jing Restaurant and shop for designer gear in the Peninsula shopping arcade.

The first super-luxury hotel in Beijing, *China World Hotel* 中国大饭店 (1 Jianguomenwai Dajie, 朝阳区建国门外大街1号, **D** Guomao, ☎ 6505 2266, 🖳 www .shangri-la.com, dbl/suite from Y1350/ Y5000) with its opulent marble lobby, offers superb service, extensive leisure and business facilities, access to the luxury retailers at the China World Trade Center and superb dining – seafood at Aria or classic Chinese cuisine at the Summer Palace. Airport transfers are included in the rate.

Where to eat

The city has no shortage of places where you can eat; the best thing to do is to simply give yourself time to wander around and see what you come across, you'll never go hungry. Unless stated otherwise places are open daily 10.30am-11pm.

Budget food is easy to find: if you wander through the *hutong*, you'll come across numerous family-run eateries serving cheap, filling noodles or dumplings, or else the evening food stalls often have things on sticks for Y1 each. Inexpensive Chinese and international food is found in the food courts of every Beijing shopping mall (the **Oriental Plaza** has a good one), where the menus are more likely to have English translations or pictures of food.

Jiugulou Dajie 旧故楼大街 (see B2 on map p392, **D** Guloudajie), leading up to the Drum Tower, is lined with inexpensive eateries specialising in barbecued meat skewers, as well as restaurants serving international cuisine.

Gui Jie 簋街 (**D** Beixinqiao), aka Ghost Street – a 1.4km strip of Dongzhimennei Dajie – is lined with over 150 Chinese restaurants festooned with red lanterns, serving a huge variety of authentic cuisines from all over China, though the street is best known for its spicy seafood and its hotpot.

Donghuamen Night Market 东华门夜市 (Donganmen Dajie 东安门大街, **D** Dengshikou or Wangfujing, 4-10pm daily) is a row of stalls lining the street, serving assorted seafood and meat kebabs, noodles, fruit on sticks, flatbread with lamb and a selection of giant centipedes, scorpions and armoured black grubs on skewers for the more adventurous (Y5-10 per skewer/Y15 upwards per dish). Yes, it's touristy, and not super-cheap, but it's worth it for the spectacle alone.

Wangfujing Snack Street 王府井小吃街 (off Wangfujing Lu, **D** Wangfujing) is another great street food market, serving the

CITY GUIDES & PLANS

likes of Yunnan noodles, Sichuan spicy soup, Uighur lamb skewers and flatbread, as well as the more exotic scorpion-on-a-stick. Prices are roughly Y10 per portion and there are places to sit and eat your noodles.

Beijing duck is, of course, the local speciality and one of the best places to try it is **Beijing Da Dong Roast Duck Restaurant** 北京大董烤鸭店 (Bldg 3, Tuanjiehui Beikou, Dongsanhuan Beilu 东三环路团结湖北口三楼, **D** Gongtibeilu, half-duck with pancakes Y140), with white linen service and chefs who train for years to carve the duck just so. Venerable **Bian Yi Fang** 便宜坊北京烤鸭 (3F, Bldg 3, New World Shopping Mall, 3 Chongwenmenwai Dajie 崇文门外大街新世界商场二期三层, **D** Chonwenmen or Cikikou, whole duck Y190), in existence since 1410, is Beijing's oldest duck restaurant and has perfected its own slow roast technique over the centuries.

An excellent choice for a wide range of Chinese dishes is **Xiao Wang's Home Restaurant** 小王府 (2 Guanghua Donglu 光华路光华东里2号, **D** Yong'anli, meals from Y90). Their spare ribs with pepper salt are outstanding, as are their hot and spicy chicken wings and Beijing duck. There's another location nearby at Ritan Park.

Wowing diners ever since coming on the scene, ★ **Black Sesame Kitchen** (3 Heizhima Hutong, Dongcheng 南锣鼓巷黑芝麻胡同3号, **D** Nanluoguxiao, ☎ 9147 4408, 🖳 www.blacksesamekitchen.com) consists of just two large communal tables (pick the one in the kitchen to watch the chefs at work); the 10-course menu consists of innovative takes on northern Chinese dishes, accompanied by unlimited wine. It costs Y300pp and dinner is served 7-10pm on Wednesdays and Fridays; the rest of the time, the chefs host cooking classes.

Muse (300m east of map, 1 Chaoyang Gongyuan Xilu, 43 Sanlitun Lu, 朝阳区三里屯北街43号同里1栋近, **D** Nonzhanguan, meals from Y50) makes excellent, fresh Vietnamese dishes, its pho, papaya salad and spring rolls simply bursting with flavour.

Café Sambal (43 Jiugulou Dajie, 旧故楼大街43号, **D** Guloudajie, meals Y100) serves delicious, authentic Malaysian food in a delightful courtyard, their curry dishes

and their Kumar lamb being particularly worthy of a mention.

For fiery Sichuan food, try this branch of **Feiteng Yuxiang** 沸腾鱼乡 (1-1 Gongti Beilu 工体北路1—1号, **D** Gongtibeilu); its *shuizhu yu* (fish chunks poached in a Sichuan peppercorn broth) or *lazi ji* (bits of fried chicken buried in a mound of dried chillies) are superb.

Right near Tinanamen Square, **Lost Heaven** 华马天堂 (23 Qianmen Dongdajie 前门东大街23号, **D** Qianmen, mains from Y45, [V]) serves flavourful Yunnan dishes in a refined setting – all dark wood and mood lighting. The salads are wonderful (try the Burmese tea leaves salad or the ghost chicken salad), as is the roast pork in banana leaf.

Yunnan Restaurant 凤凰竹 (25 Lindgan Hutong, off Jiugulou Dajie 旧故楼大街灵丹胡同25号, **D** Guloudajie, meals Y100, [V]) is an excellent place to immerse yourself in the sweet, sour and spicy flavours of Yunnan cuisine. Their tofu dishes are very flavourful, there are plenty of exotic vegetarian dishes that use vegetables and blossoms unheard of in the West, the spicy chicken is tender and beautifully flavoured, and the pineapple rice comes in a hollowed-out pineapple.

A 24-hour, three-tiered dim sum restaurant, bedecked with lanterns, **Jin Ding Xuan** 金鼎轩 (77 Hepingli Xijie 和平里西街77号, **D** Yongshegong) is a great place to try anything from fluffy char siu buns to delicate dumplings with scallops, prawns, pork, and vegetables, some coloured with spinach or carrot. No English spoken, but there's an English picture menu. Very popular, so you may have to queue outside and wait for your number to be called.

Just across the street from the top of Beijing's most popular pedestrian street, **Xiongdi Chuancai** 兄弟川菜 (121 Gulou Dongdajie 鼓楼东大街121号, **D** Beixingqiao or Nanluoguxiang) offers the best of bold, spicy Sichuan flavours. Go for the pork belly flavoured with Sichuan peppercorns, the deep-fried cumin lamb, and the garlicky fresh cucumber. Mains from Y35.

Good choices for **vegetarians** (and vegans) include *Xu Xiang Zhai Vegetarian Restaurant* 叙香斋 (26-1 Guozijian Dajie 国子监街26−1号, D Beixinqiao, buffet Y85) with its superb lunch and dinner all-you-can-eat buffet featuring veggie versions of dumplings and sushi as well as a multitude of mock-meat and mock-fish dishes prepared from soy and gluten products.

Pure Lotus 净心莲 (Metropark Lido Hotel, 6 Jiangtai Lu, Chaoyang, 朝阳区将台路6号丽都假日饭店3楼, D Sanyuanqiao, meals from Y110), run by Buddhist monks, serves vegan food as you've never seen it before – wonderfully imaginative tofu, vegetable and mock-meat dishes, exquisitely presented on mother-of-pearl dishes. There's no alcohol, but plenty of fruit juices and an extensive tea menu. Get off at Sanyuanqiao and take a taxi the rest of the way.

For sweet and savoury **crêpes**, head to French-run *Crepanini* 可百尼尼 (Nali Patio, 81 Sanlitun Beilu 三里屯北路81号, D Gongtibeilu), a cute café also specialising in paninis and waffles.

Just south of Sanlitun, ★ *Bookworm* 老书虫 (Bldg 4, Nansanlitun Lu, 南三里屯4号, D Tuanjiehu, 🖳 www.beijingbookworm.com) is a Beijing institution, where you can sip your coffee or glass of wine or enjoy a light meal surrounded by a vast library of thousands of books. This is the spot for poetry readings and quizzes and the annual literary festival.

Oasis Café (1 Jingshan Qianjie 景山前1号, Dongcheng, D Dongsi or Nanluoguxiao) is a welcoming coffee shop at the north-east corner of the Forbidden City, serving excellent brews from around the world and good sandwiches.

To stock up for your Trans-Siberian journey, check out *Super 24* (24-hour supermarket, Sanlitun Bar St/Sanlitun Lu, 三里屯路, D Gongtibeilu). *Lufthansa Center Youyi Shopping City* 燕莎友谊商城 (50 Liangmaqiao Lu 亮马桥路50号, D Dongzhimen) also has a wide selection of food. If you're missing Marmite and Tetley tea, try *April Gourmet* 绿叶子食品店 (1 Sanlitun Beixiaojie, 三里屯北小街1号, D Gongtibeilu), a small store specialising in those hard-to-find imported foods.

Where to drink

A hidden treasure in 100-year-old Qing-dynasty courtyard, ★ *Great Leap Brewing* 大跃啤酒 (6 Doujiao Hutong 豆角胡同6号, D Shichahai) is a microbrewery with a great selection of ales made mostly from local ingredients. To find it, walk west from Nanluogu Xiang along Jingyang Hutong, head right, then left, then right again and turn left into Doujiao Hutong.

Another great little hutong bar is *Za Jia* 杂家 (Hong En Temple, Doufuchi Hutong 豆腐池胡同宏恩观, D Guloudajie), with split-level seating that lets you sit practically up on the roof and a friendly, low-key vibe. Its unique feature is that it's built into the gateway of a 600-year-old Taoist temple.

At *Paddy O'Shea's* 爱尔兰酒吧 (28 Dongzhimenwai Dajie 东直门外大街28号, D Dongzhimen), a genuine Irish pub and sports bar, you can enjoy the rugby and Premiership football on its many screens while imbibing Guinness and Kilkenny on tap. For superb German beers made from a 700-year-old Bavarian recipe, head to the *Drei Kronen 1308 Brauhaus* microbrewery (1F Bldg 5, China View, Gongti Donglu, D Dongsishitiao or Gongtibeilu, 🖳 www.dreikronen1308.com), while *Tree* 树酒吧 (43 Sanlitun Bar St 三里屯北街43, D Tuanjiehu) dispenses an excellent selection of Belgian beers and great wood-fired pizzas to a discerning mix of expats, locals and visitors.

The Drum and Bell 鼓钟咖啡馆 (41 Zhongluowan Hutong 钟楼弯胡同41号, D Guloudajie) has an attractive rooftop patio where you can drink your beer and watch the sun set over the *hutong*, while at nearby *Bed* 床吧 (17 Zhongwang Hutong, off Jiugulou Dajie 旧故楼张旺胡同17号, D Guloudajie) you can recline like a Roman and enjoy Asian finger food at one of the best-loved chill-out spots in the city.

Contempio (4 Zhangwang Hutong, off Jiugulou Dajie 旧故楼张旺胡同4号, D Guloudajie) is an ultra-cool café by day and bar by night, its low lighting, mellow soundtrack, comfy seats and great service adding to the atmosphere. *Salud* 老伍 (66 Nanluogu Xiang 南锣鼓巷66号, D

Andingmen), one of the liveliest bars in Sanlitun, serves great sangria and homemade infused rums in test tubes, and hosts live acts.

The pick of the hotel bars includes the sumptuous *Happiness Lounge* (Pangu 7 Star Hotel, 27 Beisihuan Zhonglu, 朝阳区北四环中路 27号, **D** Huixinxijiebeikou), 3km to the north, where you can sip a cocktail while looking over the Bird's Nest and the Water Cube (see box p391).

Nightlife & entertainment

Beijing nightlife is alive and kicking every night of the week, while weekend nights get going around midnight and carry on until dawn. Check listings for the latest happenings (see p397).

Clubs To window-shop for your party venue, good areas to head are **Sanlitun** ('Sanlitun Bar Street') and the **Houhai** 什刹海 lake district, both filled to bursting with bars and clubs that carry on late; Sanlitun' offers a more upmarket, international scene.

At the opium den lounge chic of the *World of Suzie Wong* (700m east of the map, 1A Nongzhanguan Nanlu, Chaoyang Gongyuan Ximen west gate of Chaoyang Park 朝阳区农展馆南路甲1号(朝阳公园西门, **D** Gongtibeilu, 🖳 www.clubsuzie wong.com), you can chill out on one of the Ming dynasty beds if you get there early enough, join the dancers on the second floor, or mix with the hipsters on the rooftop terrace.

At *Salsa Caribe* (Area 4, Gongti Beilu, 朝阳区工体北路4号凯富酒店旁机电研究院院内(三里屯南街, **D** Gongtibeilu, 🖳 www .salsacaribebeijing.com) you can strut your stuff to great live Latin music on their sweaty, packed dancefloor.

Beijing's premier gay club, *Destination* 目的地 (7 Gongrentiyuchang Xilu 工人体育场西路, **D** Chaoyangmen), is perpetually packed at weekends.

Mix 密克斯 (inside the north gate of the Workers' Stadium 工人体育场, **D** Dongsishitiao) heaves with hip-hop clubbers at the weekend and hosts quality international DJs. Nearby *Vics* 威克斯 is another dance giant, playing reggae, hip-hop, R&B and soul, with a separate chillout zone playing trance; Wednesday is ladies' night, with free drinks before midnight.

Live music The ever-popular *What? Bar* 什么酒吧 (72 Beichang Jie 北长街72号, **D** Tiananmen West, north of the west Forbidden City gate) hosts up-and-coming musicians and bands and the music ranges from rock to psychedelic to ska. Best nights to attend are Friday and Saturday.

Mao Livehouse 光芒 (111 Gulou Dongdajie 鼓楼东大街 111号, **D** Nanluoguxiang) is another popular live music venue, with a large stage and separate bar area. The bands can be hit-and-miss, but on occasion international acts play here and the entrance fees rocket.

Another place to consider is *Salud* (see Where to drink).

❏ It's opera, but not as you know it...

Forget the mellifluous voices and stilted tragedies of the European stage and instead prepare yourself for an epic spectacle with a soap opera plot that may involve ghosts, cross-dressing nuns, clowns, kung fu fights, acrobatics, low-brow humour and even live animals. Beijing opera is far older than its tamer European cousin; its roots reach back to the 10th century when popular legends were acted out in teahouses by travelling performers to entertain working-class folk. Since then it has evolved into an elaborate and distinctive art form – as much a visual spectacle as aural – with costumes, makeup and colours used to define a character. You can tell the importance of a character by how elaborate their headgear is; the sound of the gong and the reaction of your fellow opera-goers alerts you to important scenes coming up, and the surtitles in English and Chinese allow you to follow the convoluted plot.

❏ **The three golden rules of shopping**
● **Haggle** Even in some shopping centres, and particularly at markets. Figure out how much you're prepared to pay, ask the seller 'Can you go cheaper?' (*Neng zai pianyi yidian'r ma?*) and then if the price is too high look suitably shocked and kick off the haggling by offering no more than half of the seller's suggested price, then working your way up to the price that you're prepared to pay.
● **Don't make your interest obvious** If you're salivating over a particular item, it'll make haggling all the more difficult.
● **Walk away** If you're still not getting the price you want, shake your head sadly and pretend to be walking away in disappointment. Be convincing, though; there's no use looking at the item longingly and repeatedly saying, 'Okay, I'm going to leave now' without moving from the spot. If you execute the walk-away correctly, odds are, the seller will chase after you or call you back and you'll get the price you wanted.

Beijing opera Even though Beijing Opera (see box opposite) was originally intended to be watched outdoors, you could do worse than catch it at **Chang An Grand Theatre** 长安大戏院 (Chang An Bldg, 7 Jianguomennai Dajie 建国门大街7号, Ⓓ Jianguomen, ☎ 5166 4621, tickets Y90-800).

Acrobatics & martial arts These two arts have been practised in China for over two millennia and your visit to Beijing is not complete without seeing one (or both!). One of the best places to catch an acrobatics show is **Beijing Chaoyang Theatre** 朝阳剧场 (36 Donsanhuan Beilu 东三环北路36号, Ⓓ Hujialou, Y200-400, performances daily at 7.15pm), which combines hoop jumping, tumbling, bicycle tricks and plate spinning with impressive feats of strength, contortion and balance. At **Tiandi Theatre** 天地剧场 (10 Dongzhimen Nandajie 东直门南大街10号, Ⓓ Dongsishitiao, Y150-380, performances daily at 7.15pm) you'll witness some of the same acts, but with one crucial difference – they are all performed by children and teenagers and are all the more moving since you sense that there's a greater potential of things going wrong.

To observe the punishing stage show of the Shaolin Warriors, combined with a cheesy but enjoyable story, head to **Chaoyang Culture Centre** 朝阳文化馆 (200m east of the map, 17 Jintaili 朝阳区小庄金台里17号, Ⓓ Guanghualu, Y200-400, performances daily at 7.20pm).

Shopping
Shops are generally open daily 10am-10pm.

Head to **Bookworm** for the best selection of English-language books in town (Bldg 4, Nansanlitun Lu, Ⓓ Tuanjiehu); there's a terrace *café* (see Where to eat) here with wi-fi.

The **Foreign Languages Bookstore** 外文书店 (235 Wangfujing Dajie 王府井大街235号, Ⓓ Wangfujing) is a great place for books, maps and postcards about China, and has extensive English-, German- and Spanish-language sections.

Swish shopping malls stocking Mango, Zara and other international brands abound in the city, but **Oriental Plaza** 东方广场 (1 Dongchang An Jie 东长安街1号, Ⓓ Wangfujing) is one of the best, both for shopping and for eating (p401).

If, however, you're looking for something more unique, check out some local designers: **Feng Ling**, at 4 Jiuxianqiao Lu 酒仙桥路4号, 4km north-east in the 798 Art District (see p391) stocks dresses and jackets with Mao's face and propaganda slogans; **Plastered T-shirts** (61 Nanluogu Xiang 南锣鼓巷61号, Ⓓ Beixinqiao) is the place to come for unusual T-shirts featuring Beijing icons; **SQY-T** (85 Wudaoying Hutong, Dongcheng 五道营胡同85号, Ⓓ Andingmen or Guloudajie) designs limited edition concept T-shirts, such as the 'Skin of The City', as well as canvas-print bowls and more; **In** (11 Yandai Xiejie, 烟袋斜街11号, Ⓓ Guloudajie) sells beautiful silk dresses, while **Hong Ying** (11 Gongti Donglu 工体东路11号, **D** Dongsishitiao) combines hippy chic with traditional style, resulting in very affordable Mandarin-collar tops and colourful skirts and bags.

For souvenirs such as porcelain, tea sets, Buddhist statues and jewelry, try the four floors of **Beijing Curio City** (1.3km south of map, 21 Dongsanhuan Nanlu 东三环南路21号, **D** Maizizhanxilou). Avoid the tourist trap of the Friendship Store on Jianguomen Dajie and the pedestrian Qianmen Dajie, just south of Tiananmen Square, where prices are laughably high.

One of the best pedestrian shopping areas is **Yandai Xiejie** (off Di'anmenwai Dajie 地安门外大街烟袋斜街), where you can find clothes, tea, porcelain and other gifts.

Shops along **Liulichang Lu** 琉璃厂路 (**D** Hepingmen) have sold artists' materials, calligraphy and paintings for centuries, and even now you can buy calligraphy materials, scroll paintings, antique maps, art books and ceramics.

Antiques can also be found at **Panjiayuan Market** 潘家园古玩市场 (1km south of map, **D** Panjiayuan, 8.30am-6pm Mon-Fri, 4.30am-6pm Sat & Sun) where you can find anything from Cultural Revolution memorabilia, scroll paintings and Yuan dynasty vases to life-size terra-cotta warriors. The market is at its biggest and best at the weekend; for the best bargains go early in the morning and bear in mind that some vendors may ask ten times the actual price for an object, so compare prices before purchasing (see box p405).

Moving on

By rail Beijing Zhan Railway Station 北京站 The K23 train to Ulaanbaatar leaves on Tuesday or Saturday mornings (30hrs) year-round and on Mondays or Saturdays in summer. The Chinese Trans-Mongolian train K3 to Moscow (100hrs) leaves on Wednesday morning, arriving in Moscow on Monday afternoon, while the Russian Trans-Manchurian train to Moscow K19 (120hrs) departs on Saturday night and arrives on Friday evening.

There are also T5 departures to Hanoi, Vietnam (Sun & Thur evening, 40hrs), and

four weekly K27 departures for Pyongyang, North Korea (26hrs). Also five daily T-series and D-series trains run to Harbin (8-12hrs) and two T-series to Shanghai (14hrs).

Beijing West Railway Station (Xi Zhan) 西站 The Q97 train to Kowloon (Hong Kong) runs daily at 1.08pm (24hrs). There are also two nightly hard sleepers to Xi'an (10-12hrs), and the T27 departure for Lhasa, Tibet (45hrs) every evening.

Beijing South Railway Station (Nan Zhan) 南站 There are several super-fast G-class departures to Shanghai daily (5½hrs) and numerous C-series departures to Tianjin (30 mins).

From **Beijing North Railway Station (Bei Zhan)** 北站 trains run frequently to Badaling (see opposite).

● **Getting a ticket Domestic tickets** can be bought from Beijing Zhan station. There is no longer a designated Foreigners' Ticket Office, but there's usually an English-speaking window amongst the ground floor ticket windows. Alternatively, your accommodation, Monkey Business (see p398) or CITS (see p399) will book a ticket for you for a small fee, saving you the queuing.

International tickets (see also pp130-4) must be booked with CITS or Monkey Business (see p398): CITS can book both Trans-Mongolian and Trans-Manchurian trains; Monkey Business can also book tickets for journeys starting in Beijing.

● **At the station** You will have to put your luggage through an **X-ray machine** and walk through a metal detector at the entrance to any railway station.

The **electronic departure board** in the main hall states the train's type (ie Z or T), number, and time of departure, and you can use that information to find the correct departure lounge (there are several) from which to board your train.

Tickets are checked upon entering so you will know you're in the correct lounge. In the departure lounge the board shows all departures from that lounge; most trains are shown as 'on time', immediate departures are shown as 'waiting', and when a train is ready for boarding (30 mins before departure), it is shown as 'check in'. **Departure announcements** at the big railway stations are made in English as well as Chinese.

By air Many airlines serve Beijing Capital International Airport (📧 en.bcia.com.cn) and there are direct flights from Beijing to most major cities in the world. Connections with a number of destinations in South-East Asia are relatively inexpensive, thanks to budget carriers such as Air Asia.

If you'd like to fly the first leg of your Trans-Siberian journey, **Mongolian Airlines** (MIAT; 📧 www.miat.com) has direct Beijing–Ulaanbaatar flights (4-5/

week). **Air China** (📧 www.airchina.com .cn) also flies to Ulaanbaatar (5/week), as well as to Irkutsk, Khabarovsk, Vladivostok, Novosibirsk and Moscow. **Aeroflot** (📧 www.aeroflot.com) has daily Beijing–Moscow flights, while **S7** (📧 www.s7.com) has thrice-weekly flights to Novosibirsk, Krasnoyarsk, Irkutsk and Vladivostok.

By bus Services from **Dongzhimen Wai (Long-distance) Bus Station** include: Huairou for Mutianyu (see p408) or Huanghuacheng (see p409), or to Miyun for Simatai (see p408). There are also services to Harbin.

DAY TRIP TO THE GREAT WALL OF CHINA 长城

China's most famous attraction makes an ideal day trip from Beijing. The Wall itself was not built in one massive construction project as many believe; in fact the original scheme, under Emperor Shih Huang (1st century BC), was simply to join extant stretches of individual defensive walls together.

It was hoped that the resulting fortification would protect China from marauding foreigners but this was not the case. The Wall – an awe-inspiring construction feat that stretches for 6200km, starting in Jiayuguan in Gansu and ending at the Bahai Sea at Shanhaiguan – is responsible for drawing more visitors than ever, as those who visit at Badaling or Mutianyu will see. Those expecting an easy stroll along the Wall may be surprised because different sections are in various states of repair; the Wall comprises crumbling battlements, steep climbs and descents as it snakes up and down the hills.

Wear good shoes (sturdy trainers will suffice) and be prepared for persistent refreshment and souvenir sellers, even on the less touristy sections. Most hotels and hostels offer day tours to different sections of the Wall, though each is also reachable by public transport. Though it's possible to appreciate the beauty and sheer magnitude of the Wall at the locations near Beijing, if you have time, it's well worth travelling further out, in order to see the Wall away from the crowds.

Badaling 八达岭
(7am-7pm daily, adult/student Y45/25, cable car one-way/return Y65/85) Closest to the city (72km from Beijing), this busy section was completely restored in the 1980s, robbing it of the authenticity that other sections still possess. It has a cable car, museum and theatre and is usually overrun with tourists, though the views of the wall snaking over the surrounding hills are nonetheless impressive.

Go here on a weekday if you don't have much time, or in the colder months, to avoid the crush of humanity. Take bus 877 (Y12, 60 mins, 6am-5pm), 880

(Y12, 1½hrs, 7am-5pm) or 919 (Y12, 1½hrs, 6am-6.30pm) from the north side of Deshengmen Gate 德胜门 (see map p385); a tour bus from Beijing Hub of Tourist Dispatch 北京旅游集散中心 by Arrow Tower (Line C costs Y120 and includes entry to the wall; 9.30-11am, while Line A costs Y180 and takes in the Ming Tombs 十三陵 as well as Badaling, departing between 7 and 9.30am). High-speed suburban trains run from Beijing North Railway Station (Y8-15) every 1-2 hours. The Wall is a 10- to 15-minute walk from Badaling station.

Mutianyu 慕田峪

(7am-6.30pm daily, adult/student Y45/25, cable car one-way/return Y60/80) A popular alternative to Badaling, this 2250m-long section, 90km north-east of Beijing, boasts stunning views and numerous Ming dynasty guard towers, with one particularly steep climb if you head west along the wall.

Take bus 916 (1h, several daily, Y8) from Dongzhimen long-distance bus station to Huairou International Conference Centre, alight at the Mingzhu Giangchang bus stop 明珠广场车站 and take a first right to change for a minibus to Mutianyu 密云 (45 mins, several daily Y20); the last minibus from Huairou back to Beijing leaves at around 7pm.

Simatai 司马台 and Jingshanling 金山岭

(8am-5pm daily, adult/student Y40/20, cable car one-way/return Y30/50) Perhaps the most picturesque section of the Wall, the 19km stretch between Simatai and Jinshanling is a less-developed section featuring 24 watch-towers; Simatai lies 108km north-east of Beijing. The four-hour hike between the two is the highlight of many a visit to Beijing. Note that the Simatai section was closed for renovation at the time of writing, but should reopen within the lifetime of this book.

The Simatai section is particularly steep, with crumbling battlements and watchtowers; you'll need both your hands for uphill/downhill scrambles, so bring a day pack for your belongings. Make sure you're wearing sturdy shoes, and don't underestimate the strenuousness of the hike, especially on a hot summer's day. You'll be able to buy refreshments from vendors along the way. This section features walls-within-walls – obstacle walls used for defence against enemies who'd already infiltrated the Great Wall, and a zipline for thrill-seekers which descends from the halfway point to the car park (Y40).

The Jinshanling section is not as steep as Simatai and it's the only section where it's possible to camp overnight in a designated camping ground.

Many hostels operate tours which start in Jinshanling and end in Simatai, but if you're travelling out there independently, it's easier to catch public transport back from Jinshanling, so do the hike in reverse.

To get to Simatai independently, catch bus 980 from Dongzhimen long-distance bus station to Miyun 十三陵 (several daily, 1½hrs, Y15) and then switch to a Simatai-bound minibus (1hr, Y15) or taxi (return Y120).

To reach Jinshanling, catch the daily Tourist Bus from Dongzhimen Wai (long-distance) bus station 东直门外车站 (Y120, 2hrs) that departs at 8am and returns at 3pm.

Huanghuacheng 黄花城

(8am-5.30pm Mon-Fri, 7am-6pm Sat & Sun, Y25) is a beautifully preserved and relatively 'untouristy' section of the wall stretching high above a natural spring lake and overgrown with wild flowers in the summer. Here you see some great examples of Ming beacon towers and wide ramparts.

Some sections of the wall are very steep and slippery where the stones have been worn smooth, with no guardrails. You may have to pay a small fee (Y2) to peasants who guard the gates to reach some sections of the wall. Take bus 916 from Dongzhimen long-distance bus station to Huairou 怀柔 (Y12, 1hr), alight at the Nanhuayuan Sanqu bus stop 南华园三区车站, walk on for 200m or so, crossing a road, to get to the Nanhuayuan Siqu stop 南华园四区车站 and then catch a minibus to Huanghua 黄花长.

Bratsk
Братск

[Moscow Time +5; population: 241,273] About 470km north of Irkutsk on the BAM (Baikal Amur Mainline) lies one of the world's largest dams. The hydroelectric power station at Bratsk, Russia's third largest after the two along the Yenisei river, is the chief (and pretty much only) attraction of the unpretty town that consists of several spread-out living suburbs. Founded in 1631, Bratsk remained a tiny village until dam construction started in 1955 and drowned the village in the 1960s. The station is reputedly capable of generating 4500 MW (the world's biggest hydroelectric project is the 12,600 MW Itaipu Dam on the Brazil–Paraguay border), though lack of customers means it has never run at full capacity. Unless you're riding the BAM anyway, or are especially interested in dams, it's not worth the effort to leave the comfort of the train.

WHAT TO SEE AND DO

The main sight is the impressive **Bratsk Hydroelectric Station Братская ГЭС** and dam. The giant dam, holding back the waters of the reservoir known as 'Bratskoye More' (Bratsk Sea), is certainly an impressive sight. As the BAM runs right across the top of the dam anyway, you will see it briefly even without getting off the train. However, if you want to get up close and personal with it, you can contact **Taiga Tours** (Hotel Taiga, 2nd flr, ☎ 416 513, 🖳 www.taiga-tours.ru) in Energetik in advance to arrange a tour.

Between Energetik and Tsentralny, at Angara village, you'll find an open-air **museum Музей** (10am-5pm Wed-Sun, until 7pm in summer, R150) containing a reconstructed Evenki camp, a wooden watchtower and a fort, as well as other buildings rescued from the original Bratsk, drowned by the dam. In the forest there are several shaman sites and examples of Evenki teepees. Since the museum is off the public transportation route, at an out-of-the-way lakeside site, it's best to take a taxi or go with Taiga Tours.

CITY GUIDES & PLANS

PRACTICAL INFORMATION
Orientation
Bratsk is not one town but a ring of connected settlements around the so-called Bratsk Sea, the reservoir created by the hydroelectric dam. From the south in a counter-clockwise direction, the towns are Port Novobratsk, Bratskoye Morye, Bratsk Tsentralny (the administration centre), Padun, Energetik on the dam's west bank and Gidrostroitel on the east bank.

Padunskie Porogi railway station, serves the suburbs of Padun and Energetik. Padun is the most attractive part of Bratsk as it has a pleasant promenade with an old log watchtower and the city's only church, but the most convenient place to stay, as far as services are concerned, is in Tsentralny.

Bratsk airport is to the north of Padunskie Porogi and can be reached by a 40-minute bus trip from the station.

Where to stay
Hotel Taiga Гостиница Тайга (ul Mira 35, Tsentralny, ул Мира 35, Центральный, ☎ 414 710, 🖳 www.hotel-taiga.ru, sgl/dbl from R2600/2800, wi-fi) has basic rooms that are stuck in the 1980s, good, modern bathrooms, an on-site sauna, a couple of cafés and a bar. Some English is spoken. Taiga Tours (see p409) is on the 2nd floor.

Hotel Shvedka Гостиница Шведка (ul Mira 25, Tsentralny, ул Мира 25, Центральный, ☎ 412 520, sgl/twin from R800/1200) is a good-enough budget option for a provincial Russian town, with rooms ranging from very basic cheapies with shared facilities to clean and comfortable singles and twins. Breakfast not offered.

Moving on
In summer, you can take one of two hydrofoils a week to Irkutsk from the river station in southern Tsentralny. Between early June and late September, hydrofoils depart Bratsk at 8am on Wednesdays and Sundays, arriving in Irkutsk at 8pm. Return journeys take place on Tuesdays and Saturdays at 8.30am. Departures are weather-dependent and subject to cancellation. Check 🖳 www .vsrp.ru for up-to-date timetables.

You have to transfer at Anzyobi Анзёби station to/from a bus or elektrichka to Tsentralny. The 071 and the 347 trains (17-24hrs) run between Bratsk and Irkutsk, while the 075 and the 091 run on alternate days to Novosibirsk (27hrs) and Krasnoyarsk (20hrs). Eastbound departures include Severobaikalsk (1-4/day, 14-16¼hrs), while the 098 runs to Tynda (41hrs) on alternate days.

> The telephone code for Bratsk is ☎ +3953.

Severobaikalsk
Северобайкальск

[**Moscow Time +5; population: 24,449**] Severobaikalsk, on the BAM railway, is the 'capital' of the northern end of Lake Baikal. The town provides excellent access to north Baikal attractions, which include trekking and mountaineering in the Baikal Mountains, the northern parts of the Great Baikal Trail (see box p308), sailing, hot springs, expeditions with the indigenous Evenki and their reindeer in winter/spring, and a Stalin-era Gulag.

The town itself is lined with cloned multi-storey apartment buildings, their foundations specifically designed to work on permafrost and they are built to withstand the constant seismic activity in the Baikal area. See pp414-15 for details about visiting Nizhneangarsk, Baikalskoye, Goudzhekit, Dzelinda, or Akikan Gulag.

WHAT TO SEE AND DO

The biggest attraction is, of course, **Lake Baikal**. Its remote northern shore is very dramatic-looking, with steep, forested cliffs, snow-peaked mountains visible across the lake, and pebble beaches completely devoid of the visitors who crowd the shores at the lake's southern end.

The easiest way to appreciate the lake is to walk south along ul Studencheskaya, cross the bridge and then descend to the shore along the dirt road past a summer café that sells shashlyk. Alternatively, cross the railway bridge directly behind the main railway station building and take the road leading straight through the forest; either will allow you to pick up the narrow cliffside path that meanders in and out of the forest.

There's more walking to be done along a specially constructed **nature trail Тропа** in the northern part of the city, the trailhead reachable by taxi. It's only 2km long, but the steep ascent and descent and the views can keep you occupied for a few hours. Ask at the Baikal Trail Hostel (see p412) for details.

As for railway-related attractions, if you turn left out of the railway station and head west along pr 60 Let SSSR, you'll shortly come across a **Locomotive P36 Паровоз П-36** on a plinth on your left-hand side, with a star at the front and marked with the letters 'CCCP'.

Other sites of interest include **BAM Museum Музей БАМа** (per Proletarsky 2, пер Пролетарский 2, 10am-1pm & 2-6pm Tue-Sat, R80), with memorabilia relating to the town's creation. If you speak some Russian, the curator will bring it to life with her impassioned storytelling.

Adjoining it is the excellent **BAM Art Museum Художественный Музей БАМа** (same opening days/hours, R80), which sometimes hosts quite wonderful, unique exhibitions. One such was by Valeri Kondakov, an internationally acclaimed artist from nearby Nizhneangarsk, whose works drew on traditional Evenk culture for inspiration and consisted of intriguing wooden sculptures and intricate woven works incorporating Evenki kilim (rugs). The staff here are also wonderfully enthusiastic, though again it helps to speak at least a little Russian to get the most out of the experience, or to go with an interpreter.

PRACTICAL INFORMATION
Orientation and services
Everything in Severobaikalsk is within walking distance with the exception of the **hydrofoil port причал ракеты**.

Bus No 1 runs between the port and the central bus station, which is in front of the railway station. Buses and marshrutkas to other destinations, such as Nizhneangarsk and Goudzhekit, also run from in front of the railway station.

There's a handy TransCreditBank **ATM** inside the railway station, a **post office** at Leningradsky pr 6, and inexpensive **internet access** both at the post office and at the public library (Leningradsky pr 5, 10am-6pm Mon-Thur & Sat, 10am-2pm Fri).

Information and tours
A particularly good website on the area, full of helpful information and listings and

run by the local tourism association, is **Warm North of Baikal** (🖳 www.privet-baikal.ru). Another helpful **website** is 🖳 www.sbaikal.ru and there's a **tourist information booth** in front of the railway station in summer (9am-6pm) where you can also get some information on the area.

Alternatively, **BAMTour БАМТур** (ul Oktyabrya 16/2, ул Октября 16/2, ☎ 921 560, 🖳 www.gobaikal.com), run by Rashit Yakhin who worked on the railway in the early 1970s but was partially disabled by a stroke, can help you arrange multi-day boat cruises along the northern shore of Lake Baikal, trekking, rafting and horse-riding. His latest idea is a ski tour with the participants sleeping in special winter tents right on the lake, taking all necessary equipment with them on sledges.

The **Maryasov family** – Anya at Baikal Trail Hostel (see below) and her father Yevgeny – are indispensable when it comes to arranging Baikal adventures. They are both deeply involved in the work around the Great Baikal Trail and Yevgeny works with a nearby Evenki community that offers excursions into the mountains with their reindeer; contact the Maryasovs at 🖳 baikalinfo@gmail.com with any questions.

Where to stay and eat

The best place for budget travellers is undoubtedly the 5-bed ★ *Baikal Trail Hostel* (ul Studencheskaya 12, apt 16, ул Студенческая 12, кв 16, ☎ 23 860, 🖳 www.baikaltrail hostel.com, dorm R600, WI-FI), run by the ultra-helpful, English-speaking Anya. She can help organise trips to the Great Baikal Trail and other local places of interest, there's a kitchen that guests may use; you tend to meet an interesting mix of Baikal Trail volunteers and adventurous travellers here.

A good choice if you're travelling in a group is the friendly *Zolotaya Rybka* **Золотая Рыбка** (ul Sibirskaya 14, ул Сибирская 14, ☎ 22 231, 🖳 www.baikal goldenfish.ru, R1200-2800). It consists of

three cottages with views of Lake Baikal, each with three rooms that share a bathroom with a good shower, two toilets, a mini-lounge and a kitchen.

In a central location, *Hotel Olymp* **Гостиница Олимп** (ul Poligrafistov 26/1, ул Полиграфистов 26/1, ☎ 23 980, 🖳 www.hotelolymp.ru, rooms R1300-3300, WI-FI) offers comfortable rooms with cable TV and a good café in the basement.

A short walk from the lake, *Dom u Baikala* **Дом у Байкала** (pr Neptunsky 3, пер Нептунский 3, ☎ 23 950, 🖳 www.bai kal-kruiz.narod.ru, sgl/dbl R900/1800) consists of cosy en suite rooms in the house and some cosy summer huts made of pine (same price) which share bathrooms. Guests have use of a kitchen and room (but not cottage); prices include breakfast.

Severobaikalsk's eating options are limited. The **central market Рынок** is a good place for fresh produce, including smoked *omul*, as well as smoked meats, cheese, bread and dairy. On the north side of the market there are several basic **eateries столовые** serving Central Asian plov (rice with meat) and Russian standards.

Café Olymp **Кафе Олимп** (at Hotel Olymp, see above) serves good, home-cooked food and there are usually a couple of lunchtime options to choose from, such as meat cutlets stuffed with egg. Just don't expect nectar and ambrosia.

In summer, you'll find a café serving **shashlyk шашлык** near the beach off ul Olkhonskaya and there are several basic **eateries столовые**, along pr 60 Let SSSR from the railway station towards ul Studencheskaya, that serve shashlyk and *pozy* **позы** – large meat-stuffed steamed dumplings.

For self-caterers the best **supermarket** is **Supermarket Vist Супермаркет Вист** (Leningradsky pr 5, Ленинградский пр 5).

Moving on

By boat Between late June and late August a hydrofoil departs Nizhneangarsk

BAMTour (БАМТур), 400m
Nature Trail (Тропа), 2km
Ул Студенческая

Ul Studencheskaya

Hotel Olymp
Гостиница Олимп

Café Olymp
Кафе Олимп

Ul Studencheskaya
Ул Студенческая

Ul Promyshlennaya
Ул Промышленная

★ trailblazer

BAM Art Museum
Художественный
Музей БАМа

Proletarsky Per
Пролетарский Пер

Ul Poligrafistov
Ул Полиграфов

BAM Museum
Музей БАМа

Baikal Trail
Hostel

Dom Kultury 'Zheleznodorozhnik'
Дом Культуры «Железнодорожник»

Eateries
Столовые

Central market
Центральный Рынок

Tsentralnaya Pl
Центральная Пл

Post Office/Internet
Почта/интернет

Pr 60 Let SSSR Пр 60 Лет СССР

Eateries
Столовые

Ul Olkhonskaya Ул Ольхонская

○ **Shashlyk**
Шашлык

Library/Internet
Библиотека/
интернет

Leningradsky Pr
Ленинградский Пр

Ul Olkhonskaya Ул Ольхонская

0   200m

Supermarket Vist
Супермаркет Вист

Bus Station
Автовокзал

Tourist
information booth

Railway Station & ATM
Железнодорожный
Вокзал

Locomotive P-36
Паровоз П-36 ●

$

Zolotaya Rybka (Золотая Рыбка), 100m,
Dom u Baikala (Дом у Байкала), 200m

Hydrofoil port
(причал ракеты)

Lake
Baikal

Severobaikalsk Северобайкапьск

CITY GUIDES & PLANS

for Irkutsk via Severobaikalsk, Olkhon Island and Port Baikal on Wednesdays and Saturdays at 7.40am, arriving 25 minutes later at Severobaikalsk and then in Irkutsk at 8.10pm.

From Irkutsk the hydrofoil makes the return trip on Tuesdays and Fridays arriving in Severobaikalsk at 9.10pm. The journey from Severobaikalsk to Irkutsk costs R4600 and the timetable is weather-dependent.

By train Westbound, the 075 and the 091 run to Moscow (every other day, 90hrs) via Krasnoyarsk (26½hrs), Novosibirsk (40hrs) and other major cities. The slower 347 runs to Krasnoyarsk (35hrs) on alternate days, originating in Severobaikalsk. The 071 and the 347 run to Irkutsk via Bratsk and Tayshet on alternate days (32hrs and 37hrs, respectively).

Heading **east**, the 076 runs to Tynda (alternate days, 26½hrs), with additional services to Tynda with the 098 (Mon only, 25½hrs).

By air There are flights from nearby Nizhneangarsk to Ulan-Ude (4/week) and Irkutsk (3/week) in summer, though they are weather-dependent and thus subject to delays and cancellations. Buy tickets at **Aviakassa Авиакасса**, in Dom Kultury 'Zheleznodorozhnik' Дом Культуры «Железнодорожник» (Tsentralnaya pl, Центральная пл, 9am-noon & 1-4pm daily).

By bus Half-hourly buses run to ul Pobedy in Nizhneangarsk (50 mins, R40), continuing on to the airport.

AROUND SEVEROBAIKALSK

Nizhneangarsk Нижнеангарск

Nizhneangarsk, 40km east of Severobaikalsk, is wedged on a narrow strip between Lake Baikal and steep mountains. The 20km-long town has a large port for a small fishing fleet. The harbour was built for construction of the BAM to the east but the railway arrived from the west before the harbour was completed. Although the regional airport is located here, Nizhneangarsk is smaller than neighbouring Severobaikalsk and was rather isolated until the arrival of the railway. The town is pleasant to stroll around with its mainly wooden buildings. At ul Pobedy 37 ул Победы 37 you'll find the **Regional Museum Краеведческий Музей** (10am-5pm Mon-Fri, R100), worth a glimpse for the Evenki exhibits. An architectural oddity is the wooden boat-rental and water-rescue station on the lake's edge. The **fish-processing factory** can be visited and gives an insight into Russian methods and working conditions. The plant makes delicious smoked or salted *omul*. You can also walk the length of the **Yarki Island Яркий Остров** spit at the eastern end of town; its length protects the vulnerable Verkhnyaya Angara delta from the lake's powerful waves.

Nizhneangarsk is linked to Irkutsk by hydrofoil (see pp412-13). The last bus from here to Severobaikalsk (see p413) leaves at just before 6pm on weekdays, 6.50pm at the weekend.

Baikalskoye Байкальское

On Baikal's western shore, 45km south of Severobaikalsk, is the picturesque fishing village of Baikalskoye, which makes for a pleasant day trip from Severobaikalsk. This is also the starting point of an 18km section of the Great Baikal Trail, that heads north from the village towards the radio mast along a cliffside path, from where you get amazing views of the village below. The trail runs through cedar and spruce forest, ending at Lake Slyudyanskoye, where you can stay at the basic *Echo turbaza* (R600), though you need to arrange that in advance with Baikal Trail Hostel (see p412).

There are two marshrutkas daily to Baikalskoye at 8am and 5pm (45mins), returning at 9am and 6pm. To get back from the Echo turbaza, you have to pre-arrange transport, or else take the dirt track that runs through the forest to the Baikalskoye/Severobaikalsk road and hitch a lift.

❏ **Frolikha Adventure Coastline Track (F.A.C.T.)**
In 2009 and 2010, Russian and German volunteers worked on and completed a stunning 100km-long trail that runs from the ranger station at the delta of the Verkhnyaya Angara River to the rustic Khakusy spa, situated on Baikal's eastern shore. This trail skirts long, sandy beaches and isolated coves, climbs cliffs and descends to Ayaya Bay. It's a challenging trail that involves fording the Frolikha River halfway along, scrambling up rocks and potentially meeting local wildlife, such as the brown bear. Your rewards are the pristine forests, incredible views of Baikal and a soak at the rustic Khakusy hot springs at the end of the trail. For more info and trail maps, check 🖥 www.baikalplan.de.

Goudzhekit Гуджекит
Goudzhekit is famous for its hot springs, which were discovered during the course of the construction of the BAM. The little spa (7am-3am), 300m from the tiny railway station, is very popular with locals, particularly when the weather gets cold.

There are also three marshrutkas a day from in front of Severobaikalsk's railway station (9am, noon, 3pm; 45mins) that return at 10am, 1pm and 4pm. If you get stuck in Goudzhekit, however, there are a couple of basic lodgings by the spa.

Dzelinda Дзелинда
With waters believed to have curative properties, tiny Dzelinda has an even more attractive spa than Goudzhekit, set in a beautiful forest location, though it's further away (92km from Severobaikalsk). The waters, a constant 44°C, are best enjoyed in cold weather, as in summer the mosquitoes can be a pain. Since the number of elektrichka (suburban train) services has been cut, your best bet is to arrange a tour via Baikal Trail Hostel (see p412).

Akikan Gulag Акикан Гулаг
Akikan Gulag was a mica mining camp in the late 1930s. The residue of those terrible years consists of several collapsed wooden and stone buildings, towers and barbed wire fences, as well as a mini railway with little bucket wagons, abandoned by the entrance of a collapsed mineshaft. The camp is a two-hour walk from Kholodnoye village (itself an hour by bus or train from Severobaikalsk); BAMTour (see p412) can help arrange a guide.

Yakutsk
Якутск

[Moscow Time +6; population: 286,456] Though not on the BAM as such, Yakutsk makes for an out-of-the-way attraction for adventurous travellers.

This is the capital of Sakha, the vast Yakut Republic (see box p471). Lying only 600km south of the Arctic Circle, it is one of the world's coldest cities (average temperature in January is -32°C) although summers are pleasantly mild (19°C in July). It is also one of Siberia's oldest settlements, founded in 1632 on the banks of the mighty Lena River as a base for exploration and a trading centre for gold and furs. There is little left of historic interest in this polluted city, but it is worth visiting for the excursions on the Lena and to see the effects of permafrost. All the buildings here have to be built on massive stilts or they would sink into the ground as their heat melts the permafrost.

Only about 30% of the people are ethnic Yakuts, most of the rest being Russians and Ukrainians. Like other minority groups in Russia the Yakuts are now making themselves heard in Moscow. In 1991 an agreement was signed between the presidents of Russia and Sakha, giving the latter a certain degree of autonomy within the Russian Federation and more control over the proceeds from gold and diamond mining in this immensely mineral-rich region.

See opposite for details about trips on the River Lena.

WHAT TO SEE AND DO

A unique place to visit in Yakutsk is the **Permafrost Institute Институт Вечной Мерзлоты** (ul Merzlotnaya 36, ул Мерзлотная 36, ☎ 334 912 or ☎ 334 969; call in advance for a tour in Russian). You are taken 12m underground to see part of the old river bed, where the temperature never varies from -5°C. Permafrost is said to affect 25% of the planet and 50% of Russia. Outside is a model of a baby mammoth found almost perfectly preserved in permafrost in 2007. The original, thought to be around 40,000 years old, is in St Petersburg's Natural History Museum.

Museum of the History and Culture of the Peoples of the North Музей Истории и Культуры Народов Севера (pr Lenina 5/2 пр Ленина 5/2; 10am-1pm & 2-5pm Tue-Sun, 🖳 www.sakhamemory.ru/museum.aspx, free entry) is said to include over 140,000 items illustrating Yakut flora, fauna and anthropology, starting from prehistoric times and ending with the 1990s. The natural history section includes one of the world's few complete woolly mammoth skeletons.

For an even-closer look at those great beasts, check out the **Mammoth Museum Музей Мамонта** (ul Kulakovskogo 48, 4th floor, ул Кулаковского 48, 4-й этаж, 10am-1pm & 2-5pm Mon-Sat; free entry), with its star exhibit being a cryogenically preserved head of a woolly mammoth. The museum's collection also includes a diverse collection of objects from the Ice Age.

Those with an interest in the region's diverse ethnic population shouldn't miss the **Museum of Archaeology and Ethnography of Yakutsk State University Музей Археологии и Этнографии Якутского Государственного Университета** (10am-1pm & 2-5pm Tue-Sat), located in the same building and focusing on the culture, mythology and everyday life of the Yakuts, Evenki, Sakha and other Yakutian ethnic groups.

The **National Art Museum Национальный Художественный Музей** (ul Kirova 9, ул Кирова 9, 10am-6pm Wed-Sun, closed 1st Wed of month, 🖳 www.sakhamuseum.ru, R300) is particularly worthwhile for its rich collection of Yakut arts and crafts, as well as an enormous display of art by Yakuts, Russians and international artists from the 16th century to the present day.

❏ **Ysyakh Festival**
The best time to visit Yakutsk is during the two-day fertility festival, held on or around the Summer Solstice. The festival involves traditional Yakut sports, such as wrestling, archery and stick fighting, as well as costumed revelry, competitions to create the best national dishes and traditional folk concerts. The most important parts of it are the blessing of the harvest by the White Shaman and the sacred rites of the second day's sunrise.

PRACTICAL INFORMATION
Getting to Yakutsk

Until the rail services start (see below) the best way to get to Yakutsk is by air. Yakutsk's international airport (🖳 www.air port-yakutsk.ru) is served by regular flights from Moscow, St Petersburg, Novosibirsk, Krasnoyarsk, Irkutsk and Khabarovsk.

Railway tracks to Nizhny Bestyakh, across the Lena River from Yakutsk, are in place and the Nizhny Bestyakh railway station was opened with great fanfare in August 2013. Building work has also commenced on the bridge that will connect Nizhny Bestyakh and Yakutsk; passenger services are due to be fully operational by September 2014. Until then you have to take a train to Neryungri and then take a passenger van or jeep to cover the remaining 810km up the Amuro-Yakutskaya Magistral highway (15-20hrs) from the railway station car park; jeeps and vans tend to meet morning train arrivals.

Two ferries – *Rukavishnikov* and *Stepan Vasilyev* – make return trips between Nizhny Bestyakh and Yakutsk; nine in each direction daily (R250).

In the summer months regular passenger boats connect Yakutsk to Lensk, Olekminsk and other riverside towns in Yakutia itself; while there haven't been any passenger boats to Ust-Kut on the BAM for years, this may change as Yakutsk has recently invested in several new passenger ships.

Services

Tour Service Centre Гостиница Полярная Звезда (ul Yaroslavskogo 30/1, office 66, ул Ярославского 30/1, к66, ☎ 351 144, 🖳 www.yakutiatravel.com) is a reputable tour agency that can organise a variety of excursions in the area and also provide interpreters, book accommodation, organise homestays within Yakut communities and arrange onward travel.

Where to stay and eat

Soviet giant *Hotel Lena* **Гостиница Лена** (pr Lenina 8, пр Ленина 8, ☎ 424 892, 🖳 www.lena-hotel.ru, sgl/dbl/lux from R2400/3400/7800, WI-FI) is centrally located and offers comfortable en suites, a money-changing facility and a café which is only good enough for breakfast. Rooms are non-smoking but smoke from the corridors can seep in.

Tygyn Darkhan **Тыгын Дархан** (ul Ammosova 9, ул Аммосова 9, ☎ 435 109, 🖳 www.tygyn.ru, sgl/dbl/suite from R4700/5300/12,000, internet access) offers comfortable but rather overpriced rooms that could use renovating. The English-speaking front desk is helpful enough; perks include a swimming pool, fitness centre, sauna and a restaurant specialising in traditional Sakha dishes, such as *oiogos* (baked foal ribs).

The city's top place to stay is ★ *Hotel Polyarnaya Zvezda* **Гостиница Полярная Звезда** (pr Lenina 24, пр Ленина 24, ☎ 341 215, 🖳 www.alrosa-hotels.ru, sgl/dbl/suite from R5750/7900/25,000, WI-FI); as befitting a hotel of its calibre, the rooms are luxurious and tastefully decorated and a full range of facilities is included, such as a tour agency, excellent restaurant, swimming pool, sauna and fitness centre. A couple of the de luxe rooms have their own Jacuzzis. Cruises on the Lena River arranged on request.

At pr Lenina 8a, пр Ленина 8а, you'll find *Tamerlan* restaurant (meals R600-1000), serving up Yakut and Central Asian cuisine, with the chefs cooking their dishes on the heated table in front of you.

The Yakutsk telephone code is ☎ +4122.

Excursions from Yakutsk on the Lena River

The geological formations known as the **Lena Pillars** have fascinated travellers here since the 17th century. About 140km upriver from Yakutsk, the rock of the cliffs alongside the river has been eroded into delicate shapes of a reddish brown colour. Two-day cruises leave each Friday evening in summer. From the landing it's an hour's strenuous climb to the top, for a magnificent view of the river and the cliffs. Tour groups are sometimes brought here on hydrofoil day trips from Yakutsk, leaving early in the morning and getting back after dark.

The cruise ships *M/S Demyan Bedny* and *M/S Mikhail Svetlov* do 36-hour cruises to the Lena Pillars and back (sgl/dbl from R8500/14,000). It's also possible to make a trip down the Lena from Yakutsk to Tiksi on the Arctic Ocean (tickets from R1000). Check up-to-date schedules at 🖥 www.lenaturflot.ru. Trips can be booked at the Tour Service Centre (see p417).

Tynda
Тында

[Moscow Time +6; population: 34,785]   Formerly the headquarters of the BAM – 'the road built with love' – and still its capital, Tynda is a no-nonsense, functional railroading town with a handful of attractions. It sits at a major junction of the BAM, and the AYaM (Amur-Yakutsk Mainline) and Little BAM.

WHAT TO SEE AND DO

In front of the railway station you'll find a **freight locomotive YeA-3246 Паровоз Еа-3246** on a plinth dedicated to the founders of the BAM, placed there to celebrate the railway's 30th anniversary.

The excellent **BAM museum Музей БАМа** (ul Sportivnaya 22 ул Спортивная 22, Tue-Sun 10am-6pm, R120) covers the early history of the railway, with the Gulag prisoners used as the chief labour force; there are photographs and a final letter from one such prisoner to his family. Other exhibits chart the railway's later development, with models of volunteers' barracks (there's an actual one right outside the museum), photos of grinning volunteer brigades and an adorable model railway.

The history of Tynda is explored, from its beginnings as early as 1917, when gold was discovered in the area, to the present-day mining centre; you can see examples of the riches of the local earth, from different types of coal to semi-precious stones, such as charoite (see p276) and jasper. There's a modest natural history section and a superb exhibition dedicated to the Evenki, items ranging from reindeer saddle, baby crib and wide, fur-covered hunting skis to horned shaman headgear and a container made of reindeer skin for holding holy ritual objects. There's also an Evenki hunting calendar on the wall, with an ingenious use of holes and pegs. You'll get the most out of the museum if you understand some Russian.

Just off ul Krasnaya Presnya, inside the attractive little park, you can see the **Cathedral of the Holy Trinity Церковь Святой Троицы**, the plasticky-looking Orthodox cathedral built several years ago and the source of some controversy: some felt that the money could've been better spent elsewhere.

If you head east along the main street, Krasnaya Presnya (named after the Moscow street of the same name since Moscow is the capital of the country and Tynda is the capital of the BAM) to the end, you reach the little square that used to have a dramatic statue of a BAM worker памятник рабочему БАМа wielding a sledgehammer as its centrepiece. The monument was removed around a decade ago overnight under mysterious circumstances.

At the intersection of ul Krasnaya Presnya and ul Profsoyuznaya, you'll find a **giant hammer and sickle Серп и молот** – a Soviet relic that hasn't been removed.

You can also visit the nearby **Evenk village** of **Zarya/Pervomaiskoye деревня Заря/Первомайское**, where there is a large local school that teaches Evenki students from surrounding villages, thus enabling the survival of the Evenki language and culture. In March the Evenki celebrate the Reindeer Hunter and Herder Festival, while early June sees reindeer rides, traditional food, song and dance in the form of the Evenki Bakaldin Festival. Buses run to Zarya from the railway station several times a day.

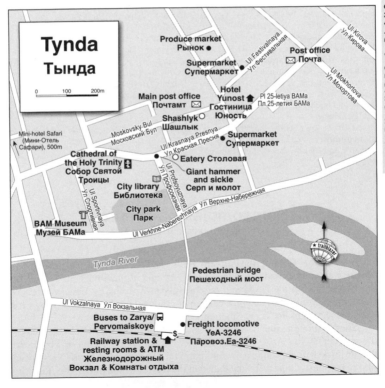

PRACTICAL INFORMATION
Orientation and services

To get to the town from the railway station, you have to cross the pedestrian bridge over the Tynda river, flanked by some industrial-sized metal pipes, and then keep walking straight until you hit the main ul Krasnaya Presnya, where you'll find a couple of places to eat, as well as Hotel Yunost.

There's a TransCreditBank **ATM** at the railway station.

Where to stay and eat

The railway station *resting rooms* комнаты отдыха (komnaty otdykha, ☎ 73 297, bed per 6/12/24 hours R400/650/1200) are clean and comfortable.

Otherwise, your central options are limited to *Hotel Yunost* Гостиница Юность (ul Krasnaya Presnya 49, ул Красная Пресня 49, ☎ 43 534, sgl/dbl from R1600/2000), where *Through Siberia By Accident* author Dervla Murphy ended up staying after she'd injured her leg, and the new *Mini-hotel Safari* Мини-Отель Сафари (ul Krasnoarmeyskaya 7, ул Красноармейская 7, ☎ 33 100, sgl/dbl R2600/3500), with sparkling en suite rooms and free wi-fi; Tynda has now joined the 21st century.

There are two **supermarkets** Супермаркет, one along ul Krasnaya Presnya and another on ul Festivalnaya, where you can stock up on basic staples, and a **produce market Рынок** along the street behind Hotel Yunost, with a couple of informal cheap eateries. At Krasnaya Presnya 29, there's an *eatery* (café) offering Central Asian food, such as plov, buuzy and pelmeni.

In summer, good *shashlyk* is available at makeshift cafés in front of the main post office.

Moving on

Heading **west**, the 075/097 serve Severobaikalsk (27hrs); the former leaves every other day, continuing on to Moscow. There are also slower trains to Moscow that run south via Little BAM, connecting with the Trans-Siberian and running via Irkutsk. The 363/364 runs to Komsomolsk-na-Amure (daily, 36½hrs), while the daily 325/326 heads south to Khabarovsk (29hrs).

There are daily trains **north** to Neryungri and Tommot on the AYaM line (5½hrs) and by September 2014, the AYaM is due to open for passenger services up to Nizhny Bestyakh, across the Lena river from Yakutsk.

> The telephone code for Tynda is
> ☎ +41656.

Komsomolsk-na-Amure
Комсомольск-на-Амуре

[**Moscow Time +7; population: 257,891**] Built in 1932, Komsomolsk-na-Amure was a city closed to foreigners until the end of the Soviet era. It remains the largest city on the BAM and is relatively prosperous by Eastern Siberian standards. The city's located on a convenient railway junction, which allows for easy connection to the Trans-Siberian via Khabarovsk.

Your first impression of Komsomolsk-na-Amure is likely to be coloured by the weather. If you arrive on a bleak, overcast day, bitterly cold in winter and the air thick with mosquitoes in summer, you might think that you've stepped into some ghastly time warp and ended in the Soviet Union of the '80s, the grim multi-storey buildings marginally enlivened by colourful shop signs. On a sunny day, however, the city seems transformed: you can appreciate the wide boulevards and the attractive main square; even the deserted waterfront with the sagging river terminal building – such a contrast with the lively Khabarovsk promenade – won't seem so depressing.

In summer and early autumn 2013, Komsomolsk was seriously affected by the flooding of the Amur river (see box, p337), with thousands made homeless and the city's buildings bearing the scars of the natural disaster.

WHAT TO SEE AND DO

Soviet mosaics

You'll find some striking Soviet mosaics in the city centre, most of them the work of artist Nikolai Dobilkin, resident in Komsomolsk in the '50s and '60s. Ones to look out for include the **WWII mosaic** at the *dom cultury* building at **Park Sudostroiteley Парк Судостроителей** (pr Mira & ul Truba, 2nd fl, пр Мира & ул Труба, 3-й этаж), the **science-themed mosaic** at the Polytechnic Institute on pr Lenina пр Ленина and the **electrician mosaic** on the side of an electric station along alleya Truda аллея Труда at the southern end of pr Mira.

Museums

The surprisingly good **Museum of Regional Studies Краеведческий Музей** (pr Mira 8, пр Мира 8, 9.30am-4.30pm Tue-Sun, 🖳 www.kmsgkm.ru, R120) charts the birth and development of the modern city, which you can just about follow in spite of the lack of English captioning. Other exhibits are devoted to the native Nanai and Evenki culture, Komsomolsk's participation in WWII, as well as the Khetagurova Movement, which encouraged women to move to the Far East in the 1930s to improve the gender balance. Though 70,000 girls originally volunteered, it's not clear how many got married and stayed. There are numerous dioramas and one exhibit is devoted to Gulags in the area.

The **Fine Arts Museum Музей Изобразительных Искусств** (pr Mira 16, пр Мира 16, 10am-6pm Tue-Fri, to 5pm Sat & Sun, 🖳 www.kmsmuseum.ru, R150) features absorbing collections of home-grown art, Russian art pre-1917, contemporary art, and some Western works. There's a particularly good section on indigenous art – with carvings, embroidery and creations made of fish skin, fur and feathers, courtesy of the Nanai, Even, Evenk, Udegei and Ulch peoples. The staff are enthusiastic about their museum's contents.

Memorials

To the north-west of the river station, you'll find the **Great Patriotic War Memorial Памятник Великой Отечественной Войне**, consisting of three stone obelisks above an eternal flame, with seven granite heads facing it and the names of the dead carved behind them. Other monuments include the **Stalinist Repression Memorial Stone Памятник Жертвам Сталинских Репрессий**, next to the City Court on pr Lenina; it was erected by the local government after being pressured by Memorial, the NGO specialising in searching for information on repression victims to see what their fate was and whether they had been posthumously rehabilitated, which is some comfort to their relatives. There are also 16 **Japanese PoW memorials Памятник Японским Военнопленным** around the city, the most central being on pr Mira beside Hotel Amur, since it was built by the PoWs.

In the Lenin District Ленинский район north-east of the centre you'll find the **Yuri Gagarin Aircraft Factory Авиационный Завод имени Юрия Гагарина**, even though he never worked there. In front of it is the **Yuri Gagarin Memorial Памятник Юрию Гагарину**, consisting of him holding a book on the Laws of the Cosmos. The book looks remarkably like a brick with a towel wrapped around it, earning it the local name of 'Brick and Towel Memorial'. Tram Nos 4 and 5 go to the Lenin District.

Also north-east of the city is **Komsomolsky Nature Reserve Комсомольский Заповедник**, where you'll find several ethnic Nanai settlements; it is best visited through Nata Tour (see below). Nata Tour can also arrange **cruises on the Amur** and **trips to Sakhalin Island** (departing from the River Station) with a particular emphasis on native cultures.

PRACTICAL INFORMATION
Orientation and services

Tram No 2 runs from the railway station to the waterfront past the main Sudostroiteley Park. The main **post office** (pr Mira 27, 8am-6pm Mon-Fri, until 5pm Sat, until 3pm Sun) is large and modern and has good **internet access** (R70/hour) and there's a TransCreditBank **ATM** at the railway station. **Nata Tour Ната Тур** (ul Vasanina 12, room 110, ул Васанина 12, офис 110, ☎ 201 067, 🖳 www.komsomolsknata.ru) is an experienced tour operator that does anything from 3-hour city excursions to multi-day ventures into the surrounding area (see above).

Where to stay

The *resting rooms* комнаты отдыха (*komnaty otdykha,* ☎ 284 193, sgl/dbl R2800/3800 for 24 hours) are clean and comfortable and are located on the east side of the railway station. Showers are R100 extra.

All clean lines, contemporary décor and thoroughly modern bathrooms, ★ *City* Сити (ul Kirova 2, ул Кирова 2, ☎ 333 338, 🖳 www.inkms.ru, sgl/dbl from R2000/2800, WI-FI) is dragging Komsomolsk-na-Amure into the 21st century. And we're very happy about it. Rooms can be rented for 12 hours overnight for half the price.

Biznestsentr Бизнесцентр (ul Dzerzhinskogo 3, ул Дзержинского 3, ☎ 521 522, sgl/dbl/suite from R2400/2600/4700, WI-FI) is a modern hotel aimed at business travellers. Some staff speak English and the spacious rooms come with flat screen TVs.

Soviet megalith *Hotel Voskhod* Гостиница Восход (pr Pervostroiteley 31, пр Первостроителей 31, ☎ 535 131, 🖳 www.hotel-voskhod.ru, dbl/suite from R2750/11,000, WI-FI) has had a facelift and the results are astonishing. Clean, bright, comfortable rooms, friendly staff, an excellent buffet breakfast and themed suites? Yes, indeed!

Where to eat and drink

On tiny pl Lenina you'll find *U City* (pr Lenina 19 пр Ленина 19, meals R300), the hangout of the young and trendy, that sells lukewarm pizza by the slice as well as Russian salads, blini and burgers.

Sushi City Суши-сити (pr Lenina 21, пр Ленина 21, mains R370) does decent enough sushi, whereas *Sholnya* Штольня (pr Mira 50, пр Мира 50, mains from R250) is a German-style beerhouse that serves decent meat dishes; their weekday business lunch is a bargain at R140. The *café* at Biznestsentr serves a combination of European and Asian dishes.

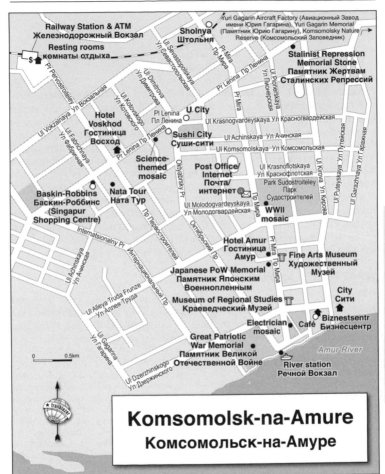

Komsomolsk-na-Amure
Комсомольск-на-Амуре

CITY GUIDES & PLANS

There's a **Baskin-Robbins** Баскин-Роббинс in **Singapur shopping centre** (corner of pr Lenina and ul Vasyanina, угол пр Ленина и ул Васянина).

Moving on

From Komsomolsk-na-Amure there are daily services to Khabarovsk with the 351/352 (10hrs) and to Vladivostok (27hrs). On the BAM, the 351/352 also runs a daily service to Vanino/SovGavan (13-14hrs). Westbound departures include Tynda (daily, 36½hrs on the 963), where you can change for a service to Severobaikalsk.

The telephone code for Komsomolsk-na-Amure is ☎ +4217.

Vanino
Ванино

[Moscow Time +7; population: 16,496] Founded in 1944, Vanino is a busy port that was originally used as a transit camp. The prisoners typically stayed here for several days, with representatives coming from various Gulags to select the strongest and fittest – a 20th-century equivalent of the slave trade. From Vanino they would be taken to Kolyma, Magadan, Sakhalin Island, Kamchatka and other parts of the inhospitable Siberian north. A great many of them, together with prisoners-of-war, helped to build the railway that reached Vanino in 1945.

Today Vanino is a commercial port, with freight ships heading for Japan, Sakhalin Island and the disputed Kuril islands. You'll only really come here to catch a ferry to Sakhalin Island, off the East Siberian coast. Its main attraction is the great variety of wildlife which visitors may photograph, study, ride amongst or hunt, with Russia's densest population of brown bears.

WHAT TO SEE AND DO

If you have a little time to while away, you can peek into the small **Regional Museum Краеведческий Музей** (ul Matrosova, ул Матросова, behind the big blue building to the east of the railway station, 2-7pm Tue-Fri, 10am-2pm Sat, free entry) covering Russian and Japanese history in the area.

PRACTICAL INFORMATION
Where to stay and eat

You have the choice of staying either in the *resting rooms* комнаты отдыха (*komnaty otdykha*, sgl/triple R1200/700pp, shower R100 extra), which are perfectly comfortable and located inside the light blue railway station building, or else there's *Hotel Vanino* Гостиница Ванино (ul Liniya 1-ya 1, ул Линия 1-я 1 ☎ 71 319 or ☎ 74 773, rooms from R2000), with basic but comfortable rooms with dated furniture, and a *café* on the ground floor.

Moving on

If you're heading to Sakhalin Island there is technically at least one freight ship daily,

year-round, to Kholmsk on Sakhalin. However, whether or not it sails depends on the amount of freight and the weather; freight takes priority over passengers, so if there isn't enough of a load, the ship won't sail. If you speak some Russian, call the day before to reserve a seat and find out whether the ship leaves the following day (☎ 8233 66 098 or ☎ 8233 66 516).

As for trains, from Vanino, the 351/352 runs daily to Vladivostok (40hrs) via Khabarovsk (24½hrs) and Komsomolsk-na-Amure (13½hrs).

The telephone code in **Vanino** is ☎ +42137 and the code for **SovGavan** is ☎ +42138

Sovetskaya Gavan
Советская Гавань

[**Moscow Time +7; population: 26,642**] Sovetskaya Gavan ('Soviet Harbour', often shortened to SovGavan) lies 36km east of Vanino and is the final stop for BAM completists. The end of the line. It was originally called Imperatorskaya Gavan ('Imperial Harbour') but its name was changed in 1922. Since the Japanese ruled the lower half of Sakhalin Island from 1905, this strategic deep-water harbour would have been the ideal place for a potential Japanese invasion and therefore had to be defended at all costs. During WWII, the Soviet Union gained control of the whole of Sakhalin Island, but the harbour continued to have great military importance during its heyday of the 1950s and 1960s as one of the three most important ports of the Pacific Fleet. As with Vanino, the railway reached here in 1945 and was built with the blood and sweat of thousands of prisoners-of-war.

WHAT TO SEE AND DO

Today, commercial activity has replaced military activity and there's a good **Regional Museum Краеведческий Музей** (ul Sovetskaya 29, ул Советская 29, 10am-5pm Tue-Fri & Sun), where you'll find information on the revolutionary and Civil War era activity in the region, as well as exhibits on local native culture and a nature section where the most impressive exhibit is a giant Siberian tiger. Though the Far East was dotted with Gulags, information on them is conspicuously absent. You can also head to the coast to check out **Krasny Partizan Lighthouse Маяк Красных Партизан**; beside the lighthouse there's a memorial dedicated to the partisan fighters who were tortured to death here by the White Army in 1919. To get here, catch a bus from Sovetskaya Gavan to Mayachnaya and walk from there.

PRACTICAL INFORMATION
Arrival
If SovGavan is your destination it's best to get off at Vanino and take a bus (R100, 60 mins, 4-5/day) to SovGavan from in front of the railway station. Even though trains may display 'SovGavan' as their final destination, they actually arrive at Sovetskaya Gavan-Sortirovka – the marshalling yards, from where you have to make your own way to the town by bus.

Where to stay and eat
The renovated *Hotel Sovetskaya Gavan* **Гостиница Советская Гавань** (ul Pionerskaya 14, ул Пионерская 14, ☎ 46 612, 🖳 www.sovg.biz, dorm/sgl/dbl from R700/2000/2800) has clean, comfortable rooms and cheap, basic dorms with shared facilities. *Café Cappucino* **Кафе Каппучино** on the ground floor is a good spot for a meal.

SovGavan is the place to stock up on red caviar, produced by the city's cannery.

Moving on
From SovGavan, the 351/352 runs daily to Vladivostok (40½hrs) via Khabarovsk (25hrs) & Komsomolsk-na-Amure (14hrs).

CITY GUIDES & PLANS

ROUTE GUIDE & MAPS

Using this guide

This route guide has been set out to draw your attention to points of interest and to enable you to locate your position along the Trans-Siberian line. On the maps, stations are indicated in Russian and English and their distance from Moscow is given in the text.

Stations and points of interest are identified in the text by a kilometre number. In some cases these numbers are approximate so start looking out for the point of interest a few kilometres before its stated position.

Where something of interest is on only one side of the track, it is identified after its kilometre number by the approximate compass direction for those going away from Moscow; that is, on the Moscow–Vladivostok Trans-Siberian line by the letter **N** (north or left-hand side of the train) or **S** (south or right-hand side), and on the Trans-Mongolian branch and Trans-Manchurian branch by **E** (east or left-hand side) or **W** (west or right-hand side).

The elevation of major towns and cities is given in metres and feet beside the station name. Time zones are indicated throughout the text (MT = Moscow Time). See inside back cover for **key map and time zones**.

Kilometre posts
These are located on the southern or western side of the track, sometimes so close to the train that they're difficult to see. The technique is to press your face close to the glass and look along the train until a post flashes by.

On each post, the number on the face furthest from Moscow is larger by 1km than that on the face nearest to Moscow, suggesting that each number really refers to the entire 1km of railway towards which it 'looks'.

Railway timetables show your approximate true distance from Moscow, but unfortunately the distances painted on the kilometre (km) posts generally do

Points of interest and stations in this guide are identified by the nearest kilometre post visible from the train

not: indeed on the Trans-Siberian they may vary by up to 40km, the result of multiple route changes over the years. Distances noted in the following route guide and in the timetables at the back of the book correspond to those on the kilometre posts.

Occasionally, however, railway authorities may recalibrate and repaint these posts, thereby confusing us all! If you notice any discrepancies, please write to the author (see p4).

Station name boards
Station signs are sometimes as difficult to catch sight of as kilometre posts since they are usually placed only on the station building (over the last couple of years, RZD have replaced most station signs with bright new ones in Russian and English) and not always along the platform as in most other countries. Rail traffic on the line is heavy and even if your carriage does pull up opposite the station building you may have your view of it obscured by another train.

Stops
Where the train stops at a station the duration of the stop is indicated by:

● (1-6 mins) ●● (7-14 mins) ●●● (15-24 mins) ●●● + (25 mins and over)

These durations are based upon timetables for the 001/002 Moscow–Vladivostok (*Rossiya*), 003/004 Moscow–Beijing (Trans-Mongolian) and 019/020 Moscow–Beijing (*Vostok*, Trans-Manchurian) services. Actual durations may vary widely as timetables are revised, and may be reduced if a train is running late.

Route timetables that hang somewhere near the provodnitsa's office tell you exactly how long each train stop should be. Provodnitsas do not let you get off

---

❏ Speed calculations
Using kilometre posts and a watch you can calculate how quickly, or more usually how slowly, the train is going. Note the time that elapses between one post and the next and consult the table below. The average speed over the 7-day journey between Moscow and Vladivostok is just 70km (43.5mph).

Seconds	kph	mph	Seconds	kph	mph
24	150	93	52	69	43
26	138	86	54	66	41
28	129	80	56	64	40
30	120	75	60	60	37
32	113	70	64	56	35
34	106	66	68	53	33
36	100	62	72	50	31
38	95	59	78	46	28
40	90	56	84	43	27
42	86	53	92	39	24
44	82	51	100	36	22
46	78	49	120	30	18
48	75	47	150	24	15
50	72	45	180	20	12

ROUTE GUIDE & MAPS

if the stop duration is less than five minutes. At longer stops, don't stray far from the train as it will move off without a whistle or other signal (except in China) and passengers can be left behind. If the train is running late, longer stops can be cut short.

Time zones

All trains in Russia run on Moscow Time (MT). **Siberian time zones** are listed throughout the route guide; major cities include Novosibirsk (MT+3), Irkutsk (MT+5), Khabarovsk (MT+7) and Vladivostok (MT+7).

Moscow Time is four hours ahead of Greenwich Mean Time (GMT+4) year-round, as Russia currently does not observe Daylight Savings Time. Note that **China** has a single time zone, GMT+8, for the whole country and for the whole year. **Mongolian Time** is GMT+8 year-round, as Mongolia also does not observe daylight saving time.

TRANS-SIBERIAN ROUTE

Km0: Moscow Москва

Yaroslavsky Station Ярославский вокзал   Most Trans-Siberian trains depart from Moscow's Yaroslavsky station (see p203), on Komsomolskaya pl (**M** Komsomolskaya). Yaroslavsky station is very distinctive, built in 1902 as a stylised reproduction of an old Russian *terem* (fort), its walls decorated with coloured tiles.

Km13: Los Лось   Just after this station, the train crosses over the Moscow Ring Road. This road marks the city's metropolitan border.

Km15: Taininskaya Таининская   A post-Soviet monument here, dedicated to Russia's last tsar, Nicholas II, says, 'To Tsar Nikolai II from the Russian people with repentance'.

❑ **Dacha**
A dacha is much more than a country cottage or holiday home: it provides its city-dwelling owners with somewhere to grow vegetables, a base for mushroom and wild berry collecting operations as well as being a place to relax away from the urban environment. Growing fruit and vegetables and collecting mushrooms and berries are not just pastimes for Russians but provide a means of survival during lean years and a supplement to their winter diet during better times. People also pick mushrooms and berries to sell in street markets in the cities. Russians are generally very knowledge-able about preserving techniques, food value and homeopathic remedies.

As one approaches a city on the train, the dacha colonies become larger and more frequent. Each privately owned house will be set on a large wood-fenced lot. The design of the house is very eclectic: small greenhouses abound and many properties have a sauna building. The earth closet of classic design is at the foot of the garden. Electricity is supplied and there is water from a community well or tap. There may be chickens; other livestock such as a goat or milk cow would belong to permanent residents. Some of the outlying villages contain a mix of small farmsteads and old houses that have been rehabilitated into dachas.   **Nancy J Scarth** (Canada)

❏ **Important note on km posts – Moscow–Kotelnich**
The km posts on this 900km section of the route, between Moscow and Kotelnich (near Vyatka), were originally calibrated from Kursky station. Now that most Trans-Siberian services no longer run on the line via Yaroslavl but via Vladimir and Nizhny Novgorod, there's a chance that the posts may eventually be updated and repainted with the distance from Yaroslavsky station, 19km further away than Kursky. When that happens you'll need to increase all kilometre readings from Fryazevo (Km54) up to the station before Kotelnich. At Kotelnich (Km870) you rejoin the old route.

Km18: Mytishchi Мытищи is known for three particular factories. The railway carriage factory, **Metrovagonmash**, manufactured all the Soviet Union's metro cars and now builds the N5 carriages to be seen on Moscow's metro. **Mytishchinsky monument factory**, the source of many of those ponderous Lenin statues that once littered the country, has at last been forced to develop a new line. It now churns out the kind of 'art' banned in the Soviet era: religious statues, memorials to the victims of Stalin's purges and busts of mafia bosses. Some of its earlier achievements displayed in Moscow include the giant Lenin in front of Oktyabrskaya metro station, an equestrian statue of Moscow's founder, Yuri Dolgoruky, on Tverskaya Ploshchad, and the Karl Marx across from the Bolshoi Theatre.

Production has also slowed at the **armoured vehicle factory**, one of Russia's three major tank works, the others being in the Siberian cities of Kurgan and Omsk.

The smoking factories and suburban blocks of flats are now left behind and you roll through forests of pine, birch and oak. Amongst the trees there are picturesque wooden *dachas* (see box opposite) where many of Moscow's residents spend their weekends. You pass through little stations with long, white-washed picket fences.

Km38: Chkalovskaya Чкаловская On your right-hand side (**S**) you'll see an **aeroplane monument** with the Russian inscription: 'Glory to the Soviet conquerors of the sky,' commemorating Chkalov, a famous pilot and Soviet hero (see p241) who was the first man to fly nonstop from Moscow via the North Pole to Vancouver (Washington, USA, not Canada) in 1937.

ROUTE GUIDE & MAPS

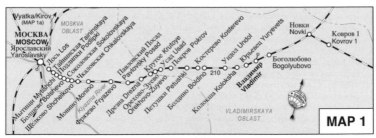

MAP 1

Km41: Tsiolkovskaya Циолковская Close to the station lies **Zvyozdny Gorodok (Star City)**, the space research centre where Russian astronauts live with their families and where they have trained for various space missions from the 1960s onwards. This part of Russia was off-limits to foreigners until 1989.

Km54: Fryazevo Фрязево This is the junction with the line to Moscow's Kursky station. Although km posts here say 54km you're actually 73km from Moscow's Yaroslavsky station (see box p429).

(Turn to p505 if you're travelling via Yaroslavl).

Km68: Pavlovsky Posad Павловский Посад This ancient town is a centre of textile manufacturing.

Km90: Orekhovo-Zuyevo Орехово-Зуево The town, at the junction with the line to Aleksandrov, is also the centre of an important textile region. It gained its pre-revolutionary credentials in 1885 with the Morozov strike, the largest workers' demonstration in Russia up to that time.

Km110: Pokrov Покров It was in the nearby village of **Novoselovo** that Yuri Gagarin, the world's first astronaut, died in a plane crash in 1968. He was piloting a small aircraft when another plane flew too close. The resulting turbulence forced his aircraft into a downward spin which he was unable to correct.

❏ The Golden Ring

You are now passing through The Golden Ring, a cluster of historically important cities surrounding Moscow and the ancient birthplace of the mighty Russian state. Major Golden Ring towns on or near the current Trans-Siberian route are Vladimir, Suzdal and Nizhny Novgorod (formerly Gorky). Along the older route via Yaroslavl are Sergiev Posad (73km from Moscow; see pp206-10), Rostov-Velikiy (224km; see pp211-16) and Yaroslavl (284km; see pp217-24).

Following the collapse of Kievan Rus, the first feudal state in Eastern Europe, its capital was shifted in 1169 from Kiev to Vladimir. At that time Vladimir and the other Golden Ring towns were little more than villages but over the next two centuries all of them grew rapidly into political, religious and commercial centres.

The typical Golden Ring town of the 11th to 18th centuries consisted of *kremlin*, *posad* and *sloboda*. The Kremlin (fortress), usually in an elevated position, was ringed by earth embankments topped with wooden walls. Watch-towers were positioned strategically along the walls. Over time the earth and wooden walls were replaced by stone and brick. Inside the Kremlin were the prince's residence, plus religious and administrative buildings. Outside the Kremlin was the undefended posad, which was the merchants' and artisans' quarter. Often next to the posad was a sloboda, a tax-exempt settlement established to attract a new workforce.

After the Tatar-Mongol invasion in 1236 Moscow (Muscovy) became the invaders' centre for tax collection and its prince was granted the title of Grand Prince. Gradually Moscow's influence eclipsed that of the Golden Ring principalities and they were soon annexed, their economic and military power used to expand Moscow's own domination. By the end of the 16th century Moscow was on its way to becoming the capital of Russia. While several Golden Ring towns retained their commercial importance due to their location on major trading routes, their golden era was over.

Km126: Petushki Петушки If you ever see a Communist-era film with bears in it, chances are it was shot in the countryside around Petushki. The town's best-known attraction is the nearby zoo, source of many animals used in Russian movies. Petushki sits on the left bank of the Klyazma River.

Km135: Kosterevo Костерево The 19th-century painter Isaak Levitan lived near here. His house has been moved into Kosterevo and opened as a museum.

Km161: Undol Ундол The station is named after Russian bibliographer V M Undolsky, who was born near here. The town is known as **Lakinsk** after M I Lakin, a revolutionary killed here in 1905. But the area is probably best known for its brewery, a Soviet-era Czechoslovak joint venture. Lakinsk beer, very popular in the 1990s, is now under strong competition from Western brands.

Km191: Vladimir Владимир (●●●)   [see pp224-9]
Vladimir (pop: 347,930) was founded in 1108. In 1157 it became capital of the principality of Vladimir-Suzdal and therefore politically the most important city in Russia. It's worth visiting for its great Assumption Cathedral, its domes rising above the city as you approach, and as a stepping-stone to the more interesting town of **Suzdal** (see pp230-7), 35km away, and the wonderful **Church of the Intercession on the Nerl** (see below), 10km from Vladimir.

Km202: Bogolyubovo Боголюбово   [see pp229-30]
Visible from the train **(N)** about 1.5km east of Bogolyubovo is the Church of the Intercession on the Nerl, one of Russia's loveliest and most famous churches. Built in 1165, the single-domed church sits in the middle of a field at the junction of the Nerl and Klyazma rivers. It was constructed in a single summer on the orders of Andrei Bogolyubsky, in memory of his son who died in battle against the Volga Bulgars. It was built on this prominent spot to impress visiting ambassadors. To symbolise Vladimir's inheritance of religious authority from Byzantium and Kiev the church was consecrated and a holiday declared without permission being sought.

Km240: Novki Новки This large town at the junction of the line to Ivanovo boasts one of Russia's ugliest stations. The original building is about a century old. In the 1980s, in an attempt to make it appear contemporary, it was encased in pink and fawn tiles. The result is a monumental eyesore.

About 13km eastward the train crosses the wide Klyazma River. The original bridge, built in the 1890s, was washed away in a flood. To avoid the problems of extending a new bridge across the river, engineers came up with a clever alternative. They built a bridge on dry land, on the inside of a bend in the river 1km to the west, then dug a canal beneath the bridge, detoured the river through it and filled in the old river bed. As you pass by you can see the old river course on each side of the bridge's eastern embankment.

Km255: Kovrov I Ковров I This ancient town gets its name from *kovyor*, the Russian word for 'carpet'. During the Mongol Tatar's reign in the 14th century, the local tax collector accepted carpets as one of the tributes. The town's best-known son was engineer Vasili Alekseyevich Degtyarev (1879-1949), father of the Soviet machine-gun. The **Degtyarev factory**, founded here in 1916, now manufactures motorcycles, scooter engines and small arms. In the town centre there is a monument to Degtyarev, holding an engineering micrometer rather than a gun. His grave is nearby and his house, at ul Degtyareva 4, has been turned into a museum. Kovrov is also famous for its excavator **factory** founded in the mid-19th century to build and maintain railway rolling stock. Its claims to fame include the world's first steam-heated passenger carriage (1866) and Russia's first hospital carriage (1877). The factory's importance is illustrated by large, colourful murals of digging machinery on the sides of Kovrov's nine-storey accommodation blocks.

Km295: Mstera Мстера The village of the same name, 14km from the station, is known for its folk handicrafts and has lent its name to particular styles of miniature painting and embroidery. Mstera miniatures, notable for their deep black background and warm, soft colours, usually depict scenes from folklore, history, literature and everyday life. They are painted in tempera (from pigments ground in water and mixed with egg yolk) onto papier-mâché boxes and lacquered to a high sheen. Mstera embroidery is characterised by two types of stitch, called white satin stitch and Vladimir stitch.

Km315: Vyazniki Вязники The name means 'little elms', after the trees on the banks of the Klyazma River among which this ancient village's first huts were sited. The town got on the map when pilgrims started flocking here after 1622 to see the miracle-working Kazan Mother of God icon. Vyazniki became famous for its icon painters, with two local masters invited in the mid 17th century to paint cathedral icons in Moscow's Kremlin.

Km363: Gorokhovets Гороховец One of the smallest of the Golden Ring towns, Gorokhovets (about 10km from the station) is worth visiting as it gives a different perspective on these ancient towns while allowing you to observe life in what is now a quiet Russian village. Gorokhovets was first mentioned in 1239 when it was burned down by the Tatar-Mongols. A fortress was built on top of the hill overlooking the town but this was destroyed in 1619 by marauding Ukrainian Cossacks under Polish command.

Architectural highlights include the Purification of the Virgin Monastery (1698) and the St Nicholas Monastery (1681-6), both of which have high, open

ROUTE GUIDE & MAPS

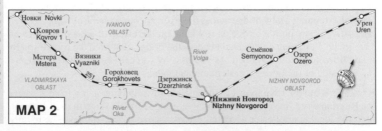

stairways, pilasters at the corners and intricate window frames. There are also several unusual two-storey stone houses from the second half of the 17th century which were designed to imitate traditional Russian wooden mansions. Also of interest is the former *ostrog* complex, used as a stopping-point for prisoners on their way to Siberia.

Km442: Nizhny Novgorod Нижний Новгород (●●/●●●: ●● for Trans-Manchurian) [see pp237-43] With a population of 1,259,921, Nizhny Novgorod, formerly known as Gorky, is Russia's fifth-largest city after Moscow, St Petersburg, Novosibirsk and Yekaterinburg.

East of Nizhny Novgorod the train crosses the mighty **Volga River**, which is about 1km wide at this point. In times gone by Russians held this river in such esteem that train passengers would stand and take off their hats to Mother Volga as the train rattled onto the first spans of the long bridge. Rising in the Valdai hills, Europe's longest river meanders 3700km down to the Caspian Sea. It is to Russia what the Nile is to Egypt: a source of life and a thoroughfare.

Km509: Semyonov Семёнов Settled in the 18th century by Old Believers (see p58 and box p321), Semyonov still boasts many buildings from that period, identified by the five or six windows on each façade, walls covered with intricate carvings, high surrounding fences, wicket gates and large prayer rooms. In the 19th century the town became famous for rosary beads and other products of its woodworkers. It was later known for a particular form of *khokhloma* painting – fine golden patterns of flowers on a red or black background. A khokhloma school was founded here in 1925.

Km531: Ozero Озеро To the left of the station (whose name means 'lake') is shallow Svetloyar Lake, at the bottom of which, according to legend, is the invisible village of Kitezh.

Km623: Uren Урен The town was founded deep in the forests by Old Believers fleeing from persecution in the 18th century.

Km682: Shakhunya Шахунья This town near the Shakhunya River derives its name from the Russian word *shag* ('step') as the river was so narrow here that it could be crossed in one jump. The town grew in the 1930s when the railway line between Nizhny Novgorod and Vyatka was built. Most buildings are

ROUTE GUIDE & MAPS

two- and five-storey apartment blocks from the 1950s, but 1930s wooden work-ers' barracks can still be seen.

Km743: Sherstki Шерстки On the border between Nizhny Novgorodskaya and Kirovskaya oblasts, this station also marks the first step away from Moscow Time.

───────────── **Km 743-1266 TIME ZONE MT + 1** ─────────────

Km870: Kotelnich Котельнич This station sits at the junction of the Trans-Siberian (Moscow–Vladimir–Nizhny Novgorod–Vyatka) line and the Moscow–Yaroslavl–Vyatka line. For Yaroslavl this is not the place to change lines; instead go 87km east to the major city of Vyatka (Kirov) where tickets are much easier to get. Kotelnich is an ancient commercial centre on the right bank of the Vyatka River, a major trading route between Arkhangelsk and the Volga region. Finding your way around the town is not easy as it lies in three ravines with only the town centre laid out in an orderly fashion. Here the major thoroughfare is ul Moskovskaya and along part of it are a number of buildings built in Vyatka Provincial Style between 1850 and 1880. Sights include the John the Baptist (Predtichi) Monastery and the Presentation of the Virgin (Vvedenski) Nunnery.

After leaving the station, the train crosses over the **Vyatka River**. This is the 10th longest river in European Russia, meandering for 1367km, and the Trans-Siberian crosses over it several times. When the train reaches the Vyatka River basin a few kilometres to the east of Kotelnich there is a noticeable change in the landscape as forests give way to fields and more frequent villages.

Km890: Maradykovski Марадыковский The nearby air force base has in the past been used for the storage of chemical weapons' agents (mustard gas, lewisite, hydrocyanic acid and phosgene). Ironically, the name of the settlement around the station is **Mirny Мирный** which means 'peaceful'.

Km957: Vyatka/Kirov Вятка/Киров (●●●) Vyatka (pop: 483,176), for-merly known as Kirov, was founded on the banks of the Vyatka River in 1181, as Klynov. It developed into a fur-trading centre entirely dependent on the river for transport and communication with the rest of the country. In the 18th cen-tury it fell under the rule of Moscow and was renamed Vyatka, soon gaining a

❑ **The Udmurt homeland**
Udmurtia Republic is one of 16 republics of indigenous peoples within the Russian Federation. The population of Udmurtia is about 1.5 million, only one third of them Udmurts. They are descendants of Finno-Ugric peoples who in turn were descended from Neolithic and Bronze Age people living in the area. Udmurts started cultivation and stock raising in the 9th century AD, and from 1236 to 1552 were dominated by the Golden Horde and the Kazan khans. In 1558 Russia incorporated the entire Udmurt area and it was only in 1932 that the indigenous inhabitants were acknowl-edged with the declaration of an Udmurt Autonomous Oblast. Today the Udmurts are the largest Finno-Ugric language group in Russia.

reputation as a place of exile. In 1934 the name was changed once more, this time to Kirov, in honour of the Communist leader assassinated earlier in the same year. Sergei Kirov was at one time so close to Stalin that most people assumed he would succeed him as Party General Secretary. But he subsequently broke away, and it is more than likely that Stalin had a hand in his death, and moreover used it as an excuse for his own Great Purge in the mid-1930s, during which several million people died in labour camps. Modern Vyatka is a large industrial and administrative centre with an attractive river front.

A branch line runs north to the Kotlas area, setting for Alexander Solzhenitsyn's *A Day in the Life of Ivan Denisovitch,* describing 24 hours in the life of a Siberian convict.

Km975: Pozdino Поздино   The town around the station is called **Novovyatsk** and boasts one of Russia's largest ski factories. During Soviet times the factory produced 20% of the nation's skis.

Km995: Bum-kombinat Бум-комбинат   This town gets its unfortunate name from its principal employer, a paper factory.

Km1052: Zuyevka Зуевка   Zuyevka was founded in 1895 during construction of the railway; during WWII hundreds of Leningraders settled here, and today their descendants manufacture swings and see-saws.

Km1127: Yar Яр   About 20km before this station you leave Kirovskaya Oblast and cross the administrative frontier into the heavily industrialised **Udmurtia Republic** (see box opposite). Yar is the first town here and it has a number of Udmurt speakers. It also sits on a steep river bank (*yar*). There has been a metallurgical plant here for over two centuries.

Between Yar and Balyezino you pass vast fields of grey-green cabbages, and rows of greenhouses covered in plastic sheeting line the track in some places.

Km1136: Balyshur Балышур   Just before arriving at the station, you pass a steam train storage depot.

Km1165: Glazov Глазов (● for Trans-Manchurian eastbound only) Originally an Udmurt village, Glazov soon became infamous as a desolate and impoverished place of exile. All this was to change with the arrival of the railway and by 1900 there were over a hundred enterprises. Within a few more

ROUTE GUIDE & MAPS

MAP 4

years the town grew into the region's largest flax, oats and oakum trading centre (oakum is a fibre used for caulking the seams of ships). There are still a few
Udmurt log huts remaining. Known as *korkas*, they are positioned along an
open paved courtyard. The courtyard had a massive gate which, like the hut,
was often decorated with carved geometrical and plant designs.

Km1194: Balyezino Балезино (●●●) A change of locomotive gives you a
chance to stock up from the traders on the platform.

Km1221: The line crosses the **Cheptsa River** which the route has been following for the last 250km. The train begins to wind its way up into the Urals.

Km1223: Cheptsa Чепца Between Cheptsa and Vereshchagino is the frontier between the Udmurt Republic and **Permskaya Oblast**. Permskaya's
160,600 sq km are, like those of Kirovskaya Oblast, lost to the swampy forests
of the taiga. But Permskaya has greater prizes than its millions of pine and birch
trees, for the region includes the mineral-rich Ural Mountains. The main industries include mining, logging and paper-making.

─────────── **Km 1267-2496 TIME ZONE MT + 2** ───────────

Km1310 (S): Vereshchagino Верещагино Vereshchagino was founded at
the end of the 19th century as a railway depot, and its main industry is still railways. There is a preserved **FD21 steam locomotive** on a plinth about 1km west
of the station near the main rail depot. The town is named after Russia's greatest battlefield painter, V V Vereshchagin, who stopped here on his way to the
Russo-Japanese War front in 1905. It was his final and fatal commission.

Km1340: Mendeleyevo Менделеево The town is named after the chemist
Dmitri Mendeleyev (1834-1907), who developed the Periodic Table. He often
visited this town during his inspections of the region's metallurgical plants.

Km1387: Chaykovskaya Чайковская This station is named after the composer Pyotr Ilich **Tchaikovsky** (1840-1893), who was born 180km south-east of
here at a factory settlement around the Kamsko-Votkinsk industrial plant.

  Until recently it was believed that Tchaikovsky died of cholera but historians have now concluded that he was blackmailed into taking poison to prevent
his liaison with the nephew of a St Petersburg noble being made public. The
nearby town (a construction settlement for the hydroelectric dam) is called
Maiski.

  From here to Perm there are some opportunities to get photos of the train as
it snakes along the winding railway.

Km1410: Overyata Оверята An 11km branch line leads south to the dirty
industrial town of Krasnokamsk, which was founded in the 1930s. Near the
town is the popular **Ust-Kachka health resort**, with medicinal mud baths.

Km1429: Perm Sortirovochnaya Пермь-Сортировочная This is one of
Russia's largest freight yards, handling up to 135 trains simultaneously.

Km1432: Kama River Река Кама Just before the train reaches Perm, you cross over the Kama River. From the 900m bridge which was built in 1899 you can see Perm stretching away to the left. The mighty Kama River, flowing over 2000km from the Urals to the Volga, is one of Russia's great waterways. Near the bridge the river banks are lined with cranes and warehouses.

A short distance west of Perm station (N) there's a turntable and beside it an ancient green 'O' Class locomotive (OB 14). Engines of this type were hauling Trans-Siberian trains at the end of the 19th century.

Km1436: Perm 2 Пермь 2 (●●●)   **[see pp244-9]**
Perm, now a city of 1,013,887 inhabitants, was founded in 1723 when copper-smelting works were established here. Because of its important position on the Kama River, the Great Siberian Post Road and later the Trans-Siberian Railway, Perm quickly grew into a major trading and industrial centre.

In the days before the railway reached Perm most travellers would arrive by steamer from Nizhny Novgorod and Kazan. R L Jefferson (see pp95-6) cycled here from London in 1896 on his Siberian bike ride and was entertained by a Mr Kuznetsoff, 60-year-old president of the Perm Cycling Club, and 50 enthusiasts. On 20 July 1907 the cyclists came out to escort an equally sensational visitor, the Italian Prince Borghese, who had just driven across Siberia from Peking (now Beijing) in his Itala and was on his way to Paris, to win the Peking to Paris motor rally. One of the wheels of the car was damaged and after the Prince's chauffeur had replaced some of its wooden spokes he declared that the wheel must be soaked to make the wood expand before the repair could be completed. A local official suggested sending it to one of the bathing establishments along the Kama River. A bathing-machine (of the type used by Victorian swimmers at English seaside resorts) was hired and the wheel spent the night taking the waters.

Shortly after leaving Perm 2 the train crosses a small bridge over a busy street. This street was once part of the Siberian *Trakt* (Great Post Road) which passed through Perm from 1863.

Km1460-1777 Between Perm 2 and the Europe–Asia border the train winds its way up to the highest point in the Urals. You might expect the mountains dividing Europe from Asia to be rather more impressive than these hills but they rise up not much more than 500m (1640ft) above sea level here. Colin Thubron (*In Siberia*) describes them as 'a faint upheaval of pine-darkened slopes'.

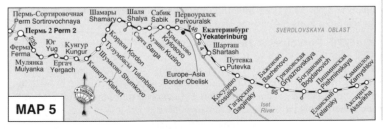

ROUTE GUIDE & MAPS

R L Jefferson wrote in 1896: 'The Urals certainly are not so high or majestic as the Alps or the Balkans but their wild picturesqueness is something to be seen to be appreciated.' Their wild picturesqueness is somewhat marred today by **open-cast mines** at Km1507 (N) and Km1509 (N). There is a large **timber mill** at Km1523 (N).

Km1534: Kungur Кунгур Just outside the town is a fascinating and almost unknown tourist attraction, **Kungur Ice Cave** (see pp249-50). The stockade town of Kungur was founded in 1648, 17km from its present site. By the 18th century the town was one of the largest centres in the Urals as it was a transit point on the Siberian Trakt. It had three big markets a year, numerous factories and the first technical college in the Urals, which opened in 1877.

Soon after leaving Kungur you see the steep banks of the Sylva River which mark the start of the Kungur Forest Steppe. This area is characterised by rolling hills which reach 180-230m (600-750ft), a landscape pitted with troughs and sinkholes, and copses of birch, linden, oak and pine interspersed with farmland.

Km1537-1650 (N): A picturesque church at **Km 1537 (N)** stands alone on a hill across the Sylva River. The railway line follows this river up the valley to **Km1556** where it cuts across a wide plain. The trees close in again from about **Km1584** but there are occasional clearings with villages and timber mills at about **Km1650 (N)**.

Km1672: Shalya Шаля Fifty kilometres to the east of this forestry town you enter **Sverdlovskaya Oblast**, covering 194,300 sq km, taking in parts of the Urals and extending east onto the Siberian plain. Like most of the other oblasts you have passed through, this one is composed almost entirely of taiga forest. From rich deposits in the Urals are mined iron ore, copper, platinum, gold, tungsten, cobalt, asbestos and bauxite as well as many varieties of gemstones – the source of both local wealth and local folklore.

Km1729: Kuzino Кузино East of the large marshalling yard here the line rises once more, passing a little town built around a whitewashed church with a green dome.

After about 10km the train reaches one of the Urals' most attractive rivers, the **Chusavya**. The line follows the course of the river for some 30km.

Km1748: Krylosovo Крылосово A large factory with rows of workers' apartment blocks looks a little out of place amongst the forests up here in the Urals. From **Km1764** east the area becomes quite built up.

Km1770: Pervouralsk Первоуральск The city's name translates as First Ural City as it was here in 1727 that the Urals' first factory was opened. Following the success of its cast-iron works dozens of other factories sprang up and today the city is home to numerous heavy engineering complexes including one of Russia's largest pipeline factories. In the current economic climate many are either facing closure or have already closed.

ROUTE GUIDE & MAPS

You can see Pervouralsk's main tourist attraction, the **Europe-Asia border obelisk** from the train so there's no reason to get off. People begin collecting in the corridor long before you reach the white stone obelisk which marks the continental division at this point in the Urals.

Km1777 (S): Europe–Asia Border Obelisk
The obelisk is about 15m to the east of the small **Vershina Вершина** railway platform. From nearby Yekaterinburg, tour companies run trips to the obelisk if you want to get up close and personal.

Km1816: Yekaterinburg / Sverdlovsk Екатеринбург / Свердловск
(●●●+)   **[see pp251-61]**
As soon as you reach the suburbs of Yekaterinburg (pop: 1,396,074) you see a large lake on the right (Km1807-9) which feeds the Iset River running through the city. There's a **locomotive depot** west of the station. The train halts here in the largest city in the Urals, for a change of engine.

After the train leaves the station, on the right along the Iset River a mass of chimney stacks pollutes the horizon. This is Yekaterinburg's main industrial region. For about 70km east of the city the train winds down and out of the Urals to the West Siberian plain. You are now in Asia (though not quite in Siberia yet).

Km1912: Bogdanovich Богданович
The clay quarries around this town produce fireproof bricks.

About 16km from Bogdanovich are the **Kurinsk mineral springs**. The *1900 Guide to the Great Siberian Railway* states, 'They are efficacious for rheumatism, paralysis, scrofula and anaemia. Furnished houses and an hotel with good rooms are situated near the baths. There is a garden and a promenade with band; theatricals and concerts take place in the casino'. Such frivolous jollities are hard to imagine in this rather gloomy region today.

Km1955: Kamyshlov Камышлов
The town was founded in 1668 as a fortress and is one of the oldest settlements in the Urals. The original buildings have all gone and today the architecture of the town is predominantly late 19th and early 20th century. There is a museum here dedicated to the locally born poet S P Shchepachev and the writer P P Bazhov, who lived here on and off between1914 and 1923.

About 6km to the west of the town, on the banks of the Pyshma River, is the **Obukhov sulphur and chalybeate mineral water sanatorium**, which has been famous since 1871.

Km2033: Talitsa Талица
The town is known for its **Mayan Маян brand of bottled mineral water**, believed to be good for stomach disorders, and for its sanatoriums, which use the above mentioned water as part of medical treatments. The town, which is 3km south of the station, is also known for another drink which is less beneficial: watered-down industrial alcohol which is sold as rough vodka.

❑ The U2 Affair: USSR 1, USA 0

The U2 affair represented an unprecedented Cold War embarrassment for the West. On 1 May 1960, an American U2 spyplane was shot down from a height of 20,700m (68,000ft), some 45km south of Sverdlovsk (as Yekaterinburg was then known). Its pilot, Gary Powers, baled out without activating the plane's self-destruct mechanism for fear that he would blow himself up (criticisms were later raised in Congress that he had not killed himself, either by destroying the aircraft or by pricking himself with the poisoned needle so thoughtfully provided by the CIA). He was picked up shortly after reaching the ground.

Four days later the USA announced that a U2 'meteorological aircraft' had 'gone missing' just north of Turkey after its pilot had reported problems with his oxygen mask. In a detailed press announcement it was speculated that he had fallen unconscious while the plane, automatic pilot engaged, might possibly have flown itself over Soviet territory. Shortly after this announcement, Khrushchev told the Supreme Soviet that a U2 'spyplane' had been shot down over Sverdlovsk. US presidential spokesman Lincoln White commented that 'this might be the same plane', and did his best to cool the situation by explaining the oxygen-supply theory again. He concluded: 'there was absolutely no deliberate attempt to violate Soviet airspace and never has been', and he grounded all other U2s to 'check their oxygen systems'.

On 7 May Khrushchev addressed the Supreme Soviet again: 'I must tell you a secret. When I made my first report I deliberately did not say that the pilot was alive and well ... and now just look how many silly things they (the Americans) have said'. Khrushchev exploited his position, revelling in the details of the American cover-up: he was in possession of the pilot ('alive and kicking'), the 'plane, the camera, and had even had the photographs developed. He also had Powers' survival pack, including 7500 roubles, other currencies and gold rings and gifts for women. 'Why was all this necessary?' he asked, 'Maybe the pilot was to have flown still higher to Mars and was going to lead the Martian ladies astray?' He laughed at the US report that the U2 had a maximum height of 16,700m (55,000ft): 'It was hit by the rocket at 20,000m. And if they fly any higher we will also hit them'.

The U2 Affair brought the 1960 Paris Summit to a grinding halt. Following the arrival of the first U2s in England in August 1962, Moscow remarked that they ought to be 'kept far away from us'. In the USSR, Powers was sentenced to ten years but released in exchange for Rudolph Abel, a KGB spy, in 1962. The Soviet press maintained that Powers had been sent home as an 'act of clemency'. No mention was made of the exchange. A few pieces of the aircraft, plus photos of the wreckage and items from Gary Powers' survival kit are on display in Yekaterinburg's Military History Museum (see p255).   **Dominic Streatfeild-James** (UK)

Km2064: Yushala Юшала The sailors from the battleship *Potemkin* were shot here and buried at nearby Kamyshlov station.

Km2102: Siberia Сибирь officially begins here. The border between Sverdlovskaya and Tyumenskaya oblasts is the frontier between the Urals and Siberia. **Tyumenskaya Oblast** comprises 1.44 million sq km of flat land, tundra in the north, taiga in the south. Until oil was discovered in the region, inhabitants were engaged in reindeer herding in the north and farming in the south. Many people have been brought into the oblast in recent years to work in the petroleum and construction industries.

South of the railway line, the point where the Great Post Road crossed Siberia's frontier was marked by 'a square pillar ten or twelve feet in height, of stuccoed or plastered brick', wrote George Kennan (on his way to research *Siberia and the Exile System* in 1887). He added: 'No other spot between St Petersburg and the Pacific is more full of painful suggestions, and none has for the traveller a more melancholy interest than the little opening in the forest where stands this grief-consecrated pillar. Here hundreds of thousands of exiled human beings – men, women and children; princes, nobles and peasants – have bidden good-by (sic) forever to friends, country, and home ... The Russian peasant even when a criminal is deeply attached to his native land; and heart-rending scenes have been witnessed around the boundary pillar ... Some gave way to unrestrained grief; some comforted the weeping; some knelt and pressed their faces to the loved soil of their native country and collected a little earth to take with them into exile ... Until recently the Siberian boundary post was covered with brief inscriptions, good-byes and the names of exiles ... In one place, in a man's hand, had been written the words "Prashchai Maria" (Goodbye Mary!) Who the writer was, who Mary was, there is nothing now left to show ...' (see p85).

Km2144: Tyumen Тюмень (●●●)   [see pp262-6]

Tyumen (pop: 634,171), founded in 1586, is Siberia's oldest town. It was built on the banks of the Tura River, site of the former Tatar town of Chingi Tura, said to date back to the 14th century. The Russian settlement was named by Tsar Feodor Ivanovich after Tyumen Khan, who once ruled this region. It grew quickly as a trading centre, with goods arriving and being shipped on from the large port on the Tura River.

At least one million of the people who passed through this town before 1900 were convicts and exiles. Many were lodged, under the most appalling conditions, in the Tyumen Forwarding Prison. When George Kennan visited the prison in 1887, he was horrified by the overcrowded cells, the dirt and the terrible smell. He wrote: 'The air in the corridors and cells ... was laden with fever germs from the unventilated hospital wards, fetid odors from diseased human bodies and the stench arising from unemptied excrement buckets ... '. After a miserable two-week stay here, convicts were sent on prison barges to Tomsk. Conditions were not much better for the 500,000 emigrants who flooded through the town between 1883 and 1900, but they at least had their freedom. When the new railway reached Tyumen in 1888 prisoners from Russia were no

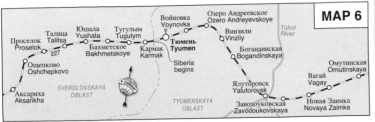

longer herded over the Urals in marching parties but travelled in relative luxury in box-cars used also for the transport of cattle and horses. Tyumen is becoming increasingly important because of oil and gas discoveries in the oblast.

Km2214: Yalutorovsk Ялуторовск The town sits on the bank of the wide, 1591km-long Tobol River. In 1639 it was the most easterly fortress of the Tsar's expanding empire. It later became one of the places of exile for Decembrists, who opened the first Siberian school for girls here.

After crossing over the **Tobol River (Km2216)**, you will see dozens of small, mostly salt lakes on both sides of the railway.

Km2431: Ishim Ишим (••) The town sits on the left bank of the **Ishim River** which was a major trading route before the arrival of the Trans-Siberian. The town's strategic location made it a natural site for one of Western Siberia's largest trading fairs. The Nikolsk Fair was held every December and attracted more than 2000 traders, some from as far away as China. The town, founded in 1670 as Korkina, became Ishim in 1782.

North of Ishim, up the Ishim and Irtysh Rivers, lies the city of **Tobolsk** (see pp266-7), one of Siberia's oldest settlements. Yermak (see pp82-3) reached the area in 1581 and established a fort here. The Tsar hoped to develop the region by encouraging colonisation but to the Russian peasant, Siberia was as far away as the moon and no voluntary mass migration over the Urals occurred. A policy of forced migration was rather more successful. The first exiles arriving in Tobolsk were former inhabitants of the town of Uglich who had been witnesses to the mysterious death of Tsarevich Dmitry. With them came the **Uglich church bell** which rang the signal for the insurrection that followed the death. The bell was reconsecrated in Tobolsk church but, in the 1880s, Uglich Town Council decided it would like it back. Tobolsk Council refused and the case eventually went to court. The judge ruled that as the bell had been exiled for life and it was still calling the people to prayer, it had not yet completed its sentence and must therefore remain in Tobolsk. It was finally returned to Uglich during the Soviet era.

Km2497:   This is the administrative frontier between Tyumenskaya and Omskaya oblasts. **Omskaya Oblast**, on a plain in the Irtysh River basin, occupies 139,700 sq km. Thick taiga forests cover the northern part of the oblast. In the south there is considerable agricultural development, the main crops being spring

❏ **A German spy in Ishim?**
George Kennan recounts an amusing incident that occurred in Ishim in 1829, when Baron von Humboldt was conducting a geological survey for the Tsar. The famous explorer (who gave his name to the Humboldt Current off the west coast of South America) was growing more than a little annoyed by the petty Siberian officials who kept him from his work. He must have been rather short with the police prefect in this little town for the man took great offence and despatched an urgent letter to his governor-general in which he wrote 'A few days ago there arrived here a German of shortish stature, insignificant appearance, fussy and bearing a letter of introduction from your Excellency to me. I accordingly received him politely; but I must say I find him suspicious and even dangerous. I disliked him from the first. He talks too much ... despises my hospitality ... and associates with Poles and other political criminals ... On one occasion he proceeded with them to a hill overlooking the town. They took a box with them and got out of it a long tube which we all took for a gun. After fastening it to three feet they pointed it down on the town ... This was evidently a great danger for the town which is built entirely of wood; so I sent a detachment of troops with loaded rifles to watch the German on the hill. If the treacherous machinations of this man justify my suspicions, we shall be ready to give our lives for the Tsar and Holy Russia.' Kennan adds: 'The civilized world is to be thanked that the brilliant career of the great von Humboldt was not cut short by a Cossack bullet ... while he was taking sights with a theodolite in that little Siberian town of Ishim.'

wheat, flax and sunflowers. As well as sheep and cattle farms, there are numerous dairy farms. This has been an important butter-producing region since the 19th century, when butter was exported as far as Turkey and Germany. It is said that butter-making was introduced to the region by the English wife of a Russian landowner. There are many swamps and lakes in the oblast which provide habitat for a multitude of water birds including duck, coot, grey goose, swan and crane.

——————— Km 2497-3478 TIME ZONE MT + 3 ———————

Km2565: Nazyvayevskaya Называевская (●) Founded in 1910 with the arrival of the railway Nazyvayevskaya grew rapidly with the influx of new agricultural workers during Khrushchev's Virgin Lands campaign. The plan was conceived following years of chronic grain shortages after WWII and involved the cultivation of 25 million hectares of land in south-western Siberia and northern Kazakhstan. To put the size of this massive undertaking into perspective, the total surface area of the UK is only 13 million hectares.

ROUTE GUIDE & MAPS

MAP 8

By the 1960s over-intensive farming had reduced five million of these hectares to desert. The Trans-Siberian runs through the northern part of the area; this, unlike the more fragile south, is still fertile. The area is famous as much for its insects as for its agriculture. In 1887 Kennan found travelling through this marshy region a singularly unpleasant experience. He wrote: 'We were so tormented by huge gray mosquitoes that we were obliged to put on thick gloves, cover our heads with calico hoods and horse hair netting and defend ourselves constantly with leafy branches.'

Km2706: Irtysh River Река Иртыш The Irtysh rises in China and flows almost 3000km into the Ob River. It's joined here by the Om. The 650m-long bridge is built on pillars of granite from the Urals which had to be brought 1000km by river to the construction site.

Just before reaching the suburbs of Omsk, you see the airport on the left. The first suburban station you pass is **Karbyshevo Карбышево**; this is where the railway from Chelyabinsk joins the Trans-Siberian line. The train then crosses the 500m-wide **Irtysh River** which gives a view of Omsk to the left. The old centre of Omsk is on the right bank (eastern side). After the bridge, the train makes a left turn and on the right passes an old brick water tower, built for steam engines in the early 20th century. This has been preserved as an architectural monument.

Km2712: Omsk Омск (●●●)   [see pp271-4]

Omsk (pop: 1,160,670) is Siberia's second largest city and a great deal of effort has gone into making it the greenest. The 2500 hectares of parks and gardens

---

❏ The Kyrgyz

South of Omsk and the Baraba Steppe region lie the **Kyrgyz Steppes**, the true home of the Kyrgyz people. The area extends from the Urals in the west to the mineral-rich Altai Mountains in the south. The Kyrgyz are direct descendants of the Turkic-Mongol hordes that joined Genghis Khan's armies and invaded Europe in the 13th century. When S S Hill paid them a visit in 1854 they were nomadic herders who professed a mixture of Shamanism and Islam and survived on a diet of boiled mutton and *koumiss* (fermented mare's milk). They lived in *kibitkas* (felt tents or yurts), the doors of which were arranged to face in the direction of Mecca. Fortunately this alignment also kept out the southern winds that blew across the steppe. Of these people Hill wrote: 'The Kirgeeze have the high cheek bones ... of the Mongol Tatars, with an expression of countenance that seemed at least to us the very reverse of agreeable.' However, he warmed to his 'new half-wild friends' when they shared their 'brave mess of *shchi*' (soup) with him.

George Kennan found them equally hospitable in 1887. Inside the tent he was offered a container filled with about a litre and a half of koumiss. For fear of causing offence he swallowed the lot and to his horror, his host quickly refilled the container. Kennan wrote 'When I suggested that he reserve the second bowlful for my comrade, Mr Frost, he looked so pained and grieved that in order to restore his serenity I had to go to the *tarantas*, get my banjo and sing "There is a Tavern in the Town"'. This did not have quite the desired effect and they left shortly afterwards.

❑ **The West Siberian Railway (Km2716-3343)**
The original line started in Chelyabinsk, south of Yekaterinburg, and ran through Kurgan and Petropavlovsk (both south of the modern route) to Omsk. Work began in July 1892 under the direction of chief civil engineer Mikhailovsky. He was beset by problems that were also to be experienced along other sections of the line: a shortage of labour and animals, a complete lack of suitable trees for sleepers, and inhospitable working conditions (eg swamps that swarmed with insects). But in 1894 the first section from Chelyabinsk to Omsk was completed, and the Omsk to Novo-Nikolayevsk (now Novosibirsk) section opened in October 1895.

The total cost of the line was 46 million roubles, a million roubles less than the original estimate.

cannot, however, disguise the fact that it is essentially an industrial city. The line between Omsk and Novosibirsk has the greatest freight traffic density of any railway line in the world.

For the next 600km the train runs through the inhospitable **Baraba Steppe**. This vast expanse of greenish plains is dotted with shallow lakes and ponds, and coarse reeds and sedge grass conceal swamps, peat bogs and rare patches of firm ground. From the train it appears as if there is a continuous forest in the distance. However, what you are actually seeing are clumps of birches and aspen trees spaced several kilometres or more apart. The lack of landmarks in this area has claimed hundreds of lives. In spring this place is hell as the air is grey with clouds of gnats and mosquitoes. The Baraba Steppe is also a vast breeding ground for ducks and geese and every year hunters bag about five million birds from this area. Below the steppe is an enormous natural reservoir of hot water.

Km2760 (S): There is a locomotive storage depot here (mostly electric) and 3km east of it is the station of **Kormilovka Кормиловка**.

Km2795: Kalachinsk Калачинск One of the more attractive towns in Omsk Oblast, Kalachinsk was founded in 1792 by Russian peasants who were distinct from other settlers because of their unusual dialect – *kalachon* means 'a sharp bend in a river'; *kalach* in modern Russian means 'a small padlock-shaped white bread loaf'. There's a useful bit of information.

Km2840: This is the administrative frontier between Omskaya and Novosibirskaya oblasts. The 178,200 sq km of **Novosibirskaya Oblast** extend across the Baraba Steppe region of swamps and lakes. Some of the land has been drained and is now extremely fertile. Crops include spring wheat, flax, rye, barley and sunflowers, with dairy farming in many parts of the Baraba region.

Km2885: Tatarskaya Татарская Tatarsk is a humdrum small town of apartment blocks and log cabins. The *1900 Guide to the Great Siberian Railway* was not enthusiastic about the place: 'The country is swampy and infested with fever. The water is bad, supplied by a pond formed by spring and bog water.' There was a church, a centre for emigrants, a school and 'the butter manufactures of

Mariupolsky, Padin, Soshovsky, Popel and Weiss, producing annually about 15,000 *puds* (250,000 kg) of cream butter'.

Km2888 (N): An attractive group of colourful log cabins. About 50km south of the line between **Chany Чаны** and Barabinsk lies Lake Chany (Oz Chany), the centre of a local fishing industry. Catches are smaller now but in the 19th century the lake was famous for its abundant stock of large pike (weighing up to 14kg/30lbs) and carp.

Km3040: Barabinsk Барабинск (●●●+ for *Rossiya* ●●●+/●●● for Trans-Mongolian and ●●●/●●●+ for Trans-Manchurian) Founded at the end of the 19th century during the construction of the Trans-Siberian. About 12km northwards is the bigger and older town of **Kuybyshev (Kainsk-Barabinski)**.

Km3212: Chulymskaya Чулымская A large railway junction.

Km3322: Ob Обь On the left, just before reaching this station, you can see Tolmachyovo airport which is one of two airports serving Novosibirsk. The city of Novosibirsk is visible to the north-east.

Km3332: The Great Ob River Bridge After nearly a century of operation, many of the steel bridges of the early Trans-Siberian are still in use today. Known as **hog-backed bridges** because of the hump in the middle of each span, they are supported by massive stone piers, each with a thick buttress that slants upstream to deflect the huge ice chunks that float down the river in the spring thaw. The 870m-long Ob Bridge is a classic hog-backed bridge made up of seven spans.

The writers of the *1900 Guide to the Great Siberian Railway* were clearly impressed by the Ob Bridge, which at the time had only just been completed. They devote almost a whole page to it, beginning: 'At the 1,328 *verst*, the line crosses the Ob by a bridge 327.50 *sazhens* long, having seven spans, the I and VII openings are 46.325 *sazhens*, the II, IV and VI, 53.65 *sazhens*, and III and V, 53.15 *sazhens*. The upper girders of the bridge are on the Herber's system.' For those unfamiliar with Russian Imperial measurement, a *verst* is 1.06km or 3500ft and a *sazhen* is 2.1m or 7ft.

Work on the bridge started in 1893 with the construction of wooden falsework which supported sections of the permanent steel structure until they could be riveted together. Bridge-building proceeded year-round and was an extremely hazardous occupation in winter. Gangs were perched 30m or more above the

❏ **The Mid-Siberian Railway (Km3343-5191)**
Work began on the Mid-Siberian Railway starting at the Ob River in the summer of 1893. Since Tomsk was to be bypassed, part of the route had to be hacked through the thick forests of the taiga regions around the station, which was aptly named Taiga. It would have been far easier to have followed the route of the Great Siberian Post Road through Tomsk but some of that city's administrators wanted nothing to do with the railway, since it would break their trade monopolies and bring down prices, damaging the economy as far as they were concerned. By the time they realised that the effect was quite the opposite it was too late to change the route. Besides, the engineers had discovered that the bypass would save 90km. The tiny village of Novo-Nikolayevsk (now Novosibirsk), situated where the railway crosses the Ob, grew quickly and soon eclipsed Tomsk as an industrial and cultural centre. This was difficult territory to build a railway across. The swampy taiga is frozen until mid-July, so the building season was barely three months long. There was the usual labour shortage and 1500 convicts had to be brought in to help. In 1895 a branch line from Tayga reached Tomsk. Although only about 80km long, it had taken a year to build, owing to the virtually impenetrable taiga and the terrible swamps. In 1896 the line reached Krasnoyarsk and work began on the eastern section to Irkutsk. Numerous bridges were needed in this hilly country but by the beginning of 1898 the mid-Siberian was complete and the first trains rolled into Irkutsk. The total cost was about 110 million roubles.

frozen river, bolting and riveting without safety lines or protective hoardings. More than a few dropped to their death below.

The Ob River is one of the world's longest, flowing more than 4000km north across Siberia from the Altai Mountains to the Gulf of Ob below the Arctic Ocean. As you are crossing over the Ob River, you can see Novosibirsk city centre on the left and Oktyabrsky port on the right. The passenger river station is a further 800m upstream from the port. On reaching the right bank the train turns northwards, passing the city's long-distance bus station. About 800m onwards on the right you pass a **steam locomotive** on a plinth.

Km3335: Novosibirsk Новосибирск (●●●)   [see pp274-81]
Novosibirsk (pop: 1,523,801) is the capital of Western Siberia. Most trains stop long enough for you to get a good look at Siberia's largest station, an impressive glass-vaulted building that took from 1929 to 1941 to complete.

Travelling east you pass through a flat land of fields and swamps with the dachas of Novosibirskians in little groups amongst the trees. The line traverses an area of thin taiga to **Oyash Ояш (Km3424)**.

Km3463: Bolotnaya Болотная
The town was founded in 1805 as a stop on the Siberian Trakt, at the junction with a 250km road south to Barnaul. The town's name means 'swampy', which is certainly appropriate for this area.

───────────── **Km 3479-4473 TIME ZONE MT + 4** ─────────────

Km3479:
The **administrative frontier** between Novosibirskaya and Kemerovskaya oblasts.

ROUTE GUIDE & MAPS

Km3491: Yurga 1 Юрга 1 The station of **Yurga 2 Юрга 2** is 7km to the south of Yurga 1. A few kilometres to the east the train crosses the **Tom River**, flowing an unimpressive (by Siberian standards) 700km (or twice the length of the Thames) from the Kuznetsk Basin into the Ob River.

Km3570: Tayga Тайга (● but not for Trans-Manchurian) This town once stood in the midst of dense taiga forest. Nowadays the closest taiga is far to the east. RL Jefferson was here in 1897 and wrote later: 'This little station was bang in the midst of the most impenetrable forest I had ever set eyes on ... in the centre of a pit it seemed, for the great black trunks of pines went up all around and left only a circular space of blue sky visible.' Annette Meakin wrote a few years later that she 'thought Taiga one of the prettiest stations in Siberia. It is only a few years old, built something after the style of a Swiss chalet.' Unfortunately it has since been replaced by a building that is rather more substantial but aesthetically less pleasing.

Tayga station sits at the junction of a 79km branch line to the ancient city of **Tomsk Томск** (see pp282-8), and in retrospect the site of the junction was badly chosen. The problem is that there are no rivers or large reservoirs near Taiga so water had to be carted in to feed the steam engines. Tomsk was founded in 1604 on the Tom River and developed into a large administrative, trading and gold-smelting centre on the Great Siberian Post Road. When it was originally bypassed by the railway, Tomsk began to lose out to the stations along the main line. It is still, however, a sizeable city of half a million people, the administrative capital of Tomskaya Oblast and a large centre of industrial engineering.

Tomsk was visited by almost every 19th-century traveller to Siberia. The city was an important exile centre and had a large forwarding prison. Having almost succumbed to the stench from the overcrowded cells in 1887, Kennan wrote: 'If you visit the prison my advice to you is to breakfast heartily before starting, and to keep out of the hospital wards.' By the time Annette Meakin visited Tomsk 14 years later the railway had removed the need for forwarding prisons and she could write: 'It was not unlike a group of alms houses. We found very few prisoners.' Tomsk achieved international notoriety when at nearby Tomsk-7 on 6 April 1993 a radioactive waste-reprocessing plant blew up, contaminating an area of 120 sq km.

Near the station is a **steam engine**, P-360192, built in 1956.

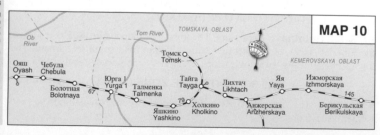

Km3602: Anzherskaya Анжерская   This ugly coal-mining town is at the northern extremity of the giant **Kuzbass (Kuznetsk Basin) coal field** which contains a massive 600 billion tons of high quality, low sulphur coal. The town, formerly called Anzhero-Sudzhensk Анжеро-Судженск, was founded in 1897 during the construction of the Trans-Siberian and in the early days of coal mining here. From the late 19th to early 20th centuries, 98% of all coal from the Kuzbass came through Anzherskaya. Most of the original miners were Tsarist prisoners, whose short and brutal lives are documented in the town's Museum of Local Studies.

A railway branch line leads south from here to **Novokuznetsk** which is the heart of the Kuzbass. In the early 1900s a plan had been put forward to link these coal fields with the Ural region where iron-ore was mined and coal was needed for the blast furnaces. The plan was not put into action until the 1930s when the so-called Ural-Kuzbass Kombinat was developed. Trains bring iron-ore to Kuzbass furnaces and return with coal for the foundries of the Urals. You will have met (or will meet if you're going west) a good deal of this traffic on the line between Novosibirsk and the Urals.

Km3715: Mariinsk Мариинск **(●●●+)**   Founded as Kisskoye in 1698, this place was nothing more than a way-station for postal riders who carried messages on the Moscow–Irkutsk postal road. In 1826, however, news of a massive gold find brought tens of thousands of fortune seekers. The gold rush lasted for decades and between 1828 and 1917 more than 50 tons of gold were extracted from the region. The town was renamed Mariinsk in 1857 after Maria Alexandrovna, the German wife of Tsar Alexander II.

Just west of the station there are large **engine repair yards** (S). Two kilometres east of the town you cross the Kiya River, a tributary of the Chulim. East of the river the line rises to cross the watershed at Km3760, where there are good views south. The line descends through the market town of **Tyazhin** Тяжин **(Km3779)** to the river of the same name and then climbs over the next watershed, descending to **Itat** Итат, another agricultural town.

Km3820:   This is the administrative frontier between Kemerovskaya Oblast and Krasnoyarsky Kray. A *kray* is a large oblast, usually established in less developed areas of Siberia. This is also the border between Western and Eastern Siberia. **Krasnoyarsky Kray** covers 2.34 million sq km (an area the size of

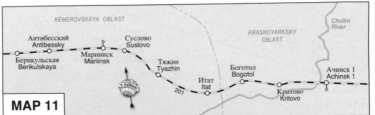

MAP 11

Saudi Arabia) between the Arctic Ocean and the Sayan Mountains in the south. Most of it is covered with taiga, although there is tundra in the region within the Arctic Circle and some agricultural land in the south. The economy is based on timber processing but there are also important mineral reserves.

Km3846: Bogotol Боготол (●, *Rossiya* **only**) The town was founded in 1893 as a station on the Trans-Siberian although there is a much older village of the same name 8km away. Near Bogotol are lignite (brown coal) deposits. Open-cut mines can be seen from the train, scarring the landscape.

About 30km eastwards the line begins to descend, crossing the **Chulim River** at **Km3916**. RL Jefferson arrived here in the winter of 1897, describing the river as 'rather a small stream when compared to the Obi, Tom or Irtish but still broad enough to make two of the Thames River at London Bridge'. At the time the bridge was unfinished but engineers had the brilliant idea of freezing the rails to the thick ice, thus allowing the train to cross the river.

Km3917: Achinsk 1 Ачинск 1 (● **for** *Rossiya*; –/● **for Trans-Mongolian; not a stop for Trans-Manchurian**) (214m/700ft) Achinsk was founded in 1642 as a stockaded outpost on the banks of the Chulim. It was burnt down by the Kyrgyz 40 years later but soon rebuilt. In the 18th and 19th centuries this was an important trading centre, linked by the Chulim to Tyumen and Tomsk. Tea arrived by caravan from China and was forwarded in barges. To the north, in the valleys around the Chulim basin, lay gold mines.

Km3932-33 (S): This is the halfway point on the line from Moscow to Beijing (via Mongolia). There's a **white obelisk** to mark it on the south side of the line but it is difficult to see.

The line continues through hilly taiga, winding round **sharp curves (Km4006-12)** and past picturesque groups of **log cabins (Km4016)**. There are good views, both at **Km4058 (N)** and, after the village of **Minino Минино (Km4072)**, at **Km4078 (N)**.

Km4098: Krasnoyarsk Красноярск (●●●)   [see pp282-96]
This major industrial city (pop: 1,016, 385) was founded in 1628 beside the Yenisey River. (Yenisey is also the name of the Moscow–Krasnoyarsk Express which you may see standing in the station). The original fort was named Krasny Yar. As an important trading centre on the Great Siberian Post Road and the

MAP 12

❑ **Evenki National Okrug**
About 900km due north of Krasnoyarsk lies the town of Tura, capital of the Evenki
National Okrug, 745,000 sq km of permanently frozen land, specially reserved for the
indigenous population. The **Evenks** belong to the Tungus group of people (the names
are often used interchangeably), who were originally nomadic herders and hunters.
After the Buryats and the Yakuts they form the largest ethnic group in Siberia but they
are scattered in small groups right across the northern regions. They once lived in wig-
wams or tents and survived off berries and reindeer-meat (a great delicacy being the
raw marrow sucked straight from the bone, preferably while it was still warm). They
discovered that Christianity fitted in well with their own Shamanistic religion and worshipped St Nicholas as deputy to the Master Spirit of the Underworld. After the
Revolution they were organised into collective farms; although most of the population
is now settled, there are still some reindeer-herders in the extreme north of the region.

Yenisey waterway, the town grew fast in the 18th century. The railway reached
Krasnoyarsk in 1896, some of the rails for this section having been brought
from England by ship via the Kara Sea (within the Arctic Circle) and the
Yenisey. Murray would not now recognise the town he described in the 1865
edition of his *Handbook for Russia, Poland and Finland* as 'pleasantly situated
and sheltered by hills of moderate elevation'.

A former governor of Krasnoyarsk was the late hardline General Alexander
Lebed, who stood against Boris Yeltsin in the 1996 presidential elections but
finally stood down and supported Yeltsin.

Km4100-2: Yenisey River Река Енисей Good views (N) and (S). Leaving
Krasnoyarsk to the east the train crosses the great river that bisects Siberia. The
Yenisey (meaning 'wide water' in the language of the local Evenki people) rises
in Mongolia and flows into the Arctic Ocean, 5200km north of its source.

The river is crossed on a bridge opened only in 1999. The old bridge, almost
1km in length, dated from the 1890s and had to be built on heavy granite piers
to withstand the huge icebergs which steamroller their way down the river for a
few weeks each year. The cement was shipped from St Petersburg, the steel
bearings from Warsaw. It took 94,000 workers three years to build it. The old
bridge was awarded a gold medal at the World Fair in Paris in 1900 (the other
engineering feat to win a gold medal in that year was the Eiffel Tower).

The Yenisey is the traditional border between Western and Eastern Siberia.
For several kilometres after you've crossed it, lumber mills and factories blight
the countryside.

Km4117: Bazaikha Базаиха There is a branch line northwards from here to
the closed city of Zheleznogorsk, formerly known as Krasnoyarsk-26, where
weapons-grade plutonium used to be produced and where JSC Information
Satellite Systems, Russia's biggest satellite manufacturer, is a significant
employer. The line goes through Sotsgorod station and terminates at the
Gorknokhimichesky Chemical complex. Neither this line nor the city appeared
on Soviet-era maps.

Open-cast mining has created ugly gashes in the hills around **Km4128 (N)**.
Between Krasnoyarsk and Nizhneudinsk the line crosses picturesque hilly
countryside, with the train climbing in and out of successive valleys. There are
numerous bridges on this section. There are good places for photographs along
the train as it curves round bends at **Km4165-4167** and **Km4176-4177**.

Km4227: Uyar Уяр At the western end of the station is a strategic reserve of
working **steam locos** and also a dump of about 10 engines rusting away
amongst the weeds. This town's full name is something of a tongue-twister: try
saying 'Uyarspasopreobrazhenskoye' after a few glasses of vodka. In 1897 the
name was changed to Olgino in honour of grand duchess Olga Nikolayevna,
and in 1906 to Klyukvenaya, after the railway engineer who built this section
of the line. In 1973 it again became Uyar.

Km4262: Zaozyornaya Заозёрная A branch line runs northwards from
here to the once-secret city of **Krasnoyarsk-45** (also known as **Zelenogorsk**)
where there's a space centre and where the production of low-enriched uranium
takes place. East of the station there are huge open-cast coal mines beside the
track.

Km4343: Kansk-Yeniseysky Канск-Енисейский (●, *Rossiya* only) This
big town, usually called **Kansk**, had an inglorious start. Its original wooden
fortress was built in 1628, 43km from the present site. The location was badly
chosen and in 1640 the fortress was moved. It was almost immediately burnt
down by local Buryats, and after being rebuilt it was burnt down again in 1677.
Over the following two centuries the town became a major transit point for
peasants settling in Siberia. Russian author Anton Chekhov wasn't very
impressed, writing that Kansk belonged among the impoverished, stagnant little towns famed only for an abundance of taverns. It's unlikely he'd change his
view if he visited today.

Km4375: Ilanskaya Иланская (●●●) The site of the town of **Ilansky
Иланский** was selected in 1734 by the Danish-born Russian naval explorer Vitus
Bering (after whom the Bering Straits are named) during the Second Kamchatsky
Expedition to explore the coast of America. It may seem strange that Bering was
surveying central Siberia but he was under orders to make himself useful as he
crossed to the Russian Far East. This station is one of the best places along the
Trans-Sib for purchasing hot and cold home-cooked food on the platform.

MAP 13

Km4453: Reshoty Решоты (–/●, *Rossiya* only) This is the junction for the line south to Abakan, an industrial centre in the foothills of the Sayan Mountains.

──────────── **Km 4474-5780 TIME ZONE MT + 5** ────────────

Local time is now Moscow Time + 5 hours. The line gradually swings round to the south-east as it heads towards Irkutsk. For the next 600km you will pass through one of Russia's biggest logging areas. Many of the rivers are used to transport the logs and you can often see log packs being towed down the river or piles of loose logs washed up on the banks. This section of the line is very impressive, the train constantly climbing and descending as it crosses numerous rivers and deep ravines.

Km4501-02: The river here conveniently marks the **halfway point** for the Moscow to Beijing (via Manchuria) run.

Km4516: Tayshet Тайшет (●, *Rossiya* only) This town is at the junction of the Trans-Siberian and BAM (Baikal Amur Mainline) railways. The 3400km BAM line (see pp498-504) traverses Siberia from Lake Baikal to the Pacific Ocean and is the gateway to a rarely visited region known as the BAM Zone. The single-track line is about 600km to 1000km north of the Trans-Siberian Railway, running parallel to it through pristine taiga, mountain tundra and wide river valley meadows. Before the 1970s the BAM Zone was virtually uninhabited taiga, dotted with indigenous villages. Today it has a population of about 300,000 involved in extracting natural resources from the region's enormous reserves. Only about 100 Westerners visit the region each year.

Tayshet was founded when the Trans-Siberian arrived in 1897 and is famous in Soviet 'Gulag' literature. Tayshet was a transit camp for Stalin-era prisoners heading east or west, and was a major camp of Ozerlag, the Gulag complex whose prisoners built the Tayshet–Bratsk section of the BAM. Construction of this section started in earnest after WWII. At the height of the work there were over 300 camps dotted along the line's 350km, with a total population of 100,000 prisoners. In *The Gulag Archipelago*, Alexander Solzhenitsyn writes that Tayshet had a factory for creosoting railroad ties (railway sleepers) 'where, they say, creosote penetrates the skin and bones and its vapours fill the lungs – and that is death'.

Km4555 (S): Razgon Разгон A small, poor-looking community of log cabins.

About 1km east of Razgon the line rises and there are views across the taiga at Km4563 (S), Km4569 (N) and Km4570.

Km4631: Kamyshet Камышет It was here that George Kennan stopped in 1887 for repairs to his tarantass. While the wheel was being replaced he watched the amazing spectacle of a Siberian blacksmith shoeing a horse. 'The poor beast had been hoisted by means of two broad belly-bands and suspended from a stout frame so that he could not touch the ground', he wrote. Three of the horse's legs had been secured to the frame and 'the daring blacksmith was fearlessly putting a shoe on the only hoof that the wretched and humiliated animal could move'.

ROUTE GUIDE & MAPS

Km4640-4680: The train snakes its way through the foothills of the Eastern Sayan Mountains. The Sayan Range forms a natural frontier between Siberia and Mongolia. At Km4648-9 you are at the **half-way point** between Moscow and Vladivostok. There are several chances for photographs of the whole train as it winds around the valleys. The best spots are around Km4657 (S), Km4660 (S), Km4662-5 and Km4667.

Km4680: Nizhneudinsk Нижнеудинск (●●) The area is known for sawmills, swamps and insects. Of the mosquitoes, Kennan complained, 'I found myself blotted from head to foot as if I were suffering from some eruptive disease.'

Near Nizhneudinsk is a famous Siberian beauty spot, **Ukovsky Waterfall**; it's 18km upstream along the Ude River which flows through Nizhneudinsk. About 75km further upstream, the **Nizhneudinsky Caves** contain ancient paintings.

Siberia's smallest indigenous group, numbering less than 500, is the Tofalar (Tofy), living in and around the isolated settlement of **Tofalaria**, 200km from Nizhneudinsk. There are no roads to this village and its only regular link with the rest of the world is a helicopter service from Nizhneudinsk.

Between Nizhneudinsk and Irkutsk the country becomes flatter and the taiga thins out. The train passes through numerous timber-yards.

Km4789 (S): There is a large, well-maintained **graveyard** with a blue fence around it, standing close to the line. Some of the graves are topped with red stars, some with red crosses. Kennan wrote in 1887: 'The graveyards belonging to the Siberian settlements sometimes seemed to me much more remarkable and noteworthy than the settlements themselves ... Many graves (are) marked by three-armed wooden crosses and covered with narrow A-shaped roofs.'

Km4794: Tulun Тулун (●, *Rossiya* **only)** Tulun sits at the junction of the M55 Moscow–Irkutsk Highway and the main road to the city of Bratsk, 225km to the north. The town's centre, near the station, still consists mainly of wooden houses.

❏ **The Tunguska Event**
About 800km due north of Nizhneudinsk, on 30 June 1908, one of the largest (pre-atomic era) explosions in human history took place, in the Tunguska River region. Some 2000 sq km of forest were instantly destroyed in what came to be known as the Tunguska Event. The sound of the explosion was heard up to 350km away, the shock waves were registered on seismic equipment right around the world, and the light from the blast was seen throughout Europe. Newspapers of the time proposed all kinds of theories to explain it, from the testing of new explosives to crash-landing Martian spaceships. Scientists now believe that it was caused by a fragment of Encke's Comet, which disintegrated as it entered the Earth's atmosphere, creating a vast fireball. In September 2002 it was reported that a meteorite hit a forest area north of Lake Baikal. On a Siberian scale this was a blip compared to the Tunguska Event but it still managed to destroy an area of 65 sq km.

The line follows the river, crossing it at Km4800 and passing a large sawmill at Km4804 (S). For once there are no wires to get in the way. At Km4809 (S) there is a large open-cast mine.

Km4875: Kuytun Куйтун The town's name means 'cold' in the language of the Buryat people (see box p458). There are cold springs in the area.

Km4940: Zima Зима (●●●+) (460m/1500ft) Zima means 'winter' and at the beginning of the 19th century this was a place of exile for members of the Sectarian sect. When Tsarevich Nicholas visited Zima on 8 July 1891 the Buryats presented him with a model yurt cast in silver.

About 3km to the east of the town the railway crosses the 790km-long **Oka River**. The river runs brown as it cuts through seams of coal and *copperas* (ferrous sulphate). The mineral-rich water and earth have their benefits as the water was used to blacken tanned animal skins and, during epidemics of cholera, the copperas earth was used as a disinfectant. But it also causes goitre, which many locals suffer from today. Down the Oka near the riverside village of Burluksk are 1000-year-old petroglyphs of cattle, horses and riders.

As the line crosses the watershed you get several reasonable views: Km4958 (S), Km4972 (N), Km4977 (S) and Km4990 (S).

Km5000-5040: You pass through the **Ust-Ordinsky Autonomous Okrug**. There's another **graveyard** close to the track at Km5010 (S).

Km5027: Kutulik Кутулик This station is the biggest railway town in the **Ust-Orda Buryat Nationality District**. The Ust-Orda Buryats are related to the Buryats to the east of Lake Baikal and to Mongolians but have a different language and culture. The best time to be here is during the harvest festival of Surkharban when there are races, archery competitions and the Ust-Orda's peculiar brand of wrestling.

Km5061: Cheremkhovo Черемхово The town revolves around the Cheremkhovo coal deposit, and various mining and industrial complexes are dotted along 10km of the railway. The first mine can be seen from the railway about 20km east of the station.

Km5087: Polovina Половина The station, whose name means 'half', was once the halfway point on the Trans-Siberian between Moscow and Vladivostok.

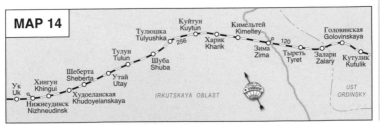

Today Moscow is 5090km away and Vladivostok 4212km. The reason for this discrepancy is that the station was named at a time when the Trans-Siberian ran to Moscow via Chelyabinsk and not Yekaterinburg, and to Vladivostok through Manchuria, rather than along the banks of the Amur.

Km5100: Malta Мальта It was in a house in Malta, in February 1928, that farmer Platon Brilin was helping a comrade to build a cellar. As he was digging his spade struck a white object which turned out to be a mammoth tusk carved into a female form. Excavations revealed dwellings with walls made from mammoth bones and roofs of antlers. He had discovered the remains of an ancient settlement, dating from the 13th millennium BC. A grave yielded the body of a child, still wearing a necklace and headband of bones. The child may have been a young shaman (see box p299) for the gods were thought to select their earthly representatives by branding them with some kind of deformity: the boy has two sets of teeth. Numerous figurines made of ivory have been found at Malta and also at a site in **Buret**, 8km from here. Many of the excavated artefacts may be seen in museums in Irkutsk. The oldest settlement so far discovered in Russia (1-2½ million years old) is at **Dering Yuryakh** in northern Siberia, near Yakutsk.

Km5124: Usolye-Sibirskoye Усолье-Сибирское This city on the left bank (western side) of the Angara River is the salt capital of Siberia. Don't, however, expect to find Siberian salt mines here. Until 1956 all salt was produced by pumping salty water from shallow wells into pans and leaving it to evaporate. These can still be seen on the left bank of the Angara River and on Varnichnoe Island. Nowadays the salt is produced at a **salt factory**, the biggest in Russia. Nearby, **Usolye Health Resort** offers salt, sulphur and mud baths to cure afflictions of the limbs.

Across the river is the nearly abandoned village of **Aleksandrovskoye** which was renowned for the particularly brutal conditions of its Tsarist prison founded in 1873. In 1902 a failed revolt led by Felix Dzerzhinsky broke out here. Many of the participants in the failed 1905 Revolution were imprisoned here.

Km5130 (N): There is a large oil refinery here.

Km5133: Telma Тельма Siberia's first textile mill opened here in 1731.

Km5160: Angarsk Ангарск (●, *Rossiya* only) Although primarily an industrial city, Angarsk is well planned and attractive as its industrial and civic parts are

MAP 15

❏ **How the post was sent to Siberia**
The building of the Trans-Siberian Railway revolutionised postal services across the vast Siberian steppes. By 1902 a letter could be carried from St Petersburg to Vladivostok in less than two weeks instead of several months as previously.

The first Siberian letter on record was carried to Moscow in 1582 by Yermak's Cossacks, and informed Tsar Ivan the Terrible that Siberia was now his. A regular postal system had been established in Siberia by 1600, Russian peasants being encouraged to emigrate to Siberia to work as Post House keepers and post-riders or *yamshchiki* (see p91). The post always had priority when it came to horses and to right-of-way on the new post roads. Each Post House keeper had to keep some horses permanently in reserve in case the post should arrive, and on the road a blast of the courier's horn was enough to make other road users pull over and allow the post to pass. Indeed the yamshchiki were not averse to using their whip on the drivers of carts which were slow to move out of the way.

In April 1829 the German writer Adolph Erman, travelling down the still-frozen Lena River from Irkutsk to Yakutsk, wrote that he had 'the good luck of meeting the postman from Yakutsk and Kamchatka. At my desire he waited until the frozen ink which I carried with me had time to thaw, and a few lines to friends in Berlin were written and committed to his care. The courier, or paid overseer who attended the mail from Yakutsk to Irkutsk carried, as a mark of his rank and office, a sword and a loaded pistol, hanging by a chain from his neck. In winter he obtains from the peasants the requisite supply of sledges and horses; and when the ice-road is broken up he takes boats, sometimes, to ascend the Lena' (*Travels in Siberia*).

By the time Annette Meakin travelled along the Trans-Siberian Railway in 1900 she was able to send letters home speedily by train, but she had evidently heard about dishonest postal officials and took pains to register all her letters. In *A Ribbon of Iron* she wrote 'If you do not register in Siberia there is every chance that the stamps will be taken and the letter destroyed long before it reaches the border. You cannot register after 2pm, in which case it is advisable to use a black-edged envelope. Superstition will then prevent its being tampered with'. Black-edged envelopes were used during a period of mourning. Much of the mail still goes by train, though sadly the travelling post-office coaches formerly attached to passenger carriages are no longer widely used.   **Philip Robinson** (UK)

Philatelists may be interested to know that Philip Robinson is the co-author of *Russian Postmarks* and author of *Siberia – Postmarks and Postal History of the Russian Empire Period*. He has since published a collection of railway postcards, *The Trans-Siberian Railway on Early Postcards*. Many of these postcards date from the 1890s and show scenes of railway construction and tunnel building.

separated by a wide green belt. From the station the industrial part is to the north-east (left side if you're heading away from Moscow) and the civic area to the south-west. Angarsk's major industry is oil refining; oil is pumped here by pipeline from the West Siberian, Tatarstan and Baskir oil fields. This pipeline can occasionally be spotted alongside the railway. The city has a river port and from here hydrofoils travel downstream to Bratsk. Ferries also run between Irkutsk and Angarsk.

Km5170: Meget Мегет Just north of Meget there's a strategic reserve (N) of L and Ye 2-10-0s **steam engines**.

ROUTE GUIDE & MAPS

Km5178: Irkutsk Sortirovka Иркутск Сортировка (●●●, *Rossiya* only)

This marshalling yard was once a small station called Innokentievskaya, in hon-our of St Innokent, Archbishop of Irkutsk, said to be Siberia's first miracle-worker. The nearby **St Innokent Monastery of the Ascension** was founded in 1672.

The Tsar stopped here on his tour of Siberia in 1891 and the visit was thus described: 'After having listened to the singing, the Tsarevich (sic) knelt at the shrine of the Siberian Saint, kissed the relics and received the image of Innokent, presented to him by Agathangelius, Vicar of Irkutsk.

At the same time a deputation from the Shaman Buryats expressed the desire of 250 men to adopt the orthodox religion and to receive the name of Nicholas in commemoration of the Tsarevich's visit to Siberia, which was thus to be preserved in the memory of their descendants. The Imperial traveller gra-ciously acceded to this request.'

Km5182: Irkutny Most Иркутный Мост Just east of this little station the
railway crosses a bridge over the Irkut River, from which Irkutsk takes its name.

Km5185: Irkutsk Иркутск (●●●+)   [see pp297-307]

Once known as the 'Paris of Siberia,' Irkutsk (pop: 606,137; 440m/1450ft) is the cultural heart of the Baikal region and is also just 64km away from the beau-tiful Lake Baikal. From the railway you cannot see much of central Irkutsk,

---

❏ The Buryats

The largest ethnic minority group in Siberia, Buryats are of Mongolian descent. When Russian colonists first arrived at Lake Baikal the Buryats were nomads who spent their time herding their flocks between the southern shores of the lake and what is now northern Mongolia, in search of pastureland. They lived in felt-covered yurts and practised a mixture of Buddhism and Shamanism.

The Buryats lived on lake fish, bear meat and berries, although their favourite food was said to be *urme*, the thick dried layer of scum skimmed from the top of boiled milk. They hunted the Baikal seal for its fur and in winter, when the lake was frozen, they would track these animals on the ice, wearing white clothing and push-ing a white sledge as a hide.

Back in their yurts the Buryats were not the tidiest of tribes, lacking even the most basic hygiene as the Soviet anthropologists Levin and Potapov point out in *The Peoples of Siberia*. Describing an after-dinner scene, they wrote: 'The vessels were not washed, as the spoons and cups were licked clean. An unwashed vessel was often passed from one member of the family to another as was the smoking pipe. Customs of this kind promoted the spread of various diseases.' It seems likely, however, that most of these diseases were brought by Russian colonists.

Although at first hostile to the Russians, the Buryats became involved in the fur trade with the Europeans and a certain amount of inter-marriage occurred. Some gave up their nomadic life and their yurts in favour of log cabins in Verkhneudinsk (now Ulan-Ude) or Irkutsk. The Buryats, who now number about 350,000, have their own **Buryat Republic** around the southern part of Lake Baikal. Its capital, Ulan-Ude (see pp319-25), was opened to tourists in 1990 and makes an interesting stopover.

located on the other side of the Angara River. In the distance, however, you can see the large Church of the Elevation of the Cross.

Km5214: Goncharovo Гончарово The town around the station is named **Shelekhov Шелехов** after a Russian merchant who led several trading expeditions to North America in the 1780s. He was made governor of the Russian settlement in America and become one of Siberia's richest merchants, with an empire based in Irkutsk. Passing through Goncharovo you can see the town's main industry, the giant Irkutsk Aluminium Complex, founded in 1956.

The train soon begins climbing into the Primorsky Mountains. Winding through valleys of cedar and pine and crossing numerous small streams, it passes **Kultuk Култук**, junction for the old railway line from Port Baikal.

At Km5228 (N) a **giant etching of Lenin** waves nonchalantly from a hill. The line climbs steeply to Km5254 and then snakes downwards, providing your first glimpse of **Lake Baikal Озеро Байкал** from Km5274 to Km5278. After a **tunnel** at Km5290 there is a splendid view over the lake at Km5292 (N).

Km5297-8: Through **another tunnel** the line curves sharply round the valley and descends to the water's edge.

After a junction and goods yard at **Slyudyanka 2 Слюдянка 2 (Km5305)** the train crawls along a part of the line that is prone to flooding from the lake.

Km5312: Slyudyanka 1 Слюдянка 1 (● for *Rossiya*; ●/●● for **Trans-Mongolian**; ● for **Trans-Manchurian**) The station is only about 500m from the lake and the stop may give you just enough time to nip between the log cabins down to the water (see box below). Only speedy sprinters should try this (in case the train leaves early) and only if the carriage attendant confirms that the train is stopping for more than 10 minutes. Some people have been left behind doing this! ('The provodnitsas were horrified at your suggestion that it is possible to run down to Lake Baikal from Slyudyanka 1.' Howard Dymock, UK).

The station building was constructed of marble in 1904 to commemorate the building of the Circumbaikal Railway. There are usually interesting things to buy on the platform – sometimes even Baikal's own *omul* fish and boiled potatoes, or raspberries and bags of *orekhi* (nuts, here meaning cedar nuts, the classic Siberian snack).

❏ **Time for a dip in Lake Baikal?**
'Last night, I paced out the distance between **Slyudyanka-1 station** and Lake Baikal. It takes **four minutes** at normal walking pace to reach the water. There is a path leading down from the left-hand side of the main station building, before the low row of vendors' shacks. Follow it downhill (passing the church to your right) and when you reach the last road, continue on the track to the lake's edge. A handy gap has been knocked in the lakeside fence, so you can plunge in quite happily before heading back to your train. Just watch out for all the broken glass left by previous beach partygoers'.
Simon Calder (UK)

Slyudyanka is the starting point for hikers and rafters travelling into the
Khamar-Daban Mountains to the south. Fur-trappers hunt sable and ermine in
the forests here. From Slyudyanka the 94km **Circumbaikal Railway** (see box
below) branch line runs along the shore of Lake Baikal to Port Baikal.

❏ The Circumbaikal Line

The original line from Irkutsk did not follow the route of the present railway but ran
to Port Baikal. Until 1904 passengers crossed Lake Baikal on ferries which took them
from Port Baikal to Mysovaya. In 1893 it had been decided that it would be impossi-
bly expensive to build the short section of railway along the mountainous southern
shore of the lake and the idea was shelved in favour of a ferry link. From the British
company Armstrong and Mitchell a specially designed combined ice-breaker and
train-ferry was ordered. The 4200-ton ship, christened the *Baikal*, had three pairs of
rails laid across her decks for the carriages and could smash through ice up to four
feet thick. A sister ship, the *Angara*, was soon brought into service. The *Angara* has
now been converted into a museum and is moored in Irkutsk (see pp301-2).

The ferry system was not a great success, however. In mid-winter the ships were
unable to break through the ice and in summer the wild storms for which the lake is
notorious often delayed them. Since they could not accommodate more than 300 people between them, many passengers were subjected to long waits beside the lake. The
Trans-Siberian Committee realised that, however expensive it might prove, a line had
to be built to bridge the 260km gap between the Mid-Siberian and Transbaikal railways. Further surveys were ordered in 1898 and in 1901 10,000 labourers started
work on the line. This was the most difficult section to build on the entire railway.
The terrain between Port Baikal and Kultuk (near Slyudyanka) was virtually one long
cliff. Thirty-three tunnels and more than 200 bridges and trestles were constructed,
the task made all the more difficult by the fact that in many places labourers could
only reach the route by boat. Work went forward simultaneously on the Tankhoy to
Mysovaya section.

The labour gangs hacked out embankments and excavated 7km of tunnels but the
line was not ready at the time it was most needed. On 8 February 1904 Japan attacked
the Russian Navy as it lay at anchor in Port Arthur on the Pacific. Troops were rushed
by rail from European Russia but when they arrived at Port Baikal, they found the
Baikal and *Angara* ice-bound in the severe weather. The only way across the lake was
a 17-hour march over the ice. It was then that the Minister of Ways of
Communication, Prince Khilkov, put into action a plan which had been successful on
several of Siberia's rivers: rails were laid across the ice. The first train to set off across
the frozen lake did not get far along the 45km track before the ice gave way with a
crack like a cannon-shot and the locomotive sank into the icy water. From then on
engines were stripped and their parts put on flatcars pulled over the ice by gangs of
men and horses.

Working as fast as possible, in all weathers, labourers completed the
Circumbaikal Line in September 1904 at a cost of about 70 million roubles. The first
passengers found this section of the line particularly terrifying, not on account of the
frequent derailments but because of the tunnels: there were none in European Russia
at that time. In the 1950s a short-cut was opened between Irkutsk and Slyudyanka,
which is the route followed by the train today. The line between Irkutsk and Port
Baikal is now partly flooded and no longer used. The Port Baikal to Kultuk section,
however, is still operational and makes an entertaining side-trip. See box p311.

The train passes through a **short tunnel** and runs within sight of the water's edge for the next 180km. Some of the best views on the whole trip are along this section of the line.

Km5358: Baikalsk Байкальск The skiing here is said to be among the best in the country. The town also makes a good base for walks and rafting in the Khamar-Daban Mountains.

About 3km past the town on the left is the **Baikalsk Cellulose and Paper Combine**, source of a strong cellulose used in aircraft tyres. Until recently its chlorine-contaminated waste water was dumped directly into the lake, causing the number of crustacean species within a 50km radius to drop from 57 to 5. Not surprisingly the factory was the brainchild of that environmental vandal Khrushchev, who wanted to 'put Baikal to work'. This was by far Lake Baikal's biggest environmental problem, and because of the enormous cost of upgrading the plant and fitting filters, it continued its destructive operations well into the 1990s. Despite a recent upgrade, rumours persist of leaks of waste material into the lake.

Km5390: Vydrino Выдрино The river just before the station marks the border of the **Buryat Republic**. This region, which is also known as Buryatia, comprises an area of about 351,300 sq km (about the size of Italy). It was originally set aside for the Buryats (see box p458), an indigenous ethnic group once nomadic but now adapted to an agricultural or urban life.

Km5426: Tankhoy Танхой Tankhoy sits in the middle of the 263,300-hectare **Baikalsky Nature Reserve** which was created to preserve the Siberian taiga. Occasional ferries travel from here to Listvyanka and Port Baikal.

When Prince Borghese and his team were motoring through this area in 1907 on the Peking to Paris Rally they found that since the building of the railway, the Great Siberian Post Road had fallen into disrepair. Most of the post-stations were deserted and many road bridges were rotten and dangerous. The Italians were given special permission by the governor-general to drive across the railway bridges. In fact they covered a considerable part of the journey here by driving along the railway line. Their 40-horsepower Itala was not the only unorthodox vehicle to take to the rails. On his cycling tour through south Siberia in 1896 R L Jefferson found it rather easier to pedal his Imperial Rover along the tracks than on the muddy roads.

Km5477: Mysovaya Мысовая This was the port where the *Baikal* and *Angara* (see box p301-2) delivered their passengers (and their trains).

When Annette Meakin and her mother disembarked from the *Baikal* in 1900 they were horrified to discover that the waiting train was composed entirely of fourth-class carriages. The brave ladies commandeered seats in the corner of one compartment but were soon hemmed in by emigrating peasants. When 'two dirty moujiks' climbed into the luggage rack above them, the ladies decided it might be better to wait at Mysovaya and got out. But the station-master allowed them

---

❏ The Transbaikal Railway (Km5483-6532)
In 1895 work was begun to connect Mysovaya (the port on Lake Baikal) with Sretensk, on the Shilka River near Kuenga (see p468), where passengers boarded steamers for the voyage on to Khabarovsk. Construction materials were shipped to Vladivostok and thence by boat along the Ussuri, Amur and Shilka rivers. There was a shortage of labour, for it proved impossible to get the local Buryats to work on the line. Gangs of reluctant convicts were brought in, although they became more interested in the operation after it was decided that they should receive 50 kopecks a day in return for their labour.

The terrain is mountainous and the line meanders up several valleys and over the Yablonovy Range. Owing to the dry climate, work could continue throughout the winter, although water was in short supply during these months. Workers were also faced with the problem of permafrost which necessitated the building of bonfires to thaw the ground, or dynamite to break it up.

A terrible setback occurred in July 1897 when over 300km of track and several bridges were damaged or swept away in a freak flood. The line was completed in early 1900 by which time it had cost over 60 million roubles.

---

to travel in an empty luggage-van, which gave them privacy if not comfort. The village surrounding the town is known as **Babushkin Бабушкин** in honour of Lenin's friend and Irkutsk revolutionary. Ivan Babushkin was executed by Tsarist forces at this railway depot in 1906 and an obelisk marks the spot.

Between Mysovaya and Petrovsky Zavod the line skirts the lower reaches of the Khamar-Daban mountains.

Km5504: Boyarsky Боярский The hills on the right of the station are all that remain of the ancient volcanoes of the Khamar-Daban foothills. East of the station the line leaves Lake Baikal.

Km5530: Posolskaya Посольская About 500m west of this station the train crosses over a narrow, shallow river with the odd name of **Bolshaya Rechka (Big Little Stream)**. About 10km downstream from Posolskaya the river flows into Lake Baikal at the site of the ancient village of Posolskoye. In earlier days Russian ambassadors travelling overland to Asian capitals would rest here; the rough village got a mention in the papers of Ambassador Fyodor Baikov when he passed through in 1656. In 1681 an abbot and a monk built a

MAP 16

walled monastery here but it has long since disappeared. Today Bolshaya Rechka hosts the Baikalsky Priboy (Baikal Surf) Holiday Camp.

Around **Km5536** the line enters the wide valley of the Selenga River, which it follows as far as Ulan-Ude (Km5642).

Km5562: Selenginsk Селенгинск The town was founded in the 17th century as a stockaded outpost on the Selenga River. Unfortunately its wood-pulping factories are rather more in evidence today than the 16th-century monastery built for missionaries attempting the conversion of the Buryats.

The factories here and in Ulan-Ude are notorious for the industrial waste they dump into the Selenga River, which flows into Lake Baikal. Pollution from the Selenga and from the once notorious cellulose mill at Baikalsk has affected over 60% of the lake; even if the pollution were to stop tomorrow it would take 400 years for the waste to be flushed out.

Km5596: Lesovozny Лесовозный The town around the station is called **Ilyinka Ильинка**.

At about **Km5624** the train crosses over the Selenga River, providing an excellent photo opportunity. At **Km5633-4 (N)** there's an army camp with some abandoned tanks. The train approaches Ulan-Ude along the right bank (northern side) of the Selenga River. About 1km before the station (N) is a **monument to five railway workers** executed by Tsarist forces in 1906 for revolutionary activities.

❏ American soldiers die defending Communists

During the Russian Civil War, American, Canadian and Japanese troops occupied parts of Eastern Siberia and the Russian Far East, helping White Russian forces battling the Communists. The undisciplined White Russians were often little more than bandits and murderers, and allied forces were often put in the awkward position of simultaneously supporting White Army soldiers and protecting the Russian population from them. An incident at Posolskaya station in January 1920 was just one of many unpleasant events that eventually undermined the allies' faith in the White Army.

White Army General Nicholas Bogomolets arrested the station master at Ulan-Ude and announced that he would execute him for Bolshevist activities. The American Colonel Morrow, based in Ulan-Ude, threatened to call out 2500 soldiers under his command unless the innocent man was released. Bogomolets retreated with the railway official to Posolskaya in his armoured train, where he opened fire in the middle of the night on the boxcar barracks of a small American garrison comprising one officer and 38 enlisted men. These soldiers swarmed out of their quarters, dropped into a skirmish line and blazed away. Sergeant Carl Robbins disabled the train's locomotive with a hand grenade before being killed. At the cost of two dead and one wounded on their side, the Americans captured the train, the general, six other officers and 48 men.

Bogomolets was released for political reasons and emigrated to Hollywood before being deported to Latvia. Sergeant Robbins and Second Lieutenant Paul Kendall posthumously received the Distinguished Service Cross.

ROUTE GUIDE & MAPS

Km5642: Ulan-Ude Улан-Удэ (●●●/●●●+)   [see pp319-25]

Ulan-Ude (pop: 416,079; 544m/1785ft) is the capital of the Buryat Republic.
Stretch your legs on the platform where there is a **steam loco** (Class Su) preserved outside the locomotive workshop (N) at the western end of the station.

You cross over the **Uda River** 2km east of the station. After a further 500m
you can see the **Palace of Culture** (N) and a **WWII memorial**.

Km5655: Zaudinsky Заудинский

The line to Ulaanbaatar (Mongolia) and
Beijing branches off from the Trans-Siberian here. Turn to p482 for the **Trans-
Mongolian route**.

Km5675 (N): Onokhoy Онохой

There are several **steam locos** at the west
end of the station.

From Onokhoy the train follows the valley of the River Brian. From
Zaigrayevo Заиграево (Km5696), the line begins to climb to **Ilka Илка**, on
the river of the same name. It continues to ascend the Zagon Dar range, reaching the highest point (882m/2892ft) at **Kizha Кижа**.

Km5734: Novoilyinsky Новоильинский

About 20km past this station the
train crosses the administrative frontier between the Buryat Republic and
Chitinskaya Oblast. Chitinskaya's 431,500 sq km comprise a series of mountain ranges interspersed with wide valleys. The dominant range is
the Yablonovy (highest peak: Sokhondo, 2510m/8235ft) which is crossed by the
Trans-Siberian near Amazar (Km7010).

―――――――――― **Km 5781-8183 TIME ZONE MT + 6** ――――――――――

Km5784: Petrovsky Zavod Петровский Завод (●)

Local time is now
Moscow Time + 6 hours. The name of the station means 'Peter's Factory', after
the foundry established here in 1789 to supply iron for the region's gold mines,
and still going strong today. The factory was rebuilt in 1939 next to the railway
and from the train you can see the flames from its open-hearth furnaces.

On the station platform there is a **memorial** to the Decembrists that were
brought here from nearby Chita in 1830, to work in the factory, and who were
housed in the factory prison. Princess Trubetskaya (1800-54) was the first wife
of a Decembrist to voluntarily follow her husband into exile. In doing so she
renounced her civil rights and noble privileges. Her name is immortalised in
Russian Women, a poem by Nikolai Nekrasov.

ROUTE GUIDE & MAPS

East of Petrovsky Zavod the line turns north-east into the wide, picturesque valley of the Khilok River, which it follows for almost 300km to Sokhondo, crossing the Yablonovy Range between Mogzon and Chita.

Km5883: Look out for the large graveyard of old **steam locomotives**.

Km5884: Bada Aeroport Бада Аэропорт The little town is clearly a product of the aerodrome and not vice versa: it's built around a large Soviet monument, a MiG fighter plane facing skyward. The runway (N) is interesting for the large number of old aircraft there.

Km5899 (S): Here is a good place for a photo along the train as it travels on higher ground beside the river. Another is at **Km5908 (S)**, where the train winds slowly along the water's edge.

Km5932: Khilok Хилок (●●●, *Rossiya* **and Trans-Manchurian only)** (805m/2640ft, pop: 13,700) East of this small industrial town you continue to climb gently up the valley beside the **Khilok River**. There are pleasant views over the wide plain all along the river. North of the line are the Khogoy and Shentoy mountains, part of the Tsagan Khuntei range. Near the station a granite monument topped with a star commemorates 11 Communists slain here during the Civil War.

The train now crosses the Yablonovy Mountains. The eastern escarpment is steeper than the western side and heavy freight trains travelling westwards invariably require extra engines.

Km6053: Mogzon Могзон (907m/2975ft) There's a steam locomotive dump in this dismal town, and heavily guarded prisons for several kilometres around, including one at **Km6055 (N)**.

Km6093: Sokhondo Сохондо (944m/3095ft) This station is named after the highest peak (2510m/8235ft) in the Yablonovy Range.

The line leaves the river valley and starts its climb into the Yablonovy Range. There is a long view at Km6097 (N). In the 1914 edition of *Russia with Teheran, Port Arthur and Peking*, Karl Baedeker drew his readers' attention to the '93 yard tunnel inscribed at its western entrance "To the Great Ocean" and at its eastern entrance "To the Atlantic Ocean" in Russian', here. The line has now been re-routed up onto a huge grassy plain. It then descends steeply through Yablonovaya, with several good views (Km6107-9).

MAP 18

ROUTE GUIDE & MAPS

Km6116 (S): There used to be a graveyard of steam locomotives here but now most of the engines have been dismantled. West of the town of **Ingoda** the train enters the narrow winding valley of the Ingoda River, which it follows eastwards for the next 250km. The line passes through **Chernovskaya Черновская**, where lignite is mined.

Km6125: Yablonovaya Яблоновая At 1040m/3412ft this is the **highest point on the line**.

Km6197 (N): About 2km west of Chita is the 16 sq km **Kenon Lake**. Only 6m deep, the lake is warmed by the nearby power station and at its eastern end there's a popular beach beside the railway line. Further on the train crosses the small Chita River, and about 1km before the main station you pass through **Chita 1** station where a railway factory is located.

Km6199: Chita 2 Чита 2 (●●●+)   [see pp327-31]
Founded in 1653, Chita (pop: 331,346; 655m/2150ft), the capital of Chitinskaya Oblast, stands beside the Chita and Ingoda rivers and is surrounded by low hills. A stockaded fort was built here by Cossacks at the end of the 17th century and the town became an important centre on the Chinese trade route. In 1827 a large group of exiled Decembrists arrived here and spent the first few months building the prison that was to be their home for the following three years. Many stayed on after they had served their sentence and the town's development in the 19th century into an industrial and cultural centre was largely due to their efforts.

East of the city of Chita the train continues to follow the left bank of the Ingoda River downhill for the next 250km. The line passes through **Novaya Новая**, whose original community and dwellings were wiped out in the great flood of 1897 (see p101). At **Km6225 (S)** there's a collection of log cabins which looks rather vulnerable, being built on the edge of the river flood plain.

Km6265: Darasun Дарасун Darasun is renowned for its carbonic mineral springs and the water from them has been exported to China and Korea for years. Near the station is a sanatorium where various cardiovascular and intestinal ailments are treated.

Km6270: Here you can see an army supply base surrounded by a wooden stockade.

Km6293: Karymskaya Карымская (●●● for *Rossiya*, ●●●+ for Trans-Manchurian) (605m/1985ft) This small industrial town was first settled by Buryats.

Km6312: Tarskaya Тарская Formerly known as Kaidalovo, this is the junction for the **route to Beijing via Manchuria (see p491)**.

A whitewashed church stands on a hill (S) above the village. You can catch good views along the river at Km6316 (S) and across the wide plains for the next 100km, especially around Km6332 (S) and Km6369 (S). The best views are all to the south, across to Mongolia.

Km6417: Onon Онон (515m/1690ft) A few kilometres east of here the clear waters of the Ingoda River are joined by those of the muddy Onon, on whose banks the great Mongol leader, Genghis (Chinggis) Khan, was born in 1162. The Onon and Ingoda together form the Shilka River, a tributary of the mighty Amur. The railway follows the picturesque valley of the Shilka for the next 120km.

Km6446: Shilka Шилка The adjacent village of Shilka, on the Shilka River was founded in 1897 just to serve the railway. Two years later it became a popular tourist destination with the opening of the **Shivanda Health Resort** (*shivanda* means royal drink in the indigenous language). Mineral water is still used to treat digestive and respiratory system disorders here. A few years later the discovery of gold nearby brought more visitors. In 1954 fluoric spar, a mineral essential in chemistry and metallurgy, was also discovered in the area.

Km6496: Priiskovaya Приисковая *Priisk* means mine, referring to the gold-mining town of Nerchinsk, 10km down a branch line from here.

Nerchinsk Нерчинск is where the 1689 Treaty of Nerchinsk was signed, which was to give the Manchurian emperor control over the Russian Far East and deprive the Russians of the valuable Amur region for the next 170 years. It was the centre of a rich silver-, lead- and gold-mining district in Tsarist times, although the deposits were known to the Buryats long before the Russians arrived in the 17th century. In 1700 a Greek mining engineer founded the Nerchinsky Zavod works; the first convict gangs arrived in 1722. George Kennan visited the mine in 1887 and was shown around by one of the convict labourers. Not all the mines were the property of the Tsar; some private owners became immensely wealthy. In one mansion he visited in Nerchinsk, Kennan could hardly believe that such opulence (tapestries, chandeliers, Oriental rugs, silk curtains and a vast ballroom) was to be found in one of the wildest parts of Siberia. From 1826 to 1917 the mines of Nerchinsk were a major Tsarist labour camp. Today Nerchinsk has some worthwhile sights. These include the early 19th-century Resurrection Cathedral and a house built in the 1860s in Moorish style by a rich merchant named Butin. Next door is the Hotel Dauriya (now closed), where Chekhov stayed in 1890.

On the southern side of Priiskovaya station is the small village of **Kalinino**. The 17th-century Russian explorer Yerofei Pavlovich Khabarov is buried under the walls of the old church. It is believed, however, that the corpse in the grave

is actually that of his brother, Nikifor, the last resting place of Yerofei remaining unknown.

Km6532: Kuenga Куэнга This is the junction for a line which runs 52km eastwards to Sretensk, which was the eastern end of the Transbaikal Railway.

Sretensk Сретенск is spread over both banks of the Shilka river with the centre on the eastern bank and the railway station on the high western bank. The two were joined by a bridge only in 1986. The Shilka is a tributary of the mighty Amur; the Amur forms the Chinese–Russian border for hundreds of kilometres before passing through Khabarovsk on its way north-east to the Pacific. It was this river route that put Sretensk on Russian maps. It was a thriving river-port (considerably larger than Chita) in the 19th and early 20th centuries before the Amur Railway (see box below) was opened. Passengers transferred here to ships of the Amur Steamship and Trade Company. Most of the 40 steamers that plied between Sretensk and Khabarovsk were made either in Belgium or the Glasgow yards of Armstrong and Co. Waiting here with her mother in 1900 Annette Meakin caught sight of some Chinese men with traditional pig-tails. She was not impressed and wrote, 'To me their appearance was quite girlish.' In 1916 the Amur Railway was completed and Sretensk, bypassed, became a backwater.

The line leaves the Shilka River here, turns northwards, crosses a plain and climbs towards the eastern end of the Yablonovy Range.

❏ **The Amur Railway (Km6532-8531)**
The building of the Amur Railway was proposed in the early 1890s but surveys showed that it would prove expensive, on account of the difficult terrain. More than 100 bridges and many kilometres of embankments would be needed. Furthermore much of the region was locked in permafrost. In 1894, when the government signed the treaty with China which allowed Russian rails to be laid across Manchuria from Chita to Vladivostok, the Amur project was abandoned in favour of this considerably shorter route. The change of plan proved to be false economy, for the East Chinese line, despite a considerable saving in distance, was ultimately to cost more than the whole of the rest of the Trans-Siberian Railway.

Russia's embarrassing defeat by Japan in the 1904-5 War revealed the vulnerability of the East Chinese line. Japan was as keen as Russia to gain control of the rich lands of Manchuria and if they did decide to invade, the Russian naval base of Vladivostok would be deprived of a rail link with European Russia. A line within Russian lands was needed. The Amur project was reconsidered and, in 1907, approved. Construction began in 1908 at Kuenga. For most of its 2000km the line would follow a route about 100km north of the Amur River, out of range of Manchuria on the southern bank of the river. Winters are particularly harsh in this region and consequently track-laying could only take place over the four warmer months; even in mid-summer considerable amounts of dynamite were needed to blast through the permafrost. There were the usual problems with insects and disease but as the rest of the railway was operating it was comparatively easy to transport workers in from west of the Urals. By 1916 the long bridge over the Amur at Khabarovsk had been completed and the railway was opened. Ironically the Japanese, as allies of the White Russians, in 1918 took over the running of the Amur Railway during the Civil War.

Km6593: Chernyshevsk-Zabaikalsky Чернышевск-Забайкальский (●●●) Nikolai Chernyshevsky (1828-89) was a revolutionary who toiled for years at hard-labour camps in the region.

Km6629: Bushuley Бушулей This is not the easiest area in which to build a railway, as Trans-Siberian engineers discovered. In winter it was bitterly cold and in the hot summers all surface water dried up. For most of the year the ground had to be thawed out with gigantic bonfires before track could be laid. The complex around the station is a molybdenum-ore enrichment plant. The mineral is added to steel to make it suitable for high-speed cutting tools. Scattered along the line are molybdenum and gold mines.

Km6670: Zilovo Зилово The adjacent town is called **Aksenovo-Zilovskoye Аксеново-Зиловское**. Southwards were the gold mines of the Kara region, also visited by Kennan, who found 2500 convicts working under appalling conditions. These mines were the property of the Tsar and from them and other Imperial mines in Eastern Siberia he could expect an average of 1630kg (3600lb) of pure gold each year.

Km6789: Ksenyevskaya Ксеньевская From here the line continues across the forested southern slopes of the Eastern Yablonovy Range for 200km.

Km6906: Mogocha Могоча (●●●) This unpretty railway settlement in the Bolshoy Amazar River Valley is probably one of the harshest places on the Trans-Siberian route to live because of permafrost and summer sun. In winter the top 10cm of earth that has thawed over the summer freezes again to as low as -60°C (-87°F), killing all but the hardiest plants, while the intense summer sun singes most young shoots. The town was founded in 1910 when this section of the Trans-Siberian was being built, and later became the base for geological research expeditions seeking gold in the hills.

The town of **Olekminsk** lies on the Lena River about 700km due north of here (this being no more than a short hike for a Siberian, for, as Russian guides never tire of saying, 'In Siberia a thousand kilometres is nothing to travel and a litre of vodka is nothing to drink', although these days they rarely add the rest of the aphorism, 'and a hundred roubles is nothing to spend'). Olekminsk holds the world record for the widest annual temperature range, from minus 60°C (minus 87°F) to plus 45°C (113°F).

This was also the place of exile in the 18th century for a bizarre Christian sect whose followers were known as the Skoptsy. They saw their salvation in abstinence and castrated themselves to be sure of a place in heaven. They lived in mixed communities which they referred to as 'ships', each having a 'helmsman' and 'crew'. They avoided drink and tobacco and were excellent farmers. Since Olekminsk is experiencing something of a baby-boom at present it must be assumed that the more unconventional practices of the Skoptsy have been abandoned.

Km7010: Amazar Амазар **(●●●)** The remains of a large strategic reserve of steam engines can be seen here. About 100km southwards the Shilka flows into the Amur (Heiling Chu to the Chinese). The **Amur** rises in Mongolia and flows 2800km along the frontier with China into the Pacific at the Sea of Okhotsk. If the Volga is the Mother River to the Russians, the Amur is the Father River. The river is exceptionally rich in fish and navigable for six months of the year. Russians explored the Amur region in the 17th century, but the 1689 Treaty of Nerchinsk with the Chinese was to lock them out for 150 years. Colonisation began in the mid-19th century with Cossack garrisons along the river. By 1860 the Amur Basin had 60 villages with a population of 11,000. The Amur is still a vital communications link in the area.

Km7075: The administrative frontier between Chitinskaya and Amurskaya oblasts also marks the border between Siberia and the Far Eastern Territories. **Amurskaya Oblast** covers 363,700 sq km in the middle part of the Amur basin and extends to the Stanovoy Range in the north. The southern region of the oblast is a fertile plain where wheat, soya-beans, flax and sunflowers are grown. Most of the area in the north is under thick forest.

Km7119: Yerofei-Pavlovich Ерофей-Павлович **(●●●)** The town is named in honour of the brutal explorer Yerofei Pavlovich Khabarov (see p83). At the eastern end of the station (N) is a **steam locomotive** (Em726-88) on a plinth.
    The river through the town is the **Urka**, down which Khabarov travelled with his mercenaries in 1649 to reach the Amur. The river route opened up a shortcut to the Russian Far East from Yakutsk.
    This area is particularly inhospitable, with frosts lasting from mid-October to early April and an average January temperature of -33°C. Patches of snow persist on shaded mountainsides as late as July.

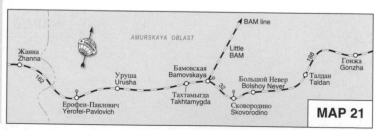

MAP 21

Km7211: Urusha Уруша Running mostly downhill for the next 100km the line passes through an area of taiga interspersed with uncultivated plains, most of it locked in permafrost.

Km7266: Takhtamygda Тахтамыгда A small settlement with a view (N) across the river valley (good views to the north continue for the next 150km). About half a kilometre east of the village (N) stands a prison, surrounded by barbed wire and patrolled by uniformed guards.

Km7273: Bamovskaya Бамовская This is a junction with the Little BAM, the line which runs north to join the Baikal-Amur Mainline (see pp498-504). It is not advisable to get off the train here without knowing when your connecting train up the Little BAM will arrive as only a few head north each day; change at Skovorodino instead.

Km7306: Skovorodino Сковородино (●/●●●) Named after a revolutionary leader killed here in 1920 during the Russian Civil War, Skovorodino is the first stop on the Trans-Siberian line for trains travelling down the Little BAM from Tynda to Khabarovsk. If you are getting off the Trans-Siberian to go up the Little BAM, Skovorodino is the place to do it. There's also a railway depot, forestry mills and a permafrost research station. You can see a lime-green P36-0091 **steam locomotive** by the station platform.

Km7323: Bolshoy Never Большой Невер On the left (N) side of the railway is the 800km long Amur Yakutsk Highway ('highway' being something of a misnomer). This terminates in **Yakutsk** (see pp415-18), capital of the Republic of Sakha, formerly known as Yakutia. This must be one of the most dismal places on the planet, for the region, which is about 13 times the size of Britain, is entirely covered with permafrost. Even in mid-summer the soil in Yakutsk is frozen solid to a depth of over 100m.

❏ **The Yakuts**

Yakuts, numbering about 400,000, form the largest ethnic group in the Far Eastern Territories. They were originally semi-nomadic herders who roamed around the lands beside the Lena River. What seems to have struck 19th-century travellers most about the Yakuts was their rather squalid lifestyle. They never washed or changed their clothes, they shared their huts with their reindeer and they preferred their meat and fish once it had begun to rot. They drank a form of *koumiss* (fermented mare's milk), which they froze, sometimes into huge boulders.

To give the Yakuts their due, they were considerably more advanced than many other Siberian tribes. Although they were ignorant of the wheel (hardly much use in such a cold climate) they used iron for weapons and tools. Most Yakut clans had a blacksmith who was usually also a shaman, since metal-working was considered a gift from the gods. The Yakuts were unique among Siberian tribes in that they made pottery. Russian colonists treated them badly and demanded fur tributes for the Tsar. Yakuts have now almost completely adopted Russian culture, and although some are still involved in reindeer-herding, most work in mining and the timber industry.

After the **tunnel (Km7343-5)** there's a long view (S) down a valley towards China, with more views (S) at Km7387 and Km7426-28.

Km7501: Magdagachi Магдагачи **(●●●)**   The train descends gently through Magdagachi, out of the taiga and onto a wide plain.

Km7566: Tygda Тыгда **(●)**   There is usually a short stop here.

Km7602: Ushumun Ушумун   The border with China is no more than 40km south-west of here. The train turns south-eastwards again, soon crossing an obvious climatic boundary and a not-so-obvious one marking the southern border of permafrost. From here on the larches grow much taller, reaching 35m, and birches and oaks spring up. These oaks are different from European oaks as they do not lose their leaves in winter but retain them even though they are stiff and brown.

Km7723: Shimanovskaya Шимановская **(●)**   Named after a revolutionary hero, this town played an important part in the development of both the Trans-Siberian and BAM railways.

Km7772: Ledinaya Лединая   Hidden away in the trees just to the north of this station is the once-secret Svobodny-18 cosmodrome that was closed in 2007.

Km7815: Svobodny Свободный **(●)**   An attractive town on the right bank of the Zeya River, Svobodny, meaning 'free', has a proud history associated with the railways. It was founded in 1912 as Alekseyevsk, in honour of the Tsar's haemophiliac son Alexei. It expanded rapidly into a major railway town, with factories building carriages, plus a hospital, schools and an orphanage all sponsored by the railways. By the mid-1930s it was headquarters for both the Amur section of the Trans-Siberian and the new BAM project.

Beyond the town the line crosses the Zeya River, the Amur's largest Russian tributary. In the rainy season the water level may rise as fast as 30cm/hour and 10m floods have been recorded. The area beyond the river, called the Zeysko-Bureinskaya Plain, is the main granary for the Russian Far East. This is the most highly populated area of the Amur region with villages every 10-20km separated by fields of barley, soya beans and melons. The similarity of the climate and landscape to parts of Ukraine attracted many Ukrainians in the 19th century. Today over half the locals are of Ukrainian descent. You can easily spot their whitewashed houses (*khatas*). The solid log constructions with overlapping log ends are Russian.

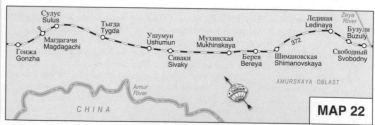

❏ Blagoveshchensk – the New York of Siberia

Blagoveshchensk, administrative capital of Amurskaya Oblast, is a large industrial centre of 217,644 people on the left bank of the Amur River; it suffered considerably in the Amur flood of 2013 but is being rebuilt. The name means 'Good News', for it was here in 1858 that Count Muravyov-Amursky announced the signing of the treaty under which China granted Russia the Amur region. The city became a centre of colonisation, growing fast in the second half of the 19th century. Locals called it 'the New York of Siberia' because its streets were laid out in a grid pattern, American style. It became the major port on the voyage between Sretensk and Khabarovsk in the days before the Amur Railway. In July 1900 Blagoveshchensk witnessed the cold-blooded massacre of its entire Chinese population (several thousand people) by Cossack forces, in retaliation for the murders of Europeans in China during the Boxer Rebellion. Annette Meakin wrote: 'The Cossacks, who were little better than savages, threw themselves on the helpless Chinese ... and drove them down to the water's edge. Those who could not get across on rafts were either brutally massacred on the banks or pushed into the water and drowned. The scene which followed was horrible beyond description, and the river was black with dead bodies for weeks afterwards. I have this from no less than five eye-witnesses.'

Good relations between the people of Blagoveshchensk and their Chinese neighbours across the river in the city of Heihe have been cemented in recent years with a rise in cross-border trade. Siberian lumber and machinery is ferried across the Amur to be exchanged for Chinese consumer goods. Heihe is connected by rail to Harbin (nightly departures; 12hrs), with onward links to Beijing. There is no bridge but ferries cross the river (12/day, 15 mins; R1200/1700 one way/return) from Passazhirsky Port east of Hotel Druzhba. There are several daily trains from Blagoveshchensk, including the 385/386 to Vladivostok via Khabarovsk and the 81/82 to Tynda.

Hotel Druzhba (ul Kuznechnaya 1, ☎ 4162 37 61 40, 🖳 www.hoteldruzhba.ru; sgl/dbl/suite R1300-2000/2000-3600/5000, WI-FI) offers decent accommodation as well as facilities such as a restaurant, swimming pool and sauna. On the premises, tour agency Amur Tourist can help arrange onward travel.

Km7873: Belogorsk Белогорск (●●●+) Some older residents of this agricultural centre must find it difficult to remember the name of their city as it has been changed so many times. It was founded in 1860 as Aleksandrovka, which stuck until 1935 when the local council decided it should be changed to the rather more impressive Kuybyshevkavostochnaya. Just when everyone had got used to this exotic mouthful it changed again, to boring Belogorsk.

There's a branch line from Belogorsk to **Blagoveshchensk** (see box above).

ROUTE GUIDE & MAPS

You can see a P36-0091 **steam locomotive** as you leave Belogorsk station.

Km7992: Zavitaya Завитая This town is famous for soya bean oil and soya flour. There is a 90km branch line to the south which terminates at Poyarkovo on the Chinese–Russian border. Only Chinese and Russian passport holders can cross there.

Km8037: Bureya Бурея (●) On the river of the same name, this town was once the centre of a large gold-mining region. It now produces tools for the coal-mining industry.

The area was once inhabited by several different tribes, most of whom were Shamanists. The **Manegres** were a nomadic people whose trademark was their shaven heads, save for one long pig-tail. The **Birars** lived in hive-shaped huts beside the Bureya and grew vegetables and fruit. North of here lived the **Tungus** (Evenki), who were hunters, and the **Orochen**, who herded reindeer.

To the east were the **Goldi**, described thus in the *1900 Guide to the Great Siberian Railway*: 'They are below average stature, and have a broad and flat face with a snub nose, thick lips, eyes shaped after the Mongolian fashion and prominent cheek-bones ... The women adorn themselves with earrings and pendants. Some of them, as a mark of particular elegance, introduce one or several small rings into the partition of the nose. The people of this tribe are characterised by great honesty, frankness and good will ... Their costume is very various and of all colours; they may at different times be seen wearing a Russian overcoat, a fish-skin suit or the Chinese dress.'

Km8088: Arkhara Архара (●) A stop at the station here is usual, with women selling snacks and fruit on the platform.

Km8118: Uril Урил On the right (S) side of the line from here to the next large station, Kundur Khabarovsky, is Khingan Nature Reserve. The reserve consists of swampy lowlands dotted with Amur velvet trees and Korean cedar pine woods with a thick undergrowth of hazel trees, wild grapes and wild pepper which is related to ginseng. It is also rich in Mongol and Siberian animals seldom encountered elsewhere, including a raccoon-like dog.

Km8184: This is the administrative frontier between Amurskaya Oblast and Khabarovsky Kray. Like much of Russia east of the Urals, Khabarovsky Kray is composed almost entirely of swampy taiga. In the far south, however, there is an area of deciduous trees. Although the kray is extremely rich in minerals, its economy is heavily based on wood-processing, fishing and the petroleum industry.

——————————— **Km8184-9289 TIME ZONE MT + 7** ———————————

Local time is now Moscow Time + 7 hours. East of this frontier you enter the Yevreyskaya (Jewish) Autonomous Oblast otherwise known as Birobidzhan, after its capital; the oblast is within Khabarovsky Kray. Because of this some stations between Obluchye and Priamurskaya are signposted in Yiddish as well as Russian.

This remote region was set aside for Jewish emigration in 1928 (and the oblast established in 1934), though it never proved popular. The oblast's Jewish population stands at about 3000 – 5% of the approximately 173,000 inhabitants of this 36,000 sq km territory. A glossy coffee-table book about Birobidzhan (written in Russian, Yiddish and English) used to be sold in the bookshops of Khabarovsk. After pages of smiling cement-factory workers, beaming miners and happy-looking milk-maids, the book ends with the following statement: 'The flourishing of the economy and culture of the Jewish Autonomous Region, the happiness of the people of labour of various nationalities inhabiting the Region, their equality, friendship and co-operation lay bare the hypocrisy (sic) of the propaganda campaign launched by the ringleaders of Israel and international Zionism, about the "disastrous situation" of Jews in the Soviet Union, about the "oppression and persecution" they are supposedly being subjected to. The working people of Jewish nationality wrathfully condemn the predatory policy of the ruling circles of Israel and give a resolute rebuff to the Zionist provocateurs.' What the book doesn't tell you is that in Stalin's anti-Jewish purges Birobidzhan's synagogue was closed and the speaking of Yiddish outlawed even here.

Km8198: Obluchye Облучье (●●●) The town is just inside the border of the Jewish Autonomous Oblast. The **tunnel** just east of Obluchye was the first in the world to be bored through permafrost.

Km8234: Izvestkovaya Известковая The name means 'of limestone' and there are large quarries in the area. The town sits at the junction of the Trans-Siberian and a 360km branch line to **Novy Urgal** (see p503) on the BAM railway. Much of this branch line was built by Japanese PoWs until their repatriation in 1949; Japanese graves litter the area. The old part of town, with its rustic wooden buildings and household garden plots, is hidden in the trees to the west.

Km8306: Bira Бира The obelisk on the platform commemorates the good works of local philanthropist Nikolai Trofemovich and his wife. The railway runs beside the Bira River for about 100km and passes through hills rich with the ingredients of cement.

Km8351: Birobidzhan Биробиджан (●)   [see pp332-4]
Originally known as Tikhonkaya, Birobidzhan (pop: 75,542), the capital of the Jewish Autonomous Region, was founded in 1928 on the Bira River. Once

ROUTE GUIDE & MAPS

famous for the bright-red, self-propelled combine harvesters made at the Dalselmash factory and exported to Cuba, Mexico, Iraq and China, the town has been hard hit by the economic downturn.

Just east of Birobidzhan on the left (N) you pass the huge **Iyuan-Koran Memorial** which commemorates a fierce Russian Civil War battle on this site in 1922. Near the memorial are the mass graves of fallen Red Guards.

Km8480: Volochayevka 1 Волочаевка 1

This small station is just a junction for the Trans-Siberian and the 344km railway to Komsomolsk-na-Amure. Volochayevka is famous as the scene of a major battle during the Russian Civil War, which took place in temperatures as low as -35°C (there is a panoramic painting of the battle in Khabarovsk's Museum of Regional Studies). The town itself is 9km from the station.

Km8512: Priamurskaya Приамурская

This small town is just on the border of the Jewish Autonomous Oblast.

After crossing 3km of swamp and small streams you reach the 2.6km **bridge across the Amur River**, the longest bridge on the Trans-Siberian and completed in 1998. It's a combined rail and road bridge, with trains running beneath the road. Before it opened cars had to cross the Amur by ferry and trains used an old bridge, completed in 1916 and now dismantled.

There is also a 7km tunnel under the Amur, built in 1937-42 for 'strategic reasons', and westbound trains sometimes use this. Khabarovsk stretches along the eastern bank of the river and the beaches here are packed with sunbathers on summer weekends. The main fishing port is 2.5km upstream.

Km8521: Khabarovsk 1 Хабаровск 1 (●●●+)   [see pp334-42]

Khabarovsk (pop: 539,636) was founded in 1858 as a military outpost against the Chinese. Today it is the most pleasant of all the Russian Far East cities. Outside the station there's an impressive statue of Yerofei Pavlovich Khabarov, the city's founder.

From Khabarovsk the line runs south to Vladivostok following the Ussuri River and the border with China. This region is a mixture of hilly country and wide flat valleys. Some 200km east of the line lies the Sikhote Alin Mountain Range, where most of the rivers you will cross have their source. In the south,

MAP 25

❏ The Ussuri Railway (Km8531-9441)

The first plans for the Ussuri Line, as the section between Khabarovsk and Vladivostok is called, were made in 1875 and the foundation stone for the whole of the Trans-Siberian Railway was laid in Vladivostok by Tsarevich Nicholas in 1891. Priority was given to the Ussuri Line as it was seen as vital for ensuring that the strategic port of Vladivostok was not cut off by the Chinese.

This was difficult territory for railway building. There was a severe shortage of labour. The local Goldi tribe, who at the time were happily existing in the Stone Age, were of no help, unable to grasp the concept of paid labour nor to understand the point of the work, never having seen a train. Prisoners recruited from the jails of Sakhalin Island were not as cooperative as convicts used on other sections of the Trans-Siberian, preferring an evening of robbery and murder in Vladivostok to the railway camps. The men here were plagued not only by vicious mosquitoes, like their fellow-workers on other sections of the line, but also by the man-eating tigers which roamed the thick forests beside the line. Siberian anthrax decimated the already small population of pack animals, and rails and equipment had to be shipped from Europe, taking up to two months to reach Vladivostok.

In spite of these difficulties the line was opened in 1897, 43 million roubles having been spent on its construction. It was double tracked in the 1930s and the branch line to Nakhodka was built after WWII.

firs and pines give way to a wide range of deciduous trees. There are good views across the plains to China.

Km8597: Here is the longest bridge on the Ussuri Railway (see box above). It crosses the Khor River, one of the Ussuri's widest tributaries, whose turbulent waters made its construction in 1897 extremely difficult.

Km8598: Verino Верино   The town around the station is called **Pereyaslavka Переяславка** and was the site of a fierce Civil War battle. In front of the station there is a war memorial.

Km8621: Khor Хор   The train crosses the Khor River again. The river here marks the southern boundary of the 46,000-hectare **Bolshoy-Khekhzirzky Sanctuary**. The indigenous Udegei people have a legend to explain why plants from both north and south Siberia are found here. Once two birds flying in opposite directions collided in thick fog and dropped their loads. They'd been sent by the Good Spirit of the South and Good Spirit of the North to throw seeds on the desert plains and mountains respectively. Since then, southern wild grapevines wind around northern pine trees and the northern berry *klukva* grows side by side with the southern spiky palm *aralia,* with its metre-long leaves.

The vegetation changes considerably with elevation. At the foot of the mountains broadleaf species dominate. On the slopes are cedar, Amur velvet ash (cork is produced from its black bark) and Manchurian nut trees while on higher slopes angular pine and fir trees dominate.

ROUTE GUIDE & MAPS

Km8642: Vyazemskaya Вяземская (●●●) This railway town was founded in 1895 and during the Russian Civil War there was fierce fighting around it. There are several memorials and a museum. To the west of the station is a plinthed **Ea series locomotive**.

Some 20km to the south the countryside changes dramatically with forests of maple, alder, willow and elm.

Km8756: Bikin Бикин (●/●●●) According to the *1900 Guide to the Great Siberian Railway* the line crossed the river here and followed it south for 30km. The book states that 'this is one of the most picturesque parts of the line offering an alpine scenery. The cuttings made in basalt rocks seem to be protected by columns of cyclopean construction. Wide expanses lying amidst the cliffs are covered with a most various vegetation, shading numerous Chinese huts. The river is enlivened by the small boats of the Golds and other natives, moving swiftly on the water's surface.' Unfortunately the line does not follow exactly the same route now, instead traversing rolling hills and marshy land strewn with telegraph poles keeling over at drunken angles.

The railway crosses the Bikin River. About 200km upstream is Krasny Yar, the largest village of the indigenous **Udegei**. Known as the Forest People for their lifestyle of fishing, hunting and gathering in the taiga, the Udegei are facing the end of their way of life because of the voracious logging industry.

Between Bikin and **Zvenyevoy Звеневой** is the administrative border between Khabarovsky Kray and Primorsky Kray. Primorsky Kray has a population of over two million people.

Luchegorsk Лучегорск (Km8773) is the largest settlement in the Far East that doesn't have the title of 'city'.

Km8890: Dalnerechensk 1 Дальнереченск 1 (●) Founded by Cossacks in 1895, this town quickly became a timber centre thanks to the region's large pine and red cedar forests. The town has a memorial to the guards killed in the 1969 border conflict with the Chinese over Damansky Island in the Ussuri River. There were several skirmishes and each country claimed the Communist high ground as being the true Marxist revolutionary state.

As both began preparing for nuclear confrontation a political solution was reached when Soviet premier Alexei Kosygin stopped in Beijing on his way home from the funeral of Ho Chi Minh. Following another round of talks in

ROUTE GUIDE & MAPS

❏ Decline of the Amur tiger
Once the scourge of railway construction workers, the largest member of the cat family, also known as the Siberian tiger, is now just another zoological statistic dwindling
towards extinction. The tigers' habitat once stretched as far west as Lake Baikal and
to Beijing in the south but now only 350 or so Amur tigers are left in the wild in an
area from Vladivostok north into the Sikhote Alin Range. Large-scale forest clearance
for timber sold to Japan and Korea forces tigers out of their territory. A male tiger can
weigh up to 380kg (840lbs), almost twice the size of a lion, and requires about 400
sq km of hunting ground. A decline in their food source (deer and wild boar) has also
reduced the population and forced remaining tigers to roam ever larger areas for prey.
  In 1987 a train just outside Nakhodka was held up by a tiger that had strayed
onto the tracks. An Amur tiger can be worth as much as US$10,000 in China, Korea
and Taiwan for the medicinal value that parts of its body are believed to have, and for
its skin. Poachers now slip across the Russian borders that are no longer tightly
patrolled.
  The animals are found in and around several nature reserves in this area:
Kedrovaya Pad (near Vladivostok), Lazo and Sikhote Alin, but your chances of seeing a live Amur tiger here are close to zero. There are far more of them in zoos around
the world than in the wild.

Moscow and Beijing in 1991, Damansky Island was given to China in its
entirety.

Km8900: Muravyovo-Amurskaya Муравьёво-Амурская This station is
named after the explorer and governor of Eastern Siberia, Count Nikolai
Muravyov-Amursky. It was formerly known as Lazo in honour of the
Communist revolutionary S G Lazo (1894-1920), who was captured in 1920 by
the Japanese when they invaded the Russian Far East, and executed at the station, allegedly by being thrown alive into a steam engine firebox.

  Two other revolutionaries, Lutsky and Sibirtsev, met a similar fate and a
monument to all three stands in front of the station.

Km8941: Ruzhino Ружино (●●●/●●) A long stop for the *Rossiya* here.

Km8991: Shmakovka Шмаковка About 29km from the station is the mostly derelict **Shmakovsky Trinity-St Nicholas Monastery**, with a very curious
history. Its land is now being fought over by two groups, both claiming to be its
original owners. The Russian Orthodox Church maintains they built the
monastery; the Russian military accept its religious past but claim that they constructed the monastery as a front for an espionage academy. It does seem more
than a little coincidental that ex-army officer and Father-Superior Aleksei, who
was commissioned to build the monastery, selected a site next to the remote
Tikhmenevo telegraph station. This was no ordinary relay station but was clas-
sified a 'top secret military object' connected to Khabarovsk by an underground
cable. And the monastery was certainly well equipped: there was even a print-
ing press and photo lab.

Km9050: Spassk-Dalny Спасск-Дальний (●) Alexander Solzhenitsyn was imprisoned in this town, where he helped build the large cement works that still operates here.

About 40km west is **Lake Khanka** which has a surface area of 4000 sq km but is nowhere more than 4m deep. The lake is famous for the lotus flower *eurea* which has giant buds and 2m wide leaves.

Muchnaya Мучная **(Km9092)** is the main railway station of the town of Chernigovka Черниговка, founded in 1886 by peasants who migrated from western Russia; it's named after the region from which they came.

Km9109: Sibirtsevo Сибирцево (●) This area is the centre of an extremely fertile region where wheat, oats, soya beans and rice are grown. Because of labour shortages these are aerially sown and fertilised. The climate of the southern part of the Russian Far East makes most areas ideal for agriculture as the warm summer rains create a hothouse atmosphere. A branch line runs from here through dairy-farming countryside to Lake Khanka.

Km9177: Ussuriysk Уссурийск (●●●) The fertile area around Ussuriysk has been inhabited for over 1000 years, first as the legendary kingdom of Bokhai and then by the Manchus. In the mid 19th century European emigrants began to settle here. At that time the town was called Nikolskoye, in honour of the Tsar. The town stands at the junction of the Ussuri and Chinese Eastern railways. When Tsarevich Nicholas visited in 1891 there were three wooden churches, a half-built stone cathedral and a population of 8000, many of them Chinese. Ussurisk is a now an agricultural and engineering centre, home of the Okean brand of refrigerator.

From Ussuriysk there are branch lines to Harbin in China via the East Chinese Railway and to Pyongyang in North Korea, though there are no passenger services currently scheduled. The scenery is very different from the Siberian taiga. The train winds through the hills in misty forests of deciduous trees (oak, elm, alder and maple) and across European-looking meadows filled with Friesian cows and willow trees.

Km9221: Amursky Zaliv Амурский Залив A branch line runs from here to the port of **Nakhodka**. For information on the line to Nakhodka, see box opposite.

MAP 27

❑ **The Vladivostok–Nakhodka Railway**
Few travellers visit Nakhodka since the Japanese ferry which connects with Trans-Siberian trains now docks at Vladivostok, which is also the location of the only airport in the region.

The journey of some 216km from Vladivostok runs through **Uglovaya Угловая** at Km34, the mining and industrial city of **Artem-Primorski Артем-Приморский** at Km43, **Novonezhino Новонежино** at Km91, **Partizansk Партизанск** at Km170, past the vineyards of the Suchan River Valley to **Nakhodka Находка** at Km206, and on to the terminus at **Tikhookeanskaya Тихоокеанская**, the port just south-west of Nakhodka.

Km9246: If you're heading east keep a lookout on the right (S) for your first glimpse of the Pacific Ocean.

Km9255: Ugolnaya Уголная (●)   The town here, called **Trudovoye Трудовое**, sits at the northern edge of Uglovy Zaliv (Uglovy Bay). Pleasant beaches and clean water make it a popular swimming spot for Vladivostok's day trippers.

East of the station the railway travels down a peninsula named in honour of the famous Russian explorer, Count Nikolai Muravyov-Amursky.

Km9262: Sadgorod Садгород   Near Sadgorod (which means 'garden city') was a station called Khilkovo, named in honour of Prince M I Khilkov, Minister of Ways of Communication in the Tsarist government and one of the main supporters of the Trans-Siberian. However, Khilkovo station has long since disappeared. The accepted date for the start of construction of the Trans-Siberian Railway was 19 May 1891, although by that time an 18km section had already been laid from Vladivostok to Sadgorod. The Tsar's son Nicholas travelled up this line and formally inaugurated the project by tipping a barrow of ballast onto the embankment at Sadgorod, then returned by train to unveil a commemorative plaque at Vladivostok.

Km9281: Vtoraya Rechka Вторая Речка   Vladivostok's **Central Bus Station** (the main long-distance bus station including buses for the airport) is here.

Km9284: Pervaya Rechka Первая Речка   According to the original 1880s plan for the Trans-Siberian this was to have been the railway's terminus, with a small branch line extending to Vladivostok. Despite the difficulties of building a multi-track railway along the steep shore, it was decided in the 1890s to extend the Trans-Siberian through to Vladivostok. Near Pervaya Rechka was a small settlement called Convicts' Hamlet, inhabited by exiled settlers who had completed their sentences.

Km9289: Vladivostok Владивосток   [see pp342-52]
Vladivostok (pop: 600,378) is one of Russia's largest and most strategically important ports.

Trans-Mongolian route

The branch line to Mongolia and China leaves the main Trans-Siberian route at Zaudinsky (see below), east of Ulan-Ude (see pp319-25). From there it takes around 5½ hours to cover the 250km to the Russia–Mongolia border. Between Ulan-Ude and the border the train travels through the heart of Buryatia, the Buryat Republic.

Note that the line turns predominantly southwards after Zaudinsky. For the entire Trans-Mongolian line we shall use (E) and (W) to show which side of the train points of interest are located. Thus if you're coming from Moscow (E) means the left side of the train and (W) the right.

Km5655: Zaudinsky Заудинский The line to Ulaanbaatar (Mongolia) follows the valley of the Selenga all the way to the border. The scenery changes remarkably quickly to the rolling green hills which make excellent pasture for the area's many cattle.

Passing through the little station of **Sayatun Саятун** (Km5677) the line crosses to the west bank of the river at Km5689-90 and continues to climb through **Ubukun Убукун** (Km5732).

Km5769: Zagustay Загустай The station sits in the shadow of an ugly factory belching out thick smoke.

About 6km from here is the mining town of **Gusinoozyorsk Гусиноозёрск**; it grew from nothing following the 1939 discovery of a huge coal basin.

Km5771-99: Gusinoye Ozero (Goose Lake) Гусиное Озеро The line passes along the western shore of Goose Lake. Until the Revolution the most important Buddhist *datsan* (lamasery) north of Ulaanbaatar was at **Selenginsk Селенгинск**, 20km to the south-east and overlooking the lake.

In 1887 George Kennan, while researching his book on Siberian prisons, arrived in Selenginsk and visited the datsan. 'We were tired of prisons and the exile system and had enough misery,' he wrote. Nevertheless he found

> ❑ **The Trans-Mongolian Line**
> This route to China is an ancient one, followed for centuries by tea-caravans between Peking and Moscow. Travelling non-stop, foreigners and imperial messengers could manage the journey in 40 days of acute discomfort. This was the route of the 1907 Peking to Paris Rally, the great motor race that was won by the Italian Prince Borghese and journalist Luigi Barzini in their 40-horsepower Itala. Until the middle of the 20th century a rough track across the steppelands of northern Mongolia and the Gobi Desert in the south was the only route through this desolate country.
> In 1940 a branch line was built between Ulan-Ude and the Mongolian border. After WWII work started on a line south from Naushki and in 1949 this reached the Mongolian capital, Ulaanbaatar. The line between Ulaanbaatar and Beijing was begun in 1953 with a workforce of Russians, Mongolians and Chinese. By early 1956 it was completed and a regular rail service began between Ulan-Ude and Beijing.

Selenginsk 'a wretched little Buriat town'. At the datsan Kennan and his companions were entertained by the Khamba Lama, the chief lama, who claimed through an interpreter that they were the first foreigners ever to visit his lamasery. They were treated to dinner and a special dance performance. The Khamba Lama had never heard of America, Kennan's native land; and, unaware that the earth was anything but flat, was nonplussed when Kennan explained that 'it lies nearly under our feet; and if we could go directly through the earth, this would be the shortest way to reach it'. Today Selenginsk datsan is operating again.

The line leaves the lake after **Km5780 Gusinoye Ozero Гусиное Озеро** (●) station and continues to climb from one valley to another, passing though **Selenduma Селендума (Km5827)** and still following the river.

Km5852 (W): Dzhida Джида (●) A large air-base, with bomb-proof shelters dug into hummocks in the ground.

Km5895: Naushki Наушки (●●●++) At this **Russian border post** the train stops for at least three hours, usually for considerably longer; the official schedule says three hours and thirty-two minutes. Customs officials collect passports and visas, returning them (often to the carriage attendant) after about half an hour. It's unwise to get off the train before you've got your passport back since guards may not let you back on the train without it.

The station tends to be crowded with black marketeers and some may get on the train and start selling roubles to travellers heading west; get rid of all your Mongolian tughriks here as it'll be impossible to do so in Russia. There's a **bank** a long way down the platform in the Mongolia direction, signposted in English, but the exchange rate is poor. The station lavatories are located in the building to the left of the station building and there's a little café in the back of the station building.

Km5900: Russia–Mongolia border (●—●●●) The border post, called **Dozorny Дозорный** (meaning 'patrolled'), is marked by an electrified fence. The landscape is rather attractive, with the impressive Selenga River (prone to flooding in late summer) to the north and hills rising to the south.

❑ **The old border town of Kyakhta**
The border post for the railway is at the modern town of Naushki, but for the tea-caravans of old the crossing was near the large town of **Kyakhta**, 20km east of Naushki, and it is still the border crossing for cars and buses heading for Mongolia. In the 18th and 19th centuries this town, together with **Maimachen** on the Mongolian side of the border, formed one of the world's most important trading centres, based almost entirely on the tea trade. Great camel caravans brought the precious leaves here from Peking (now Beijing), across the Gobi Desert. Kyakhta was a bustling town of wealthy traders and tea-barons until the Trans-Siberian provided a cheaper way to move tea from China to European Russia. Maimachen is now called Altan Bulak.

On 24 June 1907 Prince Borghese and his team roared into town in their Itala and were entertained royally by local dignitaries. The morale of the tea-merchants had sunk with the recent decline in trade but was greatly boosted by the arrival of the car and they began making plans for their own motor-caravans.

An earlier visitor to these border towns was George Kennan, who attended a banquet in Maimachen where he was served dog-meat dumplings, cocks' heads in vinegar and fried lichen from birch trees, washed down by several bottles of French champagne. He was sick for the next two weeks.

In January 1920 Kyakhta witnessed a particularly appalling atrocity when the sadistic White Army General Semenov despatched 800 people suspected of being communists, using a different method of execution each day. Today Kyakhta's many crumbling old buildings and several vast churches hint at prosperous times past.

MONGOLIA

Kilometre numbers below are based upon Mongolian kilometre posts. For approximate cumulative distances from Moscow see the timetables (pp509-10).

Km21: Sühbaatar Сухбаатар (●●●+) The customs and immigration process at this **Mongolian border town** (pop: 19,662) is a rather tame affair for foreigners, although the baggage of local travellers may be thoroughly inspected. During the procedures a diesel engine is attached. The Mongolian dining-car, however, is not added until Ulaanbaatar. Black marketeers walk through the carriages offering to change your roubles for tugrik. Since Mongolian currency is almost impossible to come by outside the country, you might want to take them up on their offer, but make sure you know roughly what the exchange rate is.

The station building is an incredible mélange of architectural styles: mock Gothic, Moghul and Modern topped with crenellations and painted what looks like lime green in the artificial light. The upstairs *café* serves basic Mongolian dishes.

Situated at the confluence of the Selenga and Orhon rivers, Sühbaatar was founded in 1940 and named after the Mongolian revolutionary leader Damdinii Sühbaatar (Sukhe Bator). It grew quickly, superseding the border town on the caravan route, Maimachen (now called Altanbulag).

It takes about eight hours to cover the 380km between Sühbaatar and Ulaanbaatar; en route the train passes through the town of Darhan.

Km123: Darhan (Darkhan) Дархан (●●●—●●) Darhan (pop: 74,738), capital of Selenga *aimag* (district). was founded in 1961 and is now the second most

---

❏ Mongolia

Mongolia is one of those countries that rarely makes headlines unless there's a dramatic change of leadership or policy. With just 2,796,000 people (almost a third of them below the age of 14) in an area the size of Western Europe or Alaska, it's a sparsely populated place. Mongolia is changing fast but the capital, Ulaanbaatar, is changing even faster. Nearly half the population lives in the capital, and it's estimated that over a third live below the poverty line.

Mongolia contains a surprising variety of terrain: a vast undulating plain in the east, the Gobi Desert to the south, and snow-capped mountains and extensive forests in the west. Most of the eastern plain is at an elevation of 1500m and the sun shines here for around 250 days of the year.

For many centuries the deserts and grasslands of Mongolia have been inhabited by nomadic herders living in felt tents (*yurts* or *ghers*). At certain times in world history they have come together under a powerful leader, the most famous being Genghis (Chinggis) Khan and his grandson Kublai Khan in the 13th century. Kublai Khan introduced Tibetan Buddhism to the country although it was not until the early 17th century that most Mongolians were converted and Buddhism gained a strong grip on the country. By the late 17th century control of Mongolia and its trade routes was in the hands of the Manchus. In 1911 the country became an independent monarchy, in effect a theocratic state since power lay with the 'Living Buddha', the chief representative of Buddhism in Mongolia, at Urga (now Ulaanbaatar). In 1921 a Communist government took power and, with considerable help from the Soviet Union, set out to modernise a country that was technologically in the Dark Ages.

In 1990 the constitution was amended to legalise opposition parties, although the first democratic elections were won by the communist Mongolian People's Revolutionary Party (MPRP). The 1996 presidential election was won by the MPRP's Natsagiin Bagabandi, but parliamentary elections the same year saw the formation of Mongolia's first non-communist government under the Democratic Union Coalition (DUC). After the DUC's pledge to introduce market reforms was stalled by former communists, the MPRP won the 2000 parliamentary election by a landslide, with Bagabandi re-elected the following year.

The 2004 parliamentary elections put in power a coalition government led by Prime Minister Tsakhiagiin Elbegdori, whose Democratic Party promised liberal market reform. President Nambaryn Enkhbayar of the MPRP was elected in 2005. Then in January 2006, crisis ensued when 10 cabinet members, all from the MPRP, stood down, citing the government's failure to curb corruption. Hundreds of protesters took to the freezing streets of Ulaanbaatar, accusing former communists in the MPRP of scuttling the government in an attempt to grab power. An uncertain truce was reached later that month when parliament approved Miyeegombyn Enkhbold, former mayor of Ulaanbaatar and head of the MPRP, as the new prime minister, though he stepped down in 2007. The MPRP, renamed the Mongolian People's Party in 2010, won the general elections in 2008, the current prime minister being Sukhbaataryn Batbold, while the presidential elections of May 2009 were won by former PM Tsakhiagiin Elbegdori of the Democratic Party. In 2013, Chinggis Khan mania in Mongolia continued with the city of Ondor Khaan renamed Chinggis Khan Khot (Khot means 'city').

The country is divided into 21 *aimags* (districts). The railway line passes through three of these (Selenga, Tov and Dornogov).

important industrial centre in Mongolia after Ulaanbaatar. It's a show town of planned urbanisation: the main sources of employment are opencast mining, food production, construction, and the production of leather and sheepskin coats.

The town is an important junction with a branch line that runs westwards to a big mining complex at **Erdenet**, and the port serves many villages along the Selenga and Orkhon rivers.

About 120km west of Darhan in the foothills of Mt Burenkhan is **Amarbayasgalant Monastery**. This vast 18th-century temple complex, which once housed 10,000 monks and drew pilgrims from many parts of Asia, was desecrated during an anti-religious movement in the 1930s but is now being restored with grants from the Mongolian government and UNESCO. Darhan is the closest railway station, but anyone interested in visiting the monastery would need a guide and their own vehicle, both of which can only be arranged easily from Ulaanbaatar (see box pp372-3). If you'd been doing this part of the journey in the not too distant past but before the railway was built, you would now be swaying back and forth in the saddle of a camel, one of many in the caravan you would have joined in Kyakhta. In the 1865 edition of his *Handbook for Russia, Poland and Finland*, Murray gives the following advice: 'It is customary for caravans to travel 16 hours a day and they come to a halt for cooking, eating and sleeping ... The Mongols are most trustworthy in their transactions, and the traveller may feel in perfect safety throughout the journey.' He also gives the following useful tips concerning local currency: 'The use of money is as yet almost unknown in this part of the country, brick-tea cut up into slices being the token of value most recognised; but small brass buttons are highly prized.'

Km232: Zuunhara (Dzhunkhara) Дзунхара (●●●) The train stops here for quite a while even though the town's only claim to fame is its alcohol factory.

Km381: Crossing wide open grasslands, dotted with the occasional cluster of yurts, the line begins to descend into the valley where Ulaanbaatar is situated. Looking south you catch the first glimpse (Km386) of ugly factories on the outskirts of the city (Km396).

Km404: Ulaanbaatar Улаанбаатар (●●●+)   [see pp352-72]
The train spends half an hour at the Mongolian capital (pop: 1,154,290, 1350m/4430ft). Outside the locomotive shed on the eastern side of the line is a collection of **steam and diesel engines** including 2-6-2 S-116, T31-011 and

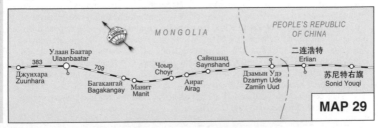

ROUTE GUIDE & MAPS

T32-508 diesels, a 750mm gauge 0-8-0 469, and a 2-10-0 Ye-0266. Black marketeers may approach you to change money.

The dining-car is attached here if you're en route to Beijing and usually removed if you're Moscow-bound. For meals and souvenirs sold in the dining-car both Mongolian currency and US$ are accepted.

Km409: Ulaanbaatar extends this far west.

At around **Km425** the line starts to climb and for the next 45km, to Km470, snakes around giving good opportunities for photos along the train.

Km507: Bagakangay Багакангай Here you can see an airfield (W) with camouflaged bunkers.

Km560: Camels are occasionally to be seen roaming across the wide, rolling plain.

Km649: Choyr Чоьɪр (●●●) Just behind this pink and white wedding-cake of a station is a statue of the first Mongolian cosmonaut, VVT Ertvuntz, who's had the all-over silver paint treatment.

Km733 (W): The pond here sometimes attracts groups of camels and antelope.

Km751: Airag Айраг The train doesn't usually stop at this small station, which is in the middle of nowhere and surrounded by scrap metal.

Km875 (E): There's a collection of old **steam locos** on display just to the west of Saynshand station.

Km876: Saynshand Сайншанд (●●●+/●●●) (pop: 20,515) This is the largest town between the capital and Dzamyn-Ude (Zamiin Uud) on the southern border.

❏ The Gobi Desert

This vast wilderness extends for 1000km north to south and 2400km west to east. Most of the part crossed by the railway is not desert of the sandy Saharan type but rolling grassy steppes. It is impressive for its emptiness: very few towns and just the occasional collection of yurts, herds of stocky Mongolian horses and small groups of camels or gazelles.

While it may not appear so, the Gobi is rich in wildlife although numbers of some species are rapidly dwindling. This is mainly the result of poaching and the destruction of habitat. There are large reserves of coal, copper, molybdenum, gold, uranium and other valuable exports. It's estimated that up to 10 billion tons of coal exist beneath the Gobi, and Japanese and Western companies are negotiating with Mongolia to extract it using strip-mining techniques, which could seriously affect the delicate environmental balance.

An American conservation group, Wildlife Conservation International, is helping the Mongolian Association for Conservation of Nature and Environment (MACNE) to monitor species at risk in the area. Among these are the 500 remaining wild Bactrian camels, the Gobi bear, the *kulan* (Asian wild ass) and Przewalski's wild horse, extinct in the wild although captive bred herds have now been reintroduced in parts of Mongolia.

ROUTE GUIDE & MAPS

Main industries include food-processing and coal-mining. Vendors on the platform sell noodles, drinks, ice cream and paintings.

Km1113: Dzamyn-Ude (Zamiin-Uud) Дзамын-Уде (●●●++) The station in this Mongolian border town looks like a supermarket at Christmas, with all its festive lights. There's a bank and a restaurant, both usually closed in the evening. Customs and immigration forms are collected. Customs officers seem to be particularly interested in inspecting the luggage of Chinese and Mongolian travellers.

THE PEOPLE'S REPUBLIC OF CHINA

The kilometre numbers below show the distance to Beijing.

Km842: Erlian (Erlyan/Erenhot/Ereen) 二连浩特 (●●●++) Chinese officials are obviously trying to outdo the evening show their Mongolian counterparts put on across the border, with a full-blown son-et-lumière. The *Vienna Waltz* blares from speakers to welcome the train and the station is decked out in red neon and fairy lights.

Chinese customs' officials come on board here. If you're travelling to Beijing you must fill in health and baggage/currency declaration forms. Passports are collected.

Bogie-changing The big decision is whether to hang out at the station or stay on the train while the bogies are changed in a shed nearby. The train spends about 20 minutes at the platform and is then shunted off to the bogie-changing shed, so you have enough time to hit the loo in the station and stretch your legs, then get back on board before the train leaves for the bogie-changing. If you decide to stay at the station take something warm with you as it will be several hours before you're allowed on board again, after the train returns to the platform when the bogie-changing is complete.

Most travellers stay on board the train until it gets to the shed where the bogies are changed. You could try to get out before the train is lifted off the ground and watch the bogie-changing from the ground, but the last time we made the trip this was forbidden and everyone had to stay on board once the train was in the shed. Still, it's interesting to watch the process from the window at the front or rear of your carriage.

The Chinese railway system operates on standard gauge (as do Europe and North America), which is 3½ inches narrower than the 5ft gauge in the former Soviet Union and Mongolia. Giant hydraulic lifts raise the carriages and the bogies are rolled out and replaced.

Back in the station you can change money at the bank (passport not necessary but you do need to know your passport number), or visit the Friendship Store (Chinese vodka, Chinese champagne, beer, noodles, sweets, fruit, tea, Ritz crackers and other snacks) and bar/restaurant (if open). Passports are returned and you depart shortly thereafter, the whole operation having taken anything from three to six hours.

ROUTE GUIDE & MAPS

❏ **Track and markers**
Chinese trains ride on the left side of twin tracks (unlike right-hand-drive Russia).
Kilometre markers come in a variety of sizes, usually like little grave-stones down at
trackside and there is some disagreement between them and the official kilometre
locations on timetables etc. The book follows these markers where possible but for
the last 70km of the journey they are not reliable, jumping at one point by 25km.

Passing through towns with Mongolian names such as **Sonid Youqi** 苏尼特
右旗 and **Qahar Youyi Houqi** 察哈尔右翼后旗, you reach Jining in about five
hours.

Km498: Jining 济宁 (●) The bulky white modernist station building is topped
by a red flag. Beside it is an extensive goods yard full of working steam engines.

Travelling due south from Jining the train leaves the province of Inner
Mongolia and enters Shanxi Province. This mountainous area was a great cultural and political centre over 1000 years ago. There are hills running parallel
to the west and wide fields either side of the line. The train follows the course
of a river which leads into a valley and more rugged countryside after Fenezhen.

Km415: Fenezhen Between this drab town and Datong you cross the line of
the **Great Wall of China** for the first time.

Km371: Datong 大同 (●●) This sprawling city (pop: 1,053,616), founded as
a military outpost by Han armies, stands in the centre of the coal-rich Datong
Basin. Its major tourist attraction is **Yungang Grottoes**, a group of Buddhist
cave temples in the foothills of Wuzhou Mountain (16km west of the city).
These caves, dating back to 460AD, are richly decorated and renowned as one
of China's three most impressive Buddhist complexes, the others being at
Luoyang and Dunhuang.

If you're stopping off here, a visit to **Datong Locomotive Works** is an interesting and educational experience. This was one of the last places in the world
where steam trains were made. In the 1980s they were turning them out at the
rate of 240 locos per year, but the manufacture of the Class QJ 8WT/ 12WT 2-
10-2 engine (133 tonnes; max speed 80kph) ceased in 1986 and the Class JS 2-
8-2 (104 tonnes; max speed 85kph) in 1989; both are used for freight haulage and
shunting work. The factory now produces parts for steam and diesel locomotives

MAP 30

ROUTE GUIDE & MAPS

❑ **Chinggis (Genghis) Khan**
For many decades the name of this famous Mongolian conqueror has been taboo in his home country. The Russians saw Chinggis Khan as a brutal invader to be erased from the history books but with their influence rapidly fading there has been a sudden rise in Mongolian nationalism. Chinggis Khan, founder of the 13th-century Mongolian Empire, is a hero once more, lending his name to the most luxurious hotel in Ulaanbaatar and also to a brand of vodka.

Along with his rehabilitation have come a number of interesting characters each claiming to be his legitimate descendant. One of the best publicised was Ganjuurijin Dschero Khan, who claimed to have been smuggled out of the country to escape the Communists when he was four years old. Mongolians were intrigued to meet him, although they didn't quite know what to make of his appearance. He arrived in a military tunic, decked out with medals inscribed 'Bazooka', 'Carbine', 'Paratroopers' and 'Special Forces', which he claimed to have won in Korea and Vietnam. Support for him waned after it became apparent that he didn't speak Mongolian.

---

and has customers in many parts of the world. Tours can be arranged through the Datong office of China International Travel Service (CITS).

At Datong the line swings eastwards to run parallel to the Great Wall, about 20km south of it as far as Zhangjiakou. About 100km west of Zhangjiakou you leave Shanxi and enter Hebei province.

Between **Km295** and Km272 (E) the **Great Wall** can be seen parallel to the line, on the hillside to the east. The best view is at **Km284** (E).

Km193: Zhangjiakou 张家口 (●) Founded 2000 years ago, this city (pop: 806,518) used to be known by its Mongolian name, Kalgan (meaning gate or frontier). It stands at the point where the old caravan route between Peking and Russia crossed the Great Wall. Luigi Barzini described it as being like one of those 'cities one sees pictured upon Fu-kien tapestries: varied and picturesque, spreading over the bank of a wide snowy river'. He would not recognise it now; it has grown into an industrial city of just under a million people. Yet he might recall the stink he'd noticed as he drove into town on 14 June 1907, for tanning and leatherwork are still major industries here. About 15km south of the city a large factory pollutes the air with orange smoke.

From around **Km175** the scenery becomes hilly and more appealing as the line climbs the mountains north of Beijing. There are small valleys full of sunflowers, poplar groves and even apple orchards. At **Km99** you cross the San Gan River, above which (E) can be seen a small isolated section of the Wall.

Km82-19: The train passes through some spectacular valley scenery, punctuated by numerous tunnels, some several kilometres long, and bridges. In the gaps between tunnels you see mountains covered with greenery, villages and the river.

Km0: Beijing 北京   [see pp383-407]
You arrive at the futuristic Beijing Zhan station of China's bustling capital (pop: 16,446,857).

Trans-Manchurian Route

For the entire Trans-Manchurian line we use (E) and (W) to show which side of the train points of interest are located. Thus if you're coming from Moscow (E) means the left side of the train, (W) the right.

Km6199: Chita Чита (●●●)   **[see Map 18 and pp327-31]**
Chita (pop: 331,346) is the last major Trans-Siberian station before Trans-Manchurian trains branch off to China.

Km6293: Karymskaya Карымская (●●●+) (see p466).

Km6305: Tarskaya Тарская Tarskaya (formerly called Kaidalovo) is where the branch line to Beijing via Manchuria leaves the main Trans-Siberian route (or joins it if you are coming from Beijing; see p466).

Leaving Tarskaya you cross the **Ingoda River** and head through open steppe-land. Some 20km further south you enter the Buryat Republic (Buryatia). The train makes brief stops at **Adrianovka Адриановка (Km6314)**, and **Mogoytuy Могойтуй (Km6370) (–/●)**.

Km6444: Olovyannaya Оловянная (–/●) The 120-flat apartment block by the station was constructed by Chinese labourers using Chinese materials. It was one of many barter deals between the Zabaikalsk (Russia) and Harbin (China) railways.

Since 1988, when the first barter contract was signed, most deals have involved Russia swapping fertilisers, old rails and railway wheel sets for Chinese food, clothes and shoes. As confidence has grown Harbin Railways has provided specialist services such as doctors of traditional Chinese medicine for railway staff at nearby Karpovka, uniforms for Zabaikalsk workers, and recon-struction specialists for Chita 2 and Petrovsky Zavod stations.

Leaving this picturesque town you cross the Onon River, which flows north of the main Trans-Siberian line, joining the Ingoda to form the Shilka. Genghis (Chinggis) Khan (see box p490) was born on the banks of the muddy Onon in 1162.

❏ THE EAST CHINESE RAILWAY 1897-1901

The route

The original plans for the Great Siberian Railway had not included the laying of track across territories outside the Russian Empire. But when surveyors returned from the Shilka and Amur valleys in 1894 with the news that the Sretensk to Khabarovsk section of the line would prove extremely costly owing to the difficult terrain, the Siberian Railway Committee were obliged to consider an alternative. Their greedy eyes turned to the rich Chinese territory of Manchuria and they noted that a line straight across this province to Vladivostok would cut 513 *versts* (544km) off the journey to the port. Since the Chinese would obviously not be happy to have Russian railway lines extending into their territory, the Committee had to think up a scheme to win Peking over to the idea.

The Manchurian Deal

It did not take wily Russian diplomats long to work out a deal the Chinese were forced to accept. After the 1894 Sino-Japanese war the victorious Japanese concocted a peace treaty that included the payment of a heavy indemnity by the Chinese. Knowing that China was unable to pay, the Russians offered them a generous loan in exchange for the right to build and operate a railway across Manchuria. They were granted an 80-year lease on a thin strip of land 1400km long and the project was to be disguised as a Chinese enterprise financed through the Russo-Chinese Bank. The rest of the world suspected Russia of flagrant imperialism, and Russia proved them right in 1897 by annexing Port Arthur.

Work begins

Construction began in 1897 but it soon became obvious that the project faced greater problems than any that had arisen during the building of other sections. There were difficult conditions (the Greater Khingan Mountains had to be crossed); there were not enough labourers; interpreters were needed to translate the orders of Russian foremen for Chinese coolies; and the area through which the route passed was thick with *hunghutzes* (bandits). It was necessary to bring in a force of 5000 policemen to protect the workers. After the Boxer (anti-foreigner) riots began in the late 1890s it became necessary to protect the rails too, for when they were not murdering missionaries the Boxers tore up track and derailed trains.

The Boxer Rebellion and other setbacks

After the annexation of Port Arthur another Manchurian line was begun – from Harbin south through Mukden (now Shenyang) to Dalni (now Dalian) and Port Arthur (now Lushun). Work was disrupted in 1899 by the outbreak of bubonic plague, although despite Chinese refusal to co-operate with quarantine procedures, only 1400 people died out of the total workforce of 200,000. In May 1900 Boxers destroyed 200km of track and besieged Harbin. The Russians sent in a peace-keeping force of 200,000 men but by the time the rebellion had been put down, one third of the railway had been destroyed. Despite these setbacks the line was completed in 1901. It would have been far more economical to build the Amur line from Sretensk to Khabarovsk, for in the end the East Chinese Railway cost the government more than the total spent on the entire Trans-Siberian track on Russian soil.

Between Olovyannaya and Borzya you cross the Adun Chelon mountain range, passing through **Yasnogorsk Ясногорск (Km6446)**, **Yasnaya Ясная (Km6464)** and **Byrka Бырка (Km6477)**.

Km6486: Mirnaya Мирная   At the western end of the station there are two small tanks whose guns appear to be aimed at the train.

Km6509: Khadabulak Хадабулак   This small village is below a large hill-top telecommunications tower. There are long views northwards across the plains to the surrounding hills.

Km6543: Borzya Борзя (●●●+)   Founded in the 18th century, with the arrival of the railway this town became the transport hub for the south-east Zabaikalsk region. A branch line runs westwards all the way to the Mongolian city of Choibalsan. Black marketeers come aboard (if you're coming from Beijing) to tempt you with army uniforms, military watches and rabbit-fur hats.

There are several opportunities for photographs along the train as it snakes around the curves between Km6554 and Km6570, and especially Km6564-5 (W).

Km6590: Kharanor Харанор   There is a branch line from here to the east which runs to the military towns of Krasnokamensk and Priargunsk.

Km6609: Dauriya Даурия   This small village is surrounded by a marsh of red weeds.

Km6661: Zabaikalsk Забайкальск (●●●++)   This town is within 1km of the border. Customs declarations and passports are checked on the train.

The train is shunted into the **bogie-changing sheds** at the southern end of the station. You can either stay at the station, remain in the carriage, or get out and watch the bogie-changing. Taking photos in the sheds was once strictly prohibited but is now permitted. You'll have to stay at the station for 2-6 hours.

There's a **restaurant** across the bridge and to the left of the station with a limited menu and a **bank** upstairs with predictably poor rates.

THE PEOPLE'S REPUBLIC OF CHINA

Note that kilometre markers between the border and Harbin show the distance to Harbin, while those further on show the distance to Beijing.

Km935 (Bei:2323): Manzhouli (●●●++) 满洲里 At this Chinese border town (pop: 181,112), once known as Manchuria Station, you must fill out currency and health declarations if you're arriving in China or, if you're leaving, fill out a departure card and present your currency declaration form.

The train spends 1-3 hours here so you can visit the **bank** and the **Friendship Store** (tins of good-quality peanuts, Chinese vodka, beer and other snacks). Puffing **steam locomotives** shunt carriages around the yard, a particularly impressive sight if you arrive in the early hours of a freezing winter morning.

Leaving the station you pass **Lake Dalai Nor** and roll across empty steppeland. You may see mounted herders, as did Michael Myres Shoemaker in 1902 when he passed through on his journey to Peking. Of the first Chinese person he saw, he wrote (in *The Great Siberian Railway from St Petersburg to Pekin*) 'these northern Celestials appear on the whole friendly, and are flying around in all directions swathed in furs, and mounted on shaggy horses.' European newspapers of the time had been filled with reports of atrocities committed by the xenophobic Boxer sect in Manchuria, hence his surprise at the apparent friendliness of the local population.

Km749 (Bei:2137): Hailar 海拉尔 (●●) Rolling steppes continue from here to Haiman. If you'd been travelling in 1914 you would have the latest edition of Baedeker's *Russia with Teheran, Port Arthur and Peking* with you and would therefore be looking out for 'the fortified station buildings (sometimes adorned with apes, dragons and other Chinese ornaments), the Chinese carts with their two high wheels and the camels at pasture'. Modern Hailar is the economic centre of the region. Local architecture is a blend of Russian and Mongolian, including log cabins, some with yurt-style roofs.

Km674 (Bei:2062): Haiman Also known as **Yakoshih**, this town stands near the foot of the Great Khingan Range which extends from the Russian border southwards into Inner Mongolia. The line begins to rise into the foothills of the range.

Km634 (Bei:2022): Mianduhe 免渡河 The train continues to climb the gently rising gradient.

Km564 (Bei:1952): Xing'an/Khingan 兴安 This station stands at the **highest point (958m/3140ft) on the Trans-Manchurian line**. The 3km **tunnel** built

ROUTE GUIDE & MAPS

MAP 33

here in 1901-2 was a considerable engineering achievement since most of the drilling was done during the winter, with shift workers labouring day and night.

Km539 (Bei:1927): Boketu 博克图 (●●) The line winds down partly wooded slopes to the town of **Balin/Barim (Bei: 1866)** and continues over the plains, leaving Inner Mongolia and crossing into Heilongjiang Province.

Km270 (Bei:1658): Angangxi 昂昂溪 (●●●/●) About 40km south of Angangxi is the ancient city of **Qiqihar (Tsitsikar)** 齐齐哈尔. By the time he reached this point Michael Myres Shoemaker had become bored with watching 'Celestials' from the windows of the train and was tired and hungry. He writes 'In Tsitsikar, at a wretched little mud hut, we find some hot soup and a chop, also some coffee, all of which, after our days in lunch baskets, taste very pleasant.'

Over lunch they may well have discussed the nearby **Field of Death** for which the city was notorious. In this open area on the edge of Qiqihar public executions were regularly performed. Most of the criminals decapitated before the crowds were *hunghutzes* (bandits). Since the Chinese believed that entry to Heaven was denied to mortals who were missing parts of their bodies, their heads had to be sewn back in place before a decent burial could take place. However, so as not to lower the moral tone of Paradise, the government ordered that the heads be sewn on backwards.

Some 20km east of Angangxi is a large area of marshland, part of which has been designated a nature reserve. The marsh attracts a wide variety of waterfowl since it is on migration routes from the Arctic and Siberia down to southern Asia. **Zhalong Nature Reserve**, 20km to the north, is best known for its cranes. Several of these (including the Siberian Crane) are now listed as endangered species.

Km159 (Bei:1547): Daqing 大庆 (●●) At the centre of one of the largest oilfields in China, Daqing is a model industrial town which produces plastics and gas as well as oil.

Km96 (Bei:1484): Song 宋 This small station is in an island of cultivation amongst the swamps.

Km0 (Bei:1388): Harbin 哈尔滨 (●●●+)   **[see pp376-82]**
Crossing the wide Songhua (Sungari) River, a 1840km-long tributary of the Amur to the north, the line reaches Harbin (pop: 3,627,483), industrial centre of Heilongjiang Province. It was a small fishing village until the mid 1890s when

ROUTE GUIDE & MAPS

the Russians made it the headquarters of their railway-building operations in Manchuria. After Michael Myres Shoemaker visited the town in 1902 he wrote: 'The state of society seems even worse at this military post of Harbin than in Irkutsk. There were seven throats cut last night, and now, as a member of the Russo-Chinese Bank expressed it, the town hopes for a quiet season.' The *Imperial Japanese Railways Guide to East Asia* (1913) recommended 'the excellent bread and butter, which are indeed the pride of Harbin' and warned travellers away from the numerous opium dens. After the Revolution, White Russian refugees poured into the town and Russian influence on the place continued. Today there are few onion-domes or spires to be seen in what is just another Chinese city: the Russian population is now small.

The city's main tourist attraction is its **Ice Lantern Festival** (see box p379) held in January and early February each year.

At the station you can get good views along the track of the numerous steam locos, from the bridges between the platforms.

Between Harbin and Changchun you cross an immense cultivated plain, leaving Heilongjiang and entering Jilin Province.

Km1260: The line crosses a wide tributary of the Songhua River. There are numerous small lakes in the area.

Km1146: Changchun (●●/●) 长春 Changchun (pop: 3,908,048) is the provincial capital. The station boasts white concrete sculptures of 'The Graces' and sellers sell snacks on the platform.

Back in 1913 the *Imperial Japanese Government Railways Guide to East Asia* was reminding its readers (all of whom would have had to change at this large junction) about 'the need of adjusting their watches – the Russian railway-time being 23 minutes earlier than the Japanese'. Between 1933 and 1945 Changchun was the centre of the Japanese puppet-state of Manchukuo. It has now grown into an industrial metropolis of almost four million people. Local industries include car production (Toyota, VW and Audi as well as the old Chinese luxury marque, Red Flag), a rail-carriage factory and film studios.

If you do get off here, local delicacies include antler broth, hedgehog hydnum stewed with orchid, and a north-eastern speciality, *qimian*, which is the nose of a moose. But Changchun is probably more popular with rail enthusiasts than with epicureans. RM Pacifics and QJ 2-10-2s are to be seen here and on the Changchun–Jilin line.

Km1030: Siping 四平 (●) This working town has lots of working steam locos in the station. About 10km further south the train crosses the provincial border into Liaoning Province.

Km841: Shenyang 沈阳 (●●●/●●) An industrial giant (pop: 6,255,921) founded 2000 years ago during the Western Han dynasty (206BC-AD24). At different times during its long history the city has been controlled by Manchus (who named it Mukden), Russians, Japanese and the Kuomintang, until it was finally taken over by Chinese communists in 1948. Shenyang is now one of the largest industrial centres in the People's Republic, but between the factories there are several interesting places to visit, including a small version of Beijing's **Imperial Palace**. The station has a green dome and the square outside it is dominated by a tank on a pedestal.

Km599: Jinzhou 锦州 (●) From here the line runs down almost to the coast, which it follows south-west for the next 300km, crossing into Hebei Province.

Km415: Shanhaiguan 山海关 (●●/●) As you approach the town from the north, you pass through the **Great Wall** – at its most eastern point. This end of the Wanlichangcheng (Ten Thousand Li Long Wall) has been partially done up for the tourists. Although the views here are not as spectacular as at Badaling (70km north of Beijing, see pp407-8), the restoration at Shanhaiguan has been carried out more sympathetically – it is restoration rather than reconstruction.

Km262: Tangshan 唐山 (●) Tangshan (pop: 2,128,191) was the epicentre of an earthquake which demolished this industrial town on 28 July 1976. The official death toll stands at 150,000 but may have been as high as 750,000. Many of the factories have been rebuilt and the town is once again producing consumer goods. Locomotives are built here at the Tangshan Works, which until 1991 produced the SY class 2-8-2 steam engine.

Km133: Tianjin/Tientsin 天津 (●●●/●) Tianjin (pop: 12.3 million) is one of China's largest ports. In the mid 19th century the British and French marched on the capital and 'negotiated' the Treaty of Peking which opened Tianjin to foreign trade. Concessions were granted to foreign powers just as they were in Shanghai. Britain, France, Austria, Germany, Italy, Belgium, Russia, Japan and the United States each controlled different parts of the city, which accounts for the amazing variety of architectural styles to be found here.

Chinese resentment at the foreign presence boiled over in 1870 in an incident that came to be known as the **Tientsin Massacre**, during which ten nuns, two priests and a French official were murdered. To save female babies from being killed by their parents (the Chinese have always considered it far more important to have sons than daughters) the nuns had been giving money for them. This had led more gullible members of the community to believe rumours that the nuns were eating the children or grinding up their bones for patent medicines.

Km0: Beijing 北京   [See pp383-407]
The exalted Chinese capital (pop: 16,446,857). You are now 9001km from Moscow.

ROUTE GUIDE & MAPS

The Baikal Amur Mainline (BAM)

Note: Local time is now Moscow Time + 5 hours.

Km0: Tayshet Тайшет (●●●+) (see p453) This town straddles the BAM/Trans-Siberian junction and marks the start of the BAM.

Km292: Anzyobi Анзёби (●) The first of the three **Bratsk** stations. This is where you'd change trains for the Tsentralny area.

Km325: Padunskiye Porogi Падунские Пороги (●●) The second of the three Bratsk stations. This is where you'd change for a suburban train to the Energetik part of town.

Km330: The Bratsk dam At this point, the railway line crosses over the top of the gigantic dam, with great views of the 'Bratsk Sea'.

Km339: Gidrostroitel Гидростроитель (●) The final Bratsk stop serves the quiet residential area of Gidrostroitel.

Km554: Korshunikha-Angarskaya Коршуниха-Ангарская (●●●) Named after the Korshunikha creek above the town, this station serves the charmless iron-ore processing town of Zheleznogorsk-Ilimsky, founded in 1948.

Km575: Khrebtovaya Хребтовая (●) This is the junction of the BAM and the Ust-Ilimsk line.

Km715: Ust-Kut Усть-Кут One of the most vibrant little towns along the BAM.

Km722: Lena Лена (●●●+) Ust-Kut hydrofoils to the Republic of Sakha and its capital, Yakutsk, used to depart from Osetrovo River Passenger Station near Lena; that service has been discontinued but may restart.

Km931: Ulkan Улькан (●) Near the town of Ulkan there are three villages whose entire male population perished at the front during WWII, turning them

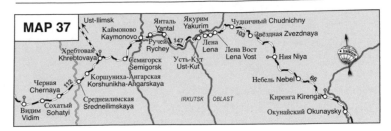

into ghost towns. At the eastern end of the Ulkan platform, there's a metallic Lenin relief and just before you reach the station, you see vast timber yards (S).

Km981: Kunerma Кунерма (●) After this stop the track does a 180-degree loop before chugging along an alpine valley with mountain views on both sides and plunging into the 6km-long Daban tunnel.

Km1004: The train passes through a long tunnel.

Km1029: Goudzhekit Гоудджекит (●) (see p415) Some trains stop at this attractive little spot with a mini-spa built around the hot spring.

Km1064: Severobaikalsk Северобайкальск (●●●+) (see pp410-13) This town (pop: 24,449) is the gateway to the beautiful northern shore of Lake Baikal and the northern sections of the Great Baikal Trail (see box p308).

Km1104: Nizhneangarsk Нижнеангарск (●) (see p414) This busy fishing village makes a good day trip from Severobaikalsk.

Km1109: Nizhneangarsk II Нижнеангарск II Here you pass the little airport from which there are seasonal flights to Irkutsk.

Km1120: Kholodnaya Холодная A 20-minute walk from the station is an indigenous Evenk village, Kholodny, which is trying to keep its traditions and culture alive in spite of the chronic alcoholism.

Km1141: Kichera Кичера (●) You may notice the Baltic influences in the architecture of this small town as it was built by the Estonian Young Communist Party.

ROUTE GUIDE & MAPS

Km1171: Dzelinda Дзелинда (see p415) One of the newer stations along the BAM, this one was built in 1996 to accommodate the tiny hot springs spa 2km into the forest.

Km1242: Anamakit Анамакит Between here and Novy Uoyan, the railway crosses over the Upper Angara River – the largest river to flow into northern Lake Baikal.

Km1257: Novy Uoyan Новый Уоян (●●●) Built in 1976 as a support base for the railway, this small town reflects Latvian influence in its architecture. Here you're often greeted by the sight of timber yards and by locals selling delicious homemade food and smoked fish.

Km1330: Kyukhelbeckerskaya Кюхельбекерская (●) This station is named after the Decembrist Wilhelm Kyukhelbecker, a friend of Pushkin's who was exiled to Siberia where he eventually died. From here, the railway goes up a series of steep valleys, climbing to 1200m above sea level.

──────────── **TIME ZONE MT + 6** ────────────

Km1376: Severomuisky Tunnel Северомуйский тоннель Here you hit the 15.3km-long tunnel – the longest in Russia – which was only completed in 2004 due to permafrost-related difficulties in the Severomuisk mountain range. The tunnel has replaced more than 50km of track which was vulnerable to avalanches.

Km1422: Ulgi Ульги This stop is named after the Buryat term for epic folk songs, in which valiant heroes battle against the forces of evil.

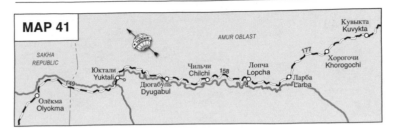

Km1474: Taksimo Таксимо (●●●+) This little town was the refuge of White Army soldiers, priests and others who fled from the Communists after the 1917 revolution. You can check out the BAM pioneer monument here.

Km1559: Kuanda Куанда (●●) In September 1984 this little town hosted the celebration of the BAM's completion, though the golden spike that joins the east and west sections of the BAM was actually hammered in around 15km to the east, at **Balbukhta Балбухта**.

Km1734: Novaya Chara Новая Чара (●●●) This is a large-ish town, the majority of whose inhabitants work for the railway.

Km1755: Kemen Кемен The noteworthy thing about this station is its proximity to the deepest permafrost on the BAM – 600 metres.

Km1851: Olongdo Олонгдо Between here and Khani lies the highest point along the BAM – 1300m above sea level.

Km1879: Khani Хани (●●●+) This is the only BAM town that's part of the Republic of Sakha.

Km2364: Tynda Тында (●●●+) (see pp418-20) One of the largest BAM towns, Tynda (pop: 34,785) straddles the junction of the BAM and Little BAM that connects it to the Trans-Siberian railway at Bamovskaya. Heading north from Tynda is the AYaM, still not completed, though you can brave an arduous 17-hour bus or taxi journey up from Neryungri to **Yakutsk** (see pp415-18). Check out the railway station's 1970s architecture and the freight locomotive on the plinth in front of the station, put there to celebrate the 30th anniversary of the BAM.

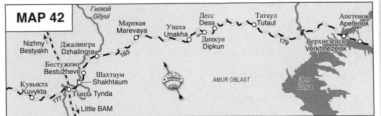

ROUTE GUIDE & MAPS

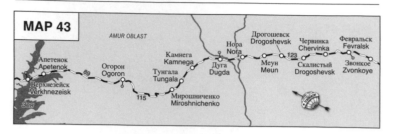

Km2391: Bestuzhevo Бестужево (●) This station is named after a Decembrist family, where all three sons were originally sentenced to death for their participation in the 1825 anti-tsar uprising, though their sentence was eventually commuted to exile.

Km2707: Verkhnezeisk Верхнезейск (●●●+) An average BAM town with little to see.

Km3033: Fevralsk Февральск (●●●+) Here the railway line crosses the gold-bearing Selemdzha river. This little town has had problems with its infrastructure due to its unfortunate location on top of a swamp.

Km3305: Bureinsk Буреинск (●) Here the line crosses the Bureya river. Building the metal bridge across this river required remarkable sacrifices on the part of the builders, who worked in temperatures of -45°C to complete it in record time in April 1975.

❏ The Dusse-Alin Tunnel

The Gulag prisoners who worked on the Dusse-Alin tunnel from 1939 onwards lived in atrocious conditions and scores died from starvation and overwork. When the chief engineer, Vasili Konserov, was shot in the back by the guard commander following a dispute, his death was deemed an 'accident' and he was buried with full honours as he'd previously received the Order of Lenin for his role in the construction of the Belomorski-Baltiiski Canal. Renowned Moscow Metro engineer Ratsbaum was recruited in Konserov's place to finish the job. Besides the atrocious working conditions, one of the problems faced by Ratsbaum was the lack of survey equipment, meaning that the tunnel had to be dug from both sides of the mountain using line-of-sight alone. Though there was a good chance that the two halves would not meet, which would have resulted in death by firing squad for the engineer, miraculously, they did meet and were only 20cm out!

Even though the tunnel was completed in 1950, it was only put to use in 1982, the work on the railway between here and Komsomolsk-na-Amure having been abandoned after Stalin's death. When work re-commenced in 1974, the soldiers unearthed grisly finds at the workers' camp here, including the frozen corpses of the previous workers.

Backblast from aircraft jet engines had to be used to melt the 32,000 cubic metres of ice that had formed within the tunnel, and in 1982, the first train passed through on its way to Komsomolsk-na-Amure.

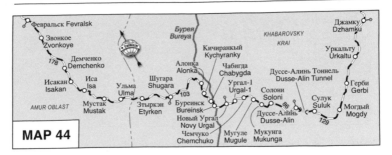

Km3315: Novy Urgal Новый Ургал (●●●+) At the coal-mining town of
Novy Urgal, you can switch to the north–south line and rejoin the Trans-
Siberian route for a shorter trip to Khabarovsk via Birobidzhan.

Km3403: Dusse-Alin Дуссе-Алин (●) This station is at the end of the 2km-
long Dusse-Alin tunnel that has a particularly tragic history (see box opposite).

──────────── **TIME ZONE MT + 7** ────────────

Km3581: Amgun Амгунь (●) Between here and the station of **Duki Дуки**
50km away, in 1989 some hikers stumbled across the wreckage of the
American-built DC-3 that crashed in this area on October 4, 1938. Its tail end is
now a monument in Komsomolsk-na-Amure.

Km3633: Postyshevo Постышево (●●●) This is the station for the town of
Berezovy, which is right near the Amgun river, considered to be one of the best
fishing spots in eastern Siberia, rich in salmon, grayling and taimen.

**Km3837: Komsomolsk-na-Amure Комсомольск-на-Амуре (●●●+) [see
pp420-3]** This is a major industrial city (pop: 257,891), founded in 1932 and
situated on the Amur river. From here, a direct railway line runs south to
Khabarovsk and Vladivostok.

Km3853: Amur Bridge Straddling the Amur river, this bridge is the longest
of all of the BAM's bridges at 1437 metres. The first train crossed in 1975.

Km3888: Selikhin Селихин (●●) From this large town, the railway line was
supposed to run north to Cape Lazarev, where it would link the mainland to

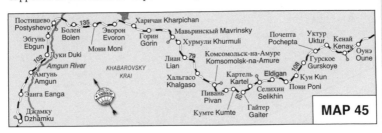

Sakhalin Island via a 9km tunnel under the strait, though this project was shelved after Stalin's death.

Km4050: Vysokogornaya Высокогорная (●●●+) Much of this town was built by Japanese PoWs, as a PoW camp was located here. The station building here resembles a Japanese temple and Japanese make pilgrimages here to visit the family graves.

Km4097: Kenada Кенада (●●) Near this stop lies the Dzigdasi village, the site of a love story between a Japanese PoW called Umoda and Marsha, a young Russian woman in exile from her native Kazakhstan. The PoW was repatriated in 1947 and never knew that Marsha gave birth to his son, who continues the search for his father.

Km4137: Tumnin Тумнин (●●) Tumnin's claim to fame is that the surrounding area is allegedly the home of the Taiga Yeti, with sightings of the creature reported on a fairly regular basis.

Km4283: Vanino Ванино (●●●) [see p424] A minor port these days, Vanino originally acted as the transportation point for Gulag prisoners who were sent to the north.

Km4291: Sovetskaya Gavan-sortirovka Советская Гавань-сортиров-ка [see p425] Since trains aren't running to Gavan-Gorod at the moment this is the final stop for long-distance passenger trains. The end of the line. Literally.

ROUTE GUIDE & MAPS

Map key

		@	Internet	☆	Police
♠	Where to stay	🛉	Museum/gallery	🚌	Bus station/stop
○	Where to eat and drink	🖪	Church/cathedral	—☐—	Rail line & station
✉	Post Office	🄰	Temple	⛴	Ferry
$	Bank/ATM	©	Mosque	●	Other
ⓘ	Tourist Information	✿	Synagogue	▩	Park
📖	Library/bookstore	⍥	Embassy/consulate		

APPENDIX A – ALTERNATIVE ROUTE

For travellers visiting Sergiev Posad, Rostov-Velikiy and Yaroslavl, the more northern rail route avoiding Nizhny Novgorod is included here. The routes follow the same track as far as Fryazevo (Km54). After Yaroslavl this route joins the main Trans-Siberian route at Kotelnich (Km870).

Km0: Moscow Москва Yaroslavsky Station Ярославский вокзал
See pp428-30 for the route as far as Fryazevo (Km54).

Km57: Abramtsevo Абрамцево
About 3km from the station is the Abramtsevo estate, one of the most important centres of Russian culture in the second half of the 19th century.

Km59: Khotkovo Хотьково
This town (pop: 22,000) has a well-preserved historic section on the high bank of the Pazha River which flows through its centre.

Km73 (N): Sergiev Posad Сергиев Посад [See pp206-10]
Have your camera ready for the stunning blue and gold domes of the cathedrals.

Km112: Aleksandrov Александров
This little-known town was, for nearly two decades in the 16th century, the real capital of Russia. From 1564 to 1581 Ivan the Terrible lived here and directly ruled the half of the country which he called the *oprichnina,* having abandoned the rest to the authority of the *boyars* (nobles) and monasteries. The oprichnina was policed by *oprichniki,* mostly low-class thugs, mercenaries and foreign adventurers. Ivan the Terrible certainly deserved his soubriquet. In his dungeons here he devised and supervised some of the cruellest tortures imaginable.

Km145: Berendeyevo Берендеево
There is a 21km branch line to the west from here to the Golden Ring town of Pereslavl-Zalesski.

Km200: Petrovsk Петровск
About 15km east of Petrovsk you will see **Lake Nero** on the right.

Km224: Rostov-Velikiy Ростов-Великий (Rostov-Yaroslavskiy Ростов-Ярославский) [See pp211-16]
Attractively located by Lake Nero, Rostov-Velikiy (pop: 34,800) is one of the most interesting Golden Ring cities.

Km240 (N):
Amidst the fields and quite close to the track is a sadly neglected but **picturesque church** with five dilapidated domes and a tower.

Km284: Yaroslavl Ярославль (●●) [See pp217-24]
Yaroslavl (pop: 608,600) was founded in 1010 by the Christian king Yaroslavl the Wise. It grew quickly into an important trading centre on the Volga shipping route. Many of the ancient cathedrals still stand in spite of the heavy fighting that went on here during the Civil War.

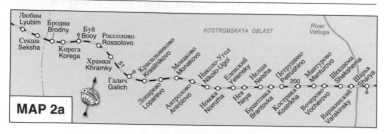

MAP 2a

About five minutes after entering Yaroslavl's outskirts you pass the suburban station of **Kotorosl Которосль** and on the left you can see the **Church of St Peter and St Paul**.

Km289: Volga River About five minutes after leaving the station, the train changes direction from north to east and crosses the mighty Volga River, which is about 1km wide here. In times gone by Russians held this river in such esteem that passengers would stand and take off their hats to Mother Volga as the train rattled onto the first spans of the long bridge. Rising in the Valdai hills, Europe's longest river meanders 3700km down to the Caspian Sea.

Km356: Danilov Данилов (•••) (pop: 19,000) There are often many platform traders here.

Km394: Lyubim Любим Lyubim's population is decreasing – down at least 10% since 1980 to about 6000 – typical of the Russia-wide migration trend from villages to large cities.

——————————— **Km 420-1266 TIME ZONE MT + 1** ———————————

Km450: Booy Буй (••) There is nothing of interest in this industrial town (pop: 28,700) specialising in cheese, flax and mineral fertilisers. Rotting silt (sapropel) is extracted from the lake and dried to be used as fuel or made into fertiliser.

Km501: Galich Галич After the station, on the right (S), you pass **Paisiev Monastery**.

Km651: Manturovo Мантурово After leaving this industrial and forestry town (pop: 21,100) the train crosses the Unzha River (Km654).

Km698: Sharya Шарья (••) Some steam locos are stored here (L and Er classes) but numbers are dwindling. Sharya (pop: 26,400) is the region's biggest timber centre.

Km818: Svecha Свеча Roughly mid-way between Sharya and Svecha you enter **Kirovskaya Oblast**. Most of this region's 120,800 sq km are within the basin of the Vyatka River. The greater part of the oblast is taiga and the main industry here is logging.

Km870: Kotelnich Котельнич (pop: 30,700) See p434.

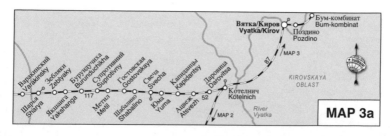

MAP 3a

APPENDIX B – TIMETABLES

Timetables for the most popular trains on the Trans-Siberian, Trans-Mongolian, and Trans-Manchurian routes are given below.

Unless otherwise indicated, departure times are shown; for arrival times simply subtract the number of minutes shown as the stopping time.

On the internet the best site for Russian train timetables is 🖳 pass.rzd.ru; alternatively try 🖳 www.realrussia.co.uk. See box p43 for more on other useful websites.

However, timetables are subject to change, so the only completely up-to-date timetable will be the one posted in the corridor of your carriage!

Table 1 Trans-Siberian: Moscow–Vladivostok (Train Nos 001 & 002: *Rossiya*)

Departures are every other day in each direction, eastbound on odd dates and westbound on even dates. Times shown are departure times – subtract stop for arrival time.

MT = Moscow Time; **LT** = Local Time; **–** = no stop

Station		Km from Mos	Stop (mins, E/W)	Eastbound No 002 MT Day 1	LT	Westbound No 001 MT	LT	Time Zone MT+
Moscow (Yaroslavsky)	Москва (Ярославский)	0	–/–	13:50	13:50	05:52	05:52	0
Vladimir	Владимир	191	23/23	17:08	17:08	02:47 Day 7	02:47	0
Nizhny Novgorod (Gorky)	Нижний Новгород (Горький)	442	12/15	20:03	20:03	23:09	00:09	0
Vyatka (Kirov)	Вятка (Киров)	957	15/15	02:07 Day 2	03:07	17:14	18:14	1
Balyezino	Балезино	1194	23/23	05:54	06:54	13:41	14:41	1
Perm 2	Пермь 2	1436	25/20	09:50	11:50	09:46	11:46	2
Yekaterinburg (Sverdlovsk)	Екатеринбург (Свердловск)	1816	28/27	15:44	17:44	04:04 Day 6	06:04	2
Tyumen	Тюмень	2144	20/20	20:16	22:16	23:05	01:05	2
Ishim	Ишим	2431	12/12	00:10 Day 3	02:10	19:10	21:10	2
Omsk	Омск	2712	16/19	03:30	06:30	15:22	18:22	3
Barabinsk	Барабинск	3040	30/30	07:30	10:30	10:37	13:37	3
Novosibirsk	Новосибирск	3335	19/19	11:29	14:29	07:01	10:01	3
Tayga	Тайга	3570	2/2	14:47	18:47	03:36	07:36	4
Mariinsk	Мариинск	3715	26/26	17:16	21:16	01:36 Day 5	05:36	4
Bogotol	Боготол	3849	1/1	19:08	23:08	23:17	03:17	4

❑ **Kilometre-post discrepancies**

Distances on official timetables do not always match those indicated by kilometre posts beside the track. Close to Moscow you may notice discrepancies of 10km or more. Beyond Kotelnich (Km870), the junction of the Trans-Siberian and Moscow–Yaroslavl–Vyatka lines, differences grow to 30-40km, largely because until a few years ago most Trans-Siberian traffic used the (longer) line via Yaroslavl.

Table 1 Trans-Siberian: Moscow–Vladivostok
(Train Nos 001 & 002: *Rossiya*) *cont'd*

Station		Km from Mos	Stop (mins, E/W)	Eastbound No 002 MT	LT	Westbound No 001 MT	LT	Time Zone MT+
Achinsk 1	Ачинск 1	3917	1/1	20:00	00:00	22:17	02:17	4
Krasnoyarsk	Красноярск	4098	22/22	23:02	03:02	19:29	23:29	4
				Day 4				
Kansk-Yeniseysky	Канск-Енисейский	4343	1/1	02:36	06:36	15:40	19:40	4
Ilanskaya	Иланская	4375	22/22	03:31	07:31	15:09	19:09	4
Reshoty	Решоты	4453	–/2			13.43		4
Tayshet	Тайшет	4516	2/2	05:38	10:38	12:41	17:41	5
Nizhneudinsk	Нижнеудинск	4680	13/13	08:18	13:18	10:13	15:13	5
Tulun	Тулун	4794	2/2	09:55	14:55	08:18	13:18	5
Zima	Зима	4940	30/30	12:16	17:16	06:20	11:20	5
Angarsk	Ангарск	5160	2/4	15:08	20:08	02:49	07:49	5
Irkutsk Sortirovka	Иркутск Сортировка	5178	2/15	15:43	20:43	02:11	07:11	5
Irkutsk	Иркутск	5185	23/35	16:20	21:20	01:45	06:45	5
						Day 4		
Slyudyanka 1	Слюдянка 1	5312	2/2	18:27	23:27	22:50	03:50	5
Ulan-Ude	Улан-Удэ	5642	23/23	23:17	04:17	18:26	23:26	5
				Day 5				
Petrovsky Zavod	Петровский Завод	5784	2/2	01:21	07:21	15:53	21:53	6
Khilok	Хилок	5932	19/15	03:59	09:59	13:27	19:27	6
Chita 2	Чита 2	6199	25/25	08:31	14:31	09:09	15:09	6
Karymskaya	Карымская	6293	18/18	10:42	16:42	06:45	12:45	6
Chernyshevsk-Zabaikalsk	Чернышевск-Забайкальск	6593	30/30	16:02	22:02	01:42	07:42	6
						Day 3		
Mogocha	Могоча	6906	15/15	21:45	03:45	19:54	01:54	6
Amazar	Амазар	7010	20/20	23:37	05:37	18:07	00:07	6
				Day 6				
Yerofei-Pavlovich	Ерофей-Павлович	7119	21/21	01:46	07:46	15:59	21:59	6
Skovorodino	Сковородино	7306	2/23	05:13	11:13	12:11	18:11	6
Magdagachi	Магдагачи	7501	15/15	08:33	14:33	09:10	15:10	6
Tygda	Тыгда	7576	2/2	09:38	15:38	07:51	13:51	6
Shimanovskaya	Шимановская	7723	2/2	11:46	17:46	05:34	11:34	6
Svobodny	Свободный	7815	3/3	13:13	19:13	04:22	10:22	6
Belogorsk	Белогорск	7873	30/30	14:34	20:34	03:25	09:25	6
Bureya	Бурея	8037	2/2	17:16	23:16	00:36	06:36	6
						Day 2		
Arkhara	Архара	8088	2/2	18:11	00:11	23:50	06:50	6
Obluchye	Облучье	8198	15/15	20:10	03:10	22:01	05:11	7
Birobidzhan	Биробиджан	8351	5/5	22:40	05:40	19:11	02:11	7
				Day 7				
Khabarovsk 1	Хабаровск 1	8521	28/30	01:10	08:10	17:04	00:04	7
Vyazemskaya	Вяземская	8642	15/15	03:11	10:11	14:37	21:37	7
Bikin	Бикин	8756	2/15	04:43	11:43	12:52	19:52	7

Table 1 Trans-Siberian: Moscow–Vladivostok
(Train Nos 001 & 002: *Rossiya*) *cont'd*

Station		Km from Mos	Stop (mins, E/W)	Eastbound No 002 MT	LT	Westbound No 001 MT	LT	Time Zone MT+
Luchegorsk	Лучегорск	8773	1/2	05:23	12:23	12:09	19:09	7
Dalnerechensk 1	Дальнереченск 1	8890	3/2	06:19	13:19	11:14	18:14	7
Ruzhino	Ружино	8941	15/12	07:17	14:17	10:25	17:25	7
Spassk-Dalny	Спасск-Дальний	9050	1/4	08:52	15:52	08:46	15:46	7
Muchnaya	Мучная	9092	1/1	09:28	16:28	08:08	15:08	7
Sibirtsevo	Сибирцево	9109	1/2	09:58	16:58	07:48	14:48	7
Ussuriysk	Уссурийск	9177	18/18	11:09	18:09	06:44	13:44	7
Ugolnaya	Угольная	9255	2/2	12:28	19:28	05:07	12:07	7
Vladivostok	Владивосток	9289		13:10	20:10	04:25	11:25	7
				Day 1				

Table 2 Trans-Mongolian: Moscow–Beijing (Train Nos 003* & 004*)

One per week in each direction: currently ex-Moscow on Tuesday, ex-Beijing on Wednesday. Times shown are departure times – subtract stop for arrival time.
MT = Moscow Time; **LT** = Local Time; – = no stop

* Note that these train numbers may be listed on some timetable sources as 0033 and 0043.

Station		Km from Mos	Stop (mins, E/W)	Eastbound No 004 MT	LT	Westbound No 003 MT	LT	Time Zone MT+
Moscow (Yaroslavsky)	Москва (Ярославский)	0		Day 1 21:35	21:35	13:58	13:58	0
Vladimir	Владимир	191	23/23	Day 2 00:53	00:53	10:40	10:40	0
Nizhny Novgorod (Gorky)	Нижний Новгород (Горький)	442	12/19	03:47	03:47	07:02	07:02	0
Vyatka (Kirov)	Вятка (Киров)	957	15/15	09:49	10:49	01:16	02:16	1
						Day 6		
Balyezino	Балезино	1194	23/23	13:42	14:42	21:45	22:45	1
Perm 2	Пермь 2	1436	20/20	17:42	19:42	17:46	19:46	2
Yekaterinburg (Sverdlovsk)	Екатеринбург (Свердловск)	1816	27/27	23:23	01:23	12:06	14:06	2
Tyumen	Тюмень	2144	21/20	Day 3 04:17	06:17	06:58	08:58	2
Ishim	Ишим	2431	12/12	08:13	10:13	03:06	05:06	2
						Day 5		
Omsk	Омск	2712	16/16	11:38	14:38	23:39	02:39	3
Barabinsk	Барабинск	3040	27/23	15:46	18:46	19:57	22:57	3
Novosibirsk	Новосибирск	3335	19/19	19:19	22:19	16:14	19:14	3
Tayga	Тайга	3570	2/2	22.38	02.38	12.24	16.24	4
Mariinsk	Мариинск	3715	26/26	01:00	05:00	10:20	14:20	4
Achinsk 1	Ачинск 1	3917	–/2	–	–	–	–	4
Krasnoyarsk	Красноярск	4098	22/22	06:47	10:47	04:12	08:12	4
						Day 4		
Ilanskaya	Иланская	4375	22/22	11:10	15:10	23:55	03:55	4
Nizhneudinsk	Нижнеудинск	4680	13/13	16:00	21:00	19:02	00:02	5

Table 2 Trans-Mongolian: Moscow–Beijing (Train Nos 003* & 004*) *cont'd*

Station		Km from Mos	Stop (mins, E/W)	Eastbound No 004 MT	LT	Westbound No 003 MT	LT	Time Zone MT+
				Day 4				
Zima	Зима	4940	30/30	20:13	01:13	15:12	20:12	5
				Day 5				
Irkutsk	Иркутск	5185	25/25	00:12	05:12	11:04	16:04	5
Slyudyanka 1	Слюдянка 1	5312	2/10	02:44	07:44	08:32	13:32	5
Ulan-Ude	Улан-Удэ	5642	30/30	08:45	13:45	03:09	08:09	5
						Day 3		
Dzhida	Джида	5852	2/2	13:15	18:15	23:15	04:15	5
Naushki	Наушки	5895	2½hrs+	16:43	21:43	22:31	03:31	5
MONGOLIA						**RUSSIA**		
Sühbaatar	Сухбаатар	5925	1hr+	23:55		22:05		
				Day 6				
Darhan	Дархан	6023	22/5	01:44		19:24		
Salkhit	Салхит	6078	– /20	–		18.43		
Zuunhara	Дзунхара	6132	20/17	03:50		17:19		
Ulaanbaatar	Улаанбаатар	6304	55/65	07:35		14:25		
Choyr	Чоыр	6551	20/21	11:50		09:19		
Saynshand	Сайншанд	7778	38/20	15:40		05:35		
Dzamyn-Ude	Дзамын-Удэ	7013	1hr+	20:35		01:40		
						Day 2		
CHINA				**Day 7**		**MONGOLIA**		
Erlian	二连 Эрлянь	7023	2hrs+	00:57		23:59		
Chzhuzhikhe	Чжужихе		2/2	03:10		18.34		
Jining	济宁 Цзиннань	7356	9/6	05:56		16:09		
Datong	大同 Датун	7483	12/12	08:11		14:16		
Zhangjiakou	张家口 Цжанцзякоунань	7661	10/6	10:46		11:26		
Beijing (Pekin)	北京 Пекин	7865		14:04		08:05		
						Day 1		

Table 3 Trans-Manchurian: Moscow–Beijing (Train Nos 019 & 020: *Vostok*)

One per week in each direction; currently both ex-Moscow and ex-Beijing depart on Saturday. Times shown are departure times – subtract stop for arrival time.
MT = Moscow Time; **LT** = Local Time; – = no stop

Station		Km from Mos	Stop (mins, E/W)	Eastbound No 020 MT	LT	Westbound No 019 MT	LT	Time Zone MT+
Moscow (Yaroslavsky)	Москва (Ярославский)	0		**Day 1** 23:45	23:45	17:58	17:58	0
Vladimir	Владимир	191	23/23	**Day 2** 02:55	02:55	14:56	14:56	0
Nizhny Novgorod (Gorky)	Нижний Новгород (Горький)	442	12/12	05:57	05:57	11:12	11:12	0

Table 3 Trans-Manchurian: Moscow–Beijing
(Train Nos 019 & 020: *Vostok*) *cont'd*

Station		Km from Mos	Stop (mins, E/W)	Eastbound No 020 MT	LT	Westbound No 019 MT	LT	Time Zone MT+
Vyatka (Kirov)	Вятка (Киров)	957	15/15	12:33	13:33	05:06	06:06	1
Glazov	Глазов	1165	2/–	15.20	16.20	–	–	1
Balyezino	Балезино	1194	23/23	16:10	17:10	01:39	02:39	1
						Day 7		
Perm 2	Пермь 2	1436	20/20	20:11	22:11	21:24	23:24	2
Yekaterinburg	Екатеринбург			Day 3				
(Sverdlovsk)	(Свердловск)	1816	27/27	01:59	03:59	15:30	17:30	2
Tyumen	Тюмень	2144	20/20	06:40	08:40	10:55	12:55	2
Ishim	Ишим	2431	12/12	10:34	14:34	07:06	09:06	2
Omsk	Омск	2712	16/17	14:03	17:03	03:45	06:45	3
						Day 6		
Barabinsk	Барабинск	3040	23/25	18:28	21:28	23:44	02:44	3
Novosibirsk	Новосибирск	3335	19/19	22:16	01:16	19:50	22:50	3
				Day 4				
Mariinsk	Мариинск	3715	26/26	04:10	08:10	13:50	17:50	4
Krasnoyarsk	Красноярск	4098	24/23	09:59	13:59	07:31	11:31	4
Ilanskaya	Иланская	4375	22/20	14:25	19:37	03:05	07:05	4
						Day 5		
Nizhneudinsk	Нижнеудинск	4680	13/13	19:06	00:06	22:20	03:20	5
				Day 5				
Zima	Зима	4940	30/30	22:55	05:55	18:27	23:27	5
Irkutsk	Иркутск	5185	30/30	02:57	07:57	14:12	19:12	5
Slyudyanka 1	Слюдянка 1	5312	2/2	05:09	10:09	11:38	16:38	5
Ulan-Ude	Улан-Удэ	5642	25/25	10:07	15:07	07:15	12:15	5
Petrovsky Zavod	Петровский Завод	5784	2/2	–	–	04:46	10:46	6
Khilok	Хилок	5932	19/15	15:30	21:30	02:19	08:19	6
						Day 4		
Chita 2	Чита 2	6199	38/25	21:10	03:10	21:52	03:52	6
Karymskaya	Карымская	6293	33/39	23:47	05:47	19:31	01:31	6
				Day 6				
Mogoytuy	Могойтуй	6370	–/5	–	–	17:05	23:05	6
Olovyannaya	Оловянная	6444	–/2	–	–	15:40	21:40	6
Yasnogorsk	Ясногорск	6446	–/2	–	–	15:20	21:20	6
Borzya	Борзя	6543	30/30	05:00	11:00	13:54	19:54	6
Zabaikalsk	Забайкальск	6661	6hrs+	14:05	20:05	10:57	16:57	6
CHINA				Day 7		RUSSIA		
Manzhouli	Маньчжурия / 满洲里	6678	5hrs+/ 3hrs+	00:10		07:01		
Hailar	Хайлар / 海拉尔	6864	8/8	02:22		01:26		
						Day 3		
Boketu	Бокэт / 伯克图	7074	11/7	05:23		22:17		
Angangxi	Ананси / 鞍钢西	7343	24/6	09:30		18:25		
Daqing	Дацин / 大庆	7454	11/8	10:48		–		
Harbin	Харбин / 哈尔滨	7613	33/21	13:17		15:10		
Changchun	Чанчунь / 长春	7855	8/6	16:00		12:14		

Table 3 Trans-Manchurian: Moscow–Beijing
(Train Nos 019 & 020: *Vostok*) *cont'd*

Station		Km from Mos	Stop (mins, E/W)	Eastbound No 020 MT	LT	Westbound No 019 MT	LT	Time Zone MT+
Siping	四平 Сюпин	7971	6/2	17:19		10:54		
Shenyang	沈阳 Шэньян	8160	15/8	19:33		08:55		
Jinzhou	锦州 Цзиньчжоу	8402	5/4	22:16 Day 8		06:15		
Shanhaiguan	山海关 Шаньхэйгуань	8586	8/6	00:22		04:13		
Tangshan	唐山 Таншан	8739	4/3	02:23		02:06		
Tianjin / Tientsin	天津 Тяньцзинь	8868	23/6	04:11		00:41 Day 2		
Beijing	北京 Пекин	9001		05:46		23:00 Day 1		

APPENDIX C – LIST OF SIBERIAN FAUNA

There are extensive displays of local animals in the natural history museums of Novosibirsk, Irkutsk and Khabarovsk but the labelling is in Russian and Latin. The following translation is given for non-Russian-speaking readers whose Latin is rusty or non-existent.

In the list below the letters given beside the animal's English name indicate its natural habitat. NS = Northern Siberia/Arctic Circle; SP = Siberian Plain; AS = Altai-Sayan Plateau/Mongolia; BI = Lake Baikal/Transbaikal region; FE = Far Eastern Territories. Where a Latin name is similar to the English (eg *Vipera* = Viper) these names have been omitted.

Accipiter gentilis goshawk (AS/SP/NS/ BI/FE)
Aegoceras montanus mountain ram (AS)
Aegoceras sibiricus Siberian goat (BI)
Aegolius funereus boreal/Tengmalm's owl (BI/FE)
Aegypius monachus black vulture (AS)
Aethia cristatella crested auklet (NS/FE)
Alces alces elk/moose (SP/BI/FE)
Allactaga jaculus five-toed jerboa (SP/BI)
Alopex lagopus arctic fox (NS)
Anas acuta pintail (BI)
Anas clypeata shoveler (SP/BI/FE)
Anas crecca teal (BI/SP/FE)
Anas falcata falcated teal (SP/BI/FE)
Anas formosa Baikal teal (BI)

Anas platyrhynchos mallard (AS/SP/BI/FE)
Anas poecilorhyncha spotbill duck (AS/BI)
Anser anser greylag goose (SP/BI)
Anser erythropus white-fronted goose (AS/ SP/BI/FE)
Antelope gutturosa/crispa antelope (FE)
Arctomis bobac marmot (AS/SP)
Ardea cinerea grey heron (AS/SP/BI)
Aquila clanga greater-spotted eagle (SP)
Botaurus stellaris bittern (SP/BI/FE)
Bubo bubo eagle owl (BI/FE)
Buteo lagopus rough-legged buzzard (NS/ SP/FE)
Butorides striatus striated/green heron (FE)
Canis alpinus mountain wolf (AS/FE)
Canis corsac korsac/steppe fox (BI/FE)

Canis lagopus arctic fox (NS)
Canis lupus wolf (SP/BI/FE)
Canis procyonoides Amur racoon (FE)
Capra sibirica Siberian mountain goat/ibex (AS/BI)
Capreolus capreolus roe deer (SP/BI/FE)
Castor fiber beaver (SP/BI/FE)
Certhia familiaris common treecreeper (AS/BI/FE)
Cervus alces elk (AS/BI/FE)
Cervus capreolus roe-buck (BI/FE)
Cervus elephas maral deer (AS/BI/FE)
Cervus nippon sika/Japanese deer (FE)
Cervus tarandus reindeer (NS/FE)
Circus aeruginosus marsh harrier (SP/BI)
Citellus undulatus arctic ground squirrel/ Siberian souslik (NS/BI/FE)
Cricetus cricetus common hamster (AS/SP/ BI/FE)
Cygnus cygnus whooper swan (SP/BI)
Dicrostonyx torquatus arctic lemming (NS)
Dryocopus martius black woodpecker (SP/ BI/FE)
Enhyra lutris Kamchatka beaver (FE)
Equus hemionus kulan/Asian wild ass (FE)
Eumentopias Stelleri sea-lion (NS/FE)
Eutamias sibiricus Siberian chipmunk (AS/ SP/BI/FE)
Ealco columbarius merlin (NS/SP/BI/FE)
Falco peregrinus peregrine (NS/SP/BI/FE)
Falco tinnunculus kestrel (SP)
Falco vesperinus hawk (SP)
Felis irbis irbis/panther (FE)
Felis lynx lynx (SP/BI/FE)
Felis manul wild cat (AS/BI/FE)
Felis tigris altaica Amur tiger (FE)
Foetorius altaicus ermine (NS/AS/SP/BI/FE)
Foetorius altaicus sibiricus polecat (SP/BI)
Foetorius vulgaris weasel (SP/BI)
Fulica atra coot (SP/BI/FE)
Gallinago gallinago common snipe (SP/ BI/FE)
Gavia arctica black-throated diver/loon (BI)
Gavia stellata red-throated diver/loon (SP/ BI)
Gazella subgutturosa goitred gazelle (AS)
Grus cinerea grey crane (SP)
Grus grus common crane (SP/BI/FE)
Grus leucogeranus Siberian white crane (NS/SP/FE)
Gulo gulo wolverine/glutton (SP/BI/FE)
Gypaetus barbatus L. lammergeyer (AS)

Haematopus ostralegus oystercatcher (SP/ BI/FE)
Lagomis alpinus rat hare (FE)
Lagopus lagopus willow grouse/ptarmigan (NS/SP/FE)
Larus argentatus herring gull (BI/FE)
Larus canus common gull (BI/FE)
Larus ridibundus black-headed gull (BI/FE)
Lemmus obensis Siberian lemming (NS/SP)
Lepus timidus arctic hare (NS/BI/FE)
Lepus variabilis polar hare (NS)
Lutra vulgaris otter (BI/FE)
Marmota camtschatica Kamchatka marmot (FE)
Marmota sibirica Siberian marmot (AS/SP/ BI)
Martes zibellina sable (SP/BI/FE)
Melanitta deglandi American black scoter (BI)
Melanocorypha mongolica Mongolian lark (BI/FE)
Meles meles Eurasian badger (AS/BI/FE)
Microtus hyperboreus sub-arctic vole (NS/ SP/FE)
Moschus moschiferus musk deer (AS/BI/FE)
Mustela erminea ermine (NS/AS/SP/ BI/FE)
Mustela eversmanni steppe polecat (AS/ SP/BI/FE)
Mustela nivalis common weasel (NS/SP/ BI/FE)
Mustela sibirica kolonok (FE)
Myodes torquatus/obensis Ob lemming (NS)
Nucifraga caryocatactes nutcracker (AS/ SP/BI/FE)
Nyctea scandiaca snowy owl (NS)
Ochotona alpina Altai pika (AS)
Oenanthe isabellina Isabelline wheatear (AS/SP/BI)
Omul baikalensis omul (BI)
Otaria ursina sea bear (NS/FE)
Otis tarda bustard (SP/BI)
Ovis ammon argalis (sheep) (AS)
Ovis argali arkhar (AS)
Ovis nivicola Siberian bighorn/snow sheep (FE)
Panthera pardus orientalis Amur leopard (FE)
Panthera tigris altaica Siberian/Amur tiger (FE)
Panthera uncia snow leopard (AS)
Perdix perdix grey partridge (AS/SP/BI/ FE)

Perisoreus infaustus Siberian jay (BI/FE)
Phalacrocorax carbo great cormorant (BI/FE)
Phoca barbata groenlandica seal (NS/FE)
Phoca baicalensis Baikal seal (BI)
Phocaena orca dolphin (NS/FE)
Picoides tridactylus three-toed woodpecker (SP/BI/FE)
Plectophenax nivalis snow bunting (NS)
Podiceps auritus Slavonian/horned grebe (AS/BI)
Podiceps cristatus great-crested grebe (AS/SP/BI)
Procapra gutturosa Mongolian gazelle (FE)
Pteromys volans Siberian flying squirrel (SP/BI/FE)
Rangifer tarandus reindeer/caribou (NS/BI/FE)
Ranodon sibiricus five-toed triton (AS/SP)
Rufibrenta ruficollis red-breasted goose (NS)
Salpingotus crassicauda pygmy jerboa (SP/AS)
Sciurus vulgaris red squirrel (SP/BI/AS/FE)

Spermophilus eversmanni Siberian marmot (BI)
Spermophilus undulatus arctic ground squirrel (FE)
Sterna hirundo common tern (BI/FE)
Strix nebulosa great grey owl (SP/BI/FE)
Surnia ulula hawk owl (SP/BI/FE)
Sus scrofa wild boar (AS/BI/FE)
Tadorna ferruginea ruddy shelduck (SP/BI/FE)
Tamias striatus striped squirrel (BI)
Tetrao urogallus capercaillie (SP/BI/FE)
Tetrao parvirostris black-billed capercaillie (BI/FE)
Tetraogallus himalayanensis Himalayan snowcock (AS)
Tetraogallus altaicus Altai snowcock (AS)
Tetrastes bonasia hazel grouse (SP/BI/FE)
Turdus sibiricus Siberian thrush (SP/BI/FE)
Uria aalge guillemot (NS/FE)
Ursus arctus bear (SP/FE)
Ursus maritimus polar bear (NS)
Ursus tibetanus Tibet bear (FE)
Vulpes vulpes red fox (AS/SP/BI/FE)

APPENDIX D – BIBLIOGRAPHY

Baedeker, Karl *Russia with Teheran, Port Arthur and Peking* (Leipzig 1914)
Barzini, Luigi *Peking to Paris. A Journey across Two Continents* (London 1907)
Byron, Robert *First Russia Then Tibet* (London 1933)
Collins, Perry McDonough *A Voyage down the Amoor* (New York 1860)
De Windt, Harry *Siberia as it is* (London 1892)
Des Cars, J and Caracalla, J P *Le Transsiberien* (1986)
Dmitriev-Mamonov, A I and Zdziarski, A F *Guide to the Great Siberian Railway 1900* (St Petersburg 1900)
Fleming, H M and Price, J H *Russian Steam Locomotives* (London 1960)
Gowing, L F *Five Thousand Miles in a Sledge* (London 1889)
Heywood, A J & Button I D C *Soviet Locomotive Types* (London/Malmo 1994)
Hill, S S *Travels in Siberia* (London 1854)
Hollingsworth, J B *The Atlas of Train Travel* (London 1980)
    An Official Guide to Eastern Asia Vol 1: Manchuria & Chosen (Tokyo 1913)
Jefferson, R L *Awheel to Moscow and Back* (London 1895)
Jefferson, R L *Roughing it in Siberia* (London 1897)
Jefferson, R L *A New Ride to Khiva* (London 1899)
Johnson, Henry *The Life of Kate Marsden* (London 1895)
Kennan, George *Siberia and the Exile System* (London 1891)

Lansdell, Henry *Through Siberia* (London 1883)
Levin, M G and Potapov, L P *The Peoples of Siberia* (Chicago 1964)
Macaulay, Lord *History of England from the Accession of James II*
Manley, Deborah *The Trans-Siberian Railway* (London 2009)
Marsden, Kate *On Sledge and Horseback to Outcast Siberian Lepers* (London 1895)
Meakin, Annette *A Ribbon of Iron* (London 1901)
Massie, R K *Nicholas and Alexandra* (London 1967)
Murray *Handbook for Russia, Poland and Finland* (London 1865)
Newby, Eric *The Big Red Train Ride* (London 1978)
Pifferi, Enzo *Le Transsiberien*
Poulsen, J and Kuranow, W *Die Transsibirische Eisenbahn* (Malmo 1986)
St George, George *Siberia: the New Frontier* (London 1969)
Shoemaker, M M *The Great Siberian Railway – St Petersburg to Peking* (London 1903)
Theroux, Paul *The Great Railway Bazaar* (London 1975)
Thubron, Colin *In Siberia* (Penguin 2000)
Tupper, Harmon *To the Great Ocean* (London 1965)
Wolmar, Christian *To the Edge of the World* (London 2013)

APPENDIX E – PHRASE LISTS

As with virtually every country in the world, it's possible to just about get by in Russia, Mongolia and China on a combination of English and sign language. English is spoken by tourist guides and some hotel staff but most of the local people you meet on the train will be eager to communicate with you and unable to speak English. Unless you enjoy charades it's well worth learning a few basic phrases in advance. Not only will this make communication easier but it will also earn you the respect of local people. You might even consider taking evening classes before you go, or teaching yourself with books and CDs from your local library.

The sections here highlight only a few useful words. Lonely Planet's pocket-sized phrasebooks in Russian, Mongolian and Chinese are highly recommended as are various apps. The following are a few of the many available: Languages, iTranslate and SayHi Translate for iPhone; Google Translate and Talking Translator for Android.

Russian

CYRILLIC ALPHABET AND PRONUNCIATION GUIDE

It's not very difficult to master the Cyrillic alphabet before you go; many letters are the same as in English and the other ones are easy enough to remember. This will enable you to decipher the names of streets, metro stations and, most importantly, the names of stations along the Trans-Siberian and Trans-Mongolian routes (Mongolian also uses a modified Cyrillic script).

The Cyrillic alphabet is derived from the Greek. It was introduced in Russia in the 10th century via a translation of the Bible made by two Greek bishops, Cyril (who gave his name to the new alphabet) and Methodius.

Cyrillic letter	Roman equiv	Pronunciation*	Cyrillic letter	Roman equiv	Pronunciation*
А а	a	**fa**ther	П п	p	**P**eter
Б б	b	**b**et	Р р	r	**R**ussia
В в	v	**v**odka	С с	s	**S**amarkand
Г г	g	**g**et	Т т	t	**t**ime
Д д	d	**d**og	У у	u, oo	f**oo**l
Е е	ye	**ye**t (unstressed: **ye**ar)	Ф ф	f, ph	**f**ast
Ё ё	yo	**yo**ghurt	Х х	kh	lo**ch**
Ж ж	zh	trea**s**ure	Ц ц	ts	lo**ts**
З з	z	**z**ebra	Ч ч	ch	**ch**illy
И и	i, ee	s**ee**k, y**e**ar	Ш ш	sh	**sh**ow
Й й	y	bo**y**	Щ щ	shch	**s**ugar
К к	k	**k**it	Ы ы	y, i	d**i**d
Л л	l	**l**ast	ь		(softens preceding consonant)
М м	m	**M**oscow	Э э	e	l**e**t
Н н	n	**n**ever	Ю ю	yu	**u**nion
О о	o	t**o**re (unstressed: t**o**p)	Я я	ya	**ya**rd

* pronunciation shown by **bold** letter/s

KEY PHRASES

The following phrases in Cyrillic script may be useful to point to if you're having problems communicating:

Please write it down for me	Напишите это для меня, пожалуйста	*Na-pi-**shi**-te e-to dlya me-nya, po-zhal-sta*
Help me, please	Помогйте мне, пожалуйста	*Po-mo-**gi**-te mne, po-**zhal**-sta*
I only speak English	Я говорю только по-английски	*Ya go-vo-**riu** **tol**-ko po an-**gli**-ski*
I need an interpreter	Мне нужен переводчик	*Mne **noo**-zhen pe-re-**vod**-chik*

CONVERSATIONAL RUSSIAN

Run the hyphenated syllables together as you speak and roll your 'R's:

General

Hello	Здравствуйте	*zdrahz-tvooy-tyeh*
Goodbye	До свидания	*Das-vee-**dah**-nya*
Good morning	Доброе утро	***Doh**-broyeh-ootro*
Good afternoon / evening	Добрый день / вечер	***Doh**-bree-**dyen** / **vye**cher*
Please / Thank you	Пожалуйста / Спасибо	*Pa-**zhal**-sta / spa-**see**-ba*
Do you speak English?	Говорите ли вы по-английски?	*Gava-**ree**-tyeh lee vy pa-an-**glee**-skee?*
No / Yes	Нет / да	*nyet / da*
Excuse me (sorry)	Извините	*Eez-vee-**nee**-tyeh*
good / bad	Хорошо / плохо	*ha-ra-**sho** / **plo**-ho*
cheap / expensive	Дёшево / дорого	***dyo**-she-vo / **do**-ro-go*
Wait a minute!	Одну минуту!	*Ad-**noo** mee-**noo**-too!*

General *(cont'd)*

Please call a doctor	Вызовите, пожалуйста, врача	*Vy-za-**vee**-tyeh, pa-**zhal**-sta, **vra**-cha*
Can I take a photo of you?	Можно вас снять?	*Mozhno vas snyat?*
Is there / are there...?	Есть ли .....?	*Yest' lee ....?*
How much / many?	Сколько?	***Skolka?***
rouble / roubles	рубль / рубля / рублей	*roobl (1), **roob**lyah (2-4), **roob**lyey (5+)*
Please write down the price	Напишите, пожалуйста, цену	*Na-pee-**shee**-tyeh, pa-**zhal**-sta, **tseh**-noo*
ticket	билет	*beel-**yet***
1st / 2nd / 3rd class	1-й / 2-й / 3-й класс	***perv**iy / **ftoroy** / **treh**tiy class*
express	экспресс	*ekspres*

Directions (see also box p80)

map	карта	***kar**-ta*
Where is ...?	Где....?	*G'dyeh...?*
hotel	гостиница	*ga-**stee**-nee-tsa*
airport / aerodrome	аэропорт / аэродром	*a-**eh**-ro-port / a-**eh**-ro-drom*
railway station	Где вокзал	*Gdeh vok-**zal***
bus station	автобусная станция	*av-to-bus-na-ya stan-tsi-ya*
metro / taxi	метро / такси	*mi-**tro** / tak-**see***
tram / trolley-bus	трамвай / троллейбус	*tram-**vai** / tro-**ley**-boos*
restaurant / café	ресторан / кафе	*re-sta-**rahn** / ka-**feh***
museum / shop	булочная / гастроном	*moo-**zey** / ma-ga-**zyeen***
bakery / grocery	булочная / гастроном	***boo**-lotch-naya / gas-tra-**nom***
ticket office (theatre)	касса (театральная)	***kassa** (te-ah-**tral**-na-ya)*
lavatory (ladies/gents)	туалет (женский / мужской)	*too-a-**lyet** (**zhen**-ski / moozh-**skoy**)*
open / closed	открыто / закрыто	*aht-**kri**-ta / za-**kri**-ta*
left / right	направо / налево	*na-**prah**-va/na-**lyeh**-va*

Numbers

1	*adeen* один	14	*chetirnatsat* четырнадцать	80	*vosyem-deset* восемьдеся
2	*dvah* два	15	*pyatnatsat* пятнадцать	90	*devya-**nosta*** девяносто
3	*tree* три	16	*shestnatsat* шестнадцать	100	*sto* сто
4	*chetiri* четыре	17	*semnatsat* семнадцать	200	*dveh-stee* двести
5	*pyat'* пять	18	*vasemnatsat* восемнадцать	300	*tree-sta* тристо
6	*shest'* шесть	19	*dyevyet-**natsat*** девятнадцать	400	*chetiri-sta* четыресто
7	*sem'* семь	20	*dvadsat* двадцать	500	*pyatsot* пятьсот
8	*vosem'* восемь	30	*treedsat* тридцать	600	*shestsot* шестьсот
9	*dyeh-vyet* девять	40	*sorok* сорок	700	*semsot* семьсот
10	*dyeh-syet* десять	50	*pidisyat* пятьдесят	800	*vosemsot* восемьсот
11	*adeenatsat* одиннадцать	60	*shizdisyat* шестьдесят	900	*devetsot* девятьсот
12	*dvenatsat* двенадцать	70	*syem-deset* семьдесят	1000	*teesyacha* тысяча
13	*treenatsat* тринадцать				

Time periods/days of the week

| What time is it? | Который час? | *katori chas?* |
| hours / minutes | часа / минут | *chasof / meenoot* |

Time periods/days of the week (cont'd)

today	сегодня	*sevodnya*
yesterday / tomorrow	вчера / завтра	*fcherah / zahftra*
Monday / Tuesday	понедельник / вторник	*pa-ni-dyel-nik / ftor-nik*
Wednesday / Thursday	среда / четверг	*sri-da / chit-vehrk*
Friday / Saturday	пятьница / суббота	*pyat-nit-sah / soo-boh-ta*
Sunday	воскресенье	*vas-kreh-sen-ya*

Food and drink

menu / bill	меню / счёт	*min-yoo / shchot*
(mineral) water / juice	(минеральная) вода / сок	*(mee-nee-rahl-naya) va-da / sok*
vodka / whisky / beer	водка / виски / пиво	*vodka / veeskee / peeva*
wine / cognac	вино / коньяк	*veenoh / kan-yahk*
champagne	шампанское	*sham-pahn-ska-yeh*
Cheers!	За Ваше здоровье!	*Zah vah-sheh zda-ro-vyeh!*
caviar / salmon / sturgeon	икра / сёмга / осётр	*eek-ra / syom-ga / ah-syo-tr*
chicken / duck	кура / утка	*ku-rah / oot-ka*
steak / roast beef	бифштекс / ростбиф	*bifshteks / rostbif*
veal	телятина	*telyahtina*
pork / ham / sausage	свинина / ветчина / колбаса	*sveeneena / vichinah / kalbahsa*
bread / potatoes / salad	хлеб / картошка / салат	*khlyep / kartoshka / sa-lat*
fruit / vegetables	фрукты / овощи	*froo-kti / o-vo-shchi*
butter / cheese	масло / сыр	*masla / syr*
eggs / omelette	яйца / омлет	*ya-eet-sa / ahmlet*
salt / pepper	соль / перец	*sol / perets*
tea / coffee	чай / кофе	*chai / kohfyeh*
milk / sugar	молоко / сахар	*malako / sakhar*
I'm a vegetarian	Я вегетариянец / вегетарианка	*Ya vegeteryanets / vegeteryanka* (m / f)

Questions and answers

What's your name?	Как Вас зовут?	*Kahk vahs zavoot?*
My name is ...	Меня зовут...	*Minyah zavoot ...*
I'm from ...	Я из...	*Yah eez ...*
Britain	Великобритании	*Ve-li-ko-bree-ta-nee-ee*
USA	США	*Seh-She-Ah*
Canada / Australia	Канады / Австралии	*Kanady / Av-stra-lee-ee*
New Zealand	Новой Зеландии /	*Novoy Ze-lan-dee-ee*
Japan	Японии	*Ya-po-nee-ee*
Sweden / Finland	Швеции / Финляндии	*Shve-tsee-ee / Fin-lyan-dee-ee*
Norway / Denmark	Норвегии / Дании	*Nar-ve-gee-ee / Da-nee-ee*
Germany / Austria	Германии / Австрии	*Germanee / Avstree*
France / Netherlands	Франции / Голандии	*Frantsee / Gollandee*
Where are you going?	Куда Вы едити?	*Kudah viy yeh-di-teh?*
I'm going to ...	Я еду....	*Yah yedoo ...*
Are you married?	Вы женаты (m) / замужем?	*Viy zhenahty* (m) / *zamoozhem* (f)?
Do you have any children?	Есть ли у Вас дети?	*Yest-li oo vas dyeh-ti?*
boy / girl	мальчик / девочка	*mahlcheek / dyehvochka*
How old are you?	Сколько Вам лет?	*Skolka vahm lyet?*
What do you do?	Кем Вы работаете?	*Kem viy rabohtayete?*
student	студент, студентка	*studyent* (m), *studyentka* (f)
teacher	учитель, учительница	*ucheetyel* (m), *ucheetyelneetsa* (f)

Questions and answers*(cont'd)*

doctor / nurse	врач / медсестра	*vrach* / *myed-sistra*
actor / artist	актёр / художник	*aktyor* / *khudozhneek*
engineer / lawyer	инжинер / адвокат	*eenzhenyehr* / *advokaht*
office worker	служащий	*slu-zhash-chi*
Where do you live?	Где Вы живёте?	*Gdyeh viy zhivyotyeh?*

Railway dictionary (Словарь железнодорожных терминов)

Ticket window
касса

for tickets after 24 hours	предварительная продажа билетов
for tickets within 24 hours	текущая продажа билетов
working from 08.00 to 20.00	часы работы с 8 до 20
open 24 hours	круглосуточная касса
break from 13.00 to 14.00	перерыв с 13 до 14
technical break from 10.15 to 10.45	технический перерыв 10.15 до 10.45

Timetable
расписание

even days (ie 2, 4, 6, ... of May)	Чёт (по четным числам)
odd days (ie 1, 3, 5, ... of May)	Неч (по нечетным числам)
weekends and public holidays	вых (по выходным)
weekdays	раб (по рабочим дням)
departure / arrival	От (отправление) / Пр (прибытие)
platform / station of destination	Пл (платформа) / станция назначения

Train
поезд

fast train / transit train	скорый поезд / транзитный поезд
passenger train / suburban train	пассажирский поезд / пригородный поезд
de luxe express train	фирменный поезд
train is late	поезд опаздывает
train does not stop	поезд не останавливается
train does not stop at the station	поезд не оставливается на станции

Station
вокзал, станция

station master	начальник вокзала
station attendant	дежурный по станции
information	справка

Carriage
вагон

SV (1st / soft), 2-berth compartments	СВ (спальный вагон)
	(or) мягкий вагон
kupé (coupé / 2nd / hard), 4-berth	купейный вагон
platzkart (open sleeping)	плацкартный вагон
obshchiy (open sitting)	общий вагон
wagon which separates and joins another train part way through the journey	безпересадочный вагон
	(or) отцепной вагон

Ticket
билет

one way / return	туда / туда и обратно
adult (full) fare / child fare	полный / детский
berth number	место
upper berth / lower berth	верхнее место / нижнее место
pass such as a monthly pass	проездной билет
discount ticket (pensioners, students etc)	льготный билет
price zones	зона

Time
Moscow Time / local time	время
	московское время / местное время

On the train
на поезде

Train Captain (head conductor)	начальник поезда
conductor	проводник, проводница
emergency stop handle	стоп-кран
baggage rack	багажная полка
blankets	одеяло
sheets	бельё
rolled-up mattress and pillow	постельные принадлежности

Useful railway expressions
Полезные железнодорожные выражения

Where is the railway station?	Где вокзал
Here is my ticket	Вот мой билет
Please show me my place	Покажите, пожалуйста, моё место
Please wake me at	Разбудите меня в ...... часов
Please wake me an hour before we arrive at	Разбудите меня, пожалуйста, за час до прибытия в ....
Where is the restaurant car or buffet car?	Где находится вагон-ресторан или буфет?
Where is the toilet?	Где находится туалет?
May I smoke here?	Здесь можно курить?
Please bring me a (another) blanket	Принесите, пожалуйста, (ещё одно) одеяло
What is the next station?	Какая следующая станция?
How many minutes will the train stop here?	Сколько минут длится стоянка поезда?
I am late for the train	Я опоздал(а) на поезд

Station signs
вход (entrance), выход (exit), переход (crossover between stations), выход в город (way out or exit to street level)

Mongolian

Westerners tend to have difficulty mastering the tricky pronunciation of the national language of Mongolia. Until recently, Mongolian was written in the same script as Russian (see p516), with two additional characters: Ө (pronounced 'o' as in 'food') and Y (with a longer, 'u', sound as in 'too'). When Mongolian is transliterated into Roman script, stress is indicated by doubling the vowels. Thus 'Ulaanbaatar' is better written this way rather than as 'Ulan Bator' as the former transliteration shows that the first 'a' in each word is stressed.

General words and phrases
Hello	*Sayn bayna uu*	Where is ...?	*Khaana bayna veh ...?*
Goodbye	*Bayar-tai*	hotel / airport	*zochid buudal / nisyeh ongotsni buudal*
Thank you	*Bayar-lalaar*		
Yes / No	*Teem / Ugu-i*	railway station	*galt teregniy buudal*
Sorry	*Ooch-laarai*	bus station	*avtobusni zogsool*
I don't understand	*Bi oilgokh-gu-i bayna*	temple / museum	*sum / moosei*
What's your name?	*Tani ner khen beh?*	lavatory	*zhorlon*
Where do you live?	*Th khaana ami-dardag beh?*	left / right	*zuun / baruun*
		How much?	*Khed?*

cheap	*khyamd*	bread / cheese	*talh / byaslag*
expensive	*kheterhiy unetiy yum-*	potato / tomato	*toms / ulaan lool*
soup	*shol*	tea / coffee	*tsai / kofee*
egg	*ondog*	beer / fermented	*peevo / airag*
mutton	*honini makh*	mare's milk	
rice / noodles	*budaar / goimon*		

Numbers

1	*neg*	8	*naym*	15	*arvan tav*	60	*zhar*
2	*khoyor*	9	*ee-us*	20	*khori*	70	*dal*
3	*gurav*	10	*arav*	21	*khori neg*	80	*naya*
4	*doroy*	11	*arvan neg*	30	*guchin*	90	*er*
5	*tav*	12	*arvan khoyor*	31	*guchin neg*	100	*zuu*
6	*zurgaar*	13	*arvan gurav*	40	*doch*	200	*khoyor zuu*
7	*doloo*	14	*arvan dorov*	50	*tavi*	1000	*neg myanga*

Chinese

The phrases below aim to give some assistance but a phrase book really is a necessity, or even a beginner's language course.

The problem with Chinese is one of pronunciation – so much depends on your tone and emphasis that if you do not get the sound exactly right you will not be understood at all. The country's main dialect is Mandarin, spoken by about three-quarters of the population. Mandarin has four tones: high tone (¯), rising (´) where the voice starts low and rises to the same level as the high tone, falling-rising (ˇ) where the voice starts with a middle tone, falls and then rises to just below a high tone; and falling (ˋ) which starts at the high tone and falls to a low one.

READING PINYIN CHINESE

Pinyin is the system of transliterating Chinese into the Roman alphabet. Pronunciation is indicated by the **bold** letters below:

Vowels

a as in f**a**r	i as in tr**ee** or as in	o as in **o**r	ü as in c**ue**
e as in w**e**re	w**e**re after c, r, s, z, ch, sh, zh	u as in p**oo**h	

Consonants

c as in e**ats**	h as in lo**ch** or the **kh** in an Arabic word,	z as in plo**ds**
q as in **ch**eap	with the sound from the back of the throat	zh as in **j**aw
r as in t**r**ill	x as in **sh**eep	

KEY PHRASES

The following phrases in Chinese characters may be useful to point to if you're having problems communicating:

Please write it down for me 请帮我写一下

Help / help me please 救命！/ 你能不能帮助我

Please call a doctor 请叫医生来

USEFUL WORDS AND PHRASES

General

Hello / Goodbye	*Nǐ hǎo / Zài jiàn*	你好 ／ 再见
Do you speak English?	*Nǐ huì shuō yīng yǔ ma*	你会说英语吗
Yes / no	*Duì / Bū duì* (literally correct / incorrect)	对 ／ 不对
No / Sorry, but no	*Méi yǒu*	没有
Thank you	*Xiè xie*	谢谢
Excuse me (sorry)	*Duì bù qǐ*	对不起
Excuse me (may I have your attention?)	*Qǐng wèn*	请问
Good / bad	*Hǎo / bu hǎo*	好 ／ 不好
I understand / do not understand	*Wǒ míngbai / bù míngbai*	我明白 ／ 不明白
UK / USA	*Yīng guó / Měi guó*	英国 ／ 美国
Canada / Australia	*Jīa ná dà / Aó dà lia*	加拿大 ／ 澳大利亚
France / Netherlands	*Fǎ guó / Hé lán*	法国 ／ 荷兰
Germany / China	*Dé guó / Zhōngguó*	中国 ／ 德国
Foreigner	*Wai guo ren / lǎowài*	外国人 ／ 老外
Translator	*Fānyìzhě*	翻译者

Directions

Where is ...?	*Zài nǎr ...?*	在哪儿？
toilet (ladies / gents)	*cè sǔo (nu / nan)*	厕所（女 ／ 男）
telephone	*diàn huà*	电话
airport	*jī chǎng*	机场
bus station	*qi chē zhàn*	汽车站
train / railway station	*huǒ chē / huǒ chē zhàn*	火车 ／ 火车站
taxi	*chū zū qì chē*	出租汽车
museum	*bó wù guǎn*	博物馆
hotel / restaurant	*fàn-diàn*	酒店 ／ 饭店
guesthouse	*bīnguǎn*	宾馆
post office	*yóu jú*	邮局
PSB / CAAC office	*Gōng ān jú / Zhōng háng gōngsi*	公安局 ／ 中航公司
What time will we arrive at ...?	*Liè chē shénme shí hou dào ...*	列车什么时候到
What station is this?	*Zhè shì nà yí zhàn?*	这是哪一站？
North / South	*Běi / Nán*	北 ／ 南
West / East	*Xī / Dōng*	西 ／ 东

Transport

ticket	*piào*	票
Hard seat / Soft seat	*Yìng Zuò / Ruǎn Zuò*	硬座 ／ 软座
Hard sleeper / Soft sleeper	*Yìng Wò / Ruǎn Wò*	硬卧 ／ 软卧
Please may I upgrade this ticket	*Qǐng nǐ huan gao yī ji de piào*	我能不能补票

Street names

Many of the street names throughout China are similar. In most of the cities you visit, for example, you will find a Renmin Lu (People's St) and Jiefang Lu (Liberation St). You will also discover that streets are named (usually) according to a system which divides them into sections: north, centre, south etc. Thus if the thoroughfare of the city is Renmin Lu, and it runs from east to west, it may well have three (or more) separate names: Renmin Rd West – Renmin Xilu, Renmin Rd Centre – Renmin Zhonglu, Renmin Rd East – Renmin Donglu. By way of an indication, the designation that is given to a particular avenue also indicates its size. Roughly the following equate to English terminology:

Street *lù* 路	Road *jiē, dàjiē* 街, 大街	Lane *xiàng* 巷	Narrow *hutong* 胡同 alleyway

Numbers

1	*yī*	一	14	*shí sì*	十四	101	*yì bǎi líng yī*	
2	*èr*	二	15	*shí wǔ*	十五			一百零一
3	*sān*	三	16	*shí liù*	十六	110	*yì bǎi yī shí*	
4	*sì*	四	17	*shí qī*	十七			一百一十
5	*wǔ*	五	18	*shí bā*	十八	150	*yì bǎi wǔ shí*	
6	*liù*	六	19	*shí jiǔ*	十九			一百五十
7	*qī*	七	20	*èr shí*	二十	200	*èr bǎi*	二百
8	*bā*	八	21	*èr shí yī*	二十一	500	*wǔ bǎi*	五百
9	*jiǔ*	九	30	*sān shí*	三十	1000	*yì qiān*	一千
10	*shí*	十	40	*sì shí*	四十	10,000	*yí wàn*	一万
11	*shí yī*	十一	50	*wǔ shí*	五十	100,000	*shí wàn*	十万
12	*shí èr*	十二	100	*yì bai*	一百	1 million		
13	*shí sān*	十三					*yì bǎi wàn*	一百万

How much?	*Duō shǎo qián?*	多少钱
That's too expensive	*Tài guì le*	太贵了

Time

One o'clock, two o'clock ...	*Yī diǎn, liang diǎn ...*	一点，两点
Ten past one (1.10)	*Yī diǎn shí fēn*	一点十分
Quarter to two (1.45)	*Yī diǎn sì shí wǔ fēn*	一点四十五分
Two thirty (2.30)	*Liang diǎn bàn*	两点半
Monday / Tuesday / Wednesday	*Xīng qī ... yī / èr / sān*	星期一，星期二，星期三
Thursday / Friday / Saturday	*Xīng qī ... sì / wǔ / liù*	星期四，星期五，星期六
Sunday	*Xīng qī rì*	星期日
Yesterday / tomorrow / today	*zuó tiān / míng tiān / jín tiān*	昨天 / 明天 / 今天

Food and drink

menu	*cài dān*	菜单
mineral water / tea / beer	*kuàng quán shuǐ / chá / pí jiǔ*	宽泉水 / 茶 / 啤酒
noodles / noodle soup	*miàn / tāng miàn*	面 / 面汤
bread / egg	*miàn bāo / jī diàn*	面包 / 鸡蛋
pork / beef / lamb	*zhū ròu / níu ròu / yáng ròu*	猪肉 / 牛肉 / 羊肉
chicken / duck / fish	*jī / yā / yú*	鸡肉 / 鸭肉 / 鱼肉
vegetables	*shū cài*	蔬菜
Do you have any vegetarian dishes?	*Nǐ zhèr yǒu shù-cài ma?*	有没有蔬菜
steamed rice	*mǐ fàn*	米饭
fujian fried rice	*fu jian chǎo fàn*	福建炒饭
fried rice	*jī dan chǎo fàn*	鸡蛋炒饭
pork in Sichuan-style sauce	*yú xiāng ròu sī*	鱼香肉丝
sweet and sour pork	*gu lao zhǔ ròu*	古老肉
pork and onion in soy sauce	*hui guō ròu*	回锅肉
beef chow mien	*niú ròu chǎo miàn*	牛肉炒面
spicy beef soup with veg	*shui zhǔ niú ròu*	水煮牛肉
chicken chow mien	*jī ròu chǎo miàn*	鸡肉炒面
chicken with cashew nuts	*yao guō jī ding*	腰果鸡丁
fried tofu with meat and veg	*jia chang dòufū*	家常豆腐
vegetable chow mien	*su chǎo miàn*	蔬炒面
hot and sour soup	*sūan là tāng*	酸辣汤
Delicious	*Hao chi*	好吃
Cheers!	*Gan bei!*	干杯

INDEX

Moscow Metro map labels:

Улица Подбельского / Ulitsa Podbelskogo
Черкизовская / Cherkizovskaya
Преображенская Площа... / Preobrazhenskaya Plosh...
...ево Chelobityevo
...ково
...ково
Сокольники Sokolniki
Красносельская Krasno...
...shkinskaya
...лово Sviblovo
Щёлковская / Shchyolkovskaya
...анический Сад / ...tanichesky Sad
Первомайская / Pervomayskaya
Измайловская / Izmaylovskaya
D E
Фонвизинская / ...я Fonvizinskaya
Butyrskaya
Партизанская / Partizanskaya
...ша Марьина Роща
Семёновская / Semyonovskaya
Алексеевская / Alexeyevskaya
Электрозаводская / Elektrozavodskaya
Рижская Rizhskaya
Пр Мира Pr Mira
Бауманская / Baumanskaya
Комсомольская / Komsomolskaya
Новокосино / Novokosino
Красные Ворота / Krasnye Vorota
Новогиреево / Novogireyevo
Тургеневская / Turgenevskaya
Курская / Kurskaya
Перово Perovo
Сретенский Бульвар / Sretensky Bulvar
Чкаловская / Chkalovskaya
Шоссе Энтузиас... / Shosse Entuziast...
Китай-Город / Kitay-Gorod
Авиамоторная / Aviamotornaya
...ральная / ...tralnaya
Марксистская / Marxistskaya
Пл Ильича Pl Ilyicha
Третьяковская / Tretyakovskaya
Римская Rimskaya
Новокузнецкая / Novokuznetskaya
Таганская / Taganskaya
...Ленина / ...enina
Крестьянская Застава / Krestyanskaya Zastava
Добрынинская / Dobryninskaya
Павелецкая / Paveletskaya
Пролетарская / Proletarskaya
...янка / ...yanka
Дубровка Dubrovka
...пуховская / ...ukhovskaya
Автозаводская / Avtozavodskaya
Кожуховская / Kozhukhovskaya
Тульская / Tulskaya
Коломенская / Kolomenskaya
Печатники / Pechatniki
Волгоградский / Volgogradsky Pr
Нагатинская / Nagatinskaya
Каширская / Kashirskaya
Волжская / Volzhskaya
Текстильщики / Textilshchiki
Нагорная / Nagornaya
Кантемировская / Kantemirovskaya
Люблино Lyublino
Братиславская / Bratislavskaya
Нахимовский Пр / Nakhimovsky Pr
Варшавская / Varshavskaya
Царицыно Tsaritsyno
Марьино Maryino
Кузьминки Kuzminki
Севастопольская / Sevastopolskaya
Каховская / Kakhovskaya
Орехово Orekhovo
Борисово Borisovo
Рязанский Прос / Ryazansky Pros...
Чертановская / Chertanovskaya
Домодедовская / Domodedovskaya
Шипиловская / Shipilovskaya
Выхино Vykhino
Южная / Yuzhnaya
Красногвардейская / Krasnogvardeyskaya
Зябликово Zyablikovo
Жулебино Zhul...
Котельники Kot...
Пражская / Prazhskaya
Алма-Атинская / Alma-Atinskaya
...стан / ...Stan
Ул Акад Янгеля / Ul Akad Yangelya
Ул Старокачаловская / Ul Starokachalovskaya
Бул Ад Ушакова / Bul Ad Ushakova
А Ул Милашенкова / Ul Milashenkova
...senevo
Аннино Annino
Ул Скобелевская / Ul Skobelevskaya
В Телецентр / Teletsentr
...невская / ...nevskaya
Ул Горчакова / Ul Gorchakova
С Ул Ак Королёва / Ul Ak Korolyova
...цевский Парк / ...itsevsky Park
Лесопарковская / Lesoparkovskaya
Бул Дм Донского / Bul Dm Donskogo
Бунинская Аллея / Buninskaya Alleya
D Выставочный Це... / Vystavochny Tsen...
E Ул С Эйзенштейн... / Ul S Eizenshteina

○ Under Construction
⚊ Transfer Station

Moscow Metro

528 Acknowledgements

[See also p6] Among the many readers who have written in with advice and suggestions, thanks to Alison (NZ), Olga Belnik (Russia), Mahmood Bhutta (UK), Alexandra Bobkov James Boyd (Ireland), John Bradford, Jonathan Brown, Simon Calder (UK), Malcolm C (UK), James Cho, Asger Christiansen (Denmark), Helen Clive, Lawrence Cotter (US Davies (UK), Lena Davigova (Russia), Christopher Downey (Australia), Laur (Netherlands), Howard Dymock (UK), Col Francis and Christine Emmo Fekkes, Jay Gary Finkelstein (USA), Penny Fitt (UK), Julia Fitzgera (Switzerland), Emmy Gengler (USA), Yiannis Gikas (Greece), Go (Australia), Jonny Googs (UK), Dmitri Gorokhov (Russia), Jo Gershon Grunfeld, Laura Hamelen (UK), Heather Hamm Reijo Härkönen (Finland), Will Harrison-Cripps (UK) (Australia), Louise Hellwig, Angela Hollingsworth (UK Benedikt Jaeger (Germany), Andy Jones (HK), Oskar Karlin Dr Mark Krebs, Valeria Kuteeva (Russia), Rowena Lambert Lonnedal Risberg (Norway), Karin MacArthur (Australia), Andr Laurie Martin (USA), Matheu (UK) & Wieteke (Netherlands), McLaughlin (UK), Richard Maxey, Thomas Morgan, Karen Mu (USA), Yuri Nemirovsky (Russia), Heather Oxley (Italy), Oded Pa Parton, Marcus Patzig (Germany), Andrea & Rocio Pellerani, Rich Perkin (Poland), Richard Pingree, Helen Revell, Paul Richards, Philip Robinson (Sandront, Nancy Scarth (Canada), Tobi Schwarzmueller (Germany), Igor Slöetjes, Rolf Smeds, Pat Smith, David Soulsby (UK), Sandra Southwell, W (Germany), Margaret Stack and Peter Munroe, Jonathan Streit, Roger Stubbin Taylor, Neil Taylor (UK), Mark Taylor (UK), Emmanuel du Teilhet (France), D Chen and Andrew van der Westhuyzen (Australia), Wim van den Hoek, Katya Voro (Russia), Julia and Chris Wallace (UK), Warren and Allison, Elizabeth Watson (UK Whitby (UK), Jan Wigsten (Mongolia), Felicity Wilcox (UK), Edward Wilson (UK), And Wingham (UK), Jennie Wogan (UK), Rashit Yahin (Russia) and Andrew Young (UK).

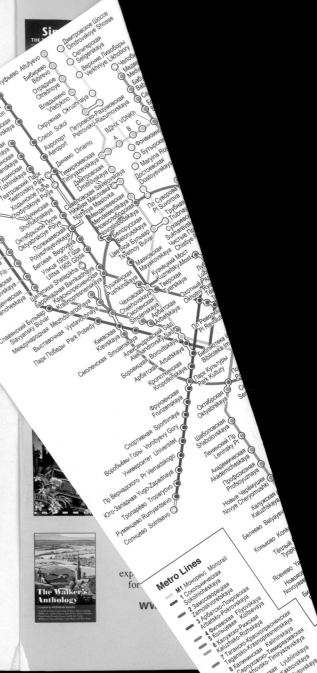

Beijing Subway

A Beihai North
B Nanluoguxiang
C Beixinqiao
D Zhangzizhonglu
E Dongsi
F Dengshikou

LINE 15
Fengbo
Shunyi
Shimen
Nanfaxin
Houshayu
Huailikan
China International Exhibition Centre
Sunhe
Maquanying
Cuigezhuang
Wangjing
Wangjingxi

Beijing Capital Airport
Terminal 3
Terminal 2

AIRPORT LINE

LINE 13
Beiyuan

LINE 6
Caofang
Huangqu
Changying
Dalianpo
Qingnianlu
Shilipu
Communication University of China
Shuangqiao
Guanzhuang

BT LINE
Tuqiao
Linheli
Guoyuan
Jiukeshu
Liyuan
Beiyuan
Baliqiao
Tongzhou Beiyuan

YZ LINE
Ciqu
Ciqu South
Wanyuanjie
Rongjingdongjie
Tongjinanlu
Rongchangdongjie
Yizhuang Culture Park
Wenhualu
Wanyuanjie
Jinghai
Yizhuangqiao
Xiaochongmen

LINE 10
Taiyanggong
Sanyuanqiao
Liangmaqiao
Agricultural Exhibition Centre
Tuanjiehu
Hujialou
Jintaixizhao
Chaoyangmen
Yonganli
Guomao
Shuangjing
Jinsong
Panjiayuan
Shilihe
Fenzhongsi
Chengshousi
Xiaocun
Songjiazhuang

LINE 5
Tiantongyuan North
Tiantongyuan
Lishuiqiao
Lishuiqiao South
Beiyuanlu North
Datunlu East
Huixinxijie Beikou
Huixinxijie Nankou
Hepingxiqiao
Hepingli Beijie
Heping lie
Beixinqiao
Zhangzizhonglu
Dongsi
Dengshikou
Dongdan
Chongwenmen
Ciqikou
Tiantandongmen
Puhuangyu
Liujiayao
Songjiazhuang

Shaoyaoju
Guangximen
Liufang
Dongzhimen
Dongsi Shitiao
Chaoyangmen
Jianguomen
Beijing Railway Station

LINE 8
Huilongguan Dongdajie
Huoying
Yuxin
Xiaokou
Yongtaizhuang
Lincuiqiao
South Gate of Forest Park
Olympic Green
Olympic Sports Centre
Beitucheng
Anzhenmen
Anhuaqiao

CP LINE
Nanshao
Shahe University Park
Shahe
Gonghuacheng
Zhuxinzhuang
Life Sciences Park
Longze
Huilongguan
Xi'erqi

LINE 2
Andingmen
Guloudajie
Jishuitan
Xizhimen
Jiandemen
Mudanyuan
Xinjiekou
Pinganli
Xisi
Lingjing Hutong
Xidan
Fuxingmen
Changchunjie
Xuanwumen
Hepingmen
Qianmen
Chongwenmen

LINE 4
Anheqiao North
Beigongmen
Xiyuan
East Gate of Peking University
Zhongguancun
Haidian Huangzhuang
Renmin University
Weigongcun
National Library
Dongwuyuan (Zoo)
Xizhimen
Xinjiekou
Pinganli
Xisi
Lingjing Hutong
Xidan
Caishikou
Taoranting
Beijing South Railway Station
Majiapu
Jiaomen West
Gongyixiqiao
Xingong
Xihongmen
Zaoyuan
Gaomidian North
Gaomidian South
Line continues 7 stations to Tiangongyuan (last stop)

LINE 1
Pingguoyuan
Gucheng
Bajiao Amusement Park
Babaoshan
Yuquanlu
Wukesong
Wanshou lu
Gongzhufen
Junshi Museum
Muxidi
Nanlishilu
Fuxingmen
Xidan
Tian'anmen West
Tian'anmen East
Wangfujing
Dongdan
Jianguomen
Yong'anli
Guomao
Dawanglu
Sihui
Sihui East

LINE 10
Bagou
Suzhuang
Changchunqiao
Cishousi
Huoqiying
Chedaogou
Xidiaoyutai
Gongzhufen
Liangshuihe
Wukesong

LINE 14
Zhangguozhuang
Garden Expo Park
Dawayao
Guozhuang
Dajing
Qilizhuang

FS LINE
Guogongzhuang
Dabaotai
Guogongzhuang
Liangxiang Nanguan
Xiju
Niwa
Line continues 10 stations to Suzhuang (last stop)

LINE 9
Baishiqiao South
Baiduizi
Military Museum
Beijing West Railway Station
Liuliqiao East
Liuliqiao
Qilizhuang
Fengtai Dongdajie
Keyilu
Fengtai Technology Park
Guogongzhuang

Fengtai Railway Station
Fengtainanlu
Fengtai Nanlu

Zhichunli
Zhichunlu
Dazhongsi
Xitucheng
Mudanyuan
Jiandemen

Yuanmingyuan Park
Wudaokou
Shangdi

LINE 6
Haidian Wuluju
Cishousi
Chegongzhuang
Chegongzhuang West
Fuchengmen
Beihai North
Nanluoguxiang
Dongsi
Chaoyangmen
Dongdaqiao
Hujialou
Jintaixizhao

Trans-Siberian Rail Routes

MT = Moscow Time (GMT+4)

Legend:
- Trans-Siberian
- Trans-Manchurian
- Trans-Mongolian
- Baikal-Amur Mainline
- AYaM
- Time zone border

■1/2■ Route map number

Scale: 0 250 500 750 1000km
0 200 400 600miles

Time zones: MT+9, MT+8, MT+7, MT+6, MT+5, MT+4, MT+3, MT+2, MT+1, MT (Moscow Time)

Seas and oceans: ARCTIC OCEAN, Bering Sea, East Siberian Sea, Kara Sea, Barents Sea, Sea of Okhotsk, Sea of Japan, Yellow Sea, Black Sea, Caspian Sea, Aral Sea

Regions: SIBERIA, FAR EAST, RUSSIA, EUROPEAN RUSSIA, MONGOLIA (GMT+8), CHINA (GMT+8), KAZAKHSTAN, JAPAN, N KOREA, S KOREA

Rivers: Ob, Irtysh, Yenisey, Angara, Lena, Nizhnaya Tunguska, Amur, Ussuri, Syr Darya

Cities and stations (selected):
Petropavlovsk-Kamchatsky, Magadan, Okhotsk, Okha, Wakkanai, Sapporo, TOKYO, Osaka, Sakaiminato, Vanino, Sovetskaya Gavan, Komsomolsk-na-Amure, Yuzhno-Sakhalinsk, Khabarovsk, VLADIVOSTOK, Nakhodka, Zarubino, Sokcho, Donghae, Birobidzhan, Fuyuan, Seoul, PYONGYANG, Suifenhe, Harbin, Changchun, Shenyang, BEIJING, Datong, Erlian, Manzhouli, Blagoveshchensk, Bamovskaya, Tynda, Neryungri, Tommot, Aldan, Nizhniy Bestyakh, Yakutsk, Lensk, Dudinka, Norilsk, Nadym, Surgut, Tobolsk, Tyumen, Chita, Ulan-Ude, Severobaikalsk, Bratsk, Taishet, Krasnoyarsk, Tomsk, Novosibirsk, Barnaul, Omsk, Yekaterinburg, Perm, Kurgan, Chelyabinsk, Petropavlovsk, Semey, Aktogay, Karaganda, Astana, Balkhash, Öskemen, Almaty, Bishkek, ULAANBAATAR (Ulan Bator), Ölgii, Ürümqi, Tashkent, Bukhara, Dushanbe, Kabul, Ashgabat, Turkmenbashi, Mashhad, Tehran, Baku, TBILISI, YEREVAN, Grozny, Astrakhan, Atyrau, Aqtau, Aqtobe, Volgograd, Saratov, Samara, Kazan, Nizhny Novgorod, Vladimir, Suzdal, Sergiev Posad, Rostov-Velikiy, Yaroslavl, Vyatka, MOSCOW, Voronezh, Rostov-on-Don, Krasnodar, KYIV, CHISINAU, MINSK, WARSAW, BERLIN, COPENHAGEN, STOCKHOLM, HELSINKI, TALLINN, RIGA, VILNIUS, Kaliningrad, Murmansk, Arkhangelsk, Vorkuta, St Petersburg, Bukhara

Countries/labels: NORWAY, SWEDEN, FINLAND, GERMANY, POLAND, BELARUS, UKRAINE, MOLDOVA, GEORGIA, ARMENIA, AZERBAIJAN, IRAN, TURKMENISTAN, UZBEKISTAN, TAJIKISTAN, KYRGYZSTAN, AFGHANISTAN, EST (Estonia), LAT (Latvia), LITH (Lithuania), Novaya Zemlya, Kuril Islands

www.trailblazer